Gower
Handbook
of
Marketing
FOURTH EDITION

GOWER
HANDBOOK
OF
MARKETING

FOURTH EDITION

edited by
Professor Michael J. Thomas

Gower

First published 1974 by
Gower Publishing Co Ltd
Second edition 1981
Third edition 1988
This edition published by
Gower Publishing Limited
Gower House
Croft Road
Aldershot
Hampshire GU11 3HR
England

Gower
Old Post Road
Brookfield
Vermont 05036
USA

Thomas, Michael J.
Gower Handbook of Marketing. – 4Rev.ed
I. Title II. Thomas, M. J.
658.8

ISBN 0–566–07441–9

Library of Congress Cataloging-in-Publication Data
Gower handbook of marketing / edited by Michael J. Thomas. — 4th ed.
    p.   cm.
   Rev. ed. of: Marketing handbook. 3rd ed. c1989.
   Includes bibliographical references and index.
   ISBN 0–566–07441–9 : $93.95 (approx.)
   1. Marketing–Handbooks, manuals, etc.   I. Thomas, Michael J.,
1933–   . II. Title: Marketing handbook.
HF5415.M2988   1995
658.8—dc20
                                            94–24812
                                               CIP

Typeset in 10pt Cheltenham by Raven Typesetters, Chester, Cheshire
and printed in Great Britain by Hartnolls Ltd. Bodmin.

Contents

PART II   ORGANIZING FOR EFFECTIVE MARKETING

The concept of logistics management – What are the costs of distribution? – Total systems management – Logistics' role in corporate strategy – References – Essential reading

List of illustrations

List of tables

Notes on contributors

Michael J. Baker (*Developing and launching a new industrial product*) is Senior Adviser to the Principal and Professor of Marketing at Strathclyde University. He is the author of numerous books and articles including *Marketing* (5th ed.), *Marketing Strategy & Management* (2nd ed.) and *Market Development* and is editor of *The Marketing Book* (3rd ed.). A past Chairman (1987) of the Institute of Marketing, he is active in consultancy and a director of nine companies.

Derek Beasley (*Staff Development, marketing education and marketing training*) is Head of Training Operations at the Chartered Institute of Marketing, where he is responsible for the largest marketing, sales and strategy training business in Europe. He recently led the team which obtained ISO 9001 registration for the Training Division.

Tim Bowles (*Information systems for marketing*) started his market research career in 1970, after six years as a research psychologist. Between 1970 and 1978 he worked with the Schlackman Research Organisation where he directed a wide range of marketing and social research projects. From 1979 to 1986 he worked with AGB Research, first as Managing Director of Research Surveys of Great Britain, AGB's *ad hoc* research company, and later as Managing Director of Audits of Great Britain, the company principally concerned with market measurement and TV audience research. In 1986 he joined MRB Group with responsibility for all of its companies outside the USA, and became Chief Executive of the worldwide group in 1990. Tim Bowles has been a member of the Council of Management of Oxfam and Chairman of the Marketing Group of Great Britain. He has published many papers on marketing research, market information systems, applied psychology and social policy research.

Tom Brannan (*Sales promotion*) graduated in Business Studies from

Strathclyde University and learned many of his marketing skills while working for Black & Decker. He spent a number of years marketing and selling capital goods before joining Primary Contact, a specialist business and financial advertising agency within the Ogilvy Group, where he is Client Services Director. Tom is a Fellow of the Chartered Institute of Marketing and a Vice-Chairman of its National Executive Committee. He is also Chairman of *Marketing Business* magazine and author of *The Effective Advertiser*. He writes and speaks internationally on marketing and related topics.

Stephen Brown *(Retailing)* is Professor of Retailing at the University of Ulster and Director of the university's retailing research unit. He has written widely on retailing issues and acted as consultant to several retail organizations. He is book reviews editor of *The Irish Marketing Review*.

Douglas Brownlie *(Analysing the environment)* has worked in management services in the British Steel Corporation. He has held research and teaching posts in the Department of Marketing, Strathclyde University, and the Department of Management Studies, University of Glasgow, before joining the Department of Management and Marketing at University College Cork. He now teaches and consults in the areas of marketing research, marketing management and strategic marketing at the University of Stirling.

Patrick Bruce *(Product design)* was Managing Director of Conran Design Pacific Limited, a multi-disciplinary sister company of Conran Design Group Limited, servicing the Asia Pacific region. He was formerly commercial director of Conran Design Group Limited. He trained originally as an industrial designer. After thirteen years of design and management experience in industry and education, he graduated from the Cranfield MBA programme prior to moving into a commercial and general management role in the design industry.

Jack Bureau *(Brand management)*, a graduate in social studies from Durham University, began his career with five years' experience of market research for several large clients of a prominent London advertising agency. He became market research manager and then group brand manager for shaving and writing products at Gillette Industries and then marketing director of the health and chemical division of Cadbury-Schweppes. He now teaches the Marketing III element of the BA degree course and postgraduate MSc and MBA classes. He is the author of *Brand Management: Planning and Control*, Macmillan, 1981.

Charles Channon *(Advertising)*, deceased, was successfully a researcher, an account director, a creative manager, and a director of account planning, starting at BMRB, moving to JWT on the account side, and then setting up the planning function at Ayer Barker. He was first chairman of the Account Planning Group and has written and spoken widely on advertising and planning. He was Director of Studies at the IPA from 1985 to 1992.

David Chapman *(Financial aspects of marketing)* had a successful career in engineering research, product design, sales and general management until the late 1970s when he joined the burgeoning ranks of management consultants. It was at this stage that he started to study the determinants of success in small and medium enterprises. Both of these studies were published by the National Economic Development Office. Arising from this he has undertaken considerable research into pricing and the consequences of the decisions made on the basis of financial information available to marketing managers. In 1983 he joined Sheffield Business School as an associate lecturer and is now Manager, Executive Programmes, an active member of the marketing subject group in both teaching and consultancy. He is also Visiting Professor of Business at the Masaryk Institute of Advanced Studies in Prague and Vice Chairman of the National Executive Committee of the Chartered Institute of Marketing.

Martin Christopher *(Physical distribution and logistics management)* is Professor of Marketing and Logistics Systems at Cranfield School of Management where he is head of the Marketing Faculty, one of Europe's largest centres for marketing teaching. His interests in marketing and logistics strategy are reflected in his consultancy and management development activities. In this connection, he has worked for major international companies in North America, Europe, the Far East and Australia. As an author, he has written numerous books and articles and is on the editorial advisory board of a number of professional journals in the marketing and logistics area. He has held appointments as Visiting Professor at the University of British Columbia, Canada, the University of New South Wales, Australia and the University of South Florida, USA. In addition he is a non-executive director of a number of companies.

Donald Cowell *(Developing and launching a new service)* is Professor of Marketing and Barkers Advertising Dean of the Business School at the University of Central England in Birmingham. A graduate of Leeds University, he worked in industry before undertaking postgraduate work for his Masters degree and Doctorate at the University of Bradford Management Centre. He taught marketing at the University of Loughborough before becoming Head of the Department of Management and then Assistant Director and Dean of the Business School at the University of Plymouth. He was formerly Chairman of the Marketing Education Group (MEG) and is currently Chief Examiner of the Chartered Institute of Marketing. His current research interests include the marketing of services and he has written numerous books, monographs and articles on marketing management and the marketing of services.

Bill Donaldson *(Customer service and customer care)* is Senior Lecturer in the Department of Marketing, University of Strathclyde. His current research interests are in customer service and the characteristics of service-driven organizations. In the last few years he has worked in these areas with companies such as Honeywell, Stoddard-Sekers and Scottish Power. In addition to several publications in the area he is also author of *Sales Management: Theory and Practice*, Macmillan Press, 1990.

Martin Duffell *(Recruitment – qualifications and sources* and *Selection – media and methods)* is an alumnus of London University (where he graduated in Classics and gained a PhD in comparative linguistics), Exeter University, and the Kellogg School of Northwestern University in the USA. He joined Unilever as a marketing trainee in 1960. His career has taken him to four continents and he has managed 20 different brands, from detergents to razor blades. He has also led every size of sales team from six to 600. In 1984 he became the head of management recruitment for Unilever in the UK and he describes his present job as 'marketing Unilever at Britain's universities'.

Gordon Foxall *(Customer behaviour)* is Professor of Consumer Research at the University of Birmingham, where he is Director of the Research Centre for Consumer Behaviour at the Birmingham Business School. He holds doctorates in industrial economics and business studies (PhD University of Birmingham 1983) and in psychology (PhD University of Strathclyde 1990). He is the author of a dozen books on consumer behaviour and related themes, including *Consumer Psychology in Behavioral Perspective* (Routledge, 1990) and the best-selling text *Consumer Psychology for Marketing*, co-authored with Ron Goldsmith (Routledge, 1994). He has also authored some 150 refereed articles and papers on consumer behaviour and marketing. Professor Foxall's research interests are in consumer theory and innovativeness.

Debbie Gorski *(The marketing database)* is a senior manager with Price Waterhouse Management Consultants, and has eleven years' experience in database marketing, marketing planning and customer service. Before joining Price Waterhouse, Debbie worked for Abbey National plc, where she was responsible for setting up their large and highly successful Telemarketing and Customer Service Centre, Abbey National Direct. She also worked previously for BP in direct marketing and marketing planning. Since joining Price Waterhouse, Debbie has specialized in the strategy, selection, implementation and use of sales and marketing systems in business, and has worked for a wide range of blue-chip clients in various industry sectors. She is author of the Price Waterhouse *Sales and Marketing Software Handbook*, a regular conference speaker and writer on the subject of marketing systems, and is also Vice Chairman of the Association of Information Systems in Marketing and Sales.

Evert Gummesson *(Relationship marketing)* is Professor of Service Management and Marketing at Stockholm University and is also on the faculty of the Swedish School of Economics and Business Administration, Helsinki, Finland. His most recent book is on relationship marketing. He is a member of several editorial boards for professional journals.

Jane Hancock *(The legal framework)* graduated from Newcastle University in 1983 with an Honours Degree in Physics. She joined the West Midlands County Council and qualified as a Trading Standards Officer in 1987 gaining a wide-ranging practical experience of enforcement work. As a Trading Standards

Officer she was responsible particularly for enforcing consumer safety legislation in addition to the broad spectrum of trading legislation. She joined Law Laboratories Ltd in 1989, specializing in aspects of non-food legislation, but dealing with all areas of the consumer products industry both food and non-food. She also undertakes quality consultancy for the food and non-food consumer product industry.

Derek Holder (*Direct mail*) is Managing Director of The Institute of Direct Marketing. A graduate from Manchester University, Derek has worked in marketing for British Airways and the Ford Motor Company. Then as Marketing Manager at McGraw-Hill and Reader's Digest, he gained wide experience in consumer and business direct marketing. He has worked as a consultant/trainer for many multinational companies and has developed undergraduate/postgraduate programmes as well as creating the Diploma in Direct Marketing.

Bernard Katz (*Agents* and *Telephone marketing*) graduated in psychology from Edinburgh University. After working with a London export merchant, he subsequently founded his own import–export company and traded round the world for 20 years. Bernard Katz has published seven marketing books. He undertakes speaker assignments and conducts management training seminars regularly in the UK, and South-east Asia.

Peter Kraushar (*Launching a new consumer product*) is President of KAE Development, Partner in Kraushar and Ramsay International and Visiting Professor at Middlesex Business School. He set up KAE Development in 1969, launched Mintel and was Chairman of KAE and of Mintel International Group for 20 years. He has specialized in product and business development since 1963 and has been personally involved in over 2 000 major consultancy projects, mostly for consumer goods and services companies, in the UK and across Europe, including Eastern Europe. He has been Chairman of the Marketing Society and has been a frequent writer and speaker on business development. He has also written two books on what works in practice in development and what does not.

Simon Majaro (*Product planning*) is Visiting Professor of Marketing Strategy at the Cranfield School of Management, Director of Strategic Management Learning and also managing director of a firm of international management consultants that bears his name; graduate in law at the University of London; barrister at law; graduate in Business Administration at the IMI, the Geneva-based business school; and lectures regularly at a number of US and European business schools. His writings include *International Marketing – A Strategic Approach to World Markets* and *Marketing in Perspective*, both published by Unwin Hyman; *The Creative Gap – Managing Ideas for Profit*, McGraw-Hill; *The Essence of Marketing*, Prentice Hall; *The Creative Marketer*, Butterworth-Heinemann and co-author of *Strategy Search*, Gower. His video *Managing*   *xxi*

Creativity was recently launched by Video Management of Brussels and is being distributed by the BBC in the UK.

Derek C. Martin *(International marketing and market research)* is Chairman and Managing Director of Martin Hamblin Research, whose activities cover a wide range of consumer and healthcare markets internationally. After reading History at Cambridge, he worked in advertising agencies and the healthcare industry before founding Martin Hamblin in 1969. He is currently Chairman of the Association of Market Survey Organisations, whose members account for over 70 per cent of all research undertaken in the UK.

Martin Mendelsohn *(Licensing, including franchising)*, who is a partner in Jaques & Lewis solicitors, London, is also Visiting Professor of Franchising and Director of the NatWest Centre for Franchise Research at the City University Business School, London; Fellow of the Chartered Institute of Arbitrators; Editor of the *Journal of International Franchising and Distribution Law* and Legal Consultant to the British Franchise Association. His current publications include: *The Guide to Franchising* (now in its 5th edition) in English, Spanish and Portuguese; *How to Evaluate a Franchise* in English, Hungarian, Polish, Czech, Indonesian and Chinese (now in its 5th edition); *Obtaining a Franchise* (a guide published by the Department of Trade); *How to Franchise Internationally*; *The Ethics of Franchising*; *The Franchisor's Manual*. He is co-author of: *Franchising in the UK: How to Franchise your Business* (now in its 3rd edition) in English, Hungarian, Polish, Czech, Indonesian and Chinese; *Comment Negocier une Franchise* (now in its 2nd edition) and *Franchising and the Block Exemption Regulation* (with Bryan Harris).

Rory Morgan *(Pricing as a marketing tool)*, a psychology graduate from London University, is a Board member of Research International UK and has been with Research International for over 20 years. Rory is renowned throughout the national and international marketing industry as an expert in both qualitative and quantitative research. In particular, he is recognized for his involvement in creating new modelling techniques. He has personally designed many of the advanced techniques used by Research International. Rory is a frequent contributor to academic journals such as the *Journal of the Market Research Society*.

Stan Paliwoda *(Understanding the international environment)* is Professor and Chair of Marketing at the University of Calgary, Alberta, Canada. His most recent books include *New Perspectives on International Marketing*, Routledge, 1991, *The Essence of International Marketing* (2nd ed.), Prentice-Hall, 1993 and *Investing in Eastern Europe*, Economist Intelligence Unit/Addison-Wesley. Forthcoming are *International Marketing Reader* (with John K. Ryans Jr.), Routledge and *Marketing*, Prentice Hall (with Warren Keegan, Sandra Moriarty and Tom Duncan). Professor Paliwoda's interests lie in international and industrial marketing strategy. He is also Editor of the *Journal of East–West Business*.

Kate Prescott *(Reaching overseas markets)* is Lecturer in International Business at the University of Bradford Management Centre where she teaches courses on International Business Strategy, Multinationals in the World Economy and European Business Management to both undergraduate and postgraduate students. Before this time she was ESRC Research Assistant at the same institution studying The Competitiveness of British Industry. Her research interests principally centre on global integration – particularly the Single European Market and the North American Free Trade Area – and extend to include international competitiveness and the internationalization of financial services. She is co-author of three books and various articles on the above issues.

Shelley Radice *(Door-to-door distribution)* is Executive Secretary of the Association of Household Distributors. She began her involvement with free distribution in 1988 through the Association of Free Newspapers. She currently serves on the ASA Committee of Advertising Practice and on the Council of the Advertising Association. Her studies were originally in Social Anthropology. She then carried out research at the National Institute of Industrial Psychology, and has written a dissertation about the sizes of organizations.

Bill Richards *(Exhibitions)* is the Executive Secretary of the Exhibition Industry Federation, for whom he co-ordinates the research programme for the UK exhibition industry. He is also responsible for the promotion of UK exhibitions in overseas markets and public relations within the UK. He is the senior partner of Tourism Research & Marketing who specialize in feasibility studies for tourism projects including exhibition and conference developments. He writes regularly for international trade magazines on tourism and exhibition subjects and is the author of a textbook on marketing tourist attractions, festivals and special events.

John Saunders *(Analysing the competition)* is National Westminster Bank Professor of Marketing, Loughborough University Business School. Previously he has worked for Bradford Management Centre, the University of Warwick, the Pacific–Asian Management Institute (Hawaii) and the Hawker Siddeley Group. He is an editor for the International School of Research in Marketing and an assistant editor of the *British Journal of Management*. As a senior consultant he has worked with many companies and institutions. These include Unilever, ICI, TI, THF, Dixons, Woolworth, Nestlé, the Asian Development Bank and the Singapore Government. He has published several books and over 100 refereed articles in the *Journal of Marketing, Journal of Marketing Research, Marketing Science, International Journal of Research in Marketing, MIS Quarterly* and so on.

Bill Stewart *(Packaging as a marketing tool)* gained M. Inst. Pkg (Dip) in 1970 while working at PIRA. He joined S. Maws & Sons Limited and gained a broad sense of commercial experience. In 1972 he was appointed packaging engineer with 3M UK and during a ten-year working period became manager, packaging engineering. He established a freelance consultancy prior to his appointment as technical packaging manager at Siebert/Head. He is widely experienced in finding economic and technically creative solutions to the many kinds of practical problems encountered in corporate identity and packaging. He was appointed a director of the company in 1985. Having spent nine years as Technical Design Director with London-based packaging design specialists, Siebert/Head, Bill Stewart is now pursuing his career as a freelance design consultant and writer.

Michael J. Thomas *(The marketing function and its organization* and *Customer service/customer care)*, having worked for the Metal Box Company in the 1950s, emigrated to the United States where he spent 11 years teaching on postgraduate courses in the School of Management, Syracuse University. He joined the Department of Marketing at Lancaster University in 1972, was appointed a Professor of Marketing at Strathclyde University in January 1987 and Head of the Marketing Department 1988–92. He is on the National Council of the Chartered Institute of Marketing, currently National Chairman. His *Pocket Guide to Marketing* was published by *The Economist*/Basil Blackwell in 1986 and *The Marketing Digest* by Heinemann in 1988. *Marketing Management* (with Julius Onah) was published in Nigeria in 1993. He edits *Marketing Intelligence and Planning*.

David Tonks *(Market segmentation)* is a lecturer in the Department of Marketing at the University of Lancaster. He has strong interests in market segmentation and marketing simulations. He also works as a marketing consultant and has been involved in over 30 large assignments for a variety of clients. He was formerly employed as a marketing manager in port services and as a brand manager in food products. He belongs to Acorn Group AOI and is a light user of brown sauce.

Norman Waite *(Staff development, marketing education and marketing training)* is the Head of Education at the Chartered Institute of Marketing. He has held that position since 1980, during which time the International Student Body has more than doubled to well over 33 000 students. He is also Chairman of the Education Committee of the European Marketing Confederation and has written and contributed to several books and journals on marketing.

Mike Wilson *(Sales management)* is Chairman of Marketing Improvements Group plc, the leading marketing consultancy and training organization and of the EuroMarketing Group SC which, through its network of consultancy members, covers all European markets and languages. His books, *Managing a Sales Force* and *The Management of Marketing*, are standard texts, and he is widely known through hundreds of seminars on all aspects of marketing. He has a high reputation for creative and perceptive advice given to companies large and small.

Preface

Is marketing facing a mid-life crisis? A number of soothsayers are trying to persuade us that this is the case.

> '. . . why does marketing lack direction today? One answer is that the environment has changed so dramatically that marketers are simply not picking up the right signals any more. Past experience is no longer a reliable guide to what today's concerns should be. Marketing has been struggling to respond to several environmental forces that have been at work since the mid-1970s. Of these, none has been more powerful than the rise of retailers.'

> 'Marketing departments have become tremendously averse to risk. Despite the accelerating rate of product launches, few genuinely new products are emerging. Of the top 50 brands in the United Kingdom, for example, only nine have been introduced in the past 18 years.'

> 'Fairly or unfairly, many consumer goods CEOs are beginning to think that marketing is no longer delivering.'

> Source: John Brady and Ian Davis (1993), 'Marketing's Mid Life Crisis', *McKinsey Quarterly*, No 2, pp 17–28.

Another source, drawing on qualitative research:

> 'Poor image and poor integration are two of the criticisms that have been levelled at marketing in the past . . .
> The problem of poor image seems to arise where marketing has allowed itself to become merely a sales support function, or where companies have tried and failed to implement certain aspects of marketing. Marketing also seems to develop a poor image where it becomes a proxy for market research and information gathering and is not seen to have an impact on decision making.
> Marketing has a much better image within organisations who adopt a 'top down' approach to marketing and use it to shape and influence strategy, not just tactics . . .
> Marketing . . . is now about customer service in a very special sense. The excellent companies are talking not just about satisfying present customer needs, but about anticipating the customer's needs of the future and delivering them today . . .
> The excellent companies are having to reorganise to become more customer

facing . . . They are looking at the end-to-end process and the total relationship with the customer and then reshaping organisation to reflect these end-to-end processes.'

Source: *Marketing – The Challenge of Change*, Chartered Institute of Marketing, 1994, pp 14–15.

Let me quote again, this time from Regis McKenna's book *Relationship Marketing*, a quotation that begins to explore the new agenda:

'not a "do more" marketing that simply turns up the volume on the sales spiels of the past but a knowledge- and experienced-based marketing that represents the once-and-for-all death of the salesman . . .
These two fundamentals, knowledge-based and experience-based marketing, will increasingly define the capabilities of a successful marketing organization . . .
Successful companies realize that marketing is like quality, integral to the organiza-tion. Like quality, marketing is an intangible that the customer must experience to appreciate . . .'

These criticisms notwithstanding, I remain confident that the increasing profes-sionalism of marketers will ensure that marketing, both as a philosophy – as a concept, as a strategic vision – as well as a function, will continue to fashion the future of organizations both profit and non profit oriented.

This Handbook is designed to keep senior management informed about the current state of marketing knowledge. This is the fourth edition, reflecting our confidence that it has been widely adopted as a source of reference. We trust that the new edition will continue in this tradition.

All chapters have been updated by their authors. Some chapters from the pre-vious edition have been deleted. New chapters include the Marketing Database (Chapter 2), the International Environment (Chapter 5), Relationship Marketing (Chapter 6), Staff Development (Chapter 10), Financial Aspects of Marketing (Chapter 13), The Role of Research in International Marketing (Chapter 15), Developing and Launching a New Product (Chapter 20), Retailing (Chapter 24), Reaching Overseas Markets (Chapter 27), Sales Promotion (Chapter 30), Direct Mail (Chapter 31), and the Legal Framework (Chapter 36).

Masculine pronouns have been used throughout, but these should be taken to refer equally to the feminine gender, except that in Chapters 8 and 9 feminine pronouns are used throughout and should be taken to refer equally to the mas-culine gender.

I am confident that this new edition will continue to serve the marketing pro-fession as well as its predecessors.

I wish to record my gratitude to my secretary Gillian Maddock who has mas-terminded the logistics of putting this new edition together whilst I have contin-ued to spread the gospel of marketing professionalism around the world.

Michael J. Thomas
Professor of Marketing
National Chairman, The Chartered Institute of Marketing

Introduction: The future of marketing and the marketing profession

The status of marketing is under scrutiny and in this introduction I will attempt, not to provide all the answers, but to raise some of the questions that face the marketing profession as we approach the millennium.

THE CRITICS

First, a flavour of some of the criticism:

> Whatever the reality behind marketing's vaunted contribution to corporate success, the large budgets it has enjoyed for decades are finally beginning to attract attention – even criticism. So much so, in fact, that doubts are surfacing about the very basis of contemporary marketing: the value of ever more costly brand advertising, which often dwells on seemingly irrelevant points of difference; of promotions, which are often just a fancy name for price cutting; and of large marketing departments, which, far from being an asset, are often a millstone around an organization's neck. . . . why does marketing lack direction today? One answer is that the environment has changed so dramatically that marketers are simply not picking up the right signals any more. Past experience is no longer a reliable guide to what today's concerns should be. Marketing has been struggling to respond to several environmental forces that have been at work since the mid-1970s. Of these, none has been more powerful than the rise of retailers.
>
> Marketing departments have become tremendously averse to risk. Despite the accelerating rate of product launches, few genuinely new products are emerging. Of the top 50 brands in the United Kingdom, for example, only nine have been introduced in the past 18 years.
>
> Fairly or unfairly, many consumer goods CEOs are beginning to think that marketing is no longer delivering.
>
> Marketers need also to develop a deeper understanding of the details of the consumer goods value chain. This involves purchasing, logistics, and key features of the buying process, where new technologies (such as EPOS systems) and new market research techniques (such as product attribute trade-off analysis) can be used to great effect. In future, what will matter will be the ability to under-

stand the behaviour of consumers both at the moment of purchase and during consumption; the flexibility to make trade-offs within a company's business system; and the determination to make a proactive response to retailers' strategies.

It is clear that many of today's marketers may not make it. In some companies, CEOs are already reorganizing marketing to reflect the increasing priority of product innovation. Elida Gibbs, Unilever UK's personal care division, is testing a new approach: marketing directors no longer have advertising, sales and promotion as their primary responsibilities. Innovation and product improvement take precedence instead. In fact, there will not be a marketing director in future. The reformulated role will carry the title of brand development director.

Among others, Procter & Gamble has introduced the concept of category management, which combines the management of all brands in the same segment to ensure greater coherence in strategy. In the era of marketing now emerging, new divisions may be needed to separate tactical from strategic activities, just as there is likely to be a rethink about which aspects of marketing are best handled from the center, and which on a devolved or local basis.

Some marketing practices are certain to need reform. One approach is to treat marketing as a process, rather than as a department. Here the organization is not divided by function – into marketing, sales, and production – but by its core processes, such as brand development and delivery system fulfilment. Under this structure, key issues can be tackled wherever they occur, rather than being stalled between functional boundaries (John Brady and Ian Davis (1993), 'Marketing's Mid Life Crisis', *McKinsey Quarterly*, 2, 17–28).

From another source, recently published:

Our survey of managing directors and marketing directors within large FMCG, retail and service sector organisations concludes that marketing departments are simply not fulfilling this role.

Marketing as a discipline is more vital than ever, marketing as a department is increasingly failing to match up to expectations. The marketing department is critically ill; only urgent treatment will enable it to fulfil the role that is now clearly staked out in the minds of top management.

- Marketing departments undertake an ill-defined mixture of activities. . .
- Marketing departments have been over-indulged. . .
- Marketing departments rarely lead the drive to enhance business performance. . .
- Marketing departments are often too short-sighted. . .
- Marketing departments are being marginalised. . .
- Marketing directors and managing directors disagree. . .
- Marketing directors overestimate their contribution. . .

But at the beginning of the '90s two things happened. Firstly, with the onset of the recession, the very conditions which led to the growth of marketing departments rapidly disappeared.

Segmentation, exemplified by 'lifestyle' marketing failed to sustain profitability and recession focused attention on harder, more accountable concepts. Long-term expansion and planning was replaced by short-termism and the demand for immediate sales results.

Secondly, the new business environment made the classical role of marketing (identifying and meeting of customer needs) even more crucial to company success.

Product life cycles continued to shorten . . . . Markets continued to segment . . . .

Conclusions:

The emerging picture of marketing departments is ominous.
They are not responsible for any outputs: for example, they are responsible for the development of advertising, but not for the strategy on which it is based. They are not responsible for the generation of sales revenues at the sharp end, although they are supposed to support this process (see Figure I.1).

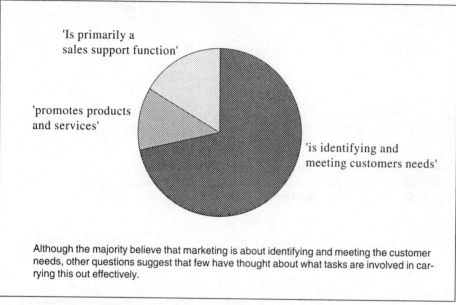

'Is primarily a
sales support function'

'promotes products
and services'

'is identifying and
meeting customers needs'

Although the majority believe that marketing is about identifying and meeting the customer needs, other questions suggest that few have thought about what tasks are involved in carrying this out effectively.

Figure I.1   What is the role of marketing in your organization?

Marketing departments are fundamentally a spending function. Caught in a period of cost-saving and redundancies, they have few roles that are uniquely their own or decisions which fall clearly within their remit.

Marketing directors overestimate the contribution of marketing departments to key business activities which should underpin all marketing plans. *Marketing at the Crossroads*, Coopers and Lybrand, 1994).

Some comments on the organizational reality of the 1980s:

The new organizations emphasized partnerships between firms; multiple types of ownership and partnering within the organization (divisions, wholly owned subsidiaries, licensees, franchisees, joint ventures, etc.); teamwork among members of the organization, often with team members from two or more co-operating firms; sharing of responsibility from developing converging and overlapping technologies; and often less emphasis on formal contracting and managerial reporting, evaluation, and control systems. The best visual image of these organizations may be a wheel (see Figure I.2) instead of a pyramid, where the spokes are 'knowledge links' between a core organization at the hub and strategic partners around the rim (Badaracco 1991). These forms were pioneered in such industries as heavy construction, fashion, weapon systems contracting, and computers, where markets often span geographic boundaries, technology is com-

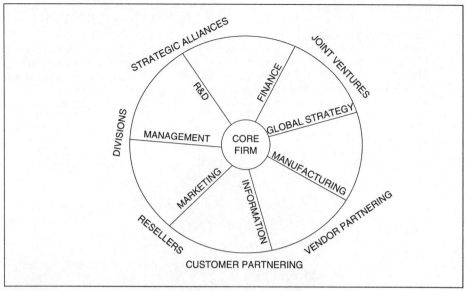

Figure I.2   Network organizations

plex, products change quickly, and doing everything yourself is impossible. Such organizations today are found in businesses as diverse as glass, chemicals, hospital supplies, book publishing, and tourism.

They depend on administrative processes but they are not hierarchies (Thorelli 1989); they engage in transactions within ongoing relationships and depend on negotiation, rather than market-based processes, as a principal basis for conducting business and determining prices, though market forces almost always influence and shape negotiation. The purpose of these new organization forms is to respond quickly and flexibly to accelerating change in technology, competition, and customer preferences (F.E. Webster (1992)), 'The Changing Role of Marketing in the Corporation', *Journal of Marketing*, October, 4,5,9).

Let me quote again, this time from Regis McKenna's book *Relationship Marketing,* a passage that begins to explore the new agenda:

not a 'do more' marketing that simply turns up the volume on the sales spiels of the past but a knowledge- and experience-based marketing that represents the once-and-for-all death of the salesman . . .

These two fundamentals, knowledge-based and experience-based marketing, will increasingly define the capabilities of a successful marketing organization. . .

Knowledge-based marketing requires a company to master a scale of knowledge: of the technology in which it competes, of its competition, of its customers; of new sources of technology that can alter its competitive environment; and of its own organization, capabilities, plans, and way of doing business. Armed with this mastery, companies can put knowledge-based marketing to work in three essential ways: integrating the customer into the design process to guarantee a product that is tailored not only to the customers' needs and desires but also to the customers' strategies; generating niche thinking to use the company's knowledge of channels and markets to identify segments of the market the company can own; and developing the infrastructure of suppliers, vendors, partners, and users whose relationships will help sustain the company's reputation and technological edge...

The other half of this new marketing paradigm is experience-based marketing, which emphasizes interactivity, connectivity, and creativity. With this approach, companies spend time with their customers, constantly monitor their competitors, and develop a feedback-analysis system that turns this information about the market and the competition into important new product intelligence...

It is a fundamental shift in the role and purpose of marketing: from manipulation of the customer to genuine customer involvement; from telling and selling to communicating and sharing knowledge; from last-in-line function to corporate-credibility champion...

Successful companies realize that marketing is like quality, integral to the organization. Like quality, marketing is an intangible that the customer must experience to appreciate...

We are witnessing the obsolescence of advertising. In the old model of marketing, it made sense as part of the whole formula: you sell mass-produced goods to a mass market through mass media...

First, advertising overkill has started to ricochet back on advertising itself... The second growth development in advertising's decline is an outgrowth of the first: as advertising has proliferated and become more obnoxiously insistent, consumers have gotten fed up...

The underlying reason behind both of these factors is advertising's dirty little secret: it serves no useful purpose. In today's market, advertising simply misses the fundamental point of marketing – adaptability, flexibility, and responsiveness. The new marketing requires a feedback loop; it is this element that is missing from the monologue of advertising but that is built into the dialogue of marketing. The feedback loop, connecting company and customer, is central to the operating definition of a truly market-driven company: a company that adapts in a timely way to the changing needs of the customer.

The line between products and services is fast eroding. What once appeared to be a rigid polarity now has become a hybrid: the servicization of products and the productization of services (Regis McKenna, *Relationship Marketing*, Addison Wesley, 1991).

These highly critical comments suggest that we urgently need to draw up an agenda for change.

THE AGENDA FOR CHANGE

Here follows an attempt to draw up such an agenda:

Customers

(Consumers, business end-users, and distributors are included in this category.)

1 How do customers define value and satisfaction? Do we have access to any methodology that really explores these issues?
2 From what base do you build customer loyalty?
3 How do customers trade off quality and price?

4 Can you any longer reach customers by mass advertising?
5 What implications does globalization have for local identity? Does local identity have any meaning in a world of global brands?

Markets

1 Have we begun to understand the implications for markets of the information based, post-industrial society?
2 Market saturation is a common characteristic of Western developed economies, too many goods and services chasing too few discretionary spending customers – can marketers find solutions to this problem?
3 Too few discretionary spending customers – is this the beginnings of bipolar society, with high-income knowledge workers as a small minority, surrounded by a low-income proletariat?
4 If markets are dominated by global producers and/or distributors, will there be any space for small- and medium-sized enterprises?

Technology

The convergence of computing and telecoms may have far-reaching results.

1 Will there be a dominance of direct marketing at the expense of national advertising?
2 Efficiency drives in producing companies may result in real-time productivity analysis exposing unprofitable products, customers and outlets. Will outlets quickly de-list unprofitable brands?
3 Customer-based market analysis may have a redundancy risk for data-based analysis (based on aggregate census data). Will lifestyle analysis come to dominate consumer market analysis?
4 The distance between suppliers and their customers may be reduced by way of electronic data interchange, electronic mail, voice mail, video conferencing and videophone. Who will become the communicators?
5 If cable reaches 25 per cent of the estimated 50 per cent of all UK households with satellite/cable (expected by AD 2000), then interactive marketing, voting, home shopping and game playing will touch a significant proportion of all householders. Who will be the interaction managers?
6 New product development and testing will have new interactive/response mechanisms. What are the implications for co-designing and co-makership? Where does marketing fit in?

Communications

Technology is already revolutionizing both information access and communications.

6 1 What are the marketing implications of interactive marketing – dealing

directly with the human face of the customer? Multimedia is the human face of electronic information!

2   The advertising industry is showing the same globalizing tendencies as manufacturing. What are the implications for marketing of a global oligopoly in advertising – eight or ten world conglomerate communications companies?

Distribution

The concentration of ownership in UK distribution raises a number of questions.

1   Has the rise of retailer power begun the process of destroying national brands? Is brand management, which in the past has been the apprenticeship route of many marketing directors, coming to the end of its life?
2   Will competitive advantage lie with those marketing organizations that are really close to the customer, i.e. retailers?
3   Will retailer brands and corporate brands dominate markets?

Marketing organization

Is the current criticism of marketing due to all (or some) of the following factors?

1   A failure to distinguish between the marketing concept and marketing function.
2   A failure to decide whether marketing is a holistic concept or a specialist subject.
3   A failure to see that the only thing that really matters is that strategic thinking is dominated by marketing imperatives.
4   A failure to match the claims of finance and manufacturing/engineering/research and development in respect of sovereignty over boardroom decision making.
5   A failure to discern that marketing and sales are inseparable.
6   A failure to understand that internal marketing must precede external marketing.
7   A failure to realize/understand that the marketing concept is the only strategic vision that can forge value-added relationships with customers, employees and suppliers.

RECENT RESEARCH

Recent research by the Cranfield School of Management, commissioned by the Chartered Institute of Marketing (*Marketing: The Challenge of Change,* 1994), sets down a marker in terms of where we are now:

- Academics strongly reject the claim that marketing is failing as a discipline.
- Finally marketing has become accepted as a dominant business philosophy.
- Implementation of the philosophy has proved the largest stumbling block of recent years.
- The hierarchical, functional nature of organizational structures has severely hindered its uptake till now.
- As companies restructure around core processes, it gives them greater opportunity to become customer-oriented.
- Given the challenges that businesses currently face, companies are placing greater emphasis on developing and strengthening relationships with customers.
- They are also becoming more future- and innovation-driven.
- At the operational level, marketing is becoming more sophisticated in the ways in which markets are evaluated and market performance is being assessed.
- Marketing is becoming more accountable for its actions and expenditure.
- Marketers need to become more professional in the tasks that they perform and need to develop their own skill base.

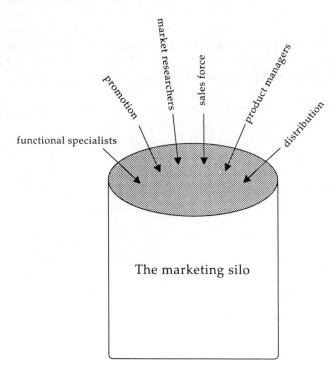

Figure I.3   The functional silo

THE CHALLENGES AHEAD

It is not my intention here to detail the changing environment; it is necessary however, to stress some dimensions of this environment, since these dimensions will most certainly dictate the future nature of our profession. Figure I.3 indicates how historically, talented and frequently well-trained people have been poured in the marketing silo, which is where marketing power has traditionally resided.

Marketers have, in some respects, become the victims of their own success. If we differentiate between the marketing concept and the function of marketing, there is evidence that senior management in most British companies have at last absorbed the concept. Companies have understood that they must be market-driven, hence everyone in the company (or organization) must be market driven. Thus the ownership of the ideological resource known as marketing knowledge now extends beyond the marketing specialism (function) and threatens to dissolve its distinctiveness and its identity.

I believe, however, and the Cranfield research supports my belief, that corporate management, though claiming to understand the marketing concept, still confuses trappings with substance. The new marketing weapon places marketing alongside finance and operations, and drives the desire to be close to customers (Figure I.4). Further, I believe that accountants, and the finance function in general, engineers and the operations function in general, and human resources managers, neither fully understand, share nor endorse the marketing concept. Ask any of them if they know how to segment a market, and why it should be done! How many accountants monitor not just budgeted profit and return on investment targets, but performance at product line and market level?

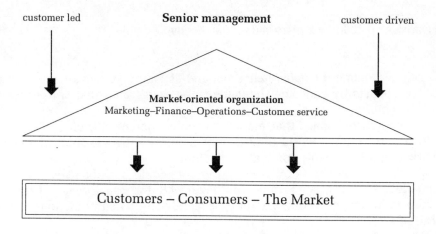

Figure I.4   The new weapon

Thus, the challenge facing our profession is to demonstrate, both within the corporation and at the highest political levels, that we are not only masters of our information-based technology, but that the precise skills of marketing, namely planning, logistics and creativity, based on superior understanding of the market place, of market forces, and the need to deliver superior value, are the crucial foundation for future corporate survival and success.

We can demonstrate that in the current global market, marketing strategy is primary. We should set the course. As Figure I.5 illustrates, market analysis defines objectives, hence sets the course.

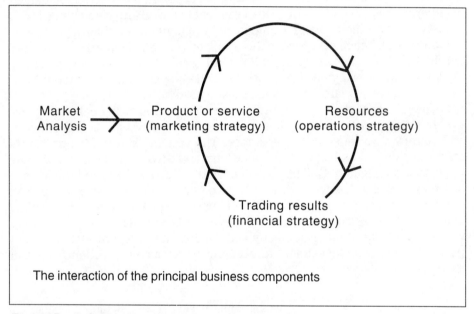

Figure I.5   Defining objectives and setting the course

We should define the value delivered, and as Figure I.6 demonstrates, value delivery starts by choosing the value to be delivered – that is a marketing responsibility.

We should recognize that market relationships are changing (Figure I.7), and that the simple world of transactions is evolving and that relationship marketing will probably dominate in the future.

We must however, recognize that our role could be subsumed within the imperatives of strategy formulation. Figure I.8, the usual image of the new organization, suggests that marketing is merely one of many functions, with no lead role.

The strategic environment we will face will need to embrace such concepts as those that appear in the right-hand column, not in the left-hand column, shown in Figure I.9.

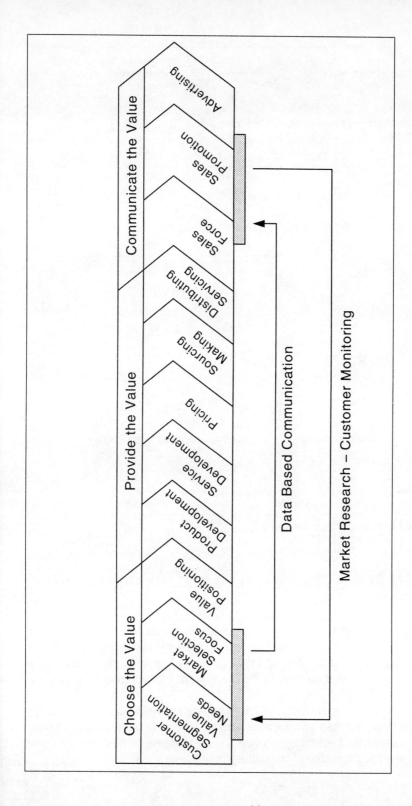

Figure I.6   The value delivery sequence

11

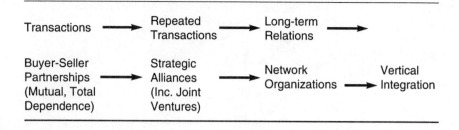

Figure I.7   The range of marketing relationships
Source: F.E .Webster (1992).
This figure should not be seen to imply that vertical integration is the ultimate goal.

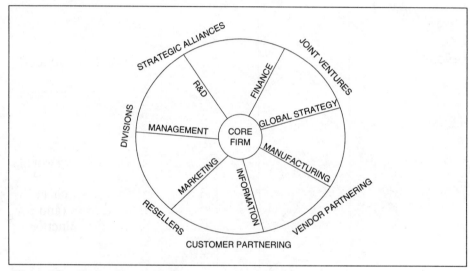

Figure I.8   Network organizations

WHAT MARKETERS NEED TO DO TO BECOME MORE PROFES-SIONAL

1   We need to come to terms with finance. We need to be able to argue effectively with the accountancy profession to persuade them that profit is not merely the bottom line but the residual effect of successful dealing with customers, and that most marketing activities are an investment, not a cost.

2   We need to demonstrate that we are the professional experts in respect of marketing information and, as a consequence, we must come to terms with Information Technology, since we are the people best equipped to exploit the facilities that IT capability provides.

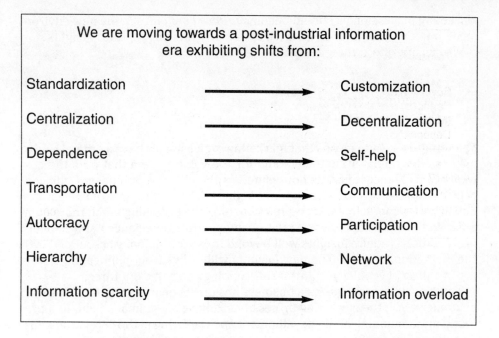

We are moving towards a post-industrial information
era exhibiting shifts from:

Standardization	Customization
Centralization	Decentralization
Dependence	Self-help
Transportation	Communication
Autocracy	Participation
Hierarchy	Network
Information scarcity	Information overload

Figure I.9   Post-industrial information era

3   We must play an active role in driving TQM, since TQM can only work in
a customer driven culture.
4   We must think strategically, from the top, and recognize that in the
future companies will be structured according to customers (and perhaps customers' customers), not to product, geography or function as
has been traditional.

Marketing has a reputation which, let us be willing to admit, is not always to
our advantage. Indeed it must be said that we will not become more professional until we address these issues. Our critics will argue that markets are
organized for purposes of exploitation not fulfilment, that marketing as a function does not possess a monopoly of understanding human wants and values,
that *'marketing's rapacious orientation to consumer needs is more plausibly
attributed to the dynamics of capitalism than it is to the development and application of marketing expertise'*. If marketing remains associated with hype and
manipulation, we will have a problem.

MARKET MARKETING!!

As a profession we have an unparalleled opportunity. We must demonstrate
by our professionalism that we are crucial to the development of the economy.
    We must be much more forceful in transmitting our professional knowledge.   *13*

Marketing professionals should become *primus inter pares* in the new environment, but it will not happen if we fail to demonstrate our superior insights.

We can operate at three levels:

- Marketing as culture.
- Marketing as strategy.
- Marketing as tactics.

Marketing as culture means that marketing professionals have a critical role to play as advocates for customers and for the value system that puts the customer first. The customer is not defined as the ultimate purchaser – the concept of internal and external marketing defines the customer as any downstream contact. Marketing relationships are becoming much more complex, and mutual dependency relationships, strategic alliances and network organizations require insights well beyond those traditionally associated with the marketing function. The new insights will derive from political economy, organization psychology, cultural anthropology, to name but three.

The most important assets a business has are its ongoing relationships with customers. We, the marketing professionals, have a legitimate claim to a profound understanding of the development and nurturing of those relationships. Though increasingly it is claimed that everyone in the corporation must be charged with this responsibility, understanding it and interpreting it is the domain of the marketing professional.

Marketing has a powerful rhetoric; we do not lack ideological materials. It is more than a set of techniques for the management of external markets. Our flexible ideology, well disposed to coping with change, would however, be hijacked by others, for quite different purposes.

If however, we are to challenge the hegemony of the accounting profession we must strengthen our own professional body. We must improve our reputation as a knowledge generator, through strategic linkages and alliances with leading-edge knowledge generators.

We expect that an increasing number of recruits to the marketing profession will be university graduates – the source of most brand managers in fmcg companies. These graduates will find that brand management will be modified or disappear altogether, a victim of changing marketing relationships. Replaced by project management, by account management, by market management, by direct mail management? The only constant will be change. These new managers will constantly need both new marketing knowledge and a range of managerial skills – particularly financial, human resource and IT skills.

More urgently perhaps, marketing managers must recognize that in addition to high standards of objectivity, integrity and technical competence, they must, in responding to the changing environment, demonstrate that they can and will serve society in general. This requires clear and articulate demonstration of their ability to be relevant in the political sense. Accountants have been successful in part because they have been so obviously servants of Anglo-Saxon capitalism with its historical focus on finance. Though here may not be the correct forum to discuss this, we could develop an argument that this historic focus has served us poorly in competition with the Japanese. In the global economy, and in the face of the competitive forces within it, it is the company and the country that delivers value to the market-place that will survive. If marketing remains tied to the forces of manipulation and hype, if it is seen merely to be the servant of capitalist masters, it will remain marginal and untrustworthy. If it can demonstrate that it has the keys to the knowledge base that will benefit society as a whole, then the marketing profession may prosper. The profession must carry that message into the corridors of power.

Part 1
DEVELOPING A MARKETING STRATEGY

1 Information systems for marketing

Tim Bowles

When I wrote this chapter for the previous edition some four years ago, it was necessary to preface my remarks by saying:

> The scope of marketing information systems, and the interest in these systems has certainly grown in the 1980s, driven by the availability of more information and by the development of computer techniques for its manipulation. Much of the available information is, however, still difficult for market management to use effectively, without considerable computer skills.

At the time of writing many companies produced all their management information on mainframe computers. The primary functions of these computers were payroll, financial analysis and stock control. Marketing data were often included but took second place when competing for overloaded computer resources.

A dramatic change has taken place over the past four years. Market research suppliers are making increasing use of electronic means for data collection and transmission, information on supermarket sales being available within a few days of collection. Marketing statistics on tape or disk are replacing traditional printed reports. In marketing led companies, product managers now have personal computers on their desks, and can employ user-friendly, menu driven programmes to gain instant access to information as it comes in. Cheap processing power has liberated the data user from past restrictions on speed of processing and data storage. (One of my own company's services uses a disc of 700 megabyte capacity which provides 20 years of product data for trend analysis).

One is tempted to report that the marketer and planner can now have easy access to all the information they require, but the reality is not so simple. We appear to be reaching a situation where the sheer volume of information creates problems in itself. The challenge for the 90s will be to manage this information for the effective support of marketing decisions.

MARKETING DATA SOURCES

A wide variety of types of data can be useful to marketing management. Sources include both textual and statistical material, which may originate from inside or from outside the company. The information may be general in nature, with relevance to broad strategic issues, or it may be quite specific and be applied in day-to-day decisions about pricing, distribution, and promotional spend.

Some of the main data sources are described in the following paragraphs.

Desk research

Readers starting with few facts on their market should not despair. There is much information available, often for little more than the cost of a phone call. Trade associations, such as the Brewers Society or the Institute of Grocery Distribution, often publish summary statistics to help their members and these are also available to other users. The Central Statistical Office publishes regular UK social and business statistics, price trends, and indices of production for products as diverse as spectacles, railway engines and surgical appliances. The London Business School Information Service covers a wider geographical spread, with topics as diverse as 'Stats. on the States' and financial data on Finnish companies.

If your information needs are more specific and detailed, assessments of individual markets are produced from time to time by Mintel International, the Economist Intelligence Unit and Euromonitor. These assessments are usually based upon published statistics, trade interviews and, sometimes, specially commissioned market research. Providing you can find a recently compiled report on your market, this type of broad market assessment can be very useful for strategic planning purposes.

Internal company data

Leading marketing companies now place great emphasis on providing internal data on product performance. The scope of internal marketing information will vary widely both between different industries and between different companies in the same industry. Internal marketing data should in most cases cover at least the following types of report:

1 Sales levels – national and by sales territory.
2 Revenue, cost and profit performance of product lines or brands.
3 Comparison of revenue and costs with budget.
4 Seasonal indices of product sales.
5 Stock and distribution levels among major customers (both wholesale and retail).
6 Product warranty returns.
7 Customer complaint analysis.
8 Marketing and advertising cost reports.

The pace of development in market information systems has nowhere been more evident than in the growth of internal company databases. This growth has been accelerated both by the spread of PCs and by the increasing capacity and power of decision-support systems, which are described in a later section of this chapter.

Market measurement

Market measurement is perhaps the most vital kind of external information for the marketing department. Whereas internal data can tell us a great deal about the performance of our own products, external data are required to tell us how our own performance measures up against that of our competitors and to give us clues on how we might improve our performance through product development, distribution, pricing and promotion. There are many sources of market measurement data, each with its own strengths and weaknesses. Each method will provide information on market size, product or brand share, prices paid and retail structure of sales. This information helps manufacturers to monitor their own market performance and the effect of their marketing strategies. It also forms a basis for negotiation between manufacturer and retailer, as manufacturers compete for shelf space in stores. The main methods of data collection are described below.

Retail audits

Retail audits involve the measurement of markets via retail sales. Retail audit interviewers call regularly at a representative sample of retail outlets to record information on consumer sales offtake, retail purchases and stocks, distribution, and retail selling prices. This information can be aggregated statistically to give total market estimates and can be analysed nationally and by region. The strength of retail audit data lies in their coverage of stock and distribution, and the fact that they do not rely upon consumers recording or remembering what they have bought. Such data cannot, of course, tell one anything about the people who buy the goods which are sold.

   In the UK the provision of retail audit information has been led for many years by the A. C. Nielsen Company which offers retail audit measurements covering groceries, drugs, alcoholic drinks, tobacco and other products.

Consumer panels

The main alternative method of measuring consumer markets. Until the late 1980s panel members, recruited to be representative of the buying population, either kept a diary of their purchases across a number of product fields or retained packs as evidence of these purchases, to be collected regularly by market research interviewers. The availability of portable barcode scanners has revolutionized data collection from consumer panels in recent years. The modern panel member now records purchases electronically, by reading the *21* barcodes on products he or she has bought with a scanning 'wand', or entering information on purchases which are not barcoded via a small keyboard. Purchase information is stored in the scanner memory and transmitted to the research company's computers by telephone, overnight. Accuracy and speed of availability of market reports have therefore been radically improved. The sample data from consumer panels are, like those from retail audits, grossed up statistically to give total market estimates in terms of product volume and expenditure.

A special strength of consumer panels is that the same people are monitored over time. This means that market trends can be tracked very accurately and individual consumer purchasing behaviour can be tracked through time. Analysis of panel data can throw light on such issues as the customer profile for different products and brands, brand share variation between different retail outlets, brand switching, and the rate at which new products penetrate the buying population. The markets measured by consumer panels include groceries, consumer durables, toiletries, cosmetics, fresh foods, alcoholic drinks and motoring expenditure.

Consumer panel market measurement is carried out in the UK by Taylor Nelson AGB. More recently Nielsen has also started to provide consumer panel data to complement its retail data services, and to enable its clients to analyse detailed consumer behaviour.

Industry data pools

Industry data pools involve the collection of information on sales volumes via trade associations or other groups of manufacturers. By pooling their internal data on product sales, for analysis by an independent statistical agency, each member of the manufacturing group can compare its own sales volume against that of other members. While such information is useful, it is generally not capable of detailed analysis and is restricted by the level of participation among significant manufacturers. Data pooling arrangements do not normally permit the separate identification of individual manufacturer performance. Each participating manufacturer can therefore compare his own data only against the total market, rather than against individual competitors.

Retail scanning

Retail scanning of the barcodes printed on the majority of packaged products has become increasingly important in the provision of market measurement information. The introduction of EPOS (electronic point of sale) equipment at supermarket check-outs has opened new possibilities for market measurement, at a level of precision which has hitherto been impossible. Access to UK scanner data from retailer check-outs is controlled via the ANA (Article Numbering Association) which represents manufacturers' and retailers' interests. With bar codes covering an ever-increasing range of products, faster and more accurate data on consumer purchases are becoming available. In the UK, in 1993, 74 per cent of grocery spend could be scanned. This was expected to rise to 80 per cent in 1995. Nielsen's grocery Scantrack already provides weekly sales data which permit the prompt evaluation of tactical marketing campaigns. During the 1990s scanner data is almost certain to replace the traditional retail audit, as the main means of market measurement at the retail level.

The user of market measurement information may be puzzled by multiple sources of what is apparently the same information. In practice, each market measurement source will produce slightly different market size estimates because of the different data collection method employed. An account of these variations and how they may be reconciled can be found in Bowles and Blyth (1985).

Media audience measurement

Consumer goods manufacturers spend large amounts of money on media advertising and need to evaluate the effectiveness of this spending, in terms of the audience their advertising reaches. Media audience data tend to be handled, on behalf of manufacturers, by their advertising agencies. There is a good reason for this in that the advertising agencies are generally responsible for buying advertising time and space. Information on the audience levels for different media, and the structure of these audiences, is essential in media planning and provides a basis on which advertising time and space can be bought and sold.

Marketing departments in some leading manufacturing companies do themselves become involved in the analysis of audience data. In any event, executives concerned in marketing management will need a broad understanding of the source and uses of audience data, even if these data are not formally incorporated into their market information systems.

In the UK, audience measurement for the different media is usually controlled by bodies which represent media owners, advertising agencies and the leading manufacturing companies. These bodies lay down the technical specification for audience measurement and act as a channel for sharing the cost of collecting and analysing audience information. The principal audience measurement services and their controlling organizations are:

1 Television – BARB (Broadcasters' Audience Research Board).
2 Press and magazines – NRS (The National Readership Surveys) and JICREG (The Newspaper Society).
3 Radio – RAJAR (Radio Joint Audience Research).
4 Posters – OSCAR (Outdoor Advertising Association).
5 Cinema – CAVIAR (Cinema Advertising Association).

The actual task of audience measurement is awarded, through the controlling organizations, to market research companies which undertake to meet the technical requirements laid down. Access to the data is obtained via subscrip-   *23* tion to the governing body. Addresses for these organizations are provided at the end of this chapter.

Single-source surveys of markets and media

Single-source surveys of markets and media are also a key source of information for market and media planning. Market measurement services and media audience measurement are normally conducted through quite separate data collection exercises. They offer no facility to relate people's purchasing habits to media exposure. This facility is provided in the UK by the TGI (Target Group Index) single-source survey carried out and marketed by BMRB International. It offers a unique opportunity to target media advertising so that it reaches users of particular products or brands. This is possible because people's product usage patterns can be cross-analysed with their reading, TV viewing, and radio listening habits, since both kinds of information are collected from the same survey respondents.

While the industry-controlled audience-research studies provide continuous and detailed information on exposure to a single medium, TGI provides less detailed information but covers the whole range of media. It is therefore widely used in media selection and the planning of advertising campaigns. TGI covers special samples of up-market consumers and children, as well as the main adult sample.

Magazines and the press

Magazines, and the daily and weekly press, are also important sources of marketing information. The trade press, in particular, provides a valuable source of competitive intelligence covering all aspects of marketing activity from brand launches to advertising campaigns for existing brands. The financial press and the financial pages of the daily press provide valuable reports on competitive activity.

In the past, companies have had a choice between maintaining their own press-cutting services or employing one of the commercial services which will select material relating to particular topics, products or companies. The development of computerized text-retrieval systems has given rise to commercial services which provide on-line access to computerized databanks drawn from the press. Many of these services are too general for detailed marketing application but a number of database services have been introduced directly aimed at the marketer. These are dealt with at greater length in the section on database services.

Social and economic data

Information on social and economic trends has limited application in the implementation and control of marketing policy. It is much more significant, however, in the stage of strategy development. Important social trends, such as changes in the employment level, increases in the proportion of working housewives and the altering age distribution of the population, all have significant implications for the long-term planning of products and services.

The richest source of such information lies in government statistics and the publications of the Central Statistical Office. A useful overview, which also refers to the major government surveys on which it is based, is the regular HMSO publication, *Social Trends*. This is a unique source for those wishing to keep in touch with the changing profile of our population and associated social conditions.

The CSO Databank contains over 30 000 annual, quarterly and monthly time series from the CSO itself, other government departments and the Bank of England.

Most of the information published by the government statistical services covers behaviour rather than attitudes and, for information on attitudes and values, the marketer must commission his or her own private surveys or identify a suitable source of syndicated survey information. The MONITOR survey, run by Taylor Nelson AGB, is employed by many manufacturing and service companies to track changing consumer values and attitudes over time.

Outside the realm of official statistics there is a wide range of other statistical sources which may prove valuable from time to time. A review of such sources has been compiled by the Statistics Service at the University of Warwick and published as *Sources of Unofficial UK Statistics* (Mort and Siddall, 1990). These sources include trade associations, professional bodies, local authorities, development corporations, and financial and economic forecasting organizations.

Specially commissioned market research

Most of this chapter is concerned with published sources of market information which can be obtained by subscription. The more sophisticated market information systems users will also incorporate their specially commissioned studies in their databanks of information. These privately commissioned studies have a broad coverage which includes product testing, new product development, advertising evaluation and other forms of communication research. Useful directories of companies offering market research services are published both by the Market Research Society and by AMSO, the Association of Market Survey Organizations.

ACCESSING AND MANIPULATING MARKET INFORMATION

Market information in statistical form, both from internal and external sources, has traditionally been published in the form of detailed printed reports. Since many market and audience measurements are analysed and reported on a weekly or monthly basis, this has meant that the information user would quickly accumulate large volumes of data which had to be accessed in the manner of a vast telephone directory. Any special analysis   *25* required had to be requested via specialist data-processing departments, which would then often deliver the analysis long after the management decision, to which the information was relevant, had been taken.

The evolution of computer software in the last 20 or so years has changed all that. Software developments, together with the quite astonishing advance of personal computers, have already begun to have a dramatic impact on the market place.

On-line data systems

On-line access to market and media information has been an active area for development. In such systems, the user obtains access to a central databank of information, held on a central mainframe computer, via a computer terminal and a special enquiry language. These developments were most rapid for media research because of the large volumes of data generated, particularly from TV audience measurement, and because of the need of media planners to estimate the audience reach (how many people saw or heard the advertising) and frequency of advertising exposure achieved by different media schedules. This led to the development of commercial on-line services which offered their subscribers access to most of the main media audience databanks. Such on-line systems are offered in the UK by IMS, Donovan Data Systems and Telmar, amongst others.

Recent developments have concentrated on easier and faster retrieval of such information and have used the benefits of personal computers to achieve this. Instead of holding large databases on central computers, thereby creating the need for expensive and often slow telephone connections, large databases can now be held on a PC, giving the user instant access. The recent advent of CD-ROM has meant that huge numbers of files can now be stored and thus accessed by a PC. Specialist media packages such as BMRB International's CHOICES and comparable systems from Telmar and IMS are taking full advantage of recent technological advances. With the PC market place moving over to graphical interfaces such as Windows, these software packages are no longer exclusively used by data-processing departments and computer boffins.

On-line access to the market measurement databases has been much slower to develop although several leading manufacturing companies have created their own software for the analysis of market measurement data, the data being delivered in computer tape form, rather than printed form, from the company conducting the source research. Many users of market measurement data, however, remain dependent on printed reports. Decision-support systems provide an alternative for those who have not developed bespoke systems themselves.

Decision-support systems

Decision-support systems are computer systems which enable management to access and manipulate data to help them make better decisions. The term is variously used to describe systems ranging from spreadsheets, such as Lotus 123 or Supercalc, to large integrated modelling programs. There are, however, a number of proprietary decision-support systems which are specially designed to assist marketing management. The more sophisticated examples will provide:

1 Terminal or PC access to a central database of internal and external information.
2 Menus or enquiry languages for selecting the desired data from the array and transforming it.
3 Graphics and presentation facilities.
4 Modelling facilities to examine various 'what if' propositions and for forecasting.

ACUSTAR, distributed by MacDonnell Douglas Information Systems, is more directed at marketing decision support than many of the alternatives. It is specifically designed for the interrogation, analysis and reporting of time series data from different marketing information sources.

EXPRESS, distributed by Information Resources Inc. (IRI Software) offers a very wide range of facilities for data analysis and presentation. EXPRESS can be used by executives with varying degrees of data-processing skill, from those who want to select from a simple menu to those who are familiar with programming personal computers. This system also offers an efficient language for the development of tailor-made systems for applications in individual companies.

In the past, decision-support systems of this type have required the storage capacity and power of large minicomputers or mainframe systems. Information Resources has now launched pc EXPRESS, which brings decision support within the reach of a PC user. This is an important development as the mainframe version of EXPRESS has, since its introduction in 1975, been successfully employed by several leading manufacturing companies to structure their market information requirements.

The growing choice of delivery options for information users was reviewed at a recent ESOMAR seminar 'Do new technologies help or hinder decision making'. Interested readers will find details on the major papers among the references and further reading suggestions at the end of this chapter.

Expert systems

Most decision-support systems are designed for the retrieval, analysis and reporting of statistical data. To this extent they impose a relatively structured approach upon the user. Perhaps the most promising development for the future arises from the study of artificial intelligence, the attempt to simulate human thinking processes in a computer. Expert systems use techniques of artificial intelligence to support decisions in complex real-life situations which *27* call upon different kinds of expertise. Expert systems are able to reason and infer, rather than simply store and analyse statistics.

These systems work by combining a databank of information in a subject area with rules of thumb which enable conclusions to be drawn. These rules of thumb are normally developed by programming into the computer the views and judgements of recognized experts in the field. This approach allows a company to maximize the value of the experience and judgement of senior executives, by programming the rules and methods which they use to make decisions into computer software, which can then be used to support decisions by less skilled executives.

Expert systems are distinguished from decision-support systems by their inclusion of rules for decision making and by the fact that they are interrogated in something approaching natural language, rather than through a structured menu of analyses, or a complex computer language. Kastiel (1987) gives some interesting examples of the development of expert systems for various marketing applications, including customer need assessment, financial modelling, direct marketing, pricing and telemarketing. Davis (1986) provides a useful review of how expert systems are assembled and gives concrete examples of two marketing applications. Morgan and Bond (1989) reviewed artificial intelligence and its application.

Developments in AI (Artificial Intelligence) and ES (Expert Systems) are likely to be rapid and impinge on marketing and market research. Already, in the UK, manufacturers such as H.J. Heinz, and retailers such as the Iceland Frozen Food group, amongst many other major companies, use EDI (Electronic Data Interchange) to process invoices automatically and to trigger stock transfers automatically once certain pre-agreed criteria are met.

GEODEMOGRAPHICS AND MARKET ANALYSIS

Geodemographics and their application in market analysis provide an information source of increasing importance to marketing companies. Market analysis is based upon the very reasonable proposition that people's purchasing and product usage behaviour is strongly related to the kind of neighbourhood in which they live. Geodemographics provide a systematic method of classifying residential neighbourhoods.

Most geodemographic systems are based upon the small-area statistics which are generated from the census and other government surveys. Geodemographic analysis involves the manipulation of this information to develop a topology of neighbourhoods, characterized by the type of housing and other characteristics of the area.

The best known, and still the most widely used geodemographic system is ACORN (A Classification Of Residential Neighbourhoods). This system, developed by CACI, clusters neighbourhoods into a series of types, based on census information.

There are now a number of competing market analysis systems in the UK, the most directly competitive being PINPOINT. A special feature of the PIN-POINT system is its computerization of the Ordnance Survey system, which provides a highly accurate geographic location for each individual address within neighbourhood types. The recent publication of the 1991 UK census has enabled all companies to both update their products and develop new variants.

The early applications of geodemographics were in direct mail, where there was an obvious opportunity to improve the efficiency of mailshots by sending only to those addresses where the occupants were likely to be interested in the product being promoted. More recently, the approach has been adopted by retailers, who recurrently face the task of locating new stores in those areas where they have the highest chance of attracting their target customers. The site location potential of market analysis systems has also been exploited by the clearing banks, by local authorities and by public utilities, again using the data to optimize the location of outlets and resources in relation to consuming households. A useful review of ACORN, PINPOINT and alternative market analysis systems has been carried out by Garrett (1987).

The whole subject of geodemographic systems is dealt with in detail in Chapter 28.

DATA FUSION

The 1980s saw the growth of a completely new way of exploiting databases. Through statistical fusion, information contained in two separate databases can be cross-analysed as if it belonged to a single database. The process depends upon statistical modelling, based upon known characteristics of the members of each database, to 'marry' any individual in one database to the person most similar in the other database. The matching process may be based upon such obvious characteristics as age, sex, occupational grade and upon less obvious characteristics such as TV viewing habits or shopping behaviour. The creation of the fused database avoids the need to collect any new information and provides a new way to create single-source data.

The methodology of data fusion is still short of general acceptance among database users but some successful examples exist. BMRB's Target Group Index has been fused with the BARB television audience measurement ratings (see section on media audience measurement). Another example is MAI's fusion of its Financial Research Services survey with the National Readership Survey.

As confidence in the use of data fusion grows, the opportunity will be opened to increase the value of any individual database by linking it with others.

GENERAL MARKETING DATABASES

Decision-support systems, such as EXPRESS and ACUMEN, are primarily designed for the storage, manipulation and presentation of statistical marketing information. Since 1980 there has been a proliferation of on-line database services which offer search and retrieval of information in text form. This information may be drawn from the general or specialist press or from published market research reports. While many database services are extremely general in nature, some are particularly aimed at marketing management.

TEXTLINE, distributed by Finsbury Data Services, began as a general press and magazine database. It now offers a specialist database for marketing, media and retailing. Two significant competitors for TEXTLINE have been launched: MAGIC, distributed by Datasolve, and MAID, distributed by Mail Systems.

MAGIC is targeted at the advertising and marketing business, and claims to contain the complete text of hundreds of newspapers, magazines, research reports and specialist data. MAID offers more signposting to the user, the information being structured into a series of report types. MAID is particularly distinguished by its inclusion of Jordan's company profiles and topline market data from A.C. Nielsen. All four databases include advertising expenditure analysis from Register MEAL, the most widely used source of this information.

SUMMARY

There is no shortage of information for marketing management. The problem is to select the most useful from a diverse array of external data sources and to integrate this with internal information to provide support for marketing decisions. The best current way to achieve this integration is to employ one of the proprietary decision-support systems which have been designed with the needs of marketing management in mind. In this way it will be possible to provide a framework to access internal data, market measurement data, media audience data and information on social and economic trends, which can be included in the database. In addition to historic reporting on market data, these systems offer facilities for modelling and forecasting. In the course of strategic market planning it may also be useful to establish a link with one of the commercial database services which offer search and retrieval of press information, and of some published market and company reports.

Finally, since this is an introductory chapter to the Handbook, perhaps one general word of warning on quality of information should be added. The quality of any information system is only as good as the quality of the data it contains. Before basing marketing decisions on a computerized information system, the user should satisfy himself or herself that data have been properly compiled, with due attention to the reliability of the source and to the statistical reliability of the estimates obtained.

ACKNOWLEDGEMENTS

I would like to acknowledge the invaluable help of Bill Wilson in conducting the research to update this chapter and in drafting possible additions to the text.

REFERENCES

Bowles, T. and Blyth, B. (1985), 'How do you like your data: raw, al dente or stewed?', *European Research*, **13**, (4), October, 170–78.

Central Statistical Office (1993), *'Social Trends'*, London: HMSO.

Davis, E. J. (1986), 'The use of expert systems in marketing', *Proceedings of the ESOMAR Congress*, September, 281–98.

Garrett, A. (1987), 'How to home in on the target market', *Marketing Week*, **10**, (14), May, 57–60.

Kastiel, D. L. (1987), 'Computerized consultants', *Business Marketing*, March, 52–73.

Morgan, R.P. and Bond, J.R. (1989), 'Methods of artificial intelligence – some applications for market research', *Proceedings of The Market Research Society Conference*, March, 49–63.

Mort, D. and Siddall, L. (1990), *Sources of Unofficial UK Statistics*, Aldershot: Gower.

ESSENTIAL READING

Beys, O. and Müller, S. (1992), 'Analysis of retail audit data with expert systems', *ESOMAR seminar*, 'Do new technologies help or hinder marketing decisions', May, 95–112.

Vog, J. (1986), 'Information systems for planning and control', *Management Decision*, **24**, (5), 17–19.

Whitten, P. (1991), 'Using IT to enhance the role of market research', *Journal of The Market Research Society*, **33**, (2), 113–25.

USEFUL ADDRESSES

ANA (Article Numbering Association)
6 Catherine Street
London WC2B 5JJ

Association of Market Survey Organisations Ltd
Fenchurch House
101–111 High Road
South Woodford
London E18 2QP

BMRB International
Hadley House
79–81 Uxbridge Road
London W5 5SU

Broadcasters' Audience Research Board Ltd
Glenthorne House
Hammersmith Grove
London W6 0ND

CACI Ltd
9–62 High Holborn
London WC1V 6DX

Central Statistical Office
Great George Street
London SW1P 3AQ

Cinema Advertising Association
127 Wardour Street
London W21V 4AD

Economist Intelligence Unit
40 Duke Street
London W1M 5DA

ESOMAR
J J Viottastraat 29
1071 JP Amsterdam
The Netherlands

Euromonitor Publications Ltd
87 Turnmill Street
London EC1M 5QU

IRI Software Ltd
Unit 5A
Foundation Park
Roxborough Way
Maidenhead
Berkshire SL6 3WD

London Business School Information Services
Sussex Place
Regents Park
London NW1 4SA

Datasolve Ltd
99 Staines Road West
Sunbury-on-Thames
TW16 7AH

Maid Systems Ltd
18 Dufferin Street
London EC1Y 8PD

The Market Research Society
15 Northburgh Street
London EC1V 9AH

Mintel International Group
18–19 Long Lane
London EC1A 9HE

The National Readership Surveys Ltd
44 Belgrave Square
London SW1X 8QS

The Newspaper Society Ltd
Bloomsbury House
Bloomsbury Square
London WC1B 3DA

A. C. Nielsen Co. Ltd
Nielsen House
London Road
Headington
Oxford OX3 9RX

Outdoor Advertising Association
77 Newman Street
London EC1A 1DX

Pinpoint Analysis Ltd
Tower House
Southampton Street
London WC2E 7HN

Radio Joint Audience Research Ltd
44 Belgrave Square
London SW1X 8QS

Register MEAL
2 Fisher Street
London WC1R 4QA

Taylor Nelson AGB Plc
Taylor Nelson House
44–46 Upper High Street
Epsom
Surrey KT17 4QS

Textline
Finsbury Data Services Ltd
68–73 Carter Lane
London EC4V 5EA

2 The marketing database

Debbie Gorski

The use of information technology (IT) to support sales and marketing activity is one of the most topical issues currently for companies. Faced with increasingly competitive markets, more demanding customers and squeezed margins, organizations need to find new ways to achieve competitive advantage at a profit. Many are realizing that the use of systems to support sales and marketing can help to increase sales, cut costs and enhance customer service and loyalty. At the same time, such systems are relatively new, difficult to specify and develop, and numerous pitfalls exist along the way for the inexperienced. This chapter will help organizations to understand the following:

- What sales and marketing systems are and how they can be used in support of the business.
- What types of systems are available, and the common issues encountered when implementing them.
- What benefits are achievable as a result of successful systems developments.
- The trends and characteristics of the packages and their suppliers in this new, fast-moving market.

The Price Waterhouse Marketing Information Consultancy conducts an annual research survey into the sales and marketing systems market to keep abreast of the changes in the market place and to assist in the production of their annual publication, the *Price Waterhouse Sales and Marketing Software Handbook*. The survey reviews the UK market for sales and marketing software from the suppliers' perspective and questions these companies about their product, their company, their customers and their views on the trends and developments in the market place. This chapter includes some of the findings from the most recent research.

THE NEED FOR MARKETING DATABASES

The sales and marketing function within a company is invariably the last department to be computerized, but growth in this area has been enormous in the last ten years, as organizations have realized the potential benefits that can be achieved through the use of IT as a sales and marketing tool. The recent Price Waterhouse survey found that, despite the recession, most companies consider the marketing database to be a more important business tool than ever before. Figure 2.1 shows the perception of the importance of these systems.

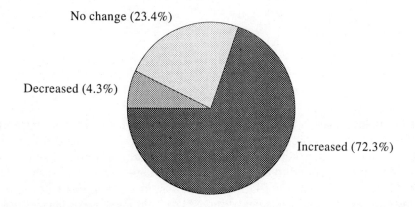

Figure 2.1   Clients' perception of the importance of sales and marketing systems

Marketing databases can now be used to support an enhanced understanding of the market place, your position within it, and the activities of your competitors by capturing data and analysing it in various ways. Customer and prospect databases can be compiled and analysed to give a full picture of the customer's relationship with an organization. Analysis of this aggregated information can help an organization to understand its customers better, segment the customer base and develop product and service offerings which are more tailored to customer needs. On a more tactical level, as customers become more sophisticated and discerning, and one-to-one relationship marketing becomes more important, systems can be used to plan, produce and monitor the effectiveness of more targeted and relevant communications campaigns with customers.

Systems can also be used to reduce costs and improve sales and marketing productivity. One of the most important areas where this is possible is in the management of a field-based sales operation. Systems can be used to help streamline administration, improve sales and profitability through better management of the customer relationship, and increase the productive time that a salesperson can spend actually dealing with customers and prospects.

THE BENEFITS OF MARKETING SYSTEMS

The benefits from using sales and marketing systems can be substantial. Some organizations have experienced productivity improvements exceeding 30 per cent within three months of giving their salesforce laptop computers running sales management software. Other organizations have achieved payback on their system through the incremental sales achieved from their first direct mailing using the new system. Generic business benefits generally fall into two main areas: cost savings and increased sales/profitability. The golden rule is that the marketing database must help you to conduct your sales and marketing activity more profitably, more cost-effectively or in any other quantifiable, successful way. Specific benefits, such as an improved understanding of customer needs, are also possible with particular types of database marketing activity and are explained in more detail below.

Excited by the possibility of such substantial benefits, many organizations are now choosing to develop sales and marketing systems. However, there are many potential pitfalls and problems for the uninitiated in a market that is fast-moving and competitive. There are many examples of organizations who have unsuccessfully attempted sales and marketing systems developments in the mid-1980s and, through inexperience and lack of understanding of what technology was available and how it could be effectively harnessed for use in their own organization, have had to abandon their old systems in favour of investment in more suitable technology. Some of the problems arise from users' lack of experience in using and specifying sales and marketing systems. Other reasons why systems are being replaced are changes in available technology and the emergence of many new software packages to replace bespoke systems.

THE SYSTEMS AVAILABLE

There is no 'best' sales and marketing system available – indeed the enormous range of functions and facilities available in the different systems make the purchase decision very much an individual choice. Many organizations will also find that they need more than one package to meet their needs fully. Some of the different types of functionality available are shown in Figure 2.2 and the typical functions of the main types of system are outlined in more detail below.

The marketing customer database

At the centre of any sales and marketing system is the core repository of data. This database will contain consolidated information on all customers and prospects, and data relating to all marketing and campaign activity. For the purposes of this chapter, the generic title of *customer database* is used. Whether this is a single physical database or a number of integrated systems depends on the specific implementation, but one thing is certain – the data that it contains should be viewed as a single entity and in order to gain the maximum benefit from the information available, it must be possible to obtain

37

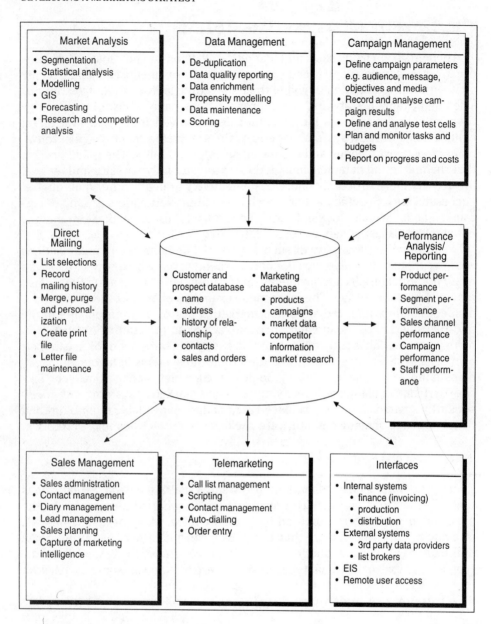

Market Analysis
- Segmentation
- Statistical analysis
- Modelling
- GIS
- Forecasting
- Research and competitor analysis

Data Management
- De-duplication
- Data quality reporting
- Data enrichment
- Propensity modelling
- Data maintenance
- Scoring

Campaign Management
- Define campaign parameters e.g. audience, message, objectives and media
- Record and analyse campaign results
- Define and analyse test cells
- Plan and monitor tasks and budgets
- Report on progress and costs

Direct Mailing
- List selections
- Record mailing history
- Merge, purge and personalization
- Create print file
- Letter file maintenance

- Customer and prospect database
  - name
  - address
  - history of relationship
  - contacts
  - sales and orders
- Marketing database
  - products
  - campaigns
  - market data
  - competitor information
  - market research

Performance Analysis/ Reporting
- Product performance
- Segment performance
- Sales channel performance
- Campaign performance
- Staff performance

Sales Management
- Sales administration
- Contact management
- Diary management
- Lead management
- Sales planning
- Capture of marketing intelligence

Telemarketing
- Call list management
- Scripting
- Contact management
- Auto-dialling
- Order entry

Interfaces
- Internal systems
  - finance (invoicing)
  - production
  - distribution
- External systems
  - 3rd party data providers
  - list brokers
- EIS
- Remote user access

Figure 2.2   Overview of sales and marketing systems

consolidated information on markets and customers from each of the separate physical systems.

Many organizations will not have the need for all of the systems that are shown in Figure 2.2, but it is almost certain that even if they have only one sales and marketing system, it will contain some of the same customer data as another in-house system, often the billing or accounts receivable system.

Although many organizations have not yet managed successfully to combine customer data from various sources in a central sales and marketing system, experience shows that more and more companies are embarking on complex and lengthy projects to deliver powerful integrated customer databases.

Marketing customer database functions

Given that the customer database is the central repository for customer and prospect information, it can be used to perform a number of very useful functions. As Figure 2.2 clearly shows, all sales and marketing applications use the data in the customer database, but there are also some functions which are best delivered as specific features of this system. These include the following:

- Prospect list import. The customer database is the obvious entry point to the sales and marketing systems for information on all externally sourced prospects.
- De-duplication and address verification processing. Along with the other data management capabilities shown in Figure 2.2, these functions identify customers and prospects for whom one or more main record exists and verifies that address details are correct. If the customer database system is the central focus for customer data and it is used as the entry point for prospect information, then it makes sense to do all de-duplication processing using the data on this system.
- Scoring and propensity modelling. The customer database should contain all demographic and behavioural data (for example, purchase and response history in summary form) on all customers and prospects, and is therefore the most suitable application for performing any propensity modelling or score-card techniques.
- Bottom-up market segmentation. The customer database can be designed to contain all of the information required to define primary and secondary segmentation of the market place. With this data it is then possible to measure penetration in a particular segment, identify cross-selling opportunities by examining behaviour of individual customers against their segment and to target direct marketing activity.
- Maintenance of a full customer history. Summaries of all customer contacts that a company may have with customers or prospects should be captured by the feeder systems and sent to the customer database. This will ensure that a single coherent customer history is available on a central system for everyone to use.
- Direct mailing. A key requirement for sophisticated direct mailing activity is that it should be possible to use any part of a customer's history or basic profile data to determine whether they should be included in a particular mail programme. Given this, and the fact that direct mailing functions are generally batch processes when system response times are not critical, it is therefore appropriate to deliver direct mailing functionality using the central customer database. This will allow for sophis-

ticated list generation functions, and will ensure that adequate processing capability exists to create large scale mailing files.

- Reporting. The customer database is the core repository for all data on customers, on sales and marketing activity and on the market place as a whole. It therefore makes most sense for this application to deliver the performance reporting requirements of senior sales and marketing staff, particularly those who tend to be based in the office rather than on the road.

The customer database will therefore act as the main focus for sales and marketing applications. That is not to say that this application has to be in place for other systems to operate successfully, just that it makes most sense to consider the need for a central, co-ordinated customer database at the same time as you plan for the implementation of any other sales and marketing applications.

Marketing customer database implementation issues

The single most important implementation issue in the delivery and maintenance of customer database systems relates to the development and operation of interfaces to and from internal feeder systems. Typically there will be a large number of interfaces and the feeder systems will provide data in a range of different formats. It is also more than likely that the feeder systems will not have been developed with the need for a consolidated picture of customer activity in mind. As a result, the data modelling and database design for a new customer database is likely to be highly complex.

Approximately three-quarters of all sales and marketing packages available are based around a customer database, containing large quantities of data about customers and prospects. However, due to the often complex and unique data needs of some organizations (for example, Price Waterhouse have worked with a number of organizations who need their database to support both business-to-business and consumer marketing activity, often with the same individuals) customer database developments are often bespoke systems. All the risks and issues typically associated with bespoke developments are therefore frequently encountered when a marketing customer database is developed.

Marketing customer database benefits.

The key benefit of a consolidated customer database application is that it provides a single picture of the relationship with a customer or a group of customers. From this single picture of customer activity, it will be possible to develop a much improved understanding of customer and market behaviour and to start to use this to influence sales and marketing activity.

A consistent picture will help to ensure that every member of sales and marketing staff has the same view of individual customers and customer groups. It will also ensure that day-to-day tasks such as direct mailing, customer analysis reporting, prospect list sourcing and de-duplication can all be performed with maximum efficiency. There will be less wastage of poorly targeted mailing packs, reports will be available without the need to manually cross-refer data from a number of systems and the database will contain the minimum number of duplicates.

Sales management systems

One of the more obvious groups of sales and marketing staff who benefit from a system is the salesforce, particularly if they are highly mobile. The effectiveness of the sales operation is one of the most important determining factors in the performance of any organization and, as such, anything that can be done to help the selling process is more likely to deliver tangible benefits.

It is now becoming almost fashionable to consider giving all salespeople a laptop computer and some form of sales management support software. As a result, this is the area in the packaged software market which is currently most advanced. The recent Price Waterhouse survey showed that sales management is the business area that is supported by the widest choice of software, with sales management facilities available in 59 per cent of all packages. Most can operate on laptop personal computers and support communications software which allow remote users to link to the central office system.

Sales management functions

At the centre of any good sales management system is a contact management capability. This function allows a salesperson to record the details of any communication with a customer in standard format and to identify all of the follow-up actions that must be taken as a result of that communication with a customer. The contact management functionality will help in the following ways:

- It will enable a comprehensive picture of historical and future activity with each customer to be built up.
- It will make sure that each salesperson tracks and completes all scheduled actions.
- It will automatically record all of the information that a sales manager requires to monitor the activity of the sales staff and hence remove the need for manual weekly sales reporting activity.

For these functions to operate successfully, the salesperson will need the system to hold full customer information including the following:

- Customer name and address, including details of all subsidiary-to-parent relationships and details of all sites from which the company trades.
- The names of all appropriate contacts (that is, customer employees).

41

- The customer order history, along with details of any service or maintenance contracts.
- Any marketing programmes aimed at the customer and how they responded.
- Any known competitor activity with the customer.
- Any non-sales interaction with the customer, such as service activity.

If the salesperson is to have a reasonably up-to-date version of this information available at all times, then facilities will be required to allow the laptop computer to exchange data with a central database. There is therefore a need for a remote communication function which allows the salesperson to dial-up to the central database to obtain new or changed customer information and for the remote system to send back any updates that have been made in the field.

Sales management implementation issues

For many organizations, the sales management application is the first sales and marketing system that they consider for implementation. This can bring a number of specific issues to light which will need careful management.

The salesforce will need to change the way in which they work in order to gain the maximum benefits from the system. This will require a change in attitude from each individual salesperson and a period of high quality training to develop new skills and an understanding of the new procedures that accompany the system. The sales staff must also be convinced that the new system is going to deliver very real benefits because if they are not motivated to use the system, they will not maintain the data it contains and the application will soon fall into disrepute.

The project team entrusted with the delivery of the new system will generally encounter three main technical issues. First they will probably have to manage the process of choosing a new system. This task applies to all packaged applications, but is particularly difficult given the wide choice of sales management applications available – more than 60 in a recent survey by Price Waterhouse.

The second key technical issue is the development, testing and implementation of the remote communications mechanism for the field-based sales staff. In order for this part of the system to operate, the application software must successfully track all changes made to the database by all sales staff and ensure that these changes are available for communication around the system. It is also vital that the actual physical components of the system (for example, communications servers and modems) and the file transfer mechanism all interact together correctly, and that they are able to move the changes tracked by the application from one point to another with absolute certainty of success. This is the most technically complex and potentially most time-consuming part of the system development process. It should be fully tested well before the first salesperson goes live on the new application.

The final technical issue relates to data conversion and is particularly relevant if this is the first sales and marketing system to be implemented in an organization. The quality of data available from the feeder systems will dramatically affect the quality of data in the new application. Any hidden problems over customer identification standards and numbering procedures in current systems will also come to light. Again, substantial time and energy will have to be invested in the development and testing of these interfaces before the new application goes live.

Sales management benefits

A successful implementation of a sales management application can deliver real benefits in terms of reduced costs and increased sales. These are generally achieved in four main areas:

- Improved information. If the salesperson has a complete picture of the company's relationship with a customer available on their laptop computer, they will have a better understanding of their potential relationship with each customer. This is particularly important for organizations which have large sales operations and where the interface with the customer includes other internal departments such as customer service or telemarketing.
- Improved management control. If the sales managers are able to track the activity of their sales staff on a day-to-day basis through a computer system rather than on a week-to-week basis using a manual or paper-based system, then management control will be improved. It will be possible for sales managers to react much more quickly to customer problems and, if the system is used effectively, possible even to anticipate a problem and ensure that it does not arise.
- Improved customer service. If the salesperson has a computer system to support activities such as generation of quotations, order entry and planning next actions to respond to customer requests, then they will be able to offer an improved level of customer service.
- Reduced costs. If the support to the salesforce is provided by computer systems rather than head office or regional office administration staff, then there is a clear opportunity to reduce costs. It is also possible to make a substantial reduction in stationery costs by replacing paper-based sales reporting systems.

In order to get real value for money from a sales management system, it is necessary to plan how the benefits of the new application and new working practices will be measured. This will help to ensure that the new system captures the information required to allow management to monitor the value of the benefits. If it is determined that the benefits are not being achieved – for example, if there is resistance from a small number of staff to using the new application – then action can be taken to improve use of the system.

43

Telemarketing systems

Telemarketing is one of the fastest growing marketing media in Europe with many companies now using the telephone as their major sales channel. To support this growth, an increasing number of systems have been developed to assist in the effective use of the telephone for marketing, sales and service purposes. Whilst many companies still manage with manual systems, computer systems are essential to support those organizations with high call volumes and large numbers of customers.

Telemarketing functions

The primary aim of most telemarketing systems is to effectively support and facilitate interactive communications with customers over the telephone. To do this, links to a telephone system or Automatic Call Distributor (ACD) are often required, together with a range of features to support interactive customer communication. Such software functions include the following:

- Contact management. In common with the sales management application, this is one of the most important areas of functionality and involves maintaining a detailed history of all contacts with a customer, including date and time of contact, who spoke to the customer, what subjects were discussed and what the outcome was. Any follow-up actions should also be recorded. This enables telephone staff to be able to talk knowledgeably to a customer with full details of their background and recent dealings in front of them.
- Call list management. Any scheduled follow-up calls need to be prompted so that staff can call back the customer at the agreed time. Many systems have powerful functions to allow telemarketing supervisors to compile lists of calls for their operators to complete, based on detailed customer profile and customer history information.
- Scripting. Many telemarketing systems provide facilities to set up scripts and prompts for telemarketing staff to use during a call. This can include information and help screens to assist staff in handling queries or objections which deviate from the normal script. The scripts are generally designed on a question-and-answer basis so that data collected by the telemarketing staff is automatically placed into the correct field in the customer's database record. Even experienced staff find such facilities a useful aid to ensure that all information is collected during the call.
- Fulfilment. Most good telemarketing systems provide facilities for the production of personalized letters, which can be produced by merging details from the customer record with text from a library of standard letters. This allows the operator to produce a personalized letter immediately after the call, and for it to be recorded in the customer's contact history.
- Call management. Automatic Call Distributor (ACD) telephone systems

are specially designed to manage the routing and allocation of in-bound calls according to user-defined rules. Other facilities, such as messages or music for calls waiting, are also provided by the ACD. It is often important that the telemarketing software and the ACD are linked together to support auto-dialling for outbound calls and so that a call and accompanying screen can be transferred from one member of staff to another.

- Reports and statistics. For a high volume telemarketing operation it is important to have operating statistics such as number of calls per hour, calls per day, calls per operator or in total. This allows for effective supervision of the telemarketing resources.

The recent Price Waterhouse survey identified that one in three packages available in the UK supports some form of telemarketing activity, although the sophistication of this functionality varies. Some packages are straightforward customer contact management or sales management systems which have basic telemarketing facilities; others are fully fledged telemarketing systems such as those used by large telemarketing bureaux.

Telemarketing implementation issues

The users of a telemarketing system are unusual in that they will spend most of their working day interacting with a computer system and, as such, the performance of that system will dramatically affect their performance as a sales channel. It is therefore important that the telemarketing system provides the users with a good service including, for example, the following:

- Screen update and refresh times should be fast, and must not obstruct the dialogue with a customer. Detailed consideration of the performance capabilities of the chosen hardware platform and operating environment are therefore key areas of activity during the system implementation.
- The system must be easy to use, with information presented as it is needed and in an easily readable format – the use of large numbers of short reference codes and complex classifications should be avoided.
- The system should provide staff with all the information required – there will be a significant loss of productivity if staff have to log-in to one system to deal with one type of call and then log-in to another system to deal with another problem or query.

Telemarketing system benefits

As telemarketing continues to grow in importance, systems are becoming increasingly powerful and more widely used. The benefits of a successful telemarketing system implementation can be substantial, and include the following:

- Increased sales and productivity gains. A good system can help to increase staff productivity substantially, enabling more calls to be made per operator, and a higher sales:call ratio to be achieved. Systems which have good support for the day-to-day administrative processes, such as fulfilment, will also improve team productivity.
- Customer service improvements. The use of a telemarketing system will help staff give higher quality, more immediate assistance to customers over the telephone. Fulfilment material will be received more promptly, and the ability to look at and use customer data during the call will make any conversation or marketing offer more relevant.
- Staff morale. In telemarketing, more than many other business activities, staff morale is vital. A happy team provided with suitable systems and administrative support will achieve higher call and sales rates.

Market analysis systems

The principal capability of market analysis systems is that they can manipulate large volumes of data from a range of disparate internal and external sources for use in the development of models of market segments and market behaviour. Reports and analysis can be easily generated, modelled and saved for future use, and business plans and scenarios developed and refined.

Market analysis functions

A market analysis system requires three basic functions: the ability to get data in; the ability to manipulate and analyse the data in any way the user sees fit; and the ability to report on the results of any analysis. The following are therefore basic functions:

- Data import. In order to use the data obtained from any number of different sources, a market analysis application will need to be able to import and verify data quickly and easily. It should also be possible to set up new sources of data for loading by providing a simple mapping between the import file format and the main application database structure. The system should also support the manual entry of data.
- Market analysis systems should provide a full range of data manipulation techniques to allow for models of market behaviour to be built. Examples of the types of data analysis facilities required are listed below – it is important that any one of these techniques can be used in isolation or in a series of analyses to form a more complex model.

  - Top-down segmentation, that is, the ability to cut multi-dimensional data on the market place in any manner that the user requires.
  - Basic mathematical functions including addition, multiplication and division.
  - Statistical analysis including deviations and distributions.
  - A range of forecasting techniques.

- – Regression analysis.
- • Output. A good market analysis system should be able to provide output in a range of different formats including:

  - – Tables and lists.
  - – Graphs and charts.
  - – Spreadsheet format.

Market analysis implementation issues

There are some generic data-related issues that exist for the development and use of market analysis systems. These include the following:

- • The quality of the underlying data that drives these applications is critical to the value of the information that is derived from the system. There are many sources of such data, including commercially available data, government statistics, industry body data, internal systems, customer surveys and market research studies. The decision on which sources to use will be critical to the success of the final system.
- • The users must have a very good understanding of the data in the system if they are to use it successfully. If they are not fully conversant with the underlying data structures, then they may perform pieces of analysis that are meaningless or which produce results containing serious errors.
- • As far as possible, the functions of the system should be developed to be independent of the data and the data structures that the system holds. If system programs are written to be dependent on the data, then every new data source that is used will require programming revisions, hence significantly increasing the long-term costs of the system.

Market analysis benefits

The key benefit that a market analysis application delivers is that users can quickly develop a more detailed understanding of the market place. Once this has been achieved, the information that is derived from the system can be used to improve market planning and product development decisions that affect the performance of the whole organization.

According to the recent Price Waterhouse survey, around one-third of all packages available in the UK have market analysis and segmentation facilities for flexible, user-defined analysis of multi-dimensional data for planning, targeting and reporting purposes. Many of these packages have statistical analysis and modelling functions (such as cross-tabulations, regression analysis and forecasting) and a report generator, which allows user-defined reports to be prepared, formatted and saved for future use. Most products also have a range of standard reports which cannot be changed by the user.

PACKAGE VERSUS BESPOKE

Historically, companies wishing to develop a sales or marketing system had little choice but to develop their own software. In the last five or six years, however, the choice of packaged software has increased dramatically, from around 30 products in 1980 to over 200 today. Even those systems that have been around for a long time have undergone several transformations during their life to keep pace with this rapidly evolving market. Companies now wishing to develop a sales or marketing system are faced with an almost bewildering range of packaged solutions (none of which fully meet their needs), or a bespoke development. So, when is a packaged system preferable, and are bespoke systems still a truly viable option?

The case for bespoke development

It is a commonly held belief that competitive advantage can only be obtained by developing bespoke systems. However, if competitive advantage is possible, it is not the technology that will deliver it but the use of the information delivered by the technology. Another common misconception is that bespoke solutions can deliver more flexibility and provide a closer match to user requirements. In many cases, though, bespoke development projects have run into difficulties and delays and, by the time the system is delivered, the business requirements have moved on.

Bespoke solutions are now far less popular but can still have a particular role to play. The key advantages of bespoke marketing systems development are:

- 100 per cent fit is possible (though it can be difficult to achieve if user requirements change rapidly). Flexibility needs to be built in or delivered using end-user toolkits so that future needs can be accommodated. Advances in IT, such as relational databases, fourth generation languages (4GLs) and Computer Aided Software Engineering (CASE) are also making bespoke solutions easier to deliver now.
- If the requirements are very unusual and cannot be met by a package, or the amount and cost of package customization would be substantial, a bespoke development is normally justifiable. In particular, in certain technical environments, the number of packages available is still rather limited and a bespoke system is the obvious choice.
- Bespoke solutions force the IT and marketing departments to go through a rigorous specification and development process. Although time-consuming, this can help to build ownership, commitment and detailed understanding of the way the system will support the business. This is essential in any sales and marketing systems development, whether packaged or bespoke, and the failure to go through this process is a major reason why some packaged systems fail.
- There are also many tools now available which blur the edges between

packaged and bespoke solutions. These systems provide a useful functional core which gives access part of the way up the development curve very quickly and provides a useful base for modifications and tailoring to specific needs. Around half of the packages available have some ability to be tailored in this way.

The case for packaged software

Packages can deliver real business benefits quickly, and often at limited cost. The key advantages of sales and marketing packages are as follows:

- The availability of a wide choice of proven solutions for common marketing or sales requirements, hence the learning curve is minimized through the use of a suitable package.
- Functionality can be delivered more quickly by using the package facilities as a core upon which to build.
- Risk is reduced by building on the past experience of package suppliers and other package users, rather than trying to 're-invent the wheel'.
- For all the above reasons, the packaged route is often much cheaper than bespoking, especially given the current competitiveness of the package market.

However there are issues to be addressed:

- The choice of package suppliers is critical. This chapter later highlights some of the potential risks and problems with package suppliers. Involvement of an independent consultancy can minimize the substantial risk of making a wrong choice in a confusing market.
- 100 per cent fit is impossible; an 80 per cent fit unlikely. Compromises may be necessary with a package, but where and how important are the compromises?
- Many companies will require more than one system to meet their needs. How they will work together must be considered, and any technical considerations taken into account.

The reality is that, for most situations, a packaged solution can be considered a real option and there is often little justification for the higher cost and more lengthy time-scales of a bespoke development, especially given the choice of packages now available. Even if requirements are highly complex and unusual, and a bespoke solution is preferred, packages could play a useful role as a short-term partial solution while a more comprehensive bespoke system is developed.

THE PACKAGE SUPPLIERS

Most organizations are now opting for the package route and, especially given   *49* the wide range of choice now available, some wrongly assume that choice of the right product is the only important consideration. In fact, selection of a good supplier is equally vital.

Small, young companies dominate this new and rapidly changing market, with approximately 80 per cent of companies having started in business since 1980, most of them selling a product that they have developed themselves. Since most companies are so newly formed and have relatively few (or sometimes no) customers, they also have few staff (the recent Price Waterhouse survey found that 60 per cent of package suppliers have 20 staff or less). This can cause some of them problems in honouring client commitments or meeting deadlines. They also tend to have a fairly low turnover (one in three has a turnover of less than £0.5 million) which can cause potential purchasers concern about their financial stability.

The choice of the right package supplier is therefore very important to purchasers of a packaged system. It is important to be convinced not only that the product has suitable capability, but that the supplier will provide appropriate resource, advice, technical skills and day-to-day support throughout the lifetime of the system. Obviously the time between system selection and implementation is one of the most critical periods, and you need to be reassured that the supplier will work with you for this period to ensure that the final version of the system really does meet the users' needs and do all the things that the supplier said it would. In this respect, choice of the right supplier is as critical as choice of the right system.

THE USERS

A wide variety of companies are now using sales and marketing systems in a range of different ways. The chart in Figure 2.3 shows the breakdown by industry sector of companies using sales and marketing systems.

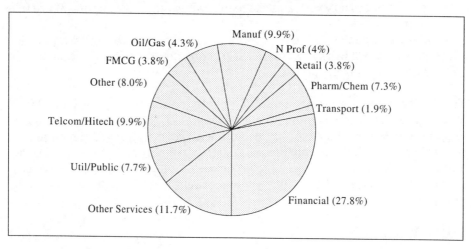

Figure 2.3   Breakdown of use by industry sector

The largest group of users are in the financial services sector and comprise 28 per cent of all companies with a sales and marketing system. One of the most important marketing activities in this sector is direct marketing. Marketing systems to support targeting and profiling are also widely used. Other service companies are also major users in this area. Use of systems in manufacturing, pharmaceutical and chemical companies is also increasingly important as markets become more competitive and they need to become better at business-to-business marketing. Another major application in the business-to-business sector is the use of sales management systems to improve the efficiency of the salesforce.

Utilities and public sector organizations have recently become significant users of sales and marketing systems, resulting from the fact that many newly privatized industries purchased systems in the late 1980s. Fast moving consumer goods (FMCG) companies also use marketing systems, particularly market analysis systems which are used for detailed business analysis and brand planning.

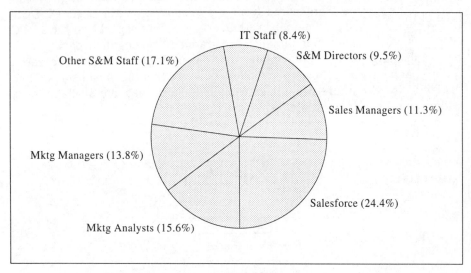

Figure 2.4   Breakdown of use by type of user

As Figure 2.4 shows, the largest group of management of end-users work in a sales role and are often field-based, using a sales system running on a laptop computer. Other sales and marketing staff, such as administrative staff providing marketing and sales support for the salesforce, are also significant users of sales and marketing systems. Marketing analysts are another group for whom marketing systems are becoming essential, as they are required to provide analysis and reports for senior management and brand managers. Extensive and increasing use of sales and marketing systems is made by senior managers and executives, who comprise 35 per cent of all users, compared to 32 per cent last year. As senior executives continue to move towards a philosophy of   *51* 'management by fact', their information requirements are increasing. It is becoming easier to have computer access than to wait for staff to provide paper-based reports, hence 'technophobia' is gradually being overcome at senior levels. This is an important development as experience shows that the success or failure of a system can often rest on the degree of support and commitment to change given by senior executives.

The use of sales and marketing systems by IT staff is relatively small, comprising only 8 per cent of users. This reflects the importance of ownership and responsibility for the system within the user community. IT staff are often used as technical administrators, providing back-up and maintenance support for the users and often working alongside the 'expert user' or system administrator who is invariably a member of the sales and marketing team.

THE TECHNOLOGY

Sales and marketing systems are now available to run on a wide range of platforms, although most originated from a personal computer base. PC DOS-based packages still predominate, with over 80 per cent of packages having PC DOS versions available, but suppliers are gradually moving their packages on to a wider range of technology platforms. Recent Price Waterhouse research found that nearly 60 per cent of suppliers believed that the most likely technical trend for the future was for existing systems to become available on a wider range of technology platforms (see Figure 2.5).

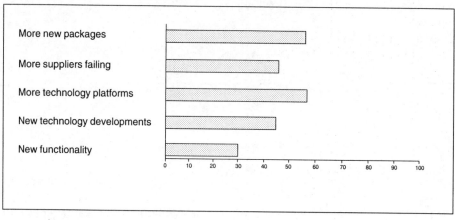

Figure 2.5   Likely developments in sales and marketing packages

In line with general systems trends, sales and marketing packages are increasingly being developed to run in the Windows environment. As a first step down this route, many suppliers have changed their products so that they can run as DOS applications under Windows. Open systems technology is also becoming more popular with over 50 per cent of packages having a UNIX version available. A newly emerging trend, which is likely to become increasingly important for the future, is for packages to run using relational database technologies. Whilst many organizations are keen to move in this direction, they are currently constrained by supplier experience in this area.

CONCLUSIONS

The growth in the use of sales and marketing systems in the last ten years has been enormous and the industry has undergone huge changes to keep pace with the demands of their clients. The use of systems has become more sophisticated and the functionality of packages has kept pace. However many mistakes have been made, largely due to the newness of the market and the inexperience of system purchasers and developers. System purchasers have not always known exactly what they wanted, and system suppliers have struggled with limited resources to introduce new functionality, new technology platforms and to understand their clients' complex business requirements. Figure 2.6 shows some of the most common problems identified by the recent Price Waterhouse survey.

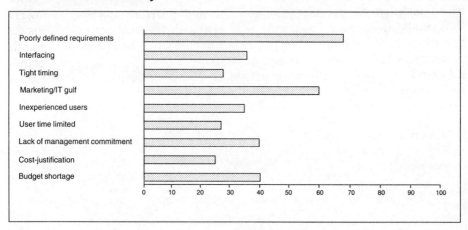

Figure 2.6   Marketing systems development problems

Despite the problems, it is clear that sales and marketing systems are here to stay. In recent Price Waterhouse research, over 70 per cent of package suppliers said the interest in sales and marketing systems from their clients and prospects appeared to have increased despite the recession. In such competitive markets, systems are now being seen as a real way to achieve competitive advantage and to manage and maintain profitable customer relationships. Another advantage for system purchasers is that they are now able to benefit from the market developments that have taken place. Software functionality has become far more flexible and powerful, and both software and hardware costs have fallen substantially as market competitiveness has increased. Companies now have an improved understanding of how systems can be used to support sales and marketing activity and better assistance in the form of expert consultancy advice is now available. The end result for system purchasers is better value for money and a better chance of success in obtaining a flexible, powerful systems solution to meet the needs of their sales and marketing staff, both today and in the future.

REFERENCES

Gorski, D. and Ingram, J. (1994), *Price Waterhouse Sales and Marketing Software Handbook 1994*, London: Pitman Publishing.

ESSENTIAL READING

Gorski, D. and Ingram, J. (1994), *Price Waterhouse Sales and Marketing Software Handbook 1994,* London: Pitman Publishing.

Rapp, Stan and Collins, Thomas L. (1986), *Maxi Marketing*, New York: McGraw-Hill.

The Journal of Database Marketing, published quarterly by Henry Stewart Publications.

3 Analysing the environment

Douglas Brownlie

This chapter begins by presenting an argument in favour of formal and systematic environmental analysis. It goes on to describe a general approach to analysing the environment which may be used by corporate and marketing strategist alike; what benefits it brings to practising firms; what management problems are likely to be encountered; and how possibly to surmount them.

BACK TO BASICS

Firms and other commercial organizations owe their existence to the market environment. Like people, they are creatures of their environment and participants, albeit unwilling, in its processes. They, too, spend much of their life learning how to cope with the complexity, hostility, unforeseen traumas, vagaries, and opportunities generated by their environment. Indeed, the market environment can be thought of as an ever-changing sum total of the facts of life with which firms have to come to terms. Their survival and prosperity is conditioned by the demands imposed by this environment. Thus, in the midst of an environment where frequent and major change is becoming the rule, firms must stay at the forefront of changes which will affect their markets and their positions within them.

The market environment consists of the external forces that directly or indirectly influence the firms' goals, structure, plans, procedures, operations, performance, and so on. Environmental analysis is the study of these forces, the relationship among them, and their effects and potential effects on the organization.

The term environmental analysis is often used interchangeably with others such as environmental scanning, environmental forecasting, competitive intelligence gathering, external search, environmental surveillance, strategic marketing information retrieval, and so on (Brownlie, 1991). I use the term 'environmental scanning' to encompass the varied information gathering, analysis and dissemination activities that firms pursue in order to keep up to date with changes in the market environment. Clearly the purpose of those activities is not merely to keep track of environmental changes. Without environmental analysis and forecasting, there is no basis for strategic planning. Environmental scanning involves activities ranging from highly structured and regularly conducted reviews and forecasts of major trends, issues and events in the business environment, to the irregular 'tip' acquired by means of insider access to a network of private and personal contacts, or even by means of espionage (Taylor, 1992).

Environmental scanning is responsible not only for generating an up-to-date database of information on the changing business scene. It also has the job of alerting management to what is happening in the market-place, the industry and beyond by disseminating important information and analyses to key strategic decision makers and influencers. However, the conversion of the awareness such dissemination will create into interest, and ultimately to some form of action, is an overtly and covertly political process which can emasculate the most penetrating analyses – particularly where vested interests are threatened and top management support absent. It is widely appreciated that the realization of a marketing orientation is, in practice, often inhibited, not by failures of the systems, technology or methodologies of marketing, of which environmental analysis is one, but by disabling management attitudes which often express themselves as resistance to change, conservatism, suspicion and prevarication.

The preceding paragraph asks the reader to take a step outside the realm of the environmental analyst and to enter that of the strategic decision maker. The tasks of gathering, analysing and disseminating information are often organized as discrete activities. The environmental analyst is likely to be a member of the corporate or marketing planning staff, or a top management aide, that is a decision influencer, but rarely a decision maker. Indeed, the 'boffinesque' role in which the analyst often finds himself cast may do little to enhance the credibility and esteem attributed to him by leading-edge strategic decision makers. They will be keen to place their own interpretations on what the expert analyst has to say – unless, of course, he has an impeccable track record in which case the expert may find himself being elevated to the status of a 'delphic oracle'. But, in the absence of any other intelligence gathering activity, whether systematized or personal, the environmental analyst and forecaster will, by means of the perceived importance of the information he generates, be in an enviable position to influence strategic decision makers' perceptions of the firm's competitive position and the options available to it. Students of history will recognize that many a bloody political intrigue was spawned by the jealously guarded, and often misused privilege of proximity to the seat of power which was conferred on privy counsellors and advisors. Thus, in addition to the technical skills demanded of the environmental scanning staff, political skills could be said to be the hallmark of an effective scanning team.

Management attitudes have a vital role to play in creating an organizational climate that enables the firm, not only to operate what should in effect be an 'open window of perception' on the past, present and prospective business scene, but also to act on the insights it provides. Readers will therefore be disappointed if they expect the methodology of environmental scanning to be described herein as a panacea for the problems of understanding and coping with the increasingly competitive and turbulent environment of the 1990s. Methodology alone will not guarantee success. Indeed, method is less important than the thinking it stimulates. Methodologies can be implanted and replicated with much less difficulty than can ways of thinking.

WHAT CAN ENVIRONMENTAL SCANNING CONTRIBUTE?

Whatever is achieved by environmental scanning will largely depend on the purpose the firm has for it. Small firms may require to be kept up to date with local regulatory and economic trends likely to have an immediate impact on their day-to-day business prospects. Larger organizations will share this requirement, but will also expect information broader in scope and of a futures orientation.

Corporate-level environmental scanning is likely to be charged with the responsibility of monitoring, interpreting and forecasting issues, trends and events which go far beyond the customer, market and competitive analyses that most firms perform as a matter of routine. In this context, environmental scanning will be expected to provide a broad but penetrating view of possible future changes in the demographic, social, cultural, political, technological and economic elements of the business environment. In so doing it should seek to arm the firm's strategic decision makers and influencers with the information, analyses and forecasts they consider pertinent to the formulation of the strategies and plans. It should also provide a basis for questioning the assumptions which underpin the firm's strategic thinking and for generating new assumptions.

In an empirical study of environmental analysis in 90 American corporations, Diffenbach (1983) reported that participants found there to be seven types of pay-offs from the activity, as follows:

1 Increased awareness by management of environmental changes.
2 Better strategic planning and decision making.
3 Greater effectiveness in government matters.
4 Better industry and market analyses.
5 Better results in foreign business.
6 Improvements in resource allocation.
7 Better energy planning.

DEFINING THE MARKET ENVIRONMENT

It has been argued that the ability to exercise control in the firm's current   *57* product markets is derived, at least partly, from a comprehensive and reliable knowledge of customers, suppliers, competitors, regulators and investors. The successful development and upkeep of the knowledge base is thought to be the principal task of formal environmental scanning – one to which the functions of marketing, R&D, purchasing, sales and finance have a major contribution to make. However, in the long term more is expected of it. For instance, as the firm looks away from its existing product markets for future growth opportunities or acquisition candidates within and outwith its current sphere of operation, knowledge will be required of a new and unfamiliar business environment having its own unique set of technological, economic, political and social trends. In so doing greater demands will be made of environmental analysis.

Churchman (1968) defines the environment of a firm as 'those factors which not only are outside the system's control but which determine, in part, how the system performs'. In theory at least the market environment is thought to include all those factors that exert any perceptible direct or indirect influence on the firm. Given such an unbounded definition, one could argue that the rest of the world then constitutes the firm's business environment. Clearly, to take such an undiscriminating view has no practical value. The task of environmental scanning can only be made manageable by taking a very selective and carefully considered view of the environment. It must eliminate much of the rest of the world from the firm's immediate attention.

The breadth of the view an organization chooses to take of its business environment has implications for the complexity of the tasks of environmental analysis and forecasting, and thus its resource requirements. A broadly-defined business mission is associated with a diversified, multi-product, multi-market firm. It would involve environmental scanning in a very broad arena of operation from which a perspective on international political and economic issues, events and trends may be called for by corporate planning. On the other hand, a narrowly-defined business mission may focus the efforts of environmental scanning more on domestic issues concerning immediate events and trends in proximate product markets. The firm's environmental scanning activities should cover as many relevant aspects of the business environment as the available resources will permit, particularly those aspects having an impact on the assumptions being used by the firm in its strategic planning and decision making.

The boundaries of the market environment must therefore be structured in such a way as to enable the analyst to identify the important from less important factors and to determine an appropriate time-scale for forecasting changes. One would expect there to be factors that deserve to be continuously monitored because of their immediate impact on the industry; these would include users, distributors, suppliers, competitors for customers and suppliers, workforce, government regulators, trade unions, product and process developments, and so on. The origin of such factors is known as the 'task environment'. It is defined as 'the more specific forces which are relevant to decision-making and transformation processes of the individual organisations' (Dill, 1958).

Table 3.1
Kast and Rosenzweig's (1974) framework for analysing the wider business
environment

Cultural	Including the historical background, ideologies, values and norms of the society. Views on authority relationships, leadership patterns, interpersonal relationships, nationalism, science and technology.
Technological	The level of scientific and technological advancement in society, including the physical base (plant, equipment, facilities) and the knowledge base of technology. Degree to which the scientific and technological community is able to develop new knowledge and apply it.
Educational	The general literacy level of the population. The degree of sophistication and specialization in the educational system. The proportion of the people with a high level of professional and/or specialized training.
Political	The general political climate of society. The degree of concentration of political power. The nature of political organization (degrees of decentralization, diversity of functions, and so on). The political party system.
Legal	Constitutional considerations, nature of legal system, jurisdictions of various governmental units. Specific laws concerning formation, taxation and control of organizations.
Natural resources	The nature, quantity and availability of natural resources, including climatic and other conditions.
Demographic	The nature of human resources available to the society; their number, distribution, age and sex. Concentration or urbanization of population is a characteristic of industrialized societies.
Sociological	Class structure and mobility. Definition of social roles. Nature of social organization and development of social institutions.
Economic	General economic framework, including the type of economic organization – private versus public ownership; the centralization or decentralization of economic planning; the banking system; and fiscal policies. The level of investment in physical resources and consumption.

The concept of the task environment opens the environmental analyst's 'window on the world' on to the organization's immediate product and supply markets, and on to current influences on its position within them. But, a wider view   *59* would also cast attention towards remote areas where developments could be underway which in the longer term would impinge on the firm's position in its current product and supply markets. For instance, substitute products and processes often originate as spin-offs from technological developments that have been made by firms outwith the task environment. Clearly it is important to look further afield than the task environment. Kast and Rosenzweig (1974) have suggested a framework by means of which the wider market environment can be divided into areas for study and analysis (see Table 3.1). Table 3.2 outlines some of the broad social issues that firms might expect to impinge on their European activities in the 1990s. Environmental scanning would be expected to follow developments of these issues (and others of a technological, political, cultural and economic nature) and evaluate the impact they are thought likely to have on the firm.

Table 3.2
Key European social issues for the 1990s

Issues	Characteristics
Low economic growth	Political instability; rising energy costs; growing unemployment; growth in international capital flows; trends to international protectionism if GATT fails; decline of basic industries; rising inflation; shortages of basic materials; falling productivity; emergence of new market economies of Eastern Europe. Increasing national indebtedness and monetary growth; European currency disorder; falling investment.
Political uncertainty	Political fragmentation in Europe; expansion of EC; trend towards decentralizing government; growth in terrorism and armed conflict; failure of EC foreign and international trade policy; rise of nationalism/tribalism; regional convergence on trade and investment policy; decline of liberal democratic values; urban conflict.
Rise of the multi-locals	Large firms decentralize, downsize and form loose federations by devolving responsibility to autonomous units; growth in smaller enterprises; more cross-border networks/partnerships.
Environmentalism	Growing influence of environmentalist lobby; enactment of EC-wide legislation

	on pollution and product liability; closer scrutiny of firms' environmental track record; growth in environmental audit requirements.
Lobby politics	Rising power and influence of lobby groups on issues such as gender, age, consumer protection, health, housing, pollution, materialism, consumer choice, representation, social responsibility, race, poverty, discrimination, access to education.
Growth of government	Closer EC integration and convergence brings with it more bureaucracy and democratic institutions.
Accountability and participation	Demands for greater accountability and transparency in the activities and decisions of government, public and business institutions; greater access to local government and participation in it; greater access to information; more disclosure of information and scrutiny of decisions and activities.

THE NEED FOR INFORMATION

Organizations subject themselves to the inconvenience, expense, rigour and pain of strategic planning in order to acquire more control over the outcome of any course of action they choose to pursue. Thus, in accordance with Bacon's dictum that 'knowledge itself is power', it could be argued that a knowledge of the business environment must precede the acquisition of any degree of control over it.

The reader is likely to have witnessed the popularization of terms such as espionage, infiltration, moles, security leaks, early warning, electronic surveillance, counter-intelligence, insider dealing, and the like (Wright, 1987). Although evocative of the anxiety and duplicity of our age, the popularization of the vocabulary of the spy lends some credence to the view that the possession of information is itself a factor endowment, and as such it should be treated as a valuable national asset. It is only one small but logical step to argue that since the gathering of information precedes its possession and dissemination, then this activity also contributes to the generation of wealth.

To the student of military strategy, the preceding view will represent a familiar and even hackneyed line of thought. After all, history offers many examples of battles which could be said to have been fought and won on the basis of 'superior' information. In planning the deployment and employment of their armies' resources, generals rely on the intelligence provided by lines of com- *61* munications which may have a political origin in their own states, but will certainly infiltrate enemy territory and institutions (James, 1985). By means of the intelligence so provided the general hopes to better prepare himself for the ensuing conflict and to enhance the likelihood of his victory – that is, to gain some control over the outcome of the conflict.

In the corporate context, the tasks of intelligence gathering, surveillance and monitoring are overseen by environmental scanning. It is responsible for managing lines of communications by means of which a flow of information is maintained between important elements of the business environment, the environmental analysts and the organization's strategic decision makers and influencers. As in the military context, the corporate intelligence service will also provide early warning and careful tracking of possible environmental threats in order that a timely response is conceived and executed. Table 3.2 indicates corporate sources of information on the business environment; Table 3.4 comments on their relative importance. Table 3.4 also suggests that to enhance the impact of its work, environmental scanning should not only seek top management support, but also its involvement in order to implicate or consult all key decision makers and influencers at corporate and divisional level.

Table 3.3
Sources of information on the business environment

Type of information	Sources of information on business environment
Inside the company	
Written	Internal reports and memos, planning documents, market research, MIS.
Verbal	Researchers, salesforce, marketing, purchasing, advisers, planners, board.
Combination	Formal and informal meetings, for example working parties, advisory committees.
Outside the company	
Written	Annual reports, investment reports, trade association publications, institute yearbooks, textbooks, scientific journals, professional journals, technical magazines, unpublished reports, government reports, unpublished papers, abstracts, newspapers, espionage.
Verbal	Consultants, librarians, government officials, consumers, suppliers, distributors, competitors, academics, market researchers, industry bodies, journalists, spies, bankers, stockbrokers.
Combination	Formal and informal meetings, membership of government working parties and advisory boards, industry bodies, trade associations.

Table 3.4
The relative importance of sources of environmental information

1 Verbal sources of information are much more important than written sources: 75 per cent of information cited by executives was in verbal form.
2 The higher the executive in the organization, the more important verbal sources became.
3 Of the written sources used, the most important were newspapers (two-thirds), followed by trade publications, and internal company reports.
4 Subordinates are the principal source of verbal information, followed by friends in the industry and, very infrequently, superiors.
5 Information received from outside an organization is usually unsolicited.
6 Information received from inside the organization is usually solicited by the executive.
7 Information received from outside tends to have a greater impact on the decision maker than inside information.
8 The outside sources used varied according to the job of the manager. Thus marketing managers talked more to customers.
9 The larger the company, the greater the reliance on inside sources of verbal information.

Source: Aguilar (1967).

The emergence of information technology has encouraged firms to carefully re-examine the purpose, structure, productivity and accessibility of their management information systems, including those governing elements of the business environment. The outcome has often been to reorganize databases which involves further systematization of the tasks of collecting, analysing and disseminating information on the business environment. The demanding task of organizing a database governing important elements of the firm's environment is made more so by the character of pertinent information – which will often possess several of the following characteristics:

- Poor structure.
- Irregular availability.
- Provided by unofficial sources.
- Qualitative in nature.
- Of questionable credibility.
- Ambiguous definitions.
- Opinion-based.
- Difficult to quantify.
- Based on insecure methodology.
- Likely to change.

63

THE EVOLUTION OF ENVIRONMENTAL ANALYSIS

Management systems would seem to have evolved in response to two trends: the increasing discontinuity, complexity, and novelty of the environmental challenges firms face, and the decreasing visibility of the future changes in the business environment. The growing impact of these trends is largely responsible for the widespread following which the strategic planning credo acquired in the wake of the trauma of the post-1974 oil shock. This led, first, to draw attention to environmental analysis as an important element of strategic planning, and second, for environmental analysis, or scanning, itself to evolve in response to the challenges confronting the firm and its planning system.

Diffenbach (1983) traces the early evolution of environmental analysis to the mid-1960s when, he claims, the market environment was generally being studied only for the purpose of making economic forecasts. Only in more recent years does he consider there has been an appreciation of the need to look beyond short-term market conditions to the wider technological, economic, political, social, cultural and demographic elements of the environment. He identifies three distinct evolutionary phases, each of which marks a growth in the scope, systematization, future-orientation and top management recognition of environmental analysis activity. Changes first began to occur during what Diffenbach terms the appreciation phase.

A pioneering investigation of environmental analysis was conducted by Aguilar in 1967. In this now classic study, the process of environmental scanning was originally conceptualized. Aguilar interviewed 137 managers from 41 chemical firms in the US and Europe. He found a lack of a systematic approach to environmental analysis which is still being reported in the more recent research of Thomas (1980), Fahey et al. (1981), Stubbart (1982), Jain (1984), Lenz and Engledow (1986), West and Olsen (1989) and Taylor (1992).

Aguilar's research revealed that the participants collected 16 types of information about their business environment. He classified them into the five groupings in Table 3.5. He reported that 52 per cent of environmental information that was gathered concerned market tidings; 17 per cent and 12 per cent concerned technical tidings and broad issues respectively. Aguilar identified two principal sources of information on the market environment, i.e. internal and external to the firm. Table 3.3 classifies sources of information according to Aguilar's scheme. Table 3.4 summarizes his views on the relative importance of several sources of market information. He found there to be four broad approaches to the collection of this information:

1 *undirected viewing*: exposure to the elements of the business environment without there being a specific purpose in mind.
2 *conditioned viewing*: directed exposure, but without undertaking an active search.
3 *informal search*: collection of purpose-oriented information in an informal manner.
4 *formal search*: a structured process for collecting specific information for a designated purpose.

Table 3.5
What information do managers need on the business environment?

1 **Market tidings**

Market potential	Supply and demand consideration for market areas of current or potential interest: for example, capacity, consumption, imports, exports.
Structural change	Mergers, acquisitions and joint ventures involving competitors, new entries into the industry.
Competitors and industry	General information about a competitor, industry policy, concerted actions in the industry, and so forth.
Pricing	Effective and proposed prices for products of current and potential interest.
Sales negotiations	Information relating to a specific current or potential sale or contract for the firm.
Customers	General information about current or near-potential customers, their markets, their problems.

2 **Acquisition leads**

Leads for mergers, joint ventures, or acquisitions	Information concerning possibilities for the manager's own company.

3 **Technical tidings**

New products, processes, and technology	Technical information relatively new and unknown to the company.
Product problems	Problems involving existing products.
Costs	Costs for processing, operations, and so forth for current and potential competitors, suppliers, and customers, and for proposed company activities.
Licensing and patents	Products and processes.

4 **Broad issues**

General conditions	Events of a general nature: political, demographic, national, and so forth.
Government actions and policies	Governmental decisions affecting the industry.

5 **Other tidings**

Suppliers and raw materials	Purchasing considerations for products of current or potential interest.
Resources available	Persons, land, and other resources possibly available for the company.
Miscellaneous	Items not elsewhere classified.

Source: Aguilar (1967).

They differ along the dimensions of the scope of the environment to be analysed, the impetus for the analysis, the degree of active search involved, the formality of the environmental scanning process, and the task orientation of the activity.

Aguilar's study concluded that for environmental scanning to make an effective contribution to the formulation of strategy, it must be conducted in a systematic fashion. He frequently found environmental scanning effort to be fragmented and inhibited by the failure of participating managers to gather and disseminate information that users considered important, and to make use of accessible information that already resided within the firm. His proposals for overcoming the 'fractionalization' of environmental scanning effort called for top management involvement in the definition and execution of analysis activities, greater co-ordination and integration of these activities with strategic planning, and greater support for these activities, not only from top management, but also from line managers.

Despite the considerable body of strategic planning literature which addresses environmental scanning, scepticism still surrounds the extent to which it is finding application in firms. The purpose of Diffenbach's (1983) study was to make some progress towards answering the doubts of the sceptics. The earlier work of Fahey et al. (1981) shared this motivation. As a result of their in-depth study of the environmental scanning practices of 12 large American firms, they proposed three broad models of environment analysis systems which represent increasing degrees of systematization, sophistication and resource intensity:

1 *Irregular systems* respond to environmentally generated crises. They are found in firms where the strategic planning culture is not well established. Their emphasis is on finding solutions to short-term problems. Little attention is paid to evaluating future environmental changes.

2 *The periodic model* is more sophisticated, systematic, proactive and resource-intensive. It entails a regular review of the task environment and some elements of the wider environment. A forward view is taken.

3 *The continuous model* emphasizes the ongoing monitoring of the business environment, rather than specified issues or events. It draws on the expertise of marketing, sales, purchasing, and so on. It operates a clearing-house for environmental information and uses regular information systems for analysis and dissemination. A long-term view of environmental change is taken.

Fahey et al. have acknowledged that the models they propose have not found widespread application in US corporations. They have noted a trend towards greater sophistication, but add that the impact which continuous environmental scanning has so far demonstrated does not appear to substantiate the major deployment of resources it requires. Of course, the empirical studies of Thomas (1980), Diffenbach (1983) and Lenz and Engledow (1986) provide evidence that persuades these researchers to take the opposite view.

Environment sector	Event/issue	Threat	Opportunity	Weighting[1]	Importance[2]	Impact on firm's strategies[3]			$\Sigma-$	$\Sigma+$
						S1	S2	S3		
Technology	1									
	2									
Political										
Economic										
Social										
Etc.										
					$\Sigma-$					
					$\Sigma+$					

Notes

1 Indicates the degree to which the event is judged to be a threat or opportunity. On an ordinal scale from 1 to 5, 1 represents a weak T/O, and 5 a strong T/O

2 Indicates the degree to which the weighted event has, or will have, an impact on the firm's strategies. On an ordinal scale from 1 to 5, 1 represents a little impact, 5 a great impact.

3 The impact each event has on each of the firm's strategies is calculated by multiplying the weighted score by the importance score. A large positive (negative) score represents a strong opportunity (threat).

The value in constructing an ETOP profile is largely to be found in the debate that follows the planner's environmental appraisal, when the firm's managers assimilate, debate and develop their own ideas of the organization's threats and opportunities.

In the profile the row sums indicate the degree to which each event/issue is thought to enhance (+) or inhibit (−) the success of the firm's strategies. The column sums indicate the degree to which each strategy is itself thought to pose a threat or opportunity to the firm, given its predicted environment.

Figure 3.1 Displaying the firm's environmental threat and opportunity (ETOP profile)

The paradox of environmental scanning is that by the time sufficient information has been collected to enable a well-informed environmental analysis to be made, it may be too late for the firm to respond before the threat strikes, or the opportunity passes. Ansoff (1984) proposes an approach to strategic management (see Figure 3.1) which in his view overcomes the paradox by enabling the firm to develop a timely response to partially predictable events that emerge as surprises and develop very quickly. At its heart is the continuous monitoring of the firm's external and internal environment for signals of the evolution of strategic issues which the firm considers able to influence its operations. Ansoff's unit of analysis is, then, the strategic issue rather than the conventional elements of the business environment. Issue-driven approaches to environmental scanning have also been developed by Nanus (1982) and Murphy (1989).

Ansoff's solution to the paradox is a 'graduated response' based on the amplification of and flexible response to weak signals. As he contends, 'instead of waiting for sufficient information to accumulate, the firm should determine what progressive steps in planning and action are feasible as strategic information becomes available in the course of the evolution of a threat or opportunity'.

ANALYSING THE ENVIRONMENT: PROCEDURES AND PROBLEMS

The organization's environmental scanning procedures will evolve over time as its commitment to them and experience of them change. It is unrealistic for a firm about to embrace environmental scanning for the first time to expect to operate a foolproof system from the outset: several technical and managerial constraints will impede progress (see Table 3.6). Of course, the evolutionary period can be shortened by ensuring top management involvement in the commissioning of the system. Top management support throughout the evolutionary period helps ensure that a *viable* system emerges from early efforts which are likely to be directed towards the installation of a system modelled on an ideal scanning procedure such as that shown in Table 3.7. An established strategic planning culture should also help expedite matters by providing a receptive organizational climate. But this cannot be guaranteed. Even strategic planners are apt to react to a threatening newcomer in a way that ensures their territorial boundaries and organizational prerogatives are preserved – particularly if the newcomer is to be funded from the existing strategic planning resource base.

Top management involvement in the commissioning of the environmental scanning system should focus on the definition of the following system parameters:

1 The boundaries of the task and business environment.
2 The appropriate time horizon for future studies.
3 The allocation of responsibility for environmental scanning.
4 The degree of formality circumscribing environmental scanning.
5 The use of environmental analyses in strategy making.

Table 3.6
Diffenbach's (1983) deterrents to effective environmental analysis

Interpretation
The problem is that of interpreting the results of environmental analysis into specific impacts on the company's businesses and into specific responses to be made by the businesses. Included is the problem of the results not being in useful or sufficiently precise form.

- Difficulty of structuring studies in a way that results can be seen to be relevant and meaningful to decision makers today.
- Difficulty of reacting because information from environmental analysis is so intangible with regard to timing and impact.
- Difficulty of assessing the implications of general environmental trends for our specific businesses before they exert themselves.
- Difficulty of translating environmental analysis into relevant business terms, e.g. ROI impact.
- Difficulty of quantifying the impact of major threats and developing alternatives to these threats.
- Difficulty of developing the path from assumption to implication to action, e.g. the tendency to relax or stop after stating the assumption, rather than follow through to an action programme.
- Difficulty in seeing the impact of environmental trends on short-range operations, i.e. the gradual, accumulative nature of trends can be deceptive.
- Lack of sufficient involvement by top management for them not only to understand the conclusions of environmental analysis but also to internalize them and change behaviour accordingly.
- Difficulty of translating potential opportunities into action plans, e.g. conversion of traditional furniture ideas into new lifestyle furniture concepts.
- The time and analysis required to apply information to our specific situations, e.g. impact of probable energy shortages or price increases on our market for motor car components.
- Difficulty of institutionalizing environmental planning into the formal planning processes of the company so that division strategies reflect the process.
- Difficulty of follow-up planning, e.g. we have pushed ahead on programmes in spite of warning signals that should have alerted us to severe problems.
- Identifying impacts on businesses, particularly when negative.

Inaccuracy/uncertainty
The problem is that either the output of environmental analysis is inaccurate, too uncertain to be taken seriously, or both.

Table 3.6 continued

- Uncertainty due to the dynamics of the market-place.
- Inaccurate depicting of environmental events.
- So many false predictions.
- Inability to predict the future, e.g. past experience revealed inability of experts to predict the extent of inflationary forces.
- Difficulty of properly characterizing uncertainties in understandable and meaningful terms.
- Difficulty of forecasting the magnitude of the impact of a future trend.
- The moving target syndrome, e.g. especially regarding government activity.
- Difficulty of predicting social aims, e.g. no-growth versus continuing growth, etc.
- Discontinuities in environmental forecasting for which no company can make satisfactory assessments.

Short-term orientation

The problem is that the preoccupation with short-term matters preempts attention to environmental analysis.

- Pressure of short-term events, which tend to soak up some of the resources nominally or usefully committed to environmental planning.
- Dislike for spending money today to help solve a speculative problem tomorrow.
- The reluctance to consider more than the short term because that is where the rewards are.
- Competition between short and long term, i.e. most environmental problems emerge slowly and require solutions which become effective only over similarly long periods of time.
- Organization structures and tasks that force managers to focus on the immediate, short-run elements of their jobs, e.g. budgets are for limited periods of time and encourage concern with this year's results, and maybe next year's.

Lack of acceptance

The problem is that environmental analysis is not accepted within the company.

- Some degree of scepticism as to the possibility of success with environmental analysis - more so at lower levels than at the top.
- Lack of understanding of the usefulness of environmental analysis.
- Difficulty of environmental analysts convincing line managers that the former's output is applicable to the latter's problems.
- The 'we already know our business' attitude on the part of operating management.

Table 3.6 concluded

- A suspicion in the practical world of business decisions that scenarios and possible occurrences are impractical and somehow dangerous.
- The 'we have been successful without it' attitude.
- A resistance to change in forecasting methods.
- The presumption by too many executives that each of them can be their own expert in assessing environmental impacts upon the company.
- Lack of commitment and personal involvement of line executives.
- The difficulty of breaking the patterns of thinking in the past.

Diversified businesses
The problem is that diversified businesses mean multiple relevant environments which make environmental analysis too complex.

- Difficulty of applying corporate expertise in environmental analysis at the operating level due to the great diversity of our operations.
- Complexity due to multiple and decentralized organization.
- Need for too large a corporate staff to keep abreast of environments for decentralized, autonomous businesses, and unwillingness of line managers to support a full-time staff for environmental surveillance at the division level.

Misperceptions
The problem is one of narrow, limited or invalid perceptions of the external environment shared by executives.

- Tendency of managers to think in non-discontinuous terms.
- Unpreparedness of managers, because of education or basic interest, to deal with social, political and cultural aspects of a rapidly changing environment (many managers are knowledge reductionists rather than holistic).
- Traditional inability to think in world market terms (instead of 'plant countries') when considering trends and factors of a social, political, technological and economic origin.

Table 3.7
A typical sequential model of the ideal environmental scanning procedure

---

1 *Monitor* broad trends, issues and events occurring in the firm's task environment. This can be complemented by means of identifying a core list of relevant publications and assigning them to volunteers who report important articles to environmental analysis for further study. Selected areas of the remote environment should be reviewed from

Table 3.7 continued

time to time. External consultants may be employed, as they often are in identifying and evaluating candidate diversification or acquisition opportunities within the markets or technologies unfamiliar to the firm.

2   *Identify* trends and the like which may have significance for the firm. An analysis team of senior executives should determine and implement the criteria by means of which *relevance* is established. Weak signals may not be amenable to screening in this way.

3   *Evaluate* the impact of significant trends, etc., on the firm's operations in its current product markets. Those having a significant impact will either be *threats* or *opportunities.* Line managers should participate in the evaluation.

4   *Forecast* the possible future directions of the significant trends, etc., and *examine* the new opportunities and threats they appear more likely to generate. Both analyst and strategist should be involved in making the choice of environmental analysis and forecasting techniques (see Table 3.8).

5   *Evaluate* the impact of these threats and opportunities on the firm's long-term strategies. The output of steps 3, 4 and 5 can be summarized by means of the environmental threat and opportunity profile shown in Figure 3.1.

6   *Report* the progress of specific environmental analysis projects, in addition to the regular monitoring activities, on a periodic basis.

Defining boundaries

To define the boundaries of the firm's environments in terms of concrete measures is an almost impossible task for all but the smallest of one-product firms servicing a local market. Nevertheless, the environmental scanner needs practical guidelines to separate relevant information from irrelevant.

Such guidelines should be determined in consultation with the top management team responsible for formulating long-term strategies and plans. The user and the analyst can define the terms of reference and objectives of scanning assignments. In this way, an operational definition of a target zone of the environment is at least possible, using as a reference point the data needs of the strategists. Of course, the definition will depend on the position and abilities of the members of the environmental analysis team, their past experience in such projects and success in applying research and forecasting techniques.

But there are no hard and fast rules for making the distinction between relevance and irrelevance. Both Stubbart (1982) and Diffenbach (1983) found organizations continuously frustrated in their efforts to arrive at a workable definition of their business environment. The nub of the problem is one of achieving a balanced view of the scope of the firm's environment. To avoid misdirecting effort to peripheral and irrelevant issues it must not be too wide in scope. Neither should it be a narrow, data-dependent, econometric but relevant, if myopic, view. Clearly the problem will be worse in diversified organizations with several relevant environments (see Table 3.6). The opportunity cost of the constricted view of the firm's environment may greatly exceed the actual cost of scanning areas of the wider business environment – particularly where weak signals are to be detected.

Appropriate time horizon

Given the difficulty organizations experience in defining boundaries, it is not surprising that they tend to focus on familiar environments – preferring to study remote environments on an *ad hoc* basis, perhaps with the assistance of consultants. A similarly conservative view is often taken of the appropriate time horizon for future studies. Diffenbach (1983) found that these were considered by divisional management to be more useful the shorter the time horizon they took. Corporate management tended to take a longer view.

The time horizon should in theory be determined by the investment cycle of the industry and the nature of the product or service it provides. For example in the oil industry a scanning term of 25 years is not unusual; in the fashion industry a period of four years is more appropriate. The time horizon should, then, exceed the duration of the firm's strategic plans. If the firm operates a policy of waiting to see what the industry leaders get up to, then environmental scanning activities may be easily resourced. But they will provide a narrow, reactive view which is biased towards the short term. A proactive regime will be more demanding of middle and top management abilities, especially in multi-product multi-market firms where a variety of time horizons might apply.

Responsibility for environmental scanning

The responsibility for environmental scanning can be allocated in three different ways. First, line managers in functions such as purchasing, sales and marketing can be asked to undertake it in addition to their other duties. These managers are likely to be able to provide information on the business environment and should, therefore, contribute in some way to any environmental scanning system. But this approach suffers from disadvantages: the demotivating resentment the line managers may feel towards this additional imposition on their time, especially where no allowances have been made, resources provided, or training given; the requirement for specialist analytical, research and forecasting skills which line managers are unlikely to possess; the possibly incompatible mentalities of the roles they are asked to play – creative and far-sighted visionary on the one hand, hard-headed operator on the other (see Table 3.6).

The second approach is for environmental scanning to be made part of the strategic planner's job. The division of strategic planning in this way leads to specialization which may also have some drawbacks. Stubbart (1982) argues that the task of environmental scanning:

cannot be easily abdicated to technical specialists at corporate headquarters. Because these specialists do not have to answer for the results of business unit performance, they often do not understand the technical requirements of the unit's business. And, most importantly, these specialists do not have a system for defining, measuring and interpreting a business unit's environment more accurately than the unit's own management can.

It may thus be desirable for both planners and line managers to be involved in environmental scanning. Ansoff (1984) argues that the need for this involvement is seldom more critical than when choosing environmental analysis and forecasting techniques. In his view this choice is too important to be left to the environmental analyst, as it is often done in practice. He argues that the user of the output of environmental scanning has an overriding duty to exert influence on the choice of technique, if actionable information and understanding are desired. Knowledge of the applicability of a technique is more important to the strategist than knowledge of the details of the technique's execution. The details of environmental analysis and forecasting techniques can readily be found in a voluminous literature on the subject (see Brownlie and Saren, 1983).

Table 3.8 lists a number of the more important techniques and relates them to the environmental condition in which their application could be appropriate. Conventional methodologies such as marketing research, demand forecasting, economic indicators and industry studies are also used.

The third approach is to establish a separate organizational unit which is responsible for conducting regular and *ad hoc* scanning at all levels, and for channelling its results to those in the firm for whom they may be relevant. General Electric in the USA is known to operate such a unit and to fund its activities by charging recipients for the environmental information provided by scanning. Where large amounts of data are collected and analysed, it has proved useful to establish a special team whose task is to make recommendations for action to top management, based on the environmental analysis.

This approach may represent a theoretical ideal. However, combinations of the first two approaches are most popular with all but the very large diversified firms who can afford to underwrite the operation of a separate unit. Combinations often operate by means of a temporary scanning team, set up on an *ad hoc* basis to oversee study of the impact a controversial environmental trend, issue or event is thought likely to have on various areas of the firm's operations.

The team membership may consist of both line (divisional) and general (corporate) management: line managers consider the product market, whilst top managers scan the wider environment. Line managers may even be temporarily seconded to a staff position for the duration of the study, often as part of on-the-job training for general management. They will often be closely involved in determining the impact of environmental changes on areas of the firm's operations in which they are experienced. Consultants, either internal or external, may be used where the impact of environmental change is likely to threaten the vested interests of line managers in some way.

There is no clear agreement about the best way to assign responsibilities for

Table 3.8
Environmental analysis and forecasting techniques[*]

Technique	Percentage of companies reporting use of techniques (n=66)	Applicable environment turbulence level		
		Low	Medium	High
Expert opinion	86	•	•	•
Trend extrapolation	83	•		
Alternate scenarios	68	•	•	•
Single scenarios	55	•		
Simulation models	55	•		
Brainstorming	45		•	•
Causal models	32		•	•
Delphi projections	29			•
Cross-impact analysis	27			•
Input-output analysis	26	•		
Exponential forecasting	21	•		
Signal monitoring	12	•	•	•
Relevance trees	6		•	
Morphological analysis	5		•	

* Adapted by the author from Ansoff (1984) and Diffenbach (1983).

environmental scanning. Every organization will experience unique circumstances that merit a particular approach which an off-the-shelf environmental scanning system may be incapable of embracing. Attempts to implant an ideal approach to environmental scanning in an off-the-shelf fashion are likely to contribute to inflated, and ultimately unfulfilled expectations, and frustration. Researchers agree that firms should involve managers of various levels in environmental scanning activities and that it takes time for those activities, and the system which integrates them, to be effectively assimilated into the corporate culture. But if environmental scanning is to become an effective contributor to the firm's strategic decision making, then organization-wide commitment and integration are vital.

Clearly, attention should be given to the quality of communications between environmental analysts and managers. Formal management education and training provides ways of forming managers with analytical skills, which may serve as a basis for communication with analysts. Conversely, analysts familiar with the needs of managers will be more able to communicate with strategy makers. Job rotation may also improve communication. The top manager who has previously served as a member of an environmental analysis unit should find it easier to communicate with analysts. But for general managers, the range of desired skills is so broad as to make it virtually impossible for one person to acquire them through job rotation in one lifetime. Intermediary advisors or consultants can also be used to improve communications, particularly in organizations where the career of the strategy maker is very different from that of an analyst – as is the case where a government minister is a politician and the analyst a civil servant.

Whatever the means by which responsibility for environmental analysis is assigned, I argue that those responsible should still undertake the following tasks:

1 Monitoring trends, issues and events in the business environment and studying their possible impacts on the firm's operations.
2 Developing the forecasts, scenarios and issues analyses that serve as inputs to the firm's strategic decision making (see Table 3.8).
3 Providing a destination to which environmental intelligence can be sent for interpretation, analysis and storage.
4 Constructing a means of organizing environmental information so that a library or database on environmental developments can be easily accessed.
5 Providing an internal consulting resource on long-term environmental affairs.
6 Disseminating information on the business environment by means of newsletters, reports and lectures.
7 Monitoring the performance of environmental analysis activities and improving it by applying new tools and techniques.

Degree of formality

It is not only difficult to decide who is to be responsible for environmental scanning. The degree of formality that should apply is also a matter for top management concern. The view that the organization takes will depend on the extent to which top management feels it necessary to be able to exert some control over the day-to-day activities of environmental scanning. Control may be a problem where responsibility for these activities is devolved to line managers whose own day-to-day responsibilities are likely to take precedence over what they may consider to be marginal 'blue sky' and 'ivory tower' exercises. This problem is likely to be exacerbated where no formal system for collecting, analysing and disseminating environmental information has been agreed. The lack of commitment and scepticism that line managers will often express about environment analysis can only be dealt with by means of education, training and involvement. They need to understand the need for better-informed planning and decision making, and the role that environmental scanning has to play in making this possible. To appreciate this, they also need to understand the forces acting on the firm in its environment and the strategies it has for dealing with them.

Yet, some organizations are content to take an informal approach to environmental scanning, relying on key executives in sales, marketing, purchasing and finance to keep abreast of changes in the business environment through newspapers, trade literature, conferences, exhibitions, and personal contacts. Others prefer to organize their efforts into a series of structured and planned activities for which specified staff bear responsibility. The difference is really one of degree. Table 3.9 indicates attributes that a formal approach to environmental scanning is likely to possess to a greater extent.

Table 3.9
Attributes of a formal approach to environmental scanning

1 Environmental trends, events and issues are regularly and systematically reviewed.
2 Explicit criteria have been established which can in turn be used to evaluate the impact of environmental trends.
3 Scanning activities are guided by written procedures.
4 Responsibility for scanning activities has been clearly assigned.
5 Scanning reports, updates, forecasts and analyses are documented in a standardized format.
6 Such documentation is generated on a regular basis and disseminated to predetermined personnel according to a timetable.
7 The application of formal techniques such as delphi studies and multiple scenarios.

Source: Brownlie, 1987.

The research of Diffenbach (1983) and Jain (1984) found larger US firms to be more likely to take a formal approach to environmental scanning. This is not surprising given that such firms are also more likely to take a broad view of their business environment, competing as they will do in a number of markets with a number of products. But the informal approach is not only the prerogative of the small one-product firm. Diversified companies may prefer to take an informal approach to such scanning activities as long-term forecasting, the generation of alternative scenarios, issues analyses and the management of weak signals. These activities demand a degree of creative thinking that can best be stimulated in an informal environment – even if the output of the process is subjected to a more formal treatment.

The use of environmental analyses in strategy making

In determining the composition of the environmental scanning unit, top management should also take care to clarify the role of the participating analysts, so as to foster realistic expectations of the contribution they are able to make to strategy formulation. The persistence of unrealistic expectations has a debilitating impact on environmental scanning. Unrealistic expectations are

77

most likely to be held, by analysts and strategists alike, whilst introducing a formal environmental scanning procedure to the firm for the first time. Fortunately experience of environmental scanning puts analysts and strategists in a better position to judge each other's contribution realistically, but some unrealistic expectations may persist. Analysts cannot realistically expect strategy makers always to make full use of their analyses, or to apply their recommendations completely and without question; they should rarely have the power to prescribe strategy. Yet, where analysts are given to such expectations, as professionals might be, the reality of their engagements with strategists may be one of impotence rather than influence. In such circumstances, the unfulfilled expectations of the analyst can easily become a source of alienation, misunderstanding and ill feeling. All of which only serves to weaken communications and thereby impede the impact of environmental analysis on strategy formulation – a position made worse by the lack of any demonstrable, direct impact of environmental analyses on strategy formulation. Similarly, top management's desire to delegate strategy making to the environmental scanning unit should be treated with caution. The careful deflation of these heroic expectations will contribute to improved communications and understanding.

The data and analyses generated by environmental scanning are only some of several inputs to the strategy-making process. The major contribution is to identify environmental trends, issues, events or signals that should trigger the reconsideration and, perhaps, revision of strategic plans. Consequently, there is every chance that environmental scanning will have an important hand in initiating strategy changes. Indeed, where a staff unit for environmental scanning exists, the occurrence of such a trigger is likely to lead to a request from strategists for environmental scanning to conduct a specific study of the related issue or trend.

The indirect use of environmental analyses in strategy making is at least possible, by virtue of the quality of its work. However, its direct use requires an enabling mechanism directed to the translation of the output of environmental analyses into specific recommendations or even a plan for implementing strategy changes. Communication difficulties once again must be surmounted. The problem is not merely that a thorough understanding of environmental analysis demands skills similar to those of the analysts, which strategy makers are unlikely to possess. The vocabulary, assumptions, processes and techniques employed by the analysts will also be alien to them. One answer is not to leave the task of translation to environmental analysts alone. They too may be unfamiliar with the arcane terminology, skills, outlook and expectations of the strategists and their peers. The use of specially convened action teams staffed by advisers or consultants is often recommended as a translation mechanism. The best solution is one that brings analysts and strategists closer together, as often as possible.

CONCLUSION

Environmental scanning can make an important contribution to the survival and prosperity of the firm. The increasingly turbulent and unpredictable market environment of the 1990s will convince more and more organizations of the need to scan and analyse their market environment systematically. It is not an easy task. The organization must expect to encounter many technical and managerial problems, particularly in enabling environment scanning to contribute fully to the formulation of business strategy. Reading this chapter is no more than a first step.

REFERENCES

Aguilar, F. S. (1967), *Scanning the Business Environment*, New York: Macmillan.

Ansoff, H. I. (1984), *Implanting Strategic Management*, Prentice-Hall International.

Brownlie, D. T. (1991), 'Environmental analysis and forecasting', chapter 6 in *The Marketing Book*, (2nd edn) edited by M. J. Baker, London: Butterworth Heinemann.

Brownlie, D. T. and Saren M. A. (1983), 'A review of technology forecasting techniques and their applications', *Management Bibliographies and Reviews*, **9**, (4).

Churchman, C. W. (1968), *The Systems Approach*, New York: Delacorte Press.

Diffenbach, J. (1983), 'Corporate environmental analysis in large US corporations', *Long Range Planning*, **16**, (3), 107–16.

Dill, W. R. (1958), 'Environment as an influence on management activity', *Administrative Science Quarterly*, **13**, March, 36–54.

Fahey, L., King, W. R. and Narayanan, V. K. (1981), 'Environmental scanning and forecasting in strategic planning – the state of the art', *Long Range Planning*, February, 32–9.

James, B. G. (1985), *Business Wargames: Business Strategy for Executives in the Trenches of Market Warfare*, Harmondsworth: Penguin.

Jain, S. C. (1984), 'Environmental scanning in US corporations', *Long Range Planning*, **17**, (2), 117–28.

Kast, F. E. and Rosenzweig, J. E. (1974), *Organization and Management: A systems approach*, 2nd edn, New York: McGraw Hill.

Lenz, R. and Engledow, J. (1986), 'Environmental analysis units and strategic decision-making: a field study of selected "leading-edge" corporations', *Strategic Management Journal*, **7**, 69–89.

Murphy, J. (1989), 'Identifying Strategic Issues', *Long Range Planning*, **22**, (2), 101–5.

Nanus, B. (1982), 'QUEST – Quick Environmental Scanning Technique', *Long Range Planning*, **15**, (2), 39–45.

Stubbart, C. (1982), 'Are environmental scanning units effective?', *Long Range Planning*, June 1982, 139–45.

Taylor, J. (1992), 'Competitive intelligence: a status report on US business practices', *Journal of Marketing Management*, **8**, 117–25.

Thomas, P. S. (1980), 'Environmental scanning – the state of the art', *Long Range Planning*, February, 20–28.

West, J. and Olsen, D. (1989), 'Environmental scanning, industry structure and strategy making: concepts and research in the hospitality industry', *International Journal of Hospitality Management*, **8**, (4), 283–98.

Wright, P. (1987), *Spycatcher*, London: Heinemann.

ESSENTIAL READING

Brownlie, D. T. (1994), 'Environment scanning', chapter 6 in *The Marketing Book*, (3rd edn) edited by M. J. Baker, London: Butterworth Heinemann. This chapter provides a thorough treatment of issues of theory, research and practice concerning environmental scanning.

Makridakis, S. (1990), *'Forecasting, Planning and Strategy for the 21st Century'*, New York: Free Press. This book is written by an author who has published widely on forecasting and strategy. It provides an up-to-date and thorough coverage of techniques and their utilization in the context of strategic planning.

Diffenbach, J. (1983), 'Corporate environmental analysis in large US corporations', *Long Range Planning*, **16**, (3), 107–16; Stubbart, C. (1982), 'Are environmental scanning units effective?', *Long Range Planning*, June, 139–45; West, J. and Olsen, D. (1989), 'Environmental scanning, industry structure and strategy making: concepts and research in the hospitality industry', *International Journal of Hospitality Management*, **8**, (4), 283–98. All three of the above articles provide very good examples of empirical research into the practice of environmental scanning and the effectiveness of such practice.

4 Analysing the competition
John Saunders

Competition made humans. Humankind has succeeded because, in the hostile environment in which the species evolved, it was superior in some way, somewhere. The same laws now govern the corporate world that humankind created. The processes differ. Our evolution was unconscious: corporations hope to shape their evolution.

The analysis of competition is part of the strategic management practice of assessing the external environment (Hooley and Saunders, 1993). It is part of the SWOT analysis where a company's Strengths and Weaknesses are compared with the Opportunities and Threats in the external environment. Analysing the competition has a key role to play alongside other components of the task environment. With customer profiles, the nature of the labour market, suppliers and creditors, competition is one of the immediate factors which provide many of the challenges that a firm faces when striving to market its goods and services profitably.

Given the familiar role of competitive analysis in strategic management, why has it recently become such an important issue? The evolutionary analogy helps to explain. Post-war economic growth and the relatively small number of developed countries meant a comparatively benign competitive environment. Burgeoning consumer demand allowed companies to succeed by understanding their markets and serving them moderately well. Recently, the environment has become more hostile. Economic growth in the developed countries has declined, as has the allegiance of the colonial powers' traditional markets. New competition from south-east Asia has also emerged. While western economies were stagnating, the new competition was growing at a rate faster than the world has ever known. In a benign environment, relatively weak corporations – like the dodo – could survive, but the current environment requires better adjusted species. With the lower growth and increased competition, companies have become predators upon each others' markets. No longer does a company just have to look at its customers but, to survive, it must be stronger than its competition in some domain. Competitive posture has joined market segmentation and differential advantage at the core of marketing strategy: the task of finding a target group of customers for whom a company has a differential advantage over competition (Figure 4.1).

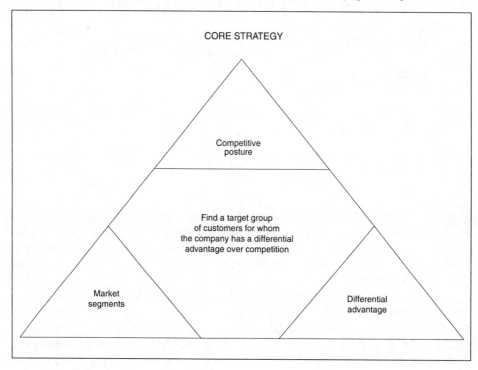

Figure 4.1   Core strategy

This chapter develops a background for analysing the competition by looking at the alternative competitive strategies and tactics that are available. Once these are understood, a framework for grading competitors is developed. The chapter concludes by describing information systems for the gathering of competitor information.

COMPETITIVE STRATEGY AND TACTICS

Porter (1985) provides three generic competitive strategies: cost leaders, differentiation and focus. He proposes, although does not prove, that companies succeed by concentrating on one or two of these, and fail by getting 'stuck in the middle' (Figure 4.2).

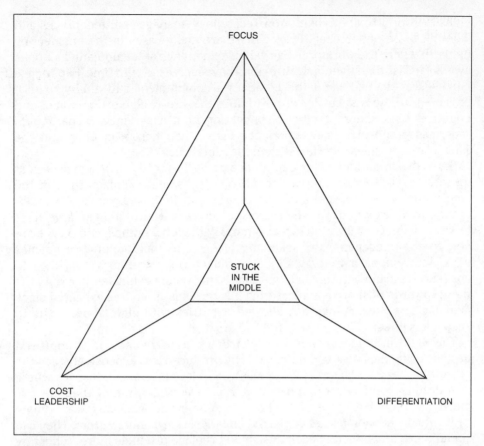

Figure 4.2   Three generic strategies
Based on Porter (1980), Figure 2-1.

Cost leadership

Cost leadership should not be confused with low price. Some cost leaders, such as Amstrad, may use a low price to achieve rapid market penetration, but many operate at the market price or demand a price premium. Boeing, Compaq and Toyota are typical of cost leaders who use their low costs to generate high contributions spent on marketing, R&D and new plant. Cost leaders use their high contribution to fund investments which help them maintain their market dominance.

The cumulative experience accruing from a high market share is frequently cited as the way to low costs. Once a company has the advantage, it can use the liberated funds to spend more on marketing or R&D and so maintain its dominance. Evidence in support of the relationship between experience and cost is strong but the pattern reflects association rather than causality. Making more products does not mean they will become cheaper; it just pro-   83 vides the opportunity to learn how technology, management techniques and labour can be better used. In fact there are many cases in the engineering industry where the workforce has gained experience at manipulating a bonus system so fast that manufacturing costs have increased with time. Experience curves also depend upon the company's commitment and ability to take advantage of the cost-cutting opportunities that are available. Companies and countries have different rates of benefiting from experience. In particular, American companies gain experience faster than European ones and the Japanese companies even faster than the Americans.

Given the limitations of the experience curve, how can a firm become a cost leader? Several opportunities depend on large-scale manufacturing. In the steel industry the Japanese and developing countries have been able to under-cut the more experienced Western manufacturers by investing in large-scale modern plant. Globalization can also help. With global brands, companies are able to obtain economies of scale unachievable by multinational companies who allow regional autonomy. Global manufacturing also allows companies to concentrate manufacturing in larger plants in low-cost countries. In reality the trend towards offshore manufacturing has been less than was expected since manufacturing technology has allowed countries with high labour costs to keep costs down.

The rapid price declines in the electronics industry show how improved designs using the latest technology can be produced less expensively than the generation they replaced. The same is true of less dynamic industries where new designs can incorporate new materials, electronic (rather than electro-mechanical) control systems can be used and new designs use fewer components. Again, economies are conferred on large-scale manufacturers. They can spend more on perfecting each design and replace products more frequently than smaller competitors.

Final sources of economy are labour and low overheads. Labour is made more efficient by investing in plant. The labour effectiveness which comes from co-operation, flexibility and commitment of the workforce is not so mechanistically achieved. Neither are the lower overheads that should come from scale and the investment in office automation. A recent American study has shown that, although blue collar workers' productivity has improved significantly over the last ten years, the productivity of white collar workers has declined. It would be surprising if the same were not true in the UK.

To achieve cost leadership, a company must focus upon tight cost controls. Some of this can be achieved by scale and appropriate manufacturing. It also needs a structured organization so that costs can be clearly allocated and controlled and a lean organization motivated by strict quantitative incentives. Experience curves are only a small part of the story.

Differentiation

Success through differentiation demands skills which differ completely from those needed for cost leadership. The differentiator wins by offering a product or service which is unique, or superior to competitors'. In the early days of the microcomputer market competition was based on who could provide the most sophisticated machine with the most facilities. This changed suddenly with the arrival of the IBM PC which became a dominant design. Immediately differentiators, such as Hewlett Packard and Sinclair, suffered as differentiation became a disadvantage. The new game became low cost and high power but with as little differentiation as possible. It certainly does not follow that a differentiation orientation becomes an unsuccessful strategy once markets mature. Until recently 35 millimetre single lens reflex cameras had become almost standardized, then the electronic cameras launched by Minolta, Canon and others stimulated new differentiation and market growth. In other mature markets design can be used to differentiate products. This approach has been exploited by Bang and Olufsen in hi-fi and Ikea in furniture.

A brand image can be used to differentiate products which are physically indistinguishable. These can be identified by the prominence of the packaging and the manufacturers' labels. Many experiments have shown that in blind tests even loyal consumers are unable to identify their favourite brand of cigarette, soft drink or beer. Without the benefit of the packaging, most also find it difficult to distinguish between such seemingly different products as whisky and brandy. Label and brand image are particularly important for prestige and designer products. In these, brand names that used to be hidden inside the jacket, back of the collar of a shirt, or on the sole of a shoe, are now displayed prominently.

Seemingly identical products can also be differentiated by distribution, for instance, Rington Tea's house-to-house distribution of tea and coffee, Avon Cosmetics' system of agents, and the distribution of some women's magazines through supermarkets or play groups. Perhaps one of the most difficult differentiation tasks is faced by airlines who, because of bilateral agreements, are all forced to fly the same aeroplanes, to the same destinations and superficially charge the same price. But, as any international traveller will know, there is wide divergence in the services offered. Singapore Airlines, British Airways and Virgin Airlines have all gained their high reputation on the basis of the inflight services they provide. Some of these are on the basis of better food with more choice, free movies, many accessories freely available to passengers, and slightly more modern aircraft, but it largely depends upon the attentiveness and professionalism of their cabin crews. The power of quality as a differentiating tool extends beyond services. In Britain, Sainsbury, and Marks and Spencer maintain a differential advantage by offering high-quality products and good customer service which, although more expensive than competitors', are perceived as being good value for money.

Sir Clive Sinclair's early successes were due to his use of innovation as a means of differentiation. It also caused his downfall. A more successful example is Sony, claimed to be world leader in the innovation of new consumer electronics. But even Sony have had to face the reality that innovation is risky. Their Betamax video recorders were the first on the market but were eventually pushed out by JVC's VHS format. Their L-caset audio format sank without trace but their minidiskette system for microcomputers is replacing the traditional floppy disk. Despite their failures, they remain innovators. Rather than bow to the dominant VHS video technology, they have introduced their own 16 millimetre system which is well suited for video photography.

The differentiating company clearly needs different skills from the cost leader. Creative people are needed rather than cost controllers. These days 'me toos' follow quickly, so a differentiator has got to move fast in order to stay ahead of the crowd. This needs close functional co-ordination, and broadly defined performance measures and incentives that encourage innovation.

Focus

Many small companies prosper by pursuing a focus strategy. Without size or resources to achieve cost leadership or overall superiority in a market, they concentrate on providing a product or service tailored to the needs of a well-defined group of customers.

After many British retailers failed in trying to follow Marks and Spencer, success came to Mothercare and Next, who succeeded by concentrating on providing for distinct market segments. Amstrad, a late entrant into the microcomputer market, was able to gain market share quickly by concentrating on two benefit segments: firstly, the market for the computer non-literate who wanted a basic machine with all the necessary facilities that they could just plug in and use; and then the word processor for people with a very specific application in mind but who also needed cheap and easy-to-use equipment. In many ways these two successful Amstrad products were inferior to other micros on the market, but for the target market segments they had clear differential advantages.

To succeed, focused companies have to keep close to the customer, and develop the marketing and design skills necessary to serve their particular needs. Also, since the target market is well defined, focused companies often find it beneficial to provide related products that serve the same market. Richard Branson's Virgin Company is an example of this.

Lastly, because survival in the long term depends upon the identification and exploitation of emerging segments, the focused company needs to be entrepreneurial and retain the spirit of the small firm. They need to follow the dictum 'Think small, stay small' in style, if not in size.

The examples show that some leading companies have not succeeded by being exclusively cost leaders, differentiators or focused. Many top companies are *both* cost leaders and differentiators. The buying power and expertise of Marks and Spencer make them a low-cost company but they trade on quality, service and their brand name. IBM is a cost leader which also trades on customer service. Boeing has lower costs than any other aeroplane manufacturer but the 747, its most profitable product, is unique. Many of the successful low-volume manufacturers complement differentiation with a clear focus, for example Jaguar, Land Rover and Morgan in the automobile industry, and J.C. Bamford in earth moving. Lastly, Amstrad's success needs to be explained in terms of both cost leadership and focus. Their success in the hi-fi market was based on integrated systems at the bottom end of the market which the major Japanese manufacturers were neglecting. Equally, although they were cost leaders, it was their identification of segment needs which enabled them to be a supplier with the audacity to challenge IBM.

COMPETITIVE ACTION

Marketing consultants Booz, Allen and Hamilton (Roach, 1981) have identified two classes of successful companies in terms of pre-tax return on sales: very large companies who can use their low cost and market dominance to achieve high profits, and much smaller companies who have found niche markets. Between the two are low performers who have lost their way. Successful competitive strategies have been identified for three classes of company across this size spectrum: the market leader, the number two company, and the nicher.

The nicher

The nicher, in fact, is a common name which is applied to successful small companies who do not all follow niche strategies. The true nicher provides a unique product or service to a segment neglected by competitors. Modern examples are such niche retailers as Tie Rack, Body Shop and Thornton's, who are not unique in terms of the products they sell but are unique in terms of their focus, product range and their store locations. They are small and yet can flourish economically because, in the market they serve, they do not face similar competitors. They exemplify three of the basic elements that Hammermesh et al. (1978) identified as necessary ingredients for successful low-market-share business: 'segment, segment, segment', think small, and have a ubiquitous chief executive. They are innovative in terms of their market offering, have grown rapidly, but have kept tightly to their target market.

Other small companies have flourished without being true nichers. These are focused companies who do not occupy a unique position in the market place, but have a clear core strategy where they focus upon a target market for whom they have a differential advantage over competitors. Many of these companies – such as Mercedes or BMW – have a strong brand image with an almost cult-like following. Too large to be niche players, yet too small to have the advantage of major suppliers in the market, they need a thorough understanding of market needs and the ability to deliver goods or services which fulfil expectations. So, in addition to their segmentation skills, they have to be able to use R&D efficiently in order to maintain their differentiation through innovation. They must also diversify cautiously and limit their growth so that they can stay close to the target markets they serve. Currently Mercedes is showing signs of having forgotten these rules, with boardroom battles following its diversification away from its automotive roots, and its cost problems.

The strong number two

The benefits of being a strong challenger are epitomized by Doyle, Dayin and Burback's powerful campaign for Avis which claimed, 'When you are only number two, you try harder. Or else.' This diabolical positioning made life miserable for Hertz, the number one. Although lower volume can make the number two company less profitable than the number one, as a challenger they can have significant combative advantages. However, there are some flawed strategies which often lead to the second, third, and lower ranks of industry dissipating their strengths and profits.

As Kotler et al. (1985) have noticed, challenging strategies lend themselves to a military analogy. There are only two basic ways in which the attacker can approach the defender: directly or indirectly. Of these, in both military and business circles, direct attacks are prone to failure. To challenge a well-established defender, by matching it product by product and expenditure by expenditure, requires resources which challenging companies rarely have. Although direct attacks on markets may be the normal mode of competition and be used to start campaigns, indirect attacks are the means of securing victory.

Whereas direct attacks have the benefit of a crude simplicity, indirect attacks on markets have a variety only limited by the creativity of the perpetrators. According to Liddell Hart, the military strategist, history shows that almost all battles have been won by flanking manoeuvres. The same seems to be true for market challenges. In this case the attacker, rather than trying to out-spend the defender in established markets, approaches those which are adjacent to the defender's but where the defender is uncommitted. An example of this is Fuji's entry into the photocopier market against Xerox. They made small machines targeted at the small users neglected by Xerox.

Another case is the Japanese motorcycle industry's attack upon the dominant western defenders. They started by marketing small machines in south-east Asia and other markets. Then, gaining strength as they attacked the market for larger and larger bikes, they were eventually able to swamp the few remaining competitors such as Norton, Triumph and Harley Davidson.

Consumer electronics is yet another market in which the Japanese have used indirect attacks. Initially, the Japanese made few market-share gains against established manufacturers of TV and audio equipment in the west. However, when technological changes occurred – such as colour TV and audio cassettes – a strategic window opened which allowed the attackers to bypass the defenders' established markets and gain a foothold in virgin territory.

The aim of the successful strategist is to avoid direct confrontation. Gains depend upon the challenger's creativity in identifying market segments which are neglected or emerging, and then having the energy to develop new offerings which destabilize the defender.

Market-leader strategies

Although defenders have a natural advantage, they are most vulnerable when they become myopic in the defence of the market they dominate. A static defence is as hopeless as a frontal attack. For years Ford tried to defend the dominant market position they gained with their Model T Ford by refining the same model and making it cheaper. This failed against the emerging General Motors who had realized that, with their new-found wealth, the American people wanted something more than a car that offered 'any colour so long as it was black'. More recently, General Motors suffered a similar fate as they tried to defend themselves against the Japanese by using the same old policies of vertical integration on the model changes and budget engineering.

Static defences do not work nor do contracting defences which depend upon retreating into seemingly easily-defended market positions. This is what the British motorcycle industry tried. To succeed, the defender needs the same agility and purpose as the attacker. Like Coca Cola, the successful defender has to use flanking manoeuvres to guard against potential weaknesses. Coca Cola's launch of Cherry Coke, Diet Coke, New Coke, and so on may have made the company less operation-efficient than if they had stuck to their core product, but they strengthened the company's market position against Pepsi and other challengers. Kelloggs displayed a similarly active defence when faced by the potential challenge of brand products. Rather than waiting until the market had grown to economic proportions, Kelloggs peppered the market with a wide range of brand products in a reactive defence.

The key to a successful defence is, therefore, the maintenance of the energy and initiative that made the company dominant in the first place. It is easy to become lazy once market dominance is achieved, but successful defenders have often avoided such a loss of impetus. Many leading western fast moving consumer goods companies such as Unilever, Procter and Gamble, and Johnson and Johnson have achieved this, as have many pharmaceutical companies and the Japanese market leaders in consumer durables. Contrast these with several western companies who have cash mountains and yet are forced to compete with the Japanese by licensing technology from the very companies who are taking their markets from them.

Although the position of the nicher, the market challenger and the market leader are different, a thread runs through the competitive strategies for all three. That is to create an identification of target markets and the avoidance of such unsubtle strategies as static defences or direct confrontation. However, there is a difference in the long-term aims of the companies in terms of the segments they identify. For larger companies, a shift into flanking segments is a tactical move which they hope will give them an advantage in confrontations. In contrast, smaller companies are seeking market positions where they will be left to achieve their moderate ambitions.

Table 4.1
Competitor assessment grid

Factor	Issue	Rating*				
		1	2	3	4	5
Product/technology	Breadth of line					
	Relative quality					
	Modernity					
	New product development skills					
	Core technology					
	Other					
Marketing	Market share					
	Structural advantages					
	Key account strengths					
	Distribution strengths					
	Geographical coverage					
	Price competitiveness					
	Sales competitiveness					
	Promotional competitiveness					
	Other					
Manufacturing	Location					
	Newness					
	Capacity					
	Productivity					
	Cost					
	Flexibility					
	Other					
Financial	Cash resources					
	Risk aversion					
	Access to capital					
	Other					
Organization	CEO quality					
	Depth and quality of management					
	Energy					
	Flexibility					
	Other					

*5 = very strong competitive position, 4 = strong, 3 = average, 2 = weak and 1 = very weak.

ASSESSING COMPETITION

An understanding of the competitive alternatives is basic to assessing competitors' capabilities. Rather than conducting an abstract analysis of company characteristics, the investigator is looking for evidence of a company's ability to respond and the nature of response expected. This process of competitor analysis can be broken up into two stages. The first looks at the elements which constitute a company's strengths or weaknesses. This can follow closely a matrix proposed by Ansoff and McDonnell (1990). The second stage then evaluates the likely behaviour of competitors.

An infinite number of issues could be included in a competitive assessment grid (Table 4.1). It is also likely that key issues will depend on the market and the company being investigated. The use of scales to rate competitors is contentious, so it should not be used in isolation nor given too much credibility. The zigzag of ratings given to each issue provides an easily assimilated assessment of each competitor's strengths and weaknesses and draws attention to critical areas. It needs to be backed by a description of how each of the ratings was derived. Once the limitations of such summary measures are understood, it is safe to go a stage further and provide an overall weighting for a competitor along the lines used in General Electric's multifactor portfolio matrix (Hormer 1982). This (shown in Table 4.2) provides an overall score for each company by multiplying a rating for each function by a weighting. The weightings are arbitrary and could be changed to fit the perceptions of the users but such tinkering has surprisingly little effect upon final scores.

Table 4.2
Competitor profile

Factor	Weight	Rating*	Weighted score
Product/technology	0.2	3	0.6
Marketing	0.2	2	0.4
Manufacturing	0.2	3	0.6
Financial	0.2	4	0.8
Organization	0.2	4	0.8
			3.2

*5 = very strong competitive position, 4 = strong, 3 = average, 2 = weak and 1 = very weak

Competitive imperatives

The competitive imperatives focus upon the key issues of competitor analysis. They add flesh to the abstract competitor profiles and assessment grid. The assessment is essentially subjective but demands statements about competitors' core skills, competitive posture and competitive reflexes.

- *Core skills* look at the main skills of the competitor. These take two forms: comparative internal measures which judge the strength of elements relative to its other abilities, and comparative measures which look at the competitors' capability relative to the industry.
- *Competitive posture* evaluates the stance of the company in terms of its aggressiveness. Is it proactive or reactive? Is it aggressive or complacent when faced with new competition? Is it quick or slow in the grasping of initiatives?
- *Competitive reflexes* refer to the competitor's ability to respond quickly to threats. It questions the available resource of the company, the ability of the company to learn new skills quickly, and to overcome inertia once it is threatened.

The components of the competitor assessment provide a broad picture of competitors and their likely responses to threats. Competitor profiles give an overall grading of each competitor. These are backed by the competitor assessment grid which draws attention to key strengths or weaknesses, and directs attention to supporting background material. The final stage provides an analysis of the core skills of the company and an assessment of how a company is likely to behave when threatened. This last stage is critical, since many companies have failed, not because they lack resources and skills, but because they lack the commitment to succeed and the energy to pursue new campaigns.

COMPETITOR INTELLIGENCE SYSTEM

It is surprising that systematic collection and communication of competitive information rarely exists in firms. Marketing executives usually depend upon their own reading of newspapers and their contacts to gather information. This can lead to valuable insights into competitors but is casual, and valuable information can be lost or arrive too late. A competitor intelligence system is a logical part of a marketing information system. There are four steps a company should take to improve the quality and quantity of this intelligence (Argyris 1990):

Train and motivate staff to spot and report new developments, particularly sales people, merchandisers, product support and new product development personnel. The importance of this process must be sold to the people concerned and facilitated through a system that makes reporting easy.

Motivate distributors, retailers and suppliers to pass along important information about the competition. This often means key managers maintaining close contact with intermediaries and feeding back the intelligence they gather. These initiatives need to be supported by a formalised clippings service which scans literature and maintains an active or passive information system.

The purchase of information from outside intelligence suppliers, such as consumer panels, etc.

The establishment of an information centre to collect and circulate marketing intelligence. The staff can scan major publications, abstract relevant news, and disseminate a news bulletin to marketing managers. Two communication channels are necessary: an express channel for urgent information and files for the retrieval of background data.

CONCLUSIONS

Greater international competition and limited growth have increased the importance of competitive strategy. It is no longer sufficient to base strategies upon markets. A company must be able to evaluate its own strengths and weaknesses and compare them with its competitors. The ability to identify and establish viable competitive strategies is fundamental to survival. A company must understand this and be able to evaluate its own capability in terms of adopting a strategy of either cost leadership, differentiation, or focus.

To avoid unwinnable battles, companies need to appreciate the tactics that can lead to marketing gains. They must be able to identify segments where they have an advantage over competitors, and make them a platform for further growth.

The growing importance of competitive strategy means that competitive intelligence must be a significant part of any marketing information system. Although a formal system could be an invaluable contributor to marketing decision making, it is less important than the exchange of information which occurs in organizations whose culture allows frequent and intensive *ad hoc* communications between people. Flexible organizations also have an advantage in their pursuit of competitive strategy. As in battle, victory does not always come to those with the most resources. It often comes to the side with the best training, the best skills and the will to win.

REFERENCES

Ansoff, I. and McDonnell, E. (1990), *Implanting Strategic Management*, London: Prentice-Hall.

Argyris, C. (1990), *Overcoming Organisational Defences: Facilitating Organizational Learning*, Boston: Prentice-Hall.

Hammermesh, R.G., Anderson, M.J. and Harris, J.E. (1978), 'Strategies for low market share businesses', *Harvard Business Review*, May–June, 95–102.

Hooley, G. and Saunders, J. (1993), *Competitive Positioning: the Key to Marketing Success*, London: Prentice-Hall.

Hormer, L.R.T. (1982), *Strategic Management*, Englewood Cliffs, N.J.: Prentice-Hall.

Kotler, P., Fahey, L. and Jatusripitak, S. (1985), *The New Competition*, Englewood Cliffs, N.J.: Prentice-Hall.

Porter, M.E. (1980), *Competitive Strategy: Techniques for Analysing Industries and Competitors*, London: Free Press.

Porter, M.E. (1985), *Competitive Advantage: Creating and Sustaining Superior Performances*, New York: The Free Press.

Roach, J.D.C. (1981), 'From strategic planning to strategic performance: closing the achievement gap', in *Outlook*, New York: Booz, Allen and Hamilton.

ESSENTIAL READING

Hooley, G. and Saunders, J. (1993), *Competitive Positioning: the Key to Marketing Success,* London: Prentice-Hall.

Ansoff, I. and McDonnell, E. (1990), *Implanting Strategic Management*, London: Prentice-Hall.

Porter, M.E. (1985), *Competitive Advantage*, New York: The Free Press.

5 The international environment

Stan Paliwoda

OPTING IN OR OPTING OUT?

Operational excellence, customer intimacy and product leadership are goals to which companies of all sizes should indeed aspire but, unfortunately, few succeed (Treacy and Wiersema, 1993). They require selling value to customers by providing reliable products at competitive prices, segmenting and targeting markets precisely and tailoring offerings to match exactly the demands of those niches. Companies that excel in customer intimacy combine detailed customer knowledge with operational flexibility so they can respond quickly to almost any need, from customizing a product to fulfilling special requests. Product leadership means offering customers leading-edge products and services that consistently enhance the customer's use or appreciation of the product, thereby making rivals' goods obsolete (Treacy and Wiersema, 1993).

The reason few succeed may well lie in their home market being too small to afford them the opportunity to compete on a larger scale. Or perhaps they have not yet woken up to the fact that they compete in a global market. A small printing firm in Calgary, Alberta, Canada, which is entirely landlocked, was shocked to find a contract that it had expected to conclude went instead to Singapore. Nothing had prepared the management of this small company to think in terms of competitors not just outside their region but globally. To many in high technology industries, the situation may seem to be predictable but printing is a mature technology which has been further weakened by computerization that brings the quality and control of desktop publishing within almost everyone's reach. The final product is no longer print on paper but may be stored on a diskette or transmitted electronically via a computer modem. Technology has changed the entire process of printing while telecommunications has effectively dismantled geographical barriers which today exist only in the minds of those who should be exporting. The international market today has much to do with survival. In days gone by, international markets may have been seen as jam on the bread and butter, but today they have become the basic bread and butter of business.

Indeed, too many suppliers chasing too few clients is a feature of a recession but in many markets it was a constant characteristic before the advent of recession which simply restored market equilibrium. There is indeed a new Industrial Competitiveness Division at the Department of Trade but what exporters need of government is support that ensures that they as exporters are able to compete with their rivals from other nations on a level playing-field. Nations today are driven by global trade and their ability to control it is long gone. While they themselves have not wakened to this fact, their national exporters and international competitors are only too well aware. It is up to individual companies and their management, as always, to fend for themselves. The decision to go international, like any other decision, is not a particularly easy one. It will require time, patience and the commitment of scarce resources for an outcome that is uncertain. However, as we view the global market today, the decision not to go international but remain simply a domestic oriented company may be seen as even bolder.

Importer 'pull' or exporter 'push'?

Many studies have been undertaken on the basic differences between exporters and non-exporters and between passive and active exporters. There have been several studies also on the phases or stages through which an exporter passes on the road to becoming an international firm. It is always assumed that the exporter is the initiator, driving forward aggressively in a dynamic market. No one has studied the role which the importer plays in this process. This is not to say that there is not one, just that it has never been properly quantified or satisfactorily investigated. The 'demonstration effect', whereby a new innovation will quickly become known in foreign markets ahead of its availability, is well known. What is still unclear is the role of importers, whether essentially active or passive in such situations. In countries like Poland, newly liberated from generations of communist scarcity, the advent of the market created many new opportunities for imported goods. Evidence is not clear as to who took the lead role. On the one hand, there are now one and a half million small businesses registered in Poland. On the other, new brands which have been introduced have become national brand leaders, for example, Panasonic, which took over as leader in televisions from the Russians, by studying the market and planning an appropriate product strategy, offering a television set that had sufficient resistors to withstand voltage surges between 220v and 440v without melting. The support and expertise of the manufacturer is therefore an important variable in market success especially when the channels of distribution are new and the distributors themselves unknown.

As regards internationalization, not everyone shares the same degree of motivation. Today, small domestic markets are being enlarged by international agreements. In the case of the European Union, this calls for complete harmonization as the objective. In the case of the North American Free Trade Agreement (NAFTA), it is free trade which is the focus. National governments have been forced to act, not because politicians believe in free trade as they do not and cannot if they wish to respond to trade unions and local readjustment effects which may have quite serious economic consequences in any one parliamentary constituency including their own. Politicians believe in free trade only in times of prosperity, their political conscience or economic understanding is insufficient to support free trade in times of recession, and this applies to the politicians of all trading nations.

However, markets today are international, and companies sell international products and often brands across national frontiers to international consumers who are better educated than ever before. The dangerous mistake a company makes is to believe that by making their product available in a certain market they are doing the local populace a great favour. Such an attitude is contemptuous of the customer to whom the product is directed and will be recognized as such by the target market. Arrogant ethnocentrism may lead to standardization of product and promotion internationally but it treats foreign managers and foreign customers as automatons without a mind of their own. While managers may have to tolerate this, customers need not and will not. Increasing worldwide competition for like products has created a situation where service becomes often the main differentiating factor between competitive offerings.

WHAT DO YOU SEE WHEN YOU LOOK?

Is the bottle of whisky half-full or half-empty? Some are risk averse, some risk receptive. Countertrade is such an international phenomenon embroiled in risk, and estimates as to its significance vary. Miller (1992) cited an estimated 40 per cent of world trade and stated a General Electric source – one of the key players in countertrade worldwide – as saying that it was worth $15 billion for that company alone. Be sure then of the corporate attitude that your company wishes to adopt as regards becoming international and of the sacrifices that it will demand, for there will be a number of opinions to be canvassed internally, and later much will depend on people pulling together in a common effort especially when things do not go as planned. Whenever something new is planned, it is a significant boost to the chances of success if there is a common focus and vision of what is to be achieved.

Next, have a look at your current sales history and examine the prospects long and short term for the profitability of each of your product lines. If you are presently engaged in exporting, examine closely the export rate and the rate of return relative to your other business. Profitability is not synonymous with exporting (Liouville, 1992). It may take time to cultivate an export market. At the same time competitiveness is known to have several levels, as shown in Table 5.1.

Table 5.1
Levels of competitiveness, taking Canada as an example

Level	Example
1 Major trade zone	Japan & South-east Asia, Western Europe, North America
2 Country	Ranking of Canada versus OECD countries, in broad economic measures (political stability or inflation)
3 Region	Location within several North American regions (Southern Ontario/Northeastern US or British Columbia/Western US)
4 Industry	World market share, as measured by import/export ratios
5 Company	Value added by products
6 Department or activity	Benchmarking the relative cost per transaction or order
7 Employee skills	Education and literacy levels

Source: Sokol (1992).

A cursory look at statistics is insufficient. By their very nature, statistics are only current on the day on which they were collected. Far more important is the examination of underlying trends. In demographic shifts, much has been written about the 'greying of America', a phenomenon happening simultaneously throughout Western Europe where the post-war 'baby-boomers', who still constitute the largest section in the population, are coming closer to retirement. This poses problems for pensions but presents market opportunities in that now there is a new age segment sufficiently young and affluent to still enjoy themselves, so new leisure pursuits, holidays and so on become viable products to target at this new segment. If we look at population statistics, we see also that China has the largest population as we would expect, but India has a middle class which China has not and India's population will soar from 897 million to 1.3 billion by the year 2025. Meanwhile, as Table 5.2 shows, the developed world will account for even less then than now (Population References Bureau, 1993).

More information is available than ever before but there is also the technology to interpret it more meaningfully than ever before. An enterprising company will therefore recognize segments ahead of his competition. Technology will allow marketers to get closer than ever before to their customers (Schmitz and Rovner, 1992).

Table 5.2
World's countries ranked by population size

1993		Population (1000s)	2025		Population (1000s)
1	China	1 178 516	1	China	1 546 301
2	India	897 443	2	India	1 379 556
3	United States	258 328	3	United States	334 716
4	Indonesia	187 638	4	Indonesia	278 170
5	Brazil	151 989	5	Pakistan	275 108
6	Russia	149 001	6	Nigeria	246 030
7	Japan	124 767	7	Bangladesh	211 224
8	Pakistan	122 398	8	Brazil	205 250
9	Bangladesh	113 882	9	Iran	161 913
10	Nigeria	95 060	10	Russia	152 280
11	Mexico	89 998	11	Ethiopia	140 800
12	Germany	81 064	12	Mexico	137 483
13	Vietnam	71 788	13	Japan	125 806
14	Philippines	64 648	14	Vietnam	107 225
15	Iran	62 847	15	Egypt	104 607
16	Turkey	60 705	16	Zaire	104 530
17	Egypt	58 292	17	Philippines	100 845
18	United Kingdom	58 030	18	Turkey	98 744
19	Italy	57 837	19	Thailand	76 403
20	France	57 678	20	Germany	73 201

Source: Population Reference Bureau's 1993 World Population Data Sheet in Hamish McRae (1993).

What are you looking for?

Adventure? Instant profitability or planned growth? Companies spend too much of the time looking in the mirror instead of out the window. A cloned subsidiary abroad is expected to be a mirror image in all respects, organizationally, financially and in terms also of results per unit sold, but what if with organizational change, which effectively delegated power and authority, the subsidiary were then allowed to proceed freely to develop the market as it wished? Few will really allow this, to their own loss.

Do you really want some generalities?

World trade takes place between developed countries and it is the large inter-

99

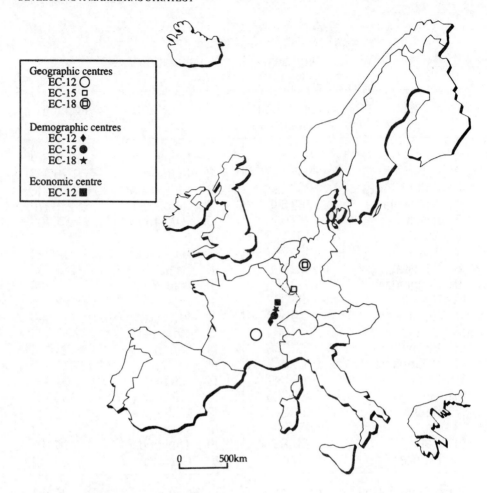

Figure 5.1   Europe's new geographic, demographic and economic centres
Source: Vandermerwe and L'Huillier (1989)

national firms which arise out of Europe, USA, and Japan that virtually dominate world trade. This does not mean to say, 'read no further if you have a
small business'. People always say that they are looking for some general
advice but their needs are usually specific. There are books available on most
things often with an accompanying video, audio cassette and maybe even
diskette as well. Yet it takes time to produce these publications: often two
years elapse between the author submitting a manuscript and the reader picking up a volume. Time is not a variable that exporters have at their command.

Information has to be current and soundly based, yet the vast majority of
this existing literature centres on the developed countries which virtually constitute world trade. Africa, India, China and South America count for very little
on a world scale although in terms of population their markets are expected to
escalate towards the year 2025, when they will account for one-fifth of the

world's population as against one-third in 1950. There are, however, significant opportunities to be had in those markets but the information is scarce and often out-of-date if it was reliable in the first place. China has now become more active in exporting and so, too, has Russia. This will create further competition but it will also create new opportunities for the sale of components, services and technologies. Equally, if your mental map is focused on a Europe of 12 nations, consider the implications of an enlarged Europe as in Figure 5.1.

A single European Market with a single product standard creates new and varied opportunities for those wishing to avail themselves of this market which then creates a new breed of Euroconsumer. Strategic alliances are a significant route for many contemplating business in this market under these new trading conditions. Add to this the market potential of increasing the size of the Union with the introduction of both EFTA and CEFTA and this would add to the Union's size as shown in Table 5.3.

Already larger than the United States, the Union is already both large and rich. It constitutes just under 40 per cent of world trade in its own right and has sovereign power to conclude agreements in its own name with individual nations. Unlike NAFTA, which is of very recent origin, the European Union now has a long pedigree dating back to 1958. Euroconsumers are now emerging who are likely to show preference for pan-European goods and services over local alternatives, and currently retailers across Europe have formed strategic alliances to create new buying centres that will seriously challenge that of the manufacturers with which they deal.

Low-cost marketing analysis

At no cost other than the opportunity cost implicit in a visit to a local library, it is possible to undertake an initial scan of the prospects for your product by region or by country.

Table 5.3
European Union expansion possibilities

EFTA (European Free Trade Agreement)	CEFTA (Central European Free Trade Agreement)
Switzerland	Poland
Austria	Czech Republic
Liechtenstein	Slovakia
Sweden	Hungary
Finland	
Iceland	

Thereafter, better quality more recent data will be required and this is where you start to incur costs. Databases are another increasingly important source of information. Some governments such as the British and Canadian make this   *101* available to exporters at no charge. All that is incurred is the connect time via the phone line. Advantages include speed, accessibility of information, helpline for searches, and the timeliness of the data provided. For small businesses, failure can result in liquidation. Market research for small businesses particularly is both expensive and difficult as owner-managers are unsure of exactly what they want, profitability aside. Knowing the data that you wish to receive helps design the survey. As the old saying goes, if you know the questions you are half-way towards solving the problem. Small businessmen particularly do not understand what they can achieve from market research and their level of relative ignorance of marketing as a function only compounds the problem (Smith, 1989). There is much more to market research than just opinion polling. Smith (1989) suggests the following:

1 Imaginative and creative desk research to include external and internal data sources as well as observation studies of competitors.
2 Use of small-scale targeted qualitative research to quickly identify the potential of a particular venture and identify any potential threats.
3 Take advantage of a number of low-cost ways of conducting large-scale surveys such as omnibus surveys through collaboration. Similarly, telecommunications technology now makes available larger-scale telephone surveys as an interesting alternative for small businesses.

The exporter like Daniel in the den of lions

Next, do exporters understand importers? This was an important question that was posed by Vernon-Wortzel, Wortzel and Deng of PRC exporters and US importers (1988). They revealed important differences in national decision criteria that were troublesome but not insurmountable barriers to trade (see Table 5.4).

Table 5.4
Importance of purchase criteria as viewed by US importers and PRC exporters

	Per cent Who Responded Criterion is			
	Unimportant	Important	Very Important	X^2
Price				
Importers	0	22	78	23.3 (R = 213)
Exporters	8	32	60	0.0001 (R = 198)
Product Quality Standards				
Product is marketable in	1	4	95	13.6
the US	3	13	84	0.001
Meets product workmanship	1	10	89	21.1
standards	3	26	72	0.0001
Meets product styling	1	12	87	17.2
specifications	5	24	71	0.0002

Meets packaging material requirements	2 / 9	29 / 36	69 / 55	15.9 / 0.0004
Has up-to-date quality control facilities	3 / 7	29 / 41	68 / 52	11.3 / 0.01
Meets product technical design specifications	7 / 4	26 / 29	67 / 67	2.9 / N/S
Meets packaging style requirements	4 / 7	31 / 41	65 / 52	7.4 / 0.02
Brand name widely recognized by consumer	33 / 10	39 / 49	28 / 41	29.8 / 0.0001

Production Capability

Can produce in the required quantity	1 / 6	26 / 35	74 / 59	15.0 / 0.001
Has good management control over production	5 / 15	30 / 37	65 / 48	16.3 / 0.001
Has demonstrated experience in making this product	1 / 11	39 / 53	60 / 36	32.2 / 0.0001
Has capable engineers to build up production/service	11 / 9	38 / 39	51 / 52	0.3 / N/S
Has labour cost relatively lower than in the US	18 / 26	32 / 32	50 / 42	4.2 / 0.05
Is known for his expertise in his industry	6 / 24	50 / 55	44 / 21	38.5 / 0.0001
Has reliable, low cost resources for raw material	14 / 33	46 / 43	40 / 24	23.2 / 0.0001
Has reliable, low cost resources for components	16 / 37	48 / 46	36 / 17	28.3 / 0.0001
Has up-to-date production facilities	9 / 12	57 / 54	34 / 34	0.6 / N/S

Delivery Capability

Delivers goods by the date promised	0 / 1	5 / 8	95 / 91	Invalid
Shipping from supplier country to the US is reliable	1 / 7	11 / 31	88 / 62	39.6 / 0.0001
Supplier fills reorders	6 / 21	31 / 50	63 / 29	50.8 / 0.0001
Supplier has a short lead time from order to delivery	3 / 6 / 21	47 / 23 / 50	50 / 71 / 29	25.8 / 0.0001 / 0.0001
Supplier has convenient access to transportation	20 / 13	54 / 49	26 / 38	7.6 / 0.02

Source: Vernon-Wortzel, Wortzel, Deng (1988).

Communications are often greatly improved with the ability to speak a few words in the local language but never sign a contract in a foreign language unless you have native knowledge of all the nuances that may be involved. Law is a crucial factor. Similarities with one's own country cannot be assumed. In fact, it is better to make no assumptions: safer instead to rely on the wording of the contract. Suppose you buy a former state enterprise and privatize it, it cannot automatically be assumed that you also take title to the land on which it is located unless this has been specifically entered into the contract. Similarly, provisions as to retention of the workforce, exposure to past debts, and to future impending taxation are yet further problems that have to be carefully negotiated at the outset as the ability to do so later with any chance of success is close to zero.

The Regulatory Environment needs close examination, especially with regard to the following:

- Environmental clean-ups relate not just to oil-spill disasters.
- Withholding taxes.
- Counterfeiting may be illegal but in any one particular underdeveloped country it is at least providing employment, and producing branded products they argue is not as harmful as drugs. Estimates for counterfeiting vary between 5 per cent and 9 per cent of world trade so it is not insignificant and could not be taking place without the government of the country concerned having some degree of knowledge about it.
- Countertrade and parallel trade is rather like talking about sex in high society. No one will admit to participating in it or getting any benefit or enjoyment from it.

Cultural awareness

Culture is learned behaviour but everywhere we see national culture under attack from an international media promoting branded goods and services that cross national frontiers. From the point of view of religion and politics, change takes place slowly. Consumers can accept change but not offence. Advertising and promotion therefore has to be thought out accordingly. While it is a task that has not changed fundamentally over the years, the environment has changed and certainly is continuing to change. In the late 1960s, the Americans appeared unstoppable in Europe, and this was summarized by the French politician Jean-Jacques Servan-Schreiber in his book, *The American Challenge* (1968). Essentially, then, what the Americans did differently was that they recognized the similarities across Europe, not the differences. The Americans practised effective mass-marketing while Europeans argued and continue to argue over their differences. Today, though, the environment has changed once again. Within nations, various peoples seek recognition which may mean:

- Country name change. Czechoslovakia split into two: Slovakia and the Czech Republic.

- Language embodies the culture of a people whether in French Canada or East Africa or Poland or anywhere else. Language is something that made us as a people and so has an important pride of place.
- Ethnic cleansing is a term of which the world was ignorant until it witnessed the atrocities in the civil war in the break-up of the former Yugoslavia.

Environmentalism has entered the language everywhere, influencing public opinion about products and about corporate policies damaging to world biosystems. There is now complete scientific consensus on the fact of global warming, the only questions remaining are how much warming will occur and when (Doran, 1990). At one level, it is a plea by the rich developed nations to save the atmosphere and climate patterns of the world. For the underdeveloped nations, it poses risks to traditional exports such as refrigerators containing CFCs known to be harmful to the ozone layer, and to timber exports of hardwoods such as mahogany that cannot be replaced as quickly as the softwoods such as pine. The underdeveloped countries see in this movement an attempt only to deny them a place in world exports. What needs to take place, of course, is a transferral (preferably free of charge) of current technologies that will replace existing practices. Without this, we have no more than an international agenda incapable of implementation. At the micro-level, however, we have real estate companies anxious now to limit their financial exposure as a result of property transactions and related industry operations by seeking answers to the pollution on the land that passes through their hands. A proactive approach to such pollution could be seen to have the following advantages (Souter, 1991):

1 Reduction of future environmental liabilities.
2 Prioritized and phased environmental liabilities.
3 Positive public relations.
4 Identification of waste minimization opportunities.

Finally, however, Alden et al. (1993) conducted a study of television advertising in Korea, Germany, Thailand and the United States, and found that, while diverse cultures share certain universal cognitive structures, the specific content of humorous advertising is likely to be variable across national cultures along major normative dimensions such as collectivism–individualism.

Cultural change

A prime example of cultural change is to be found in Eastern Europe among the former communist countries. Usually we pass on culture down through generations but since 1989 we have witnessed changes there to which national cultures could not readily respond. Democracy means little if you have never known it before in your lifetime. The very concept of a market economy presented a major challenge in Eastern Europe which knew communism after

1945 when the so-called liberating armies of the Soviet Union forgot to move on. However, in the Soviet Union it presented a really major challenge in that few grandparents or great-grandparents were around who could remember the days before 1917. An economic system had failed miserably and another had not been chosen. Into the vacuum entered the market economy. Living experience of such a system was scarce and remains scarce. In Poland, laws dating back to the 1930s and the pre-communist era were turned to, as they were still technically on the statute book since they had never been repealed, but in the Soviet Union as it collapsed there was not even this anachronistic framework on which to build. Regulation then would continue to move out of step with economic developments and political needs.

In a post-Cold War world, much rethinking has had to be done of traditional attitudes on both the East and the West as these new states merge to form a new Central Europe and vie for membership of the European Union. In the next few years some variant of market economy will settle down and become a model for Russia and the other independent republics. Meanwhile, there are young willing entrepreneurs in all of these new republics but little in the way of a supporting infrastructure to grant them the necessary funding, accommodation and business permits to start operation (Klebnikov, 1992). For cultural change to become established in Russia, for example, it will require more than just the opening of a McDonalds in Moscow.

Benchmarking for success

Who is doing sufficiently well to become a role model? The search moves outside your industry to become a search for the best in each sector of commercial and industrial activity and not just to emulate them but to learn sufficiently from them so as to surpass them. Take invoicing, for example; the costs of mistakes are high. For invoices and shipping documents it means not getting paid, or at least a delay in payment. From this perspective, the price of not getting it right first time is very high. In distribution, much of a resource may be tied up in transportation and warehousing yet has anyone asked the consumer what he/she wanted? If it is a lower price, then perhaps a lower level of service would be an acceptable compromise. Look around at what is happening elsewhere and be prepared to learn from others not necessarily in your industry. First, learn from your customers; secondly at the strategy implementation stage, learn the best practice of those in industry and commerce irrespective of which industry they happen to be in. Commercial problems are remarkably similar.

Compatible promotions?

Theoretically, good promotions promote the product but increasingly promote the company and often even the advertising agency creating the campaign. International media not only carry advertising but reports also of advertising campaigns that are distinctive enough to be brought to the attention of a public outwith the reach of this advertising.

Such an example would be first, General Motors (GM) bringing out a credit card in their name in the United States which offered the customer the benefit of discounts on a new car purchased from them in line with usage of the card (Kerwin, 1992). It also offers no annual fee and a floating interest rate currently 1 per cent lower than that of rival cards. Ford has since brought out such a card also for the American market. It underlines the strength of the financial subsidiary of both companies and the need also to differentiate and do something different to win the hearts and minds of the American buying public who have not been well-served by either. Yet for the card to be successful, it has to effect a switch in buying patterns, making card customers buy GM over the competition.

Maximizing the return from distribution

L'Oréal provides a good case in point of a company that sees different market segments within a national market and therefore plans accordingly. Examples are to be found in the positioning of their brands such as Niosome Face Cream to banish wrinkles, sold in exclusive upscale beauty shops and Plénitude, sold for one-sixth less in supermarkets and discount stores although it contains the same ingredient and is made by the same company (Echikson, 1993). L'Oréal therefore is able to span both the upscale market and the mass market with its brands to help achieve 12 per cent average annual sales growth and 15 per cent profit growth over the past decade. However, it is also worth noting that they spend twice the industry average on research. An innovation will first be launched as a luxury product then simplified and relaunched in the mass market.

Franchising is another good example of how marketing success can become a commercial asset in itself. Franchising is essentially the transfer of marketing knowhow and increasingly, it is international in character. US studies of 'Franchising in the Economy' show increasing international involvement. Between 1971 and 1988, the number of franchisors rose from 156 to 374 and in outlets from 3 365 to 35 046. McDonald's estimates for 1994 that it will earn 28 per cent of its operating profit outside the US. Franchising is not just an American phenomenon; many British companies, for example, Body Shop, Tie Rack and Prontaprint, have been successful while others would include the Italian Benetton or French Yves Rocher (Welch, 1992).

SUSTAINABLE DEVELOPMENT

The well-known management author and guru to many, Peter Drucker, has put forward his belief that the future belongs to the small- to medium-sized company with an international network of strategic alliances. The multinational has become too visible, too clearly domiciled in any one country and much too large to be able to penetrate markets imperceptibly. The costs of meeting competition are escalating, forcing former arch-rivals into collaboration on research and development for new products with forever shortening life cycles. Not only the costs but the stakes are forever increasing. Faini et al. (1992) undertook research for the export demand function of 23 less developed countries and found that for an LDC a large share of the benefits of devaluation on export revenues are made to vanish when other LDC competitors pursue similar policies. The strategy therefore is not one that is at all capable of being self-sustaining. Tseng et al. (1991) conducted a mail survey of 452 Taiwanese firms of which only 33 were found to export to Europe although the majority overall were engaged in exporting.

Market environment change

This applies to the former communist states of Eastern Europe as well as the European Union adjusting now to the harmonization measures introduced with the Single European Market, likewise to Canada, United States and Mexico as they contemplate further closer trade association under the umbrella of the North American Free Trade Agreement. Markets are dynamic and what is changing now is not only the markets themselves but national government attitudes towards the groupings to which they belong. Meanwhile national governments outside these groupings complain of the potential for creating a trade fortress as with the Single European Market. This is the accusation levelled by the United States and by Japan against the European Union but neither of the accusers is free from this sin either. Perhaps then they more readily see this facet in others. Oppenheimer (1992) highlighted certain trends that should be considered in strategic planning for the next decade:

1   A continuing crisis of economic growth.
2   Domestic absorption of major power centres.
3   Increasing role of international organizations particularly the United Nations, and collectivization of crisis intervention.

Juuti (1991) put forward the list of factors that will change working life in the 1990s as follows:

1   Automation.
2   Internalization.
3   Higher levels of education and training.
4   An ageing population.
5   Changing values and attitudes.

Speculative business

This will be short term but, while it may reap some benefit for the individual company, it may also be disruptive to the host market in which it is operating. Pricing is at the top of the list of short-term strategies, and may be predatory in nature. Dumping is one example, defined in terms of selling in the host country market for less than in the country of origin and of being injurious to local industry. Yet another speculative form of business is counterfeiting. Estimates vary widely as to the penetration of counterfeiting within world trade, some as high as 5 per cent of world trade. Countertrade with its more sophisticated variants of barter has become the new generic term for what is still erroneously termed 'barter', as what takes place is payment partly in convertible currency and partly in goods, whereas payment in barter proper allows only for the payment of goods with other goods. Choosing to enter into countertrade deals can be highly speculative particularly where there is no specialist countertrade intermediary to negotiate a guaranteed discount price for goods offered in return for payment.

Beware what is imperceptibly present

1 First, as Funabashi (1992) points out, the Persian Gulf crisis showed that despite Japan's economic power, it had very little geopolitical influence. Equally, Japan is likely to emerge stronger than before from this recent recession as a result of shrewd management by the Bank of Japan (Curran, 1992).

2 If certain countries such as those in Eastern Europe are applying for membership of the European Union, it has to mean the introduction of harmonization of taxes for example, including the much hated Value Added Tax introduced for the first time in Poland at 22 per cent fuelling further inflation.

3 Russian entrepreneurs and others in Eastern Europe want now to make money. Their governments have to create the conditions for them and for Western investors to make the markets develop. Currently, they are struggling with commodity exchanges, as a first step towards a true market.

Make provision for the unexpected

Be prepared for the following:

- Legal minefields enforcing societal protection on the environment and other issues.
- Language nuances of meaning giving rise to ambiguity and conflict because a contract was not correctly worded. This can apply equally when a successful advertising campaign is transferred to another country with its own language or strong dialect. Either confusion or humiliation will result or, in extreme cases, both.
- Taxation, particularly of the retrospective kind.
- Nation competitor economic responses including trade retaliation devices such as from the USA or Japan, which may have the force of their legislature behind them.

PLANNING FOR GLOBAL GROWTH

Koepfler (1989) provides the following four essentials for global growth:

1 Identify potential markets early.
2 Analyse current and future regional markets. Think long-term and assess the strategic potential of each of these markets.
3 Maintain first-hand knowledge of the market by selecting local management with a sound understanding of the local culture and give them decision-making authority.
4 Form partnerships.

This last point ties in with what has been said by Drucker, and by others, that the future belongs to the firm which has a flexible organizational structure, is able to devolve power locally to the regions and can therefore best profit from the advantages to be gained from strategic alliances which maintain the semblance of a local organization but with international tentacles.

REFERENCES

Alden, Dana L., Hoyer, Wayne D. and Lee, Chol (1993), 'Identifying global and culture specific dimensions of humour in advertising: a multinational analysis', *Journal of Marketing*, **57**, (2), April, 64–75.

Curran, John L. (1992), 'Why Japan will emerge stronger', *Fortune*, May 11, 46–53.

Doran, Lee (1990), 'Investing in a greenhouse world', *Canadian Banker*, **97**, (2), March–April, 28–33.

Echikson, William (1993), 'Aiming at high and low markets', *Fortune*, **127**, March 22, 89.

Faini, Riccardo, Clavijo, Fernando and Senhadji-Semlali, Abdel (1992), 'The fallacy of composition argument: Is it relevant for LDC's manufacturers' exports?', *European Economic Review*, **36**, (4), May, 865–82.

Funabashi, Yoichi (1992), 'Japan and the new world order', *Foreign Affairs*, **70**, (5), Winter, 58–74.

Juuti, Pauli (1991), 'Work in the 1990's: Improving productivity and the quality of working life', *Industrial Commercial Training*, **22**, (1), 6–11.

Kerwin, Kathleen (1992), 'Can GM sell cars with a credit card?', *Business Week*, September 21, 78.

Klebnikov, Paul (1992), 'A market grows in Russia', *Forbes*, June 8, 78–82.

Koepfler, Edward R. (1989), 'Strategic options for global market players', *Journal of Business Strategy*, July/August, 46–50.

Liouville, Jacques (1992), 'Under what conditions can exports exert a positive influence on profitability?', *Management International Review*, **32**, (1), 41–54.

McRae, Hamish (1993), 'How to fit 8.5 billion people on the globe', *Independent*, 12 May, 20.

Miller, Cyndee (1992), 'Worldwide money crunch fuels more international barter', *Marketing News*, **26**, (5), March 2, 5.

Oppenheimer, Michael F. (1992), 'Challenges to planning and strategy in the 1990's', *Vital Speeches*, **59**, (5), December 15, 130–34.

Servan-Schreiber, Jean-Jacques (1968), *The American Challenge*, New York: Atheneum.

Schmitz, Robert A. and Rovner, Marc L. (1992), 'A world of diminishing distance: how information technology is collapsing the transaction barriers between marketers and consumers', *Marketing and Research Today*, **20**, (4), November, 227–36.

Smith, David (1989), 'Small is beautiful but difficult: towards cost-effective research for small business', *Marketing and Research Today*, November, 192–204.

Sokol, Reuben (1992), 'Gaining a world-class edge', *CMA Magazine*, September, 16–19.

Souter, Gavin (1991), 'Environmental cleanups gain attention', *Business Insurance*, **25**, (31), August 5, 25–7.

Treacy, Michael and Wiersema, Fred (1993), 'Customer intimacy and other value disciplines', *Harvard Business Review*, January–February, 84–97.

Tseng, Jou-ying and Yu, Chwo-Ming Joseph (1991), 'Export of industrial goods to Europe: The case of large Taiwanese firms', *European Journal of Marketing*, **25**, (9), 51–63.

Vandermerwe, Sandra and L'Huillier, Marc-Andre (1989), 'Euro-consumers in 1992', *Business Horizons*, January–February, 30–40.

Vernon-Wortzel, Heidi, Wortzel, Lawrence H. and Deng, Shengliang (1988), 'Do neophyte exporters understand importers?', *Columbia Journal of World Business*, Winter, 49–56.

Welch, Lawrence S. (1992), 'Developments in international franchising', *Journal of Global Marketing*, **6**, (1/2), 81–97.

ESSENTIAL READING

Paliwoda, Stanley J. (1993), *International Marketing* (2nd edn), Oxford: Heinemann.

Paliwoda, Stanley J. (1994), *Essence of International Marketing*, Hemel Hempstead: Prentice-Hall.

Paliwoda, Stanley J. and Ryans, John K. Jr. (1994), *International Marketing Reader*, London: Routledge.

6 Relationship marketing

Evert Gummesson

In this chapter relationship marketing (RM) is introduced, first by a definition and examples, then by listing 30 marketing relationships, the 30Rs. As RM is part of the whole management process, the marketer must understand the interdependency between marketing and organizational design, and therefore the modern network organization is presented. The benefits of RM and its implications for marketing planning are described in the next sections. The chapter ends with comments on the novelty of RM.

DEFINING RELATIONSHIP MARKETING

In this chapter, we will use the following definition of RM: 'Relationship marketing is marketing seen as relationships, networks and interaction.' *Relationships* require at least two parties who are in contact with each other. The basic relationship in marketing is that of an exchange between a supplier and a customer (see Figure 6.1).

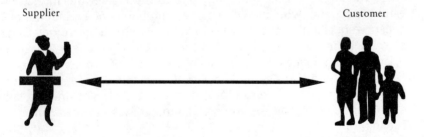

Figure 6.1   The relationship between a supplier and a customer
Source: Gummesson (1994).

Networks emerge when the relationships become many, complex, and difficult to overview (see Figure 6.2).

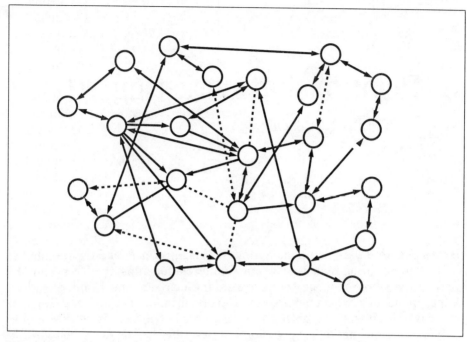

Figure 6.2   A network of relationships
Source: Gummesson (1994).

In the relationships, the parties enter into active contact with each other. This is called *interaction*. The following examples of key marketing activites show the variety of applications for relationships, networks and interaction:

- The old saying that all business is local holds true even in the era of global business. Joshua Tetley in the UK controls 1 000 pubs. In order to strengthen the personal relationship to the consumer the 100 Club was established. Staff who knew the names and habits of a minimum of 100 guests were eligible for membership. A misgiving was expressed that the club might not get any members at all. The outcome was a great surprise: 500 employees knew the names of 600 customers or more; the champion could address 1 200 customers by name. In the pub the customer seeks company, relaxation, and pleasure. It is a business relationship although it can be personal; sometimes it even turns into friendship.
- Carl Sewell of Dallas, Texas, and Stew Leonard of Norwalk, Connecticut, are both masters in creating long-term customer relationships. Sewell sells Cadillacs; Leonard fresh food. Their philosophy is similar. For Sewell a customer was worth US $332 000 in 1990 (Sewell, 1990). That is

the average lifetime Cadillac consumption of a loyal customer. When Sewell visited Stew Leonard in 1990, Leonard pointed out a customer approaching his store and said: 'Here comes 50 000 dollars.' Leonard's estimate was based on a customer kept for ten years, spending $100 weekly. Both Sewell and Leonard listen to the customers and observe them, not through questionnaires and written reports but in real life and real time. Action is taken here and now. The strategy is customer retention, and customers stay loyal because they like the provider.

- The Italian Benetton family, merchants of branded fashion clothes and accessories, has 6 400 franchised shops in some hundred countries. Its founder, Luciano Benetton, travels to the shops to exercise leadership and collect his own impressions; so do 200 of his staff. Furthermore, the Benetton shops are part of an online computer network which enables global monitoring of current sales. This is both a close and distant relationship, based on personal contact, utilization of state-of-the-art information technology, and streamlined logistics.

- Professional services are mainly marketed through reputation, personal networks and ongoing interaction in assignments. One of the world's largest management consultants, McKinsey & Company, win a substantial portion of their orders from ex-consultants. They encourage consultants to accept positions offered by their clients. They arrange beautiful exits for quitting consultants in order to make the ex-consultants feel loyal to their former employer. They offer automatic membership in an alumni association. When in need of consulting services, where else would an ex-McKinsey consultant turn?

- From its humble beginnings in 1922, the Reader's Digest established advanced relationships with its readers through the mail. The prime target was finding and keeping subscribers, and only secondarily achieving sales through retailers. Its founders, the Wallaces, realized the value of the names and addresses as well as of the record of buying behaviour of its subscribers. They used the customer base to market related products such as books and gramophone records. Their mailing lists are structured in accordance with previous buying behaviour: subscriber, subscriber who bought one special book, subscriber who bought the quarterly condensed books, subscriber who gave a gift subscription for Christmas, and so on. The ability to stay in touch through direct mail is different from the contact at the local pub; the Wallaces were early in managing the paradox of customized mass marketing. They managed this before the advent of the computer, but the computer has made the use of the customer base even more efficient.

- Deregulation in Europe and America has made it possible for national telecoms to expand their markets. But they can hardly do it on their own. Three telecom organizations from small countries – the Netherlands, Sweden, and Switzerland – have formed the Unisource alliance. British Telecom has joined forces with MCI Communications, the second largest operator of international telecommunications in the

US. In the early 1980s, because of antitrust laws, the then dominating telecom company in the US – Bell – was broken up into seven regional operators, the Baby Bells. The purpose was to stimulate competition. AT&T is prohibited by law to acquire stock in the Baby Bells, but by acquiring, in 1993, the largest operating company in mobile telephony (McCaw), AT&T can, with the help of cellular technology, bypass regional and local telecom operators. Competition thus takes new forms and old regulations are nullified by alliances and novel technology. The relationships created through these alliances provide new and necessary platforms for marketing. Alliances have succeeded mergers and acquisitions in popularity. They allow more rapid growth than is possible through the hiring of own talent and competency.

- Compared to in Japan, it is easy to become a supplier in Europe and the US, but it is just as easy to be thrown out. In Japan the relationship is more stable and long term. The word 'keiretsu' signifies sustaining personal and financial relationships between firms. For the foreign company, the 'keiretsu' links, cartels, and old-boy network represent formidable obstacles that Japanese corporations do not face when they go overseas. The personal and social networks often determine the business networks. In some cultures, business is almost solely conducted between friends and friends-of-friends.

In these examples relationships, networks, and interactions of different kinds are applied to marketing. They show the wide scope of RM. We are surrounded by relationships in our daily lives, as business people, consumers and family members. We refer to people as well-connected, belonging to the right clubs, and having influential relatives. We have girlfriends or boyfriends, go steady, marry, have an affair, divorce. Dancing is a dynamic relationship. You can invite someone to dance. It can be a smooth waltz but you also step on your partner's toes. Peters (1992, p. 17) makes it even more dramatic: 'Today's global economic dance is no Strauss waltz. It's break dancing accompanied by street rap. The effective firm is much more like Carnival in Rio than A Pyramid Along the Nile.'

Research in marketing during the past 20 years particularly points to the significance of relationships, networks and interaction. So does practice. The interest in RM is growing internationally; some books have appeared and the number of articles is growing fast. The notion of RM clearly differs from the definition of marketing suggested by the American Marketing Association (AMA, 1985), which tends to become an 'official' international definition:

Marketing is the performance of planning and executing the conception, pricing, promotion and distribution of ideas, goods and services to create exchanges that satisfy individual and organizational objectives.

This definition is based on the traditional marketing mix theory, referred to as the 4 Ps (Product, Price, Promotion, and Place). It sees marketing as the active manipulation of the Ps in order to make the customer buy. It is primarily concerned with mass marketing of standardized consumer goods, but is incorrectly promoted as a general approach to marketing. The strongest criticism of the marketing mix theory and the AMA definition is the lack of consideration for relationships (Grönroos, 1994).

Unfortunately there are indications that the basic values of the manipulative marketing mix theory have not changed. RM is too often presented as a bag of smart tricks that help you trap customers. The relationship then becomes that of the fisherman to the fish: 'Get them on the hooks and make sure they don't escape!' True RM must be based on a strategy where both parties voluntarily remain loyal to each other, but are also free to leave.

THE 30Rs: MAKING RELATIONSHIPS TANGIBLE

The philosophy of RM and the examples have to be converted into more tangible and systematically defined relationships that can become part of a company's marketing planning. Through practice and research, I have defined 30 relationships – the 30Rs. These are listed and briefly explained in Table 6.1. With the exception of the first relationship which is the foundation of marketing, the Rs are not in rank order. Their significance will vary between companies and markets. In reading the list keep RM in mind by posing the question: If we view marketing as relationships, networks and interaction, what do we see and how do we use what we see?

One might inquire about the logic behind the 30Rs listing. The basic logic is that each is essential in building functioning customer relationships. Although the logic is not one-dimensional and sequential, some patterns can be discerned.

Table 6.1
The 30 relationships – 30Rs – of relationship marketing
Source: Gummesson (1994).

R1   *The classic dyad: the relationship between the seller and the buyer.* This is the parent relationship of marketing, the ultimate exchange of values which constitutes the basis of business.

R2   *The many-headed customer and the many-headed supplier.* Marketing to other organizations – industrial marketing or business marketing – often means contacts between many individuals from the supplier's and the buyer's organization.

R3   *Megamarketing: the real customer is not always found in the marketplace.* In certain instances, relationships must be sought with a 'non-market network' above the market proper – governments, legislators, influential individuals – in order to make marketing feasible on an operational level.

R4   *The classic triad: the customer–supplier–competitor relationship.* Competition is a central ingredient of the market economy. In competi-

117

Table 6.1 continued

tion, there are relationships between three parties: between the customer and the current supplier; between the customer and the supplier's competitors; and between competitors.

R5 *Alliances change the market mechanisms.* Alliances mean collaboration between companies. Competition is partly curbed but collaboration is necessary to make the market economy work.

R6 *Market mechanisms are brought inside the company.* By introducing profit centres in an organization, a market inside the company is created and internal as well as external relationships of a new kind emerge.

R7 *The service encounter: interaction between the customer and front-line personnel.* Production and delivery of services involve the customer in an interactive relationship with the service provider's personnel.

R8 *Inter-functional and inter-hierarchical dependency: the relationship between internal and external customers.* The dependency between the different tiers and departments in a company is seen as a process consisting of relationships between internal and external customers.

R9 *Relationships via full-time marketers (FTMs) and part-time marketers (PTMs).* Those who work in marketing and sales departments – the FTMs – are professional relationship-makers. All others who perform other main functions yet influence customer relationships directly or indirectly are PTMs. There are also contributing FTMs and PTMs outside the organization.

R10 *Internal marketing: relationships with the 'employee market'.* Internal marketing can be seen as part of RM as it gives indirect and necessary support to the relationships with external customers.

R11 *The non-commercial relationship.* This is a relationship between the public sector and citizens/customers, but includes also voluntary organizations and other activities outside of the profit-based or moneterized economy, such as those performed in families.

R12 *Physical distribution: the classic marketing network.* The physical distribution consists of a network of relationships and is sometimes totally decisive for marketing success.

R13 *The electronic relationship.* An important volume of marketing today takes place through networks based on information technology. This volume is expected to grow in significance.

R14 *Mega-alliances.* EU (The European Union) and NAFTA (The North America Free Trade Agreement) are examples of alliances above the level of the single company and industry. They exist on a government and supranational level.

R15 *Quality providing a relationship between production and marketing.* The modern quality concept has built a bridge between technology and marketing. It considers the company's internal relationships as well as its relationships to the customers.

R16 *Personal and social networks.* Personal and social networks often deter-

Table 6.1 continued

mine business networks. In some cultures, business is solely conducted between friends and friends-of-friends.

R17   *The two-dimensional matrix relationship.* Organizational matrices are, common in large corporations, above all in the relationships between product management and sales.

R18   *The relationship to external providers of marketing services.* External providers reinforce the marketing function by supplying a series of services, such as those offered by advertising agencies and market research institutes, but also in the area of sales and distribution. It is often a matter of outsourcing previously internal services.

R19   *The relationship to the customer's customer.* A condition for success is often the understanding of the customer's customer, and what suppliers can do to help their customers become successful.

R20   *The owner and financier relationship.* Owners and other financiers can determine the conditions under which marketing works. The relationship to them influences the marketing strategy.

R21   *Parasocial relationships via symbols and image.* Relationships do not only exist to people and physical phenomena but also to mental images and symbols such as brand names and corporate identities.

R22   *The law-based relationship.* A relationship to a customer is sometimes founded primarily on legal contracts and the threat of litigation.

R23   *The criminal relationship.* Networks built on a 'criminal business mission' - organized crime - exist around the world and are often invisible, sometimes disguised in legal businesses. They are apparently growing, but are not observed in marketing theory. In more normal business networks, there can be instances of systematic criminal behaviour.

R24   *The mental and physical proximity to customers v. the relationship via market research.* In mass marketing, where the closeness to the customer is lost, the customer relationship is based on surveys, statistics and written reports.

R25   *The customer as member.* In order to create a long-term sustaining relationship, it has become increasingly frequent to enlist customers as members of various loyalty programmes.

R26   *The relationship to the dissatisfied customer.* The dissatisfied customer perceives a special type of relationship, more intense than the normal situation, and often badly managed by the provider. The way of handling a complaint - the recovery - can determine the quality of the future relationship.

R27   *The green relationship.* Environmental, ecological and health issues have slowly but gradually increased in importance and are creating a new type of customer relationship through legislation and the voice of opinion-leading consumers.

R28   *The knowledge relationship.* Knowledge can be the most strategic and

Table 6.1 concluded

> critical resource and 'knowledge acquisition' is often the rationale for alliances.
>
> R29 *The mass media relationship.* The media can be supportive or damaging to marketing. Sometimes relationships to the media are crucial for success or failure.
>
> R30 *The monopoly relationship: the customer or supplier as prisoners.* When competition is inhibited, the customer may be at the mercy of the provider – or the other way around. They become prisoners.

Some relationships are primarily externally oriented and involve a direct contact with customers: the classic dyad between supplier and customer (R1), the relationship between the many-headed seller and the many-headed buyer (R2), the classic triad of customers, suppliers and competitors (R4), the service encounter and the interaction between the customer and front-line personnel (R7), and the interaction between the part-time marketers and the customers (R9). Some of these relationships primarily concern consumers and others are intercorporate relationships. These are all market relationships, applicable to the market proper.

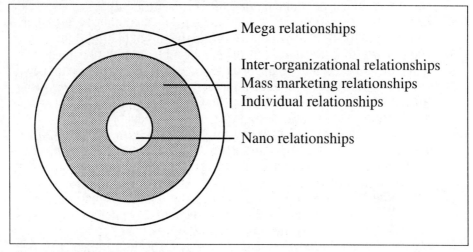

Figure 6.3   RM ranges from relationships below the market to market relationships and relationships above the market
Source: Gummesson (1994).

Certain relationships are nano relationships (from Greek 'nanos', dwarf). These are primarily internally oriented and indirect, providing support to the market relationships. Among these are the market mechanisms that have been brought inside the company (R6), the inter-hierarchical and inter-functional dependency (R8), internal marketing to reach the 'employee market' (R10),

120

quality as a bridge between technology and marketing (R15), and the two-dimensional matrix relationship (R17).

Other relationships are mega relationships on levels above the market proper. Megamarketing (R3) and mega-alliances (R14) belong here, and to a certain extent also personal and social networks (R16), and the relationship to the mass media (R29).

Figure 6.3 shows marketing relationships as concentric circles, starting with the supplier and the nano relationships. The shaded circles signify the actual market relationships. The mega relationships of the outer circle envelope the nano and the market relationships. Both the nano and mega relationships are necessary to make daily marketing work; they are supportive from below and from above.

Organizational issues unite some of the Rs: alliances change the market mechanisms (R5), the relationship to external providers of marketing services (R18), and the owner and financier relationship (R20). There is a series of special relationships to customers: the non-commercial relationship (R11), the relationship to the customer's customer (R19), relationships to symbols and image (R21), the proximity to the customer v. the relationship via market research (R24), the customer as member (R25), the relationship to the dissatisfied customer (R26), and the monopoly relationship taking the customer or supplier prisoner (R30).

The relationships also concern form and content in varying ratios. The form – the conduit – is emphasized in the classic marketing network of physical distribution (R12) and the electronic relationship (R13). In the green relationship (R27) and the knowledge relationship (R28), focus is on content.

Some relationships do not exist in the marketing literature at all, although they are practised in everyday operations. Among these are the electronic relationship (R13), the law-based relationship (R22) and the criminal relationship (R23). Others display aspects that are particularly topical and urgent but are not observed in the marketing literature, notably the green relationship (R27) and the knowledge relationship (R28).

RM AND THE MODERN CORPORATION: MANAGING THE NETWORK

RM concerns every employee. Some employees influence customer relationships as full-time marketers working in a marketing or sales department. The main job of others is not marketing, but part of their time they influence – directly or indirectly – relationships to customers; they are part-time marketers (Gummesson, 1991). Marketing is embedded in the whole management process which makes it more appropriate to speak of marketing-oriented management than of marketing management. In order to understand RM, therefore, it is necessary to understand the 'soul' of the new corporation.

Companies are more and more being seen as networks and dynamic entities that change their shape continuously. There are many names for the new corporation: the network organization, the virtual organization, the boundaryless *121* organization, and even the imaginary organization. RM could be viewed as the marketing aspect of the new organizational structures.

The basic notion of the network organization will be explained below, first with a series of illustrative cases, then in a more generic way.

- *Financial services.* AFS (Assurance and Financial Services), a subsidiary of the Skandia insurance company, describes its organization as consisting of 500 000 customers, 12 000 active and independent brokers, 1 200 employees dispersed over the globe, and a corporate staff of no more than 20 people. Information technology is crucial, the borders to customers and outside providers are indeterminate, and the core organization is kept at a minimum.
- *Manufacturing.* In 1991, ABB (Asea Brown Boveri), producing electrical equipment and services connected with design, installation, maintenance and so on, had 215 000 employees. They were divided into 8 major segments, 65 business areas, 1 300 subsidiaries, 5 000 profit centres and innumerable teams. ABB wants to be global and local, large and small, centralized and decentralized, hoping to get the best out of each extreme.
- *Professional services.* Ernst & Young is one of the world's largest firms of accountants. In Chicago it has established a 'virtual office' for 500 of its 1 300 employees. The accountants work from their homes and from cellular phones in their cars, in the offices of their clients, in hotel rooms and conference facilities, in airports and on board flights. If they plan to work at the office, they book a room the day before ('hotelling') and the room is prepared for them with their telephone connection and other personalized facilities. To perceive Ernst & Young as the same as their office building and organizational chart would obviously be a serious mistake. It is a living amorphous organism that keeps changing continuously.
- *Retailing.* IKEA has 120 huge furniture stores around the world. Its concept is based on customers buying packaged furniture which they themselves transport to their homes, unpack and assemble, and dispose of the packaging material. If their car is unsuitable for furniture transportation they can buy a rack to put on top of it and vans are available for rent on favourable terms. The customers' work has extended into the service delivery, taking over the furniture assembly and transportation.
- *Internal services.* Within the oil company BP (British Petroleum), the design department works as an in-house consulting company. Its designers co-operate within a network of organizational units, first and foremost including the manufacturing, marketing and purchasing functions. They work in temporary projects with people who change from one project to the other.

Badaracco (1991, p. ix) describes the transition away from the clearly defined traditional corporation, 'the citadel':

Firms were. . . islands of managerial coordination in a sea of market relation-ships. . . Companies are now breaking down barriers which, like the Berlin Wall, have endured for decades. Their managers are now working in a world that con-sists not simply of markets and firms, but of complex relationships with a variety of other organizations.

Gradually we are accepting that companies are not clearly defined citadels and objects. Organizations are fuzzy sets which take amoeba-like forms. They become borderless entities. They live [alleged] paradoxes by simultaneously attempting to be centralized and decentralized, large and small, global and local. They continuously change shape by changing the customer relation-ships and other relationships on which they are built, and by changing the interaction within these relationships. They quickly adapt to changing needs and provide 'instant' products and services in large varieties so as to cater for individual needs. 'Any time, any place' has become a guiding principle. They are difficult to describe and overview.

The network company keeps control of a core business, where it can add value better than anybody else, while outsourcing other activities. Its core is intellectual capital rather than equipment, land and raw material. Information technology and other innovations, faster travelling and better education pro-vide the basis for network developments. The core is usually associated with a unique product or service, an ability to innovate, a unique marketing method, or a financial strength. From the core, a texture of alliances and contacts can be woven. The strength is the ability to combine own resources with resources from other organizations and the ability to grow and shrink more quickly than the traditional organization. It becomes possible for new breeds of small knowledge-based companies to stay small and yet operate with large resources.

The network organization is a transition from a solid structure to a bundle of processes. The currently popular notion of 'business reengineering' (Hammer and Champy, 1993) has a process orientation. So does quality management which is manifested in the methodology of 'process management', in the ISO 9000 (BS 5750) standard series which requires applicants for certification to document their processes, and in the national and international quality awards, such as the Malcolm Baldrige National Quality Award in the US.

In summary, organizing a network business requires continuous creation, transformation and maintenance of dynamic processes and organizational structures which consist of relationships and interactions. Management must defend a new type of citadel which successively changes character and whose boundaries change depending on which stakeholders look at the organization. The organization becomes a project. Traditionally, a project is limited in time, and based on the resources of a stable organizational structure. Today, the whole organization is a project. Figure 6.4 contrasts the traditional hierarchy to the new network format. The hierarchy is clearly delimited. It does not include the customer nor any other actor outside its jurisdiction. The network organization is open to include any pertinent relationship, whether internal in the traditional sense or external. The black node in the network diagram sym-

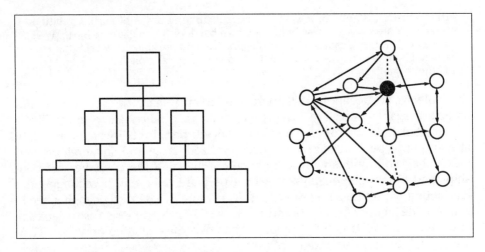

Figure 6.4   The traditional hierarchy and the new network corporation.
Source: Gummesson (1994).

bolizes the core of the organization. The company becomes a network of relationships in the larger networks of relationships constituted by the market and society in general.

BENEFITS OF RM

Three main benefits can be derived from RM. First, RM helps to keep the customer for a longer period, thus lowering marketing and sales costs. Second, having close relationships adds to the security and stability of a business. Third, RM contributes to the efficiency of the market economy which is beneficial both to business firms and citizens.

Keeping the customer

RM aims to create a long-term interactive relationship between providers and customers, along with profitability. It reflects a current trend expressed in terms such as 'captive customers', 'retention marketing' and 'zero defection'. The distinction between RM and transaction marketing (Jackson, 1985) points to the fact that RM is not always the solution. In transaction marketing, each sale is single with no promises for the future; only price and convenience counts.

A popular adage states that it costs five to ten times as much to get a new customer as to keep one. In industrial marketing there may sometimes only be one or a few customers in each country, such as in marketing defence products, passenger aircraft or telephone switching equipment. It is obvious then that a supplier has to handle those customer relationships with great care and patience and look at the long-term profits.

Not only the longevity but also the quality of a relationship must be taken into account. Either the customer or the seller can be the active party or both can be active; the frequency of transactions can be high or low; the interaction can be close and last long; it can be distant and brief, complex or simple, regular or occasional and so on. Berry and Parasuraman (1991) have suggested three levels of relationships with different degrees of dependency between providers and customers. Level One relationships are the closest to transaction marketing; they are primarily based on price. At Level Two, the relationship has deepened to include social aspects; they become more personal and communication is important. Level Three includes a structural bond between the provider and the customer, for example in industrial marketing through a computer-based order system in which both parties have invested. A Level One relationship does not differentiate a company from the competition. It is easy to imitate, while the higher levels gradually become harder to imitate.

Increasing security and stability

Companies need a basic degree of security and stability. Security and stability are associated with promises, honesty, reliability, predictability, freedom from fear of being swindled or let down, and reduction of uncertainty and risk.

Relationships provide security and stability. People with a close relationship trust each other. They want to do repeat business. They create a plus sum game and the strategy becomes win–win, thus making the relationship beneficial to all parties. Without relationships, it is easy to fall into a 'find a sucker' and 'be smart' mentality. Manipulative marketing can be compared to the use of artificial fertilizer and pesticides which increase short-term harvests but impoverish not only the soil but the whole of nature, for short-term greed.

Relationships and security can be dependent on the business culture and ethics existing in a particular industry or market. There can be clear rules and ethical codes telling what is right and wrong. There can be clear rewards and punishments. Business becomes close to the rules of the parlour game; if the dice shows five, you move five steps and this is not negotiable. Growing global competition and mass markets create anonymity and insecurity about the rules of the game and the confidence one can place in others. Swindlers are often successful just because they manage to fake the confidence and trust of close relationships; these are the con men.

Security can also be derived from the law, but legal security may be illusory. A written contract can seldom cover all aspects of a business deal, particularly when business transactions are complex. It can be costly to enforce if broken. The US is an example of legal dominance and weaker relationships, while Japan is the opposite.

If the knowledge of the customer or supplier is superior, security can be derived from this knowledge. For most of us, buying a used car poses a problem as we do not have sufficient knowledge to evaluate the quality of the car. In today's society (often described as a knowledge-based society) knowledge is highly fragmented. We are increasingly dependent on narrow specialists and on products and service systems that we may not readily understand. We either have the knowledge ourselves, or we deal with companies we trust and with whom we are prepared to maintain a sustaining relationship.

Making the market efficient

In market economies, competition is hailed as the driving force for progress and welfare. In its idealized and theoretical form in economics, a market equilibrium is achieved when supply and demand meet, price being the referee. Innumerable decisions and actions taken by individuals – and today also by computers – accumulate and lead to market equilibrium.

However, competition is not enough to create a viable market. It is time to acknowledge a business-oriented type of equilibrium – the marketing equilibrium – based on three forces: competition, collaboration, and institutions/regulations. Collaboration through relationships, networks and interaction is the core of the contribution from RM. There is no market without collaboration between suppliers, customers, competitors and others. This is obvious from the list of the 30Rs. Used wrongly, co-operation curbs healthy competition, but used with good judgement it provides enhanced efficiency.

RM needs institutions/regulations, too, even if business people tend to complain about their existence. The global wave of privatization and deregulation is a consequence of markets having become stifled by misguided state interference and obsolete regulations. Today's important contribution to deregulation is actually re-regulation, abandoning inadequate institutions and regulations and providing supportive ones. The belief that competition will do the whole trick is just as naive as the communist belief that a planned economy, controlled by institutions/regulations, would do the trick. In the former Soviet Union and its colonies, where total regulation of the markets was replaced by free competition, the result is chaos, misery, unfairness, bribery and violence. There is need for 'good institutions' which support economic activity.

We continuously need to challenge and revise the balance between the three forces of the marketing equilibrium.

IMPLICATIONS FOR MARKETING PLANNING

How does RM affect marketing planning? There are two issues to be observed and which may be supplementary to other issues of a traditional plan:

1 Establish which relationship portfolio is essential to your specific business for the planning period, and make sure it is being attended to. Not all of the 30Rs are important to all companies all the time. Some may already be handled well, whereas others may be important but neglected. Therefore a relationship portfolio – a combination of those relationships that are selected for priority treatment – should be compiled.

2   Estimate the cost and revenue and the contribution of profits from the
    direct customer relationships and the supportive relationships. As 'the
    language of management is money', a good question is how the relation-
    ship portfolio pays off. The profitability issue first concerns the outcome
    of the direct exchange relationships with customers and raises ques-
    tions such as: How long does it pay to interact with the customer? Do we
    want all customers, or should we get rid of some? Which new relation-
    ship should be established? Both Stew Leonard and Carl Sewell see long-
    term relationships in terms of profit. Second, the estimates also concern
    the investment in supportive relationships, such as internal marketing
    and lobbying. By defining a relationship profitability equation for a spe-
    cific business, the revenue and cost of the relationships can be better
    understood and determined. For example, there has long been a ten-
    dency for companies to move away from multiple sourcing towards sin-
    gle sourcing; getting the customer to increase our share of the total
    purchasing may increase revenue without increasing cost.

IS RELATIONSHIP MARKETING NEW?

Finally, one can ask how new RM really is. Is it the emperor's new clothes, the
fashion of the 1990s for executives, consultants and business school professors? Or does RM really add novel insights into marketing? My answer is both
yes and no. RM provides fresh lenses and puts emphasis on important areas
that are missing or are given scant attention in traditional marketing. It suggests underpinning values for marketing. This justifies calling RM a new paradigm and the beginnings of a new marketing theory. In essence, marketing
should be systematized common sense. However, common sense easily gets
lost in the complexity of the modern world of business. Successful business
people have probably always understood the significance of relationships,
networks and interaction. It is obvious how much weight companies and consumers give to relationships and how little weight has been given to them in
the marketing literature.

REFERENCES

American Marketing Association (1985), 'AMA Board approves new marketing
    definition', *Marketing News*, March 1, 1.

Badaracco, J. L. (1991), *The Knowledge Link*, Boston, MA: Harvard Business
    School Press.

Berry, Leonard L. and Parasuraman, A. (1991), *Marketing Services: Competing
    Through Quality*, New York: The Free Press.

Grönroos, C. (1994), 'Quo vadis, marketing? Towards a relationship marketing
    paradigm', *Journal of Marketing Management*, **10**, (4).

Gummesson, Evert (1991), 'Marketing revisited: the crucial role of the part-time marketer', *European Journal of Marketing*, **25**, (2), 60–75.

Gummesson, Evert (1994), *Relationship Marketing: From 4Ps to 30Rs*, Stockholm: Stockholm University.

Hammer, Michael and Champy, James (1993), *Reengineering the Corporation*, New York: Harper Business.

Jackson, Barbara B. (1985), *Winning and Keeping Industrial Customers*, Lexington, MA: Lexington Books.

Peters, Tom (1992), *Liberation Management*, New York: Alfred A. Knopf.

Sewell, Carl (1990), *Customers for Life,* New York: Doubleday.

ESSENTIAL READING

Christopher, Martin, Payne, Adrian and Ballantyne, David (1992), *Relationship Marketing*, London: Heinemann.

Gummesson, Evert (1994), *Relationship Marketing: From 4Ps to 30Rs*, Stockholm: Stockholm University.

McKenna, Regis (1991), *Relationship Marketing*, Reading, MA: Addison-Wesley.

Part II

ORGANIZING FOR EFFECTIVE MARKETING

7 The marketing function and its organization

Michael J. Thomas

Marketing as a function is dynamic, and may presently be undergoing a transformation that will change its nature in a radical way. If everyone in the organization understands that customer orientation must involve them, not just the marketing team, then marketing's place in an organizational sense will be changed. Relationship marketing is now being discussed as the new wave development – combining marketing, total quality management and customer service. Relationship marketing (Christopher, 1991, McKenna, 1991, Gummesson, 1995 and Chapter 6 in this volume) will only work if internal marketing is successful. Internal marketing is about persuading everyone, from the telephone operators to people on the shop floor, that they are an essential element in the marketing team.

What follows does not attempt to propose radical organizational change, for it would be premature to advocate and describe the new marketing organization.

Organizations should serve the purposes for which they have been created. This chapter is firmly based upon the assumption that the purpose of any marketing organization is primarily to serve customer needs. At the same time it is recognized that the marketing organization is a vehicle for the company, and in particular for the chief marketing executive, to achieve the goals and objectives of the company.

Marketing executives have two parallel responsibilities. They have to make operating decisions whereby short-term marketing programmes are implemented, and they have to make a vital contribution to the strategic decisions which guide the company into the future and which ensure its long-term survival in the face of social, technological, environmental and, in particular, competitive change. Good marketing organization must accommodate and be responsive to the needs of both operating and strategic decision making.

Very few companies in the UK are marketing companies. Though many chief marketing executives will happily state that they have embraced the marketing concept, such evidence as we have about marketing organizations in the UK suggests that only a minority of companies are organized to implement it effectively.

Too many chief marketing executives are preoccupied with operating decisions, when they should be concentrating on strategic decisions. Too many marketing executives are concerned with the short term rather than with the long term, with individual customers rather than with market segments, with sales volume rather than with long-term profit. Marketing organizations in the 1990s must be focused on long-term survival, on exploiting long-run opportunities. They must examine how these can be turned into new products and markets, and how strategies can be developed that will ensure long-term growth in markets both at home and overseas.

There is no substitute for market orientation as the ultimate source of profitable growth, and the only way to be market-orientated is to make sure that the organizational structure of the company concentrates on its major markets.

Most companies, even some sophisticated companies, think with some conviction that they are market-orientated, whereas in reality they are product- and production-orientated. There is no guarantee, for example, that a company which uses the product management system (see 'Product management organization', below) will be market-orientated for, not surprisingly, many product managers can be very product-orientated. In contrast with companies which think they are market-orientated are those which have been forced into new organizational orientation as a result of pressure from very large customers such as retail grocery chains which require that the companies they buy from use a specialist approach. Such an approach is referred to variously as national account selling, special accounts marketing or trade marketing. Similarly, companies which do business with the government, particularly with the Ministry of Defence, have had to develop specialized marketing approaches in response to the unique buying and contracting procedures of the customer.

The logic of such changes in organization can easily be applied to other markets, both consumer and industrial. A number of companies have made an initial step towards market orientation by differentiating between consumer markets and institutional or commercial markets, developing marketing units to deal with each type of market. Some companies differentiate between distributors and original equipment-manufacturing customers. Some companies differentiate between classes of distributors, organizing their approach to distribution on the basis of the different markets served by different classes of distributors. Ironically, some companies are product-orientated in their approach to the home market but market-orientated in their approach to overseas markets, an organizational approach forced on them by the special requirements of overseas markets and customers.

There is no one best way in organizational terms to implement the marketing concept, and what follows is not simple prescription. Rather, a series of questions about the marketing organization will be posed and explored; questions that should enable the chief marketing executive of any company to explore the extent to which his marketing organization is marketing-orientated. It should be said that market orientation is first and foremost a state of mind and the chief marketing executive plays the key role in developing strategies, plans and organization to implement the marketing concept.

The chief marketing executive is responsible for guiding his company into market orientation. He is responsible for serving the needs of established markets, for serving new needs in established markets, and for searching out new opportunities in new markets. What type of marketing organization might best serve his needs?

WHAT SHOULD DETERMINE THE NATURE OF YOUR MARKETING ORGANIZATION

The basic principles of organization

Eleven principles of organization are frequently cited as general guidelines for any organization. They are not immutable but provide a sound basis for organizing any management task. They are classified into four basic elements:

1 *Objectives*. The objectives of the enterprise should be clearly stated and understood.
2 *Activities and groupings*. The responsibilities assigned to a position should be confined as far as possible to the performance of a single leading function. Functions should be assigned to organizational units on the basis of homogeneity of objective.
3 *Authority*. There should be clear lines of authority running from the top to the bottom of the organization, and accountability from bottom to top. The responsibility and authority of each position should be clearly defined in writing. Accountability should be coupled with corresponding authority. Authority to take or initiate action should be delegated as close to the scene of action as possible. The number of levels of authority should be kept to a minimum.
4 *Relationships*. There is a limit to the number of positions that can be effectively supervised by a single individual. Everyone in the organization should report to only one supervisor. The accountability of higher authority for the acts of subordinates is absolute.

The specific properties of an organization

The specific properties of an organization, all of which need to be in harmony with one another, are as follows (Spillard, 1985):

1 People.
2 A mission and set of objectives which together define their tasks.

133

3   Specialization and a separation of skills.
4   A hierarchy of authority as a means through which power is exercised.
5   A control system to secure resources and outcomes.
6   Information flows to enable decisions to be made.
7   Procedures for undertaking defined tasks.
8   A system of rewards and punishment to secure compliance.
9   A set of values to bind the whole thing together.
10 A boundary which defines the limits of the organization.
11 Linking mechanisms through which to relate to other organizations.

The external environment

Markets

The nature of a company's markets will help to determine the nature of the organization. Where there are relatively few markets, a market-orientated, functional or market management-orientated organization is appropriate. Where the number of market groups is large, and none is very powerful, a product-orientated, product management system is appropriate. A geographically dispersed market, particularly one involving overseas markets, will require some form of geographical organization, though this will be combined with product or market management. Customer rather than market orientation may be appropriate, particularly when customers are few in number, requiring negotiated sales and/or a high level of after-sales service.

The business environment

The type of business engaged in will influence decisions about appropriate marketing organization. A company producing fast moving consumer goods is not likely to be similar in organization to a firm selling high technology products to a small number of industrial consumers. The role of advertising, for example, will differ greatly between two such environments, and in so far as the marketing organization will to a degree reflect the relative importance of each of the sub-functions of marketing (sales, advertising, new product development, after-sales service and so on) we would expect each marketing organization to differ. Finally, if the rate of change in the markets being served is high, we would expect a marketing organization to be flexible and responsive to change. And, since there are very few mature, unchanging environments around, most organizations must have this flexibility.

Customer requirements

The buying practices of customers become a crucial influence on marketing organization. Where large customers buy through a central purchasing office, when large retail and wholesale chains negotiate 'deals', and where the government is a principal customer, then market orientation is required – the customer is the market.

The internal environment

Management style

Management style influences organizational design and structure, and history cannot be treated as bunk in thinking about the redesign of organizations. Implicit and explicit top management attitudes will to a degree determine the pattern of individual and group action, of centralization and decentralization.

Product policy

As product lines proliferate, simple functional organization must give way to product and market orientation.

People

Organizations are living things, and human attitudes help determine what an organization does. People and not organization charts give life to an organization. One reason why few companies have implemented (in any meaningful way) the marketing concept, is that the same people who held management positions during periods of production or sales orientation have remained in positions of responsibility when the marketing concept has been embraced. The organization charts in many companies have changed, job descriptions have been rewritten, but the same people are in place. Changes in organization must not ignore people, but must be designed to achieve their objectives through effective management of people, sometimes requiring painful shifting or removal of people if the organizational change is to be meaningful.

Organizational choices

The organizational choices available depend to a degree on the impact various contingencies might have on the organization. A fundamental debate over the years has concentrated on the strategy–structure argument. The traditional argument is that the choice of an organization's strategy must determine the nature of the organization, since that organization must be fitted to executing the chosen strategy. This so-called instrumental view of organization derives from the work of Chandler (1962) who demonstrated that many US corporations showed structures that reflected their chosen strategies. It seems unlikely that each time strategy is changed to cope with the exigencies of dynamic market conditions, structures will have to change in response. Few managements wish to contemplate or cope with ever-changing organizational structure. Thus, ideally an organization needs to be created which can cope with more than one strategy – to respond to changes in focus and direction. 'One cannot say with certainty that structure always follows strategy, or vice versa. What one can look for, however, is a set of contingencies which would help managers in marketing decide in what circumstances one follows the other' (Spillard, 1985; see also Bonoma, 1985).

TYPES OF ORGANIZATIONAL STRUCTURE

Functional organization

This is the most basic structure, embracing the activities of sales, advertising and sales promotion, marketing research and product planning. In large organizations, where a divisionalized structure is used, the functional marketing structure may be utilized within each division, as well as at corporate level.

The advantage of this form of organization is its relative simplicity, but its very simplicity makes it suitable for firms which sell relatively few products in relatively few markets. When products and markets grow in complexity and diversity, severe strain is put on the functional organization. A modification of the simple functional organization which does respond to our previously expressed concern for the importance of strategic market planning is shown in Figure 7.1.

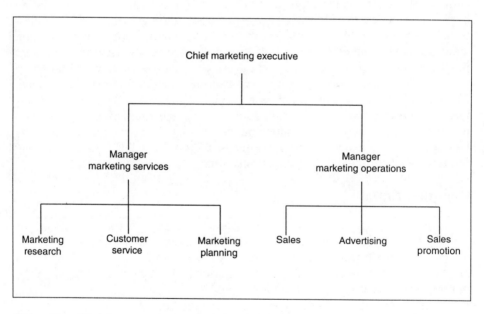

Figure 7.1   Modification of functional organization

Product management organization

The growing complexity of the product lines offered by a company is likely to reduce the effectiveness of the simple functional organization. Then a product line organization becomes feasible and relevant, and in the large fast moving consumer goods companies the use of a product manager system is of proven relevance. Such a system is by no means to be confined to such companies, however.

In the largest companies, when divisionalization takes place, each division may be organized around a major product or product group. The brand manager structure in one division of Beechams is shown in Figure 7.2. A generalized form of a product or brand management system is shown in Figure 7.3 (Thomas, 1991).

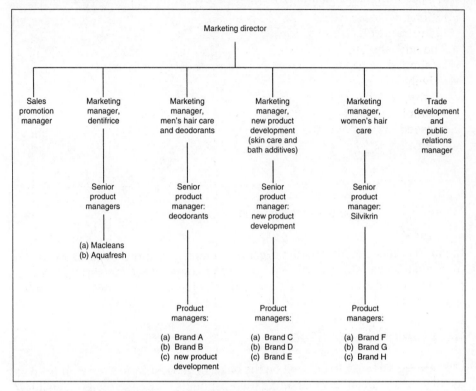

Figure 7.2   Example of brand management structure

Market management organization

It was stated initially that the purpose of any marketing organization is to serve consumer needs, which is the meaning of the marketing concept. Growing market orientation may require an organizational response as described above, namely greater attention to the product–market fit by use of a product manager system, or a system that concentrates on the needs of particular markets and use industries or channels of distribution. The term 'trade marketing' has been used to describe this organizational approach (particularly in the grocery products trade), though there is little evidence that concentration on key accounts has yet forced any fundamental change in marketing organization – the product manager system can adapt to key account orientation. However, market orientation is vital to implementation of   *137*

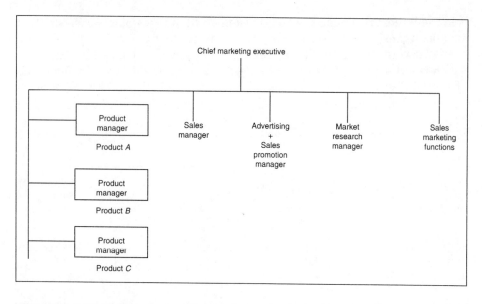

Figure 7.3   General product or brand management system

the marketing concept, and the organizational implications of market orientation must be carefully considered. Where markets are sufficiently differentiated from one another, and potentially large enough to warrant special organizational focus, some changes in organization will logically follow.

Geographical organization

Organizational units structured on the basis of geography are relevant primarily to large organizations marketing their products and/or services on an international scale. Geographic organization on this scale usually contains within each geographic entity organizations reflecting functional, product, or market-type organizations.

Customer-orientated organizations

A marketing department based on customer orientation will not differ in essentials from an organization based on markets, but where a few very large customers exist for a company's products, consideration must be given to a customer-orientated organization.

PRODUCT OR MARKET MANAGEMENT?

The most likely dilemma facing chief marketing executives is how to develop their marketing organizations beyond the relatively simple functional structure that serves so many companies. This section summarizes the main advantages and disadvantages of a product or a market management system of marketing organization.

The product manager system enables a multi-product firm to bring a total business management orientation to each product or brand it manufactures. The core responsibility of the product or brand manager is to develop an annual marketing plan geared to the needs of his or her product, and designed to enlarge its market share and profitability. The product/brand manager is the product/brand champion. The product/brand manager in his or her annual planning should be concerned with total marketing opportunity, but his or her strategic thinking will inevitably be limited in scope, since he or she is employed primarily as an operations manager. Product/brand management has limitations in the strategic sense, and characteristically brand managers are interested in their own brands, to the exclusion of much else. New product development fits poorly into the brand management system.

Only where the product defines the market, where the product manager and market manager are synonymous, is the danger of product orientation avoided. Alternatively, in markets where customers are few in number, there is likely to be little danger of product managers being out of touch with significant market developments. But, where a company's products are used by many different types of customers, or in many different ways; where customers' needs are rapidly changing, and new markets are likely to emerge; where technology is available to produce new solutions to customers' problems; and where a company's offering is a mixture of product(s) and service, then a market management orientation must be seriously considered (Thomas, 1988).

SOME QUESTIONS TO ASK ABOUT YOUR MARKETING ORGANIZATION

1 Is current marketing strategy innovative and data-based, clearly expressed and continually re-examined?
2 Does your company have a detailed annual plan, and long-range plans that are continually re-examined and updated?
3 Do contingency plans exist, and how effectively can the company react to changes in the environment?
4 Is the company organized to serve the needs of chosen markets, both at home and abroad, as the means to obtaining long-term growth and profits?
5 Is the company prepared to segment its markets and develop different product offerings for each segment?
6 Does management take a systems view of resource management – is a balance struck between the needs of the marketing mix (sales effort, advertising, product quality, service), the major functions of the company (manufacturing, finance, marketing) and the external environment (customers, distributors, suppliers)?
7 Are the main marketing functions in the company (sales, advertising,

product-line management, new product development, after-sales service) managed and controlled in an effectively integrated manner?

8   Does marketing work closely and effectively with research and development management, with manufacturing management, with the purchasing department, with physical distribution and transport management, with accounting and finance, to the end that all departments co-operate in the best interests of the company?

9   Is new product development an effectively organized unit, closely integrated with the strategic planning of the company?

10 How well informed is marketing management about its present and future markets? How recent are market research studies of customers, of buying influences, of changes in distribution channel behaviour, of competitors' performance?

11 How well and how regularly are sales potential and profitability calculated for each market segment, sales territory, product, channel of distribution and order size?

12 Is each area of marketing expenditure regularly analysed for cost-effectiveness?

If the answer is yes to questions 1 to 9 and 12, and assessments of questions 10 and 11 are positive and regular, you ought to be managing an effective marketing-orientated company. Any hesitation in answering any of them suggests that the relevant aspects of organization and marketing orientation ought to be closely examined.

REFERENCES

Baker, M.J. (ed.) (1994), *The Marketing Book*, 3rd ed., Oxford: Butterworth–Heinemann.

Bonoma, T.V. (1985), *The Marketing Edge: Making Strategies Work*, London: Free Press, Collier Macmillan.

Chandler, A.D. (1962), *Strategy and Structure*, Cambridge, MA: MIT.

Christopher, M., Payne, A. and Ballantyne, D. (1991), *Relationship Marketing*, Oxford: Butterworth-Heinemann.

McKenna, R. (1991), *Relationship Marketing*, New York: Addison-Wesley.

Spillard, P. (1985), *Organisation and Marketing*, London: Croom Helm.

Spillard, P. (1994), 'Organization for Marketing', Chapter 4 in M.J. Baker (ed.), op. cit.

Thomas, M.J. (1988), 'Product Management vs Market Management', in M.J. Thomas and N.E. Waite (eds), *The Marketing Digest*, London: Heinemann.

Thomas, M.J. (1994), 'Marketing – in chaos or transition?', *European Journal of Marketing*, **28**, (3), 55–62.

ESSENTIAL READING

Christopher, M., Payne, A. and Ballantyne, D. (1991), *Relationship Marketing*, Oxford: Butterworth-Heinemann.

McKenna, R. (1991), *Relationship Marketing*, New York: Addison-Wesley.

Doyle, P. (1994), *Marketing Management and Strategy*, Hemel Hempstead: Prentice-Hall International.

8 Recruitment - qualifications and sources

Martin Duffell

David Ogilvy (1985) advised young advertising people seeking a marketing training to get jobs as brand managers with a fast-moving consumer goods (FMCG) company. It is worth reflecting on why he chose an FMCG company when there are oil, motor, and electronics companies which are much bigger than the world's largest FMCG business. (The three largest FMCG companies in the world by dollar sales volume are Philip Morris, Unilever and Nestle; all three had sales well over $30 billion in 1993).

Ogilvy may of course be swayed by the fact that the largest single advertisers in both the USA and UK are in FMCG; but a case can also be made that FMCG is the most advanced branch of the science, or art, of marketing. Certainly FMCG marketers have to develop ultra-sensitive techniques and fast reflexes. Motor car manufacturers, for example, would have an FMCG-like relationship with their market only if motorists did not buy cars, but rented them weekly, and every Saturday could choose between keeping their car and sending it back to its maker. The FMCG marketers' consumer is theirs only until the end of the packet, tube or bottle. The need to submit their product to the consumer's choice fifty times a year is what best sharpens marketing operations and the people who work in them. Certainly, marketing managers with FMCG experience are much in demand in other fields, and files on the holders of key jobs in FMCG marketing are essential equipment for any professional headhunter.

I propose to tackle the subject of recruiting and selecting marketing people in the following way. First, in this chapter I examine what marketers actually do, particularly in FMCG, and then proceed to analyse the qualities likely to make them good at it. I then discuss where you will find people with these qualities. In the next chapter I consider how you can attract marketing applicants, and the methods available for selecting the right people for your marketing operation.

The 1990s have seen a change in the UK marketing recruitment scene which is long overdue. Women are beginning to outnumber men among the new recruits to large companies' marketing departments. Throughout the 1980s there were signs that more women graduates than men were becoming interested in FMCG marketing careers. This is logical, since the majority of FMCG purchases are made by women. The number of female applicants to companies such as mine swelled during the 1980s. In recent years we have had as many female applicants as male, and more than half our marketing traineeships are now gained by women.

This contrasts with earlier generations; of Unilever's 20 UK companies, only two have women marketing directors. This change provides me with a convenient method of simplifying and clarifying what I have to say about relationships in an FMCG marketing department. Throughout this chapter I shall refer to brand managers as *she* and the older generation of marketers – general marketing managers and marketing directors – as *he*. The present influx of new female talent into marketing in the UK suggests that within a decade or so this convention will no longer be appropriate; but for my present purpose it will save words and strained syntax.

THE NATURE OF THE MARKETING TASK

Each year I meet several hundred marketing candidates – young people who want a career in marketing – and I find that many of them have misconceptions about both marketing and management. One is that marketing managers sit in intellectual isolation, with a mass of data, making decisions. Nothing, of course, could be further from the truth. No sane company takes decisions which could cost them millions until all the relevant factors have been weighed and the points of view of all parts of the business have been taken into account. Marvin Bower is quoted as saying that marketing is objectivity (Ogilvy, 1985, p.172), but objectivity is an essence squeezed laboriously from a thousand subjective sources. In marketing, those sources are people, and *you* are always one of the most subjective. Marketers, like many other managers, have as their daily task dealing with a variety of people, and turning conflict into agreement and agreement into action. This *melée* often appears daunting to the more introverted candidate.

The question of introversion and extroversion leads to one of the paradoxes of careers in marketing. The quality on which success depends at senior levels is judgement: the marketing director's judgement can make or break the company. The second most important quality at this level is the ability to motivate subordinates. But at more junior levels persuasive power and persistence lead to success, and these two qualities are more often associated with extroversion. Thus we have the paradox that the best marketing judgement on the board of a company may be that of an introvert – who will have had to behave like an extrovert to get there!

I do indeed know a few marketing directors who are relatively introverted; the answer to the foregoing paradox is that a determined introvert can *143* develop the ability to sell ideas and can even acquire an appetite for complex people problems. For while 'introvert' and 'extrovert' are sometimes useful labels, the qualities we use these words to describe are developed rather than innate.

The task of the junior marketing manager (in FMCG, the brand manager) is at variance with the preconceived ideas of many marketing candidates. The principal decisions a brand manager has to make are what ought to happen on her brand, and how to make it happen. The brand manager's vital role in marketing decision making can be seen from two old conundrums. The first is this: what would happen to a brand if its brand manager's job were abolished? The answer is – nothing. The factory would go on putting the same old formula in the same old pack, the agency would keep screening the same old commercials, and the sales force would keep trying to sell the brand in the same old way and in the same old place. The result would be entropy: a sure recipe for killing a brand slowly in a changing market place. From this hypothetical exercise it can be seen that a brand manager is primarily an *agent of change*. Brand managers are judged and rewarded in proportion to their effectiveness as agents of change.

How brand managers bring change about can be seen from the second conundrum. How many people work for a brand manager? The answer is that if she is not very good, no one will, but if she is, everyone in the business will be working for her. Brand managers make things happen by the force of their arguments and their powers of persuasion. Only then do they discover how their ideas fare in the market place and develop the judgement to become marketing directors.

Many marketing candidates are surprised to learn that a brand manager's personal staff usually comprises from nought to three brand assistants, and the higher figure only on a very big brand. Such candidates have a faulty model of the power pyramid in a company, which looks like that in Figure 8.1.

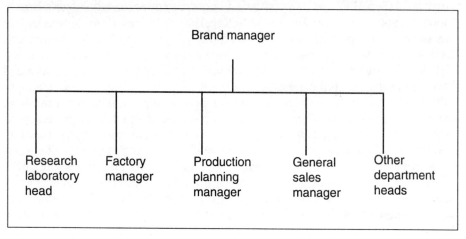

Figure 8.1   A power pyramid

The candidate becomes crestfallen when reminded that a medium-sized FMCG company probably has ten brand managers whose brands are usually formulated in the same laboratory, produced in the same factory, and so on. This renders impossible the organization chart in Figure 8.1 where each functional manager would have to report to ten people. The real organization chart is shown in Figure 8.2; it is more like Figure 8.1 turned upside down, and the lines are now broken – indicating not reporting but liaising relationships.

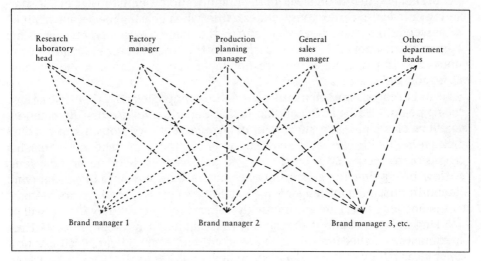

Figure 8.2   An organization chart

In the maze of relationships in Figure 8.2, giving instructions is out of the question. Each brand manager must persuade each functional manager of the priority and importance of the work he or she is doing on that manager's brand. Once our marketing candidate realizes this, she will know that success or failure as a brand manager depends on the logical rigour of her arguments and persuasive powers.

In fact, the brand management system in an FMCG company is a perfect and rare example of a self-regulating rat race. If a more effective brand manager works on a smaller brand and a less effective one on a bigger brand, the whole company's efforts and priorities become distorted. The board will ask itself why so much resource is being directed towards a small brand. If the answer is that the smaller brand has a more effective brand manager, out of self-preservation the company will have to rebalance its priorities by firing or demoting the bigger-brand manager and promoting the more effective smaller-brand manager. Since market salaries for brand managers varied in 1994 from approximately £20 000 to £44 000 a year there is plenty of scope for promotion and reward in brand management.

I have devoted considerable space to a detailed analysis of the dynamics of an FMCG marketing department because I believe that once the dynamics are   *145* understood, the qualities required in marketing recruits become clear. Before I leave the subject of the marketing task, however, I must deal with two important issues: where brand managers go when they are 30 and how marketing and sales careers interrelate in the modern market place.

How long can any individual continue being an agent of change, armed only with her own persuasive powers and competing to get to the top rung in the brand-management ladder? And where does an individual go once she gets there? I believe that the answer to the first question is until the age of 30, 35 at the most. In every career there comes a time when chasing the details of innovation seems better left to younger and fresher minds. At that point, exercising judgement developed from years spent in the front line of innovation, and motivating those younger and fresher minds become more attractive and appropriate challenges.

For this reason most marketing-led FMCG companies staff their marketing departments with 'high flyers'. Marketing departments are usually small in numbers of people, and successful companies find no problems in staffing then entirely with very able and ambitious young people who will either be promoted or leave. Even on the largest and most demanding brands, four years is a long time to be an agent of change. I know one brand manager who stayed on a brand much longer than that. But every three or four years he got a new boss, and this had an amazingly rejuvenating and innovating effect. I believe that, on balance, if anyone is to make a lifetime's career of brand management she will need frequent changes of brand, market, and possibly country to remain fully stimulated and stretched.

Because Britain, unlike the USA or France, has no fair-trading laws to prevent it, the distributive trade here is growing into a leading marketing force. A small number of very large and powerful retailers control the routes between the largest FMCG manufacturers and their British consumers, and in the last ten years retailers have learned how to flex their muscles. Distributor-owned brands (DOBs) are the main competitors of the market leaders in many FMCG markets in the UK. The British chains are not only large, they are profitable on a scale which makes their US equivalents look second-rate, and their house names are as powerful an influence on the British consumer as even the biggest manufacturers' brands. These chains are usually prepared to stock market leaders in any field, if only to make their own-label product appear aggressively priced, but also-ran brands either hand the bulk of their profits over to the retail chain or quit the battlefield.

The leading distributive chains in the UK have in effect become major FMCG manufacturers and marketers, and their marketing operations are often as sophisticated and high powered as those of even the largest traditional FMCG companies. Their management, at board and negotiating level, is also of the highest calibre and this presents a new and fascinating challenge for British FMCG marketers. If company X develops a new wonder product which all British consumers are likely to want, there is still one further marketing hurdle. Should all the leading chains object to their profit margin on this wonder product and refuse to stock it, the majority of British consumers will never get the opportunity to try it and, however good the product and its advertising may be, it will fail. Moreover, if it does gain stockists in all the major retail outlets, it will probably have 18 months at the most before DOBs which look very like it and cost 20 per cent less appear on the retailers' shelves. This new situation really stretches the ingenuity of FMCG marketers in Britain. They have to be sharper, more creative, and more efficient then they have ever been before. But this situation throws into high relief the point of contact between the FMCG marketing company and its customer – and now rival – the retail chain. The negotiator who represents the FMCG company at the chain's head office is a key figure, and there are two philosophies concerning who this figure should be.

The philosophy which is losing ground is that the key account negotiator should be a skilful, older sales executive who has known 'old What's-his-name', the buying director of Sadsco's, ever since he was filling the shelves at their Tenderham branch. This philosophy is losing ground because, increasingly, the chains' buying directors are very bright, objective people, graduates, perhaps MBAs, who passed through the Tenderham branch so quickly that no one got to know them. And in this arena the canny old sales executive is outclassed. What is more, he has no idea of the effect on company profit margins of the small concessions made in negotiation with the new buying director, and so he loses every round.

The alternative to the old sales executive as negotiator for the FMCG company is the young marketer, fresh from making a success of running her first major brand. Such people can calculate the effect of every concession they make, and can compete with the new buying director as an intellectual equal. There are only two snags. The first is that the retail chains have as much need of bright young marketers today as their suppliers do; so the young account negotiator may go in with a promotional proposition and come out with a job. The second is that the very bright, very ambitious young FMCG marketer may need extra training, not to say special psychological preparation, for this kind of contest, something which was not always on the agenda of brand managers in the past.

Despite these two snags, I have no doubt that the second model is the model of the future. Distributor power is a fact of life for British marketers, at least of FMCG. So young marketing managers should grow up to live with this and should develop the negotiating skills required for managing the new situation; and they will need to plan for this experience as one of the stages of developing a marketing career. This must clearly be taken into account when selecting and recruiting tomorrow's marketing management.

THE QUALITIES REQUIRED IN MARKETERS

From the foregoing analysis there emerges a list of qualities desirable in a recruit to marketing. The first of these is *drive*. This quality lies at the root of persuasive power, and indeed of most human achievement. The young marketer's success will depend on energy and enthusiasm combined with a deep need to influence the environment and *make things better*.

Two other important qualities are competitiveness and self-confidence. For reasons I have explained, marketers must be competitive both internally in the firm and externally in the market. They have to be hungry to succeed and this is likely to show in their record of achievement in life so far. It almost certainly means that they will also be ambitious; to succeed, this ambition must be clothed in social skills and directed into task orientation, but it must be there.

It is clearly important for marketing people to be intelligent, to outwit rather than be outwitted, to develop arguments without logical flaws, based on calculations containing no errors. It is easy to say that a marketing recruit should be of the highest possible intelligence. But we must acknowledge that there are many types of intelligence: academic aptitude, practical and 'streetwise' intelligence, the ability to think quickly and deeply. These are all important in marketing with the possible exception of the first. Some employers do set academic minima in recruiting managers, including marketing ones: at least an upper second-class honours degree, or some such qualification. The problem with this approach is that academic performance is not a reliable indicator of IQ. My company has been administering tests of logical reasoning for more than 30 years to candidates for its management traineeships and the low correlation emerges quite clearly. Different undergraduates do very different levels of work and some choose to read subjects which come easily to them while others do the opposite. Moreover, introverts tend to secure better degrees than extroverts and we have already discussed a possible correlation between extroversion and success in marketing.

My own company does not make its job offers to management trainees conditional on degree class, basically because, statistically at least, passing its selection process is more difficult than getting a first. In my own long experience of graduates in business I have observed that a much higher proportion of successful technical managers have firsts than successful marketers. What is clear, however, is that marketing managers need a high degree of numeracy if they are to persuade their company to spend millions on the basis of their calculations. They also need the ability to absorb and process vast amounts of data logically. The average reading speed among adults is about 300 words a minute. A brand manager with a reading speed of 600 words a minute can examine twice as much data in the same time as an average reader. There are courses which can improve your reading speed, and some guarantee an 80 per cent minimum improvement, but normal adult reading speeds vary from 200 to 800 words a minute and a marketer who can manage the latter has an in-built advantage.

In summary, while academic prowess and intelligence are not the same thing, it must be important to get the brightest marketers you can. They work at the competitive edge of the business and if your company's marketers are brighter than your competitors' then the market, and of course your shareholders, will feel the impact.

The last quality I shall discuss is communication skill or, as it used to be known, the gift of the gab. Marketers spend a large proportion of their time talking: to be effective they have to be good at it. We have noted the brand manager's dependence on persuasive power and while technical managers can afford to be silent guardians of their company's destiny, marketing managers cannot. A company needs the most articulate marketers it can get. Having examined the CVs of many present and future marketing managers I am aware of how many contain in their list of youthful activities 'acting' or, even more frequently, 'debating'. In fact, there is some evidence in my company's 40 years of dusty recruitment files that there is a golden virtue which marketing recruiters should be seeking: the ability to win intellectual arguments with people whose IQ is higher than your own!

Having looked at the most desirable qualities in marketing recruits, I shall now consider where those qualities are to be found.

SOURCES OF MARKETING TALENT

The principal decision to be made by marketing recruiters is whether to buy ready-trained marketing people (either by specific job advertising or via head-hunters) or whether to recruit and train their own. Both involve cost. My experience suggests that brand managers require something like 40 per cent in extra salary to lure them into the unknown from the leading marketing organization that trained them. On the other hand a marketing training such as only a handful of the biggest FMCG companies can give costs many thousands of pounds.

There is one great disadvantage to buying in, and that is the inverse relationship between current career potential and inclination to change employers. Headhunters, in particular, will contact a range of candidates for your marketing vacancy. The candidate who is about to gain a big promotion in her present company, or a glamorous posting overseas, or six months at Harvard Business School, will probably turn down the offer despite the larger salary. The candidate who resents falling behind in the race, or who has been told to pull her socks up, will probably accept. Equally, a candidate working for a train-your-own company who is really good is likely to have designs on the job currently held by her boss. Joining the company to which the headhunters introduce her may well lead to the problem that the new company will use the same headhunters to obtain her next boss. Marketers who switch companies usually learn the wisdom of keeping on good terms with the headhunters who engineered their first move – they will probably need them again.

This consideration has led to a change in practice among large FMCG companies in the UK. In the 1950s and 1960s they relied primarily on buying in marketers from just two companies famous for their training and 'grow-your-own' policies. Today most big FMCG companies recruit new graduates and train them in addition to their buying-in activities. This mixed policy, however, brings problems. Home-grown young marketers become disenchanted by the prospect of being beaten to the promotion they want by a bought-in manager.

I believe on balance that for a company that is big enough, in the UK the best policy is still grow-your-own. Doubtless the UK will follow the US trend towards executives with mobile careers. But US personnel executives, caught in the pantomime of 'golden handcuffs' and 'golden handshakes', are not *149* always happy with the short period for which they can retain the good people they recruit. They envy the employee loyalty of European companies and have admiration, and almost awe, for the very few US corporations which can maintain a grow-your-own policy.

If you decide to buy in your marketing talent there is no shortage of head-hunting firms. If you decide to recruit and train your own you have a different problem. Which people would be good at marketing if they were to be recruited and trained? Most marketing recruiters in the UK join the 'milk round', as it is known, and recruit new graduates. The reason for this is economic. People with the abilities recruiters seek are distributed in fair numbers among the graduating population. Elsewhere, people of the same age and ability are few and far between. So it costs thousands of pounds to screen graduate ranks for suitable talent; it would cost millions to search through the whole population of the same age. I am sure that many bright, forceful and competitive people do not go on to higher education, even in 1993 when a record 25 per cent of British 18-year-olds did so. But it seems highly likely that very competitive people with good brains will take up the challenge of academic competition if they can. The way that companies such as my own legislate for exceptions is by setting their qualifications for graduate trainees as 'an honours degree from a British university or equivalent level of ability'. I will, and have, accepted people as being 'of equivalent ability' – but no company would want to face the cost of considering a quarter of a million applications, and that is why most marketing recruiters stipulate graduates.

I am often asked whether following a particular degree course helps make a better marketer. The answer in technical fields is obvious: chemists are particularly suited to marketing chemicals. But in FMCG there is no proof that having a relevant degree helps. In any one year between 10 and 20 per cent of my company's graduate trainees have degrees in business studies or commerce. Although there is evidence that their studies help them in a career in industrial finance, there is nothing to suggest they can be ready earlier for their first brand responsibility if they go into marketing. In fact, it has been argued that since a brand is an abstraction, people who have learned how to handle abstractions – theoretical scientists, philosophers, pure mathematicians and classicists – make better marketers. Certainly there are plenty of examples of graduates in these subjects getting to the top in FMCG marketing.

Companies such as my own in the UK, therefore, recruit graduates of all disciplines, guided by the desire to find the qualities I described in the previous section. There is a drift towards business subjects in British higher education, but only 100 students in each undergraduate year are able to study management at our two oldest and most prestigious universities. The great majority of British students with outstanding A-level grades do not, at present, go on to study business or management. This is, however, gradually changing and a few business courses at British universities are able to demand a mixture of As and Bs at A level as entry requirements. Meanwhile, many business-school admissions tutors prefer arts, science or engineering graduates for places on their MBA programmes.

I am often asked, 'Do you recruit MBAs?' The answer is, in finance yes; in marketing, at this point in time, very few. MBA recruitment in Unilever peaked in 1971 (at nine recruits), and since then we have not deliberately set out to recruit people with this qualification. Nevertheless, each year a few MBAs win places on our management development scheme in open competition with first-degree students and holders of other postgraduate degrees. In general, we have not found that MBA entrants are able to take responsibility for a brand any more quickly than other recruits. I am, of course, referring to MBAs who do not have substantial brand experience before starting their MBA course. Those with experience are able to get jobs in marketing with or without a paper qualification.

Diehard practitioners of marketing liken marketing to swimming. If having a Bachelor's degree in aquatic locomotion does not win you a place in the Olympic swimming squad, why should having a Master's? This is perhaps a little unfair, but US experience, once again, is illuminating. In the USA 80 000 people gain full-time MBAs every year, compared with 4 000 in the UK (the latter figure contrasts with only 1 200 a year ten years ago). American businesses, however, make their target the MBAs of a few 'top-tier' business schools from which some 5 000 students get their MBAs – the remainder have problems finding jobs despite having acquired the same theoretical knowledge (Cooper and Dowd, 1987). In other words, the thing that makes the 5 000 'top-tier' MBAs desirable employees is the competition to get places in those business schools – only the very brightest make it. In Britain, when the brightest young people all do MBAs, companies like mine will recruit all their management trainees from amongst MBAs. That day may come but it is not here yet.

REFERENCES

Cooper, C. and Dowd, K. (1987), 'Mid-life crisis for the MBA', *Management Today*, April, 82–86.

Ogilvy, D. (1985), *Ogilvy on Advertising*, 2nd ed., London: Guild Books.

ESSENTIAL READING

Swasy, Alecia (1993), *Soap Opera: The Inside Story of P&G*, New York: Times Books.

Mitchell, Alan (1994), 'Marketing's New Model Army', *Management Today*, March, 42–9.

Storr, Anthony (1968), *Human Aggression*, Harmondsworth: Penguin.

9 Selection – media and methods
Martin Duffell

Assuming that you have decided to grow your own young marketers and for good economic reasons have decided to recruit graduates, you will find that there is a great deal of competition for the ablest candidates. As a marketing person you will relish this competition, because it means that there is a graduate market and you can employ your professional skills in marketing your vacancies.

While the market for graduate vacancies is much smaller than for any FMCG product in terms of numbers of consumers, it has nevertheless merited both market research and media expenditure over a number of years.

Graduate recruitment is a mature market. The numbers graduating in the UK have been increasing under the influence of the government's funding rules. In 1991 there were 119 000 new graduates; by 1994 there were approximately 180 000. The official statistics under-report the extent of graduate unemployment. The proportion of new UK graduates still seeking employment on 31 December 1991 was reported as 11.5 per cent (source: CSU). The real proportion who had not found permanent jobs was over 30 per cent because large numbers who were in temporary work, travelling, untraceable or joining the irrational boom in postgraduate study had actually failed to gain full-time permanent employment. This suggests that there is a glut of good candidates to fill your marketing vacancies; but that is not the case. The top 1 per cent of 21-year-olds, on any criterion, in 1988 was over 9 000; it then began a steady ten-year fall, which will bottom-out at 6 500 in 1998; in 1993 it was below 8 000. If you are seeking the best and brightest, they are a shrinking number in a growing undergraduate population, and there will be as stiff competition for them throughout the 1990s as there has ever been.

The chartered accountancy profession is the market leader by volume, taking up to 10 per cent of all the graduates entering employment. Since most marketers have a low boredom threshold, you will not really be in competition with the accountants. You may, however, find yourself in competition with the City's institutions. The City offers starting salaries which are on average 40 per cent higher than those paid by recruiters and trainers of marketers. The City can afford to pay more because it recruits graduates for narrower jobs; their training costs are lower and the period before productive labour is shorter. The initial salary differential may tempt marketing candidates. But since the City offers jobs which have much less variety and scope for creativity, a small secondary market is developing for marketers, consisting of people who have started a career in banking or finance and have found it hard to keep awake.

GRADUATE RECRUITMENT MEDIA

As with any mature market, regular research information can be purchased and there is a wealth of media available. For a number of years MORI (Market and Opinion Research International) has carried out a regular attitude survey based on a sample of over 1 000 final-year students at more than 20 universities. The fieldwork is done in March each year and the results published in June. The names and addresses of all the organizations and publications mentioned in this section appear at the end of the chapter.

Media used in graduate recruitment include press (national, student and specialist recruitment), posters (there are numerous noticeboards in universities), brochures (the biggest single media cost in most recruiters' advertising spend) and video (the medium with the smallest audience). The most important single graduate recruitment medium I believe to be public relations at universities, particularly with careers advisory services, but also with academic staff and student audiences which can be attracted to presentations, vacation courses, and vacation employment.

If you plan to enter this market you will find one reference book invaluable: *Graduate Careers Services Directory* (published by the Central Services Unit (CSU)). You can also get expert help from any of a number of advertising agencies which specialize in recruitment consultancy and advertising. Those whose work I know at first hand and can recommend include Associates in Advertising, Trotman and Company, and Newpoint and PRL (all in the London area) and Cambridge Flag, and Hobsons (both based in Cambridge).

The graduate recruitment market is as complex as any I have experienced, and consulting the reference books I have mentioned and a good recruitment advertising agency is a necessary preliminary to playing an effective role in it. There are, however, four organizations, three directories of graduate employers, and two national fortnightly publications which must be mentioned in even the briefest survey.

The first organization is AGCAS (the Association of Graduate Careers Advisory Services). This is the national body of professional careers advisers, university staff who provide individual and group counselling on careers to all students, maintain a comprehensive careers library, and offer a variety of other services to job-hunting graduates. AGCAS has its own publishing house based in Manchester, the Central Services Unit (CSU).

153

There is a national organization for employers of graduates, AGR (the Association of Graduate Recruiters, formerly known as the Standing Conference of Employers of Graduates), which represents the interests of graduate recruiters. AGCAS and AGR have an agreed code of practice for graduate recruitment and a new recruiter of graduates would be wise to join AGR and obtain a copy of this code.

Two student/business organizations are very active on the campuses in Britain. They are valuable allies, second only to careers advisers, and their officials are energetic students with a strong motivation towards business. AIESEC (l'Association Internationale d'Etudiants en Sciences Economiques et Commerciales) is a well-established international organization which arranges student exchanges for vacation work all over the world. It has branches in more than 20 universities in Britain where students of all disciplines can become members. AIESEC provides a wide range of training experience and business knowledge for its members and has a national committee of full-time officials based in London and an international headquarters in Brussels.

SIS (the Student Industrial Societies), the first of which was founded in the 1970s, now have branches in more than 50 universities. They arrange presentations for their members, industrial visits and events which will help develop their business knowledge and skills. The SIS have a full-time national campaign organizer, based at their headquarters in Birmingham. Both AIESEC and SIS can provide recruiters with a ready-made communication route and with student audiences, and both are well worth supporting.

If you intend to recruit any number of graduates for marketing it is worth having details of your vacancies in one or more of the three principal directories which list graduate recruiters. *Prospects* (formerly called *ROGET: the Register of Graduate Employment and Training*) is published by CSU; *GO (Graduate Opportunities)* is published by Newpoint; *GET (Graduate Employment and Training)* is published by Hobsons. All these directories are revised and published every year, usually during the long vacation, and they are distributed free to final-year undergraduates and postgraduates in Britain.

There are two important fortnightly publications in which graduate recruiters can advertise their vacancies. CSU produces both: *Prospects Today* and *Prospects Plus*, the latter offering jobs to start at the beginning of the next academic year. These are distributed free to students via careers advisory services. There are also opportunities to advertise your presence in the graduate recruitment market in the yearbooks and other publications of the SIS and AIESEC.

Having mentioned this list of media, I believe that there is no real substitute for visiting the campuses in person and learning from, as well as building good relations with, the careers advisory services.

SELECTION METHODS

Psychologists like Ruth Holdsworth of Saville and Holdsworth classify the data used in selection under a Latin square according to whether input and interpretation are subjective or objective. Figure 9.1 shows the use of a common convention (for example, Mars, 1982, p. 29) to label the four boxes.

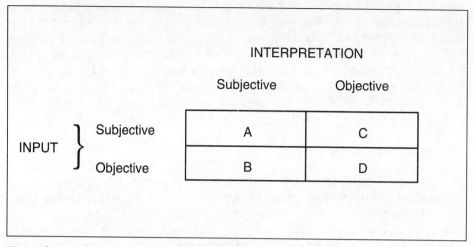

Figure 9.1   A Latin square for data classification

Clearly, behavioural scientists will want to maximize the amount of the selection process which falls in box D and minimize the part in box A. Occupational psychologists believe that the two most unreliable ways of selecting people for jobs are references and interviews (see Herriot, 1987, p. 79); not surprisingly both fall in box A. Figure 9.2 plots where each of the methods discussed in this chapter falls in the Latin square.

I have placed application forms in the centre because some parts of them, or some ways of interpreting the information in them, fall into each category.

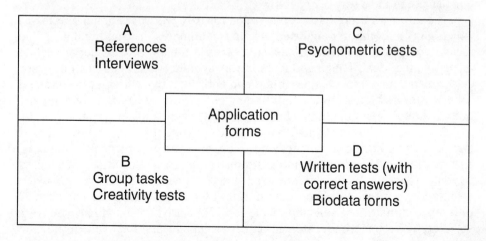

Figure 9.2   Selection methods classified in the Latin square

References

Since references are subjective statements evaluated according to the selector's subjective view of the referee's judgement, they are useless unless your aim is to find the best-connected candidate. References are used as positive criteria only by employers who are too busy or too lazy to find out which candidate would be best at the job. They are also sometimes used to avoid open competition for a post of privilege. You can use them to fill your marketing vacancies but, if you do, you should not expect your recruits to win in any open and competitive market.

Application forms

There is an AGCAS approved standard application form available in all careers services, and many employers accept applications on this form. It helps applicants: some will fill in one, photocopy it a hundred times, and send it to a hundred employers. Some employers worry that this indicates no special interest in *their* job and suggests the candidate lacks confidence in obtaining an offer by applying to only a few carefully selected employers. My own company uses a six-page 'horror' which puts many applicants off, particularly those who are not very interested in joining us. Some careers advisers run seminars on how to fill in application forms: in so far as this helps candidates not to undersell themselves this is a good thing. On the other hand, help given to a candidate in filling in an application form may not benefit him or her in the long run. I remember one candidate who was so unlike his application form that I was mystified until he confessed that his father had composed it and his mother had typed it for him. He was not offered the job and would not have been even if he had not confessed. Many application forms look 'coached', but there is one almost blank page in the form my company uses which I do not think anyone has yet found a way of coaching.

In recent years there has been a vogue for using *biodata* application forms which can be computer-analysed, so that candidates' factual details can be measured against the data for past successes in the job concerned, or against some defined ideal. The proponents of this system (which has been used for selecting tax inspectors) argue that it can entirely replace first interviews and thus pay for its high software and running costs. Some years ago my company had a leading consultant in this field examine a large sample of applicants' data which were transferable to such a form. The consultant successfully predicted two out of every three applicants who would succeed in our selection process; this was impressive. But it is interesting to compare the candidates selected by biodata but rejected by our traditional process with those who were selected by our traditional process but not identified by biodata. The striking difference is that those selected by biodata alone are very like those who were selected by both methods, at least on paper. It suggests that a fair proportion of management trainees produced by our traditional process are 'oddballs'. I would advise marketing recruiters to keep taking oddballs rather than computer clones. People are a species like any other, subject to a natural selection which is beyond their control. When the environment changes completely, it may be that only one of the oddballs is able to cope. The thought that tax inspectors might go the way of the dinosaur fails to bring tears to my eyes.

Interviews

First interviews for marketing candidates are arranged on campus at most universities in the spring term. The careers advisory services often take over the administration of this 'milk round' and as many as 30 employers may be interviewing on the same day. If you wish to see more than two or three candidates, this is likely to be more economic than paying their fares to your offices.

It can be debated whether personnel managers or marketing managers are better for this purpose. My own view is that if you are interviewing only marketing candidates a marketer is best, but only one who has attended a good interviewing course and gained some experience. Excellent interviewing courses are offered by the Industrial Society, the Institute of Personnel Development, and commercial firms of occupational psychologists such as PA or Saville and Holdsworth. Failing this, a number of good interviewing primers have been written, and one I can recommend is Martin Higham's *The ABC of Interviewing* (1979). It should always be remembered that selection is a two-way process. The candidate you are interviewing is assessing your firm as an employer. For this reason it can be an advantage to make the interviewer the youngest person qualified to do the job. It helps communicate that young people get responsibility in your business. If the interviewer is not competent this youthfulness will backfire – the unsuccessful candidate will tell everyone that the employers who were impressed by him or her in interview sent their managing directors to do it, while you sent the office junior.

Some interviewers put a lot of faith in what they call tough, that is, hostile interviewing tactics. I do not recommend if for marketers, since the hostile interview is the last place where depth of analysis or creativity will have a chance to emerge. All a hostile interview reveals are reflexes in conflict – I *can* see its use in selecting both spies and marines.

Tests

As we have noted, tests are the most objective method available to selectors but they are useful only if they are appropriate. Basic numeracy tests are unnecessary for people with a good O-Level grade in mathematics, and verbal tests are probably appropriate only for graduates whose course does not require writing essays. It must also be noted that average verbal test scores have been falling sharply ever since television came into the home. A graduate in the top 0.1 per cent of IQs would have been likely to have a vocabulary of 35 000 words (English count) some 30 years ago: today it is likely to be about 25 000.

My company employs a test in graduate selection which measures the   *157* speed and accuracy of non-verbal, non-numerate reasoning. It is useful to have as an extra piece of information when a candidate's academic record conflicts with the apparent level of intelligence in live performance, or when there are glaring inconsistencies in both. Advertising agencies often use tests of creative writing ability which are obviously appropriate. For jobs where experienced people are being examined an 'in-tray' exercise may be appropriate: candidates can be asked to sort out a heap of correspondence by priority and compose replies. To summarize, tests are good objective data if they are appropriate. One type of test I would not advise in the 1990s is spelling. From more than 3 000 application forms I receive each year, I do not expect the number without a spelling mistake to reach double figures. Since the advent of television and the demise of Latin in schools even candidates with firsts in English cannot spell.

Psychometric tests appear in one of the boxes in Figure 9.2. Occupational psychologists have done a great deal of work on both sides of the Atlantic on questionnaires which will measure a candidate's personality attributes. Some of the tests produced are very impressive, measuring several dozen attributes on a sensitive scale. It is important, however, to appreciate their drawbacks. The first is that the data are useful only if you are sure where your ideal employee lies on this series of scales. You can, of course, take one of these tests yourself and select only candidates with similar personality profiles to your own. This would bring the cloning problem I have already discussed. It is, moreover, difficult to predict results from personality traits: who would win a war between a man who was more paranoid than he was obsessive (Stalin) and another who was more obsessive than he was paranoid (Hitler)?

The second point which must be made about psychometric tests is that they measure a number, albeit a large one, of personality characteristics. But whole people are more than the sum of their parts, and we can never really be sure we have measured the right characteristics.

The third point concerns the classification of psychometric tests into box C (Figure 9.2) – subjective input/objective interpretation. People doing such a test, provided they do not cheat, are giving an accurate picture not of their personality but only of how they see themselves. Thus, for example, these tests measure how logical or persuasive people believe they are rather than whether they *are* logical or persuasive. The input is thus subjective; the interpretation, on the other hand, is an objective tool only when it is used to compare one candidate's self-perception with another's or with an ideal. The ideal may also, of course, be regarded as subjective, thus relegating psychometric tests to box A.

Despite the reservations I have expressed, a large number of businesses have used psychometric testing to select for a wide variety of jobs and are clearly satisfied with the results. Perhaps the blueprint for the ideal young marketer will one day be agreed and, if so, then the scientific tests appropriate to it will rapidly appear.

Group tasks

In the previous chapter I pointed out that young marketers work in a *melée* of people rather than in isolation, and this makes a group selection process very appropriate for marketers. Drive, competitiveness, decisiveness, self-confidence, task orientation, social skills, communication, debating skill, logic, quick thinking, imagination and speed in assimilating data can all be demonstrated in group situations. My own company was among the first to use group tasks, discussions and case studies in the selection of management trainees. Our selection boards, as we call them, were devised many years ago by Harold Bridger, a founder member of the Tavistock Institute of Human Relations, in consultation with the people at the very top of our business. Indeed, today, when many other employers have adopted group assessment, our selection system is distinguished mainly by the unique feature that the chairmen and directors of our main board, as well as those of our numerous subsidiaries, play a regular part in graduate trainee selection. A high proportion of our top management entered the business as graduate trainees and were chosen by the same system. A high proportion of them are also marketers.

In the 40 years since their inception, our selection boards have been amended, updated and refined many times. Harold Bridger has passed the baton on to professional colleagues who are now called 'The Advisors Group', but the underlying principles of the system are unchanged. The selection day contains four group activities as well as reasoning tests and interviews for candidates invited, eight at a time, to our London head office. The decision on the candidates' potential for senior management in Unilever is made by an *ad hoc* panel of senior managers usually from four different subsidiary companies. If there are marketing candidates, two of the selectors will be marketers. A senior personnel executive chairs the selectors' discussions, a younger personnel manager manages the candidates' day, and two professional behavioural scientists take part in all the selectors' discussions but have no vote in the decision.

A large number of organizations now use group assessment techniques, which are, I believe, particularly appropriate to choosing marketers. There are also a number of assessment centres run by commercial consultancy firms such as PA and Saville and Holdsworth which offer a selection board service to employers. Armed with the assessment centre results, the employer can interview a short-list and make offers. Many larger companies prefer to organize their own group assessment internally.

One important feature of Unilever selection boards is not always found in other group processes. The behavioural scientists who assist at our selection boards interview candidates individually towards the end of the selection day and offer feedback on any aspect of it the candidate wishes. Some candidates do not want to know what the selectors make of their group performance, style, or personality shown during the day, and the feedback is not forced on them. A majority of candidates, however, want to learn things which they might be able to work on for the benefit of their own personal development. Group activities under observation are often stressful, and candidates usually

159

also appreciate the calming influence of an objective look at their strengths (which are usually many) as well as their weaknesses.

AFTER SELECTION

If you have decided to recruit new graduates to staff your marketing department, and have gone through the lengthy process of selection and hiring them, you are now ready for the crucial task: training. My company has acquired a reputation over many years for training marketers. The underlying principles of a Unilever marketing training are very simple. Such a training includes a series of courses in business and marketing theory which we call our Business Education Programme. It also includes attachments to the sales force, the factories, and every department of the Unilever company concerned. It will also probably include outside attachments, to an advertising agency and a market research company, for example. Most important, a young marketer works in a brand office undertaking increasingly responsible tasks on the brand until she is ready to be appointed to manage a brand of her own. Such an internal training is not possible for every marketing employer, but there are many other alternatives, as the next chapter will reveal.

REFERENCES

GET: Graduate Employment and Training, Cambridge: CRAC.

GO: Graduate Opportunities, London: Newpoint.

Graduate Careers Service Directory, Manchester: CSU.

Herriot, P. (1987), 'Graduate recruitment – getting it right', *Department of Employment Gazette*, February, 78–83.

Higham, M. (1979), *The ABC of Interviewing*, London: IPM.

Mars, Gerald (1982), *Cheats at Work*, London: Allen & Unwin.

Prospects, Manchester: CSU.

Prospects Today, Manchester: CSU.

Prospects Plus, Manchester: CSU.

ESSENTIAL READING

Association of Graduate Careers Advisory Services (1993), *Graduate Careers Service Directory for 1994*, Manchester: Central Services Unit.

Smith, Mike and Robinson, Ivan T. (1993), *The Theory and Practice of Systematic Personnel Selection*, 2nd ed. London: Macmillan.

Strebler, Martin T. and Pike, Geoff (1993), *Shortlisting the Best Graduates*, Report 253, Brighton: Institute of Manpower Studies, University of Sussex.

ORGANIZATIONS

The Advisors Group (see also Tavistock Institute of Human Relations, below), c/o Ms Ellen Noonan, 187 Tufnell Park Road, London N7 0PU.

AGCAS: see CSU.

AGR: Association of Graduate Recruiters (known as SCOEG until the late 1980s), Sheraton House, Castle Park, Cambridge CB3 0AX; tel: 01223 356720.

AIESEC, United Kingdom, 29–31 Cowper Street, London EC2A 4AP; tel: 0171 336 7939.

Associates in Advertising, 5 St John's Lane, London, EC1M 4BH; tel: 0171 251 5554.

Cambridge Flag, Middlewhite Barn, Milton Road, Impington, Cambridge CB4 4NF; tel: 01223 233882.

CSU: Central Services Unit, Crawford House, Precinct Centre, Manchester M13 9EP; tel: 0161 273 4233.

CRAC: The Careers Research and Advisory Centre (publish through Hobsons Ltd, see below).

Hobsons Limited, Bateman Street, Cambridge CB2 1LZ; tel: 01223 354551.

IPD: Institute of Personnel Development, IPD House, Camp Road, Wimbledon, London SW19 4UW; tel: 0181 946 9100.

MORI: Market and Opinion Research International Ltd, 32 Old Queen Street, London SW1H 9HP; tel: 0171 222 0232.

Newpoint, Windsor Court, East Grinstead House, East Grinstead RH9 1XA; tel: 01342 326972.

PA Personnel Services, Hyde Park House, 60a Knightsbridge, London SW1X 7LE; tel: 0181 235 6060.

PRL, 29 Ludgate Hill, London EC4M 7NH.

Saville and Holdsworth, The Old Post House, 81 High Street, Esher, Surrey KT10 9QA; tel: 01372 68634.

SCOEG: Standing Conference of Employers of Graduates – now known as AGR (see above).

SIS (Student Industrial Societies), Quadrant Court, 49 Calthorpe Road, Edgbaston, Birmingham, B15 1TH; tel: 0121 454 6769.

Tavistock Institute of Human Relations (see also The Advisors' Group, above), The Tavistock Centre, Belsize Lane, London NW3 5BA; tel: 0171 435 7111.

Trotman and Company Ltd, 12–14 Hill Rise, Richmond, Surrey TW10 6UA; tel: 0181 940 5668.

10 Staff development
Derek Beasley

According to the *World Competitiveness Report 1993* the UK is in 19th place out of 22 developed countries for both investment in employee training and in the availability of competent senior managers. Considering all the factors that comprise the world competitiveness scoreboard, the UK is in 16th position and the companies at the top of the board all score higher than the UK on training investment and senior manager availability. The need to develop staff at all levels both in their current jobs and for future ones is no longer a soft option for when profits are exceptional, but a basic necessity for corporate survival.

The staff development process is business-driven. It prepares staff at all levels to perform better to achieve company business objectives in a world in which success depends on the ability to deliver quality, variety, customization, convenience and timeliness.

From an overall organizational viewpoint the objectives of a staff development process are to:

- Strengthen company leadership.
- Increase productivity and effectiveness at all levels.
- Strengthen communications both laterally and vertically.
- Provide a more flexible structure for the recruitment and development of staff.
- Broaden the pool of knowledge and skills.

From the viewpoint of those being developed the objectives of the process will be:

- A strengthened role in setting and carrying out the company's business strategy and objectives.

- Increased effectiveness and productivity.
- Diversified work assignments.
- Increased promotion opportunities.
- Updated skills and knowledge.

These objectives are unlikely to be met unless certain principles are in place to support staff development:

1   The process must support the company culture and management style which may well be changing as flexible networks replace large top-down hierarchies.
2   The company will provide development and training opportunities and encourage staff to share in the responsibility for their development and so create a learning culture.
3   For each business objective, staff development needs are determined and resources allocated, so that staff development and business strategy are linked.
4   Managers are actively involved in the programme, being assessed and developed themselves as well as assessing and developing their own staff.
5   The development programmes are designed and updated according to the needs and strengths, learning styles and culture of the organization.
6   The programmes are cost effective, focusing on results.

WHAT IS A 'STAFF DEVELOPMENT PROGRAMME'?

A staff development programme is not just an off-the-job training course but can include any of the following in any combination that provides an appropriate solution to meet identified needs:

- *Academic assignments*: These can vary from being a school governor providing marketing input to the Board to lecturing at the local college or university.
- *Coaching*: Regular discussions between manager and subordinate in which the former provides positive help to the latter to improve performance.
- *Formal training*: On off-the-job courses, whether in-company or on open courses outside.
- *Institute membership*: Where relevant, company pay the fees and encourage active participation.
- *Job rotation and job enrichment*: The former is a way of broadening knowledge and skills through a succession of temporary jobs; the latter involves expanding the job holders' responsibilities in the current job permanently.
- *Monitoring*: A formal approach to develop a subordinate personally or professionally by a senior from another department.

- *On-the-job training*: The improvement of skills under frequent supervision whilst working.
- *Open (or distance) learning*: This combines videos/CBT/CDI and workloads for study outside normal working hours. Weekend tutorials are often included.
- *Outward-bound training*: Unfamiliar and challenging physical and psychological activities outdoors.
- *Project management*: Increasingly companies are forming project teams which are cross-organizational to solve difficult problems or investigate new ideas, so broadening the knowledge and skills of the team members and managers.
- *Qualifications*: The encouragement through fee payment and time off to obtain relevant qualifications (see the Appendix to this chapter for details of marketing qualifications).
- *Reading*: Planned reading, a simple but under-used development method.
- *Sabbaticals*: Paid or unpaid time off (normally 6–12 months) for the staff member to do *anything* except work as normal.
- *Secondments*: Managers are loaned to another organization for a year or more. This can be a reciprocal arrangement.

WHAT IS THE ROLE OF THE MARKETING MANAGER IN STAFF DEVELOPMENT?

This will depend upon the size and philosophy of the organization. In companies with, typically, 150+ employees there are frequently shared responsibilities with the personnel department. But even in the larger organizations the effects of downsizing and staff empowerment through total quality management programmes have increased the line managers' responsibilities for staff development.

The marketing manager will certainly need to ensure there is an adequate financial budget for the development of the marketing team, whether that be held within the department or centrally. Equally important is the budgeting of time to ensure that departmental performance does not suffer whilst individuals are being developed, and that the manager can devote enough personal time to the process, whether it be subordinate development or discussions with colleagues where inter-departmental effort is required. The marketing manager must be seen to be a supporter of the process and the champion for his or her department.

Other activities are more typically conducted by the personnel function but the marketing manager may find increasing involvement in them, especially in the smaller company. These include analysis of current staff competencies against required job competencies, programme design and evaluation, advising on career paths and goals, evaluating external providers and courses, leading training sessions, and monitoring international business trends that can effect staff development.

DEVELOPMENT IN WHAT?

The knowledge and skills required for effective job performance by marketing staff, contributing to overall business performance, vary considerably according to the job itself. But there are certain core skills which, although traditionally associated with management level jobs, are increasingly becoming part of lower-level jobs as staff are given more responsibility in the flatter organization structures of today.

These increasingly common skills are:

- Interpersonal, coaching, counselling, interviewing and negotiating.
- Diagnostic, problem solving, decision making and creative thinking.
- Leadership, supervising and team building.
- Oral and written communication, including listening and foreign languages.
- Planning and time management.

Knowledge is typically required in:

- Business economics, regulations and law.
- Finance and accounting.
- Information technology.
- Marketing – the philosophy, culture and techniques.

The depth of knowledge required and breadth of skill will obviously vary from job to job, which in turn will be based upon the critical success factors of the business.

Conflicts and solutions

The dilemma marketing managers face, like all their colleagues, is how to relate the knowledge and skills required for a job with the innate strengths and weakness of the job holder. As organizations become flatter, staff need more knowledge and skills and it becomes more likely that skill conflicts arise. For example, someone who scores highly on innovation and creativity is unlikely to be equally good at practical problem solving; someone good at project control, budgeting and scheduling is unlikely to score highly at personal counselling.

The message here is that it may be best to adapt and build on existing strengths and re-design the job, rather than assume a development programme can change the individual significantly. This in turn emphasizes the need for the marketing manager to review what the organization requires of the department as a whole first, and then develop staff to meet those objectives, rather than have preconceived or rigid ideas on what each job must be.

The marketing manager needs to be a professional manager as well as a marketer, dynamic and open-minded with an entrepreneurial spirit and a vision of the future shared with his or her team. An ability to work with consensus, winning support rather than demanding it, is necessary, backed up by a sensitivity to cultural differences and an understanding of different trading conditions.

The importance of learning

The ability of organizations to capture and apply knowledge is a decisive factor in meeting the new competitive standards – an increase in the importance of learning. Constantly changing variety, plus the need to customize, accelerates the pace of change and learning to adapt. The need to market innovations more quickly requires organizations to learn even faster. The need to make quality improvements and to develop new applications from major breakthroughs increases the value of the organization's ability to learn while making the product, delivering the service and interacting with the customer. New information and communications technologies accelerate the pace of change and add to learning requirements by increasing both the volume and the flow of information.

There is a greater emphasis now on learning within the organization, rather than external research. Continuous incremental learning produces the small improvements responsible for most commercial successes. Learning is pervasive throughout the organization, which has important implications for organization structure. Internal networks allow learning to flow across functions; external networks (suppliers and customers) keep learning moving through the organization.

It is more difficult to anticipate the specific functional skills required for the future so companies can train for it today. It is one task to train to do today's work with today's skills for today's profit, but quite another to train for tomorrow's work with tomorrow's skills for tomorrow's profits – hence the supreme importance of creating a learning culture, as many of tomorrow's jobs cannot be envisaged today.

Learning Pays is the title of an important Interim Report by Sir Christopher Ball for the RSA (1991). Amongst many interesting insights are two diagrams (see Figures 10.1 and 10.2). The challenge facing most organizations is how and where to start the move from the 'vicious' to the 'virtuous' circle. I would suggest creating a learning culture within society as a whole is the essential but most difficult start point.

More realistically, organizations should be taking the initiative themselves to develop the learning ethos. From a profit point of view, this must start with learning that is totally concerned with improving skills and knowledge relevant to current and future jobs; this, ideally, should be supported by encouragement of constant learning in topics not related to work and thus, together, help create the overall learning culture we need. If constant learning, supported by frequent training resulting in high skills and knowledge, becomes the norm, all other 'virtues' should follow.

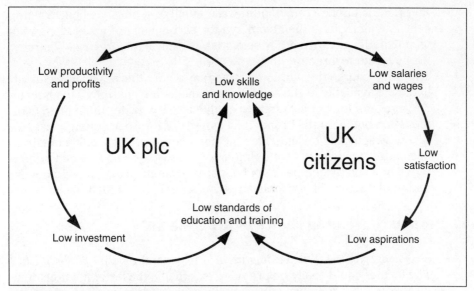

Figure 10.1   Vicious circles of the 20th century
Source: Ball, 1991.

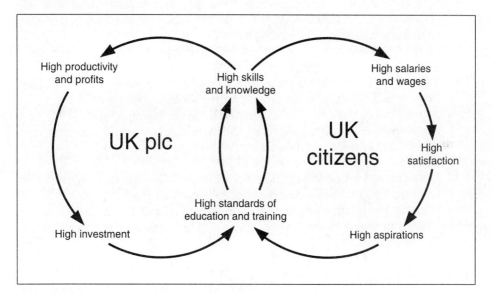

Figure 10.2   Virtuous circles of the 21st century
Source: Ball, 1991.

TRAINING

One of the most popular and effective staff development methods is a formal off-the-job training programme, a structured learning experience directly related to the job. Such programmes are of three main types:

167

- An open or public course, often residential at a purpose-built training centre, which offers the advantage for participants of exchanging relevant experiences with other delegates as well as the organized learning led by a course director.
- The same course run within the company where there is a large enough audience available at the same time to make this possible. This has the advantage of lower cost, greater confidentiality, easier timing and commonality, but lacks the broadening aspects of the open course.
- A course specially designed for the company, working from an analysis of training needs and developing tailor-made material. This can be prepared and run by company staff, external training providers or a combination of the two. This course adds the benefits of uniqueness.

Factors to consider in choice of programme

- *Knowledge and skill to be imparted*: Is it general or company-specific? The former could easily be provided externally, the latter must be done internally – but may use an external source to develop the course and material necessary, if no internal resource is available.
- *Staff to be trained*: How many share the same needs and would be available at the same time? What is the best number required on the course to make it a successful learning event? Most training events, to be good learning experiences, need around 12 participants, but this does vary according to the subject matter.
- *Timing*: Is this crucial? Is there time to design a tailor-made course internally or not? If an external course is the solution, the choice of training provider may be partially determined by the dates on offer.
- *People resources*: Do you have the necessary internal resources to design, implement and evaluate programmes? If not, you need external experts.
- *Financial resources*: What budget is available? Do you need to prioritize training programmes according to the needs of the business? Internal training is cheaper per person trained, provided the numbers to be trained in the same knowledge and skills are sufficient and available at the same time.

How to choose an external provider

Research shows that the key influence in selecting a training provider (and course) is personal recommendation from colleagues. However, in addition, it is worthwhile conducting some essential checks of your own, such as the following questions:

- How experienced are the course directors and trainers, both in their particular subject areas and in training?

- What commitment is there to customer-determined quality and how does it manifest itself?
- How varied are the training methods used (for example, lecture, group discussion, games and simulations, self-assessment inventories, CBT, panel discussions, guest speakers, films and videos, reading, projects, syndicate work)?
- Do the training facilities enhance the learning process (for example, quiet with no interruptions, trained staff and resources readily available, site dedicated to learning)?
- Details of the providers of marketing courses can be found from several sources, including the following:
  - *The Marketing Managers Yearbook*
  - *The National Training Index* (also provides a Course Assessment Service for members)
  - *European Management Education Guide*
  - The most comprehensive provider is the Chartered Institute of Marketing whose directory of residential courses will give the best overview of topics marketers need training in at various stages in their careers.

Training paths

Within the CIM directory will be found suggested training routes for those in the marketing function from graduate or sales trainee to marketing or sales director and managing director. Marketing managers should plan their own and their subordinates' development and training path, recognizing that such a plan is likely to be very changeable (see Figures 10.3, 10.4 and 10.5 for examples).

Qualifications through training

A recent development has been the interest from both individuals and their organizations in recognizing a programme of training events through a meaningful certificate. The Chartered Institute of Marketing offers a menu approach, with a choice of courses appropriate to different levels of experience. This means that, as a result of taking 21 days training over a period of several years, and passing short exams at the end of each course, individuals can obtain a Certificate in Marketing or Sales Management Practice, or a Certificate in Professional Selling. Such a certificate takes several years to obtain because training is directly related to the current job or a new position in the near future and the design of the menu ensures courses are taken at different job levels encouraging the training path approach.

The two management courses can, allied to relevant practical experience, provide the criteria for associate membership of CIM and entry to the Diploma in Marketing, the only marketing education qualification currently recognized in the EU.

MARKETING TRAINING PATH

This diagram illustrates the classical training programme for an individual working within a marketing environment. At any time during an ongoing vocational training programme, individuals may wish to enhance their personal skills and knowledge within a specialist subject and the areas available are depicted under the 'specialisms' options.

KEY:
For ease of reference events are colour coded into four main categories as follows:

- ☐ **Fundamental**
- ☐ **Implementation & Practice**
- ☐ **Advanced**
- ☐ **Strategic**

NOTE:

Figures in brackets = duration of event, e.g. (1) is a one-day event. Full details of one-day events are advised separately by post.

MARKETING THEORY & PRACTICE   STRATEGIC MARKETING

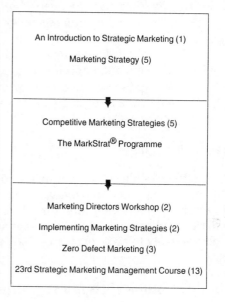

SPECIALISMS:

Advertising
- ☐ Fundamentals of Advertising (1)
- ☐ The Principles of Advertising (5)
- ☐ Effective Advertising Copy (2)
- ☐ Managing Advertising (3)

Communications
- ☐ Practical Writing and Planning for Print (2)
- ☐ Getting the Best from Agencies (2)
- ☐ Effective Marketing Communications (5)
- ☐ Market Communications Strategy for Top Management (2)

Direct Marketing
- ☐ How to use Direct Mail Effectively (1)
- ☐ Writing Successful Direct Mail Letters (1)
- ☐ Direct Marketing (2)

Europe
- ☐ European Business Strategy (3)

Exhibitions
- ☐ Successful Exhibitions (1)
- ☐ How to get Results from Exhibitions (2)

Finance
- ☐ Finance and Accountancy for Non-Financial Managers (1)

- ☐ Finance for Marketing and Sales Managers (5)

Information Technology
- ☐ Information Technology and Marketing (3)
- ☐ The Micro-computer: Its Practical Applications in Marketing (1)

Marketing & The Law
- ☐ The Legal Aspects of Marketing and Sales (1)

Market Planning
- ☐ Preparing a Marketing Plan (1)
- ☐ Marketing Planning (2)
- ☐ Advanced Marketing Planning (2)

Market Intelligence
- ☐ Market Intelligence (2)
- ☐ Know your Market (3)

Marketing Research
- ☐ Introducing Marketing Research (1)
- ☐ Marketing Research – Consumer Goods and Services (5)
- ☐ Marketing Research – Industrial Products and Services (5)

Merchandising
- ☐ Successful Merchandising in a Retail Environment (1)
- ☐ Effective Retail Merchandising (3)

Pricing
- ☐ Pricing and Profit Strategies (3)

Product Development and Management
- ☐ Developing New Products and Services (5)
- ☐ Profitable Product Management – Consumer Goods and Services (5)
- ☐ Profitable Product Management – Industrial Goods and Services (5)
- ☐ Profitable Product Management – Financial Services (5)
- ☐ Profitable Product Management Decisions (3)

Public Relations
- ☐ Fundamentals of Public Relations (1)
- ☐ Practical PR for Marketing (3)

Sales Promotion
- ☐ Fundamentals of Sales Promotion (1)
- ☐ Effective Sales Promotion (3)
- ☐ Effective Sales Promotion for Retail (3)

SALES TRAINING PATH

This diagram illustrates the classical training programme for an individual working in selling or sales management. At any time during an ongoing vocational training programme, individuals may wish to enhance their personal skills and knowledge within a specialist subject and the areas available are depicted under the 'specialisms' options.

KEY:

For ease of reference events are colour coded iinto four main categories as follows:

- ❐ Fundamental
- ❐ Implementation & Practice
- ❐ Advances
- ❐ Strategic

NOTE:

Figures in brackets = duration of event, e.g. (1) is a one-day event.
Full details of one-day events are advised regularly by post.

SELLING THEORY & PRACTICE

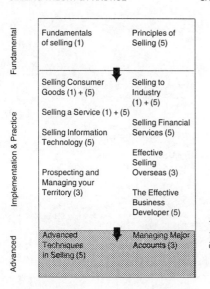

SALES MANAGEMENT

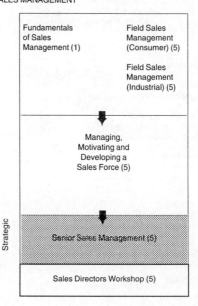

SPECIALISMS:

Finance
- ❐ Finance and Accountancy for Non-Financial Managers (1)
- ❐ Finance for Marketing and Sales Managers (5)
- ❐ Finance for Sales Representatives (2)

Forecasting
- ❐ Scientific Forecasting for Improved Results (1)
- ❐ Sales forecasting using a Micro-computer (2)

Negotiation
- ❐ Fundamentals of Negotiation (1)
- ❐ Effective Sales Negotiation with Major Accounts (Consumer) (5)
- ❐ Effective Sales Negotiation with Major Accounts (Industrial) (5)

Office Management
- ❐ Sales Office Management and Administration (5)

Sales and the Law
- ❐ Legal Aspects of Marketing and Sales (1)

Telephone Selling
- ❐ Techniques of Telephone Selling (1)
- ❐ Telephone Selling Skills (2)

Sales Training
- ❐ Sales Training Techniques (5)

Figure 10.4   Sales training path

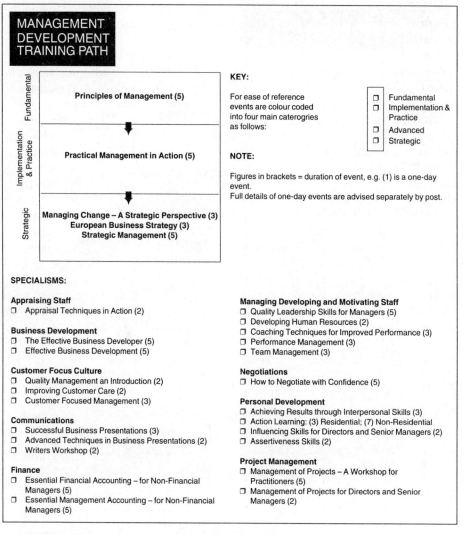

MANAGEMENT DEVELOPMENT TRAINING PATH

Fundamental

Principles of Management (5)

Implementation & Practice

Practical Management in Action (5)

Strategic

Managing Change – A Strategic Perspective (3)
European Business Strategy (3)
Strategic Management (5)

KEY:

For ease of reference events are colour coded into four main caterogries as follows:

☐ Fundamental
☐ Implementation & Practice
☐ Advanced
☐ Strategic

NOTE:

Figures in brackets = duration of event, e.g. (1) is a one-day event.
Full details of one-day events are advised separately by post.

SPECIALISMS:

Appraising Staff
☐ Appraisal Techniques in Action (2)

Business Development
☐ The Effective Business Developer (5)
☐ Effective Business Development (5)

Customer Focus Culture
☐ Quality Management an Introduction (2)
☐ Improving Customer Care (2)
☐ Customer Focused Management (3)

Communications
☐ Successful Business Presentations (3)
☐ Advanced Techniques in Business Presentations (2)
☐ Writers Workshop (2)

Finance
☐ Essential Financial Accounting – for Non-Financial Managers (5)
☐ Essential Management Accounting – for Non-Financial Managers (5)

Managing Developing and Motivating Staff
☐ Quality Leadership Skills for Managers (5)
☐ Developing Human Resources (2)
☐ Coaching Techniques for Improved Performance (3)
☐ Performance Management (3)
☐ Team Management (3)

Negotiations
☐ How to Negotiate with Confidence (5)

Personal Development
☐ Achieving Results through Interpersonal Skills (3)
☐ Action Learning: (3) Residential; (7) Non-Residential
☐ Influencing Skills for Directors and Senior Managers (2)
☐ Assertiveness Skills (2)

Project Management
☐ Management of Projects – A Workshop for Practitioners (5)
☐ Management of Projects for Directors and Senior Managers (2)

Figure 10.5   Management development training path

Open learning

Mentioned above as one of the methods of staff development, open learning, however, is probably best considered as a training method. It is now appreciated that for maximum effectiveness open-learning solutions include face-to-face sessions (often at weekends), and the material is also often used in part on more traditional interactive courses.

Distance learning, flexible learning, resource-based or materials-based learning are other terms used to describe open learning, and in themselves indicate the attributes of this form of learning, in which the course director becomes less the focus of learning, and rather more a mentor and facilitator. In essence the learning takes place at the convenience of the individual, and can be cost-effective if there is a suitable generic package available and this type of learning suits the individual.

The Open Learning Directory, published annually by Pergamon, is the best guide to what is available, and has a section devoted to marketing, sales and distribution. Equipment requirements vary from audio cassettes through videos and PCs to CDI.

Larger organizations can, of course, develop their own open learning material using internal or external resources. The initial up-front costs can be high, but if the population to be trained is large, and the time-scale short enough to prevent the material becoming outdated, the cost per person can be cheaper than for conventional training – provided the staff concerned learn effectively this way.

Whilst there is considerable enthusiasm on the part of government at present for this form of training, mainly on cost grounds, it has to be said that from the customer's point of view, open learning appears most successful when part of a total programme that includes study weekends, group work sessions, tutorials and on-the-job training. Open learning packages, therefore, are best considered as another resource for trainers to utilize in designing effective and efficient training programmes.

REFERENCES

World Competitiveness Report (1993), annual publication, IMD and World Economic Forum.

Ball, Sir Christopher (1991), *Learning Pays: the Role of Post-Compulsory Education and Training*, London: RSA.

Lever, Karen (annual publication), *Marketing Managers Yearbook*, London: AP Information Services.

Steverink, Leo (annual publication), *European Management Education Guide*, Netherlands: IMEC.

Whitehead, Christine (twice yearly: January and July), *National Training Index*, London: Graduate Group Ltd.

ESSENTIAL READING

Garratt, Bob (1990), *Creating a Learning Organization*, London: Director Books.

Margerison, Charles J. (1990), *Making Management Development Work: Achieving Success in the Nineties*, Maidenhead: McGraw-Hill.

Sheal, Peter R. (1992), *Staff Development Handbook*, London: Kogan Page.

Appendix: The Chartered Institute of Marketing

N. E. Waite

MARKETING QUALIFICATIONS

The CIM originated the professional vocational courses and examinations which have been offered on a regular basis since 1928. The whole purpose behind this was to provide staff development for employees on a part-time evening-class basis. In 1965 the Institute of Marketing was responsible for funding the first Professional Chair in marketing in the UK at Lancaster University. Nowadays university business schools, almost without exception, have at least one or more professors of marketing. (See Table 10.1 for courses in Marketing in British universities.)

Syllabuses currently available from the CIM and taught by college providers throughout the world provide the essential knowledge and understanding necessary to underpin practical competence. These include the Certificate in Marketing and Certificate in Selling, Advanced Certificate in Marketing, Advanced Certificate in Sales Management which lead on to the Diploma in Marketing, a three-year post A-Level part-time course for marketing managers. These courses are available to all who meet the entry criteria. Distance learning courses and self-study texts are also available together with other publications designed to help students prepare for the Institute's qualifying examinations. There are currently some 33 000 students throughout the world studying for these qualifications. Holders of the Diploma in Marketing are automatically eligible for election to graduate membership with full membership (MCIM) available to those who also have the required marketing management experience (see Figure 10.6). This qualification is also recognized under EU directive 89/48/EEC which resulted from the European Union's move to harmonize qualifications across all member states. Furthermore as a chartered body's qualifying examinations, the Diploma in Marketing is also recognized as an alternative to a first degree for those who wish to pursue postgraduate

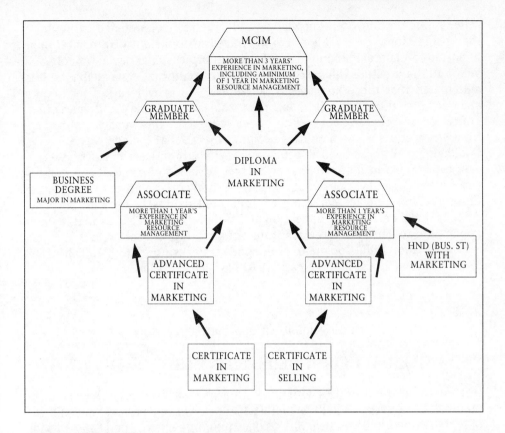

Figure 10.6   Membership of CIM: the qualifications route

courses such as an MBA, other Masters degrees or a further/higher education teachers qualification. The Institute aims to ensure that these courses are designed so that successful candidates will be adequately prepared for the demands made on both sales and marketing executives who wish to be successful in this important and vital function of business.

The CIM is also at the forefront of the development of National Vocational Qualifications in sales and marketing and has played a leading role in creating the industry standards against which practitioners will be measured and certificated. The Chartered Institute of Marketing has also been made an awarding body for the Sales NVQ Levels 2–4 and Marketing NVQ Levels 2–4, targeted for introduction during 1993 and 1994, with NVQ Level 5 being developed during 1995. These certificates in practical competence will be offered alongside the traditional underpinning knowledge courses for which the CIM has an international reputation.

However, education and training does not stop when you become a qualified member of the Chartered Institute of Marketing. The CIM emphasized this fact by the introduction of a continuing professional development scheme from July 1993 which is designed to ensure that all practising members keep themselves up-to-date in both knowledge and practical competence throughout their professional career. Members will have the opportunity to register their intention to maintain a minimum of 35 hours professional development each year and the Institute will carry out selective monitoring of participants. It is anticipated that these 'Registered Marketers' will provide a further quality standard for those who practise the profession of sales and marketing. Education and training courses to be accredited for this purpose will range from short courses, such as those offered by the CIM College of Marketing, Cookham, to MBAs and will also include other study and learning activities.

In today's world more than ever before, evidence of professional competence is a must and various education and training programmes offered by the Chartered Institute of Marketing are designed expressly for this purpose. Further details of the CIM education and training courses are available upon application to The Chartered Institute of Marketing, Education and Training Services, Moor Hall, Cookham, Maidenhead, Berkshire SL6 9QH; tel: 01628 524922; fax: 01628 851493 (Education), 01628 526045 (Training).

Table 10.1
Marketing qualifications from Universities*

UNIVERSITY FIRST DEGREES IN BUSINESS STUDIES

Degrees in business studies with marketing specialization – sandwich course one year in industry – widely available at the newer universities and colleges of higher education. Entry qualifications: minimum of two good GCE A-levels (minimum of five GCE subjects, two of which must be at A-level).

UNIVERSITY FIRST DEGREES IN MARKETING

Bournemouth: BA Hons International Marketing Management; Leisure Marketing.
Central Lancashire: BA (Hons) Marketing; BA (Hons) BSc (Hons) Combined Hons Marketing.
De Montfort: Combined Studies Marketing.
Edinburgh Queen Margaret: BA Hons Applied Consumer Studies; Food Product Management; BSc Applied Food Science with Marketing.
Glamorgan: BA Hons Marketing; Marketing with Languages.
Glasgow Caledonian: BA/BA Hons Marketing & Communications.
Greenwich: BA/BA (Hons) International Marketing.
Heriot-Watt: (studies at the Scottish College of Textiles): BSc Hons Textiles with Marketing.
Huddersfield: BA/BA Hons Marketing.

*NOTE: This list indicates some of the courses available but new ones are being added every year.

Table 10.1 continued

Humberside: BA Hons European Marketing.
Lancaster: BA Hons Advertising & Marketing: BSc Hons Marketing.
Leeds Metropolitan University: BA/BA Hons European Marketing Public Relations.
East London: BA/BA Hons Business Studies (Marketing); BSc/BSc Hons Biomarketing & Management.
London Guildhall: Joint Degree Subjects Marketing; Minor Subjects Marketing.
North London: BA Hons International Marketing/Business Management.
London South Bank: BSc Hons Consumer Product Management.
Manchester: BSc Hons Management & Marketing of Textiles with a Modern Language.
Manchester Metropolitan: BA Hons Retail Marketing.
Newcastle upon Tyne: BSc Hons (Agriculture & Biological Sciences) Agricultural & Food Marketing.
Northumbria at Newcastle: BA Hons Modern Languages & International Marketing.
Paisley: BA/BA Hons Business Economics with Marketing Management; Marketing.
Plymouth: BA Hons Marketing.
Salford: BSc Hons Modern Languages & Marketing Studies.
Sheffield: BEng Hons Mechanical & Manufacturing Engineering; BSc Hons Food Marketing Management.
Southampton Institute: BA (Hons) Marketing; BA (Hons) Marketing Design.
Staffordshire: BA Hons Marketing.
Stirling: BA Hons Marketing; Marketing-Financial Studies: BSc/BA/BAcc General Marketing.
Strathclyde: BA Hons Marketing; BSc in Technology & Business Studies Marketing & Management Science.
Teesside: BA Hons Design Marketing; Marketing.
Wales: Aberystwyth BSc Single Hons Agricultural & Food Marketing.
Wolverhampton: BA/BSc and BA/BSc Hons Marketing.

HIGHER DEGREES AWARDED BY UNIVERSITIES/COLLEGES

Aberystwyth University: MSc Agricultural and Food Marketing.
Bournemouth: MA Consumer Marketing; Advertising; Public Relations.
Brighton: MA in Marketing.
Bristol UWE: MSc/Postgraduate Diploma in Marketing.
Buckinghamshire: MA European Marketing Mgt.
City: MBA Marketing.
Cranfield: (Silsoe) Marketing and Product Mgt for Food & Agriculture.
Dundee: MBA Marketing.
Hull: MBA Strategic Marketing.
Kingston: MA Marketing.

Table 10.1 concluded

Lancashire (UCL): MA Export Marketing.
Lancaster: MPhil Marketing.
London Guildhall: MA Marketing.
London Southbank: MSc International Marketing.
Manchester: MBA Advanced Marketing Management; Research for Marketing Decisions; MEd Education Marketing; MSc Marketing.
Middlesex: MA Marketing Management.
Newcastle upon Tyne: MSc/MPhil International Agricultural Marketing.
Nottingham Trent: MSc Marketing Management.
Northumbria at Newcastle: MA Marketing.
Paisley: MSc Marketing.
Salford: MSc Marketing (PT).
Sheffield Hallam: MSc International Marketing.
Southampton Institute: MA Marketing.
Staffordshire: MSc Marketing.
Stirling: MSc Marketing.
Strathclyde: MSc International Marketing; Marketing.
Sunderland: MA International Marketing; Marketing.
Ulster: MA Business Strategy; Marketing.
UMIST: MSc Marketing.
Wales: Aberystwyth MSc Agricultural & Food Marketing.
Westminster: MA Marketing.

DIPLOMAS AWARDED BY UNIVERSITIES

De Montfort: Graduate Diploma Computer Systems – Sales & Marketing.
Humberside: Postgraduate Diploma Fisheries-Marketing.
Kingston: Postgraduate Diplomas Marketing.
Liverpool John Moores: Postgraduate Diploma Marketing Management.
Manchester Metropolitan: Postgraduate Diploma Marketing Management.
Napier: Postgraduate Diploma European Marketing & Languages.
Newcastle upon Tyne: Postgraduate Diploma Agricultural Marketing; International Agricultural Marketing.
Northumbria at Newcastle: Postgraduate Diploma Marketing.
Paisley: Postgraduate Diploma Marketing.
Stirling: Postgraduate Diploma Marketing.
Strathclyde: Postgraduate Diploma International Marketing; Marketing.
Sunderland: Postgraduate Diploma International Marketing; Marketing.
Ulster: Postgraduate Diploma Business Strategy; Marketing.

CERTIFICATES AWARDED BY UNIVERSITIES

Manchester Metropolitan: Postgraduate Certificate Marketing Management.
Ulster: Postgraduate Certificate in Marketing.

ESSENTIAL READING

Hart, N. and Waite, N. (eds) (1994), *How To Get On In Marketing: A Career Development Guide*, 2nd ed., London: Kogan Page.

CIM (1994), *Education and Training for the 90s*, Maidenhead: CIM.

CIM, *Marketing, Sales, Management and Strategy Training Courses Prospectus*, annual publication, Maidenhead: CIM.

11 Sales management
Michael Wilson

THE JOB OF THE SALES MANAGER

The sales manager must first and foremost be a manager. Like other managers in the company he or she is responsible for getting things done, through other people, towards economic objectives. This simple definition has many implications.

'Getting things done' implies that the sales manager must be action-orientated and must be concerned with results rather than means. He or she will be judged by what is ultimately achieved rather than by the processes he or she manages. 'Through other people' suggests that the results will, in fact, be achieved by others. The sales manager is not there to do their job for them although this is what far too many sales managers do. It is often easier to handle difficult customers personally than to develop a sales executive to cope with them. 'Towards economic objectives' means that the sales manager must constantly consider the financial implications of his or her actions.

The six basic functions of the sales manager

To fulfil his or her basic duty as a manager of the company, the sales manager must carry out six specific functions:

1 Plan objectives and strategies for his or her team.
2 Develop an organization structure capable of achieving the objectives.
3 Recruit and select staff who can perform the jobs laid down in the organization structure.
4 Train them in the further knowledge and skills required to perform the jobs.
5 Motivate them to perform their jobs to the best of their abilities.
6 Evaluate and control them to ensure the objectives are achieved.

Particular problems of sales management

In performing the six functions the peculiar difficulties of sales management must be recognized. Unlike any other body of staff in the company, the sales force is normally geographically well spread. Thus they cannot be supervised as closely as in other departments. This causes particular problems of motivation, communication and control for the sales manager and feelings of isolation for the sales executive.

Again, unlike other sections of the company the sales force spends the vast majority of its time with people other than company employees, usually, of course, with customers and prospects whose viewpoints are very different from those of the sales executive. This can cause attrition whereby the sales executive's attitudes and skills are worn down by constant contact with opposing views. For example, it is difficult for a sales executive to maintain that his or her product has a particular advantage when buyer after buyer, month after month (whether correctly or not), says that it is not better than the competing products.

Furthermore, the kind of people who choose this isolated and wearing life are often, paradoxically, those least capable of coping with it. Those who choose selling as a career are normally gregarious individuals, yet the structure of the job ensures that they spend a minimal amount of time with their colleagues.

Need for leadership and training

Sales management must provide strong leadership and training to overcome the particular difficulties of the sales job. The training programme must be powerful enough to inculcate methods of working which will be followed despite the lack of close supervision. Training must also be continuous to counter the attrition of dealing with customers. The leadership shown by the sales manager must be clear and strong enough to support staff who are widely spread and whose nature requires a high level of social contact. Some of the problems can be eased by skilful organization, careful selection and attractive commission systems. However, the basic conditions of the sales job make it imperative that the sales manager places great emphasis on leading and training his or her team.

HOW TO PLAN THE SALES OPERATION

The sales manager will begin by considering the marketing objectives, policies and strategies and control criteria. He or she will probably have a forecast of sales by revenue and volume, a forecast of gross and net profit required, perhaps an expense budget ceiling, a description of the product range available with additions and deletions, price structure, promotional support and so forth.

Forecasting sales

In many companies the sales manager will be involved as a member of the marketing team in the definition of sales forecasts. The process will normally start by forecasting sales for the next period. This is the most critical prediction in the company as it will determine the production schedule, raw material and finished stocks, promotional expenditure and so on. It is best to approach the forecast in two stages. First, what will sales be, assuming all variables in the situation are the same in the future as they have been in the past? Second, which variables will change and what will the impact be? Some of the variables will be internal factors which management decides to change, others will be external factors which are uncontrollable by the company but whose effect must be predicted.

The sales forecast forms the hub of the sales manager's objectives. It will, of course, influence and in turn be influenced by the plans he or she formulates. It also represents the heart of each individual sales executive's objective in that the total forecast should equal the summation of the individual sales targets.

Developing the sales plan

Having set the sales forecasts and targets, the manager must now consider how they will be achieved. In formulating objectives, obviously some thought will already have been given to the plan. After the plan is written it might well be necessary to reconsider the goals which have been previously identified.

Basically, the sales manager must ponder five questions:

1 What is to be sold?
2 To whom?
3 At what price?
4 By what methods?
5 At what cost-effectiveness?

In some of these areas, notably the product range and pricing structure, the sales manager may well have limited influence; they are often controlled by the marketing planning department, through a brand or product management structure. In respect of all five facets he or she will certainly have to consider the inputs from other parts of the business: what stocks will be available from production; what money is available from finance; what advertising and sales promotion support is planned and so on.

What is to be sold?

This is the product range definition, and here the sales manager can at least advise his or her marketing planning colleagues on the saleability of the various items in the range as well as new product requirements. From a sales management viewpoint he or she will have to decide whether the full range should be sold to everybody. In some capital equipment markets where the distributor has to make a heavy investment in stock it may not be in the interests of the company to supply dealers whose financial resources may be overreached if they purchased the more costly products. Likewise, companies which have to make after-sales service arrangements may well decide not to sell products to customers who are geographically isolated.

To whom?

The sales manager must next consider the customers and prospects for the company's products.

He or she will first study the existing markets and decide whether business with them is likely to increase, decrease or remain static. This judgement will be based on a study of previous buying records. By analysing customers in terms of their potential and actual purchasing of the various products the sales manager has to offer, the areas to be attacked can be identified. Prospective customers can be analysed in the same way.

By what methods?

Having identified from the product/market analysis the segments to be attacked, the sales manager can now consider the methods most likely to achieve the objectives set.

The main promotional tool is the sales force. The first question to be answered is: what sort of service should the sales force provide in order to influence the buyer? If, for example, the manager of a food firm has identified supermarkets as an area of great potential, this will lead him or her to consider how best to persuade supermarkets to buy more of the firm's products. The best way to approach any problem of selling to a distributive network is to consider what help the dealers need in order to sell the product; in this case, supermarkets will buy more only if they can sell more. One way of selling is to merchandise the product in-store, so the sales manager may well organize the field force towards that objective. Obviously such a conclusion will have important implications for the selection, training, organization and control of the field force. The same thinking applies to companies in other industries. For example, a crop protection firm pondering how to increase sales to agricultural merchants will have to consider how the merchant will market the product to farmers. Perhaps the job of the sales force in this case will be to help the merchant develop his own marketing skills.

Even where distribution networks are not involved, the sales manager must still give thought to what service to provide to the buyer. For example, a packaging company must consider whether the buyer needs sales people who are technical experts in the packaging itself, the packaging process and the machinery required, or the particular packaging problems of individual industries. On the other hand, perhaps sales executives should be more of a design consultant or maybe have a high degree of financial knowledge so that they can discuss the cost-effectiveness of their products. Most important of all in selling packaging, salespeople will need an appreciation of their customers' own marketing problems. Thus the successful industrial sales executive selling packaging to, say , a food company will certainly have an awareness of the problems of the food company selling to the retail trade, and, moreover, the retail trade's problems selling to the housewife.

Such an analysis of what kind of sales effort is needed will lead to identification of the sales methods that are appropriate. The complexity of seller/buyer relationships becomes rapidly obvious. It is only by such definition that the sales manager can develop the presentational approach that will create success in the face of product/price parity.

Having identified the nature of the sales method, the sales manager can then consider the scale of effort required. He or she must calculate how many customers and prospects should be called on and how often. The customers are relatively easy to specify because they are known by name to the company. However, it may be uneconomic to have very small customers visited personally, except very seldom. The level of prospecting is more difficult to calculate as in many companies potential customers cannot be identified by name. At least, however, the sales manager can indicate the characteristics of likely prospects. Such a profile can then be used by the sales force to select prospects to be called upon. Alternatively, the sales manager can plan simply to allow a certain percentage of time or calls for the process of looking for new business, giving the sales executive the responsibility of using the time or calls wisely.

How often calls should be made is always difficult to assess. Obviously different categories of accounts will require or demand different call frequencies. In some trades where there is an established buying frequency, usually little is gained by calling at a different frequency. For most companies, however, the call frequencies have to be decided by management and the best rule of thumb to follow is to call as infrequently as possible without jeopardizing the business. Many companies over-call because they fear that if they are not on the customer's doorstep as often as possible they will lose business. It is worthwhile to experiment with call frequencies to see if slowing down the frequency does actually affect sales. Even marginal changes can have a dramatic impact on cost. If, for instance, a sales force is calling on average every four weeks and this could be altered to every five weeks, the company could possibly save up to 25 per cent of its sales costs.

The support of the field force will also be covered by the sales manager's study of the methods required to achieve his objectives. It is often the case that various parts of the supplier/buyer relationship can be more economically handled by techniques other than personal visiting by representatives. Telephone selling is one method that is successfully used to handle routine ordering, thus freeing the sales staff's costly time for more creative work. In the consumer goods trades, where point-of-sale display work is common, many firms have split their field forces into sales executives and merchandisers. In industrial selling, the sales force has often to be supported by technical staff who can advise more expertly on the product and its applications. In the computer market the sales executive is usually backed by a team of experts who can advise the customer on systems design, programming and installation.

Furthermore, parts of the sales task may be better handled by other non-personal promotional techniques. For example, it may be more economic to generate prospects for a life assurance company by advertising and direct mail than by cold canvassing by the sales force. Customer education in using the product may be better handled by producing videos than by individual tuition from the sales executive.

In other words, the sales manager's task in deciding the nature and scale of the methods necessary to achieve objectives should not be limited to a simple consideration of how to deploy sales executives. The criteria for selecting techniques must not only be effectiveness and use of the sales force but also cost and use of total company resources. Obviously the majority of the effort will be through the sales force in most companies; this should not lead, however, to ignoring other possibilities.

At what cost-effectiveness?

The planning focus of most companies has been traditionally on growth, particularly profit growth coming naturally from sales volume or at least revenue increases. However the situation facing many industries is one of stagnant, even declining markets, prices under pressure and most costs rising rapidly. In such circumstances the planning focus has to change from one of simple growth to a search for increased productivity.

Productivity is the measurement of the interrelationship between inputs and outputs, well acknowledged if not totally understood in production processes, but far less well explored in sales because of historic assumptions about year on year sales increases. Improving productivity is not simply a question of cost reduction, the dreaded 'head count' exercises for example. Paradoxically such efforts often actually reduce productivity as senior, highly paid sales management have to do the work left behind when junior, lower paid jobs are eliminated.

To analyse and subsequently to increase productivity there must be a clear understanding of what outputs are desired, what inputs are necessary and the nature of the relationship between the two in terms of causation (i.e. what effects result from what causes) and correlation (i.e. how much a change in input will affect the output). Typical desired sales outputs include volume, revenue, product range, mix, market share, gross margin, and net margin. The relative importance and achievability of these will of course vary from company to company and situation to situation. Thus a company which has traditionally sought volume increase may now have to concentrate on margin protection.

Sales inputs are characterized by the type of sales activity used (for example, field force, telesales, van sales), the number of sales personnel (both in the field and in the sales office) and the type of person employed (management: staff ratios, calibre, pay and so on).

185

There are so many different measures of sales productivity that a sequential approach is needed to concentrate management attention on the key figures and, what is more important, their underlying causes.

A good starting point is to measure the ratio of sales to sales cost. Sales will normally be taken as revenue, but should be analysed by volume, price and mix relative to target. Sales cost will usually include not only field force costs, but also the costs of the sales office, sales management, training and so on. This overall measurement can be further analysed as shown in Figure 11.1.

Ratios	Comments
1 Sales: sales costs	What is the trend?
2 Sales per sales executive, explained by:	Are there big differences?
3 Number of customers/contacts per sales executive	Are there big differences?
4 Number of calls per day	Relationship to sales?
5 Face-to-face time: total time	Enough time with customers?
6 Orders: calls	Trends in 'strike rate'?
7 Average order value	Differences between sales executives?
8 Field sales costs: total sales costs	Too much 'indirect' cost?
9 Percentage of labour turnover	Is the salesforce stable?
10 Most successful sales executive: average sales executive	Difference gives some indication of improvement potential

Figure 11.1   Assessing sales productivity: ten key ratios

Such quantitative assessments of current productivity will usually highlight areas for improvement and at the same time indicate the underlying causes which must be modified if results are to be improved. Furthermore, evaluating sales performance in this way forms a sound basis for the whole planning process.

Major customer planning

Most companies' sales exhibit strong 80:20 tendencies, that is, a small percentage of large customers taking the bulk of the sales and vice versa. These major customers are so important that they require special planning attention from sales management and, usually, special handling.

In planning this important aspect of the business, the sales manager must first consider the maximum proportion of sales revenue the top customers should account for. One service company, for example, will not allow its top five accounts to represent more than 40 per cent of the sales revenue because above that level it considers itself too vulnerable. An industrial components company decided that no single market should account for more than 15 per cent of its output and that each market segment ideally should consist of no more than five organizations controlling 80 per cent of purchases. Of course, it is not always easy or even possible to control the customer/sales mix in this way, but it is a good start to have a sales policy on this important issue so that if and when major customers are predicted to become too dominant appropriate action can be taken, for example to broaden the customer or market base of the company.

Second, the profitability of business with major customers should be analysed as it is too facile to assume that because they produce most of the sales they must inevitably produce most of the profit. In fact, because large customers demand large discounts, tend to take longer credit, need more stock back-up, expect considerable promotional support and so on, the costs of servicing them are usually disproportionately high. To analyse and control major customer profitability an increasing number of firms produce profit and loss accounts for each top customer. At first, these usually show to the horror of management that the principal customers produce much less profit than had been believed, and in many cases actually show a net loss. However, only by analysing performance in this detail can a realistic basis be laid for future planning and negotiation.

HOW TO ORGANIZE THE SALES FORCE

Many sales organizations have developed without regular, objective analysis of their purpose or structure. Today they are out of date and unable to fulfil the purposes for which they were originally designed. This is because the traditional hierarchical structure is based upon conditions which no longer hold true in a great number of firms. Such organizations assume that there is a large number of relatively small, geographically separate and independent buying points all with similar requirements, and that these can be serviced by a large number of geographically separated sales executives who can perform similar tasks and who represent the main promotional activity of the company.

Changes in buyer/seller relationships

These suppositions have been made obsolete by a number of fundamental changes in the buyer/seller relationship. First, as has been discussed, the buying power in many industries is no longer evenly distributed. In many markets a few big companies (either distributors or end-users) control the majority of the purchasing. Because of their buying power and importance it is not usually feasible to delegate sufficient responsibility and authority to the sales executive in whose territories they happen to be located. Furthermore, the large customers themselves are increasingly centralizing their purchasing so that branches or subsidiaries which might at one time have been direct customers for sales executives in different territories are no longer allowed to buy.

Second, the development of new marketing techniques has meant that some tasks traditionally performed by the sales force can be more economically or efficiently handled by other methods. The growing use of telephone selling, contract ordering, broking, auxiliary or commando sales forces and even franchising is having a significant impact on the nature and scale of the field sales effort required.

It is evident that the sales manager must consider these influences in planning his or her organization. To fit the sales team to the needs of the customers the sales manager must identify:

1 the task of the sales force;
2 how many sales executives are needed;
3 how they should be organized;
4 how they can be managed;
5 how the sales force can be integrated with the rest of the company.

Task of the sales force

It is an oversimplification to say that the job of the sales force is to sell and therefore its members are salespeople. In many industries this is not true within the normal concept of the function – collecting an order. For example, the representative for a pharmaceutical house calling on doctors never takes an order. The grocery sales executive calling on branch stores of a multiple chain may not be able to take an order as the store manager often does not have the authority to buy. The executive selling plant hire will only occasionally receive an order when calling on a construction firm which happens to have an urgent need that day.

The sales force structure should also be scrutinized. A geographical split may be most economical in that travel time is minimized. It may not, however, be the most effective. In one glass container company it was seen that the prime service to be provided to the buyer was a technical knowledge of bottling as applied to the customer's particular industry. Thus the sales force was regrouped on an industry basis, changing the organization structure from its traditional geographic basis. Obviously there was some increase in travel costs because each industry group worked nationally but this was more than offset by the increase in sales.

Number of sales executives needed

Many sales managers can give no logical explanation of why the sales force is the size it happens to be. Even when explanations are forthcoming, such as that the sales force is based on population distribution, county boundaries or sales revenue per person, the rationale must still be in question. Such criteria often bear little relationship to the amount of sales effort required. Counties differ greatly in size; population density will seldom correlate directly with sales or potential. Even the assumption that each sales executive should be able to handle a specified amount of sales revenue is very suspect. Generating £100 000 of business in one part of the country can be far harder than it is in another. The amount of sales force effort required to handle 100 customers spending £10 each is likely to be far greater than servicing one account of £1000.

Sales force workload analysis

The aim of building an organization from the bottom up is to give the appropriate level of service to each customer and the appropriate amount of work to each person. The only common factor between sales executives is the number of working hours and this should be the starting point for a workload analysis, which is the only logical way of constructing a sales force. The amount of work per person can then be calculated by assessing the elements of the sales job. If a sophisticated approach is needed, work study and method analysis can be used to establish these elements and the time taken on each. Typically, they include prospecting, travelling, waiting, selling and writing reports. If the number of actual and potential accounts to be visited and the frequency of visiting can be assessed, it is possible to calculate the size of sales force needed (see Figure 11.2).

NUMBER OF ACTUAL AND POTENTIAL CUSTOMERS × CALL FREQUENCY

AVERAGE DAILY CALL RATE × NUMBER OF WORKING DAYS PER YEAR

Customer categories and call frequencies
Category A (over £50 000 a year)   500 × 12 visits p.a. = 6 000
Category B (over £25 000–£50 000 a year)   2 000 × 9 visits p.a. = 18 000
Category C (£10 000–£25 000 a year)   5 000 × 6 visits p.a. = 30 000
Category D (under £10 000 a year)   7 000 × 2 visits p.a. = 14 000

       68 000

Average daily call rate = 8

Number of working days
Total days in year   365
Weekends   104
Holidays   15
Sickness   5
Training   10
Conferences   5
Meetings   11   150
Number of working days   215
Call total per sales executive 215 × 8 = 1 720

Number of sales executives required = $\dfrac{68\,000}{1\,720}$ = 40

Figure 11.2   Calculating sales force size

Territory organization

The organization of each sales executive's workload can now be considered to ensure the territory is covered as effectively as possible. Customers to be called upon have been identified, call frequencies have been set and call rates calculated. Using these three factors the territories can be built up to form appropriate workloads per person. How the workload is handled will have an impact on achievement and cost and, if left to their own devices, many sales executives will work in almost random fashion round the territory, 'territory' in this case implying a group of customers, not necessarily a discrete geo-graphical area, so the comments are applicable to industry-based territories as well as geographical areas. Some will tend to call more frequently than is necessary on customers near to home and will ignore accounts in distant parts of their areas. Others, particularly industrial sales executives, may give too much attention to customers whom they find technically interesting or from whom they get a pleasant reception rather than allocating their time in accor-dance with sales potential. The prime aim of territory organization analysis is to maximize selling time by minimizing travel time in particular.

How the sales force should be managed

Having assessed the nature and scale of sales force required, the type and number of managers needed can be decided. Again, following the basic con-cept of looking at the organization from the bottom up, the first question to be answered is: how many sales executives can the first-line manager manage?

Organizational theorists have long pondered this problem and arrived at dif-ferent answers by a variety of techniques. Generally, their views range between four and eight to a manager. Because of the variety of different man-agerial situations, any generalization may well be highly inaccurate and there-fore it is more sensible to approach the question by assessing the workload to be handled. There are four principal elements that should be considered:

1   The division of responsibility between line field management and other company staff. For example, how much responsibility and therefore how much time does the field manager need to spend on recruitment, sales promotion, market research and the like? What staff support is available from other departments? How much time must the manager spend in meetings other than with his or her own staff?

2   The nature of the sales task to be supervised. Different sales jobs require different degrees of involvement by the manager. For example, a pioneer sales force is likely to need far more time from the manager than a rou-tine order-taking team.

3   The amount of personal selling undertaken by the manager. Some indus-tries demand a large amount of personal sales time from the manager, operating either alone or as part of a sales team. It is common practice, for instance, in capital equipment selling for the manager to lead a team on important sales projects.

4   The degree to which field training is necessary. This will depend on the type of sales executive and the sales activity as well as on the seniority of the people concerned. A recently recruited speciality sales executive

– say, in office equipment – is likely to need far more field training than a senior van sales executive who has long experience of the job. However, because of the attrition process all salespeople undergo, some field training is necessary in virtually every situation.

How the sales force can be integrated within the company

For the sales force to function efficiently it must be viewed as an integral part of the total company effort. To achieve this there must be a clear concept of the role of the sales force in the total communication process with the market place. In far too many companies the various promotional tactics are seen as separate units. Thus it happens that the first time the sales force hears about a product modification (which they should be using to sell with) is when a customer comments on it. Even more important is the relationship between the sales force, which is basically an implementational weapon, and the marketing planners. Unless great care is exercised, particularly in companies with product management structures, the sales organization is continuously torn between different brand objectives and plans.

The best way to overcome these difficulties is to involve sales management in the marketing planning process and for the marketing plan to be the basic operating document for everybody in marketing.

HOW TO STAFF THE SALES ORGANIZATION

Sales performance factors

The performance of a sales executive will depend upon three basic factors: innate character traits, training and motivation. The objective of the staffing process is to choose people whose inborn characteristics are suited to the sales job and who can then be developed and motivated. Obviously there are some individuals whose intrinsic personalities are such that little or no training or incentives are required. These are the 'born' salespeople. However, they tend to be few and far between and gravitate towards those industries where their outstanding sales skills are directly rewarded by high commission rates, such as life assurance, office equipment and other forms of speciality selling.

Most sales managers must plan not only to pick staff with the appropriate characteristics but also to train and motivate them. To choose good sales staff, it is necessary to understand some basic concepts of the staffing process and to have a system for handling recruitment and selection.

Basic concepts of staffing

A sales manager needing to recruit somebody new is faced with a predictive problem. How will a person the manager knows little about perform in a job that person knows little about? By some means the manager must match the one with the other, and the failure to achieve congruence causes many of the staff problems in the industry. The manager must therefore appreciate that he or she is not simply looking for a 'good' person, but someone who is appropriate for a particular job: a case of trying to pick horses for courses.

The first stage in the process will be to define carefully the job to be performed. From the organization study that has already been conducted, the general framework of the position will have been delineated. Now it can be specified in the form of a written job description.

From this document the manager can identify the characteristics a successful incumbent would possess, and thus construct a profile.

These two statements contain the criteria against which candidates will be assessed and present incumbents appraised. If new people are required, applications can now be generated by recruitment techniques using one or more sources such as internal staff, newspaper advertising, consultants and so on. To begin to assess applicants, the manager must first gather information about them and, second, have some methods for evaluating and checking these data.

Whenever a prediction must be made of how someone will perform in the future, it is wise to examine in depth what that person has done in the past. Psychological research indicates that in terms of basic behavioural patterns, people do not change very much particularly after the age of maturity. (In fact some psychologists argue that fundamental personality patterns are settled by the age of seven. As most salespeople are well over this age, the precise data does not really matter.) The selection process is therefore concerned with collecting detailed information about the applicant from as far back as possible, verifying that the facts are as stated and then analysing them to identify repetitive behavioural traits.

The techniques which can be used for this collection, verification and analysis process are the application form, psychological tests, reference checking, the structured interview and the placement analysis.

There are eight steps in a systematic staffing procedure:

1 Writing the job description.
2 Constructing the profile.
3 Recruiting candidates.
4 Assessing application forms.
5 Checking references.
6 Psychological testing.
7 Structured interviewing.
8 Evaluating and placing successful candidates.

HOW TO DEVELOP JOB SKILLS

Planning skill development

The art of selling is the presentation of product benefits in such a way that buyers are persuaded that their needs will be satisfied. To be successful the sales executive must not only be knowledgeable about the product and the customer but also skilful in the presentation of this knowledge. Otherwise, the most knowledgeable people would be the most successful at selling. Increasingly, companies are discovering the lack of correlation between technical knowledge and sales results. For example, for many years it was traditional in the drug industry to employ pharmacists, rather than salespeople, to call on doctors. Both here and in general , an increasing number of companies are finding that staff who are basically salespeople tend to be more successful. Obviously they must be given some technical training but the emphasis is now firmly on the sales aspects of the job.

The training programme must aim to achieve the objectives of giving knowledge and developing skills. The nature and scale of both areas should be specified in advance so that the programme can be directed towards definite goals.

Setting development objectives

This should be approached by identifying the gap between the level of performance expected of the sales force and its current standards. The desired level of achievement can be defined by analysing job requirements of the job specification. For example, if it is noted in the job description that a sales executive will make presentations at trade conferences or be responsible for in-store promotions, the development programme must include training in public speaking and merchandising. Figure 11.3 shows extracts from typical job descriptions and the knowledge and skills required to fulfil the defined tasks. The individual goals of particular parts of the training programme can be derived from this.

Importance of field training

The most important area of sales force development is the continuous field training process. This is normally undertaken by the sales manager concerned. It is difficult to delegate because it is interwoven with other aspects of the management function such as control and appraisal. Some companies, however, do use a field trainer system. For it to be successful, the division of responsibility and authority between manager and trainer must be carefully defined, otherwise the salespeople will become confused about what guidance to take from whom. Too often, the system is introduced for the wrong reasons – to create a promotion opportunity for senior sales staff or to reward an old company servant who lacks real management potential. If the importance of field training is recognized and seen as an integral part of the sales management function, the need for field trainers seldom arises. Where the volume of field training seems to be beyond the line management capability, the first areas to be examined should be the organization structure and spans of control.

Extracts from typical job descriptions	Knowledge requirement (*What do they need to know?*)	Skill requirement (*What do they need to do?*)
In conjunction with his or her area manager, set targets by product group.	Customer records. Prospect records. Sales forecasting technique.	Ability to analyse statistics, derive trends and identify opportunities.
Must be fully knowledgeable about the products and their applications.	Product features and applications in customer circumstances.	Ability to relate product features to customer needs. Ability to find and interest new customers.
Must achieve the targets agreed by obtaining orders from existing customers and prospects.	Prospecting techniques. Preparation techniques. Sales interview techniques.	Presentational skills. Communication skills. Persuasion skills.
Must handle all customer queries and complaints.	Objection-handling techniques. Complaint-handling procedures.	Communication skills particularly with irate customers.
Must represent the company at trade shows and exhibitions and make presentations when called upon to do so.	General company history and background.	Public speaking. Visual aids.
Must monitor and report on competitive activity and state of trade in his or her area.	Market research techniques. Information sources.	Ability to ask fact-finding questions and analyse answers. Report-writing.
Must ensure the company's products are displayed to best advantage.	Merchandising techniques. In-store promotions schemes.	Display-building. Selling merchandising ideas.

Figure 11.3   Knowledge and skill requirements analysis

HOW TO MOTIVATE THE SALES FORCE

The motivation of their sales staff is probably the most common topic of conversation whenever sales managers meet. All managers have their own pet theories on how to get the best out of people. The reason why it is such a popular discussion point is because sales staff can be directly supervised only intermittently. It is therefore vital to success that they are deeply motivated to work on their own. Moreover, the nature of the sales job inevitably involves loneliness and certain customer contacts which can depress the morale of any but the most enthusiastic of salespeople.

Because of the geographical separation and the wearing aspects of the job, it is vital for success that sales managers possess or develop the ability to motivate their staff. To do so they need a clear understanding of why people work and what they wish to gain from their work. Only then can they create an environment which will cause their staff to employ their full abilities in their jobs.

Incentives and disincentives

Motivation involves providing incentives which encourage salespeople to give of their best, and removing disincentives which prevent them from devoting their whole energies to their work. Unfortunately, far too often, motivation is equated with incentives only, although it is common to find that the elimination of disincentives – for example injustices, unfair treatment – is the more powerful influence.

It must also be recognized that virtually every incentive brings with it a disincentive, either for the same person or for his or her colleagues. For example, while a commission system may provide a strong incentive for a sales executive, it may also be a disincentive if he or she feels the payments are unfairly calculated. Likewise, a competition may be a strong motivator for the winners, but it can be demoralizing for the losers, particularly if they believe that because of the construction of the contest they had no real chance of winning.

The task of managers is therefore to consider the needs of their staff both individually and as a group, and to arrange a balance of motivational influences that will encourage them to achieve the company's objectives. In essence, this is best done by ensuring that an individual's own goals in life are consistent with the company's aims. For example, there is little point in recruiting people who are highly motivated by money into a company which offers security as its major satisfaction. Similarly, if the company pays commission as a standard percentage of all turnover achieved, it can hardly complain when the salespeople concentrate on those products which are easiest to sell in volume although they may be the least profitable.

Perhaps the most amusing contradiction is those managers who bemoan the decline of company loyalty as a motivational influence while regularly poaching staff from their competitors.

Although recognizing that everyone has an individual need pattern, there   *195* are five main motivational influences the sales manager must fully understand. These are:

1 Remuneration.
2 Direct incentives.
3 Job satisfaction.
4 Security.
5 Status.

Remuneration

Remuneration and its effect on motivation are a vast and complex subject. Little research has been done, particularly in Britain, into the effects of different forms of payment systems. Nevertheless, certain principles can be identified:

1 Pay, although important, is certainly not the only and may not be the prime motivational influence.
2 Most companies will have to pay at least in part by salary and salaries should depend upon an assessment of the grade for the job and an appraisal of the employee in order to position him or her within the grade.
3 Where it is possible to pay in part by results, this will have a beneficial effect and lead to the achievement of better sales results; but certain preconditions must be met to administer commission schemes successfully.
4 The commission system likely to be most effective is payment on the basis of turnover, probably because it is the easiest to understand.

Direct incentives

This is the term used to cover all the many systems of payment in cash or in kind other than basic remuneration. It includes fringe benefits, merchandise awards, point schemes and competitions. Apart from fringe benefits such schemes do not usually make a significant difference to total earnings and their basic intention is motivational.

Use of direct incentives

Merchandise awards and competitive schemes are best used to focus short-term attention on particular aspects of the business. They are a tactical rather than a strategic motivational weapon. When employed in this way, they can be very effective to concentrate sales force attention on, for example, gaining new accounts, increasing sales of lower volume products, or even submitting call reports on time.

Job satisfaction

In most surveys of salespeople's attitudes, job satisfaction is rated as the highest motivating influence. It certainly appears that in an affluent society, the major reason a sales executive chooses and remains in a company is because he or she finds the work enjoyable and fulfilling. It is therefore, at least in part, the responsibility of the manager to create a satisfying environment.

As we mentioned earlier, however, everyone has a particular need pattern and, therefore, what constitutes job satisfaction will vary from individual to individual. Some enjoy achieving perfection in the detail of their work, others are motivated by the opportunities of working with a wide cross-section of people. Many different satisfactions can be gained from similar jobs and the manager should emphasize particular aspects for each individual. Likewise, what one finds enjoyable, another dislikes. Again, the incentive/disincentive equation must be handled by management with some care.

Job satisfaction is the most important motivating force for most salespeople. Although each individual has his or her own concept of what is required from his or her career, certain common factors are found. For a position to be satisfying:

1 It must be perceived by the individual as being worthwhile to him or herself, the company and society.
2 There must be clear and challenging goals with regular feedback of results.
3 It must contain a body of knowledge and skills which the individual is given the opportunity to learn.
4 There must be an opportunity for at least some employees to progress either to management or to more important sales tasks.
5 The efforts made by the individual must be recognized and appreciated by his or her superior.

Security

The need for security is a common if seldom admitted motive. The nature of the remuneration system and the relative importance of salary and commission will obviously affect job security and must be considered from this aspect.

However, the less obvious facets of security should not escape the sales manager's attention. First, the degree of security the company wishes to offer must be identified. If the salespeople's jobs are too secure there is a danger that the sales force will stagnate. On the other hand, a high level of insecurity normally leads to high staff turnover and although a great deal of activity might be generated, it is doubtful whether much of it will be purposeful. In companies where insecurity is a constant feature of the environment, morale tends to be low and although there is often an appearance of frenetic action, achievement is usually very limited.

Status

The social status of selling has already been mentioned in the earlier discussions on job satisfaction. By explaining the social worth of the sales function, the manager will also be upgrading its position in society. The manager can also help to improve its status within the company and the market by ensuring that the job titles given carry as much prestige as possible without going to the extremes of 'regional sales director'. The manager should also ensure that the rest of the company realizes the importance of the function so that when a customer telephones and asks for a field sales executive by name, the switchboard operator does not use descriptions such as 'only one of our sales reps' (or, worse still, 'travellers') when he or she is not in the office. Likewise, when put through to the sales department, the caller should be greeted by someone who says he or she is that sales executive's secretary or assistant. He or she can, of course, adopt a similar role for a number of other sales people as well.

Identifying motivational influence and planning motivational schemes

Motivation is the business of management. 'Getting things done, through other people, towards economic objectives' implies quite rightly a leadership function.

The sales manager's motivational task starts with setting the job specifications and salary grades of the sales force. In formulating these, he or she will begin to set the framework of motivational satisfactions the company can offer to help achieve its objectives. It is extremely important that conscious thought is given to ensure compatibility between the goals of the firm and those of its employees.

Regular objective checking of the level of motivation is thus a wise precaution, particularly in those companies whose sales forces are widespread and have insufficient contact with each other and even with their management. Opinion polls can give a sound basis, particularly in such circumstances, for positive and visible managerial action.

HOW TO CONTROL THE SALES OPERATION

In order to control any activity, there must first be objectives and a plan. Unless it is known what is to be achieved and how, whether it is being achieved cannot be assessed. Conversely, there is little point in setting goals and defining actions unless there is an evaluation procedure.

Management by exception

The problem facing all managers is that they have to achieve results from resources which are scarce. They have only a limited amount of manpower, money and facilities. In particular, they have the most severe constrictions on their own time because although other resources can be expanded where necessary, the number of hours in the day cannot. It is essential, therefore, that their time is used efficiently. One of the prime methods for ensuring this is to devote time only to those parts of the business which are not running according to plan.

The analysis of facets which are not up to standard implies a control system which indicates such variances. This whole process is known as 'management by exception' and can be operated wherever a control mechanism of this kind has been constructed. For example, if the standards set are costs, the result is a standard costing system; if they are budgets, a budgetary control system. To operate such control systems in this way requires that:

1 Standards are set.
2 Actual information is collected.
3 Variances are produced and analysed.
4 Corrective action is taken.

Setting standards of field performance

To identify appropriate standards for control, managers should ask two questions:

1 What constitutes success?
2 What affects the achievement of success?

Absolute standards

In a sales operation, success can usually be defined as the achievement of the sales targets. These serve as the prime standards of control. By themselves, however, they are insufficient. The achievement or otherwise of the annual sales target constitutes an absolute standard. It measures what has happened but it is then usually far too late to redress the balance. Moreover, it does not indicate why the performance has been poor. In a sense it is analogous to the oil pressure warning light on a car. When it glows it indicates that the pressure has fallen below the level necessary for efficient engine operation. It registers this fact after the event has taken place. If the car is being driven at high speed on a motorway, by the time correct action has been taken, damage may well have occurred. Even if that is avoided, the motorist will still not know why his or her oil pressure has decreased.

Diagnostic standards

Diagnostic standards, which help to identify why performance is varying from target are defined by asking the second question: what affects the achievement of success?

In the case of a particular sales executive failing to achieve target, the man- *199* ager must consider the actions that individual takes which should lead to the goals being met. Surprisingly, there are only four, and these can be identified by the following questions:

1　What kind of people does he or she call on?
2　How many does he or she call on?
3　How often does he or she call?
4　What does he or she do while there?

The construction of standards is the essential first element in the sales force control system. To ensure that appropriate standards have been set, the sales manager should check that they satisfy five criteria:

1　That they are quantitative wherever possible so that variances can be measured.
2　That they cover what the sales force is supposed to achieve.
3　That they measure how the sales force is progressing and help to predict the likely outcome.
4　That they help to diagnose the reasons for sales performance.
5　That they identify likely variances sufficiently early to enable corrective action to be taken.

The secret of effective control is the definition of appropriate quantitative standards. Without them, control is virtually impossible. With them, the manager's task is dramatically simplified and significant amounts of time are saved.

Collection of information

Details of actual performance must be collected so that they can be compared against standards. The better the definition of the standards, the clearer the specification of the information required. Every manager complains about the ever-increasing volume of paperwork, facts and figures that has to be handled. One of the main reasons for the explosive growth of available information is that the ability to collect and process data has generally outstripped the skills to use it. In a frantic attempt to gain some form of control management calls for more and more analysis and because of the sheer quantity of available information, believes that it thus has a grip on the situation. Nothing could be further from the truth.

Criteria for information collection

The information collection process should not be started until a clear set of standards is defined. Otherwise, faced with a lack of definition of what should happen, the manager has to search through thousands of facts on what has happened and must somehow arrive at a judgement as to the corrective action needed. The development of electronic data processing has simply worsened the situation because it has improved information capture and processing. Parodoxically, computers are best used as a tool of managerial control when they give the minimum information, not the maximum available data. Once standards have been defined, the computer can readily be used to run a management by exception system pointing out only the variances from plan for management to take corrective action.

Variance production and analysis

Variances are produced by comparing actual results against the pre-set standards. However, this simple method may need to be refined as high variances may result which reflect the forecast error of the standards. For example, although the average daily call rate is set at eight, there is probably no cause for alarm if this varies between six and ten. Because so many of the standards are produced by averaging past performance, it may well be necessary to process the actual results before comparing them against standard.

Taking corrective action

Having identified the true nature of the variance, the sales manager has to decide whether it results from faulty standard setting or inadequate performance. If the former, the standards will have to be modified. If the latter, the performance of the individual will have to be improved, usually by some form of training or instruction. If the individual is to improve, he or she must be given specific targets to achieve within specific time periods otherwise little or no change will result.

If the individual fails to improve and the manager is certain that the standards are correct, and that the appropriate legal procedures have been followed, there is no choice but to transfer him or her from the sales force or, more likely, terminate the employment with the company.

Management responsibility for corrective action

Sales managers must not shirk this fundamental responsibility although it can be extremely distressing to have to dismiss someone who may have been with the company for some years and whom a manager has come to know well. It is almost axiomatic that the worst personnel problems are found in those companies which have tried to pretend that the failure would improve. . . somehow, some time. Sales managers can be absolutely certain that staff difficulties of this nature can only get worse.

Sales managers must realize that there are four aspects to this basic responsibility. First, they are charged by the company to achieve financial objectives. Second, they have a responsibility to themselves to fulfil their tasks as managers. Third, they have a duty to the other members of their teams to ensure their efforts are not dragged down by retaining below-standard performers.

Fourth, and most important of all, they have a critical responsibility to the individual to tell him or her as soon as he or she cannot achieve the standards demanded by the company. No one can be happy in a job he or she knows he or she cannot do. The sooner that individual finds a position where his or her talents can be utilized, the better for all concerned. A company is never more culpable than when it retains someone, who is palpably incapable of achieving the desired levels of performance, for so many years that he or she becomes virtually unemployable when eventually asked to leave. Management cowardice or, at best, *laissez-faire* is one of the worst failings companies ever exhibit. Ruthlessness, paradoxically, is often the kindest and fairest attitude that a firm can adopt.

THE ROLE OF TECHNOLOGY

Another key wave of change affecting selling and sales management is the increasing spread of information and communications technology into the sales function.

At the sales executive level, this means that more and more companies are automating basic sales processes such as customer record cards, journey planning and call reporting, issuing salespeople with laptop or notebook computers, car phones, modems and even in-car fax machines. These tools enable them not only to plan their work more efficiently but also to check stock availability even whilst with the customer and to place orders directly down the telephone line into the supplier's mainframe computer.

From a sales management viewpoint, the development of lower-cost hardware and, especially, purpose-built software enables the creation and maintenance of customer and prospect databases, the planning of sales force utilization as well as the measurement and evaluation of the sales activity against criteria such as numbers of calls as well as orders gained.

Although all the necessary technology currently exists, it is still only being thoroughly utilized by a minority of the companies to whom it can apply. As the customer bases of suppliers decline and increasingly polarize so that fewer major customers dominate the business, as competitive pressures increase with the Europeanization and globalization of markets, the forward-thinking sales manager will have to use information and communications technology increasingly to keep costs under control, speed up order gaining and fulfilment processes, and more accurately and efficiently plan and control sales activities.

CONCLUSION

The nature of sales management has changed dramatically in the last two or three decades; in many firms even the last few years have seen a complete reorientation of the function. As markets become increasingly international, this process of change will not simply continue; it will accelerate as the margins of error become even finer. No longer will finger-in-the-wind management be precise enough to generate profits.

Sales management in particular and marketing management in general must become more professional and more scientific to survive in the future. The great barrier to progress at the moment is the lack of proven theory. To overcome this hurdle, sales managers must be prepared to hypothesize about better operating methods, not simply perpetuate techniques because they are traditionally accepted. They must experiment with innovative approaches and, most important of all, must attempt to validate their hypotheses by rigorous assessment.

ESSENTIAL READING

Lidstone, J. B. J. (1992), *Beyond the Pay-Packet*, Maidenhead: McGraw-Hill.

Stafford, J. and Grant, C. (1993), *Effective Sales Management,* 2nd ed., Oxford: Butterworth-Heinemann.

Wilson, M. T. (1983), *Managing a Sales Force*, 2nd ed., Aldershot: Gower.

12 Brand management
Jack Bureau

This chapter looks at the role of brand management as a management discipline. This is examined under seven headings:

1 Introduction: brands, branding and brand management.
2 The need to manage revenue.
3 Revenue sources.
4 Key revenue management functions.
5 Planning revenue management: strategy.
6 Planning revenue management: operational management and control.
7 Brand management: past, present and future.

An analysis of the way business is traditionally undertaken in organizations which do not use brand managers identifies the need for such a role. Such a need is established whether or not the business is brand-based: the case is made as a need to manage revenue. The heterogeneity of revenue sources is identified as the key factor which determines marketing planning boundaries: it is not sensible to attempt to plan two or more distinctly separate marketplace entities. Each requires individual attention from the marketing function. The chapter looks at the planning requirements for such entities, both for the long term (strategy) and the short term (operational). Finally, the chapter examines the objections which have been raised to the brand management function, and forecasts its growth as a discipline in the future.

BRANDS, BRANDING AND BRAND MANAGEMENT

One of the most persistent certainties in the history of the business enterprise is its hazardous nature. An examination of all British enterprises born in the last hundred years would yield a remarkably small number of survivors. And a primary reason for their extinction lies in the fickleness and changeability of the market-place. Death through market indifference almost certainly lies at the heart of the persistently high failure rate of 20th century organizations.

In such a dangerous environment, there are no fail-safe principles of business practice to guarantee organizational survival. Yet in the dangerous currents and storms of the market-place, a number of practices have come into being which dramatically reduce the risks of foundering. Among these is the practice of branding: the process which gives a product or service a unique identity in the market-place through an amalgamation of name, design, packaging, legal protection and the promotion of unique and desirable qualities, undertaken to make it easy for the customer to separate a product quickly and memorably from all its competitors.

Failing a simple and memorable means of identifying one product from another, the customer must fall back on personal judgement and buying experience. In such cases the customer will learn from experience to trust one supplier or distributor more than another. The regular use of such a supply source creates the missing brand identity. Thus, before the universal advent of branding and of the supermarket, it was the common experience of high-street shoppers (from earliest times right up to the 1940s) that they learned to select, for example, the provision merchant who consistently maintained a high level of quality at the prices they could afford. The individual grocer thus created a store brand in his own name, providing the solution to the consumers' brand identification needs. Today the practice continues for those high-street commodities which remain unbranded by the manufacturer/supplier – classically in the market for meat and vegetables.

Branding has thus developed in response to the combined needs of the customer and of the producer.

The customer finds great benefit in quickly and easily identifying products which previous experience has revealed provide a reliable and desirable level of need satisfaction, knowing that the producer has a vested interest in maintaining that quality in order to sustain the integrity of his reputation, thereby keeping customer enthusiasm and loyalty.

To the producer, the policy of branding provides the considerable benefits of building and sustaining the customer's interest and of creating an identity for the product which makes it much harder for competitors in the battle for market power. Branding, through the operation of laws which uphold the integrity of brand ownership, allows the producer to carve out a niche in the market-place which can belong to no one else, providing much greater certainty of employment and profit for the producer.

In the most successful cases, the policy of branding may create an entity in society which is vivid, tangible, needed and even loved by large numbers of its users and consumers, even on an international level: Coca-Cola, McDonalds, Marlborough, Christian Dior, Rolls-Royce, Gillette, Rolex, Schweppes are internationally recognized by hundreds of millions of people.

Brand names reflect the fragmented nature of most markets. Whether as a result of taste-preferences, the demography of consumer groups or of their social aspirations, the use to which the products can be put or the price which customers can afford, the multi-segment nature of most markets requires the creation of a proliferation of brands created to satisfy each segment. While the company name – Ford, Cadbury, Glaxo, General Foods, Lever Bros – may identify a powerful super-brand in a big market, it is the brand name of the segment that is bought by consumers: Mondeo, Whispa, Zantac, Maxwell House, Comfort.

The growth in the last hundred years of the brand as a means of maximizing market power has led to an understanding of the supreme value of a well-established, high-profile and successful brand in the market-place.

The 20th century trend to fewer companies, of ever-increasing size, competing in markets of growing complexity and competitiveness, has resulted in the creation of giant companies owning large clusters of well-known brands, operating in a multitude of markets. This creates a considerable problem in organizational management: how best to ensure the proper management in the market-place of those precious commodities, the company brands, and how to guarantee the constant development of new brands, to ensure growth in market power as well as to ensure the replacement of dying brands.

While brands are most commonly associated with fast moving consumer goods marketing, the concept of branding is its most important characteristic, not the market in which it may or may not be prevalent.

The concept of branding lies in the logic already identified above: that it provides the market-place with reassurance – and preferably guarantees as to the quality performance competence, reliability and the value for money of any product or service it seeks to buy, and to know that the producers will publicly stake their reputation in delivering these promises by clearly identifying each of their products in the market-place as belonging to them. Taken to its logical extreme, it would be a foolish producer who failed to put his brand on a product which meets these desirable criteria.

The value of brands: brand equity

In its determination to become larger, the business organization inevitably considers the possibility of acquiring other businesses. It does so most generally in order to obtain the products being successfully marketed by the acquisition prospect.

Now the briefest consideration of the normal failure rate level of new products makes the prospect of acquiring successful brands – without having borne the cost of their development and the other pains of their possible failure – an extremely enticing one.

To most organizations the value of the ownership of major brands is enormous. Unfortunately this value is rarely reflected in the company's balance sheet. Logically enough, financial directors and accountants generally, while recognizing the importance of brands to success in the market-place, have no easy means of placing a reliable value on such assets: after all, the value of the brand is in terms of such nebulous elements as reputation, goodwill, prestige and development potential. None of these are necessarily more than fleeting: the reputation of a brand may disappear in a very short period of time. Memories have no resale value.

However, with an increasing recognition of the heavy financial burden involved in developing new products ('growing your own products'), there is a growing willingness to accept the real – if ephemeral – value of brand reputations as corporate assets when corporate acquisitions ('buying brands off-the-peg') are being considered. The price paid by Nestlé for Rowntree-Mackintosh – many times its value, if brand equity is ignored – is a pointer to the developing recognition of the value of brands.

THE NEED TO MANAGE REVENUE

Revenue may be defined as the money the organization earns in the process of selling its products or services. The heart of all business lies in its capacity to earn revenue – at a profit. The heart of the system known as brand management lies in the concept that revenue-earning requires to be managed in just the same way as every other element of the organization. Such a statement may seem to be so obvious as to verge on the fatuous, yet the practice of truly managing revenue is not at all widespread in Britain.

At the birth of every business venture there is, of course, an immediately recognized need for some means of selling the product in order to generate revenue. To the extent that it is the salesforce that generates orders, so the salesforce is always the first marketing element created to manage revenue.

Many organizations, having created the salesforce, take no further steps to develop their revenue-managing skills, but rely solely on the skills of the salesforce to sustain pressure in the market-place to maintain the flow of orders. For such organizations, the salesforce is seen as the only system necessary to manage and obtain revenue.

As the years go by, these organizations come to recognize, of course, that a large number of marketing tools other than the salesforce is available to support revenue earning. To apply further pressure in the market-place the business organization may come to realize that 'marketing' will involve other activities necessary to provide the salesforce with the support it needs to ensure the achievement of the forecasted revenue.

Thus, from the simple first step of creating a selling function to generate revenue may grow a large body of help, guidance and expertise in the business of winning orders.

With a fairly complex structure of salespeople, advertising experts, public relations specialists, market researchers, merchandising and promotions operators, the marketing activities of the organization are now a good deal more comprehensive and sophisticated than they were before, when 'marketing' really amounted only to selling. However, even with this level of sophistication, some fundamental problems relating to revenue management still exist.

The process of co-ordinating each of these marketing activities – sales, mar-   *207* keting research, advertising, merchandising and sales promotion, public relations and so on – now assumes considerable proportions, and begins to take up more and more of the time of the head of these marketing functions. Under such circumstances, heads of marketing find themselves concentrating on the fire-fighting problems involved in the day-to-day business of administration, at the expense of planning the medium- and the long-term future of the products. (Occasionally companies resolve this problem by dividing the functions of selling and 'marketing'. In these organizations you may find a sales director and a marketing director on the company's board, each responsible for just a part of the total marketing functions.)

Each marketing specialist now has the responsibility of undertaking the detailed planning for his or her specialist activities across the full range of products: no one exists to undertake the full range of planning activities for each of the products individually. If the product requires substantial reassessment because, for example, it has problems in the market-place; because the way the product is made or presented is in need of re-examination; because the price is wrong; because its general consumer acceptance requires examination, or is found to be declining, then there is no one who is actually paid to resolve such problems. In the marketing department structure under discussion, there is no one who is expected to review each product in terms of its total effectiveness in the market-place, choreographing total marketing activity, masterminding all the marketing forces the company can bring to bear in order to maximize the success of the product.

It can be said, of course, that such a co-ordinate function already exists in as much as it is the primary function of the marketing director. Such a responsibility might even be considered to reside in the boardroom – even in the person of the Chief Executive – since full co-ordination of the revenue-earning powers of the organization must be of the utmost importance to the survival of the organization and, thus, be a principal topic for boardroom decisions.

While the logic of this argument is persuasive, the most cursory examination of the amount of work involved in revenue management will make clear that it cannot be managed either by a single person or by a committee. For most organizations, the work involved in revenue management makes it a full-time job for at least one individual, and frequently for more than one, and the pressing nature of the problems which need to be solved will require their continuous attention. In any case the members of the boardroom should not initially concern themselves with the wealth of small detail inevitable in the planning stages of revenue management.

Once an organization has perceived the logic of these arguments, it will recognize that one of the elements crucial to the continuing success of the organization – the health of its product in the market-place – requires close and continuous planning to maximize the probabilities that the product achieves maximum revenue at the maximum level of profitability.

The overwhelming majority of organizations earn their revenue from a wide spread of products and services, in a wide spread of markets, to widely different segments of the buying population. It really does not make sense for such organizations to work on the principle that revenue management can be effectively achieved by taking decisions about price, product, distribution or promotion across the full range of the organization's products, as if the market-place were homogeneous, and as if decisions taken for one product were necessarily relevant to decisions about any of the others.

Unless the organization produces one offering in the market, and only one, selling to one group of customers, having one set of pricing, promotion, place and product problems, there is a clear and profitable case to support the concept that revenue management must be undertaken at the individual product level: even the smallest organization must recognize the segmented nature of its revenue-earning activities and the heterogeneous nature of its marketing problems.

REVENUE SOURCES

While the principle central to the philosophy of brand management seems logically inescapable – that revenue requires managing and that it must be managed product by product – the ability of organizations to 'lump' their revenue into entities that are meaningful in the market-place varies considerably. At one end of the continuum lie the consumer good companies whose market offerings are in clearly unique brands, recognizable as such by producer, distributor and consumer. At the other end of this continuum lies the multitude of companies whose products are not at all clearly distinguishable in this manner, and which are certainly not branded. Producers of raw material, machinery, maintenance service, insurance policies, security services, suppliers who work exclusively in supplying original equipment manufacturers: the list of items which are less easy to parcel into revenue-manageable portions is endless. It is important, of course, to distinguish here between the problems which arise out of the nature of the market and those which exist because of the (relative) marketing backwardness of the participants.

There was a time when a great many more products than is the case today were sold as commodities because of a marketing failure among the producers: consumers were in the habit of seeking the generic product rather than any one manufacturer's brand. For example, in the 1920s and 1930s the consumer sought oranges but not Jaffa oranges, raisins and sultanas but not Whitworth's, wallpaper paste was home-made and gave no revenue to the Polycell brand. Many products today continue to sell in the market-place without any of them – in a marketing sense – 'belonging' to any one producer. There may be a variety of good reasons why this should be the case: more often the reason lies in the marketing backwardness of the producers and distributors operating in these markets. The list of markets which continue to be very largely undifferentiated in this way is surprisingly large: the market for petrol, for household linen (to use an old-fashioned but useful categorization), for a great deal of furniture, for most vegetables, for virtually all meat and fish, and so on. It is not that no 'branding' occurs in these markets, it is rather that such activity appears to be either limited or largely unsuccessful. These markets and many others remain determinedly 'commodity' markets and reflect market opportunities that have yet to be seized. It would be a brave person who asserted that such failures are due to any incompetence in applying revenue-management principles, but it would be foolish to refuse to recognize the connection between the practice of revenue management and the establishment of a clear product identity in the market-place.

By its nature, revenue management abhors a commodity market, as it abhors the economist's construct of perfect competition – and for the same reason: both speak of a supplier's inability to apply some controlling element to the environment in which he or she operates. And from this it follows that both show a higher propensity of market failure, lower levels of profitability and more uncertainty in employment.

While we may accept that many organizations fail to establish any clear identity for their market offerings because of marketing backwardness, it is now necessary to look at those which have difficulty in so doing for quite different reasons. A number of categories suggest themselves:

1   For the engineering workshop which handles everything on a one-off basis, every element of the revenue it earns is unique, tailor-made, individually costed and may never again be repeated. Marketing control systems of revenue management will not fit easily into such an organization, working in such a way.

2   Many organizations see the market segment or the customer as more dominant than the product. The centre of marketing and manufacturing attention for the maker of automobile parts may well consist of three dozen or so leading motor manufacturers around the world which dominate world demand for made-out parts. What may require to be managed is the revenue not from a product but from each customer.

3   Many organizations will sell the same range of products to different groups of customers, and it is those groups which focus marketing planning attention. For example, the market for household cleaning products (detergents, cleaners, disinfectants, bleaches and so on) lies both in the ordinary household and also in the nation's institutions – hospitals, schools, universities, business premises and factories, office blocks, prisons and so on. The household market and the janitorial market are sufficiently different to warrant separate groups to manage the revenues from each separately.

4   Organizations whose revenue-earning capabilities lie in winning contracts on multi-million pound projects will be unlikely to manage revenue in the same way as the brand manager for a company selling canned soups. Revenue management of this sort is exclusively in the domain of the boardroom and its officers.

Bearing in mind the considerable problems of directly applying the concepts of revenue management by products to these four categories, the decision to be taken is whether it is worth the effort to do so, or whether such efforts will in the end fail in the light of practical difficulties in making the new system work.

A very strong case can be made for seeking always to apply the principles of product management regardless of the difficulties initially encountered: the system has too many benefits to forgo it.

Every business operation needs to identify its market offerings into separate, homogeneous blocks of revenue-earning capability, and structure its marketing department to allow planning managers to manage each separate block of revenue. To this recommendation should be added, however, a useful proviso – it is quite unnecessary for the target of revenue-planning attention to be a product. It may quite satisfactorily and sensibly be a named customer, a group of customers, a segment of the market or any other element which can be identified as being in need of individual planning attention.

Some examples may be useful:

1   A charitable organization like the World Wildlife Fund may identify countries – or even continents – as the target for planning attention.
2   A national bank may identify different types of customers as the planning focus. Additionally, it may identify a number of sub-markets among each of its groups of customers: the small business may be planned for separately from the large institutions, the average householder may be planned for separately from the wealthier, investing individual.
3   The jobbing engineering business might identify the different markets from which it does – or could – get its revenue: tool-makers, blacksmiths, sheet-metal fabricators, civil engineering contractors, local government authorities and so on.

KEY REVENUE MANAGEMENT FUNCTIONS

So far, this chapter has attempted to establish:

1   The necessity to plan and manage revenue.
2   The necessity to break down the total revenue into identifiably homogeneous parts, whether such parts are made up of brands, product ranges, customers or markets.
3   That the process of managing the key elements of revenue planning should be undertaken by specialists who have no other organizational responsibilities.

The recognition of the importance of these three points will lead the organization to create a revenue management function. Because it will become the hub of marketing activity, this function will clearly be located within the marketing department, together with the selling, market research, promotions management, public relations and other marketing specialisms. The number of revenue managers to be appointed will depend on the complexity of the range of products or services offered in the market-place, on the one hand, and on the   *211* wealth of the organization on the other. Good revenue managers are expensive!

The name given to these revenue managers will depend largely on tradition, or on the forces that determine their areas of responsibility in the organization – products, brands, markets and so on. They are generally called product managers, brand managers or market managers. If they are at all numerous, they will be grouped, three or four at a time, under group brand/product managers – who in turn report to the head of the marketing function.

The remainder of this chapter refers to this discipline under these many titles, and the reader need not be confused, for their meaning lies in their titles: brand manager, product manager, market planner, product planner and revenue manager/planner all describe the same task and the same profession, and only the emphasis is different.

It is now possible to fill out the skeleton so far constructed by examining the function essential to the revenue management role.

Analysis

Probably the single most important function of revenue managers is that of analysis. They are hired, above all, to have a better understanding of the products for which they have responsibility than anyone else in the organization. This understanding concerns all aspects of the product as it interacts with the market-place. Gathering together data about the product, revenue managers will synthesize it into a coherent interpretation of the product's market-place behaviour. While market researchers may understand the customer better, works engineers may understand the physical performance characteristics of the product better, the salesforce may be better able to sell the product and the purchasing department may be better at buying the product's ingredients, revenue managers will see all these activities, skills and performances in terms of the need to maximize the criteria of the market-place: volume of sales, the volume of revenue and the volume of profits accruing to the product as the result of sales.

Whereas other corporate functions are concerned with one stage in the life of all the products – the purchasing stage, the manufacturing stage, the transportation and warehousing stage, for example – revenue managers are concerned with all the stages of the single product, from the forecast of its consumption (as they draw up plans for the future of the product) to its manufacture, delivery, purchase and consumption by the user in the market-place. Such a role requires that revenue managers see themselves primarily as the product's 'minder'; in constant attendance on the health and effectiveness of the product, prolonging its healthy life on its journey through its life cycle. The primary benefit of such a role to the organization is that it allows the remainder of the organization to concentrate on its specialisms (production engineering, purchasing, bookkeeping and so on) in the knowledge that someone is concerned with marrying up all their skills to the benefit of the product in the market-place.

Creating solutions

The analysis undertaken by revenue managers will invariably result in the discovery of both problems and opportunities for the product in the market-place. Probably the single most difficult task revenue managers have is to arrive at a solution for each of the problems, and to arrive at a means of maximizing each of the opportunities. It is in this area in which the 'art' of marketing lies, for to any one set of problems there are probably a thousand satisfactory and effective solutions. The difficulties are not made simpler by the knowledge that the outcome of most solutions is likely to be difficult to measure. Additionally, there is rarely enough money (not to mention courage) to make experimentation possible by testing alternative solutions. Finding a good solution to a marketing problem is the skill which marks out the good from the mediocre marketing practitioner: it is the skill that accounts for the high salaries commanded by top marketing planners.

Formalizing solutions

After a full diagnosis of the product in the market-place; after establishing the product's strengths and weaknesses there, and determining the proper course of action to take, revenue managers must now find a means of obtaining management's agreement to any changes that they are proposing to make to the marketing of the products. For this reason, among others, they will find themselves writing a formal planning document to serve as a basis for presenting their solutions to corporate management. The reasons for such formality are many:

1 *The role of revenue managers is essentially co-ordinative.* They rely entirely on other departments to enact the plan they have drawn up for the product. They will do so more easily if all the complexities of such co-operating have been formally hammered out and agreed with each of the co-operating departments. Documentation makes more certain that all the i's have been dotted and t's crossed.
2 *Revenue-managing documents generally contain elements which are too fundamental to the running of the company for such documentation to be acceptable on an informal back-of-the-envelope basis.* Such crucial elements as unit sales forecasts, profit and loss accounts, pricing structures and media schedules require to be formally as well as very precisely detailed.
3 *Marketing planning is much more an art form than a matter of scientific competence.* If that were not true, there would be no way to account for the widespread failure of new product launches. Because of this high level of uncertainty and risk which normally accompanies most marketing ventures on the one hand and, on the other, the considerable costs associated with marketing activities (selling, promoting, distribution and so on), it is a normal requirement for all major changes recom-

mended by marketing, and most minor ones as well, to require formal, documented review by the corporation's senior managers. Hence the formal documentation.

4 *Great uncertainty in the market-place requires diagnostic tools to give the best chance of reliable post-mortem analysis of failure and success.* Whether the marketing activity recommended turns out to be successful or otherwise, planning documentation provides the opportunity to measure changes against forecasts of changes. (This is the reason why vaguely worded and fuzzy objectives should be avoided in the compilation of planning documents.) There is also great value in looking back to yesterday's plan against which to check today's: to re-read yesterday's ambitious targets in the light of today's ignominious failure is a salutary remedy for marketing smugness.

Plan approval and authorization

Having pulled together a complete plan for the product in the market-place, it will now be necessary to persuade the organization to accept the validity of the plan. It is the task which will make the greatest demand on the persuasive and diplomatic powers of the revenue manager.

The personnel to whom the plan requires 'selling' are to be found in the boardroom: the organization's senior management will want to approve the marketing planning activities of the marketing department. Crucially, it is this formal approval of revenue managers' plans for their products for the year to come which provides them with the authority they require to enable them to undertake their daily work. For the brand management system to work requires that the brand managers' plans are supported by the clear and overt approval of the boardroom.

Such support and such approval may be most simply systematized through the annual approval of plans. Brand managers for their part lay out in detail what they recommend for the product, and corporate management for its part – perhaps after suitable modifications to the plan – provides the approval which then enables brand managers to go to every company department to obtain their co-operation in bringing the agreed product plan to a fruitful conclusion. Brand managers take their plans to the marketing director and, on receiving approval, emerge with a marketing department plan. The marketing director and each brand manager now take their plan to the board and, if the board agrees with the plan, emerge from the boardroom with a company plan for the product.

The authority which is vested in the boardroom is now the authority vested in the product plan.

Co-ordination and execution

For the fullest co-operation between the marketing planning function and other personnel who are crucial to the plan's successful outcome, the planner will also need fully to persuade the salesforce, the manufacturing facility and other functions of the organization of the good sense and value of the solution proposed for the marketing problem.

Much of the day-to-day life of revenue managers is spent in co-ordinating all the activities necessary to bring the plan to a fruitful outcome.

Monitoring and analysing the result

Once the marketing plan is being executed in the market-place, revenue managers will want to know whether it is meeting the plan's objectives. The planner will have called for whatever system and surveys are necessary to enable such measurements to take place, co-ordinating with the marketing information managers to ensure some measurements take place.

The availability of such measurements brings revenue managers full circle to a new analysis of forces and trends in the market-place, which in turn may identify new problems and new opportunities which may suggest the need for new solutions and new plans.

PLANNING REVENUE MANAGEMENT: STRATEGY

The circle of activity outlined above describes the circle which is common to all good management. Relating this to the market-place does not define the activities of the revenue manager. The areas of responsibility of brand and product managers may be examined under the headings of strategic requirements and operational requirements. By strategic is meant, simply, the longer-term planning horizon. By operational is meant, in contrast, the shorter-term planning horizon. Longer and shorter are, of course, relative terms, and may vary widely from market to market and from organization to organization. To simplify matters, longer term may be considered as always over two years but nearly always less than ten years. Consequently, shorter term will usually refer to one or two years ahead.

The marketing department does not lay down organizational strategy and, therefore, neither do the marketing department's revenue managers. Strategy is the task of the organization's most senior managers – the board. Before it can undertake any serious marketing planning, therefore, the marketing function will call for clear strategic guides from the board. It needs such guidance for particular and important reasons:

1   To manage a product or a service in the market-place the planner needs to manage the marketing tools which determine its effectiveness: those elements which Borden (1964) referred to as his 'mix ingredients':

- Product planning.
- Pricing.
- Branding.
- Channels of distribution.

- Personal selling.
- Advertising.
- Promotions.
- Packaging.
- Display.
- Servicing.
- Physical handling.
- Fact finding and analysis.

A cursory glance at this list makes clear that important decisions in most of these areas are likely to have long-term effect in the market-place. In turn that fact makes clear that revenue managers must operate within a set of strategic corporate boundaries which are clear. They need to know where the company is going and where it wants to get to, to ensure that all their recommendations fall within the organization's long-term plans.

2 Sooner or later the organization's strategic objectives will call for growth which cannot be met from its current portfolio of market offerings: it will need to seek new products and/or new markets within which to operate. The organization will turn to the managers of new product revenue to help create, launch and manage such new business. It will normally fall to the marketing function to provide the manpower to plan and co-ordinate such efforts. Under such circumstances, the marketing function requires clear strategic guidelines:

- as to scale of new business required, and the time period over which it must be brought into existence;
- as to the constraints which the organization wished to apply to limit the range of options open to it in its search for new products and markets. For example, the organization may lay down constraints as to the levels of investment maxima and minima in new product ventures or the level of risk; or it may demand that all new ventures should fall within the technological, managerial and marketing capabilities which currently exist in the organization.

3 The function of managing the revenue of a product in the market-place is intrinsically bound up with the concept of managing the product through its 'life cycle': the idea that every product is on its way to its demise and requires, therefore, constantly to be watched and worried over. Thus the very nature of revenue management is itself long term, (and strategic) as is the very nature of the product life cycle.

4 Many of the most 'creative' solutions to a product or a service in the market-place results in quite fundamental changes: a significant change in product specification, say, or a complete reorganization of a service facility. If you pay someone to plan the life of the offering in the market-place, you must occasionally expect a recommendation for radical change. Such changes often require long-term decisions and investment

on the part of other functions in the organization: the construction of new buildings, undertaking a major programme of fundamental research in the R&D department, the buying of capital equipment, the complete relocation of sources of production, the development of new distribution networks. All these marketing recommendations involve the long term for non-marketing functions, and require to be foreseen and forecast in plenty of time: the short-term horizon will not suffice.

PLANNING REVENUE MANAGEMENT: OPERATIONAL PLANNING

Largely throughout their planning activities in new product marketing, revenue managers will be involved in the development of marketing strategy, that element of corporate strategy which helps the organization to meet its corporate objectives. For the majority of their working lives, however, revenue managers are primarily concerned with the management of the existing revenue from the existing range of products. Such planning is referred to as 'operational planning'.

It should now be clear that the essence of such activity is to review each product in terms of its total effectiveness in the market-place, choreographing total marketing activity in the market-place, masterminding all the marketing forces the company can bring to bear in order to maximize the success of the product.

While the systems each organization uses to achieve those aims vary widely, a number of activities are fundamental:

1 The organization will want to set up a schedule of formal planning which ties in with its budgetary requirements. Thus there will be an annual marketing plan for each major profit earner in the organization. (Some organizations will want such a plan more frequently, calling for a product marketing plan every six months.)
2 The organization will wish to monitor the progress of activity promised in the annual plan, to measure the actual versus the predicted effects of the plan.
3 The organization will want to see recommended changes in marketing tactics when the monitoring system detects an unfavourable deviation from the objectives.
4 The organization will want to be certain that the revenue managers co-operate closely with other organization functions in enacting the plans which they have recommended, and will set up a system to guarantee that such co-ordination takes place.

The annual marketing plan

Once a year, each principal revenue and profit-earning segment of corporate business (that is identifiably different in the market-place from every other segment) will undergo its annual, agonizing reappraisal. It is, of course, misleading to give the impression that planners spend the rest of the year not planning. Quite the contrary: they plan more or less every working day. But most of the time they plan for the very short term, helping to solve very short-term problems, coping with short-term emergencies. Yet they know that once a year they must commit themselves to a concrete set of recommendations for their products for the next 12 to 18 months ahead, synthesizing all their activities into a coherent solution to the problems the product faces. Furthermore, they know that such a plan will provide the blueprint for the next year's workload.

Plan contents

Every market, and every product or service within the market, is sufficiently different to ensure that no one standard format is perfect for the annual plans of all products. Neither will it be sensible for an organization to insist on an annual product plan for every single product or service it offers in the market-place, even if it could afford the multitude of marketing planners needed. The essential need is to ensure that annual product planning is undertaken for:

- All principal revenue and profit-earners.
- All ventures recently launched in to the market-place.
- All products identified as having serious problems in the market-place.

Despite differences in markets and their products, there are a number of marketing planning fundamentals which must serve as the core for annual plans.

1 *Revenue account*: The end result of the revenue manager's planning efforts, contribution and skills are to be found in the financial contribution forecasted for the product. Such a revenue account serves as the ultimate measures of the organization's competence with the product under review. Such an account will:

- Indicate clearly the financial parameters on which the account is founded: estimated variable product costs per unit and average selling price per unit.
- Show the forecast of units to be sold.
- Clearly itemize marketing expenditure details, both for direct marketing expenditures (advertising and sales promotion expenditure, for example), and indirect marketing expenditure (the cost of the salesforce, market research and distribution for example).
- Provide comparison with previous year's revenue accounts.
- Be percentaged to make such comparisons simpler.
- Clearly show the profitability planned for the product at the gross margin level, the 'contribution after direct marketing expenses' level and at the pre-tax-profit level (always an approximation of the truth,

but nevertheless a very useful figure to the motivation of marketing planning).

2 *Sales forecast*: While the revenue accounts will have revealed the forecast of total sales, many organizational departments – manufacturing, purchasing and financial, for example – will need a detailed monthly forecast for unit sales for each product.

3 *Product specifications*: The annual plan will make clear any planned changes to be made to the product or service; why such changes are recommended; what the estimated effect will be in the market-place: how and when they will be implemented; what are the cost and the pricing implications of such changes, and what monitoring devices will be applied to measure the actual outcome of the changes.

4 *Pricing policy*: The annual product plan should recommend the pricing policy of the product together with any recommended changes to that policy, the thinking behind such changes and the effects anticipated as a result. Competitors' prices, pricing structures and their apparent pricing strategies may also need to be examined, compared with those of competitors, and policy change recommendations explained and justified.

5 *Promotional policy*: Used in the widest sense to include all aspects of sales promotion – personal selling, advertising, public relations, trade and consumer promotions, sponsorship, exhibitions and so on – the promotional policy for a product may involve a great deal of planning activity, accounting for a considerable percentage of the organization's revenue. The promotional effort applied to a product or service is the principal tool the organization uses to ensure that revenue planning is a dynamic response to the market-place, not simply a passive reaction to events. Creatively and analytically planned, product, price and promotion determine the marketing competence of the organization. Of the three, promotion is the most flexible and the most capable of rapid adaptation to rapidly changing marketing circumstances: it is possible to mount a new promotional plan from scratch in a few weeks. Such flexibility is not possible for product changes, and the options for changes to the price of the product tend to be narrower and should, unlike promotional tools, be used as little as possible. Within the umbrella of the promotional policy lie a number of areas which need to be separately described:

- Advertising policy.
- Trade promotions/sales servicing policy.
- Consumer promotions.
- Public relations.

6 *Selling and distribution policy*: The efforts both of the salesforce and of those charged with the distribution of the product to the customers will have a significant effect on the competence of the product in the market-

place. To that extent, product planners will be very concerned to re-examine sales policy and distribution policy when they come to write the annual marketing plan for their products. They will have to reconsider, for example, the level of attention given to those products by the salesforce – in as much as all the organization's products compete for the salesforce's attention – the types of aids they should provide to help the salesforce in its efforts to sell the products, and the extent to which the distribution systems employed by the organization are to the best advantage of their products or require modifications. Marketing planners, the better to know the problems and opportunities affecting their products in these areas, will take particular care to spend time with the specialists running these functions: they will regularly go out on sales calls with the company salespeople, and be sure to keep themselves fully informed about selling and distribution function activities.

Co-ordinating systems

It is clear that the role of the brand manager must interact very closely with many of the other organization's functions. Competent brand managers are sensitive to the hazards of interfering with the functional efficiency of other departments. Yet this sensitivity is no substitute for formal systems to ensure that the introduction of a brand management function does not play havoc with existing control and reporting systems. A number of areas are especially vulnerable to the enthusiasm of determined brand managers.

Production planning

Keen brand managers will have the powerful desire to make sure that their products are always available for sale, always delivered on time, always at the forefront of the organization's production schedules. For many markets a forecast of sales, in the short term especially, is likely to be less than reliable, and the person with responsibility for scheduling production efficiently will be constantly pressurized by the brand managers to change production schedules to the advantage of this or that product, to meet unexpected fluctuations in sales. Chaos (and expensive chaos) may result, together with friction and distrust between the marketing and manufacturing departments. Control systems, in the guise of good pre-planning and routine, regular meetings between the two functions require to be set up.

Technical enquiries

Because they are given responsibility for planning the life of the product in the market-place, imaginative brand managers will dream up a large number of marketing alternatives which may call for modification to the product, the product packaging, the production processes and so on. When a number of brand managers each come up with a number of what may be speculative

220

ideas, all of which require investigation by engineers, scientists, cost accountants and other corporate specialists, a great deal of time and company energy can be spent pursuing them. Systems need to be set up which cope with this work flow, and which, ideally, restrict the work to those ideas which have a real chance of being both workable and acceptable to the organization, once the details have been worked out.

Financial awareness

Brand managers must be trained to view all their activities in terms of profitability and cost-effectiveness. They will be strongly encouraged to speculate – calculator in hand – about the financial outcome of their alternative plans, in order to develop an awareness of the need to allocate limited resources effectively. The wise organization makes sure that revenue managers have close ties with, and get routine help and advice from, the financial and accounting functions of the company. Some organizations have even developed marketing-liaison accountants who devote their time to guiding, helping and double-checking the financial calculations of the marketing planners. Brand managers will need to recommend pricing policy. This, in turn, will require them to have a full understanding of product costs and of the overhead recovery requirements expected of the product. While they are not expected to be involved in capital investment programmes, or cash flow problems, they will need an understanding of both, in as much as they are both relevant to marketing decision-taking by the senior management of the organization. Brand managers will also be expected to be guardians of the budget allocated to their products for a variety of marketing expenditures – for example on advertising, public relations, point of sale material and literature and so on.

BRAND MANAGEMENT: PAST, PRESENT AND FUTURE

Past and present

This chapter has reviewed the workings of a management system which lies at the marketing heart of many of the world's most successful consumer goods companies, and a system which is beginning to be evident in industrial and service-goods companies. The system and its benefits are by no means theoretical. As a system, of course, brand management has its problems as well as its advantages. But the logic that lies behind it is inescapable, and the organizations currently using it would, by and large, strenuously resist its removal. It may be constructive, however, to examine some of the objections which have been raised to the brand management system.

Responsibility without authority

The commonest criticism in the academic literature concerning brand management as a system is to be found in the statement that the brand manager is a manager with responsibility but without any authority. A number of points need to be made:

1   The areas of the business for which the brand manager is asked to make recommendations are at the heart of the organization's ability to survive, thrive or fail. Changes to product specifications, price and promotional support may very well destroy the product and, ultimately, the company. Even the marketing director is not given delegated authority for most of the responsibilities that belong to the brand manager, hence there is no way such authority would be given to the brand manager, or should be. These responsibilities are the last the board willingly delegates: it only does so because the product-planning load could simply not be undertaken at board level. For revenue to be properly managed, someone must be given responsibility for it, *without* being given authority over line management. The alternative is that revenue should not be managed, which is plainly nonsensical; or that each revenue manager is given line authority, which is an even greater nonsense.

2   The revenue manager's lack of formal line authority is more than counterbalanced by the board approval which is given to the annual product plan on which the brand manager bases all his or her work. In a marketing-oriented organization, every other department is aware that the brand manager has the support of the board: it is this which gives the brand manager all necessary authority.

3   In any case, responsibility without authority applies to every single line manager in the organization. It is only the extent of lack of authority and the level at which it operates that differentiates one manager from another. For example, the board most certainly does not give the manufacturing director unlimited authority over capital investment projects. The board's approval will need to be sought for such expenditures.

The short-term horizon of the brand manager

It is said that brand managers, sensing the necessity to make their mark on the new range of products they have inherited, will attempt to make unnecessary changes to the product and seek to maximize short-term success in the market-place at the expense of the medium- and long-term health of the products. To this criticism is added the fact that brand managers are notoriously 'on the move', constantly seeking to go faster and higher up the promotional ladder, and that such ambitions inevitably result in a short-term focus. Of course this is true. It is equally true that the group brand manager and the marketing director must ensure that such short-term views do not prevail at the expense of success in the market. In any case, it takes no great insight for ambitious brand managers to recognize that they will seriously damage their reputation – and, hence, promotional prospects – by seeking short-term benefits to their personal advantage but to the disadvantage of the company.

Brand managers wastefully compete against each other

It is the nature of brand managers – and one of their virtues – that they quickly become fervent champions of the products for which they have been given responsibility. As such they will make every effort to get the organization to pay maximum attention to their products, and are quite indifferent to the rest of the organization's range. The effect is that of a group of managers avidly competing for the organization's limited resources, inevitably resulting in waste. Once more, this would be true were it not for the controlling forces applied to brand managers by more senior members of the marketing department. Marketing directors hardly encourage such tactics. And it is a function of other managers in the organization – the general sales manager and the production manager, for example – to balance the needs of one product with those of the others.

The future

It is likely that the brand management system will grow in acceptability and usage in the business community. It will, of course, need to adapt to changes, as it will need to adapt to being used in the new types of organization to which it will be introduced. The greatest threat to its development lie in those companies which are organizationally and emotionally not yet ready to accept the system. Many cases, if not most, of the failure of brand managers as a system – and marketing practice in general – can be traced either to a poor understanding of what is involved, a failure to develop the systems necessary to underpin the new discipline or a fundamental failure to give full support to the practitioners and their system when they are introduced.

The introduction of brand management as a new system into a business may, of course, prove to be a traumatic experience to existing systems and, above all, to the power structure of the existing managers. For this reason it can be argued that the standard procedures and goals in the recruitment of today's brand managers ought perhaps to be re-examined and reassessed. Currently the brand management structure, where it is employed, has – on its lowest rung – bright young graduates taken straight from the universities and hired to act as assistant brand managers, where they 'learn the business'. After a period of 18 months to two years, they will graduate to handling the smaller of the company's products; two or three years after that, they may achieve the stardom of a set of important, high profit earning brands.

There are problems in such a system:

1   A good deal of the goodwill towards the marketing department is routinely frittered away because, from the point of view of the usually older senior managers in all the other departments, too many important decision areas in marketing are left in the hands of 23- and 24-years-olds who are still learning the basic rudiments of business operation. (Few things are more calculated to irritate the old hand than the young marketer.)

2   To overcome this problem, the marketing function routinely protects its young brand managers and assistants with a bevy of experts, who are hired partly to take decisions (which might be better taken by the brand manager), partly to provide advice (which an older brand manager would need less). Policy here differs widely between different companies, but very young brand managers, inexperienced in the ways of business generally, are the norm in many organizations.

Some companies are beginning to take another route. They are refusing to take graduates directly into the revenue management function. Instead they are recruiting brand managers directly from young middle managers, 27- to 28-years-old, who have already had five or six years' experience with the company, who know the other company managers, already have a wide experience of another discipline (for example, sales, market research, accountancy) under their belt and who have proved their managerial competence in these disciplines to the satisfaction of the company.

The fact that even the junior brand manager is responsible for a set of brands (and their associated profit contributions), which are of importance to the company, and whose corporate health is more truly in the brand manager's hands than in that of any other company manager, suggests that the product's 'minder' should never be less than an able and experienced company executive. It might be an improvement in company recruitment policies if the post of assistant brand manager became a position at which to arrive, instead of being a post at which to start a business career.

PROBLEMS WITH INTRODUCING THE REVENUE MANAGER SYSTEM

It would be unrealistic to conclude this chapter without a brief examination of some of the hazards in brand/revenue management, which are particularly acute when the system is first introduced to an organization which has not previously used it.

Problems of transition

The advent of the brand manager inserts a new layer of management into the system. It has the effect of changing the lines of communication between managers and between departments, of providing a quite new focus of responsibility, of diluting existing power bases. For the brand manager's system to work the company's senior and middle managers need both to understand and appreciate the value of the new system. The probability that such appreciation will be felt by all the managers of an organization is remote. The system will suffer buffets and storms in the first few years of its operation.

Problems of diplomacy

Most of the working life of the brand manager is spent in persuading other managers to provide what is necessary to achieve the objectives agreed in the product plan. Not all brand managers manage this task with tact and the persuasiveness of logic. Many find that the short route to success lies in aggression and general abrasiveness. In few other functions are the selection and recruitment criteria more important than those used in the selection of brand managers.

Problems of delegation

It is an inevitable corollary of the function of brand management that there must be responsibility without delegated authority (the case for this has already been elaborated). As a result, the role of the brand manager may very well prove disheartening if care is not taken to handle such a problem intelligently. One of the most successful means of solving the problem is to make sure that, up to the highest levels, brand managers are always expected to present whatever case they have planned for the marketing of their products. So long as they have to fight for themselves, they will come to recognize that authority for marketing activity is largely dependent on their skills both as a planner and a presenter. If they are not allowed to carry out the plans they have recommended, it will be because they have failed to persuade the board of the soundness of their recommendations. Obversely, when the board agrees with those recommendations, they will know that it is their policies which are determining the marketing success of the products for which they have responsibility.

Problems of interference

Unless fairly carefully controlled, brand managers become a ubiquitous presence in all the departments of the organization, seen to be 'sticking their noses in where they have no business'. The need here is for a planner who is sensitive to the territorial defensiveness of line managers, as well as for a sound, formal control system which prevents undue interference by brand managers in the running of non-marketing functions in the organization (already discussed above).

The classic means of overcoming resentment by other managers towards such 'interference' is to train brand managers to take an active interest in the functions of those other departments under the guidance of those charged to manage them. In a manufacturing organization, for example, the brand managers should know the factory process, the people and the problems on the factory floor in order to sustain good communications and information about 'their' products where they are being made. When this is achieved, the effect may very well improve tolerance of each discipline towards the other, in the light of a real understanding of each other's operational and managerial problems.

CONCLUSION

For many business organizations, revenue management is already seen to be as useful and as necessary as any other business discipline used to improve organizational efficiency and effectiveness in the market-place.

In this chapter the case has been strongly made that revenue requires planning, controlling and managing. The chapter has examined the means of achieving such management.

Ultimately the logic of brand management lies in its capacity to generate more profits, to secure greater certainty of secure employment and to generate a sense of greater competence and professionalism in the organization which uses such management disciplines.

REFERENCES

Borden, Neil N. (1964), 'The Marketing Mix', *Journal of Advertising Research*, June.

ESSENTIAL READING

Arnold, David (1992), *The Handbook of Brand Management*, London: The Economist Books Ltd.

Chernatony, Leslie and McDonald, Malcolm (1992), *Creating Powerful Brands*, Oxford: Butterworth-Heinemann.

Hanscombe, Richard (1989), *The Product Management Handbook*, Maidenhead: McGraw-Hill Book Company (UK) Ltd.

Jones, John P. (1986), *What's in a Name?* Aldershot: Gower.

13 Financial aspects of marketing
David Chapman

Managers in marketing, and other disciplines often consider finance to be something best left to the accountants. This view is on the whole very short-sighted because it is important to differentiate between understanding the financial consequences of managerial action and properly accounting for the company's affairs.

Research undertaken by the author, reinforced by consultancy, over the last 15 years, has shown (*Make Ready for Success*, 1981) that successful firms have:

- Clear corporate objectives.
- A well-defined marketing strategy.
- A clear understanding of money and its use as a company resource.
- Good decision-making procedures based on good information systems.
- Managers working as a team and well-trained to meet the changing needs of the business.

This research shows that marketing policies which are based on a good understanding of finance hold the key to success. The research also shows that the more successful firms are those which concentrate on generating revenue and increasing value added while containing costs. The less successful firms concentrate only on managing costs.

Later research (*Measures for Success*, 1984) also shows that a concentration on marketing, even in times of recession, enables the more effective companies to sustain and indeed improve profits. Many writers argue that the managerial focus in the United Kingdom on costs, rather than market opportunities, has contributed substantially to recession because a trade deficit of £20m is indicative of the fact that British manufacturers overemphasize the management of costs.

The purpose of this chapter is to examine some of the financial issues *227* involved in making marketing decisions and measuring their out-turn. It will consider the role of marketing in improving profits, financial issues for making marketing decisions and measures for keeping track of company performance. The chapter takes a marketing rather than accounting perspective.

CORPORATE OBJECTIVES

For many years economic theory was based on the assumption of 'profit maximization', that is that the primary aim of any business organization is to make as much money as it can, within the constraints imposed by scarce resources and the commercial environment. More recently this assumption has been discarded in favour of a more fundamental one with profitability not an end in itself, but rather the means to meeting corporate objectives.

Thus the task of management has been defined as 'The organization of group activity toward the satisfaction of human need at profit'. Similarly marketing is defined as 'the management process responsible for identifying, anticipating and satisfying customer requirements, profitably'.

It can be concluded that, whilst profit is not an end in itself, the long-term viability of a company will be very dependent on profits which are determined by an exchange of satisfactions between the customer and the supplier.

The role of marketing in improving organizational profit – the absolute value of profits generated – and profitability – the rate of return in relation to another aspect, for example capital employed – is a good starting point. It is also important to note that there is often confusion between the total profit made by a company and profit per unit of output of production. This latter point will be dealt with later.

PROFIT THROUGH VALUE ADDED

An important element in both marketing management and the development of profits is the concept of 'value added'. *The Corporate Report* (1975) defined value added as:

> The simplest and most immediate way of putting profit into proper perspective vis-à-vis the whole enterprise as a collective effort by capital, management and employees is by the presentation of a statement of value added . . . In time it may come to be regarded as a preferable way of describing performance.

In other words it is the *value* which, in the eyes of the customers, the supplier adds during the transaction. For a manufacturer it is the value added to those materials and other purchases in the production of saleable goods. For a shop it is the value added as a result of stockholding, convenience and location. Good marketing has a significant impact on the perceived value of a good or service. For example a BMW is perceived as having more value than a Skoda, thus improving its value added.

Thus the aggregate value added which a firm derives from selling its products is the sales value of those products less the costs of purchase of the raw materials and other purchases which the firm had to buy in order to produce them.

Influences on value added

Value added, therefore, is influenced by the sales activity of the company through volume, price and mix of work and through the management of purchases. For example, a change of policy to buy in rather than make could have a significant effect on purchases and a sales value increase might hide a fall-off in value added. The use of this measure of 'what the company keeps' therefore compensates for value of purchases; value added rather than sales is a true measure of the commercial progress and performance of a company.

Application of value added

The amount of value added created is also important because out of it the firm pays wages and salaries to its employees, overheads to various providers of services, interest to banks, taxes to the government and dividends to its shareholders, hopefully having something left over to plough back into the business as retained earnings. The division of a sales value of £5m of a manufacturing company is typically as shown in Figure 13.1.

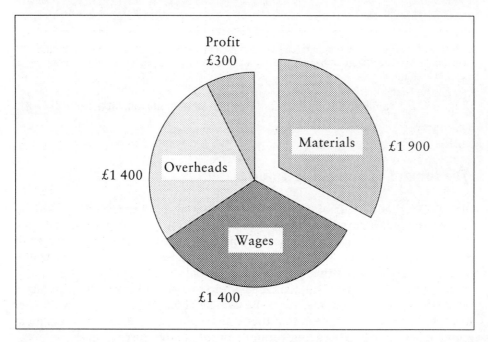

Figure 13.1   The value added cake for a typical company generating sales revenue of £5m per annum

Contribution and net profit

The second important, and more widely used, measure is that of contribution, which is the value added less the direct wages paid in a company. The use of contribution analysis is often cited as a good business measure, but its sole use can have disadvantages as will be shown later.

Net profit is what is left after overheads have been deducted from contribution. Figure 13.2 quantifies the cake shown in Figure 13.1.

	£000s	
Sales		5 000
less materials	1 500	
less sub contract	400	
= Value Added		3 100
less direct wages	1 400	
= Gross profit (Contribution)		1 700
less overheads	1 400	
= Net Profit		300

Note: Both value added and contribution can be called gross profit, depending upon the accountancy convention. In this chapter, where the term gross profit is used this is equivalent to contribution.

Figure 13.2   Value added and contribution analysis of management accounts

The impact of managing value added

Value added and contribution can also be graphically expressed on a break-even chart (see Figure 13.3). The break-even chart is typically used as a device for cost analysis but it is a very valuable tool for the marketing manager to identify the financial implications of marketing decisions. It also demonstrated the leverage that marketing activity has on profits.

In Figure 13.3, the vertical axis measures the value of sales and purchases while the horizontal axis measures the volume of output for the year at 100 per cent, but this does not mean that there is 100 per cent utilization and in most companies there is often scope for more output above current levels.

The area between the sales line and the purchases line represents value added, which for the year end at '100 per cent utilization' is £3 100 000.

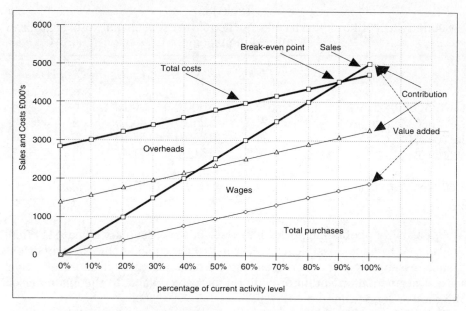

Figure 13.3   Break-even chart which shows the make-up of the cost structure and the make-up of value added and contribution

Fixed costs

Direct wages are regarded as a fixed cost, incurred whatever the level of sales during the year, and are plotted with a line parallel to that for purchases. Overheads are also a fixed cost and therefore plotted with a line parallel to the wages line. The area between the sales line and the overheads line represents net profit which only becomes positive once the sales line has crossed above the line combining purchases, wages and overheads, that is at the break-even point. Above that point any value added that is generated goes straight into net profit. It is this fact which makes the management of value added such as important issue in marketing.

The impact of changes in volume, price and cost

The benefit of using the break-even analysis is that it shows clearly the impact of an increase in sales and/or prices on the amount of value added and net profit generated. The figures shown in Table 13.1 relate to a given set of circumstances. They show the marked differences in profit improvement of revenue management as against cost management. For example a 5 per cent improvement in volume, with fixed costs held steady results in a 50 per cent improvement in profit. If wages are reduced by 5 per cent, the cost management approach, then profits improve by only 23 per cent. In both instances there has been a productivity increase of 5 per cent.

231

Table 13.1.
Changes in profit occur as a consequence of focusing on marketing rather than cost management

	£000s	Sales	Profit	% of Sales
Current budget	5 000	5 000.0	300.0	6
Increase volume	5%	5 250.0	455.0	9
Increase price	5%	5 250.0	550.0	10
Increase both price and vol.	5%	5 512.5	717.5	13
Reduce wage cost	5%	5000	370	7%

The possibility of obtaining price increases in a recessionary climate is often considered to be impossible. However improvements in value added performance, essentially price increases, can be obtained through more effective market segmentation and improving the perceived value to the customer of the good or service offered.

The effect on profit of price, volume and cost management will differ according to the particular set of circumstances for a company. From a marketing planning standpoint the development of break-even analysis is crucial to effective marketing planning.

The influence of the mix of products

The above example is, in effect, taking a global look at the results of an organization over time. As most managers know, companies do not operate in single markets nor do they have a single range of products. Thus the start point for market planning is break-even analysis. Good marketing requires that the effectiveness of each of the marketing activities, products, markets, sales regions and so forth is examined and its worth to the company identified. This involves the relationships between revenue and costs.

Pricing is dealt with elsewhere in this handbook, but John Winkler suggests that over 80 per cent of companies price on the basis of costs plus profit (Winkler, 1989). Thus to the marketer the methods used in determining costs can be important.

COSTING AND MARKETING

Impact of poor information

In normal day-to-day operation, companies incur costs and these are classified under many different headings. Normal operation costs are usually produced by management accounting systems which invariably use absorbed costs. An absorbed cost is one where non-production costs, for example overheads, are apportioned to cost centres in an arbitrary manner. Johnson and Kaplan (1991) suggest that 'these labour based arbitrary measures do not represent the demands made by each product on the resources of the firm . . . When such distorted information represents the only available data on product costs, the danger exists for misguided decisions on product pricing, product sourcing, product mix and responses to rival products.' Such distorted financial data for the marketer could be catastrophic.

The reason for this view is that absorption costing systems use facts about expenditure, estimates of utilization and opinions of apportionment of over-head. Even if such costs are calculated to the tenth decimal place they are no more than opinions and reflect the costs of a particular activity for a given set of circumstances. It is for this reason that the calculation and use of cost rates in firms causes so much conflict. Yet, in spite of all the reservations expressed by many writers as to the validity of such systems, particularly in today's rapidly changing business environment, they are used extensively, from government down, to provide the basis for fundamental business decisions. This leads to one writer asking 'How much of your business is disappearing into the cost accountancy black hole?' Nevertheless there are situations where the use of 'full cost' is appropriate, where it is better to approximate to the desired figure.

Use of cost data for marketing decisions

One of the major drawbacks to the application of the absorption costing system is when it is used to establish the profitability of products, sales activities and so forth. Very often the cost of production of a single unit of output is established and a decision as to whether to continue with production is often made on the basis of the relationship of this cost to the price available in the market. This level of profit then determines the viability of the activity.

There are a number of problems with this approach, in whichever area it is applied. First, the notional profit is totally dependent upon the arbitrary allocation of overhead and second, even if overheads are apportioned equitably, the cost of production will change depending upon the level of output. Since marketing is about the management of change, a method of identifying the consequences of change is vital in effective marketing management.

Financial analysis of marketing activities

In the earlier sections on break-even analysis, the concept of contribution was introduced. It is used widely as an alternative measure to absorbed cost to identify the financial performance of marketing activities, for example product pricing, product sourcing, product mix and sales management. However, the introductory paragraph identified the concept of value added analysis and this is introduced as an additional view of the marketer's analysis. To illustrate this the product mix of a company can be examined in four stages:

233

- Absorbed costs.
- Breakdown into variable costs and apportioned fixed costs.
- Contribution analysis.
- Value added and contribution analysis.

The following examples are drawn from real situations which the author has met in the course of consultancy projects.

Table 13.2 shows the profile of a group of products which are marketed by a company, with a total revenue of £9.25m. per annum. The total costs of the activity mean that the company is making little profit. The analysis of the product groups, using full cost, shows significantly different profit performance between the different product categories.

From Table 13.2 it could be argued that products 3 and 4 are wiping out the profit made by products 1 and 2. Logic would seem to indicate that products 3 and 4 should be discontinued.

Table 13.2
Comparative profit performance of different product groups using full absorbed costs

£000s			Product		
	Total	1	2	3	4
Sales	9 250	2 750	2 300	2 300	2 200
Total costs	9 150	1 550	1 150	3 160	3 290
Net profit	100	1 200	850	- 860	- 1 090

Table 13.3
Costs broken down into variable costs and apportioned overheads

			Product		
	Total	1	2	3	4
Sales	9 250	2 750	2 000	2 300	2 200
Variable costs	6 050	900	1 600	2 050	1 500
Apportioned Overhead	3 100	650	550	360	1 040
Total costs	9 150	1 550	1 150	3 160	3 290
Profit	100	1 200	850	-860	-1 090
% on sales	1%	43%	42%	-51%	-49%

The information available is incomplete in that the costs give no indication of their make up. Table 13.3 shows that the costs can be divided into variable costs, wages and purchases, and apportioned overheads. This then gives two elements, one which is directly attributable to production and the other which is apportioned overhead.

Table 13.3 still gives the same picture, but shows that if two products, 3 and 4, were to be discontinued, the company would make a shortfall on the recovery of overheads. This would mean a restructuring of the company if these overhead costs were to be reduced. However the shortfall would not be equal to the £1.4m. which is arbitrarily apportioned, but would be equal to the contribution to overheads and profit.

The overhead costs of a company are to all intents and purposes fixed, and can only be changed by a restructuring of the company. The American expression 'overhead burden' is a particularly apt description. If *contribution* analysis is adopted, then these overhead costs are considered as a single cost and the *'contribution'* of each activity to that cost and profit is established. To do this the variable costs established in Table 13.3 are subtracted from the sales figure, which gives the contribution (see Table 13.4).

Table 13.4
Calculation showing variable costs and contribution to overheads and profit

£000s		Product			
	Total	1	2	3	4
Sales	9 250	2 750	2 000	2 300	2 200
Variable costs	6 050	900	1 600	2 050	1 500
Contribution	3 200	1 850	400	250	700
Fixed costs	3 100				
Profit	100				
C/S %	35%	67%	20%	11%	32%

Thus from Table 13.4 it can also be seen that the financial picture of the 'worth' of the product groups is also changing if measured as a proportion of sales.

In practice, contribution is influenced by two factors: the purchases which have to be made to produce the goods, and the amount of labour which is used in production of the goods. The purchases are essentially directly variable to output, but wages, whilst often considered a variable, are often semi-variable because current employment practice means that workers have considerable security of employment. From a management standpoint the division of contribution into its constituent elements of labour and materials can enable the manager to identify the value added the company obtains from the activity. The division is shown in Table 13.5.

Table 13.5
Calculation showing the constituent costs of the products 1 to 4, and the calculation of value added and contribution, and the associated performance ratios

£000s		*Product*			
	Total	1	2	3	4
Sales	9 250	2 750	2 000	2 300	2 200
Purchases	3 515	800	1 250	720	745
(V)alue (A)dded	5 735	1 950	750	1 580	1 455
(W)age cost	2 535	100	350	1 330	755
(C)ontribution	3 200	1 850	400	250	700
Fixed cost	3 100				
Profit	100				
VA/S	62%	71%	38%	69%	66%
VA/W	2.26	19.5	2.14	1.18	1.92
C/S	35%	67%	20%	11%	32%

The table gives a full analysis of the influence on the profits of the company achieved by the different product groups. This type of analysis can be used for a wide range of marketing activities. Within the analysis three performance measures are introduced. They are:

- *Value added to sales*. This identifies the proportion of the revenue kept by the company.
- *Value added to wages*. This is a measure of productivity, which compensates for inflation,
- *Contribution to sales*. This arises from the combination of the above.

The use of these three measures tells a story which is a little different from that identified by Table 13.2 which just examined full cost.

Product 1, in both cases, is clearly the best. The product gives high value added and excellent productivity, and a marketing shift to this product would rapidly improve the financial situation.

Product 4 has high levels of value added, but is labour-intensive and, since overheads are often apportioned in relation to labour, the product attracts a high level of overhead. This labour intensity can be measured by the 'value added to wages' ratio (*Measures for Success*, 1984). In reality the product has a good level of sales, and if it were to be discontinued the company would lose £1.455m. of value added. This would be catastrophic to the company. The corporate action for this product is more effective production, through investment or production management, not closure.

Product 2, with a similar level of sales, has low value added, indicating a significant level of purchases. It is labour-intensive per unit of value added, but the proportion of the total labour bill is relatively small. Thus in full cost terms it seems profitable. The management action for this product is to improve value added by the reduction of purchases by examining the bought out element, and to improve methods of production.

Product 3 is more problematic. It gives high levels of value added but is very labour-intensive. However, discontinuing this product would reduce value added by £1.58m. which is 25 per cent of the value added of the firm. Unless the product were substituted by sales from other products, the consequences for the company would be restructuring.

The four tables which have developed the picture of how information can change depending upon the method of analysis is crucial in the development of marketing policy. In many cases the decision to discontinue products, close channels of distribution and a range of other marketing activities is based on poor information systems. It is essential that marketing managers have in place information systems which will give them information for good decision making.

Influences on value added and contribution performance

The influence of the various managerial activities are shown in Figure 13.4. Value added and contribution are directly influenced by the effectiveness of the management of the company and give true figures of resource costs. They take out any masking of apportionment of overheads. Together value added and contribution can be used to calculate some important performance measures which give the marketing manager a more coherent view of the financial performance of products and activities under review. Furthermore the information obtained in the type of analysis developed can be used to model changes in price, volume, mix, sales activity and so forth so that the consequences of marketing action can be identified.

So far the topics of this chapter have been concerned with planning and analysis but at some stage the effects of marketing action will need to be identified and this can be established from the company accounts.

THE PURPOSE AND ANALYSIS OF ACCOUNTS

The purpose of accounts

There are three main questions that the accounts of a business should answer:

1   Whether the business is operating at a profit or a loss.
2   Whether the business will or will not be able to meet its commitments as they fall due, and so do not have to close down as a result of lack of funds. This is referred to as liquidity.
3   Whether or not the assets are being maintained, so that the interests of creditors and owners are protected.

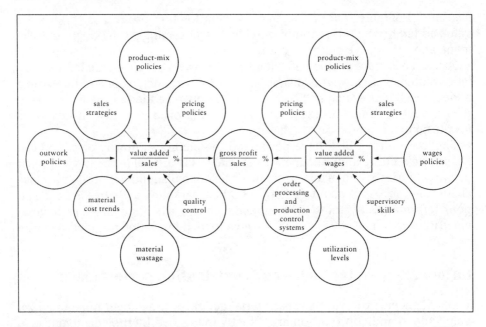

Figure 13.4   The relationships between the various influences on gross profitability
(contribution)
Source: Chapman and Hill, 1993.

Profit and liquidity

Earlier paragraphs identified the importance of profit in meeting the organization's objectives. Whilst profit is important for long-term survival, marketing
decisions should always consider liquidity to ensure that a situation where the
company runs out of cash does not arise.

Structure of accounts

The accounts should be so designed as to provide an accurate record of the
transactions of a business in terms of:

- Income and expenditure through the trading account.
- Assets and liabilities through the balance sheet.

Balance sheet

The balance sheet is a snapshot of the company's assets and liabilities at a particular point in time. It is not a picture of the results of trading over a period
but does reflect the out-turn of trading in terms of retained profits and the liquidity of the company.

FIXED ASSETS		
Buildings	£300 000	
Plant and machinery	£355 260	£655 260
CURRENT ASSETS		
Stock and work in progress	£332 250	
Debtors and prepayments	£416 110	
Cash	£290	£748 650
CURRENT LIABILITIES		
Creditors	£223 380	
Bank borrowings	£27 880	
Tax	£21 940	£273 200
Net current assets		£475 450
TOTAL ASSETS		£1 130 710

CAPITAL		
Shares	£345 000	
Capital reserve	£24 850	
Retained profit	£91 670	£461 520
LONG-TERM LIABILITIES		
Deferred taxation	£52 360	
Debentures	£616 830	£669 190
Total liabilities		£1 130 710

Figure 13.5   Indicative balance sheet 1993/4

239

Profit and loss account

The profit and loss account may be sub-divided into the following sections:

- Manufacturing account (which shows cost of manufacture).
- Trading account (which shows profit or loss on trading).
- Profit and loss account (which show net profit and loss for the period).
- Profit and loss appropriation account (which shows the net profit for the period brought down (or loss)); any balance brought forward from the previous period; how the profit is distributed, for example Corporation Tax, Transfer to Reserves, Dividends to Shareholders; and the balance carried forward to meet the next period.

Sources and uses of funds

The sources and uses of funds statement is the account which links the trading account and the balance sheet.

An example of a balance sheet is shown in Figure 13.5 and a short form trading account is mentioned in earlier paragraphs in Figure 13.2.

Security and compliance

It is also necessary to consider the following:

- *Security*: The opportunity for fraud or theft needs to be strictly limited, if not excluded completely.
- *The law*: Certain information about accounts is required by law to be filed with the Registrar of Companies (UK) and certain information is required by the Inland Revenue for tax purposes.

Measuring trends

Many managers find it difficult to understand and interpret accounting information. As a first stage in the analysis of past performance, it is useful to take the previous three years' accounts and put extracts into a standard form. This enables trends to be established.

For example, the overall turnover figure can offer a quick means of determining the state of progress. Nevertheless, as with any analysis, beware of the false figure that can be caused by inflation or a change in the mix of work which may distort the true situation. Overall figures, however, may conceal significant variations within particular product groups which affect value added, and it may be necessary to carry out a more thorough sales analysis, as undertaken in earlier paragraphs. It is also interesting to note that few financial accounts measure value added.

Financial ratios

Discrete figures in themselves are useful but the progress of an organization is better served by establishing performance ratios. Managers invariably know the performance of their car in terms of miles per gallon or speed in miles per hour. Financial performance ratios serve the same function.

Financial ratios provide the means by which trends within the company can be observed so that timely action can be taken. The key ratios which we have selected are based on the main purpose of continuation of the business.

There is considerable debate as to the key ratios for establishing business performance. Experience indicates that the corporate situation requires a number of perspectives to get a true picture.

The performance measures required are:

- The return on the investment in the organization.
- The return on the business activity.
- The utilization of assets and funds.
- The liquidity of the company.
- The efficiency ratios of the organization.

Return on assets

This measure uses data from the profit and loss account and the balance sheet. For this purpose, net profit is defined as the profit after payments of all loan interest but before tax, and the capital employed or net worth, which is the average of the capital employed throughout the year and normally extracted from the balance sheet.

$$\text{Return on investment (ROI)} = \frac{\text{Net profit}}{\text{Capital employed}} \times 100\%$$

This ratio is frequently used to identify the progression of the organization to establish whether or not it is giving an appropriate return on the capital invested in the business.

However, care needs to be observed when making inter-company comparisons because different conventions can mean differences in the calculation of both profit and capital employed. There is also another issue when making year-on-year comparisons which needs to be considered: this is the effect of inflation. The profit is taken from the profit and loss account, which is using current values and the capital employed is using historic figures which are not compensated for inflation.

Return on the business activity

The return on the business activity is obtained from the profit to sales measure. This is calculated using the profit figure above and the sales output of the company.

$$\text{Profit to sales} = \frac{\text{Net Profit} \times 100}{\text{Sales revenue}}$$

This ratio uses two current values from the profit and loss account and therefore is self-compensating for inflation.

Use of assets and funds

There are three ratios which are used here, the second of which is particularly important to the marketing manager.

$$\text{Asset turnover} = \frac{\text{Sales}}{\text{Capital employed}}$$

This ratio measures the rate of use of the capital in the organization. Again there is the problem of the use of current and historic values.

The second ratio – debtor days – measures the time it takes for customers to pay for the goods they receive. The calculation of this figure uses data from the balance sheet (debtors), and from the profit and loss account (sales).

$$\text{Debtor days} = \frac{\text{Debtors} \times 365}{\text{Invoiced sales}}$$

This figure is particularly important to the marketing manager and such information should be available for all customers. It is an important measure for marketing managers to examine when contemplating taking on a new customer.

A further calculation measures the time it takes the company to pay its suppliers:

$$\text{Creditor days} = \frac{\text{Creditors} \times 365}{\text{Purchases}}$$

If this figure is extended for a company then it can sour relations with suppliers.

Solvency

The answer to whether the business is solvent requires two more ratios: the short-term liquidity ratio and a long-term solvency ratio.

$$\text{Liquidity ratio} = \frac{\text{Liquid assets}}{\text{Current liabilities}}$$

In effect, this is the amount of money available from debtors and cash that the firm can expect to receive in the short-term period compared with the bills which will need to be settled in the same period. Stocks are not included because, in the normal way, they cannot be turned into cash quickly. This ratio is often called the Acid Test.

This ratio should be at least 1:1 for this would mean that sufficient money was coming in to meet the immediate debts, but today many companies work on a significantly lower figure.

$$\text{The long-term solvency ratio} = \frac{\text{Current assets}}{\text{Current liabilities}}$$

This ratio, often called the working capital ratio, is recommended to be maintained at 2:1. The marketing manager's influence on this ratio is that of managing debtors and stock.

Effectiveness ratios

The final ratios are effectiveness ratios and to eliminate the effect of direct purchases in total sales, the ratios are expressed in terms of value added, reflecting the opening paragraphs of this chapter.

Value Added = Sales *less* purchases (Materials and sub contract)

The ratios have already been introduced in Figure 13.4 when examining products.

Since value added is a function of volume, price and mix in terms of sales and purchasing effectiveness, the first ratio is the commercial effectiveness ratio:

$$\text{Commercial effectiveness} = \frac{\text{Value added}}{\text{Sales}}$$

The second ratio is that of production effectiveness and measures how effective the company is in producing the value added obtained:

$$\text{Production effectiveness} = \frac{\text{Value added}}{\text{Production wages}}$$

The third ratio is that of gross profit which combines the two value added ratios:

$$\text{Gross profit (contribution) \%} = \frac{\text{Gross profit} \times 100}{\text{Sales}}$$

FINANCIAL CONCLUSIONS

The aim of this chapter has been to identify those financial issues which are influenced by and most affect the marketing manager and thus has taken a   *243* marketing rather than an accountancy perspective. The chapter has identified the importance of marketing in developing organizational profit and establishing measures of performance. It has examined the importance of obtaining appropriate information on which to base marketing decisions and to identify how the costing information can identify where management action is necessary to ensure development rather than cutback.

Above all the underlying message in this chapter is that marketing has the major influence on the profits and financial continuity of an organization. Unless there is continual focus on developing revenue and, more importantly, value added, profits and losses will occur almost accidentally and under those circumstances the cost cutters run riot.

REFERENCES

Accounting Standards Steering Committee (1975), *The Corporate Report*, London: ICAEW.

Chapman, D. J. (1984), *Measures for Success,* London: NEDO Books.

Chapman, D. J. and Hill, B. (1993), *The Power of Value Added*, London: Eaglehead.

Parker, R. H. (1988), *Understanding Company Financial Statements*, Harmondsworth: Penguin Business.

Printing Industry Sector Working Party (1981), *Make Ready for Success*, London: NEDO Books.

Winkler, J. (1989), *Pricing for Results*, London: Heinemann.

ESSENTIAL READING

Johnson, H. Thomas and Kaplan, Robert S. (1987), *Relevance Lost*, Boston, Mass: Harvard Business School Press.

Ward, P. (1989), *Financial Aspects of Marketing*, Oxford: Butterworth-Heinemann.

Wilson, R. M. S. (1987), *Financial Analysis – A Management Introduction*, London: Cassell.

Part III
DEVELOPING THE PRODUCT

14 Understanding customer behaviour

Gordon R. Foxall

CUSTOMER-ORIENTED MARKETING

Marketing is fundamental. Only the simplest socio-economic systems can avoid it. Any society whose economy extends beyond subsistence or simple barter must make arrangements for orderly material exchange, that is, for the systematic creation and implementation of the marketing mix. This requires that decisions be taken with respect to the kinds of product and service that will be produced, the ways in which the availability of goods for sale will be communicated, their distribution, and their pricing – in other words, marketing mix management.

But while all exchange economies require that such marketing decisions be taken, societies differ widely in the styles with which they discharge the necessary functions. Fundamentally, they vary according to who takes these decisions. In most cases, marketing decisions have been taken by or on behalf of producers, that is, by manufacturers, distributors or governments, while customers' choice has been severely restricted by their lack of discretionary income and the absence of effective competition among suppliers. These circumstances have ensured that the managerial style with which basic marketing functions have been discharged is overwhelmingly *producer*-oriented in its outlook, aspirations and results.

Those economies – typically industrialized and affluent – in which the style of marketing management is predominantly *customer*-oriented differ primarily because, to a considerable extent, economic power lies with buyers and users. By virtue of their capacity to choose among competing firms, competing industries and competing nations, buyers ultimately influence the product, promotion, place and price decisions which determine the marketing mix.

Simple as this distinction seems, its implication is that marketing success depends upon the creation and use of marketing mixes that are more sensitive to and more considerate of the actions of buyers than those of one's competitors. Sometimes the effective matching of corporate resources to customers' revealed requirements appears to result from no more than a managerial hunch or spontaneous insight. But appeals to 'entrepreneurial insight' do little to help managers make decisions. Detailed examination of the factors which make for successful new product development – in consumer durables and non-durables, and industrial goods – indicates that those companies which consistently produce winners have managers who understand customers' needs and behaviour and work with the users of their products to develop more satisfactory innovations, rather than relying on guesswork or intuition.

Marketing management, especially marketing planning and the gathering and use of marketing intelligence, is inescapably based on some idea or other of how (and perhaps why) customers behave as they do. In the interests of effective marketing, it is necessary that those responsible for such ideas add appreciation of the subtleties and complexities of buyer behaviour to their entrepreneurial insights. The very success of behavioural science in marketing makes this emphasis important (Foxall, 1990). Over the last two decades in particular, ideas about the motivation of consumer choice have become increasingly current with the result that many unsophisticated and uninformed conclusions are frequently drawn with respect to the nature of consumers' decision processes. Someone who has just purchased an expensive consumer durable, such as a video recorder that turns out to be obsolescent, is unlikely to respond by going through an extensive decision process in which he or she calmly examines all the available alternative models and goes on to purchase one of them – but this is precisely what a recent, managerially-oriented book on marketing suggests! Similarly, there is all too often a tendency to ascribe industrial buying decisions to either unalloyed ratiocination or emotional irrationality. A little knowledge can be misleading and even dangerous.

This chapter, therefore, discusses, albeit briefly, the main ways of looking at consumer and industrial buying behaviour from the viewpoint of behavioural theory and research. It does so on the assumption that each perspective can be relevant to a particular set of circumstances but that none is universally valid.

THE CONSUMER BUYING PROCESS

Buying is a process, not a single act. It is a sequence of pre- and post-purchase activities which surround and influence purchase decisions. All the stages of buying are of interest to the marketing manager who seeks to influence prepurchase awareness of needs or wants, any ensuing search for and evaluation of information about products and brands that might satisfy them, the topography of buying (what? where? how many? how often? and so forth), and the consequences of consumption, all of which may shape patterns of purchase and repurchase. Marketing strategies have been sought from understanding of the social and psychological factors which affect consumers' decisions at each stage of this sequence on the assumption that patterns of choice can be strengthened or modified by acting upon the social identification or mental state of the buyer. The behavioural sciences have been strongly invoked in this task: social psychology supplying concepts and measures of attention, perception, motivation, personality, attitudes, intentions and so on, whilst sociology and anthropology have provided concepts of status, social class, group influence and culture. Each of these influences has inspired *ad hoc* studies of consumer choice using, for example, brand attitudes in an attempt to account for brand selection. A more sophisticated approach has attempted to organize the disparate behavioural science concepts – taking account of their interactions with one another, as well as their separate influences – into systematic models of human behaviour rather than a checklist of potential determinants of choice (Foxall and Goldsmith, 1994).

The most widely-established models of this kind depict the consumer as a processor of information who is involved in:

- receiving via the senses data from the environment (for example, an advertisement for a new brand of a fast-moving product), and perceiving and interpreting them according to experience, opinions, goals, personality structure and social conditioning;
- searching for additional information to clarify the want/need so aroused, and evaluating the alternative competing brands available to satisfy it; and
- developing the beliefs, attitudes and purchase intentions which in turn determine brand choice.

The consumer is thus portrayed as an active collaborator with the marketing system, engaged in establishing relevant cognitions (beliefs) and rationally modifying them on the basis of novel information, subsequently responding affectively (with like or dislike) to each alternative, and finally acquiring the conative (motivational) intention to buy the favoured brand (that which most closely fits the customer's goals and aspirations) which precedes choice in the market-place.

The sequence of events and accompanying mental processes and states assumed by such models is an elaboration of the cognition–affect–conation hierarchy proposed by the mechanistic models of advertising response of more than a quarter of a century ago. The resulting stimulus–organism–response (S–[O]–R) psychology of the comprehensive models is shown in simplified form in Figure 14.1.

Comprehensive modelling has played a useful, though limited, role in attempting to organize and integrate a mass of possibly explicative concepts, measures and research findings into a meaningful sequence which promotes understanding, prediction and, perhaps, control of consumer behaviour. In as much as testable hypotheses have been derived from the models, knowledge has increased; even when research has suggested that the models should be radically revised or alternative explanations sought, such modelling has

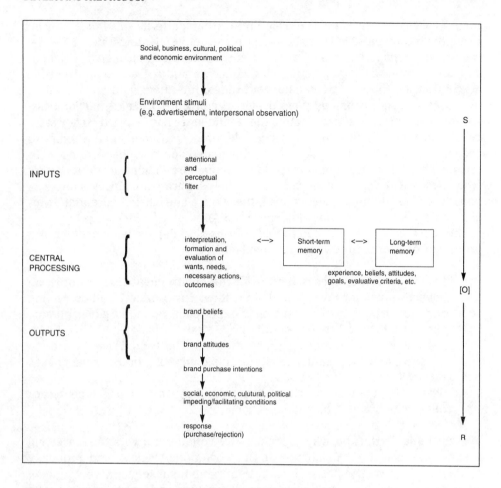

Figure 14.1   The consumer as an information processing system

played some part in stimulating systematic investigation in place of *ad hoc* enquiry. However, during the 1970s and 1980s, this approach to explanation was strongly criticized both on scientific grounds and as a practical device for the prediction of such managerially useful aspects of consumer choice as brand and store choice.

The comprehensive models have depicted the individual consumer as too rationalistic an information processor, failed to make allowance for explanations which do not demand that the consumer is inevitably a highly involved and committed problem solver, and otherwise made assumptions which have not been confirmed by observation, at least not sufficiently strongly to be of much use in marketing. Empirical evidence for the models has always been scant, but most damaging is the revelation that, except where conditions are highly conducive to a particular purchase, there is little relationship between those main determinants of attitude and intention to purchase suggested by the models and the buying decision itself (Foxall and Goldsmith, 1994).

Particularly in the non-laboratory contexts which are directly relevant to marketing, brand attitudes and brand purchase intentions may be poor predictors of buyer behaviour. Situations which intervene between the expression of a purchase intention (for example, as part of a market research investigation concerned with new brand development) and the opportunity to buy the new brand (when it eventually appears on the market) are responsible for low attitude–behaviour correspondence; this effect is, moreover, to be expected, given the limitations of the psychological theory and the research instruments employed. The implication is that analysis of the external environment within which consumer behaviour occurs, and of patterns of similar, prior behaviour, will lead to a more complete understanding of consumer choice, and some comprehensive modellers have already moved in this direction.

LOW INVOLVEMENT, LOW COMMITMENT

For others, however, the central causal chain remains information–attitude–intention–behaviour, and there is no reason to abandon the information-processing approach in its entirety simply because it is not unequivocally the key to understanding consumer choice in every circumstance.

There is much support for sequences of consumer behaviour other than the familiar cognitive–affective–conative hierarchy which underpins many textbook accounts and much market research activity. In particular, there is the suggestion that, whilst minimal cognitive learning often precedes purchase, behaviour (purchase) is the next stage in the hierarchy, and affective or attitudinal effects follow rather than precede buying and consuming. But the experimental work which played a large part in establishing the predominance of this 'low-involvement hierarchy' also led to the conclusion that cognitive information processing, while occurring far less frequently, is the viable alternative. The sophisticated view which is slowly emerging among consumer researchers is that understanding should concentrate on the circumstances to which each sequence is appropriate rather than on trying to establish one or other as the sole explanatory mechanism.

This reasonable approach is adopted here, though it is important to emphasize the pervasive nature of low involvement/low commitment consumer behaviour: as the following discussion indicates, much of what is known from direct observation about consumer behaviour is consistent with this.

First and foremost, the evidence indicates that the frequently encountered uncommitted consumer uses information in a far more *ad hoc*, less structured way than the comprehensive models claim. In the key area of consumers' comprehension and use of additional nutritional information on food packaging, empirical research demonstrates that most buyers neither understood the extra data nor employed them in making purchase choices. Although the consumers claimed to like more rather than less information and to feel more satisfied when it was provided, they did not as a result use it extensively or make more rational decisions. (This is not to argue against the provision of such information or the further education of buyers: but it hardly provides evidence of information-hungry buyers whose decision mechanisms are geared to the economically rational processing of information.)

Even when relatively expensive, infrequently-purchased consumer durables are bought, there is considerable evidence that buyers severely limit their pre-purchase searches for information. Customers in such circumstances often visit only one retail outlet and consider only one brand, using price and the reputation of suppliers as short-cut indicators of quality, and relying extensively on in-store sources of information such as sales staff, avoiding such 'neutral' sources of information and evaluations as *Which?*

This does not imply an irrational consumer but is consistent with the nature of human attentive and perceptual processes: only a small fraction of the information aimed at consumers penetrates their perceptual defences; still less is attended to, interpreted, yielded to, or allowed to exert influence over behaviour. Indeed, how else could the consumer cope with the massive volume of such information available from advertising and other sources?

Consumers, after all, shop and consume partly for fun; these leisure or semi-leisure actions have high emotional content and spring from a variety of non-work, non-intellectual motivations.

If extensive, formal information gathering, the first phase of comprehensive decision making, is absent from much consumer behaviour, the whole process falls into doubt. Indeed, the elaborate sequence favoured by the early models is strikingly difficult to detect over a considerable range of consumer purchasing. The evidence supports the view that brand choice is usually not the outcome of any detectable decision process at all, not simply because the decision process becomes compressed with repeat buying, but because in many instances there is no such process at all even at the time of the initial purchase.

Again, this is hardly surprising: the opportunity costs of extensive problem solving preclude an information-processing approach to selection within most product classes where, typically, the differences between competing brands are minimal or of little or no consequence to buyers (where, in other words, the consumer is relatively uninvolved, uncommitted and indifferent to the available substitutes). The notion of the consumer whose behaviour exhibits a narrowly-defined rationality based on discriminations born of extensive information processing is difficult to sustain as a general model in the face of evidence that in so many cases brand-level choices are determined by the social and physical environments in which buying occurs, notably the arrangement of supermarket and other store interiors which give rise to so-called impulse or unplanned purchasing on a large scale.

The concept of the information-processing consumer who is invariably an active problem solver and decision maker rests upon an exaggerated evaluation of the power of external stimuli to control behaviour, especially marketer-dominated information sources. Television advertising, widely cast as the strongest of these stimuli, far from involving its audience and creating determinative attitudes to brand purchase, effects – at most and after enormous repetition – small changes in viewers' perceptions. The viewer, far more concerned with the programmes, makes few if any connections between the advertising and his or her life, and even the minimal learning of brand names which may follow massive doses of repeated advertising is preconscious. It is the in-store opportunity to purchase the advertised brand that activates whatever perceptual learning has taken place, stimulates point-of-sale remembering and, possibly, leads to brand trial.

Any effective response towards an advertised brand expressed at the pre-purchase stage must be extremely weak and speculative, perhaps reflecting feelings towards the advertisement itself rather than the advertised item. Attitudes, likes and dislikes based on evaluation can form only after purchase when the item's performance can be judged from direct experience. Even then, brand attitudes remain so weak (absolutely and by comparison with opinions about more involving social and political issues) that some investigators have asked whether recorded brand attitudes constitute anything more than measurement artefacts.

Direct observation of sequences of consumer purchases over time bears this out. Since most product classes are composed of many brands, each similar to the others in terms of physical attributes and formulation, it is not surprising that the vast majority of buyers do not discriminate among them by preferring one brand above all others and showing 100 per cent loyalty to it in their purchasing. A small proportion of buyers of a product is completely loyal in this way, selecting the same brand on every occasion, but most are not. Most consumers purchase different brands on different occasions, selecting from a relatively small subset of available brands which are close, tried and tested substitutes. Thus, not every brand in the product class has an equal chance of being purchased – customers are not random buyers – and, while a typical consumer may purchase among the brands in his or her 'repertoire' in some systematic way (for example, choosing brands A, B and C in a series of shopping trips in the order A B C A B C A B C . . .), he or she is more likely to exhibit a fairly haphazard selection of repertoire brands over time. Strict brand switching, in the sense that a brand is totally abandoned as another is irrevocably substituted, is rare indeed. Similar patterns of consumer behaviour over time also, over time, characterize store choice (Ehrenberg, 1972).

Awareness, trial, repeat

The identification of the uncommitted consumer, apparently indifferent at the brand level (however important and involving the *product* may be), and the careful monitoring of his or her choices over long series of shopping trips, has led to the development of a much simpler model of consumer behaviour based on the sequence awareness–trial–repeat buying (ATR) (Ehrenberg, 1974). This depicts repeat buying (all-important to most consumer goods suppliers) not as the outcome of elaborate cognitive learning on the part of the individual buyer, but as a function of brand trial, the experience of buying and, more important, use of the selected brand. It is during this trial stage (which may involve several acts of purchase and consumption) that the consumer is able to make the evaluation on which the development of brand attitudes and future purchase intentions relies. Repeat buying rests upon the reinforcement of whatever positive benefits such use confers on the customer, his or her personal evaluations of its value in use, rather than on the mental conditioning inculcated by powerful marketing stimuli (which advertising is often assumed to present) and the strong, determinative mental states supposedly derived from them.

Trial itself is a function of awareness: consumers seldom purchase brands of either durables or non-durables of which they have not previously heard from acquaintances or advertising. Advertising *is* important, therefore, especially in the case of new brands, in achieving awareness of brand names. But its role is principally to arouse curiosity, at best an extremely weak positive evaluation which will lead to trial of the item.

The ATR model of purchasing and consumption, a dynamic representation of the sequence of consumer choices, does not deny the importance of the marketing mix – the advertising which creates awareness before trial and reminds the customer of any rewarding outcomes, thus reducing dissonance and encouraging repeat buying; distribution which provides brand availability for trial; pricing, the facilitating/impeding mechanism – but neither does it attribute to it the power to shape continuing brand choice before the buyer has even purchased the brand for the first time. ATR emphasizes the part played by evaluative trial, a facet of consumer behaviour which entails appraisal of the tried brand (especially in comparison with previously adopted brands within the same product class) in determining the composition of the buyer's repertoire of brands and pattern of long-term purchasing.

Further, the ATR approach, together with the painstaking empirical research upon which it rests, helps clarify the nature of consumers' commitment and rationality. At the product class level, the buyer is likely to be highly involved and committed to purchase: the very frequency of purchase and the assiduous manner in which buyers try out and evaluate the available product class members in order to construct a repertoire of suitable alternatives support this. But the similarity of these alternatives, at least in terms of their physical composition, promotes relative indifference such that the individual buyer is uncommitted as a rule to any particular brand. As long as at least one repertoire brand is available, the consumer is likely to make a purchase, though most opt for variety when it is offered in the course of several purchase occasions.

This implies not a random, indifferent consumer but a sensible, informed and experienced buyer who knows what he or she wants and which brands supply it. This buyer's sensibility is not narrowly economic, however: a few extra pence to pay for an acceptable non-durable item, a few extra pounds for a durable, will not necessarily deter purchase. But the consumer is technically aware and experienced as a result of the frequency of purchase opportunities and the large amount of trial experience gained. The consumer is knowledgeable, within the requirements that make the product purchase desirable or necessary, and hence able to be a reasoning and alert purchaser if not a rational information processor.

CONSUMER BEHAVIOUR IN NEW AND MATURE MARKETS

The conclusion that both high- and low-commitment consumer behaviours exist, though the latter predominates, alone offers limited practical insight. At the least, it is necessary to know when each is likely to occur in order that appropriate marketing responses can be decided. One approach to understanding the contributions of these distinct concepts of consumer choice is to trace buyer behaviour over the life cycle of a typical product market – at first, discontinuous in that it is founded upon a genuinely novel product whose adoption considerably modifies buyers' consumption patterns but which, as it progresses, is characterized by the emergence of a number of continuous (that is, incrementally different) product versions, which have little if any disruptive influence on the consumption behaviour of buyers who are, by this time, familiar with the established product class.

The behaviour of customers confronted by a discontinuous innovation (the first brand in an entirely new product class, for example video recorders or home computers in their initial manifestations) is described as 'extended problem solving'. In the absence of similar brands, prospective buyers compare the innovation with products as similar to the new item as exist (for example, tape recorders or hand-held calculators). This comparatively lengthy procedure occurs during the introduction and into the growth stages of the product life cycle and allows the buyer to judge the discontinuous brand on the basis of perceptions of its additional benefits. Those who buy at this stage are relatively insensitive to price, typical consumer innovators who are inner-directed, affluent compared with later adopters, and venturesome.

During the growth stage of the cycle, consumers who have become familiar with the characteristics of the product find it easier to compare the various brands which emerge. Now that potential buyers appreciate the features of the product, more manufacturers have an incentive to enter the market, offering slightly different versions, knowing that customers can make straightforward judgements of the incremental innovations, and vary their repertoire decisions accordingly. Price becomes an increasingly salient variable in the purchase behaviour of the later adopters who now enter the market.

Once a dominant product design emerges for the industry, the result of technological refinement and the alignment of production and marketing with clear knowledge of customers' requirements and purchase propensities, brands become increasingly standardized. Market segmentation based on customers' differing willingness to pay for brands of varying quality or performance emerge and, within each segment, competing brands satisfy the specific wants of buyers whose 'limited problem solving' entails a sophisticated and informed process of choice.

The mature phase of the life cycle sees the emergence of fewer new brands, but those which are launched conform closely in their formulation/construction to the design dominating the particular segment whose requirements they match. Customers are by now capable of comparing and evaluating a new version of reference to the attributes of a wide range of alternatives which make up the product class. Their purchases are accurately described as 'routine response behaviours', and the most important purchase criteria are price, availability, and the requirement that new brands reach the standard set by incumbent versions.

This life-cycle approach embraces the highly involved consumer who, when highly discontinuous brands first appear, attempts to make informed decisions through careful evaluation of the costs and benefits likely to ensue from adoption; the somewhat sophisticated buyer whose purchase of one of the competing similar brands which later appear is preceded by minimal decision making; and the apparently uncommitted consumer, involved at the product level to obtain certain well-defined benefits but less committed in advance of purchase to particular competing brands which supply them in a standardized manner.

INDUSTRIAL BUYER BEHAVIOUR

Industrial markets involve the economic transfer of products and services between businesses or other organizations. They include markets for such goods as primary produce, capital equipment, raw materials, and intermediate products such as components. They also include catalytic inputs which facilitate production without entering into products or the processes by which they are made: routine office supplies, for example, and corporate banking and insurance services. The nature of industrial buyer behaviour is somewhat different from that encountered in final consumer markets – notably because of the derived nature of demand for non-consumer goods – but the differences can easily be exaggerated.

Both consumer and industrial buying can be specialized and novel, taking on the appearance of a highly rationalized activity; both can be routinely repetitive, apparently entailing no decision process at all. Each can be socially influenced and result in group rather than individual choices. The main difference derives from the fact that industrial buying is a professional activity, undertaken on behalf of formal organizations. While purchasing by final consumers is normally a prelude only to consumption, industrial buying usually represents an early stage in a process of investment, from which economic returns, perhaps at a pre-specified rate or level, are sought. It is, therefore, an activity which forms part of the strategic management of the company and it is undertaken (indirectly if not directly) in competition with the strategic buying activities of other businesses.

As a result, industrial buying often attracts larger risks, both corporate and personal, and is marked by greater complexity and uncertainty than consumer buying. But not invariably: business organizations usually have far greater resources for withstanding risk and uncertainty, and can bear the consequences of some purchasing mistakes that would damage households. Similar

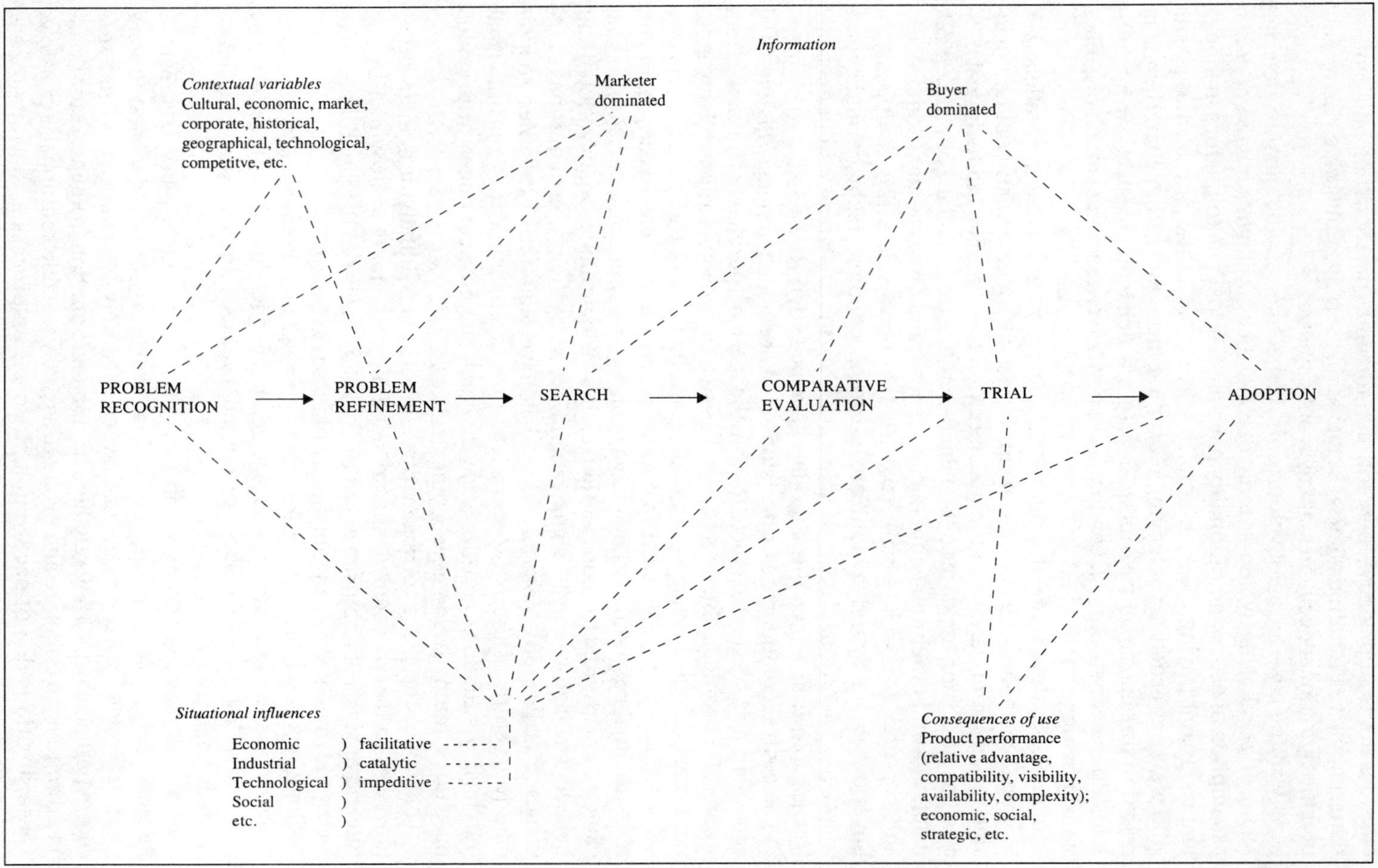

Figure 14.2 Simplified model of industrial buying

considerations of selective perception, individual personalities and motivations, cognitive limitations, social status and group dynamics give rise to only boundedly rational decision making in both spheres.

As was the case in the development of consumer buying models, determinants of purchasing which extend beyond the simplifying micro-economic assumption of economic rationality have tended to come to the fore in modelling industrial buying. Many examples – from that of the purchasing agents who were rewarded for achieving maximum discounts rather than minimum prices to the emotional and political factors which influence fleet car buying – attest to the constraints on economic logic which characterize much organizational buying.

Indeed, the development of industrial buying models closely parallels that of consumer behaviour models, from the 'task' models which confined decision makers' motivations to the maximization of economic and technical utilities, to the 'non-task' models which emphasized social, psychological, emotional and other non-economic influences, and on to the decision process and composite models which have tried to encapsulate the complexity of buyer behaviour by endeavouring to integrate economic, technical and behavioural considerations. Figure 14.2 summarizes the analytical and conceptual framework within which these models have been derived.

The central component is a decision sequence which implies a high level of economic and technical efficiency on the part of purchasing organization. Aware of a problem, the decision maker searches extensively for likely solutions, carries out thorough comparative evaluations of these, and ultimately selects that which promises the optimal returns. Empirical investigation and measurement have shown that a large proportion of purchase decision making cannot be attributed to economic and technical logic alone: organizational and behavioural factors exert a significant influence on the shape of purchase outcomes (Foxall, 1988). Most formal models have, therefore, attempted to indicate the nature of the antecedent and concurrent influences on industrial purchasing situations and the ways in which the consequences of previous purchases impinge upon new buying decisions.

This is not the place to review these models individually. It is instructive, however, to take account of the advance in understanding provided by the Buygrid analysis of Robinson et al. (1967) which describes the situational influences which help shape buying behaviour and decisions.

The Buygrid distinguishes three buying situations: the new task, the modified re-buy, and the straight re-buy (which have much in common respectively with extended problem solving, limited problem solving, and routinized response behaviour).

New task buying occurs when the purchaser's uncertainty is greatest. Because the problem in question has not previously arisen, decision makers must draw upon whatever general experience they have; because their specific experience is nil, they rely heavily upon information from marketer-dominated sources to compare and evaluate as many feasible solutions as possible.

These situations do not occur often, the decision processes they involve are thorough and careful (since not only the firm but the buyer's career may be at risk) and, frequently, the decision outcome plays a decisive part in determining future choices of supplier and make. A typical new task situation would occur when a novel make of capital equipment is introduced into a new product market at the beginning of the life cycle of an innovative technology (for example the development of advanced manufacturing techniques). In this situation, the buying decision requires a number of formal and informal stages; all the buyphases depicted in the Buygrid (Figure 14.3) are probable.

Buyphases	Buyclasses		
	New	Modified	Straight
1 Anticipation or recognition of a problem (need) and a general solution			
2 Determination of characteristics and quantity of needed item			
3 Description of characteristics and quantity of needed item			
4 Search for and qualification of potential sources			
5 Acquisition and analysis of proposals			
6 Evaluation of proposals and selection of supplier(s)			
7 Selection of an order routine			
8 Performance feedback and evaluation			

Source: Robinson et al. (1967), p. 14.

Figure 14.3   The Buygrid

Straight re-buys are the opposite of this: they are recurring purchases which can be dealt with by routine procedures. Previous suppliers are most likely to be considered at this stage and it is most probable that the present in-seller (the existing supplier) will receive the new order. Most industrial/organizational buying decisions fall into this category; there is no need for the buying organization to go through all the buyphases to reorder satisfactory products and the sequence of buyphases shown in the Buygrid is thus severely telescoped.

The out-seller (that is, not an existing supplier) is clearly at a disadvantage. His or her strategy is usually, therefore, to persuade the buyer that some element of the purchase situation has changed: he or she may offer a significant price advantage, new technology, a more extensive system or other inducement. Buyers faced with such new information normally attempt to obtain the benefits from the in-seller; the out-seller has introduced some change in their routine buying behaviour. The point is usually to alter the buyer's decision criteria in some way.

If the out-seller is successful in persuading the buyer that some important facets of his or her purchasing situation have altered, the task situation becomes a modified re-buy and the buyer is likely to reconsider a number of the buyphases depicted in the Buygrid, possibly phases 2 to 8.

THE SOCIAL CONTEXT

Both consumer and industrial buying are socially influenced but the latter differs in that it is generally undertaken within a formal organizational structure in which responsibility for buying has been consciously apportioned. At its simplest, industrial buying requires no more than a purchasing agent acting knowledgeably, perhaps on behalf of others: such straight re-buys can be safely delegated to professional buyers. At its most complex, as in the case of new task buying, it may require the multiple interactions of many executives of differing status and functional responsibility. The term 'buying centre' is used to denote the various individuals within the organization who participate in a buying decision. Its composition varies from transaction to transaction and its members are often difficult to identify in complex buying situations, for instance for a new data-processing system.

Such new task buying typically involves managers of differing status, both in terms of the executive levels and the functional areas represented. In addition, the roles and interactions found in such infrequent purchasing are complex: *gatekeepers* may facilitate or impede the flow of information, and will certainly edit it, before it reaches *deciders*; *influencers* attempt to ensure that specific features are available in the required product or that a particular supplier is favoured; *users* may be responsible for initiating the entire purchase–decision sequence, with or without taking any further interest or part in the ensuing operations, though if they do they are likely to play an important role in determining the specifications of the chosen product. The actual *buyers* in new task contexts, those who negotiate and place an order, are likely to be senior managers who are not purchasing specialists.

Establishing the precise composition of the buying centre is no simple task; researchers' ideas of who participated in a specific decision vary according to the methodology they employ. However, it is interesting to note Johnston and Bonoma's (1981) report that, on average, four functional departments, three strata of managers, and seven individuals were required to make a typical capital equipment purchase in the sample of firms they investigated; in the case of service acquisitions, four departments, two levels of management, and five individual managers participated.

Straight re-buys, by contrast, involve much simpler social relationships. Responsibility can, as has been noted, be safely delegated to the specialist buyer who may need to consult no one else in the organization. However, even in such circumstances, the buyer is subject to the attempts of some out-sellers to modify the topography of the buying situation, possibly by circumventing the buyer's authority by appealing to a senior manager.

This is a useful reminder that industrial buying is a political process and sellers' failure to consider the distribution of power within the purchasing organization has not infrequently resulted in failure to sell. The control of information and communication is central to the nature of industrial buying; the capacity to exert control over the gatekeeping role of purchasing managers is especially valuable. For important decisions, buying power does not necessarily reside with those who carry formal authority in the organization, neither is influence over the buying-decision process confined to any particular functional area. Those who wield power in the buying centre can be identified through careful observation of managers' verbal and non-verbal communications behaviour.

However, those managers who have ultimate authority to make purchases (especially in complicated new task buying) are frequently the most anonymous and least visible members of the buying centre: knowing that they alone can ratify decisions, they are often content to leave negotiations to juniors who must defer to them for the final say-so.

INDUSTRIAL MARKET SEGMENTATION

Recognition of the similarities between consumer and industrial buying, especially in mass markets, has led to an increasing use of research concepts and techniques originally developed for, and for years confined to, the former sphere in the analysis of organizational buyer behaviour. While it has been customary to segment industrial markets according to non-behavioural factors such as product, company size, geographical location and supplier, there has been steadily mounting interest in more sophisticated approaches which take purchase and consumption behaviour into consideration (Wind and Cardozo, 1974).

A particularly interesting development is the segmentation of industrial markets according to the benefits sought by buyers, a technique applied originally for consumer goods and recently exemplified by Moriarty (1983) in a study of buyer behaviour in the non-intelligent data terminal market. This market contains over 40 competing suppliers but is dominated by IBM which accounts for about two-thirds of sales. Segmentation has traditionally been based on the division of buyers into IBM and non-IBM purchasers. On the basis of an extensive survey of non-intelligent data terminal buyers, 40 per cent of which had bought IBMs, Moriarty compares such supplier-oriented segmentation with that which emerges from consideration of the benefits sought. It is instructive, in view of changing conceptualizations of industrial buyer behaviour, to follow his comparison.

261

His research indicates that IBM machines appeal disproportionately to large firms (employing more than 1 000) and firms in the distribution and financial sectors. IBM deciders emerge as low-risk purchasers, keen to please their superior managers by making a visibly 'safe' purchase, selecting a terminal which is supported by a full range of software and complementary equipment, and which is compatible with their firms' existing mainframe computers. IBM selectors have more experience than non-IBM deciders in purchasing terminals; their companies also buy significantly more terminals which may give rise to this. IBM-buyers' purchases are generally funded by their data-processing departments. Participants in the buying decision report greater need (than their opposite numbers in non-IBM buying organizations) to feel confident about what they are buying and perceive the decision as risky, but their conservatism in buying belies a high degree of self-ascribed innovativeness.

Non-IBM machines appeal disproportionately to small companies (with up to 250 employees) and companies in manufacturing. Non-IBM buyers apparently used a more formal purchase decision procedure, considering more sellers at the initial and final stages; they also attach more importance to formal information sources, significantly more than IBM-buyers to such external sources as trade advertisements, literature and trade shows (Moriarty, 1983, 99–109).

Cutting across these supplier-based categories is another basis for segmentation: the different benefits sought by relatively homogeneous groups of buyers of data terminals. Moriarty identifies two main benefit segments in this market. Both rate service and reliability as extremely important and, in addition: segment 1 seeks price flexibility, that is, a willingness on the part of the supplier to negotiate, high sales competence and ease of operation; segment 2 is concerned primarily with the quality of software available, the breadth and compatibility of the manufacturer's product line, the visibility of the chosen machine to top management and the ability and reputation of the manufacturer. This second segment is relatively insensitive to price.

Consideration of these two segments gives a rather different impression of segment structure from that suggested by a supplier-related classification. Segment 1 firms are more likely to be located in distribution and manufacturing, segment 2 in business services. Segment 1 firms are of small and medium scale (having up to 1 000 employees), segment 2 large (over 1 000), though the former are more likely to have larger operating units (employing over 1 000). The decision participants in segment 1 firms are most probably middle managers from the sales, production, and administrative functions and general managers, while those in segment 2 are more likely to be finance and data-processing specialists but senior or first-line managers. The former perceive greater risk in the decision, believing themselves to be under greater time pressure; the latter have greater need for confidence in the product and value prior experience of a supplier.

Finally, 31 per cent of segment 1 firms and 51 per cent of segment 2 firms had purchased IBM machines (Moriarty 1983, 110–120).

MARKETS AS NETWORKS

Every frame of reference has its uses and its limitations and it is worth concluding by noting the criticisms of the framework assumed in this chapter (and in most marketing publications) advanced by those academics who portray industrial markets in terms of networks of organizations which share long-term, stable relationships.

The typical 'marketing-mix-based' approach to markets assumes the viewpoint of the supplier and concentrates on a single time period; but the networks approach emphasizes their interactions over time. It is based on the understanding of the market environment as a vast network of related firms. Rather than separating the values exchanged in the market-place into the four main marketing-mix elements controlled by a marketing manager, the networks paradigm is concerned with the totality of resources and activities of seller and buyer and the resulting interdependencies. The dominant framework for understanding marketing assumes that information is usually gathered through market research, that is, separate investigations remote from normal commercial interactions. The networks approach stresses that marketing intelligence is received and interpreted during the market exchange process, that is, as part of everyday commercial relationships. While the former approach delineates the firm clearly according to its legal and constitutional boundaries, the latter is based on an open systems viewpoint in which the firm's boundaries are behaviourally determined and, therefore, cannot be fixed. While the firm is portrayed in the 'marketing-mix approach' as a self-contained entity engaged in persuading or otherwise influencing the consumers and competitors, the interaction approach emphasizes the co-operation and trust that exists between firms, their joint mechanisms for handling conflict (Mattsson, 1984).

This emerging framework, which has been applied predominantly to industrial markets but has scope for application in consumer markets too, probably applies mainly to buying situations involving straight and modified re-buys rather than those involving considerable discontinuity. But it places a valuable emphasis upon the frequent long-term relationships encountered by market participants and provides a useful antidote to the too-constrained view of the market which is the received wisdom.

REFERENCES

Ehrenberg, A.S.C. (1972), *Repeat Buying*, Amsterdam: North Holland.

Ehrenberg, A.S.C. (1974), 'Repetitive advertising and the consumer', *Journal of Advertising Research*, **14**, (1), 25–34.

Foxall, G.R. (1988), 'Markets, hierarchies and user-initiated innovation', *Managerial and Decision Economics*, **9**, 237–52.

Foxall, G.R. (1990), *Consumer Psychology in Behavioral Perspective*, London and New York: Routledge.

Foxall, G.R. and Goldsmith, R.E. (1994), *Consumer Psychology for Marketing*, London and New York: Routledge.

Johnston, W.J. and Bonoma, T.V. (1981), 'The buying centre: structure and interaction patterns', *Journal of Marketing*, **45**, 143–56.

Mattsson, L.G. (1984), 'An application of a network approach to marketing: defending and changing market positions', in N. Dholakia and J. Arndt (eds), *Changing the Course of Marketing: Alternative Paradigms for Widening Marketing Theory*, Greenwich: JAI Press.

Moriarty, R.T. (1983), *Industrial Buying Behaviour*, Lexington: D.C. Heath.

Robinson, P.J., Faris, C.W. and Wind, Y. (1967), *Industrial Buying and Creative Marketing*, Boston: Allyn & Bacon.

Wind, Y. and Cardozo, R.N. (1974), 'Industrial market segmentation', *Industrial Marketing Management*, **3**, 369–77.

ESSENTIAL READING

Foxall, G.R. (1989), 'User-initiated innovations', *Industrial Marketing Management*, **18**, 95–104.

Foxall, G.R. and Goldsmith, R.E. (1994), *Consumer Psychology for Marketing*, London and New York: Routledge.

Foxall, G.R. (1990), *Consumer Psychology in Behavioral Perspective*, London and New York: Routledge.

15 The role of research in international marketing

Derek Martin

This topic is sufficiently large to be difficult to contain in a brief chapter without potentially giving a distorted view of the context and driving forces in international marketing today. Because of this it will not attempt to be a brief list of 'how-to's' but concentrate on some of the main themes which affect marketing decision making on a worldwide basis, and the information requirements which are engendered by these forces.

It was possible, 10 to 15 years ago, to regard international marketing as an adjunct of domestic marketing, in many companies. There were some worldwide giants, but even these maintained a distinction between their base domestic market and the international arena. Now it is almost impossible in the UK and the rest of Western Europe to ignore international marketing. Even if a product is confined to one country alone, it is likely to face competition from products manufactured or designed in other countries, or from domestic competition owned elsewhere, bringing a range of established products from other countries into the domestic market. As the Single Market develops, it should, of course, be necessary to change the designation of 'international' to 'outside the EU', since virtually the whole of Western Europe will be a domestic market, in principle. In practice, there may be many barriers to be overcome before this ideal can be achieved. The cultural differences are still considerable between the members of the EU, and these can have a substantial effect on product acceptability, requiring changes in product specification for different countries; distribution systems are different; pricing structures vary, in addition to the problems created by variable exchange rates; and the channels of communication and promotion vary considerably, quite apart from the different cultural responses to advertising and promotional messages.

If this is the picture within the designated Single Market, how much more complex is the situation for those considering marketing in the Middle East, *265* the Pacific Rim, South America, and North America, just to consider major and fast developing regions.

GLOBALIZATION

Analysis of markets in Western Europe alone identifies some quite profound differences between countries in their life style, attitudes and behaviour, but there are very powerful forces working to break down these differences. The technology of communication has advanced so rapidly that it has revolutionized the dissemination of information, both to the consumer and within company organizations. The satellite, the modem and the fax have created a distribution of information and images, and with them knowledge, understanding, and desires which spread far beyond national boundaries. The youth market, which carries less cultural baggage, accepts cheerfully that there may be the same music, clothes, and food consumed by their contemporaries in any country in the world. There is a global re-organization of services beginning where, for instance, a US insurance company can maintain its domestic claims department in Western Ireland, and added-value skills such as computer programming can be provided for Western European software companies in India.

The dramatic upheaval of the established order in the former Soviet Union, and in Eastern Europe, apart from internal political factors, reflect some of this globalization. It has become almost impossible to limit awareness of what is happening in other parts of the globe, and even more important what is the apparent life style and consumption of more 'modern' countries.

As long ago as 1983, Theodore Levitt, commenting on this process, was saying: 'The world's aspirations now level simultaneously outward and upward, with increasingly larger portions of its population greedily wanting the modernity to which they are so constantly exposed' (Levitt, 1983). Ten years later, with the progress not just of Japan, but also of South Korea, Taiwan, Thailand, Malaya, and now China itself creating not just powerful manufacturing entities but important consumer markets, with the fast-changing markets of Eastern Europe and the complex developments in the former Soviet Union looking for rapid introduction of 'western' style markets, to look at just two parts of the globe, how much more is this the case.

Levitt also envisaged in the same chapter on globalization that the future lay in globally standardized products, with former national or regional differences in preference for product or service features fading away. This developed further the concept of niche markets on a global or at least trans-national basis for products, where groups of consumers could be identified in a variety of countries having more in common with each other in their tastes and needs than they did with others of their own nationality.

SOCIAL CHANGE

From the late 1970s, there have been regular series of research studies tracing
the attitudes and behaviour of consumers across a variety of western coun-

tries. Social change research has shown that the same changes in consumer attitudes and wants can appear in different nationalities and cultures. It also identifies similar groups within those countries who share the same attitudes and wants, although such segments may be of different sizes in each.

This monitoring of socio-cultural trends has identified groups within each country who will be more susceptible to global marketing than others, but it also demonstrates in broad terms that there is no such thing as an homogeneous market, in any one country or across groups of countries. For instance, the RISC Euroscan study (Ladet and Montrelay, 1993), covering a sample of 12 500 European individuals, identifies:

- Open to change: 30 per cent.
- Mainstream: 40 per cent.
- Resistant to change: 30 per cent.

Within this broad structure RISC identify ten sub-groups of European consumers, with for instance those in the 'open to change' area being identified as the most favourable target for global products; another group with strong ethical convictions can be a target for environmentally friendly offerings; while there are still several groups who are self-centred, impulsive and pleasure-seeking, who are the principal users of luxury, fashion, and international brands. Again the size of these groups varies between the countries in the sample.

THE MOVE TO INDIVIDUALISM

An alternative theme to Levitt's concept of global homogenization, with major brands making a single standard offering of product, pack, advertising, and price positioning, has been that of utilizing technology for increasing individualization of product offerings. The growth of specialist publications, produced relatively inexpensively and designed to target quite small groups with particular leisure, hobby or professional interests, is one example of where technology has opened up product possibilities which did not exist economically before. There has even been talk of newspaper or magazines designed for the individual reader, by matching a set of specific individual reader interests against a portfolio of written material – the designer newspaper, faxed through to you each day. Technology can provide the back-up to maintain detailed records of individual requirements, for example in your taste in furnishings, hotels, sports equipment, or the weekly grocery shopping to provide an individual service – the list is only as long as your imagination. The key is providing individual service of the sort which was supplied before mass marketing drove out the small shopkeeper, and provides choice in a world which has become increasingly similar and choiceless.

It seems likely that while the global product, undifferentiated in formulation or design, or promotion by country, will be a feature of international marketing, alongside it will exist an even greater diversity of offerings, probably also   *267* benefiting from economies of scale, but capable of customization to sub-groups in each population who will be identifiable trans-national segments. One of the complexities of this situation will be that each individual may fit different segments, depending on the product field, and that there will be strong cultural issues requiring further customization of offering within each country.

Kenichi Ohmae (1990) has postulated that global brands have not come about because of the incipient demand for a standard product which appeals worldwide to the thirst for modernity, but more because the costs of marketing and technology are so great that such businesses have become high-fixed-cost operations who must seek global markets. In this way globalization is the direct result of internal corporate economics. If this is the case, such brands provide formidable competition, but may nevertheless have difficulty sustaining themselves against a tide of more individually designed products in future years. The quality and value label which such global products can claim could equally be taken up by smaller, more customized products, which would have the added benefit of being for the individual.

The difficulties of sustaining a brand across many markets are illustrated by Richard Lynch (1990) in looking simply at the opportunities in Europe, and the options of developing Euro-Brands, a considerably less arduous task than that envisaged by global marketing. He draws the conclusion that many major companies have failed as yet to develop Euro-brands, and even where they have a substantial European presence, many have achieved this with a variety of nationally based brands. He makes one simple calculation which puts the Euro-brand concept in context: 'it will be necessary to have an advertising and promotions budget of at least US$50 million for three years. . . As an order of magnitude this means sales of the order of US$500 million per annum to justify this type of resource allocation.' One further point which he makes is that all successful Euro-brands deliver consistent quality and that 'procedures to ensure that this is maintained are an essential element of the cost of a European launch'.

QUALITY

This touches upon another recent theme in marketing, that of 'relationship' marketing and total quality. This, expressed simply, is the concept that marketing exists to find, service and keep customers, not just sell product. Once again the emphasis is on the individual: specific marketing designed to reach the customer through producing customized product, delivered through a relevant channel of distribution, identified and promoted through selective media, competing on quality design and service, and with pricing based on customer-perceived value. The development of marketing along these lines has been forecast by Kotler and Stern, and has been taken up with enthusiasm by some promoters of 'new wave' marketing such as John Fraser-Robinson in his book *Total Quality Marketing* (where he quotes these privately supplied forecasts).

The quality concept has been a major force in manufacturing for some time but has now reached all areas of company activity and spread out into services companies as well. Its application to marketing implies a better management of the relationship between the customer and the supplier, and a change of thinking from quantity of sales, to a long-term and profitable relationship.

MARKET RESEARCH IN THE FRONT LINE

It is clear from the brief analysis above that international marketing is a far more complex issue now than it used to be. Managing brands, or looking for brand opportunities, across a variety of markets, with changing patterns of consumer behaviour and attitude, and finding potentially profitable niches across markets, or re-interpreting a product offering to maximize its appeal in a different culture, or altering a product formulation or design to meet local requirements – all require a combination of clear overall strategy and sensitivity to local issues. This is only likely to come from the collection of relevant and interpretable information specifically designed to provide solutions to the company's problems. Information is only as good as the use made of it, and the era of greater internationalism in marketing is going to have to place more reliance than ever on research providing the understanding which will make for successful brands.

In turn, it is noticeable that the research industry itself is recognizing this fact. International research is the fastest growing sector of the industry and increasingly by consolidation, alliances, or by providing standard services around the world, research suppliers are seeking to meet the needs of clients on an international basis.

Research spend has been driven in the past largely by the twin factors of consumer expenditure, and corporate profits, much the same as advertising spend, although in a rather different relationship (Martin et al., 1992). The implication of this is that it has more often been used in a reactive way to check market performance than to examine and test new opportunities. The fact that when consumer expenditure slows or declines, research rapidly follows suit, indicates that manufacturers are not using it for serious planning across the economic cycle, or to set their strategy for the next five years.

In international markets, the need to plan ahead to spread risk and develop large new markets demands research that can aid understanding of the product offering which a brand can make in different markets. Such research has to be able to deliver decision-related information, not discursive, background, 'interesting' data.

The research should be focused on providing the marketer with information which will interpret that careful balance which needs to be kept in international marketing – between the international common denominators of the product, and the necessary local interpretation of the opportunity – and which will maximize the chances of success. Ways of demonstrating the trade-off between overall pan-European, or even global opportunity, and the local requirements are critical to making good marketing judgements.

Overall, research should supply the marketer with consistency of data across countries, and this does not always mean using exactly the same question or technique; instead it implies standardization and harmonization of often different data-collection procedures. In some ways this is easier to do when dealing with qualitative data than with the apparently more reliable quantitative information where what is behind the figures is important. Comparing numbers collected from different countries may be misleading if they do not represent data with the same meaning.

IDENTIFYING MARKET DEMAND AND OPPORTUNITY

There is available to the international planner a substantial amount of basic data about markets, concerning their volume, brand shares, and distribution patterns. In the case of major product fields, this may be in a suitably comparable form, such as Nielsen data, or consumer panel information (for an example, see Betman and Leuba, 1991). In smaller product fields, however, it may be necessary to undertake specific desk research to establish the nature of the market-place in each country. Searches of international research databases should always be completed before specific research is undertaken, since there is a wide range of standard studies available on many markets on an annual basis. These may only provide basic data, but will provide a first stage screening mechanism in looking for market opportunity.

The opportunity in a national market for product introduction, extending a brand or service available elsewhere needs, most importantly, at the second stage, to be analysed in terms of competitive opportunity. The assumption that a successful brand in one country, backed by a major multinational organization can effectively claim a position in another market needs to be examined closely. Blanchard and Macrae (1988) report, from an analysis of some 2 000 product-introduction exercises using Simulated Test Market research, that in 25 per cent of cases the market was so crowded that there was no opportunity for a new brand and any introduction was destined to fail. Their work also defines a number of criteria which will determine the strategy of introducing a product into a new market.

Market structure is seen to be more important than product category, and successful performance in one market, even with product quality which can be transferred to another, may not predict success. The same performance may not compete adequately against the established competition, and achieved trial may need to be much higher to arrive at an acceptable long-term brand share.

Van Herk (1993) describes the need to understand whether existing brands in a market-place are there because they tapped generic need. Research to establish the role which the brand plays in relationship to the product category is critical in these circumstances. The history of a product category, the extent to which the end-user market can be segmented, the number and position in the consumer's hierarchy of brands all need to be investigated before opportunity can be quantified, and strategy set.

When this has to be checked across a large number of markets, it is clear that the planner needs the support of research tools which enable complex issues to be simplified. Comparability needs an understanding of the cultural framework even at the level of how respondents will answer questions. Scaling techniques present particular problems since different cultures will respond with superlatives or mid-point scores, buying intention questions may be treated differently, and attitudinal and image data (on which much may depend in analysing market opportunity) cannot always be translated directly between languages. Qualitative research may have the benefit of speaking directly to the concerns of the marketer and is often an invaluable introduction to the complexity of cultural differences, and clues as to the commonalities between markets, which need to be examined further in quantitative research.

Quantitative research, to be valuable in supporting decisions about market opportunity, has also to provide the competitive context. Ideally, norms for response in each market would aid such a process but will frequently not be available. The large amount of research material which can be collected from a multi-national project will need sifting and simplifying. Here multivariate analysis can be a considerable help in focusing attention on the main driving issues when comparing markets and looking for key points of similarity or difference.

It is also likely that companies which are already present internationally will have substantial internal resources of information which could prove useful both in establishing key criteria for market entry with specific products, and also in maintaining longer-term tracking of market trends, and competitive activity, strengths and weaknesses. Internal information systems need to be set up on a planned and structured basis to achieve full use of such information, and can also act as a significant factor in widening perspectives about the company's product offerings, and competitive performance.

PRODUCT

The ideal of a global product, which presents exactly the same product features in all countries, is difficult of attainment. In the case of products where the sensory elements are important – such as food and drink, toiletries and fragrances – the response to odour and flavour and to the visual appearance of a product can vary considerably across cultures. This may not be only a cultural response but can be rooted in physical characteristics. Different skin types may be predominant in one country, resulting in different response to skin care, fragrance, or hair products. Different dietary regimes may result in different perceptions of the same flavour. Amendments to the salt or sugar content of a product may be vital to obtain its acceptance, but will have corresponding interactions with other flavour elements.

The fitness for purpose of products in all categories may vary because of environmental factors, such as temperature, type of dwelling, or the context of use.

The user-friendliness of the product will also be important, as will be how comprehensible it is. This is, of course, to say that products must meet consumer needs in the particular market-place either in terms of established needs, or in terms of indirect needs which can be met but to date have not been established.

Researching product response internationally again requires care in ensuring that the product is presented in the right context, and that the forms of measurement are comparable. Sensory research can establish where modifications to flavour and odour may optimize product acceptance, and such work should routinely be conducted, even if the subsequent strategy determines a standard formulation internationally (Williams, 1989). It may not be possible economically to meet every country's optimal formulation, but the information on what that is will enable an informed assessment of the best compromise internationally to be made.

Product is, of course, only a part of the offering to the end-user. The branding and positioning of the product is at least as important. In measuring consumer response to a product unbranded, we are simply undertaking an artificial exercise to enable analysis of any product weaknesses and strengths to be identified as to their origin, in formulation or design. The branded, identified product is the one which is ultimately to be marketed, and it is critical to examine at an early stage in the development process how the consumer perception of the product in this final form may vary from the unbranded version. Perception of product qualities will demonstrate interaction between image and physical characteristics on some counts, while other features may be predominantly physical or image. The perception of the branded competition needs to be identified to help understand market-place opportunity, and what the product offering should be (Martin, 1989).

In comparing product measurement internationally, it is important to ensure that the product features being measured are being compared correctly. Simple translation of descriptions can be a minefield resulting in a failure to understand what might be a key strength or weakness in a product, especially important if a brief is to be given to R&D for product amendment. Detailed qualitative analysis of product descriptors and multivariate analysis of product performance against a variety of competitors is desirable to avoid these problems.

A further issue to be examined in international product work is the virtue or otherwise of indicating a country of origin. Increasingly, there is a market for ethnic products, whether Thai food, English Burberries, or Australian wine. In other instances, the country of origin may provide an overall image at odds with the product, its pricing, or perceptions of reliability or quality. Such perceptions should be tracked regularly for international marketing since they are undoubtedly changing as the world shrinks.

DISTRIBUTION

Varying patterns of distribution in different countries obviously need to be researched before proceeding with a marketing plan. One of the difficulties in an increasingly pan-European market is for retailer purchasing itself to be conducted multi-nationally. This can result in traditional measures of ex-factory or even wholesaler sales being less than accurate for a particular marketplace. The emphasis may have to switch further to consumer panels as a measure of product distribution (Betman and Leuba, 1991).

The growth of direct marketing has also been significant. The establishment of databases of consumers in a wide range of product fields has stretched research from a sample-based analytical tool to one which is involved in identifying target markets, and delivering them to the marketer. This has created some ethical concerns within the market research community, which commits itself internationally to preserving respondent confidentiality, and the data protection legislation within EU countries tends to support this approach. Where database, and list-generation activities take place, often by means of a form of 'survey', this is usually undertaken by companies specifically devoted to such activity, not market research suppliers. There is nevertheless a move to try to link information about target markets collected from market research studies to database information by means of comparable profiles of the characteristics of the target market consumers. This is legitimate since it preserves confidentiality of the original research respondents. Further EU directives are being prepared which may make direct marketing subject to further restrictions, but it continues to be a burgeoning area of distribution.

CUSTOMER SATISFACTION RESEARCH

The growing emphasis in marketing on managing the relationship between manufacturers and their customers, which was discussed above, has resulted in a rapid growth of customer satisfaction research. In the USA, where much of this work originated, it is the fastest growing area of research activity over the past three years.

It has been directed to fields where customer service is a critical part of the total offering – such as telephone services, banking, and health care – but is also strong in the automotive field, where maintaining a customer over the several years before another purchase is made is clearly important. It is steadily being taken up in more fast moving consumer goods areas, as well.

In some instances, the initial impetus was to provide a measurement tool of employee performance, and a guide to payment and bonus. It has developed further into analysis of methods of customer retention (Cottrell, 1993), which is clearly relevant to the concept of total marketing quality which was touched upon earlier in this chapter.

The development of customer satisfaction research methods has been rapid, and the size and continuous nature of the work has understandably attracted many major research practitioners. There is rather more debate about the effectiveness of such work in demonstrating how companies have used it to maintain customers, and this has led to other programmes being introduced which promote action ahead of discovering problems in customer satisfaction. The measures within customer satisfaction studies can include product or service performance and quality, and pricing as well as the 'ongoing relationship between customer and supplier'. In this way it can act as a brand tracking system. On an international basis, it should be able to identify whether a company's performance overall in the market-place is consistent, and this can be valuable for internal management evaluation. It can also generate very considerable amounts of data, which need to be reviewed regularly for critical changes in performance, and also analysed for predictive ability.

PRICING

Brief mention has been made above of the varying opportunities which a brand may have in individual markets, depending on the history, and current performance of the competition. This can mean making a different offering with the same product in different markets. This is also true of pricing, which creates further complication.

While it may be possible to identify an optimum price in each market-place, the increasing internationalization of markets and of retailer buying make this a hazardous exercise. Within the EU there can rapidly develop the problems of parallel importing where wholesalers seize on a lower-priced country to import branded product for distribution in another higher-priced one. The manufacturer can do little to prevent this under EU regulations. In setting prices, therefore, it may be desirable to take an international viewpoint, rather than a local one, since pricing structures with considerable imbalance between neighbouring countries may confuse and undermine the marketing opportunities within all of them. Analysis of Nielsen retail audit data or of international consumer panel data will help in establishing where such problems may exist for competitors, or within one's own organization.

Pricing research is also critical in helping to understand the opportunity for any product, especially on an international basis. The end-user's perception of the price and value of the product should be the baseline from which pricing strategy is developed. Questions such as what quality, and what other features and values the product delivers for a certain price, compared with competition, can best be checked using some form of brand/price trade-off analysis. The elasticity of demand in the market should also be checked to see if opportunities for segmentation by price exist. Further work modelling sales levels against price in the market-place can establish whether a brand is driven by absolute or relative price relationships, and the marketing strategy adjusted accordingly.

Simulated test market analysis can also look at price in the context of the total offering by the new product, but this will be undertaken most effectively when the overall strategy for the product, including price, has been decided. Since price can be such a critical factor in determining market opportunity, and overall risk, it should be researched in detail in the development process.

PROMOTION

Some of the earliest applications of global branding have been in the use of international advertising campaigns, seeking to provide a single identity around the world. This has been successful in a limited number of cases in fast moving consumer goods – Coca-Cola and Marlboro cigarettes are obvious examples. In targeted markets such as business travellers, airlines have tried the same approach, as have computer manufacturers.

However, it does seem that, aside from the potential savings in advertising origination costs, this is a difficult area in which to demonstrate that standard images have universal appeal. Research is needed to explore within individual countries whether or not there may be common themes, and how well certain images work in providing a metaphor for the product in that particular culture. A different positioning for the product, or a different tone to the advertising may be required. This implies careful exploratory qualitative research to help understand what the associations may be, before proceeding to pre-testing of completed advertising. Here again considerable differences in research technique may be required depending on the country. Even within Europe, the emphasis will vary from group discussions, to extended depth interviews, or even weekend-long groups. Projective techniques to establish an emotional content to images or themes are often used, and hands-on participatory groups or interviews where the client and agency change the material as the research proceeds are also popular. This demonstrates the complexity of different cultures to be considered (and this can even affect the accepted format of the research) whenever an international advertising campaign is being developed. The temptation to voice-over a commercial from another country may be considerable, but is likely to provide a poor quality promotional vehicle, and one recognized by the consumer as such.

Pre-testing systems, for TV and for press advertising, utilizing standard research procedures, are widely available. While these can provide excellent comparisons of standard advertising campaigns across countries, and also norms for advertising performance by different material between countries, they should be treated with care. The diagnostics of advertising performance may be quite a small part of the research, and therefore guidance on how to change a campaign which is not performing well may need to come from further research, for which there is often little time.

Advertising tracking, or in its more extended form, brand performance tracking, is becoming increasingly used on an international basis. The value of regular monitoring of brand performance against consumer usage, awareness, and attitude measurements is considerable in establishing future strategy, and in evaluating current promotional performance in a competitive context. It is sometimes easy to forget that promotion of a brand in a particular market works both on that brand and on its competitors, and vice versa. Understanding the absolute and relative performance of a campaign leads to a truer assessment of promotional effectiveness. Advertising or brand tracking, ideally, is continuous since this allows for analysis of everything which is hap- *275* pening in the market-place, from competitive activity to retailer action, to economic policy. However, for many brands this may be too expensive, and there are tools for measuring promotional performance within single studies.

Within the heading of promotion comes sales promotion activity – competition, coupon offers, special prizes, money-off other products and so on. More emphasis has been placed on these exercises in recent years, which has resulted in the level of spend rising much faster than for advertising itself. Pre-testing of such offers is desirable, especially to examine the impact on image, as well as comparison of the appeal of alternatives. Tracking studies can identify the success of such campaigns overall, as well as that of advertising, and how various promotional activities work together or not. Internationally there can, of course, be economies of scale in running promotions which are essentially similar, providing the marketing purpose is the same.

Packaging is a major factor in promotion, and also needs to be researched on an international basis. Different cultural responses to colour, design, and images or icons on packs can be considerable. International testing for shelf impact (how well the packs stand out in a typical display), and for image and communication of brand qualities is essential if standard packaging is to be used internationally. This has become increasingly the case as production has been centred in particular countries serving an international market.

CONCLUSION

The principal point of tension in determining how a brand is to be marketed internationally is on the often fine line of maximizing the common features, which can work across borders and cultures, and the degree of amendment which should be undertaken to meet the requirements of those local cultures and markets. There is no substitute for research at the market analysis stage, when strategy is being defined, and in testing all elements of the marketing mix, against competition, to help understand what the opportunity and risk is for the brand.

REFERENCES

Betman, R. and Leuba, D. (1991), 'The importance of pan-European marketing information for international marketing strategy' in *International Marketing Research*, Amsterdam: ESOMAR (European Society for Opinion and Marketing Research).

Blanchard, J. and Macrae, C. (1988), 'Detecting opportunities and risks to global branding – the value of a global marketing databank' in *Seminar on International Marketing Research*, Amsterdam: ESOMAR.

Cottrell, Richard J. (1993), 'Proactive Relationship Management: The Next Step to Long Term Customer Loyalty' in *Seminar The Ideal Product, the Ideal Customer, The Ideal Company? New perspectives in Customer Satisfaction Research*, Amsterdam: ESOMAR.

Fraser-Robinson, John (1991), *Total Quality Marketing*, London: Kogan Page

Ladet, Michel and Montelay, Francois (1993), 'How to meet clients' needs' in *Seminar on Marketing and International Research*, Amsterdam: ESOMAR.

Levitt, Theodore (1983), *The Marketing Imagination*, New York: The Free Press.

Lynch, Richard (1990), *European Business Strategies*, London: Kogan Page.

Martin, D.C. (1989), 'How marketing influences sensory perception and how sensory perception should influence marketing', *Seminar on Research for Flavours and Fragrances*, Amsterdam: ESOMAR.

Martin, Derek C. and Hagan, Laurence W. (1992), 'The market research market in Europe, the USA, and Japan and the major economic factors influencing it' in *Joint ESOMAR/ARF/JMA conference,* Amsterdam: ESOMAR.

Ohmae, Kenichi (1990), *The Borderless World: Power and Strategy in the Interlinked Economy*, London: Collins.

Van Herk, Martin C. (1993), 'Multi-cultural marketing: The Asian experience', *Seminar on Marketing and International Research*, Amsterdam: ESOMAR.

Williams, A.A. (1989), 'Optimising Flavours and Fragrances for International Markets' in *Seminar on Research for Flavours and Fragrances*, Amsterdam: ESOMAR.

ESSENTIAL READING

Birn, R., Hague, P. and Vangelder P. (1991), *Handbook of Market Research Techniques*, London: Kogan Page.

Worcester, R.M. and Downham, J. (1986), *Consumer Market Research Handbook*, Amsterdam: North Holland/ESOMAR.

Papers from Seminars on international research in 1991 and 1993, European Society for Opinion and Marketing Research (ESOMAR), JJ Viotastraat 29, 1071 JP Amsterdam, Netherlands.

Market Research Society (15 Northburgh Street, London EC1V 0AH) publishes country notes, providing basic information on demographics, sampling methods, research procedures and sources of information. Regional volumes cover Western Europe, the Far East, North America, Eastern Europe, and Latin America.

Also published by MRS: *International Directory of Market Research Organisations*, covering 80 countries.

16 Product planning

Simon Majaro

Simple concepts are not always easy to translate into practical programmes. What can be simpler than the 'marketing concept'? I have been teaching marketing for many years and have spent enormous time and effort in striving to convert companies from being technology-led or production-orientated to market-led enterprises.

Yet after so many years I still encounter many companies that only pay lip-service to the underlying philosophy of marketing. Having a marketing director and/or a marketing department do not *per se* turn a company into a marketing-orientated enterprise. Too many organizations are still convinced that a genuine adhesion to the marketing concept is simply manifested by the establishment of a marketing function. What many such companies forget is that the true converts to the marketing creed take a more holistic approach. The whole organization must be prepared to focus its thinking and acting in response to customers and their needs and expectations. Easy notion to preach; a most difficult concept to apply.

The firm's attitude towards its products and product planning can provide a most valuable acid test of the extent to which it has adopted the marketing philosophy as part of its corporate shared values.

The first point to remember is that no product exists in a vacuum. I recently met a CEO of a large company who expressed deep frustration at the fact that one of the firm's major new products was not moving. 'It is a wonderful product but nobody seems to want it!' was his *cri de coeur*. His chagrin was increased even further when I told him that in fact he had no product. All he had was a cluster of raw materials assembled into what looked like a product. No product exists until the customer derives a utility from it. A product is designed to provide utilities and satisfaction to the customer and if the latter cannot perceive their value, no product exists.

If this statement is acceptable to the reader, one should now attempt to respond to the very fundamental question: 'What is my product?' This question represents a very subtle shibboleth. The reader may recall the biblical story of the Gileadites who could identify their enemies by asking them to say 'Shibboleth.' Whoever responded by saying 'Sibboleth' with a soft 'S' was an enemy and was slain. The inability to pronounce the test word correctly betrayed the person's tribal affiliation. Now, ask a person: 'What is your "product"?' The answer should help you to judge the level of understanding and commitment that the interlocutor has towards the marketing creed.

THE VARIOUS FACES OF THE 'PRODUCT'

A product has many faces. What the manufacturing person sees can be different from what the marketing person should be seeing. Let us consider an example. A company manufactures ball bearings and roller bearings in a vast assortment of sizes, alloys and configurations. The production manager will respond to the question: 'What is your product?' by simply saying: 'Ball bearings and roller bearings'.

Members of the marketing team should be reprimanded if they give the same answer. To them the product or products are 'anti-friction' devices. They are aids to the reduction of friction in a number of machines or instruments such as motor cars or machine tools. To those who have no friction problems, ball bearings are not products but simply a load of junk. On the other hand to those who have a significant friction problem to overcome, bearings provide a vital added-value solution. To them, bearings are certainly important products. The true marketer would know, and in great detail, the various sectors of the Standard Industrial Classification that have friction problems to overcome. Moreover he or she would be able to identify the sectors which represent prime targets for exploitation and those which represent secondary and tertiary opportunities. The day that all functions in the organization, and not only marketing people, talk or think like this would be the day that the firm could truly call itself marketing-orientated.

This example is quite simple. Let us now look at more complex situations. A pharmaceuticals company manufactures a number of drugs. By the nature of the industry and its level of technology, the drugs represent complex chemical compounds. The production people and the research and development people are very tempted to define the product in units of the 'wonder drug' that the firm produces. The enlightened marketing person will describe the product in terms of the illness which the drug combats or the discomfort which it alleviates. The production-orientated man will boast about the units of the antibiotics which the firm manufactured in a given period; the truly marketing-orientated person will talk about the number of pneumonia sufferers who were cured by 'our product' and, when attempting to measure the firm's market share, will do so in relation to his or her perception of the market, namely the number of pneumonia cases that occur in the course of the year.

Normally the more intricate the product and the more sophisticated the technology, the greater the chasm between the perceptions of the product *279* among the various functions of the enterprise. Obviously the research and development person who has been instrumental in the development of a highly innovative analgesic would prefer to talk about the complex chemical molecule of the product, rather than its headache alleviation characteristics. They are of course both right, but the research and development person talks about the physical properties of the product; the marketer talks about what the product does for the consumer. In marketing terms the latter utility is the one that really matters. Unless you have a headache you are not in the market-place and the product has no relevance to you. If you do have a headache you become passionately interested in the product, not because it contains the x or y wonder ingredients but simply because it will alleviate your condition.

A manufacturer of diesel engines will tend to talk about the number of units, the size of the units and the number of cylinders produced in the course of the year. 'What is your product?' will inevitably be answered with 'Diesel engines of 50 h.p. or 75 h.p. etc. configuration'! The marketer should say: 'We manufacture energy-producing units of a particular design as an auxiliary facility in process plants, or ships or hospitals and at a cost per unit of electricity of x pence etc.' The marketing person must respond to the question as if he or she were the buyer of the product.

The message should be quite clear. Companies that have adopted the marketing creed with its full implications always seek to define their products in terms of what the customers buy and the cost/benefit which they derive from them. The products are seen as solutions to problems or as enhancements to consumers' lifestyles and/or general well-being. This philosophy should apply, with equal rigour, to all consuming environments, be they for industrial goods or consumer products. Clearly this implies that the marketing organization understands fully what satisfies the customer/consumer either in terms of tangible benefits or less quantifiable intangibles.

THE 'PRODUCT' - A NEW DIMENSION

Much has been written about the product life cycle and what happens to sales and profitability during its course. The concept is a useful one but one of its pitfalls is the fact that we often forget to identify the product in terms that are really meaningful to the marketing process. The product may be progressing well towards 'growth' in the context of its technology or manufacturing processes, yet it may have reached its 'saturation' point in terms of its market or segment penetration. The two levels of performance are not necessarily congruent. Let us take an example.

A manufacturer of running shoes supplies the fraternity of professional and quasi-professional joggers with specially designed shoes that provide arch support when running or sprinting. The sales follow a classical pattern which indicates that a 'product life cycle' is in operation. As a result of the ravages of competition and the fact that the product has reached the saturation point in the cycle, pressure on margins is heavy and erosion of profitability is taking place. Nonetheless, rather unexpectedly the life cycle takes a twist upwards and sales are starting to boom again. The obvious implication is that the laws of gravity have been defied and that the theory of the product life cycle should be relegated to academic manuscripts only.

What has really happened is that the 'marketing ecology' has changed. A new market has sprung up for the firm's product: the amateur joggers, people of all ages who have read about the health value of jogging and decided to join the throng of early morning enthusiasts. In truth what has happened is that a new market has developed and to all intents and purposes the product has acquired a new face and should be treated as a new product. On this basis one would have one product for the professional runner and one for the enthusiastic jogger. The physical product may be the same but the marketing product will be different and each will deserve its separate analysis *vis-à-vis* the life cycle evaluation.

In the light of this, it is instructive to re-examine the earlier example from the pharmaceuticals industry. Imagine that Stanton Chemicals manufactures an antibiotic product, Stantalyn, which is used effectively in the treatment of a wide range of infections. If the product is looked at as a technological package, its life cycle could be traced on the basis of its total sales and profitability. On the other hand, we can rightly assume that each infection type represents a separate market with the result that one can plot the life-cycle performance in relation to each sickness. Thus, without getting too involved in the technicalities of a complex industry, one can have a product life cycle in respect of each identifiable 'indication': infections of the throat, ear, lungs, bile duct and so on. Each 'indication' will have its own product (with or without different brand names) and each one of these products will have its own life-cycle.

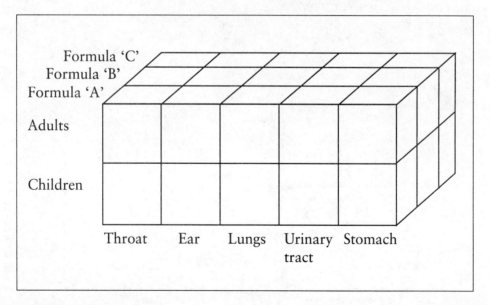

Figure 16.1　Product/market/segment vectors

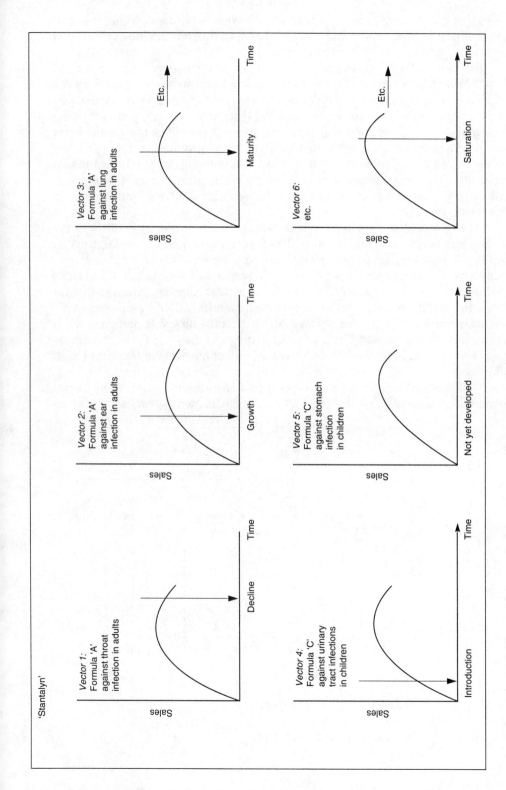

Figure 16.2 Vector life cycles

The situation can be further embellished by saying that the drug used by children in relation to one kind of illness is a different product from the one used by adults. Thus we finish by getting a three-dimensional matrix of product/market/segment *vectors* (see Figure 16.1).

It is quite possible that the product will need to undergo a slight differentiation process, such as the production of a sweetened syrup for children, to facilitate absorption or swallowing, but essentially the product characteristics in technical terms are probably unchanged. Thus this illustration would suggest that we have many products as shown in Figure 16.1, and not just one. If this is so, we can now look at the new dimension of the product life cycle by plotting the cycle of each 'vector' in turn, as illustrated in Figure 16.2.

This kind of analysis is much more meaningful within a truly marketing-oriented environment than talking about a product life cycle in a commercial vacuum, as most marketers tend to do. This concept opens a new perspective for the marketer inasmuch as one can now ascribe a more practical dimension to life-cycle analysis. The product becomes the instrument of satisfaction for each market segment rather than a cluster of raw materials bunched together into a physical assemblage that one calls a 'product'. It is now possible to monitor the level of satisfaction that one achieves in each market niche and establish whether the satisfaction is progressing well or is declining. Furthermore it is much easier to react to a decline in satisfaction by applying the most appropriate marketing tools for each stage of the 'vector' life cycle than a technology-based product life cycle.

'Vector' in mathematics means a quantity having direction as well as magnitude, denoted by a line drawn from its original to its final position. By applying a certain amount of lateral thinking I use the term 'vector' to mean the market segment which is 'satisfied' by a specific product offering. Thus if a segment is capable of being satisfied by a number of products offered by the firm, each 'product/segment' unit of activity is a vector. In other words, what is being suggested is that instead of talking about the progress of a product or a brand along the life cycle, it is much more sensible to talk about the progress of the vector life cycle, namely the 'utility rendered to a specific market segment'. A diesel engine manufacturer who has designed a small power generating plant that can supply energy for a factory and also propel vessels has two distinct 'vectors': the supply of energy to a plant; *and* the supply of propulsion for ships. The physical and technical product may be the same but in marketing terms two separate vectors exist and their life cycle may be totally different.

Top management often expects the identical performance from all its products. In many instances this is neither possible nor justifiable. Different vectors have to cope with totally different marketing environments and to expect the same level of results from such environments just because the physical product is the same is illogical. The level of competition, the cost/benefit requirements and the distribution problems can tilt the balance in favour of one product/segment and make the other look unattractive. Marketing people understand this much better than accountants or production people. The latter feel that a machine is a machine and the level of profit it provides to the selling company is the same irrespective of who uses it and what it is being used for.

I have been preaching this message for many years. In fact it formed the main theme of my contribution to earlier editions of this Handbook. The most rewarding feedback that one can receive in response to challenging philosophies is when one encounters companies that have applied the concepts propounded. The notion that segment managers are more important than product managers seems to gain ground in an increasing number of companies. Clearly it is a concept that calls for considerable pluck on the part of those responsible for organization development. It departs from the established and well-trodden 'mindset'. Nonetheless if one accepts that a cleverly-designed structure can provide the firm with a competitive advantage, here is an opportunity to pursue creative avenues for exploitation.

MARKET SEGMENTATION REVIEWED

The theory of market segmentation has taught us that very often a company does better by devoting its efforts and creativity to developing a marketing programme specifically designed to appeal to a segment of the market rather than to the market as a whole. The theory goes on to say that having studied the firm's strengths and weaknesses in some depth, the marketer decides to seek to satisfy a selected part of the market rather than attempt to be all things to all people. However, when approaching the market with a segmentation policy it is necessary to recognize that it is essential to gain a significant portion of the sub-market whilst a small market share of the whole would have sufficed.

Segmentation policies often fail for the simple reason that having decided to segment the market and concentrate one's effort in that area, one has acquired too small a share of the segment in question. It is therefore vitally important that the person who decides to concentrate on a segment should seek to dominate or obtain a significant part of that segment. The would-be segmenter should carry out thorough market measurement studies to establish beyond all reasonable doubt that the selected segment justifies the firm's attention. After all, having opted for a part of the market instead of its totality, one takes the risk of 'placing all one's eggs in one basket' and before taking such a decision one must be satisfied that the strategy selected is right.

Market segmentation offers considerable scope for creativity. It is an area in which the innovative marketer can identify opportunities which competitors have missed or have decided to ignore. Thus, when one looks at the more successful car manufacturers in the world such as BMW, one soon recognizes that the real reason for their success was the fact that they had identified a very attractive, albeit small, unexploited market segment. However, in selecting one's target segment for marketing development one must ensure that three fundamental conditions are adhered to: the segment must be measurable; it must be sufficiently substantial to justify the effort to be invested in it; it must be accessible in the sense that the institutional systems that facilitate the marketing process (for example channels of distribution, media availability) exist.

These three conditions are of course interrelated and perfectly logical. Yet it is sad to watch how often fairly experienced marketers fall into the trap of selecting segments which do not meet one or more of these conditions, and consequently fail. A further pitfall lies in attempts to 'cheat old age' of a declining product by simply differentiating it *vis-à-vis* a specific segment which happens to be on the decline as well.

In our modern and very competitive environment, it is not enough to assume that a segmentation policy is *per se* a formula for success. One must refine the concept beyond what we have attempted to do in the past. Before indulging in product planning we must break down the market into consumer-oriented and cost/benefit-oriented sub-markets or 'vectors'. Obviously there is nothing to stop the marketer from standardizing a product for a cluster of 'vectors', but it must be by design and not by accident. This is not dissimilar to the kind of problem one encounters in international marketing where the effective marketer seeks to identify the needs of each country but then attempts to standardize the product for as many countries as lend themselves to such standardization.

For example, suppose a large transport company has decided to specialize in the field of carrying very heavy cargoes (over 150 tonnes per cargo). This is in itself a segmentation policy in as much as the company has opted out of the very competitive field of transporting ordinary cargoes. One hopes that before embarking on this strategy, which demands a very heavy 'infrastructure', the company has gone through the process of measuring the size of the market for heavy cargoes and found it to be substantial in marketing terms. Furthermore, the company should have established that the segment in question is accessible.

The strategy may prove to be successful but if the company wishes to pursue the logic of this argument a step further, it must undertake a vector analysis. That would help to ensure that the marketing effort is more directly geared towards the real marketing opportunities and that the product is totally congruent to the needs of each vector.

How should the company go about it? It should analyse, step by step, in quantified terms who needs to carry very heavy cargoes. The Standard Industrial Classification offers a useful division of the industrial scene. Thus the mining/quarrying and the chemical and shipbuilding industries are all relevant vectors, and each one probably needs a different product. Moreover, some of these many vectors will offer better marketing opportunities than others.

If one could plot all these opportunities on a 'dart-board' type chart (see Figure 16.3), the best will fit into the 'bull's eye' centre, the next on the adjacent circle and so on. Once the implications of this philosophy are grasped by the creative marketer, he or she will have acquired an excellent tool for planning. First, the product will be more directly designed to meet the best vector's needs. Second, the promotional mix can be geared towards the most attractive target audience. Third, the salesforce can be directed towards the 'bull's eye' buying environment. It is a totally different story from sending a salesforce in search of people who need to transport very heavy cargoes.

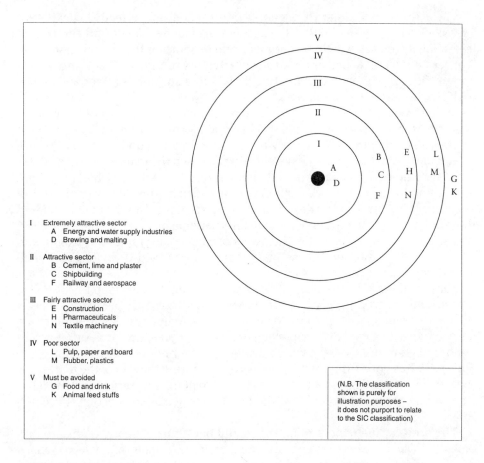

Figure 16.3   The relative attractiveness of 'sub-markets' for a 'heavy-cargoes' transporter

ORGANIZATIONAL IMPLICATIONS

It is worth exploring the organizational implications of what has been suggested. Many companies have so-called product managers or brand managers. Quite a few of these firms must reflect upon the real role of these managers and its appropriateness to a truly marketing-orientated business. In many situations these managers are the hidden manifestation of a bias towards the product as seen by production people rather than the one seen by marketing people. What, for instance, is the marketing relevance of a flooring product manager in a firm that manufactures and supplies flooring for domestic, industrial and institutional markets? Surely what such a company needs is a domestic flooring *market* manager, an industrial flooring *market* manager and an institutional flooring *market* manager.

The word 'market' is emphasized because the product as such does not exist until such time as the market/segment/vector in question exists. It is the needs of the market which the manager has to satisfy and not the needs of the product. In seeking to meet the needs of the market, the marketer has to develop a total marketing mix and not only a product. By calling him or her a product manager we simply fog the issue and detract from the importance of the job.

It is not suggested that the role of product managers has disappeared. In many firms such managers are most appropriate and their role is an important one. At the same time it is recommended that, before opting for a structure that encompasses the product management concept, top management must explore the alternatives and consider the relative merit of each in relation to the marketing aims of the firm. In fact in certain circumstances one can envisage solutions which embrace both product management and market management in a matrix combination (Majaro, 1988).

The whole essence of the matrix approach to organization development is based on the theory that two vital, albeit slightly overlapping structures can coexist. One of the structures is traditional, hierarchical and results-orientated. The other structure is co-ordinative, integrative and in many instances seeks to impart a truly marketing-orientated dimension to a system which by its very nature is less capable of being dynamically so. Referring back to the earlier example of Stanton Chemicals, one can envisage a matrix type organization like the one shown in Figure 16.4.

A structure like this may well prove to be the best way of combining the more traditional way of managing the product with the much more progressive, albeit more complex, marketing-orientated approach.

Finally, a simple checklist for the more enlightened reader:

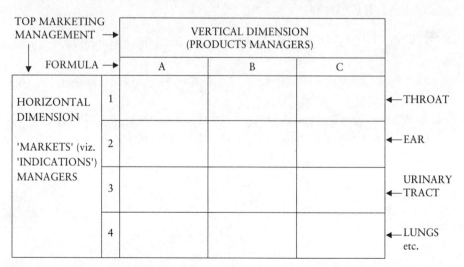

Figure 16.4   Matrix organization for Stanton Chemicals

1   Do not attempt to structure your organization until you have established clearly what your products are.
2   Before defining what your products are, attempt to identify the size and accessibility of the various market vectors that your company is best equipped to satisfy. The 20 per cent of the vectors that offer 80 per cent of the results for your firm will direct you towards the most sensible and effective structure.
3   Maintain enough flexibility in your structure to enable you to cope with the dynamism of the market-place. The matrix approach to organizational structuring can offer such a flexibility in some situations.
4   Never forget that the most successful marketing takes place when the company knows exactly who it is trying to satisfy.

The approach described in this chapter is somewhat unorthodox. It places the emphasis upon markets and segments rather than on the products themselves. It is based on the theory that a product does not exist until the moment that somebody needs and wants it. The logic underlying such a principle is indisputable. Yet in practice many companies are reluctant to adopt it insofar as it departs from the more traditional way of organizing for product planning. It is not a suitable model for the faint-hearted, but perhaps the more plucky reader will look at the ideas put forward in a more positive way.

REFERENCES

Majaro, Simon (1993), *'International Marketing – A Strategic Approach to World Markets',* London: Routledge.

ESSENTIAL READING

Kotler, Philip (1991), *Marketing Management: Analysis, Planning and Control,* Hemel Hempstead: Prentice Hall.

Majaro, Simon (1993), *The Essence of Marketing,* Hemel Hempstead: Prentice Hall.

Moore, William and Pessimier, Edgar (1993), *Product Planning and Management: Designing and Delivering Value,* Maidenhead: McGraw-Hill.

17 Product design

Patrick Bruce

The objective of this chapter is to establish the need within organizations to adopt a considered approach to design in the development of new products and the redesign of existing ones.

Product design is seen here in the context of classical marketing thinking and is identified as a critical tool in matching the firm's resources to market opportunities. The skills of the designer are discussed, and the characteristics of a design hierarchy described. It is argued that it should have the close attention of senior management, and should be directly and independently represented at this level.

It is suggested that subordinating design to the management of other business disciplines will inhibit the use of design as a competitive weapon in the market-place. As design affects almost every area of organization from production through to finance and distribution, it is identified as a necessary aid to the management of change both inside and outside the firm.

To gain maximum benefit from a product design facility, either in house or consultancy-based, the explicit consideration of resources required and provision for their sound management are necessary. Some of the issues surrounding the choice between in-house and consultancy-based design are explored and the benefits examined.

Finally, the need to approach product design in a structured way is supported by a method developed through many years of consultancy work by a design practice in the unique position of servicing both members of its own holding company and a substantial external client-base. The method breaks the design process down into distinct stages, using client involvement to help eliminate perceived and actual risk. Each phase is examined showing the importance of adequate research before the process starts, and the need to use the integrative skills of the designer to seek solutions across company divisions, not simply within them.

THE SCOPE OF THIS CHAPTER

There is no shortage of literature on the subject of design, and arguably an over-abundance of attempts to define it through the written word. It is clear that, however it is defined, design as a business tool affects a bewildering array of issues from the corporate image or identity of a company; through the tangible aspects of its product range; the means of communication used to reach end-users, financial institutions and employees; the appearance and performance of its means of distribution, including vehicles, warehousing and final outlets; and so on. To keep this section to manageable proportions, product design will be considered here as it applies to tangible goods aimed at consumer and commercial end-user markets.

Despite this closely defined area, product design will have had some impact earlier in the development cycle, for example in shaping the components and sub-assemblies that make up the finished product.

Many of the issues relating to goods design will also apply to the intangibles of service industries, to fashion products and to food products. The reason for keeping to design of end-users products is that it allows for a clearer discussion on how design fits into the business environment and how the process works.

PRODUCT DESIGN AND MARKETING

When considering the subject of product design the key question is why it matters at all. The marketing literature is a fruitful source of arguments justifying new product development, or the redevelopment of existing product. Product life-cycle theory indicates a finite time-span during which a product can be expected to be profitable, and gives a clear description of the need for initial expenditure to support the development of the product market.

It also highlights the need to support the development of new product with the proceeds of successful products currently on the market to ensure that continuity of income and profit is maintained. The work of the Boston Consulting Group further underlines product life stages, and their cash-generating or cash-absorbing implications.

Judging the finite life of products is, of course, the key to the successful use of such models. It is the one issue which is, perhaps, simplest to understand but most difficult to measure before the event. Plotting sales will allow some measure of life-cycle progress at a given point, and will allow a commercial view on whether the redesign of an existing product should be undertaken, or when a new replacement product needs to be introduced.

However, the underlying assumption is that the generic product form is still appropriate in the market-place. One might question whether a typewriter manufacturer should be redesigning or developing new typewriter products on the basis of a life-cycle plot, or whether the generic form itself is under threat from low-cost word processors. Clearly a much wider view of what is happening in the market-place is required, including serious evaluation of substitute products arriving from an industry sector outside traditional industry competition.

The typewriter example shows life cycles curtailed by technological change. There are also circumstances where national and cultural differences impose limits on potential market growth. All the direct and indirect influences should be evaluated before product development takes place to ensure the differences are accommodated, and the market size implications clearly understood.

One variable not often made explicit is the influence of fashion on product design and development. Taste has always influenced the end-user, and with the advent of global marketing and exposure to ever wider varieties of cultural and visual choice, this has become an issue of critical importance in many areas of industry and commerce. Lifestyle marketing in consumer goods has sought to address this factor, clearly targeting defined segments.

It would be dangerous to assume that taste has no effect on products targeted at commercial purchasers. The office furniture industry has had to adopt domestic influences in the appearance of their products in terms of colour, texture, fabric usage and style, as well as the ever-changing functional requirements imposed by office electronic equipment. Manufacturers of heavy goods vehicles have readily accepted many elements of design from saloon car manufacturers who, in turn, are bowing to the demands of corporate image and domestic influence.

What this means is that without a thorough audit of company resources and the wants and needs of the market, and working towards matching resources and opportunity, no amount of product development and design will ensure success in the market-place.

DESIGN AND THE CORPORATE MANAGEMENT STRUCTURE

Professor Bruce Archer (1974) in his book *Design Awareness and Planned Creativity in Industry* described the need for design and its management in the context of the total business entity. He suggested that design should be considered a business tool, and that its use and proper management could be shown to affect the whole business operation. The question of what constituted good design was posed by asking who it should be good for. Good design would consider many corporate issues: the generation of profit over the product life; the satisfaction of consumer needs; the ability of the company to produce, market and distribute the product; and the contribution of the product in visual and functional terms to the environment.

He argued that while good design did not, by definition, create any visual offence, neither did it set out to be fine art. Its purpose must be to optimize and accommodate the often conflicting requirements of the business enterprise.

The influence design has on so many aspects of corporate and end-user life is underlined by Mark Oakley (1984), author of *Managing Product Design*. He argues that as a business discipline product design should be independently represented at senior level within the management structure. If it becomes *291* subordinate to any other traditional business discipline it cannot achieve optimal solutions to satisfy the multitude of conflicting interests in the business.

Christopher Lorenz (1986), in his book *The Design Dimension*, identifies a number of international companies which have established that design is no longer to be considered 'a low level creature of marketing'. He quotes Professor Philip Kotler's view that the only way for corporations to ensure market success is to design better products. Among the companies Lorenz identifies as having elevated design to 'fully fledged membership of the corporate hierarchy' are Olivetti, John Deere, Ford, Olympus, Sony, and Philips. They have recognized the value of design as a competitive weapon and integrated it into their corporate structure.

Lorenz's list of a designer's skills and attributes includes imagination, creativity, the ability to demonstrate three-dimensional relationships, communication skills in words and sketches, and the ability to synthesize multi-disciplinary factors into a coherent whole.

It is because of this combination of skills, and the ability to comprehend and work across traditional business disciplines, that Peter Gorb of the London Business School believes that designers have high potential in the role of general management. Gorb refers to the conservative nature of organizations which correctly seek to preserve the assets of their shareholders and their employees, and who will therefore resist change. However, the increasing globalization of markets and shorter product life cycles have meant that companies must cope more and more with the issue of change, both internally and externally.

The development and implementation of new products are for many companies disruptive activities and underline the perception of designers as change agents. Oakley points to the incidence of organizations which have resisted such change to the point where their very survival has been at stake. He points out that many firms pay lip-service to the need for design while laying down internally inconsistent policies which prevent product innovation. He quotes twelve reasons established by J. R. Bright in a 1964 publication explaining why companies and their employees resist change. Among these are the protection of status or habit, the protection of the capital base of the company, and preserving the equilibrium of the business atmosphere and society.

While most commentators believe that change is a necessary fact of business life in order to protect the survival of the business entity, one does not have to look far to see the conflict caused within organizations which seek to introduce changes to working habits, manufacturing techniques and product ranges. In the examples quoted by Lorenz earlier it is clear that the need to change has been grasped, and the integrative synthesizing nature of the designer's skills have been adopted at senior level.

Oakley (1984) shows examples where design, having been made subordinate to another discipline, failed to produce optimum results. Seen as an agent of change, design becomes an overt threat, and the firm loses the opportunity to use available skills constructively as a competitive weapon.

292   The case made here, then, is that to provide the greatest potential to an organization in managing its way into the future, the design function should not be considered a subdivision of some other business discipline. As an integrative discipline it should receive the attention of top management. It is an area of key importance in the whole range of the company's activities. It straddles all the traditional business functions within an organization, and acts as the interpretative interface between the organization and its markets. Without it the company will not generate new products. Put in the wrong hierarchical relationship, it will not ensure that opportunities in the market-place are matched to internal resources, present and future.

THE ORGANIZATION OF PRODUCT DESIGN

This subject is dealt with succinctly by Oakley (1984) and it is not intended to deal with it in great detail here. Oakley points out some of the essential differences in hierarchical relationships between design departments in relation to other traditional business divisions. The design hierarchy tends to be flat, with decisions being taken on a team basis, not top down. Expertise is distributed throughout the organization, and authority is assumed by the knowledge holder, not necessarily the hierarchical head. All members of the team will contribute to decision making, with tasks and roles being frequently redefined to suit the prevailing needs of the situation. This organic style of management structure is contrasted with the mechanistic style which is formal, hierarchical and bureaucratic. Most situations will demand a mix of the two styles located along a continuum from one extreme to the other. This would roughly equate to the need for design expertise along a continuum from pure engineering design to pure appearance design. Figure 17.1 shows this in diagrammatic form.

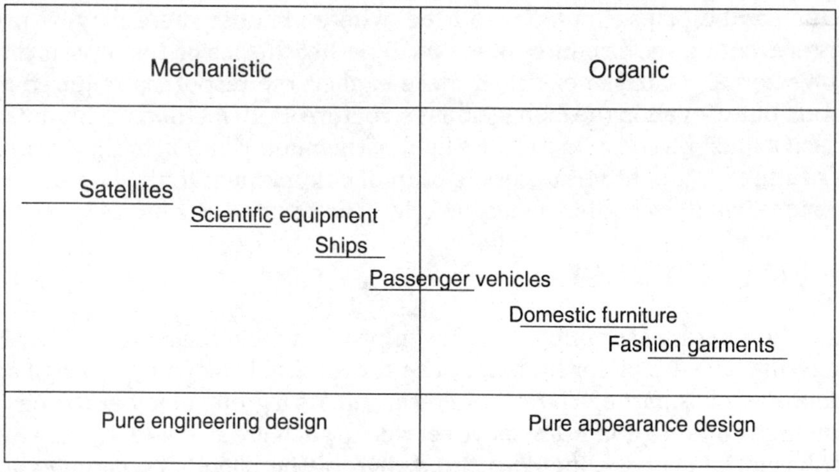

Mechanistic	Organic

Satellites
  Scientific equipment
    Ships
      Passenger vehicles
        Domestic furniture
          Fashion garments	

Pure engineering design	Pure appearance design

Figure 17.1   Organic and mechanistic management structures

Clearly the organization must decide on its own management needs and style depending on the match of internal resources with external opportunity. What is of critical importance is the decision to use an internal resource or an external consultancy to meet its design needs. There are strong arguments in favour of both approaches. Those organizations which establish in-house teams make a substantial commitment to the direct use of management time, the ongoing associated staff and space costs, equipment allocation, and so on. This commitment forces explicit recognition of the issues surrounding design.

The decision to use an external consultancy, however, is often not considered as explicitly. Because it is felt to be a low-risk option allowing a quick exit if something goes wrong, there tends to be less commitment to the design function. However, to maximize the match of resource to opportunity demands commitment to make the process work. Designers, while having a broad range of skills and attributes, do not possess a magic wand. They need to work within defined parameters which can be established only by the careful investigation and evaluation of the matching process, and this can be done only with the explicit input of the commissioning company. This means an appointment at senior level to establish and control the necessary budgets, co-ordinate the information from all departments within the firm, establish time-scales and monitor the design programme against agreed criteria.

Decisions on how the external consultant is to be used must be made explicit. Is it necessary to concentrate on purely conceptual ideas? This may be the case where the company has become so production-orientated that it assumes internal constraints. Is the company too small to support the necessary staff on a full-time basis? Can the consultancy offer a range of skills unavailable in-house? Will an external consultant produce consistently better results 'because his life depends on it'? With a consultancy an unsuccessful scheme can be dispassionately aborted, where in-house there may be pressures preventing such a course of action. Whether the design resource is internal or external, management must make explicit the resources required and responsibility levels in the management structure. Both methods of organizing for design must be considered in the light of their contribution to the organization's future. Competitive success is born of commitment to the key issues in all senior management disciplines including the design function.

THE DESIGN METHOD

What follows is a description of a design process which has grown from the need to manage design for both in-house and external clients by a design consultancy which is part of a large holding group. As a group member the design consultancy offers a comprehensive service to each group company on a long-term basis. The service includes the design of the client's communications (both corporate and trading), the retail environment (architectural, interior and merchandising), the selection and design of the product as well as related packaging and graphics, and its fashion goods requirements. The result of this consistent commitment to design can be seen in the group's extraordinary expansion through organic growth and acquisition and merger, and its consistent level of profit despite the needs of a business in an expansionary phase of its life. The design skills on which this business rests were established over 30 years ago when the consultancy was the only element of the group in existence. The aspect of non-group consultancy was developed and expanded at the same time as the group business grew, reaching the point where it now offers a fully developed range of design skills to both group and non-group clients. As a result of this experience it has been able to develop a design method made up of several clearly identifiable stages, each complete in itself. This method is used to ensure that the design programme is kept on track, that it starts with the right information, that it suits the particular requirements of the individual company and that wherever possible risk is eliminated.

Risk limitation

Perceived risk is of central importance to the client using a design consultancy. Like all service businesses, the service cannot be stored, and the nature of the whole process is intangible. For all the success stories of similar clients with similar problems, there is always the doubt of possible failure. V. A. Zeithaml (1981) comments on the high level of perceived risk in services marketing. The article describes a continuum ranging from high search qualities (those attributes which can be established with certainty before purchase) through high experience qualities (those which cannot be determined before purchase but which can be evaluated afterwards) and high credence qualities (those which cannot be evaluated even after purchase). Risk increases from easy evaluation in the former case to difficult evaluation in the latter. Zeithaml places professional services in the difficult to evaluate (high credence qualities) sector where perceived risk in purchases is high. It is suggested that methods of risk reduction are critical in service businesses.

This is a most important factor to the consultancy, and leads to the involvement of the client as closely as is practicable in the whole process. Risk reduction should start before the client contacts the consultancy, with the definition of the problem and evaluation of resources and opportunities as the first step. Once the client has established the basic criteria he or she is in a position to discuss the formulation of the brief and to evaluate the correct consultancy to undertake the work.

The brief

The brief is all-important. It establishes the boundaries of the problem, the methods and extent of the work to be done, and the time-scales and budgets within which results are expected. It is in the context of the brief that a sound estimate of time expenditure and therefore cost can be evaluated, and critical decision points can be established. Substantial input from the client is required at this stage and understanding of the problem is reflected back from the designer. Clear understanding of the problem, the manufacturing constraints, the market objectives and the timing, eliminates the first element of perceived risk.

Orientation

This stage is the development of an appropriate 'visual language' to be used to guide the designer's hand. Orientation is a useful method of visually interpreting qualitative market data which describe several different 'segment opportunities' in terms of appearance and consumer lifestyle. The client can see his or her research in pictures. It is important because it imposes agreed constraints on the problem in terms of appearance and materials. In terms of ranges of appropriate products available off the shelf it identifies product gaps very early in the programme. This eliminates an endless search for ill-defined ideas and starts to manage the process in a disciplined way. It also seeks the direct involvement of the client at an early key decision point, ensuring that the programme does not put the company beyond its ability to cope with the change inherent in product development and design. It is also reassurance that the designer has fundamentally understood the brief.

Sketch design

Following agreement on which visual language should be adopted to suit the now explicit characteristics of the end-user, the next stage is the generation of design concepts. These must meet the objectives of both the identified customer base and the organizational resources available. Commonly known as 'sketch concepts', the ideas are generated in volume with detail limited to critical areas. The ideas must conform to the criteria agreed in the previous stages and give the client the widest variety of choice and stimulus. Despite the focusing effect of earlier work, the designer will still produce a bewildering array of conceptual work conforming to the criteria laid down. Depending on the nature of the programme there may be several decision points during this stage, forcing client and designer continually to target or refocus the design effort, evaluating and refining earlier ideas and directions.

Often the client will be starting preliminary costings now to ensure that those ideas widely off target can be eliminated. So further risk is removed through the creative collaboration of both client and designer. At the end of this phase there will be no unexpected shocks or utterly impossible propositions, although through the collaboration the client's view of the end-product may well change substantially as alternatives are generated and evaluated.

The working relationship between designer and client enables the decision-making process to be approached in a dispassionate manner when selecting the concepts to be taken to the next phase. The origin of the ideas becomes submerged and the decisions are made jointly, avoiding conflict and maximizing the likelihood of a productive end result.

Design development

Following agreement on the appropriate concept, the next element in the programme is the detailed development of the design. This stage deals with the
refinement of all the external, user-orientated aspects of the product. Given
the designer's knowledge of the manufacturing system the product idea is
developed both in general form and in detail. This stage reconciles the needs of
the manufacturing process and the end-user. It is an integrative stage, developing the best match of resources to opportunity and incorporating cost constraints, profit requirements and so on. It is at this stage that the client's
technical personnel have a greater input into the process, advising on technical feasibility and cost, while the designer works to ensure that the original
concept is not lost to purely technical expedience. A product which satisfies
the perfect operational manufacturing criteria but which will not sell is value-
less.

As an aid to evaluation it is often useful and necessary to produce a sketch
model. This is a three-dimensional representation of the product which allows
assumptions about size and proportion of the drawn form to be checked thoroughly. It is extremely cost-effective in that it prevents too much detailed
development taking place in the wrong area or according to the wrong dimen-
sional criteria. The combination of sketch model and detailed visuals allows a
proper assessment of the product's physical and visual characteristics, having taken into account all the critical manufacturing and financial criteria.
Once again the emphasis is on eliminating perceived risk. The committed
input of technical personnel now starts to limit actual risk in manufacturing as
well.

Measured drawings and model-making

The final design stages involve the production of fully measured drawings
and the building of a finished model or prototype. Here again, the input of the
manufacturing company is crucial in controlling costs of design and product
manufacture. While the designer is capable of producing toleranced piece-
part drawings, this usually proves unnecessarily expensive, and where possible the task should be undertaken by the manufacturer. The production
of general arrangement drawings, showing all key control dimensions of the
fully assembled product, is in most cases adequate and relatively inexpensive.
The choice between model-making and prototyping will depend on the manufacturing method. Where there is a substantial tooling commitment, modelling
the product in its finished form is the only method to adopt. This will allow the
highly finished model to be used in final market testing and appraisal before
committing to tooling and other associated launch costs.

Implementation

Following the final costings of piece parts, sub-assemblies, final assembly and the amortization of tooling, the final stage is to commit to production and implement the new product. Once again, it is essential that there is commitment from the designer to protect the marketable idea from excessive manufacturing constraints which might dilute it and make it unsaleable. The support and appraisal during the implementation phase by both the designer and manufacturing staff are extremely important in ensuring the maximization of the product's value in the market-place. The design industry is littered with examples of time and effort wasted due to the lack of resources for this phase. The successful product sells, performing well against all criteria laid down. The product lacking implementation resource can only fail.

Packaging

One might think that at the successful conclusion of the implementation phase the role of design is over. This is not the case. Very few products can be transported or displayed or even sold without some form of packaging and branding, ticketing, guarantees, instructions and so on.

These aspects must also be considered explicitly in terms of costs and benefits. A good product with poor shelf presence ceases to attract the end-user in the competitive environment. At an early stage therefore it is necessary to establish what routes of distribution are to be used, and the criteria for the packaging and two-dimensional design work. Is the packaging to be protective, or is it decorative? What competitive products exist, and what is their market presence? What information about the product must be displayed, and how? The opportunity to use these elements to add value, to influence the purchase decision, and reinforce the choice of the end-user should not be missed.

However, it is often ill-conceived, and not considered part of the whole bundle of benefits made available to the customer. It is an area where the integrative skills of the designer can maximize the marketing opportunity by ensuring a product solution which meets the user's needs and aspirations, and is internally consistent in every aspect.

CONCLUSION

This chapter has attempted to confront some of the issues surrounding the role of product design within the company. It has examined the interface between design and marketing, arguing that it allows a visual assessment of marketing criteria, and that its proper management will often cause necessary shifts in marketing thinking.

It has shown that the design process affects all areas of corporate life. To achieve maximum benefit from the integrative skills of the designer, the place of design in the management hierarchy must be at senior level. If the discipline is to be subordinated to any other business function, this will impose severe limitations on the design function, preventing it from seeking product solutions which adequately match company needs and resources with market opportunity.

Whether the company chooses to use an internal team or an external consultancy, the need for management and other resources must be made clear. No amount of product design expertise will guarantee success if commitment in terms of time, money and information is not made at senior level.

Finally, a well-tried design method was discussed. This breaks the design process down into distinct and manageable phases, encouraging client input at all key decision points, thereby reducing perceived and actual risk.

The design process touches every aspect of corporate existence, from production to finance, marketing, distribution and so on. If it is to work effectively across all business disciplines, the approach to design must consciously deal with the issues of its place in the company hierarchy, its resourcing, management and design method.

An increasingly global market and shortening product life cycles put great pressure on companies to change. A key element in the management of change is the use of the creative and integrative skills of the designer, to ensure that competitive new products reach the market in a form which clearly matches the ability of the company to produce them at a profit with the desire of the consumer to buy them.

REFERENCES

Archer, L. B. (1974), *Design Awareness and Planned Creativity in Industry*, London: The Design Council.

Lorenz, C. (1986), *The Design Dimension: Product Strategy and the Challenge of Global Marketing*, Oxford: Blackwell.

Oakley, M. (1984), *Managing Product Design*, London: Weidenfeld and Nicolson.

Zeithaml, V. A. (1981), 'How consumer evaluation processes differ between goods and services', in *Marketing of Services*, Chicago: American Marketing Association.

ESSENTIAL READING

Gorb, P. (ed.) (1990), *Design Management*, London: ADT Press.

Hollins, W. and Pugh, S. (1991), *Successful Product Design: What to Do and When*, Oxford: Butterworth Heinemann.

Lorenz, C. (1990), *The Design Dimension*, Oxford: Basil Blackwell.

The Design Management Journal, published quarterly by The Design Management Institute, Boston.

USEFUL ADDRESS

The Design Council, Haymarket House, No. 1 Oxendon Street, London, SW1Y 4EE. Offers a range of services to industry including help on design problems, defining design opportunities, training requirements and guidance on support schemes.

18 Packaging as a marketing tool
Bill Stewart

Packaging is becoming increasingly recognized by marketing professionals as one of the most powerful tools available to them. The days when pack design could be relegated to a purely functional role are long gone. In this chapter we shall consider why packaging justifies marketing attention, the tasks packaging must perform and the potential for maximizing this performance.

THE IMPORTANCE OF PACKAGING AS A MARKETING TOOL

Packaging in one form or another has been part of human civilization for a long time. Historically, its use was restricted to being the medium for collating produce. We may assume that archaeological artefacts such as pots and jars were indeed items of packaging designed to hold powders and liquids. No doubt less durable materials were used but did not stand the test of time – early biodegradable packaging! While the containment role of packaging, therefore, has long been recognized, it is only in recent times that the promotional aspects have begun to be fully appreciated. Until around 25 years ago, there were no specialist packaging designers in the UK although they were already playing a part in marketing activities within the USA. In Britain, there were graphic designers, packaging engineers specializing in the technical aspects of packaging and packaging suppliers who also offered design services restricted to their particular packaging medium.

As the level of marketing sophistication grew, so the need for true specialists increased. Taking a lead from the pattern established in the USA, in-house packaging engineering departments offering a limited design role and packaging consultancies were established to service the expanding needs of the marketing function. Even then, few organizations could offer a total service combining graphic and technical disciplines. Today, with packaging accounting for around 3 per cent of the UK gross national product, its importance is firmly established. Design, in general, has now been accepted as a means of increasing sales, albeit rather late in the day for much of British industry. Nevertheless, the increasingly high calibre of marketing personnel recognizes that imaginative packaging design, if used correctly, forms an integral part of marketing strategy. Consultancies too have recognized the need for change and many now provide a full service from graphic and structural design through to computer-generated 'artwork'.

There is little doubt that, historically, the most important influence on packaging has been the rise of self-service outlets. Often the pack is the only sales aid available at point of purchase. Informed assistants are generally not available to explain the product's attributes; the pack itself must do this, and, if the product is to be successful, do it better than the competition. The UK retail grocery sector currently operates on around a 96 per cent self-service basis. The picture varies throughout Europe with Italy, for example, changing rapidly from traditional retail outlets to the supermarket pattern of shopping found in the UK and France.

It would be wrong to suggest that packaging is the only tool to assist the marketing function. Amongst others, advertising plays a major role although it is significant that many adverts feature the packed product, often, in the case of TV commercials, as the closing shot.

Although the retail grocery area accounts for a huge slice of consumer spend, there are other areas to self-service where packaging plays an equally important part. Out-of-town superstores, the so-called 'sheds', sell a wide variety of prepacked goods, with car spares and DIY materials being of prime importance. Here, where goods often require complex and technical selection, the pack must work even harder.

So far, we have mentioned the retail trade. Wholesale operations too have been affected by the trend to self-service. Cash-and-carry outlets are a further example of the selection of goods being influenced by pack design. After all, in some respects the wholesale pack must perform the same functions as its retail derivative, even though in collations of prime units.

WHAT PACKAGING MUST DO

All packs must meet several criteria although the degree of emphasis on individual aspects will vary according to the product nature and markets envisaged. All aspects should nevertheless be considered. Failure to do so is likely to result in packaging problems which ultimately reflect on the product itself and could create lack of faith in that product and possibly the brand itself.

Containment

The first function of packaging is to contain the product. Instances of pack failure – leaking bottles and bags – are becoming increasingly rare. The negative impact on repeat purchase and damage to the brand have become well recognized. Tamper-evident features are now incorporated into many packs as a result of much-publicized cases of product adulteration. While this no doubt acts as a deterrent and a safeguard, sadly those who wish to contaminate products for malice or gain have become more skilful at gaining access to products despite tamper-evident measures. Theft from prepacked goods, 'shrinkage' as the trade would term it, is yet another unsavoury feature of modern retailing. Many multiples are critical of pack styles which permit goods to be removed while the pack appears intact. Currently there is a conflict concerning small products, commonly blister-packed on to a relatively large backcard designed to prevent goods being slipped into a pocket or bag. From an environmental viewpoint, this is overpacking. Retailers do not necessarily agree. In Germany, the use of larger than necessary backcards for preventing theft is specifically disallowed under the Packaging Ordinance of May 1991.

The use of child-resistant closures has become mandatory for some product categories, to make access to hazardous products difficult for children. It often makes it difficult for adults too, and, in particular for those with arthritic or muscular problems.

Packs need to contain product effectively, maintain product integrity, perhaps incorporating tamper-evident features, yet allow ease of opening, product dispensing and subsequent re-closure. Consumer research shows a marked aversion to packs which are difficult to open. Biscuits are the most often cited in this respect. The standard response from the packaging industry has been that the consumer has a choice: soggy biscuits or a pack that may be slightly inconvenient to open. Furthermore, the industry has been rather too ready to suggest that the problem is due to the consumer's lack of training. After all, argues the industry, a tin of beans needs a tin opener and the consumer accepts this without question; in the same way, some packs require the use of common household equipment to open them. The implication is that the answer is to 'educate' consumers.

While this may have been the case when the consumer was faced with little choice, this attitude will not win sales where multiple choice is now often the norm. We ignore the consumer at our peril. Insufficient attention to the consumer's needs is not only arrogant but short-sighted in today's competitive climate. Manufacturers seem to be waking up to these realities and we see, in the instance of our biscuit example, the incorporation of tear tape to assist opening.

Protection

Protection is a basic technical requirement applicable to all packaging. Products must be presented to the consumer in pristine condition or hard-won brand values will be jeopardized. Additionally, the energy invested in the product and the pack will have been wasted which, in environmental terms, represents a misuse of resources, materials and energy. It is important that the hazards likely to be experienced by the product are identified throughout the distribution chain. These can be broadly divided into two categories: transit and climatic hazards.

Transit hazards are those physical hazards encountered during the product's journey from manufacture, through storage and distribution to the point of sale and, ultimately, to the end-consumer. Inevitably, multiple handling will be involved during this cycle, the extent and severity of which will depend upon the nature of the journey, methods of handling, and weight and size of the product. Collations of unit packs are also a factor in determining the level of handling likely to be encountered. Transit damage results from impact brought about by dropping, crushing through excessive stacking, and vibration during transport. Pack design must take such hazards into account, initially by use of material and pack-style performance data, tempered by design experience with similar products and distribution cycles. Subsequent testing, either using simulated transit conditions or an actual test run, will soon reveal problems.

Climatic damage is likely to result from damp, excessive heat or cold, or indeed any combination of these. Remember that, even if the product withstands such climatic variations, the pack may not. A weakened pack may lead to transit damage in these circumstances.

Legal compliance

Packaging must of course comply with the law in all respects. The requirement will vary considerably depending upon the nature of the product, the countries of sale and type of transport used. With greater attention being paid to safety, legal requirements are becoming increasingly more complex. Greater consumer awareness, governmental actions and the trend to more international trade have all played a part in this. While, in the past, some manufacturers may not have adopted quite such a responsible attitude as they should have done, the move towards strict liability has encouraged greater compliance. Disasters directly attributable to packaging are, in these circumstances, likely to attract prison sentences in addition to huge financial penalties. In the extreme, leaking chemicals which are a contributory cause of, say, an aircraft crash, could have serious repercussions for even the largest of companies. Aircraft are not cheap! It is not appropriate here to detail the many legal requirements which require consideration; this is itself becoming a specialist area of the packaging operation. Suffice it to say that legal clearance should be obtained as a matter of course.

Environmental considerations

Packaging has assumed a high profile within the environmental debate, partly because it is a very visible form of waste and partly because packaging is an everyday experience for most of us. While there has been a notable lack of governmental action in the UK, most countries within the EU have already put in place some form of legislation. The EU Commission has produced a draft directive in an attempt to harmonize environmental action throughout the community. It is not anticipated that this will be ratified by the UK and others much before the turn of the century.

Germany has assumed the lead role in Europe with a dramatic piece of legislation specifically aimed at reducing packaging levels and encouraging recycling and reuse. In fact, packaging waste can only be disposed of by recycling or reuse. There are no other options such as landfill or incineration. The German experiment has largely been successful and there is little doubt that the rest of Europe will eventually adopt many of the same tactics, which are being reflected in the draft EU directive. It is likely that energy recovery through controlled emission incineration will be allowed, possibly even Germany rethinking this option.

Until the UK introduces an infrastructure on a national basis for the sorting and disposal of household waste packaging, the environmental problems of packaging will be tackled on an *ad hoc* basis. In the meantime, exports have to meet an array of national legislation in other countries. Happily, by meeting German requirements, we can be fairly sure that we will be complying with those of the rest of Europe.

In outline, packaging should meet the following criteria:

1 Establish whether packaging is necessary.
2 Remove secondary packaging if possible.
3 Do not overpack.
4 Use the most energy-efficient materials appropriate to the task.
5 Consider recycling where this is a cost-efficient option.
6 Use recycled material.
7 Try to use one material throughout the pack structure.
8 Mark packs with an indication of material nature.

Packaging should not be considered as having only a negative impact on the environment. We should remember that packaging also prevents product spoilage, extends consumer choice and provides convenience for busy lifestyles.

Identification

Packaging must identify the contents. This is applicable to all types of packaging, whether it be military equipment, car components or cornflakes. In many instances, text is supplemented by machine-readable barcodes and, increasingly, either covert or overt security marking to prevent counterfeiting. Identification has legal significance through Trade Description legislation and other product-specific requirements.

Promotion

Promotion in this context means the pack acting as a positive selling agent, promoting the product. It does not mean special offers. The first task of packaging is to stand out visually against competing brands. Shoppers rapidly scan shelves: successful packaging has to arrest attention. It must achieve this in the prevailing lighting conditions at point of sale and must be distinctive when compared to other products in close proximity. These are likely to be competitive products but may also be other classes of goods.

The principal tools available here are shape, colour and texture. Individual circumstances will dictate which of these will be most effective. It is worth noting that shape is often the most potent feature and yet is often most neglected. Some products are instantly recognizable by shape alone – the Perrier bottle can be recognized at distances well beyond the ability to read the label. Shape can be used in this way to create a unique brand identity, promoting the brand without recourse to graphics.

Cost

The criteria outlined above must be achieved in a cost-effective manner. It is important that the total cost be considered, not simply the cost of the pack itself. This should include labour in assembly, storage and transport as well as material cost, if a true picture is to be obtained.

WHAT PACKAGING CAN DO

By use of good design, both graphic and structural, the opportunities provided by packaging can be exploited to the full. The product, however, must live up to the expectations conveyed by the pack. If the anticipated promise suggested by the packaging remains unfulfilled, the product will ultimately fail.

A good design is one which meets the objectives laid down in the marketing brief. It can be judged by these criteria and, if the brief is correct, by the sales generated. Other judgements are subjective and of relatively little value. The aim should be not to win design awards or to be clever for its own sake, but simply to be on target with marketing requirements.

The designer, nevertheless, should exercise his or her ability by challenging the brief, moving outside it to explore fresh areas and then narrowing down to the demands of the brief once more. In this way, both designer and client can be sure that all design directions have been adequately explored. Those directions which, clearly, are inappropriate can be rejected, allowing design time to be concentrated on those candidates showing most potential.

Imagery

Packaging is a superb medium to create product imagery through the use of shape, surface graphics, colour and texture. It is vital that marketing management is clear about the image they wish the product, and hence the pack, to project. Often, it can be very useful to have an input from the advertising agency. They may have a slightly different perspective to that held by marketing, itself of value but, importantly, their views tend to focus on imagery as a vital advertising ingredient. Where imagery is not clear or, worse still, incorporates conflicting imagery, the pack will need to work much harder to convey more than one message. The result often has the effect of diluting each individual imagery component and introducing blandness or mixed messages in the design. This should be avoided if pack strength, in imagery terms, is a fundamental requirement for product sales. It is a marketing responsibility to identify imagery and to communicate it clearly to the designer.

When the required imagery has been identified, the designer's role will be to achieve it within the parameters of the brief. Most design studies are a compromise between conflicting requirements. Practical considerations must inevitably assume greater importance as the study progresses. There is little point in meeting imagery targets when the cost of production, for example, is well above the budget set or indeed impractical in any other way.

It is important to recognize that shape is significant in aligning the pack with its imagery, an area often neglected in favour of surface graphic treatments alone. If, for example, the product is a luxury shower gel aimed specifically at the female market, then the pack may need to be 'soft' in image terms. Clearly, features such as hard edges may be inappropriate. This often poses a problem for the designer who may, for several reasons, be limited in the choice of packaging media. There simply might not be sufficient latitude to select materials or processes which allow the use of soft curves, although it should be stressed that every opportunity should be taken to try to incorporate a medium which does reflect the imagery requirements. In this instance, the only available options may be to use texture or surface graphics to achieve the desired effect.

It would be misleading to conclude from the above that graphics represent a fall-back position when shape options are exhausted. The optimum design solutions are achieved when structural pack design and graphics are developed in tandem, each augmenting the other. Indeed, the twin disciplines of technical and graphic design can never truly be separated. Technical designers know the limitations of the processes and materials with which they are working while, largely unfettered by such constraints, graphic designers can visualize the desired end-effect. Between them, imaginative and practical solutions emerge with physical shape and graphics in harmony.

Every opportunity should be taken to build consumer benefits into the packaging. This is one way of differentiating your pack from the competition and providing a further reason for purchase. Be warned, however, such benefits must actually work in a practical sense. Consumers quickly learn to avoid packs which do not function as well as expected. Ideally, any consumer benefit should be readily perceived without recourse to printed explanations. If, for example, it is thought that a liquid product which is poured in use requires a handle to ease dispensing, the container should be designed so that 'pourability' is visually communicated at a glance. The pack has not only to perform well but also look as though it has been designed for performance. The total design should indicate how the product works.

Table 18.1
Checklist 1 – General information

This checklist covers the points to be checked with regard to the product and the market.

1   The market:

- Total size – volume and value – trends – brand fragmentation and shares.
- Regionality.
- Seasonality.
- Wholesale distribution breakdown.
- Consumer profile:

    - Age.
    - Sex.
    - Socio-economic groups.
    - Special characteristics.

2   The product:

- History.
- Brand share.
- Description and usage.
- Frequency of purchase.
- Sizes.
- Prices.
- Advantages and disadvantages against competition.
- Brand loyalty.
- Regionality.
- Seasonality.
- Wholesale distribution breakdown:

    - By outlet type.
    - By counter versus self-service.
    - Direct.

- Prospect profile (existing/future):

    - Age.
    - Sex.
    - Socio-economic groups.
    - Special characteristics.

- Copy strategy.
- Planned advertising and promotion.

HOW TO USE PACKAGING AS A MARKETING TOOL

We have seen, in outline, the criteria that packaging must meet, and have looked at some areas where packaging is uniquely positioned to assist the marketing strategy. In this section, we can now begin to consider how the full potential of packaging as a marketing tool can be harnessed. There are no short cuts. Only by following a disciplined series of events, can you be sure that all opportunities and potential pitfalls have been given full consideration.

Conduct of the study

The study should be structured to follow a series of logical steps, the first of which consists of gathering further information.

No two design studies are the same. Each will vary according to the product type and the market to be entered. The activities described below must be regarded as the ideal pattern, one indeed typical of many studies.

Developing the brief

To direct packaging design work with the greatest possible accuracy, it is necessary first to build the fullest possible brief. Checklists 1 to 7 (see Tables 18.1 to 18.7) show the type of information which is needed, and will help build such a brief. Not all the points listed will be relevant to every study but they should all be considered. Checklist 1 covers the general information on the market and the product's position in that market, which will be applicable to any study. Checklists 2 to 6 deal separately with the facts required for a technical design on the one hand and a graphic design on the other. Finally, checklist 7 (Table 18.7) covers administrative information.

The information demanded by the checklists is typical of that needed by packaging design agencies, but is equally applicable for briefing other groups servicing market requirements such as, for example, advertising agencies.

Table 18.2
Checklist 2 – Technical design requirements

The points refer to the requirements of the consumer and the product.

1 Design objectives:

(Here list specific design objectives)

- New design/revolutionary/evolutionary.
- Design continuity/analysis of existing elements.
- Imagery.
- Standout.
- Range integration/extension.
- Competitors.
- Countries of sale.

Table 18.2 continued

2   *Consumer requirements:*

- Ideal quantities, sizes, weights.
- Size/value for money impressions.
- Importance of:

  - Style.
  - Shape.
  - Colour.
  - Texture.
  - Product visibility.

- Requirement of consumers to inspect and handle prior to sale.
- Need for storage.
- In-use life required.
- Opening/closing/re-sealing requirements.
- Child-resistant/tamper-evident.
- Dispensing/extraction.
- Measuring.
- After use.
- Protection of the consumer against hazard from the product.

3   *Environmental considerations:*

- Appropriate pack for product.
- Minimum energy use in total life cycle.
- Minimum depletion of raw material resources.
- Waste at each stage of manufacture.
- Impact of post-consumer waste.
- Ability to be recycled/re-used.
- Absence of toxic material content.
- Compatibility with recycling/disposal infrastructure.
- Avoidance of overpacking.
- Single material or ease of segregating different materials.
- Materials properly identified.

4   *Product requirements:*

- Compatibility of materials and product.
- Product life/deterioration characteristics.
- Shelf life.
- Product size/weight/volume.
- Protection against:

  - Liquid/moisture.
  - Microbiological contamination.
  - Gases/odour.

Table 18.2 concluded

- Temperature extremes/thermal shock.
- Infestation.
- Light; UV/artificial.
- Mechanical damage:
    * Crushing.
    * Dropping.
    * Squeezing.
    * Puncture.
    * Additional transit hazards.

Table 18.3
Checklist 3 – Further technical design requirements

The points in the checklist refer to production and legal requirements.

1   Production requirements:

- Need for use of existing plant.
- Machinery, lines and manpower available.
- Opportunity for introduction to new processes and machinery.
- In-plant facilities for:

    - Material manufacture.
    - Package/component manufacture.
    - Printing/decoration.

- Tied or favoured suppliers.
- Suppliers who definitely should not be approached.
- Contract packaging.
- Cost breakdowns of existing packaging.
- Forecast sales quantities.
- Forecast purchasing quantities.
- Pack cost budget.
- Processes:

    - Sterilization.
    - Pre-weighing/metering.
    - Filling.
    - Closing/sealing.
    - Checkweighing/headspace.
    - Labelling/printing/decoration.
    - Overprinting.
    - Inspection/quality control.
    - Collation.
    - Outer packaging.

- Storage:

    - Methods.
    - Time requirements.

311

Table 18.3 concluded

- Stack weight/height restrictions.
- Pallet size/type.
- Despatch methods.

• Opportunities for standardization and cost reduction.

2 Legal requirements:

• UK.
• EU.
• National country of sale.
• UN.
• Transportation (local and international).
• Weights and measures.

Table 18.4
Checklist 4 – Further technical design requirements

The points in the checklist refer to the distribution and merchandising aspects of the technical design brief.

1 Distribution requirements:

• Methods of distribution:

- Mail order.
- Wholesaler.
- Retailer.
- Direct.

• Estimated length of time stored at:

- Warehouse.
- Wholesaler (including cash and carry).
- Retailer.
- Consumer.

• Method of:

- Transportation.
- Loading.
- Warehousing.
- Wholesale storage (including cash and carry).
- Retail storage.

• Importance of divisibility at all stages.
• Transportation weight requirements.
• Requirement of standardization for range.
• Anti-pilfering/tamper-evident requirements.

Table 18.4 concluded

2   *Merchandising requirements:*

- Size with own/other display fixtures.
- Use of planograms.
- Hanging slot configuration.
- Carded products:

    - Radius/square corners.
    - Price mark area.
    - Product orientation.
    - Product visibility.
    - Need for tactile product examination.

Table 18.5
Checklist 5 - Pack graphic design

Areas to be considered for graphic design projects.

1   *Design objectives:*

- New design.
- Redesign/updating:

    - Design continuity/analysis of existing elements.
    - Range intergration/extension.

2   *Consumer requirements:*

- Size impression.
- Appropriate pack for product.
- Importance of pack appearance in use.
- Preferred/associated colours.
- Usage instructions.

3   *Retail display requirements:*

- Shelf size.
- Estimated display life.
- Position of display:

    - Shelf.
    - Counter.
    - Dispenser.
    - Check-out.
    - Window.

Table 18.5 concluded

- Position in relation to purchaser:

  - Eye-level.
  - Above/below.
- Display by brand/product group.
- Panels most often seen:

  - Facings (front, back, top, sides, bottom).

- Lighting levels at point of display.
- Proximity:

  - Competitive products.
  - Other product lines.

4   *Wholesale display requirements (including cash and carry):*

- Need for coding/labelling on outer case.
- Degree of branding necessary.
- Need for subdivisible sales units.

5   *Production requirements:*

- Number of colours/varnish.
- Size of print area.
- Method of reproduction.
- Materials.
- Quantity.
- Run size.
- Artwork requirements.
- Cost limitations.

Table 18.6
Checklist 6 – Special graphic requirements

Additional considerations which apply specifically to graphic design studies.

1   *Special requirements:*

- Anticipated future copy changes.
- Foreign/multilingual copy.
- Price flashes.
- Promotional flashes.
- Barcodes.
- Need to tie in with advertising/point of sale.

Table 18.6 concluded

2 Legal requirements:

- Cautionary information to be included.
- Legislation to be observed:
  - Correct size and style of copy.
  - Content weight/volume declaration.
  - Ingredients copy, order and size.
  - Maker's/supplier's name and address.
  - Special claims.
  - Warning symbols
  - Use of EU symbols.

3 Restraints:

- Materials.
- Processes.
- Inks.
- Pack style/form.

Table 18.7
Checklist 7 – Administrative requirements

Administrative information which should be considered at an early stage of the project and at interim points throughout.

1 Time requirements for development and completion.
2 Availability of existing research.
3 Packaging research and testing planned for the project.
4 Need for additional shipping case or associated point of sale.

(Acknowledgement: The author acknowledges permission from Seibert/Head Ltd to reproduce, in modified form, the 'Checklist for a packaging brief' from which Checklists 1 to 7 are abstracted.)

Intake of additional information

Designers, however imaginative, are working to a brief and the results of their work will be measured by their success in meeting the design objectives. To understand fully what these objectives are, the designers' first task is to familiarize themselves with the market, the environment in which the product will be sold. While a casual stroll around a supermarket, for example, might yield some information, it really is insufficient. One of the most successful methods is to organize a structured store survey. This should be conducted in a number of outlets, representative of the product's distribution. The list of outlets to be visited needs careful selection in conjunction with the marketing depart-

315

ment. Allowance should be made for regional bias or variation, outlet sizes and degree of sophistication, location (out of town, high street and so on) and any other factors of importance to the product's sales pattern. International studies require similar detailed consideration for each country of sale.

A store survey looks for opportunities and limitations at point of sale. To assist in identifying these, measurements are required. Lighting levels at point of sale are of prime importance. If the product is often displayed in poor lighting conditions, any design will have to take this factor into account if the pack is to stand out. Stores are unlikely to alter their arrangements simply to assist you to sell your product. If, therefore, your product is going to be relegated to a poorly-lit area of the store, dark pack colours may be a poor choice. Lighting can be measured by using a camera set on one-thirtieth of a second, using a film speed of 200 ASA. The aperture required to allow photography at this setting can be recorded. Using these settings, experience shows that lighting levels of f4 and below are progressively poor, while those above f4 indicate good lighting.

It may also be important to know what facings are being displayed. For example in the case of a breakfast food cereal packed in a rectangular carton, the survey may indicate that more ends than fronts are displayed on the shelf. While the designer may concentrate on decorating the large main panel, he or she ignores the end at his/her peril. These should at least be branded and not, as is often the case, show barcodes only. We are not in the business of selling barcodes!

The third measurable factor in the store survey is to chart goods which are in proximity to our product, or its likely position should it be a new product. This involves charting those products which are above, below and to each side of our product in each of the locations being researched. In this way we can learn what packs our product needs to stand out against. In some instances, this might mean direct competitors but can often be products from our own company or totally different product lines. We may wish to make use of the association of surrounding products in a positive sense by deliberately designing in a link between our product and, say, the brand leader – a 'me-too' product – or concentrate on brand name being shared with another product in the range. Alternatively, we may wish to distance our product from all those around it, deliberately making it different in pack form and decoration. The choices are presented when the facts are available.

The store survey can be disciplined by the use of a simple form, an example of which is shown in Figure 18.1. In practice, the use of photography and colour slides in particular assists enormously with the analysis of store survey data. It is surprising how much more detail can be appreciated viewing slides in the relative calm of the office, rather than when caught up in the hustle and bustle of a busy supermarket.

Photography also enables a complete design team to participate and become familiar with the product's environment. It would be difficult to take a complete team of designers around each location; apart from the logistical problems, store managers are likely to object. Commercially too, there are obvious advantages to photography. Film is cheap, design time is expensive.

STORE SURVEY
CANNED READY MEALS

LIGHTING LEVEL | 1/30th sec: 200 ASA

BRAND	FACINGS	BRAND	FACINGS

PROXIMITY TEST

BRAND

GENERAL OBSERVATIONS

OUTLET NAME ....

OUTLET ADDRESS ....

CLASSIFICATION
Grocers
Multiple/Co-op/Independent Symbol/Independent
Self-Service/Counter Service

Figure 18.1   Simple store survey record form

In practice, it is not always easy to carry out photography in stores. Management actively discourage it unless specific permission has been granted, which takes time to obtain and often results in the store being artificially spruced up prior to the survey, not at all representative of normal conditions. Sadly, most store surveys have, through necessity, become rather furtive affairs although, in truth, stores have really nothing to hide.

Interviews with buyers are increasingly becoming a feature of many studies. This is true at both retail and wholesale level. With a large proportion of business in the hands of five or six companies, particularly in the retail grocery trade, it is nonsensical to commit to a repackaging programme without consulting the appropriate buyers at an early stage. Contrary to many marketing managers' fears, buyers are generally most helpful and willing to express their expert knowledge. Perhaps it is a refreshing change to be given the opportunity to comment on the pack forms they admire, what their stores wish to see in packaging terms for now and the future, and what packaging they definitely would not wish to see – rather than be subjected to a sales pitch. Also importantly, buyers can advise on merchandising requirements and arrange for planograms to be made available.

Factory visits are essential to understand the practical limitations and opportunities at the point of manufacture. Some information will have probably been included in the initial brief but there is no substitute for seeing the filling and packing lines at first hand. Again, photography can be a useful aid in analysing production methods after completing a factory visit. The total production process from goods inward through to the despatch bay needs to be studied. Of particular importance will be the condition and storage of packaging materials, the filling/packing lines, handling and warehousing of packed stock, and transport methods. Projects vary in character but where central distribution warehouses or wholesale warehouses play a role in the distribution chain, these also merit a visit. At each stage the opportunity should be taken to obtain information directly from those involved with the product and packaging. Typically, this might include production, quality assurance, warehousing and distribution staff, all of whom are likely to have an in-depth knowledge of the problems encountered. They will also have opinions on improvements together with practical experience of trying to cope with or introduce new ideas.

We have assumed that the original brief was a full one. Most studies will still require further input as the project progresses. It can be rewarding to include, for example, information from sales management which, after all, is at the forefront of the business. Sales and account managers know their markets and, in addition, may have to 'sell' any pack changes to their team. They will certainly have a view and it should be listened to .

By now, we will be in possession of a vast store of information, some fact and much opinion. It would be a mistake to regard the opinions of all those we have consulted to be correct. There will be contradictions, departmental defences, budgetary protection and company politics all playing a part. Surprisingly, there is usually a consensus of opinion on the leading issues. It is in the detail and implications of change that most companies find difficulties. Often, it is easier for someone removed from the day-to-day operations of the company to gain a fresh perspective, enabling them to set rational design parameters for the study.

The design stage

The design director must decide how much information the team needs to start the project. Too much information too early in the study may impair creativity; too little information too late may cause wasted time in pursuing unworkable solutions.

Where packaging studies involve both structural and graphic disciplines, it is preferable to identify first the technical design solutions, those pack forms and materials having most potential. This, however, should not be done in isolation. The most potent pack designs result from exploiting the harmony of both structure and graphics from an early stage, rather than considering graphics as an afterthought.

Stage 1, therefore, sees mainly conceptual technical work, often originating as sketches but fairly quickly progressing to three-dimensional mock-ups or computer-generated 3D images. While there is little doubt that computer technology has advanced rapidly, there really is little substitute for mock-ups which can be viewed and handled in the same way as the real thing. There is rarely one solution to a design problem so, at this point, there may be several candidates worthy of further development. Design is a combination of creative and analytical thought. Each creative solution requires analysis, checking against the brief and the requirements established from earlier store surveys, factory visits and discussions.

Once technical directions are established, graphic design can start to explore the options, probably concentrating on the main display panel but with a view to how the design can be interpreted on other pack surfaces. Research from store surveys will indicate how and where the pack is likely to appear on shelf. This is the time that such information must be put into practice, remembering always that the first duty of the pack is to stand out on shelf.

It is normal to present the full scope of work to the client together with the rationale for excluding some design routes and recommending others. The rationale must take account of all the factors involved in the project, including an indication of cost, environmental performance – practicalities as well as issues concerning imagery, standout and so on. We should also remember that at this point we may have the opportunity to produce a unique brand identity, established through shape alone.

Stage 2 of the design process will see further development of those directions agreed as having potential at the end of stage 1. Technically, we may see extensions to the range being progressed and, almost certainly, draft specifications established. Extensive graphic experiments take place, building on the outline directions from the previous stage. If a range of products is to be packed, a representative selection will probably be tackled to establish broad guidelines applicable to later implementation across the total range.

At the conclusion of this stage, the work is reviewed and presented together with firm recommendations. Should market research be required, it is generally introduced at this point of the study, probably requiring the production of highly finished models.

The third stage sees design refinement and fine tuning following the results of market research. Specifications will now become firm and final costings obtained. Any need for the incorporation of graphic variants to accommodate language changes, for example, are likely to take place at this point.

As a check, and before artwork proceeds, it is often worthwhile pausing to reflect on the attributes we are aiming to achieve:

- Standout – on shelf.
- Containment – of the product.
- Imagery – appropriate to the product and brand.
- Differentiation – from competitors.
- Adaptability – across ranges and language varients.
- Suitability – for the intended use of the product.
- Legalality – meets legal requirements.

If the pack meets all these criteria in full, it stands a fair chance of being successful.

Finally, as the fourth stage of our idealized study, artwork would be prepared to the printer's requirements. With computerized systems now being the norm, traditional artwork has largely been superseded by its electronic equivalent. Most design studios will prepare artwork on disc or transmit artwork via a modem link directly to the printer. Proofs are still necessary for most print applications, requiring sign-off by the client. Where required, quality control procedures and corporate design manuals may follow.

By tackling the problems in a logical sequence, as outlined in this chapter, the packaging project can be tailored to a critical path analysis plan, ensuring that no deadlines are missed and no areas overlooked.

USEFUL ADDRESS

Institute of Packaging, Sysonby Lodge, Nottingham Road, Melton Mowbray, LE13 0NU. The Institute of Packaging is the only UK organization for individual packaging professionals.

19 Pricing as a marketing tool
Rory Morgan

In a competitive enterprise system, price flexibility is an essential enabling mechanism that stimulates the creation of desired goods, and removes gluts caused by over-production. In every price-controlled system, two views exist: that of the *producer,* and that of the *consumer.* From the earliest societies that used money rather than barter as a basis for the exchange of goods, setting the correct price level – the level that balances the interests of both parties – has exercised the greatest minds. The satirist Juvenal, speaking in classical times, noted that 'here in Rome, all things can be had', but added the wry consumerist aside 'at a price'.

Nevertheless, before the development of modern economic theory, price setting by the producer relied almost entirely on practical experience, 'gut feel' and the immediate feedback of market outcomes. While many would argue that this still remains the basis of many marketing price decisions, there is no doubt that the usefulness of the economic tradition, first expounded by Adam Smith and David Ricardo nearly two centuries ago, has been to stimulate the investigation of markets for *systematic* relationships between the price of goods and the subsequent demand for them (or vice versa).

THE THEORY

A fundamental notion in classical economics is that of the *demand function.* In its simplest form, the argument is that in a given market, and for a given price, there is a level of quantity demanded. This level of demand can be expressed as sales volume, brand share and so on, but ultimately represents the degree to which the 'consumer' is prepared to accede to the prices imposed by the 'producer'. A possible graphical representation of this relationship is shown in Figure 19.1 which shows a linear function. Since every line has its mathematical equation, the equation that expresses the relationship between price and

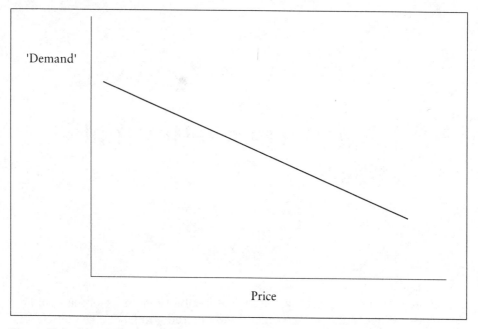

Figure 19.1   Linear demand curve

demand is known as the *demand equation,* and the resulting graph the *demand curve.*

There are a few points to note about this curve. First, as can be seen the slope of the curve is downwards, or *negative,* implying that demand decreases as prices rise (or conversely, that demand increases as prices fall). Most markets comply with this, although it is worth pointing out that some do not: for example, products with great 'snob' appeal, or luxury markets in general often reverse the slope so that demand rises as prices rise.

Clearly, there must be a point on the price axis where this relationship no longer holds, generally at the extremes of very low and very high price. Nevertheless, the rule may well apply within the price bounds normally encountered in the market. (This reversal is also true for markets with negative slopes to the demand curve – if a huge price were charged, it may instil in consumers' minds the notion that there must be something special about the product, and hence increase its value.) An important point about demand curves is that they refer to local phenomena of pricing, and should not be extrapolated too far.

The slope of the demand curve is of great interest, therefore, since it indicates the magnitude of response to price changes. This rate of response is termed the *elasticity of demand.* If the curve were perfectly horizontal, there would be no demand for notionally a very large change in price, and the demand in the market would be described as being perfectly *inelastic.* In contrast, a vertical (or near vertical) curve suggests dramatic changes in demand for very little change in price, that is, demand is *elastic.*

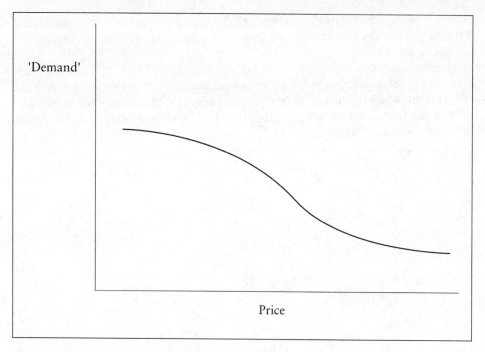

Figure 19.2   Curvilinear demand curve

However, in real life, many markets do not possess linear demand curves, and the relationship between price and resulting demand is less regular. This is particularly true when the demand for particular products is considered. For example, Figure 19.2 shows the typical 'S'-shaped curve found in many branded markets. As can be seen, at the extremes of low and high price, the demand is considerably more inelastic, but quite elastic in between.

This is explained as follows: in many competitive markets, a very low price will not attract all the possible buyers to the product, since there will be some who are not aware of it, or do not have it available, or who are strongly attached to other products. Further decreases in price therefore attract diminishing numbers of customers – hence the curve at the low price end will tend to the horizontal. At the other extreme of high price, the loyal buyers of the product will be more resistant to switching as high prices are encountered – hence the curve in this region will again tend to the horizontal. The region in between represents the switching in and out of more price-sensitive consumers, and the curve in the mid-price region will therefore show greater elasticity of demand.

In these curvilinear situations, there is no single measure of a product's price elasticity, since the slope of the curve depends upon the point at which price is measured. It is usual therefore to agree a band either side of a particular price, and define the *price elasticity* of that price as the percentage change in demand resulting from a percentage change in price. Since slopes are commonly downwards, elasticities are generally negative in value. For example, if a 1 per cent increase in price results in a 4 per cent drop in demand, the elasticity would be −4.

The significance of this figure can be best seen in revenue terms. If the elasticity is −1, sales will rise or fall by the same percentage as prices change, and total revenue will therefore be unaffected. However, an elasticity greater than −1 implies that revenue will rise if prices rise, and conversely fall for cases where the elasticity is less than −1.

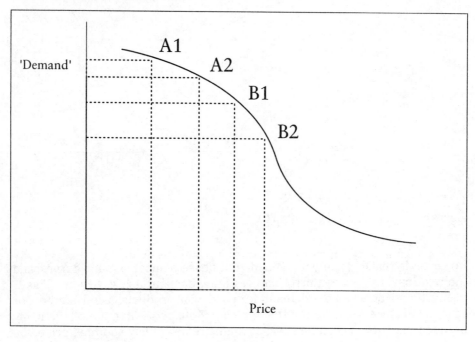

Figure 19.3   Evaluating price changes

It should be clear that knowledge of the shape of the demand function is essential for price setting. For example, in Figure 19.3, a product priced at point A1 is in a quite different situation from one priced at point B1. The demand curve at price A1 represents a 'plateau' situation where an increase in price to A2 would incur only a small drop in demand. However, a product priced on the 'cliff' at B1 would suffer a considerably greater loss in demand if it increased its price to B2, even though the price increase were the same in both cases.

Note also that in some markets, *thresholds* exist, often involving the 'next rounded value', such as £1, or even 10p intervals for some low-priced products. These thresholds exhibit themselves as local discontinuities in the demand curve, or 'steps'.

THE PROBLEM FOR THE PRODUCER

While it is true that some markets are exempt from concern for correct price setting (for example, highly competitive markets at one extreme, and highly oligopolized markets at the other), most marketing concerns have some latitude in setting prices, and therefore must face continual pricing decisions. This is as true for non-manufacturing organizations (such as those providing services) as for manufacturers. While in many cases the need is the simple one of maximizing sales (and/or profits), it is clear that this must be done in the context of the particular constraints facing the marketing organization, together with its strategic objectives.

While this chapter concentrates on method rather than objective, it is worthwhile noting that the objectives of price setting can vary considerably.

'Internal' objectives

For example, the need may be to *reduce* price to gain product trial among customers (penetration), or, in stark contrast, to *raise* price where the increase in line profits more than offsets the likely loss in sales volume.

Moreover, price alteration strategies may be undertaken in differing contexts. Thus the marketing goal may reflect needs as different as that of promoting a new product recently launched, or of treating an ageing brand or product as a 'cash cow' to fund other parallel developments.

Equally, pricing policy may reflect the need to meet internal organizational targets such as a satisfactory rate of return on the investment made. What is almost certain is that different pricing policies will be required for products at different points in their life cycles.

'Competitor' objectives

In addition to 'internal' constraints, pricing decisions frequently reflect the constraints facing the competitors, in a fixed market within which a number of marketing organizations operate.

Perhaps the simplest objective of a pricing strategy here would involve the need to maintain, grow, or control the decline of a particular product's or brand's share of the market, whether this be expressed in volume (for example thousands of cases, or tonnage) or monetary value (for example 'sterling' share).

In competitive situations, price setting is frequently complicated by differing production overhead costs encountered by different organizations, leading to differing profit levels for similar products. Here the decision making frequently incorporates some notion of the capacity of a competitor to respond to a price change initiated by one organization. This is one of a number of scenarios which can lead to long and protracted pricing wars: the threat of rapid retaliatory price cutting acting as a barrier to the entry of new competitors, or as a means of waging a lengthy war of attrition against a less-favoured competitor.

In general, competitive markets provide some of the greatest problems for price setting, since theoretical demand analysis conducted at the consumer level often does not provide for an estimate of competitor reactions. Frequently, the 'room for manoeuvre' on pricing is less than expected, since the market may well have formed a dynamic equilibrium that will tolerate only small price movements before 'self-correcting' price reactions are triggered among competitors.

Consumer objectives

In some cases, pricing strategy may react to the knowledge that sensitivity to price can vary considerably between consumers: that is, there are those consumers who are very *price conscious*, and who would be very likely to switch products in the event of a price change; and those who are particularly attached – or loyal – to a particular product or service, and who would tolerate quite large changes in price before contemplating switching. Clearly, not everyone can be described in such black-and-white terms, and this distinction represents the two extremes of a dimension upon which most consumers can be positioned.

Nevertheless, knowledge of the composition of the consumer market-place expressed in these terms is invaluable for some pricing policies, since it allows the producer to target a product or service to particular segments, possibly in the light of current production or distribution constraints. For example, a 'skimming' policy would price a new product high to gain a premium from likely loyal buyers, even at the expense of failing to attract price-conscious buyers who would require a lower price before buying. Later in the product life cycle, perhaps when production capacity has been built up, greater distribution achieved, and competitors have entered the market, the price can be reduced both to appeal to a wider group, and to present greater difficulties to competition.

Strategies such as these, however, obviously require a good knowledge of the segmentation of the market in these terms, and the sizes of relevant groups. While this can be acquired by the trial-and-error method, specific research techniques have been developed to quantify this issue.

'Trade' objectives

While the consumer is the ultimate arbiter of success or failure of a pricing strategy, the growing trend of the concentration of the retail trade (in the fast moving grocery sector as well as the durables sector) in most developed countries means that the modern producer has, in practice, an intermediate customer, and by *force majeure* has relinquished to the retailer a good deal of control over end-pricing. This has a number of consequences.

In some cases the retailer in effect sets the end-price, and has taken over the role of the producer. Many of the arguments made above therefore now apply to the retailer and it remains for the manufacturer to negotiate (possibly via volume discounting) satisfactory distributor margins. Of course, since the interest of the retailer is ultimately concerned with the *volume* of sales (at a given margin), the manufacturer is faced with presenting convincing arguments (for example from market research, previous track record, support media expenditure and so on) that satisfactory sales volume will in fact be achieved. Given that failure to meet retailer objectives in these situations can lead to de-listing, and that an unprecedented proportion of sales in some markets is now concentrated in the hands of a progressively smaller number of retailers, one outcome is that responsibility for trade negotiations is becoming increasingly centralized, and less the function of a salesforce.

In other cases, the manufacturer can heavily influence the end-price, or even dictate it. Alternatively the retailer is allowed the flexibility to alter the end-price by offering the consumer discounts. In either case, the manufacturer has determined the price to the trade, but needs to ensure that sufficient margin exists to provide a reasonable incentive to the distributor. This can lead to pricing policies which have more to do with maintaining trade margins, than presenting the end-consumer with consistent prices (the motor car industry is an example).

THE PROBLEM FOR THE CONSUMER

It takes two parties to make a contract, and if the producer has one viewpoint, the other side of the price-setting coin is the final purchaser. Underlying the 'demand' stimulated by a particular pricing strategy lie the large number of individual consumers who have chosen to accept the price, or who have chosen not to. Moreover, the average elasticity of demand in a market may or may not be a good representation of the many individual consumers who will have widely varying degrees of price sensitivity.

In this context, price plays a psychological role to the consumer. There are a number of aspects to this, and as we shall see later, these have a considerable impact on the research methodologies designed to assist price setting (Morgan, 1987a).

Price as information

To the producer, changes in price represent deliberate responses to marketing pressures, and priced products are therefore, in legal terms, unemotional 'propositions to treat'. To the consumer, however, prices often represent more than cold economic utility. Work originally carried out by Stoetzel in 1954 suggested that price possesses a psychological *information content* to would-be purchasers, as do pricing movements. For example, a price reduction may well reflect general price trends in the market, but may signal to the customer a variety of other messages: the item may be faulty; or about to be superseded; or the price will fall further; or that the quality has been reduced. Similarly, a price rise could suggest scarcity (and hence desirability) or higher quality (Oxenfeldt, 1961, p. 28).

Judging price

Extensive research carried out in the 1960s and 1970s into the psychological processes consumers undergo when evaluating price established an important principle: most consumers in most markets do not make absolute judgements about brands or products in isolation. Instead, *relative* judgements are made about products within a person's repertoire. Moreover, this comparative basis for assessment typically extends beyond an evaluation of performance or image characteristics, into the area of price judgement. For most purchasers, it is the relative price considerations when compared with alternatives that convey the most information, and which therefore by extension contribute to purchasing decision making.

To some extent, this issue of the relativity of price perception is exacerbated in markets where prices vary considerably by distribution channel. For example, in some fast moving consumer goods markets, the price of the same product can vary by as much as 100 to 200 per cent between cut-price multiples and corner shops. To a consumer, a fixed reaction to a specific price would be less than useful in situations where the product might be purchased from a number of outlets.

Familiarity with price

Possibly as an extension of the above, consumers may be unfamiliar with prices, and unaware of the price of alternatives not immediately on display at the point of sale. One research project in the USA, which involved intercepting shoppers emerging from supermarkets and asking in detail how much they had paid for items they were carrying in their shopping baskets, found an astonishing lack of recall of prices paid. Of course, this does not imply that prices are unimportant, since the displayed prices on the shelves may well prompt discrimination on the part of the buyer, rather that the decisions are often made locally and prices not stored in long-term memory for future reference and comparison.

It is clear from a number of recent studies, however, that in many low cost/outlay grocery markets the *involvement* of the consumer with the decision task itself can be very low indeed in developed countries. While this could reflect the boring and repetitive nature of buying in these fields, an alternative (or supplementary) view might be that the quality differentials within many product fields have grown smaller, so that the consequences of making a 'wrong decision' are much less. The development of retailer own-labels, with assurances on quality (and therefore value for money), may well have contributed to this.

In some cases, especially in the purchasing of consumer durables, research has shown that the purchasing decision can extend a considerable period before the actual purchase. This *information-gathering* period will of course include the collection of information on price, as well as product performance criteria. In the six months prior to the typical purchase of a motor car, the average consumer will progress from a situation of very vague pricing aware-ness to detailed 'on the road' costs, including a knowledge of possible trade-in deals and dealer discounts.

Repertoires

A common finding from consumer panel data in repeat purchasing markets is that the proportion of product buyers who are 'solus' (that is, have bought the same product – and no other – a defined number of times) is very small, and typically less than 8 per cent. In most markets involving repeat purchasing, it is clear that consumers maintain 'repertoires' of products, between which they are prepared to switch periodically. This does not mean that all products within an individual's repertoire have equal likelihood of purchase; in fact they can each be thought of as having their own probability of purchase greater than zero and less then one (except in the case of single brand repertoires, where the probability for that brand is therefore one). A number of factors may contribute to this switching.

The most obvious example in the area of household purchasing arises when a *single consumer* is making purchasing decisions to satisfy the tastes and needs of others in the same household. The degree of independent decision making allowed by these other members may be wide (as in most foodstuffs) or more restricted (for example alcoholic beverages). The decision made by the actual purchaser may not therefore be totally autonomous.

In some markets (for example confectionery, breakfast cereals or snacks) there can be a distinct search for novelty or variety, which can overcome a price barrier by prompting an 'impulse' purchase.

In other markets, a number of products can be purchased with a view to use on a number of *occasions*. Examples here can range from personal toiletries to alcoholic beverages: the important point is that a single consumer is acting in effect as a number of different consumers, depending on the occasion. Again, this can have an important implication on price setting, since the same person can be extremely price-sensitive for some occasions – everyday perfumes for example – and much more price tolerant in others – for example fragrances for special occasions.

The perception of price

Finally, but by no means exhaustively, there is the issue of how the consumer actually evaluates the effect of the 'magnitude' of a price. For example, in the case of multiple purchasing where more than one unit is bought at the same time, does the buyer think (and hence make decisions) in terms of the unit price, or of the total outlay? Or indeed, in terms of pack price, or price per 100 grams?

At this point, the role of the psychologist takes over from that of the econo-mist, and the concern is more to do with the understanding of *individual* choice processes than of their aggregated effects.

This can be a relevant issue when products are sold 'unbundled', that is, where the purchaser must put together a number of individually priced components to satisfy his or her needs. In consequence, should the marketing organization concentrate in its price-setting policy on the price sensitivity of the individual components, or on the 'gestalt' of the total price? A good knowledge of the real price premium that customers would be prepared to pay for products can lead to a pricing policy that is more in line with consumer expectations, than a production-based 'cost plus' system. Moreover, premiums gained in one area can support losses made in others. For example, most car manufacturers charge more for larger engine options, even though the cost difference is rarely justified by the extra production costs – simply because there exists a consumer expectation that this should be the case. Different paint finishes, however, are often given parity costing even though production costs may vary significantly.

RESEARCHING DEMAND RELATIONSHIPS

In the event, the marketing organization will need some systematic research to determine the nature of price relationships in the market. In view of the considerations noted above, it is not surprising that most research methods in some way attempt to derive the demand curve for a product, or for a market.

In broad terms, there are two different ways of doing this.

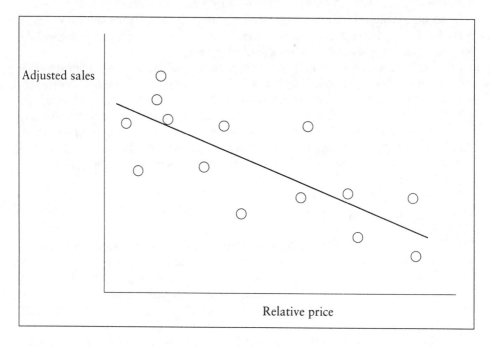

Figure 19.4   Scatterplot of demand at various relative prices

Econometrics

The most obvious way of establishing price-demand relationships is to examine past sales data, and note the way in which patterns – or correspondences – exist between pricing movements and sales. Thus, for example, one might plot the average selling prices of a product in a number of successive sales periods against cases sold. In fact, because of random effects, the relationship would be unlikely to be perfect, and some means would be needed to make a 'best estimate' of the relationship between the two variables.

It is possible to use mathematical curve-fitting techniques to derive a 'best fit' for data of this sort. For example, the method of linear *regression* would calculate a line through the data points that was 'best', in so far as the sum of squares of distances of each point to the line was at a minimum. This is shown in Figure 19.4. This line, represented by an equation, could be used to assess the elasticity of demand in the market, and also to predict the outcome of possible pricing movements.

In reality, this statistical approach, known as *econometric analysis*, is considerably more complex than this simple example suggests.

To start with, as noted earlier, most demand relationships are non-linear and possibly discontinuous, so that considerably more sophisticated mathematical models (such as Box-Jenkins, or ARIMA approaches) must be fitted to past data. Just a few of the problem areas encountered in this area are discussed below.

Data points

Most economic techniques require a large number of data points before reliable models can be constructed from them. As a general rule of thumb, at least 20 measurements are required as a minimum, or around two years' monthly (or four-weekly) sales periods. This naturally poses problems in new markets, so that this approach is difficult to use for the price setting of innovatory new products prior to launch.

However, the large number of data points required brings its own problems. Markets change over time – and great care must be taken to avoid merging data from periods where different circumstances applied: for example, different competition, or tax rates.

Variables

So far, just one variable has been suggested that could have an effect on sales – that of price. In reality, of course, there are a large number of 'independent' variables which can affect a 'dependent' issue such as sales: for example, advertising activity (both for the product, and for competitors), promotional campaigns, trade incentives, facings, out-of-stocks, changes in retail distribution levels and so on, to name just a few. Complex econometric models may well incorporate a large number of factors, all designed to 'explain' apparent

331

changes in demand, or sales, and often at a regional level, or by grocery multiple.

Some of these factors are not continuous, that is, they are of very short duration. For example, a short but intense burst of TV advertising is designed to have an effect long after the campaign finishes. This may need to be modelled also, as will any variables that are 'lagged', or whose effects linger on after they have themselves ceased. In some case, it is possible to specify the degree of lagging to the model, which will then optimize the 'fit' with the data. In other cases, the modelling procedure will itself suggest the pattern of lagging in the data.

Variable definition

In addition to specifying the number of variables in the model, great care must be taken to define these in the most appropriate manner. For example, 'price' may be expressed as absolute average retail selling price (RSP), or RSP relative to other products.

The measurement of sales effect may come from ex-factory sales, an industry deliveries audit, consumer panel data, or retail audit, and each of these has its own advantages and disadvantages. Moreover, the expression of the level of sales may be simply in terms of absolute volume, or adjusted for variations in distribution, as in 'rate of sale'.

In some markets, care should be taken to discriminate price-demand relationships between different variants or pack sizes of the same brand. This is especially true when sales fluctuate, or exhibit seasonality, since in peak periods there is a natural tendency for larger pack sizes to be bought.

Patterns or trends

A particularly confounding feature of some markets (at least where econometrics is concerned) is that there may be distinct trends, stemming either from the growth of the market as a whole, or its decline. If prices have changed systematically through this period of change, false premises can be deduced from the apparent relationship, and need to be corrected for.

The most frequently occurring periodic trend is shown by seasonality of demand, where the cycle is often annual. In some cases this can be anticipated as an effect of known magnitude (for example, sales of lawn mowers), while in others the amplitude of the effect can vary (ice cream sales and weather are an example).

Competitive reaction

Where the econometric model is used to predict the outcome of possible price changes, care must be taken to take full account of the potential reactions by competitors, since the model will often not have taken these into account if they have not featured in the past periods on which the model was based.

In general, econometric models can be a useful tool in the marketing armoury, for calibrating markets and as a basis for prediction. Nevertheless, they suffer from a fundamental philosophical shortcoming. By placing great emphasis on the apparent correlation of variables, they may stimulate misleading conclusions about the nature of the relationships between them. In short, 'just because A occurs with B, does not mean that A causes B'. Very little can be said about why A or B happen anyway.

Another cause for caution arises from the inescapable nature of the data themselves, which are of course exclusively derived from past events. In many cases, and in many stable and mature markets, this 'historicality' of the data is perfectly acceptable for short-term tactical planning. But in others, rising on the tides of fashion or requiring long-term strategic planning, a reliance on the pattern of past events to predict the future may be at best irrelevant, and at worst dangerous.

Ad hoc methods

If the origins of econometrics arose from the methods of classical economic theory, those of the *ad hoc* approaches derived from consumer psychology. In these methods, the aim is not to look at past aggregate sales data, but to adopt an experimental approach by recruiting a sample of consumers and asking them to undertake a specific task that will uncover their reaction (and hence, by inference, the reactions of the universe of consumers as a whole) to particular pricing options.

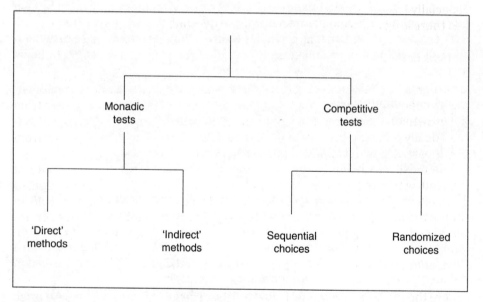

Figure 19.5   Classification of *ad hoc* methods

There are a number of distinct advantages to these approaches. First, they avoid the 'historicality trap' of using past data (noted earlier), and can be adapted to new markets where no data exist. Second, they are particularly suitable for new product development concepts or prototypes which have yet to be launched. Third, because they involve the recruitment of specific samples of consumers (which can be defined in particular ways), they allow the market to concentrate on target consumers that have been defined elsewhere. Finally, they are the only way to identify the extent to which individual consumers in a market vary in terms of price sensitivity, and therefore provide a means of performing market segmentation.

In recent years, this area has witnessed a considerable growth in the number of methods available, all of which have their advantages and disadvantages in particular situations. Nevertheless, they fall into distinct 'schools' of thought, as shown in Figure 19.5 (Frappa and Marbeau, 1982).

Monadic approaches

In monadic methods, respondents who are recruited to take part are exposed to a *single* concept or product, and asked to deliver an opinion about their inclination to purchase at one or several prices.

The simplest (and oldest) system involves asking just that: 'Would you buy the product at price X?' and obtaining a 'Yes' or 'No' answer. In fact, this 'direct' approach is rarely used, since consumers are often reluctant to commit themselves in such a strong fashion during a market research interview; and if the stimulus is an unknown product or service, there may need to be a period of familiarization before a purchase decision is made.

Therefore, a more usual approach is to use a 'buying intention' scale, which allows the respondent to make a more graded reply. Such a scale might be as follows:

I would definitely buy	5
I might buy	4
I am not sure	3
I probably would not buy	2
I definitely would not buy	1

The number of responses from the study given to each category would be summed, and a mean score calculated by using the category weights shown (in this case, 5 to 1). Although the mean score generally has no intrinsic meaning in itself, experienced researchers can compare the scores achieved with those from previous studies, and judge how well the product has performed in stimulating purchasing intentions among consumers.

Although scaling approaches clearly require back data (or 'norms') for comparison, they have been shown to be well correlated with actual purchasing (Riddle and Wilkinson, 1979).

A more 'indirect' approach dealing with the presentation of a single product stimulus was developed by Gabor and Granger (1965). In this, respondents are presented with a series of prices in random order, and for each price asked whether they would buy or not. If they respond in the negative, they are asked whether this is because it was too cheap (that is, dubious quality), or too expensive. From these data, cumulative response curves can be charted for the proportion of likely buyers at any price (that is, those who thought the product was neither 'too cheap' nor 'too expensive'), thus generating a quasi-demand curve to which pricing-setting principles can be applied.

Van Westerndorp (1976) proposed a similar approach in his 'price sensitivity metre', which attempts to increase the precision of the response by collecting it on a five-point scale, although the methodology is essentially similar.

While these monadic techniques have been extensively documented – and are particularly appropriate for ill-defined markets (where the nature of the competition is difficult to specify) or genuine 'innovation products' – they can be criticized for not taking into account some of the findings mentioned earlier about the way in which consumers evaluate price. In particular, monadic approaches make no allowance for *relative* judgements which consumers might make between alternatives at different prices, or indeed that a given 'price' might itself *vary* in distribution. What might be an 'expensive' price for a hypermarket shopper might after all be a 'cheap' price in a village store.

The first point was addressed by Gabor and colleagues in their 'randomized shop situation' method (Gabor et al., 1970). In this, respondents are shown a number of prespecified scenarios of products at particular prices. A typical scenario would consist of more than one brand, which would therefore allow the respondent to make relative judgements. Faced with a scenario, respondents can either select a single product as the one most likely to be purchased under those conditions, or specify the proportions of each they might buy over time (for example in repertoire situations) (Morgan and Godfrey, 1985).

While this approach is clearly more appropriate for well-defined markets, the researcher must spend some time in advance designing the specification of the scenarios to be presented.

Perhaps the most advanced methodology currently available for use in well-defined markets using competitive scenarios is the 'brand/price trade-off' (BPTO) method, developed by my company in the late 1970s (Morgan, 1987b). In this system, respondents are faced with a scenario of competing brands, which can be tailored for each individual's repertoire, or availability at his or her usual source of purchase. The elicitation method proceeds by starting all items at given prices, and successively asking the respondent to examine the priced items and state the one he or she would be most likely to purchase. The 'chosen' item is then increased to a higher price, and the question asked again. The interview stops when either the respondent refuses to purchase any of the brands at the prices they have reached, or when the range of prices under review is exhausted.

A practical advantage of this method is that scenarios do not need to be specified in advance, and the only pre-specification required is the actual range of prices to investigate. However, there are a number of other advantages to the approach.

Typically, the data collected from each respondent in a BPTO exercise are subjected to 'conjoint analysis' to derive weights representing the relative desirability of the product items to that respondent, as well as the relative sensitivity to price levels. This allows a computer model to be built that is capable of 'simulating' respondent 'choices' for any combination of brand and price. This analysis is conducted at an individual level (technically known as 'micro-modelling') before aggregation, and so in theory offers the most sensitive way of handling individual differences in brand appeal and price tolerance. Moreover, since the analysis is conducted at the individual level, the individual predictions can be weighted for heaviness of consumption to provide *volume* share estimates, in addition to *usage* shares.

The advantage to the market is that the resulting computer models can be used in a totally flexible way to predict market outcomes, often via an interactive session at his or her personal computer. For example, a single simulation could be conducted to examine the effect of a single brand's price change, or changes to a number of brands, or even the effect of a competitor reaction. This is shown in Table 19.1 where the 5 percentage point gain in brand share experienced by Brand B has been achieved at the expense of a 2 per cent loss in share for Brands A and D, and a 1 per cent loss for Brand C.

Table 19.1
BPTO simulation of a price increase for brand B (brand shares)

	Current market %	Simulation
Brand A	22	20 (– 2%)
Brand B	13	18 (+ 5%)
Brand C	42	41 (– 1%)
Brand D	43	21 (– 2%)

Alternatively, a series of simulations can be conducted in which the price of a target brand is systematically changed, with the remaining brands kept constant at their 'market' prices. A graphical plot of brand share movements resulting from this will reproduce the 'demand curve' for the target brand, as well as the gains/loss from competitors. From the example in Figure 19.6, it can be seen that the result of price increases for brand B reproduces the expected 'S' demand shape, and also shows that brand A is much less likely to benefit (that is, to compete) than brand C.

In general, BPTO modelling represents the 'state of the art' in *ad hoc* methods, where competitive product displays can be employed.

CONCLUSION

This chapter presents a general review of pricing problems in marketing. Of necessity much has been omitted, both in terms of general theory as well as

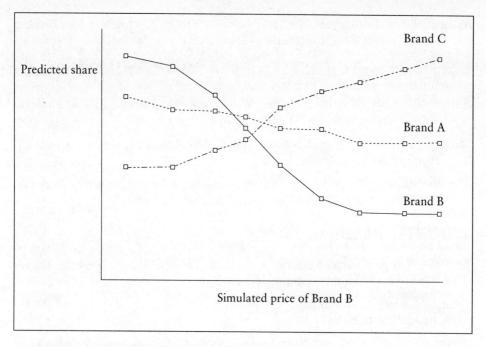

Figure 19.6   BPTO simulated brand shares

details of case practice. Nevertheless, the References and Essential Reading sections below should provide the interested reader with further sources.

As in most branches of marketing, the most useful asset remains common sense. While the old adage 'There ain't no brand loyalty that two cents off can't overcome' may not hold in all circumstances, it still remains a good rule of thumb until proven otherwise.

REFERENCES

Frappa, J. P. and Marbeau. Y. (1982), *Pricing New Products at Better Value for Money,* Vienna: ESOMAR Congress.

Gabor, A. and Granger, C. (1965), 'The pricing of new products', *Scientific Business*, **3**, August, 141–50.

Gabor, A., Granger, C. and Sowter, A. (1970), 'Real and hypothetical shop situations in market research', *Journal of Marketing Research,***VII**, August, 355–9.

Morgan, R. P. (1987a), 'Ad hoc pricing research – some key issues', *Journal of the Market Research Society,* **29,** (2), pp.109–21.

Morgan, R. (1987b), *Brand/Price Trade-Off – Where We Stand Now,* Munich: EMAC/ESOMAR Symposium on Micro and Macro Modelling.

Morgan, R. and Godfrey, S. (1985), *The Role of Pricing Research In New Product Development,* Brighton: Market Research Society Conference.

Oxenfeldt, A. R. (1961), *Pricing for Marketing Executives,* San Francisco: Wadsworth Publishing Company.

Riddle, M. and Wilkinson, J. (1979), *New Product Development in an Evolving Market,* Dubrovnik: ESOMAR Seminar.

Stoetzel, J. (1954), 'Le prix comme limite', 184–8, in P. L. Reynaud (ed.) *La Psychologie Economique*, Paris.

Van Westendorp, P. (1976), *Price Sensitivity Meter: A New Approach to Study Perception of Prices,* 139–67, Venice: ESOMAR Congress.

ESSENTIAL READING

Birn, R., Hague, P. and Vangelder, P. (eds) (1990), *A Handbook of Market Research Techniques,* London: Kogan Page.

Crimp, M. (1990), *The Marketing Research Process* (3rd edn), Hemel Hempstead: Prentice-Hall.

Clifton, P., Nguyen, H. and Nutt, Susan (1992), *Market Research – Using Forecasting in Business,* Oxford: Butterworth-Heinemann.

20 Developing and launching a consumer product

Peter Kraushar

DEVELOPMENT TRENDS

Approaches to product development have changed very significantly since the 1960s. Companies 30 years ago regarded product development as almost synonymous with diversification, being quite prepared to consider 'blue sky' projects; the consumer was king or queen so, if somehow it had been possible to find a consumer need or to improve on a current product, little else mattered. Companies were perfectly happy to consider new brands, so new product development was also new brand development in many cases. The scope of the project was usually just the country where it was being developed except for durables which even then were marketed across frontiers. Internal development based on products coming out from the company's R&D was the norm, and much reliance was put on regional test markets.

What a difference from today's situation!

- 'Stick to the knitting' based on focus on the core business and understanding of the company's competitive strengths has at last become the key to development in most companies all over the developed world.
- The trade is as important as the target consumer. Companies have realized, to their cost, that however good the consumer proposition, the project will fail if key retail chains do not give it distribution because, for example, it does not fit in with their trading policies.
- Very few new brands are now being developed. Product development so often is no more than brand extension or product extension; much of the activity is concentrated now on 'old product development' to revitalize current products – all cheaper and less risky activities.
- Many countries are now the objective for any one project, only small- and medium-sized companies restricting its scope to one country.

339

- Use of outside technical facilities, contract packing, brand licensing, joint ventures, even acquisitions as vehicles for achieving specific development aims have made development a much more flexible activity.

WHAT IS A NEW PRODUCT?

The problem of definitions is formidable. A new variety in the Heinz soup range, the redevelopment of an Elida Gibbs shampoo, a new international car model for Ford, the transfer of an ethical Reckitt & Colman pharmaceutical product to over-the-counter applications, the Mars move into ice cream, a new financial service for Prudential, private-label soap for Aldi, a new range of chilled sauces for Covent Garden Foods, Racal's entry into cellular radio – these are all examples of obvious new consumer products, yet the difference between them is obviously huge in both scope and in type.

Not surprisingly, there is no magic formula ensuring success for all types of product development and for all product categories. Anyone naive enough to think that there is one deserves to fail! However it is possible to establish a number of useful guidelines and approaches which can be adapted to specific situations. It is on this basis that a general article on product development is worthwhile.

General guidelines

Whatever the company or the market, there are guidelines which are valid in each case.

Understanding of company and market position

Whether the company is one shop or a small dairy or a multinational, it is still possible and important to seek to understand its strengths, its weaknesses, how they compare with competitors, its position in the market-place. Obviously, large companies will base their assessment on market research and relatively sophisticated competitive comparisons, while small ones will need to rely on 'feel' and word of mouth, but it is amazing how much such information can be obtained at no cost, if one is keen to obtain it.

Development strategy

As a result of the above, each company needs to arrive at a development strategy including:

- Need, if any, for additional developments – in product or geographical terms – as compared with growth of the current business.
- Assessment of how far, if at all, to depart from the defined core business.
- Possible development options – internal development, joint ventures, acquisitions, and so on.

340

- Financial criteria – short, medium and long term.
- Other criteria to be considered – time-scales, competitors to be avoided, high v. low volume, seasonality, utilization of current branding, use of current distribution channels, and so on.

Communication of strategy

It is amazing how often companies arrive at a strategy which is then not communicated within the company to the people who should know it! The most successful companies are those who enthuse the total workforce by making everyone feel that they are participating in the enterprise, so surely it can do no harm and might do much good to circulate and indeed discuss future development strategies as widely as possible, even if some confidential details need to be excluded.

Allocation of necessary resources

Even the most sophisticated companies have been guilty of splendid intentions and strategies without following through by providing the necessary resources – financial, organizational, technical. Unless this happens, wishful thinking finishes up as wasteful and even counter-productive exercises.

Development organization

One of the most common truisms in business is that priority problems bedevil all development; no one has ever run a business without everyday problems which by their nature require urgent solutions and so today's business always wins priority over tomorrow's.

In practice, it is not possible to solve this problem unless the person running the current business has enough time to work on the future or unless someone else who has no responsibility for today runs tomorrow. Companies, therefore, need to find the most suitable organization which takes care of this point if they need to succeed.

General commitment

One can almost smell in some companies the sense of general commitment to the future, to change, to development, which permeates throughout all departments at all levels, whereas in others nothing will do except the status quo. Even when there are specific people or departments with responsibility for future development, there is real need for positive commitment in the whole company, otherwise it is easy for other departments, for example finance or sales to give inadequate priority to the new project. Over the years a plethora of promising projects has died when the salesforce was not adequately motivated to sell and develop sales of new products in comparison with the company's current ranges.

Vision

Western companies, particularly British ones, have been rightly criticized in many cases for their complete lack of development vision – restricting their interest to very short-term activities with minimum risk and almost no financial investment. That kind of approach is clearly justified when a company has no resource to do anything else or in times of real recession, but so often powerful organizations have refused to take any other view and then have been surprised by the lack of new development opportunities! By comparison, some continental companies and certainly Far Eastern competitors take a much more far-sighted view. It is worth quoting John Smale who said, when Chairman of Procter & Gamble in 1989:

> Procter & Gamble entered Japan in 1973. For a number of reasons our company lost money in Japan and we were in an investment phase until 1986, thirteen years later. We now have major products in 13 different categories in Japan and last year made a good profit. In the years ahead Japan could become our largest and most profitable international subsidiary.

Obviously not every company can afford such a level of commitment, or even needs it, but too many believe that such results can be achieved almost automatically, without putting in the right kind of effort, including investment. Everyone should remember Smale's words before adapting them to their circumstances and then should arrive at the company's future vision – visionary but realistic!

Creativity

Everyone can be creative, everyone can have good ideas. The receptionist or the factory worker could have as good an idea as the Chairman. The vital point is to establish an environment for the generation of such ideas, as well as continuous search for relevant ideas and developments throughout the world, and then to use rigorous prioritization systems to focus on the most significant and the most suitable ideas. These then need to be developed as far as is possible, to be appraised by market research or by other means as relevant.

Obviously, the greater the risk, the more it is worthwhile spending money on evaluation and usually companies rightly go for many evaluation stages.

Implementation

In practice, poor or inadequate creativity is not usually the reason for failure; the reason much more often is poor implementation, because companies think that, once they have a good development idea which has had positive evaluation, they are home and dry. Yet to translate that idea or concept into a real product produced by standard production, sold and marketed through real distribution channels and achieving the planned product quality sales volume and profitability demands high levels of management expertise, leadership, persuasion, planning and luck!

There is no doubt that a few companies can take a mediocre idea and make it into a world beater, whereas there are innumerable companies all over the world that have proved themselves quite incapable of successfully commercializing some very exciting ideas. The difference in performance between the two types of company is startling.

Monitoring and learning

Finally, every development needs careful monitoring after commercialization, so that it can be frequently assessed and even amended as necessary. In some cases, of course, it needs to be aborted – the more successful companies have learnt when to stop putting more money in and cut their losses as early as possible.

Such monitoring and relevant documentation also enable the company to learn more and more from each development project; development practice is so much more important than theory, yet it is amazing how often even sophisticated organizations do not seem to make an effort to learn from their past projects as well as from those of competitors. Those that learn and learn are likely to become tomorrow's best implementers.

Small companies

Most companies in every country are, of course, small or very small, while books on all aspects of business including new product development concentrate almost invariably on huge multinationals! The Shells, Unilevers, General Motors and so on are clearly very important and have huge innovation needs, which will be discussed later, but let us dwell first on the small companies which, by definition:

- have limited financial resources.
- operate in narrow geographical areas.
- have little management.
- are often dominated by one or two persons.
- have little R&D.
- have limited marketing and market research expertise, quite apart from limited resources in these areas.

Yet their development needs can be very great and pose a real challenge, because many of them just cannot afford to make a bad mistake, unlike the multinationals. They need to adapt to their own situation and resources the points made earlier, but need to concentrate in particular on the key areas shown in Figure 20.1.

Very few have a clear strategy; for example do they really want to grow significantly? This is by no means an automatic need in the absence of financial institutions clamouring for ever-higher earnings and, with hindsight, many owners would prefer to have grown only slightly, retaining control of their   *343*

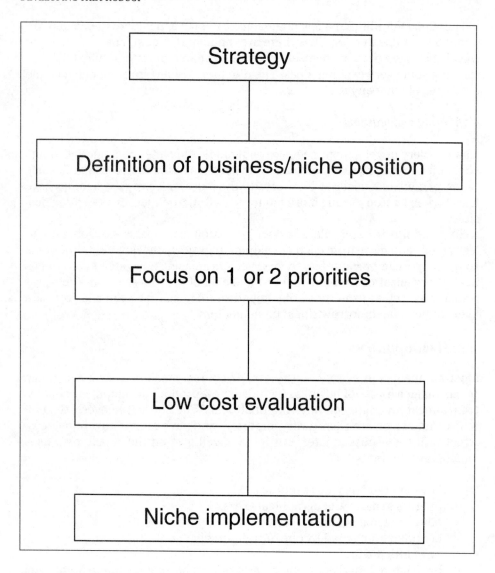

Figure 20.1   Key points for product development by small businesses

company and their destiny, instead of going for headlong growth with significant risks, which, even when successful, tends to finish up with a situation
where acquisition by a larger company takes place. If the latter event is to be
the final objective, it is perfectly justifiable, but it needs to be considered much
earlier, as it has considerable effect on product development.

Whatever the strategy, the company must have a strongly defined competitive position compared with any larger direct or indirect competitors; if it does
not, it is bound to have real problems against companies with much more
resource.

Some examples of niche positions

1 Wilkin with its Tiptree brand of jams competes against large competitors in the notoriously tough food market through high quality, premium-priced products.

2 Merrydown concentrates on strong vintage cider, letting Bulmers, Taunton and Gaymer dispute the standard cider market.

3 Aston Martin, which only survives by manufacturing a very small number of expensive high-quality cars, relies on its name among car enthusiasts.

4 Tetrosyl, run largely by one man, has been able, through flexibility and speed of action, to compete against much larger companies in car and household DIY chemicals.

5 McCormick has established itself in many countries as *the* company in herbs and spices – an area where the huge number of varieties and the merchandising problems make it very difficult for large food companies to enter the market.

6 Brandways Supercook has equally done a great job of developing a very wide range of cake decorations and related products in attractive packaging – there is little incentive for others to copy.

7 Prince has found ways of establishing a niche in sports equipment, particularly by using technology to develop different tennis rackets and squash rackets. Not surprisingly, it has floundered when trying to compete in related product areas with no points of differentiation, for example tennis balls.

8 Manley Ratcliffe was most successful as a honey blender run by one man, John Manley, who concentrated almost entirely on supplying own-label products. After his untimely death, the company lacked leadership and has gone through two acquisitions, being currently owned by Nestlé.

9 W.L. Housewares, an entrepreneurial houseware supplier which looks for good ideas all over the world, has them manufactured under contract and puts together interesting merchandising concepts, for example, Italian houseware ranges.

10 Covent Garden Soups has stolen a march on many large food companies by manufacturing extremely high quality, if expensive, soups, in chill distribution cartons. Interestingly, a venture into sauces was much less successful.

11 Charbonnel et Walker, the Bond Street chocolate confectioner, has the reputation of supplying much of the aristocracy in Britain as well as a few others – hardly the same market as Cadbury or even Terry's.

12 A relatively small Polish flour miller in Szymanow, west of Warsaw, has established such a reputation for its prepacked flour that it cannot meet demand at prices 7 to 8 per cent higher than competition, while most other flour mills in Poland are having terrible trouble – niche marketing and added value are as relevant in Eastern Europe as everywhere else! 345

Priorities

Because they lack resources – management, technical and finance – these kind of companies must focus very strongly on their current business, most of their development being no more than brand/product extension or updating of the current products.

Any real new product development should be looked at with a very cynical eye. If there is any danger that it would lead to problems for the current business it just must not be progressed.

If it is to be progressed, usually one priority project is plenty and, if there is no resource for proper market research, an enormous amount can still be done through informal soundings with target consumers and through discussions with current trade customers. Such companies usually have excellent trade relations between the top people in end-use and every effort should be made to exploit this to help evaluation.

Implementation

Finally, the implementation is key, as usual, and the top person/top management needs to give it all the loving care that they bestow on the current business. It must also fit well with the niche culture of the established business – if it is very different and if it is something that a large company could do and could be interested in doing, then the danger signs should be flashing – or rather should have flashed long before.

Use of third parties' technical development and/or production can well be relevant in many cases, as WL has shown, to lessen the risk and again focus on the company's strengths.

INTERNATIONAL PRODUCT DEVELOPMENT

All companies, large and small, need to innovate through old as well as new product development and the international dimension has added both problems and opportunities to this process. There are a number of different approaches which are shown in Figure 20.2.

One of the most interesting examples of the first approach is the Italian confectionery company, Ferrero, which for many years now has concentrated its R&D in Luxembourg and has conducted in this central location concept development and research work using bus-loads of market consumers from Belgium, Holland, Germany, Italy, France, so that very quickly and cost-effectively almost the whole of Europe can be covered in one piece of research. Ferrero Rocher, Rafaello and other very distributive confectionery products have emerged as a result and have succeeded quickly in many countries.

Mars, with its international production and marketing organization now spanning the whole of Europe and seeking wherever possible to find uniform European brands, is another company to go a long way towards international product development from the beginning.

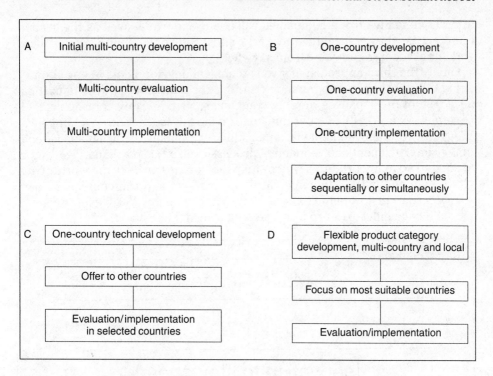

Figure 20.2   Four approaches to international product development

Other large companies are moving that way. In Unilever the Chairman, Michael Perry, stated categorically that the key to success begins and ends with innovation and the company is experimenting with innovation centres in different countries, for example in Bangkok for Asian hair, in UK for deodorants, in Italy for toothpaste, in Hamburg for skin products, in Paris for hair products. This is basically the second approach for an idea or a brand to be proved in one local market before it is rolled out across frontiers 'at the speed of light', as soon as it is successful. This speed of roll-out is crucial these days for a large multinational, to maintain its competitive position in current markets, develop new markets, and upset the status quo wherever possible.

Perry's call for pragmatism and speed of action reflects the new international competitiveness which will have much impact on international development:

> If you are strong in a market you have a vested interest in maintaining the mould. If you are the usurper, you have a vested interest in breaking the mould. What we now say to our people is, even if you are in a strong position in your market, your task is to make everything that now goes on in the company irrelevant. . . it is not your task to keep off all boarders. . . it is your task to create the successor to that, because, if you do not, somebody else will. That is stretching their minds like nobody's business!

In practice many strong companies will use the fourth as well as the second approach, as they realize that there is no substitute for flexibility as good ideas and initial success can come from anywhere.

Finally the third approach of strong technical developments in one country being offered to marketing/manufacturing subsidiaries worldwide is particularly true of the Japanese durable companies, such as Sony, Panasonic, Fuji, Olympus, Canon, which continue to provide in Japan both technological breakthroughs and refinements of existing technologies. The Japanese technology improvement and refinement process (Kaizen) is particularly strong in leading to so many products which their subsidiaries all over the world struggle to commercialize – in some cases the markets and the companies' own resources are just not able to cope as they are so many. Yet Western companies still have much to learn from the Japanese in this respect.

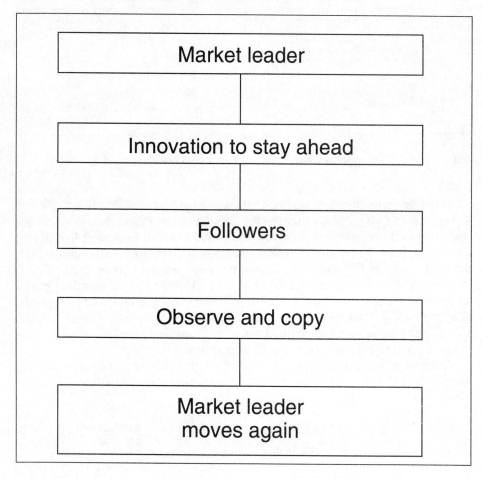

Figure 20.3   Classic market innovation

New international brands

The discussion of new international brands usually comes back to the existence of Coca-Cola, Pepsi, Lux, Levi, Mercedes, Sony, etc. etc. in most countries of the world, but how many of these are new? Mars has certainly been bold in its European branding recently, even changing local brands where necessary despite must past investment, for example changing Mr Dog to Cesar across Europe, but most companies talk about new European branding without doing it.

Large companies should certainly aim to establish new European brands, either starting in one country and then expanding them or launching in another simultaneously. It is predicted that in many product categories the Eurobrand situation will be very much more advanced within the next 20 years. This has, of course, impact on product development as it needs to be part of the original strategy if it is to succeed.

BENCHMARKING AND INNOVATION

Benchmarking has, of course, been widely used in recent years to improve companies' organization and practice in many areas, but KAE Development has particularly adapted benchmarking to product development and innovation. This is in line with Unilever's current approach, as described by Michael Perry, to seek innovation very flexibly, but very urgently.

Thus it is possible to tailor benchmarking or best practice to a company's particular situation in the context of development. It is easy and long practised by the best companies to establish best practice in their particular field, but the whole idea of benchmarking is to seek exciting and appropriate analogies in completely different areas, throughout the world, and then adapt them to a particular situation. At the moment most companies and most markets have the structural approach shown in Figure 20.3.

Such situations tend to preserve the balance of market power, no one upsets the status quo, and eventually there is often a loss of momentum, as everyone wears 'industry blinkers'. These days there is a need for a much more dynamic approach (see Figure 20.4).

Benchmarking in practice

For example, a company dealing in what seems a very simple product – bread manufacturing and marketing – could well seek very innovative developments by considering the following in its benchmarking processes:

Development strategy

* The Mars approach towards international branding as well as multi-country production centres.

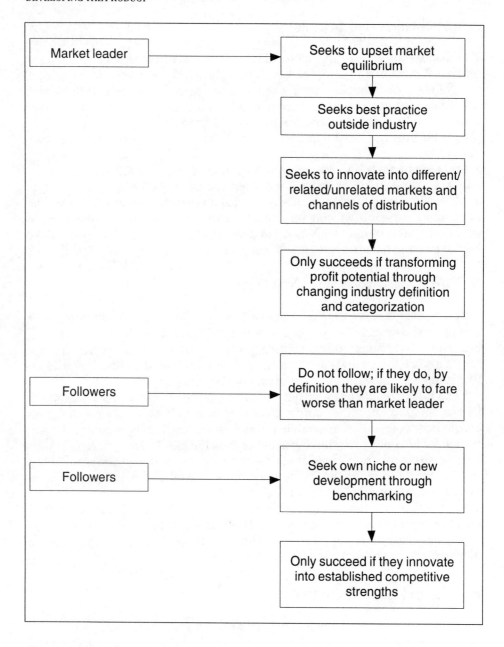

Figure 20.4   KAE benchmarking for market innovation

- Longer-shelf-life yoghurts as an example of convenience for trade and logistical reasons.
- Sony, Matsushita and Canon for financial criteria relating to development.

- The Pedigree Petfoods 'pincer movement' towards a market, attempting to have both strong brands in the upper price quartile and unsupported price brands at prices difficult for own-label to match.

Creativity

- The Ferrero multi-country development approach.
- Lessons from daily newspapers, a product even more perishable than bread.
- The Kit-Kat story from confectionery.
- The pizza success in providing both a raft and a topping.
- Famines and ways of treating them in Third World countries.
- Guinness as a 'cult' drink with its colour and many special values.
- The 3M product champion approach for innovation.
- The Hershey and Black & Decker practice in logistics – could this lead to a real innovation for a bread company?
- The Xerox or Procter & Gamble approach to customer service – could certain adaptations lead to developments in bread?
- The Marks & Spencer and Aldi models of retailing – are they applicable in some way to bread shops?

Technology

- The Japanese companies' technology approach must be of considerable interest.
- Has Hewlett Packard something to offer in its engineering excellence?
- Can the Kodak information systems lead to thoughts in bread which can again result in significant developments?
- Does the way in which General Motors or Ford assembles its cars have applications to international 'assembly' of bread components?
- Can developments in biotechnology, genetic engineering and so on lead to different and relevant raw materials for bread?

Development, evaluation and implementation

- The Procter & Gamble very focused, thorough and long-term approach must be quite applicable.
- Equally the workaholic Mars managers and executives with their dedication to try to make something work, even if they seem relatively mediocre ideas initially, must have lessons for all businesses.
- McDonald's mix of owned and franchised outlets could provide some signals for both bread shops and bread products generally.
- CPC's specialist catering organization – Caterplan – can be very applicable in the specific catering area across many countries.
- Mail order companies may provide useful implementation lessons in both distribution and credit control of new developments.

351

- Learn from the Japanese team approach in development of copiers, cameras and so on.

While some of the examples may prove quite inappropriate and others could be preferred, it is hoped that they at least serve to open one's eyes to see how broadly it is now worth looking to find real innovations for a bread company or indeed for any kind of organization.

THE IDEA AND THE CONSUMER/CUSTOMER PROPOSITION

Most companies do not have too many problems in generating ideas; what is much more difficult is to generate the right ideas, to prioritize in order to focus only on significant ones (a small idea often takes as long to progress as a large one), to transform the latter into real understandable target consumer or customer propositions which are understandable and to which consumers can react in initial small-scale market research.

Cost-effective yet accurate visualization of such concepts has long been a notorious problem. The usual hand-drawn concept boards, while very successful in some cases, have proved positively misleading in others, consumers reacting to a person's face in a usage situation rather than to the concept itself or being affected by the artist's problems in showing a product attractively on such a board. For example, anyone trying to portray the texture, the colour, the sheer appetite appeal of a new biscuit on a concept board backed by some initial rough prototypes will agree that it is extraordinarily difficult to do justice to what could be a good idea by showing, in effect, some brownish 'turds'. Many good ideas have suffered as a result!

The joint venture between the computer graphics specialist, Creative Input, and KAE Development, adapting computer graphics to concept development and research has some significant advantages:

- It is possible to show colour, texture, product format in amazing detail. Thus the idea of a chewing gum with a strip of lemon juice visualized through computer graphics can make the onlooker salivate, while it would be dead on a concept board.
- Variations and variables can be executed very accurately.
- Usage situation can be completely standard without any unwanted differences, the one variable being a different product put into the standard background.
- The computer graphics have, of course, huge advantages of speed and flexibility once one visualization has been done. Thus, if it is decided to embark on a series of group discussions, it is very easy and cheap to show say eight computer graphic visuals at the first two groups, decide which three or four are worth progressing and with what changes, change the latter accordingly for the next two groups, amend again if necessary for another two groups and so finish up quickly and cheaply, certainly very cost-effectively, with exactly what the target consumers regard as what they are interested in, to represent the detailed brief to R&D.

- Indeed an unexpected bonus of the use of computer graphics in concept development has been the interest by R&D in having such visualizations, quite apart from any marketing and market research benefits, as they can use them as benchmarks for their technical development work.

Computer graphics should also help in durable products development, to save on the initial use of very expensive and long-lead-time prototypes; obviously the latter are still very necessary, but it should be possible to focus their need only after positive results from computer graphic visuals. This is relatively uncharted testimony still, but in theory the benefits must be significant.

NEW PRODUCTS AND THE TRADE

It is a truism that in every developed country and in every market there has long been a concentration towards a smaller number of more and more powerful distribution channels, often large retail chains. The power of Sainsbury, Tesco, Tengelmann, Aldi, Boots, W. H. Smith, B&Q, Dixons and many others in their respective countries and markets has become so strong that suppliers must consider them in the early stages of development as much as they consider the consumer.

This approach was thought ridiculous 30 years ago, but trade research has since developed fast to establish:

1 The trade attitudes towards the relevant market and product category.
2 Their attitudes to possible new products from specific suppliers, both those in the market currently and others wishing to enter it.
3 Reactions to actual products or concepts including the trade's feeling whether such introductions have the potential to enlarge the total category sales in the store rather than just gain market share; this has become an increasingly important factor in recent years.

While the first two points are relatively straightforward, suppliers are not surprisingly worried by trying to address the third because of the confidentiality factor. In some cases, this may be a valid fear but, if there is the right relationship between the two parties, retailers in practice are flattered by being asked and indeed often give most useful guidance which has led in the past to quick 'death' of unviable ideas as well as to real product improvements of eventual successes. Such partnerships must be the way forward in most cases.

WHY SO FEW MAJOR NEW PRODUCTS?

Bill Ramsay, Fellow of Templeton College, Oxford, and formerly International Development Director of General Foods, has analysed for many years the number of really significant new products in grocery markets, basing this work on Nielsen data. During the period 1956–89, only 97 large new grocery products succeeded in Great Britain, though the figures exclude tobacco, alcohol, and frozen foods; thus about three a year have succeeded in a significant way. Studies in France, Brazil, Mexico, USA, Canada equally showed that between two and four grocery product successes a year have been the norm in each country.

Possibly other product areas may show higher success rates and the definition problem is difficult, though Ramsay has been as careful as he could about this. What is certain is that the success rate of development has been unsatisfactory to date and Ramsay, after over 30 years of analysis has a three-fold prescription to improve the situation:

1   We must overcome the fear of failure – the principal reason why so few products succeed.
2   We must resource new product development properly.
3   We must develop a real company strategy which copes with both consumer and distributor.

These may seem obvious precepts, but in practice the strongest and most sophisticated companies in the world have failed to observe them in the past. Those that want to survive and prosper in the future can no longer afford to disregard them.

EXTERNAL DEVELOPMENT

At first sight it may seem odd to include a few words on external development in an article on new products, but it is very important that companies should consider acquisitions and all forms of joint venture as closely related to internal development. In practice, projects may well switch from one type to another as opportunities arise; for example United Biscuits were very interested in developing new chocolate confectionery products, but found it difficult to do this in practice, so acquisition of Terry's as a development vehicle was a heaven-sent opportunity. Very recently United Biscuits sold Terry's at a good profit to Philip Morris, having decided it did not represent part of UB core business – a good illustration of how companies' development policies change and evolve over time.

Where would Rover be today without the joint venture with Honda? It has enabled Rover to survive and innovate, using Honda's technology and design resources, while Rover's branding and distribution have also contributed significantly – a case of complementary resources contributed by the respective partners; without such a complementary situation a joint venture would just founder.

NEW PRODUCT DEVELOPMENT IS FUN AND WORKS

Finally everyone must realize that new product development is a most stimulating business activity – the Jeremiahs who always moan should be expelled from it! And it can work extremely well, for example the Racal product development in cellular radio which was a bold venture a few years ago but now yields well over £100 million profit! The right approach, the right attitude, allocation of resources and a bit of luck – the ingredients for success are then there.

ESSENTIAL READING

KAE Development, *New Products in Grocers – Studies in Trade Attitudes to Development 1970–1990.*

Kraushar, Peter (1985), *Practical Business Development – What Works, What Does Not*, Eastbourne: Holt, Rinehart and Winston.

Kraushar, P. M. (ed.), (1986), *New Product Development*, ESOMAR Monograph Series, Vol. 1.

Kuvahama, Y. and Takeda, Y. (1990), 'A managerial approach to R&D cost and effectiveness evaluation', *IEEE Transactions on Engineering Management*, May.

Mitchell, A. (1993), 'The Driving Force Behind Unilever', *Marketing*, 8 April.

Nielsen, *International Food and Drug Store Trends 1988.*

Porter, M. E. (1985), *Competitive Advantage: Creating and Sustaining Superior Performance*, The Free Press.

Porter, M. (1990), *The Competitive Advantage of Nations*, London: Macmillan Press.

Ramsay, Bill (1991), 'The challenges and opportunities for new product development in the FMCG industry', paper to Management Centre, Brussels.

21 Developing and launching an industrial product

Michael J. Baker

For many years it has been argued that there are more similarities than differences between industrial and consumer marketing so that it is divisive and often counter-productive for practitioners in either field to ignore practice and experience in the other. Nonetheless, in the particular, it is clear that there are important differences in degree which merit separate consideration and treatment. In the preceding chapters a number of authors have dealt with many of the key concepts related to new product development and the same ground will not be covered again – the primary objective here is to focus attention on some of the more distinctive features associated with the marketing of new industrial products.

Clearly, within the scope of a book of this nature, it is possible to provide only a brief overview of some of the main factors and the reader is strongly recommended to consult some (or all) of the books listed in the References and Essential Reading at the end of the chapter in order to gain an appreciation of the complexity and richness of this field of marketing activity.

The chapter is organized in the following manner: first, the importance of new product development to the firm's survival and growth as the principle plank in its competitive strategy; next, the reasons why users and markets resist innovation with the result that many new products are deemed to be failures. Arising from this analysis, some guidelines are proposed for identifying early buyers so that the firm can develop the most effective launch strategy to ensure rapid penetration and the development of the market for its new product.

THE IMPORTANCE OF NEW PRODUCT DEVELOPMENT

While it is true that demand does exceed supply in certain markets, this is largely confined to new markets for new products. In more traditional and familiar markets, such as those for steel, ship-building, car tyres and even cars themselves, potential capacity far exceeds effective demand with the result that firms compete with each other for the customer's favour. Classical economics would have us believe that this competition would focus on price, but the reality is that manufacturers choose to recognize that demand is not homogeneous and so seek to differentiate their product to match more closely the needs of specific sub-groups or market segments. Clearly if manufacturers are successful in distinguishing their products in a meaningful way, then they provide prospective users with a basis for preferring them over other competing alternatives and so create a temporary monopoly which allows them a measure of control over their marketing strategy.

The desirability of exercising some control over a market rather than being controlled by it – being a price maker rather than a price taker – is self-evident. The wisdom of doing so is equally compelling, for a number of surveys have shown conclusively that while price ranks third or fourth in the selection criteria of most industrial purchasing agents, product characteristics or 'fitness for purpose' ranks first.

For these reasons product differentiation has become the basis for competition between suppliers competing for a share in a market and this explains the importance attached to product development by most companies today. It also helps to explain why new product development (or innovation) has become increasingly sophisticated and much riskier than it used to be. This is because, with so many more companies investing heavily, minor features are quickly copied or made obsolete by more radical changes. In the same way, the accelerating rate of change has had a similar effect on major innovations so that the average life of products is becoming shorter and shorter (compare, for example, valves, transistors and microprocessors as basic inputs to computing devices). Thus many companies are faced with the apparent paradox that if they do not innovate they will be left behind, while conversely if they do the probability of failure is very high and this could ruin the company too. As Philip Kotler has put it:

> Under modern conditions of competition, it is becoming increasingly risky not to innovate . . . At the same time, it is extremely expensive and risky to innovate. The main reasons are: (1) most product ideas which go into product development never reach the market; (2) many of the products that reach the market are not successful; and (3) successful products tend to have a shorter life then new products once had.

With regard to the first point it is clear that discarding products during development must impose some cost. However, a great deal of advice is available on this phase of development, and it is believed that companies have become much better at weeding out weak ideas earlier in the development cycle and so are able to minimize losses from this source. Similarly, a shorter life might be preferable to a long one if one can generate similar volumes of sales, because the discounted value of present sales is greater than future ones and early capitalization of an investment gives the company greater opportunity for flexible action. This point will be developed later.

357

Much the most important cause for concern is the fact that many products are not successful at all. In these cases not only has a company incurred all the development costs but it has also incurred the marketing costs of launching the new product, not to mention the possible loss of goodwill on the part of the users who discover the product is unsuccessful and likely to be withdrawn from the market.

THE NATURE AND CAUSES OF PRODUCT FAILURE

While claims concerning the incidence of new product failure are common-place, few such claims are based on hard evidence. Those which are usually conflict with one another, due to the absence of any agreement about precisely what is to be measured, so that trying to quantify the proportion or value of failures is largely a matter of speculation. However, managers are agreed that the number and cost of failures are high and are anxious for advice as to how they can reduce this risk. To do so it will be helpful to propose a simple defini-tion of failure and then see if at least the main causes of it can be identified.

A simple definition of failure is that this is deemed to have occurred when the innovator so decides. While this may not appear to be very helpful, it should clear the ground by making it explicit that success and failure are com-parative states and there is no yardstick or criterion for deciding when one ends and the other begins. To argue otherwise would be to claim that all com-panies subscribe to the same managerial objective – for example, a return of x per cent on capital employed – and clearly they do not. It follows that your fail-ure might be someone else's success and attempting to define the states pre-cisely is a sterile exercise.

This is certainly not true of establishing the perceived causes of failure because by so doing it should be possible to develop guidelines and tests for identifying and avoiding these in future. Unfortunately, relatively few compa-nies appear to be willing to document their failures and there is a marked dearth of case history material on the subject. In 1964 the National Industrial Conference Board in the USA conducted a survey as a result of which it offered the following list of factors underlying failure in rank order or importance:

1 Inadequate market analysis.
2 Product defects.
3 Higher costs than anticipated.
4 Poor timing.
5 Competitive reaction.
6 Insufficient marketing effort.
7 Inadequate sales force.
8 Inadequate distribution.

Over 50 per cent of all respondents cited the first three reasons.

A more recent study was carried out by Robert Cooper and Roger Calantone of McGill University in which they asked managers in 150 industrial companies in Quebec to categorize the nature of the causes leading to market failure: 'those products where sales had failed far short of expectations'. Table 21.1 summarizes the responses to this survey and reveals strong support for the findings of the 1964 study.

Table 21.1
Specific causes for poor sales performance (N = 89)

Specific cause	Percentage of product failures	
	Main cause	Contributing cause
Competitors were more firmly entrenched in the market than expected.	36.4	13.6
The number of potential users was overestimated.	20.5	30.7
The price was set higher than customers would pay.	18.2	33.3
The product had design, technical or manufacturing deficiencies/difficulties.	20.5	25.0
Selling, distribution or promotional efforts were misdirected.	15.9	23.9
The product was the same as competing products... a 'me-too' product.	14.8	25.0
Did not understand customer's requirements: product did not meet their needs or specifications.	13.6	26.1
Selling, distribution or promotional efforts were inadequate.	9.1	31.8
A similar competitive product was introduced.	10.2	22.7
Were unable to develop or produce product exactly as desired.	11.4	19.3
Competitors lowered prices or took other defensive actions.	12.5	13.6
Timing was too late.	8.0	13.6
No market need existed for this type of product.	5.7	18.2
Timing was premature.	6.8	13.6
Government action/legislation hindered the sale of the product.	2.3	3.4

These causes of new product failure have been summarized as six 'failure scenarios' as shown in Table 21.2.

By contrast, in 1982 Booz, Allen and Hamilton updated their 1960s survey and came up with seven factors contributing to new product success:

Table 21.2
Failure scenarios

Product characteristic	% of failures
The better mousetrap no one wanted (innovative, unique products rejected by the market).	28
The me-too meeting a competitive brick wall (similar to products on the market already meeting customers' needs).	24
Competitive one-upmanship (me-too products hurt by the concurrent introduction of similar competitive products).	13
Environmental ignorance (products not well-suited to customer needs).	7
The technical dog product (technically new products not performing).	15
The price crunch (products well suited to customer needs but priced too highly).	13

1 Product fit with market needs.
2 Product fit with internal functional strengths.
3 Technological superiority of the product.
4 Top management support.
5 Use of the new product process (normative theory).
6 Favourable competitive environment.
7 Structure of new product organization.

In between these studies Andrew Robertson and his colleagues at the Science Policy Research Unit at Sussex University conducted an analysis of a series of 34 new product failures and concluded that their main cause was a lack of market orientation.

While the evidence may not be as extensive as one might wish, the conclusion appears inescapable – failure is the consequence of managerial ignorance or, worse still, managerial neglect: ignorance because there is a very extensive managerial literature based on well-documented practice, which emphasizes the importance of thorough market analysis is an essential prerequisite of any new product development; neglect because it is management's responsibility to keep itself informed of the best current practice and, if one is well informed, it is difficult to conceive how one could excuse commercial failure in a variety of ways which fundamentally all come down to the same thing – inadequate market analysis.

Several other chapters in this book provide advice on aspects of market analysis and measurement, all of which is applicable to industrial marketing. Accordingly, it will be assumed that the reader is informed and responsible and will put to good use the advice contained in these chapters. Unfortunately, while this will greatly enhance the probability of success, it cannot guarantee the eradication of 'failure' for one or other of two basic reasons.

First, failure is defined in terms of not achieving a target sale volume within some prescribed period of time, usually determined on the basis of the time necessary to earn a satisfactory rate of return on the capital employed. The difficulty in applying such a criterion is that the great majority of managers tend to use a straight linear extrapolation when projecting future sales despite the fact that all the available evidence on the sales performance of successful new products points convincingly to some form of exponential growth. The theoretical expression of such a phenomenon is the well-known product life cycle concept which postulates that all products pass through a life cycle characterized by slow initial development. This is followed in turn by a period of rapid growth and a period of maturity or stability, whereafter sales will begin to decline unless management takes positive steps to extend or even rejuvenate the mature phase. Such a product life cycle is shown in Figure 21.1 together with a straightforward linear projection of expected sales. From Figure 21.1 it is abundantly clear that in the initial phases the new product will consistently underperform against the target – indeed the gap between the two will increase. Depending upon the time-scale involved, it seems quite likely that many managements will withdraw a product from the market because of its apparently deteriorating performance (the gap between 'projected' and 'actual') without ever knowing whether it would 'take off', in which case actual sales would later greatly exceed those projected.

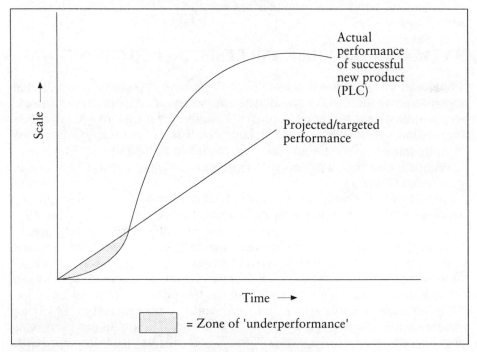

Figure 21.1   Product life cycle and projection of expected sales

Of course this is the major criticism levelled against the PLC concept – it can tell you only what the sales performance of a *successful* new product will look like – it cannot tell you if any given product experiencing difficulty in penetrating a market would be successful if you persevered with it.

The second reason why existing advice on market analysis and new product development will never result in a 100 per cent record of success is that there is another important factor which has been omitted from conventional analysis and which accounts for a significant proportion of failures. This factor has been described in a number of ways, the most familiar of which is 'resistance to change'. But, however we describe it, it is an expression of managerial attitude towards new products and it helps to explain why such products make slow initial progress when first introduced to a market.

It is vital that managers responsible for launching new products should understand why prospective customers may be slow to appreciate or accept the benefits claimed for such innovations. Clearly, if one possessed such information it might be possible to devise strategies to overcome these difficulties. Basically, the problem seems to be that while most managers feel that they can pre-identify the most receptive market for an innovation, the evidence is that by and large they are not very good at it. With the benefit of hindsight it is not difficult to see why company A could not seem to make up its mind about the benefits of adoption while company B accepted it almost immediately. The question is can we identify any patterns in the reactions of companies to new product propositions which would enable us to pick out the B companies in advance? The next section summarizes some of the factors which should be taken into account.

MANAGERIAL ATTITUDE AND RESISTANCE TO CHANGE

It has been suggested that a leading problem with economic theory is that many non-experts mistake its models for reality. Much the same problem seems to beset our attitude to industrial purchasing decisions for, while it is argued that consumers may act irrationally, it is unquestioningly accepted that companies follow the precepts of economic rationality and make decisions which maximize a price/quantity relationship in the manner prescribed by economic theory.

My own view is that *all* buyers use objective criteria in determining which purchase will give them the most satisfaction; that is, they behave 'rationally'. Unfortunately, such a process frequently fails to enable a prospective buyer to come to a decision for the simple reason that after exhausting all the available objective criteria, he or she is still left with two or more apparently equivalent alternatives and has to make a choice between them. As theoreticians we can assume away this problem by stating that if two or more products are objectively the same then they *are* the same and it does not matter which we choose. In the real world it is not like that at all – Daz is different from Omo, Rover is different from Mercedes, Goodyear is different from Dunlop, JCB is different from Caterpillar and so on. In the absence of any means of distinguishing between close substitute products life would become intolerable for we would live in a state of constant uncertainty. Thus the reason products are perceived as different is because we believe them to be so (usually with more than a little help from their manufacturers) and it is this belief or attitude which determines how we make purchase decisions.

But subjective factors do not influence only final purchase decisions when we are required to make a choice between what otherwise might be considered objectively identical products, they also influence our perception of the objective factors themselves. Thus it is not a question of what the seller claims are the attributes of a product or the benefits which will flow from its adoption that is important but the prospective buyers' interpretation of these claims, and there are numerous reasons why their views may differ. For example, James Bright (1964) cites twelve main sources of opposition to innovation and it is significant that only two of these, 3 and 6, make any pretence to economic objectivity:

1 To protect social status or prerogative.
2 To protect an existing way of life.
3 To prevent devaluation of capital invested in an existing facility, or in a supporting facility or service.
4 To prevent a reduction of livelihood because the innovation would devalue the knowledge or skill presently required.
5 To prevent the elimination of a job or a profession.
6 To avoid expenditures such as the cost of replacing existing equipment, or of renovating and modifying existing systems to accommodate or to compete with the innovation.
7 Because the innovation opposes social customs, fashions, tastes, and the habits of everyday life.
8 Because the innovation conflicts with existing laws.
9 Because of rigidity inherent in large or bureaucratic organizations.
10 Because of personality, habit, fear, equilibrium between individuals or institutions, status, and similar social and psychological considerations.
11 Because of a tendency of organized groups to force conformity.
12 Because of reluctance of an individual or a group to disturb the equilibrium of society or the business atmosphere.

There is now a considerable body of evidence which confirms beyond doubt that industrial buyers are just as subject to the processes of selective perception and distortion as are individuals making purchases for their own needs. It follows that industrial sellers should follow the example of their consumer counterparts in seeking to develop a better understanding of the factors which shape and influence the buyers' attitudes and behaviour. The final section of this chapter attempts to isolate certain guidelines which may prove helpful in this task.

363

IDENTIFYING THE INDUSTRIAL 'EARLY BUYER'

From the foregoing discussion it should be clear that:

1 Commercial failure is usually the result of delay in building up an acceptable sales volume.
2 The sales of a new product grow exponentially so that after an initial slow start successful products 'take off' and sales grow very rapidly indeed.
3 There is an inherent resistance to change and it is this which delays early sales.
4 While one may define a new product's economic and technological characteristics in objective terms these characteristics are viewed subjectively by prospective purchasers.

If we accept these conclusions it seems reasonable to hypothesize that the first person to buy must perceive the innovation more favourably than those who defer a decision or else reject the new product. It follows that if this is so there must be a significant advantage in being able to pre-identify potential early buyers for it will then be possible to target one's initial sales efforts at them. As noted above most sellers would argue that they already try to do this, but if their preselection is based upon their perception of who is likely to benefit most from purchase then it is unsurprising if this differs from the potential user's view.

For example, many innovators concentrate their sales efforts upon market leaders or those with the greatest potential demand for the new product on the basis that they have the most to gain. They also have the most to lose and it is this alternative interpretation which invariably predisposes the bigger company to proceed cautiously. This is not to say that they will not be among the first to buy, because given their scale of operations large users can often afford to buy an innovation solely to test it without any final commitment to it either way. Conversely, small companies may need only one unit of the innovation if it is a piece of capital equipment, or may have to standardize upon it if it is a raw material or component with the result that they are wholly committed and have to make the innovation work. Other things being equal, then, smaller companies have a greater commitment to any innovation they adopt and so will make strenuous efforts to make it successful.

Smaller companies are also likely to respond more quickly for the simple reason that decision making is more concentrated than in large companies and does not have to proceed through a hierarchy of committees. Further, in the smaller company it is usually simpler to discover who the key personnel are – the 'gatekeepers' who allow in or exclude information on new products, and the opinion leaders who gain job satisfaction through influencing their colleagues' views on specific matters such as the technical merits of a new piece of machinery. The benefit of being able to identify key individuals is obvious because we can then get to know them as such and achieve a much better knowledge of what conditions their perception.

Extensive research has shown that the firms most likely to respond quickly to new products are those which are experiencing some difficulties or problems of their own. For example, Jim Utterback of the Massachusetts Institute of Technology found in a study of five industries in Europe and Japan that 'successful projects were seen to be related to a fairly or highly urgent problem faced by a firm', and this conclusion is confirmed by numerous others. In broader terms, innovations are likely to appear more attractive to unsuccessful than to more successful companies. The conventional wisdom tends to favour the more successful, if for no other reason than that they will be able to pay, and this increases the probability of delay in market penetration.

A third factor of considerable help in pre-identifying the receptive companies is determination of the policy on depreciation and replacement. Most innovations are substitutes for something else and it is clear that a need to replace may give rise to the urgency discussed in the preceding paragraph. Certainly, if organizations are actively reviewing replacement possibilities there would seem to be a greater likelihood of their being willing to evaluate a new product than would be the case if they are entirely satisfied with their present supplier or installation. Most organizations have explicit depreciation and replacement policies, and time taken to determine these and the stage in the cycle at which individual companies are placed could repay handsome dividends in identifying the most receptive market segment.

A study of replacement policies may also uncover opportunities for joint product development, an approach which work by Eric von Hippel has shown to have a very high success rate. Most companies are flattered that their suppliers should take an interest in their likely future needs and are often willing to participate in joint product development, thus making it quite clear what benefits users are seeking and also providing facilities for field testing and trials. In addition, one of the most persuasive arguments to encourage the purchase of a new product is to be able to point to its successful use by someone else (another risk-reduction strategy).

Collectively all the foregoing factors emphasize the need to know your customers and to put yourself in their shoes when considering the perceived merits of an innovation.

Most new products are introduced by existing companies into existing markets and this is obviously much less difficult than is the case when developing an entirely new market. In the latter instance the same advice still applies, but much of the information will be more difficult to come by and may have to be inferred from other indicators. In such circumstances considerable benefits can be obtained by regarding the market development phase as a capital investment project (like research and development) and offering inducements to early buyers which help reduce the high perceived risk of being first. For example, it is possible to limit the financial risk by leasing or sale-or-return clauses, and running-in problems can be reduced by providing technical assistance and a generous policy on losses due to start-up difficulties. Alternatively, it is possible to join forces with a supplier/distributor with a proven track record in the market and benefit from its marketing skills.

WHO IS RESPONSIBLE FOR NPD?

Until now the emphasis in this chapter has been upon the launch phase with little or no reference to the internal process of NPD. In part this is because earlier chapters have looked at issues of product planning and product design. However, reference has also been deferred to reinforce the point that launching new products is a decidedly risky business from which it follows that those with responsibility for the activity bear a particular burden to guarantee that every possible effort has been made to ensure that the proposed product will meet the needs of a clearly defined target audience.

While these issues have been discussed in general terms earlier it might be helpful here to report some of the findings from an ongoing research project at Strathclyde University into the association between marketing and competitive success. Thus far the project has pursued two main thrusts. The first, 'Profit by design', was sponsored by the Design Council and concentrated on the specific contribution of design – both aesthetic and technical – as an element in the marketing mix. The second – 'Project MACS', funded by the ESRC and the Chartered Institute of Marketing – adopted a much broader approach and set out to evaluate the findings of populist and anecdotal accounts of the correlates of competitive success (see, for instance, *In Search of Excellence, The Winning Streak*, and the like) in a rigorous and closely controlled survey.

Given that attention to design factors and their importance in determining success have become management motherhoods it would clearly have been naïve to approach the question of the precise role and contribution of design in a direct way. Accordingly, 'Profit by design' adopted an indirect approach and purported to be an exploration of the process of new product development. Thus by bundling in design with a whole host of other considerations it was felt that specific reference to design would both be spontaneous and reflect its comparative standing *vis-à-vis* other relevant factors.

In that the full report of the study is much longer than this chapter it clearly is not possible to do justice to it here but one particular finding is felt to be particularly apposite. This relates to the involvement of different persons and functions within the process of NPD from conceptualization to launch. A diagram speaks a thousand words, and Figure 21.2 summarizes the findings.

From Figure 21.2 it is clear that marketing has an important role to play at all stages of development, that both engineering and aesthetic design are key elements and that top management involvement is significant at key stages in the process. However, the importance of the findings is even greater than appears at first sight for the data were split according to the actual *performance* of the respondent companies into successful and less successful categories. It emerged that a company's ability to be successful is determined by the range of people it employs and the involvement of these people in key decision-making areas such as new product development. The evidence suggests that the greater the functional representation and the greater the integration of functions the greater is that company's ability to develop commercially successful products. Companies in the study learned from experience that new

Stages in new product development process

	Opportunity identification	Design	Prototype development	Prototype evaluation	Introduction
Highest involvement	Marketing	R&D	R&D	Marketing	Sales
	MD	Eng. design	Eng. design	R&D	Marketing
	Sales	Marketing	Engineering	MD	MD
	R&D	Aes. design	Production	Sales	Production
	Eng. design	Sales	Marketing	Eng. design	Quality control
	Aes. design	MD	Aes. design	Engineering	Engineering
	Engineering	Engineering	MD	Production	Eng. design
	Production	Production	Sales	Q. control	R&D
	Finance	Q. control	Q. control	Aes. design	Aes. design
Lowest Involvement	Q. control	Finance	Finance	Finance	Finance

Figure 21.2 Personnel involvement in the design and development of new products

Note MD: Managing director; Eng. design: Engineering design; Aes. design: Aesthetic design; Q. control: Quality control.

367

product development is a repetitive, synthetic activity which can be continually refined and quickened to increase new product leverage over competition. This ability to shorten and refine the process of NPD is particularly important in dynamic markets where technological advances are frequent and result in new products being outdated prematurely.

SUMMARY

In the scope of such a short chapter we can only scratch the surface of an enormous subject. Hopefully the discussion will encourage reading of the specialist books, some of which are listed below, as well as underline the relevance of the other chapters in this book. Marketing is a highly complex activity in which the practitioner must combine a multiplicity of factors to meet a dynamic and continually changing situation. Nowhere is this more true than in the case of new product development, yet it is an activity which we cannot afford to avoid if we wish to remain competitive. If follows that any guidance on how to improve our success rate is to be welcomed and it is hoped that this chapter has provided some insight into the more important factors.

REFERENCES

Booz, Allen & Hamilton Inc. (1982), *New Product Management for the 1980s*, New York.

Bright, J. R. (1964), *Development and Technological Innovation*, Homewood, Illinois: Richard D. Irwin.

Utterback, J. M. (1979), 'Product and process innovation in a changing competitive environment', in M. J. Baker (ed.), *Industrial Innovation*, London: Macmillan.

Von Hippel, E. (1976), 'The dominant role of users in the scientific instrument innovation process', *Research Policy*, **5** (3).

Von Hippel, E. (1978), 'Users as innovators', *Technology Review*, **80** (3), January.

ESSENTIAL READING

Baker, M. J. (ed.) (1994), 'Innovation and new product development', *International Marketing Review*, special issue, **11** (1).

Baker, M. J. & Hart, S. J. (1989), *Marketing and Competitive Success*, Hemel Hempstead: Philip Allan.

Craig, Angie and Hart, Susan (1992), 'Where to now in new product development research?', *European Journal of Marketing*, **26**, (11).

22 Developing and launching a service

Don Cowell

The British economy is now a service economy. That is, in terms of output and in terms of employment, services have become the largest sector of the economy. Corresponding with this service revolution, marketing scholars study the subject of services marketing much more intently, systematically and rigorously.

The development and launching of new products have been important topics for marketing academics and professionals for a number of years. There is a significant volume of published literature which reflects both the extensive research which has been undertaken and the importance of the topic to practitioners. A number of potentially valuable insights, frameworks and experiences are available in this new product literature and are applicable to developing and launching a new service. However, it is increasingly recognized that there are a number of issues which are distinctive to services. For this reason the topic of new service development has been identified as an area of great importance (Cowell, 1988).

It is very likely that our knowledge of new service development and launching will increase over the next few years. The purpose of this chapter is to examine the factors that should be considered when preparing for the launch of a new service.

REASONS FOR DEVELOPING NEW SERVICES

There are a number of reasons why service organizations develop new services, including the following:

1 *Obsolescence*: service organizations cannot continue to rely on their existing range of services for their success. Sooner or later they become obsolete. They mature and then decline in their product life cycle. Change is a way of life for the innovative service organization.

2   *Competition*: new services are required to maintain present sales success and customer loyalty as well as to capitalize on changing marketplace needs in competitive markets.

3   *Spare capacity*: new services may be introduced to use up spare capacity, for example vacant theatre seats or low levels of usage at off-peak times on transportation systems.

4   *Seasonal effects*: many service organizations (tourism, for example) may have seasonal patterns of demand. New services may be introduced to even out these fluctuations.

5   *Risk reduction*: new services may be introduced to balance an existing sales portfolio where heavy dependence is placed on just a few services offered within a range.

6   *Opportunities*: new opportunities may emerge through a competitor withdrawing from a market or market research revealing unmet customer needs.

Whatever the reasons for introducing new services they are usually obtained in two ways. First, they may be obtained externally through acquisition or through licensing (for example, as in international marketing). Second, they may be developed internally through the process of new service development. Both strategies are risky and can result in failure; this chapter is concerned with the latter.

SERVICE/MARKET STRATEGIES

An important influence upon a service organization's new service development and launch procedures and processes will be its service/market strategy. This relates to decisions regarding target markets to be served and services to be offered to those target markets. The strategic options for service organizations are similar to those available for organizations marketing products. They are:

1   Attempting to sell more existing services to existing clients.
2   Attempting to sell existing services to new clients.
3   Attempting to sell new services to existing clients.
4   Attempting to sell new services in new markets.

The word 'new' can have a number of meanings attached to it in service contexts. One categorization of product innovations lends itself to service settings and identifies six groups ranging from major innovations to style changes (Heany 1983):

1   *Major innovations* are new services for markets still largely undefined. They include both new types of services (the first carphone systems are an example) as well as new service delivery systems, for example distance education schemes.

2 *Start-up businesses* are new services for a market already served by services meeting the same generic needs. Examples include telephone banking and motor manufacturer credit card schemes.

3 *New services* for the currently served market are an attempt to offer existing customers of the business a new service not available before but which may be offered by a competitor. Examples include airlines providing passengers with limousine collection and delivery services.

4 *Service line extensions* are additions to the existing service range and line. They include restaurants adding new menu items or airlines enhancing their services by adding a new route.

5 *Service improvements* involve a change in certain features for services already on offer to an existing market. They include speedier execution of an existing service through automation, an airline increasing leg room on seats or a university library extending opening hours.

6 *Style changes* represent a highly visible series of changes. They include new livery and design schemes for a transport company, refurbished interiors in a chain of opticians or new uniforms for hotel and restaurant staff.

Opportunities in the market-place are the impetus for new service development and launch policies. However new the service may be, a systematic process for new developments has its virtues.

NEW SERVICE DEVELOPMENT

It has been found that an ordered and systematic process for developing and introducing new products may help reduce the risk of product failure. Although procedures vary considerably (some procedures may be highly elaborate and formal, others informal and much less specific), where such systems exist, they tend to include a series of steps or phases between the decision to look for new ideas and their ultimate commercialization in the market-place. While the terminology of new product development and the range and order of steps included in the process vary, the underlying notions behind their use do not. These are, first, to create as many good ideas as possible and, second, to reduce the number of ideas by careful screening and analysis to ensure that only those with the best chances of success get into the market-place. One such sequence of steps is:

- Idea generation.
- Idea screening.
- Concept development and testing.
- Business analysis.
- Development.
- Testing.
- Commercialization.

Not all these steps may be necessary for all services. Much will depend upon factors such as the characteristics of the particular target market, the nature of the new service, competitive pressures, the time and resources which can be devoted to the process and the degree of innovation involved.

Idea generation

Ideas may be generated in many ways. They can arise inside and outside the organization; they can result from formal search procedures, for example marketing research, as well as informally; they may involve the organization in creating the means of delivering the new service product or in obtaining rights to the service product, as with a franchise.

The creative process of developing new ideas has long intrigued marketers although the process itself still defies detailed understanding. This has led in some cases to the adoption of techniques like 'synectics', brainstorming and lateral thinking to help improve the creative dimension of new service development.

Idea screening

This stage is concerned with checking out which ideas will justify the time, expense and managerial commitment of further research and study. Two features are usually associated with the screening phase:

1   The establishment or use of previously agreed evaluative criteria to enable the comparison of ideas generated (for example, ideas compatible with the organization's objectives and resources).
2   The weighing, ranking and rating of the ideas against the criteria used.

Screening systems range from the highly sophisticated, involving the collection and computer analysis of a mass of data, to simple checklists of a few factors considered to be vital. But it is important to stress that no single set of criteria is appropriate for all organizations – they must develop and adapt their own set of criteria to their particular circumstances.

Concept development and testing

Ideas surviving the screening process must then be translated into service concepts. In the service context this means concept development and concept testing:

1   *Concept development* is concerned with translating the service idea (where the possible service is defined in functional and objective terms) into a service concept, the specific subjective consumer meaning the organization tries to build into the product idea. Thus, in attempting to sell the idea of regular saving to young, unmarried people, a building

society might market the idea on the basis that participants would be saving towards house purchase and might later receive preferential mortgage treatment.

2 *Concept testing* is applicable in a services context as well as in goods contexts. Concept testing consists of taking the concepts developed by idea generation and idea screening, and securing reactions to them from groups of target customers.

An associated stage of the development of the service idea is that of service positioning. Service positioning is a concept increasingly widely referred to though it remains imprecisely defined, loosely used and difficult to measure. Essentially it is the visual presentation of the image of an organization's service in relation either to competitive services or to other services in its own mix. The principle underlying this method of presentation is that it enables service attributes to be compared with competitive offerings and with the customer's perceptions of services relative to his or her needs.

Some services, for example tour operators, may be positioned directly against competition. Others develop effective strategies by deliberately not confronting competition directly. For example, Avis admitted it was number two in the car rental market in the USA and advertised that it must try harder. On the other hand economy lodges and motels in the UK stress low-cost room rates and basic services in positioning themselves against rivals with more elaborate services.

Business analysis

This stage is concerned with translating the proposed idea into a firm business proposal. It involves undertaking a detailed analysis of the attractiveness of the idea in business terms and its likely chances of success or failure. A substantial analysis will consider in detail aspects like the manpower required to implement the new service idea, the additional physical resources required, the likely estimates of sales, costs and profits over time, the contribution of the new service to the range on offer, likely customer reaction to the innovation and the likely response of competitors. Obviously it is not possible to generate accurate forecasts and estimates and it is customary to build some degree of tolerance into the analysis to allow for the uncertainties and ambiguities involved. This stage may typically involve some initial technical and market research and initial timings and costing for a new service launch.

Development

This stage requires the translation of the idea into an actual service for the market. Typically this means that there will be an increase in investment in the project. Staff may have to be recruited or trained, facilities constructed, communications systems may need to be established. The tangible elements of the service will be designed and tested. Unlike goods the development stage of

373

new service development involves attention to both the tangible elements of the service and the service delivery system.

Testing

It may not always be possible to test new services. Airlines may introduce a new class of service on a selected number of routes or a bank may make a new service available initially on a regional basis; but some new services do not have such an opportunity. They must be available and operate to designed levels of quality and performance from their introduction. The American Express Bank, for example, after conducting detailed research which indicated that opening a London branch would be successful, had ultimately to take the plunge and go ahead by establishing a branch with a range of services.

Commercialization

This stage represents the organization's commitment to a full-scale launch of the new service. The scale of operation may be relatively modest, such as adding an additional service to an airline's routes, or large scale involving the national launch of fast-service footwear repair outlets operating on a concession basis. In undertaking the launch some basic decisions must be made:

1 When to introduce the new service.
2 Where to launch the new service, whether locally, regionally, nationally or internationally.
3 To whom to launch the new service – usually determined by earlier exploration in the new service development process.
4 How to launch the new service – for example, unit trusts may offer a fixed-price unit on initial investments during a certain period.

With highly novel and innovative services, organizations may be guided by the extensive literature and experience on innovation and diffusion. However, like many areas of marketing, most documented experience in this area has concentrated on tangibles rather then intangibles, and innovation in the service sector requires further empirical study.

SERVICE RANGE

Few service organizations offer only one service; they usually offer a mix of services for use or purchase. The particular range will be developed in response to internal needs or external influences. For example, high street banks now offer between 200 and 300 different kinds of services for personal customers, partly as a response to business development but partly also as a result of competitive pressures and customer demand. A typical service range has both width and depth. Width refers to the number of different service lines offered, depth refers to the assortment of items within each service line. A service line is a group of service items sharing similar characteristics in terms of customers, sales methods or price. Figure 22.1 illustrates the concepts of service range, width, depth and service line, using simple customer categories, for a local authority leisure centre.

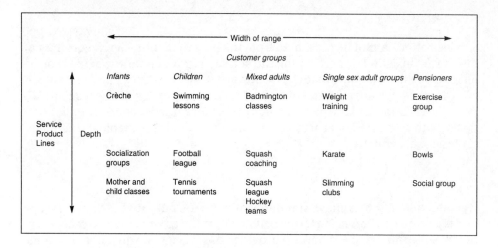

Figure 22.1   Illustrative service product range

In designing a service range careful attention should be given to the following:

1   What the optimum range of services should be. Most service organizations rely on market research evidence and trial and error in making this decision.
2   The positioning of the range of services provided against competitors' offerings.
3   The length and width of the range and how the services within it complement one another.
4   The profitability of the range where profit is a key concern, as it will be with most commercial services.

The new service development process outlined above is similar to that for new products. There are, however, a number of distinctive features of services which in turn create special considerations for service marketers. The remainder of this chapter deals with these matters.

DISTINCTIVE FEATURES OF SERVICES

Intangibility

Services are essentially intangible. It is often not possible to taste, feel, see, hear or smell services before they are purchased. Opinions and attitudes may be sought beforehand, a repeat purchase may rely upon previous experience, the customer may be given something tangible to represent the service, but ultimately the purchase of a service is the purchase of something intangible.

Inseparability

Services often cannot be separated from the person of the seller. A corollary of this is that creating or performing the service may occur at the same time as full or partial consumption of it. Goods are purchased, sold and consumed whereas services are sold and then produced and consumed. The inseparability of the creation and the performance of certain kinds of services applies particularly to some personal services, for example dental or medical treatment, professional services.

Heterogeneity

It is often difficult to achieve standardization in the output of certain services. The standard of a service in terms of its conformity to what may be prescribed by the seller may depend on who provides the service or when it is provided. So even though standard systems may be used to handle a flight reservation, book a car in for service or quote for life insurance, each 'unit' of service may differ from other 'units'. Franchise operations attempt to ensure standards of conformity but ultimately with services it is difficult to ensure the same level of quality of output as it may be with goods. From the customer's viewpoint, too, it is often difficult to judge quality in advance of purchase.

Perishability

Services are perishable and cannot be stored. Spare seats on a package tour or an empty hotel room represent capacity lost for ever if they are not 'consumed' when they are available at any point in time. In addition, considerable fluctuating demand patterns may apply to some services which aggravate this perishability feature further. Important marketing decisions in service organizations relate to the service levels they will provide and how they will respond in times of low and excessive usage, for example through differential pricing, or special promotions.

Ownership

Lack of ownership is a basic difference between a service and a good. With a service a customer may only have access to or use of a facility (a hotel room, for example). Payment is usually for the use of, access to or hire of items.

With the sale of goods, barring restrictions imposed by, say, a hire-purchase scheme, the buyer has full use of the product.

A summary of these characteristics of services is shown in Table 22.1. Also

Table 22.1
Some constraints on the management of services and ways of overcoming them

Characteristics of service	Some implications	Some means of overcoming characteristics
Intangibility	Sampling difficult. Places strain on promotional element of marketing mix. No patents possible. Difficult to judge price and quality in advance.	Focus on benefits. Increase tangibility of service (e.g. physical representations of it). Use brand names. Use personalities to personalize service. Develop reputation.
Inseparability	Requires presence of producer. Direct sale. Limited scale of operations.	Learn to work in larger groups. Work faster. Train more competent service providers.
Heterogeneity	Standard depends upon who and when provided. Difficult to assure quality.	Careful personnel selection and training. Ensure standards are monitored. Pre-package service. Mechanize and industrialize for quality control. Emphasize bespoke features.
Perishability	Cannot be stored. Problems with demand fluctuation.	Better match between supply and demand (e.g. price reductions off peak).
Ownership	Customer has access to but not ownership of activity or facility.	Stress advantages of non-ownership (e.g. easier payment systems).

shown are some implications of these characteristics and suggested means of overcoming the problems posed.

There is, however, still difference of opinion as to whether some of these characteristics do help to discriminate between goods and services. For example, some commentators provide cogent arguments why intangibility, heterogeneity and perishability at least are not of themselves sufficiently discriminating. They believe there are too many exceptions to their use for services alone and believe that what is required is not a simple product/service scheme differentiating on the basis of the characteristics of the offer itself

377

but a more complex taxonomy of offerings which differentiates on the basis of product/service characteristics and market characteristics. That said, these features of services do seem to have an influence upon creating special considerations for service marketers concerned with developing and launching new services.

SPECIAL CONSIDERATIONS FOR SERVICE MARKETERS

Some special considerations for service marketers stemming from the differences between services and products are dealt with in this section.

Table 22.2
Service characteristics and their effects on marketing research

Characteristics	Effects upon marketing research
Intangibility	• Where a dominantly intangible service, home use tests not appropriate • Often appropriate to move directly from concept testing to test marketing in new product development • 'Researchability' problem for dominantly intangible services
Patenting difficult	• Reduces incentives for large R&D investment • More focus on 'me-too' services • Tendency towards service improvement rather than innovation • Ease of competitive entry influences viability of new service concepts
Standardization difficult	• Difficult to develop accurate concept descriptions • Problems in concept testing
Direct relationship between service performer and client	• Judgements of service influenced by who performs the service and the client's involvement in performance
No clear lines of demarcation between a service and the place in which it is delivered, the process and the people	• Concept testing difficult because of need to assess impact of performer and physical evidence on service itself.

Problems in researching new services

Some differences between marketing research for new services and for new products stem from the characteristics of services themselves, some of which together with their suggested effects on the use of marketing research, particularly for new service development research designs, are shown in Table 22.2. The general problems of researching services with their often elusive, ephemeral and intangible qualities are aggravated when new services are being researched. The uncertainty and ambiguity of the service, the difficulty the customer may have in articulating what benefits are sought from a service innovation, and finalizing the elements the service should consist of, provide a 'researchability' problem for the market reseacher. One scheme represents a service offer as a constellation of tangible and intangible attributes. A particular problem in new service development is to identify, weight and rank the separate elements that make up a service offer. These are difficult judgements for researchers to obtain from customers for existing services. They become even more difficult with new services.

The very nature of services means that researchers and users must be prepared to use 'soft', qualitative data particularly in conceptualizing a service. Because services possess the characteristics of perishability and intangibility their value is more often judged in terms of benefits rather than features. This can mean that to determine what a service entity is to a market, a marketer must conduct more initial marketing research than in product marketing. Also, a tight service specification may be difficult to produce. These problems of measurement have led to the development of new techniques in marketing research. For example, they have led to attempts to clarify the concept testing process for services. One framework for concept testing has a number of steps:

1 The service idea begins with analysis of consumer needs.
2 Ideas are then generated to meet these needs.
3 These ideas are subjected to a preliminary analysis during which the competitive environment is considered.
4 The ideas are examined internally and subjective judgements are made about the market size and potential response.
5 A preliminary external reaction from potential customers and suppliers is obtained.
6 The 'positioning' of the service in the market is then considered and field studies are undertaken to present the concept specifically to a carefully selected sample of potential customers.
7 Finally the concept is evaluated and customer understanding, customer buying and usage intentions and customer benefits in particular are sought.

Unfavourable results may mean revising the concept; favourable results may mean test marketing (where applicable) or direct introduction of the service *379* (where possible). The purposes of this framework are thus to find out whether a potential customer:

- Understands the idea of the proposed service.
- Reacts favourably to it.
- Feels it offers benefits to meet unmet needs.

Concept-testing processes for services have been a relatively neglected area of marketing management. However, the growing interest in service marketing and the importance of clearer definitions of services, have made this a significant area of development over the past few years.

Compared with products, some differences experienced with services offer advantages to the marketing researcher. First, the researcher has the opportunity to evaluate services before, after the sale and during the sale (that is, during the performance of the service). Unlike a product, which is produced and then consumed, some services are consumed as they are being produced. The provider can thus obtain feedback while the service is being produced and make appropriate adjustments where these are required by customers. One study has shown that participating in a marketing research investigation on site does not actually interfere with enjoyment of a service. However, the consumer's evaluation of being a respondent is sensitive to the costs and rewards of participation and the service organization needs to maintain the respondent's goodwill. Second, direct customer involvement with many services allows the user to specify the type of service required direct to the seller or performer. Third, the relatively more recent use of marketing research by service organizations has given them certain advantages. They are able to use proven techniques developed in other contexts. They can benefit by avoiding earlier mistakes and misapplications of marketing research techniques in product fields.

Issues associated with new service features

The buyer's choice of a new service may be influenced by features associated with it. These features may be seen by the consumer as a fundamental part of the 'core' service or as 'peripheral' to it. In tangible product marketing the brand, the colour, the design or the package may be important contributory factors to the consumer's purchase decision. Generally such elements are less conspicuous features in service marketing but they may nevertheless be integral components of some forms of service planning. The relevance of some of these features is described below.

Service branding

Branding is difficult because of the problems of maintaining consistency of quality in service settings, and it would seem not to be used in services marketing as much as it should. This is surprising for, given the intangible nature of services and the difficulty of distinguishing one service from another, branding provides a significant method for achieving some degree of service differentiation.

Service patents

The intangibility of services means that there are no patents. It is thus difficult to prevent competitors from copying service innovations, even though trade names can be protected. This means that innovations may have short life cycles since they are easy to copy. Banks and airlines are examples of where the absence of patent protection has brought large-scale copying of practices, for example the classes of air travel available. The absence of patent protection is one of the characteristics which present unique problems to service organizations and their clients. The British Invisible Export Council has pointed out that with regard to certain traded services, the expertise they require makes them difficult to copy quickly.

Service warranty

The provision of a service is formally undertaken within a framework imposed by the law of contract. This framework of legally enforceable obligations is a complex combination of those undertakings which were agreed expressly by the parties precontractually and those which are imposed from outside. Terms are implied into contracts by statutes. For example, the Supply of Goods and Services Act, 1982, implies into contracts for the supply of services terms which stipulate that the service will be supplied with reasonable care and skill, within a reasonable time and at a reasonable cost (unless time and cost are expressly fixed). Indeed, other statutes (such as the Unfair Contract Terms Act 1977) severely restrict the potential for limitation or exclusion of such obligations as these. Moreover, terms can be implied into such contracts as these because they are trade usages or customs or because they have become normal between the parties over a previous course of dealings.

However, in discussions about the nature and content of what is provided in the supply of a service the marketer may overlook the essential importance and the value to increased market share of the supply of more than that which must be supplied to avoid the threat of action for breach of contract. For example, if at an airport the passengers are delayed by circumstances beyond the control of the service provider, the supply of facilities which are over and above the legally enforceable obligations may improve the profile of the service product. Thus if passengers are set to be delayed for hours, the personal attention of the service provider to ensuring the maximum practicable comfort and convenience of each of his customers becomes a marketing tool in itself. The customer is aware that more is being supplied than, in his perception, is being paid for.

After-sales service

After-sales service is usually associated with the sale of tangibles. However, it is also relevant to services markets. For example, an airline may assist passengers to arrange hire cars and book hotels as part of its service; an insurance company may advise clients on changes they should make to their policies as their personal circumstances change; a stockbroker may assist a client to readjust a portfolio of shares; a dentist may provide a check-up some time after providing dental treatment.

After-sales service can be an important element of the service marketing mix. Its availability can help to secure a sale in the first place; it can maintain and develop customer loyalty and goodwill; it can provide a means of obtaining feedback about service performance; it can provide a means for obtaining suggestions for new and improved services.

Problems associated with the design of the service process

A significant influence upon a customer's perception of service quality is how well the process of service delivery functions. The way in which service systems operate is crucial to customer satisfaction. Those which operate effectively and efficiently can give marketing management considerable marketing leverage and promotional advantage. It is clear that a smooth-running service operation offers competitive advantages particularly where differentiation between services is minimal. But effective and efficient systems do not operate by chance, they operate by design. Developing and launching a new service is as much concerned with the design of service delivery processes and procedures as with the design of the services themselves. Often the service product is the service process. Many service operations, particularly those operating multi-site operations, need to codify operations procedures to ensure some consistency in service performance. Some service operations have extensive procedures manuals to try to ensure some uniformity of operation.

The area of service design and service delivery is traditionally viewed as the responsibility of the operations manager, but in service organizations co-operation between marketing and operations is vital. In service systems the implications of operational performance and malpractice are too visible to be solely operational concerns. The customer is so often involved as a participant in the service delivery system that operational concerns about service delivery effectiveness and efficiency are marketing concerns too. Particular problems associated with the design of the service process therefore stem from the much closer relationship needed between operations managers and marketing managers. The design of service processes from a marketing perspective has received scant attention by many service organizations, but is increasingly recognized as an area in which a new service can be differentiated from competitors' offerings.

Problems associated with the use of people in new services

Service personnel are important in most organizations. They are particularly important in those situations where, in the absence of clues from tangible products, the customer forms an impression of a new service from the behaviour and attitudes of staff involved in the service delivery system. The design and launch of a new service therefore demand attention to the service product, the service process and service personnel involved. How a new service is performed will ultimately influence the image of a service organization. As with the new service process, the design of the new service employee–customer relationship should not be left to chance. Attention must be given to the people aspects of the service. Many service organizations which launch new services now recognize the importance of careful selection and training of service personnel, standardization of patterns of behaviour towards customers, ensuring consistency of appearance and conducting quality control studies through service personnel audits. The significance of the relationship between employee and customer has received the attention of academic researchers in marketing as the role of the service 'encounter' and the role of employees in new services development and delivery has been fully recognized.

CONCLUSIONS

Service marketers can benefit considerably from existing knowledge of the new product development and launch process derived from studies of new consumer products and new industrial products. However, this chapter suggests that some distinctive aspects of services may create special issues for service marketers. Since services themselves vary considerably in terms of their nature, form, processes and delivery, generalizations about new service delivery and launch should be treated with caution.

REFERENCES

Cowell, D. W. (1988), 'New service development', *Journal of Marketing Management*, **3**, (3), 296–312.

Heany, D. F. (1983), 'Degrees of product innovation', *Journal of Business Strategy*, **3**, Spring, 3–14.

ESSENTIAL READING

de Bretani, U. (1991), 'Success factors in developing new business services', *European Journal of Marketing*, **25**, (2), 30–60.
Easingwood, C. J. (1986), 'New product development for service companies', *Journal of Product Innovation Management*, **4**, 264–75.

Easingwood, C. J. (1993), Special edition on 'New Product Development in the Financial Services Sector' in *The International Journal of Bank Marketing*, **11**, (3), 1–41.

Part IV
DISTRIBUTING THE PRODUCT

23 Physical distribution and logistics management
Martin Christopher

Distribution, and the wider business philosophy of logistics, have always been a central feature of all economic activity. Yet paradoxically it is only in recent years that they have come to receive serious attention from either the business or academic worlds. One very obvious reason for this neglect is that, while the *functions* that comprise the logistics task are individually recognized, the *concept* of logistics as an integrative activity in business has developed only within the last 20 years.

What is logistics? It can be variously defined, but expressed at its simplest it is (see Bowersox, 1978):

> The process of strategically managing the movement and storage of materials, parts, and finished inventory from suppliers, through the firm and on to customers.

Logistics is thus concerned with the management of the physical flow which begins with sources of supply and ends at the point of consumption. It is clearly therefore much wider in its reach than simply a concern with the movement of finished goods – a commonly held view of physical distribution. In the logistics scheme of things we are just as much concerned with plant and depot location, inventory levels, materials management and information systems as we are with transport.

One of the features of the logistics concept – which is its greatest attraction while simultaneously being the greatest obstacle to its widespread adoption in industry so far – is that it places the emphasis on integrating activities that traditionally have been located in different functions of the business. Thus in many companies responsibility for, say, inventory on the one hand and transport on the other may be vested in the production function and the distribution functions respectively, and decisions on one will often be made without regard for the other. The logistics viewpoint, however, forces the decision maker to recognize the connections between the component elements of the materials flow system – indeed it encourages comprehensive systems thinking rather than functional tunnel vision.

It is interesting to trace the evolution of thought in the logistics activity and then to assess its importance for business today.

As early as 1915, writing from Harvard Business School, Arch Shaw took a view of the logistics activity which was radically far-sighted. He said:

The relations between the activities of demand creation and physical supply . . . illustrate the existence of the two principles of interdependence and balance. Failure to co-ordinate any one of these activities with its group fellows and also with those in the other group, or undue emphasis or outlay put upon any one of these activities, is certain to upset the equilibrium of forces which means efficient distribution.
. . . The physical distribution of the goods is a problem distinct from the creation of demand . . . Not a few worthy failures in distribution campaigns have been due to such a lack of co-ordination between demand creation and physical supply . . . Instead of being a subsequent problem, this question of supply must be met and answered before the work of distribution begins.

This view of logistics as a bridge between demand creation and physical supply is as valid today as it was when first expressed 80 years ago. However, no matter how fundamental this idea was, very little attention seems to have been paid to it and, indeed, in 1962 one of the gurus of management, Peter Drucker, writing in *Fortune* magazine, said:

Physical distribution is today's frontier in business. It is one area where managerial results of great magnitude can be achieved. And it is still largely unexplored territory.

There are signs, however, that management consciousness of the importance of logistics is growing and recent years have seen a considerable upsurge in interest in this area.

A number of factors have contributed to this growth in interest in logistics management. One is that as companies seek out areas for productivity improvement they are forced to confront the substantial corporate costs represented by distribution. Production and marketing have both been subjected to scrutiny by academic commentators and the more efficiency-conscious companies. Now it is the turn of the materials flow system that binds production and marketing to receive similar examination.

Giving increased urgency to this examination is the growth in the costs of movement and storage. Energy crises have had a direct impact upon transport costs, and soaring interest rates have made the costs of holding stocks a sizeable expense. Beyond this the vast proliferation in the size of most companies' product ranges has meant that the total stockholding investment of these companies has increased dramatically. When one considers that ten years ago a typical frozen food company offered a range of only 200 items whereas now it has a total range of over 500, it can be appreciated how important a factor in the corporate balance sheet inventory has become.

Changes in the channels of distribution have themselves forced many manufacturers and distributors to take a fresh look at their distribution systems. Grocery retailing in the UK is a prominent example of how power in the marketing channel has dramatically changed hands. Twenty-five years ago there were 150 000 retail grocery outlets; today there are only 60 000. Clearly the size of these outlets in physical and turnover terms has increased considerably and so too has the centralization of retail buying power. For example, Tesco and Sainsbury together account for over 25 per cent of the UK sales of groceries. The impact this has had on manufacturers, and in particular on their distribution systems, has been far-reaching.

Similar changes in channel relationships have occurred in many other industries too.

The combination of all these factors has brought the distribution problem into sharp focus. In particular, awareness is growing both of the impact of logistics upon corporate profitability and, underlying this, its impact upon the national economy.

THE CONCEPT OF LOGISTICS MANAGEMENT

As we have already noted, the logistics concept is based on a total systems view of the materials and goods flow activity from the source of supply through to the final point of consumption. It recognizes the interrelationships between the multitude of functions involved in this movement from source to user and in so doing forces management to think in terms of managing the total system rather than just one part of it.

The specific functional areas encompassed by logistics might be termed the 'logistics mix' and could be summarized as follows:

- *Inventory*, for example:
    - Service level decisions.
    - Materials requirements planning.

- *Information*, for example:
    - Order processing.
    - Demand forecasting.

- *Warehousing and handling*, for example:
    - Depot location.
    - Unitization and packaging.

- *Transport*, for example:
    - Mode decisions.
    - Scheduling.

The logistics management task is concerned with the integration and co-ordi-   *389* nation of these activities in such a way that end-markets are served in the most cost-effective manner.

The whole purpose of the logistics activity is to provide 'availability'. Everyone will be familiar with the cliché: 'The right product in the right place at the right time.' If one adds 'at the least cost', that is precisely the objective of logistics management.

Another way of defining the objective of logistics management could be in terms of 'customer service', which is in effect an elaboration on the notion of 'availability'. The idea of customer service encompasses all the points of contact between the customer and the supplier in terms of physical fulfilment of orders. Customer service is the output of the logistics system and it results from the combined effects of the activity centres within the 'logistics mix'. All these activities are important in establishing a desired level of customer service performance. They are also interdependent: if one activity fails, the system fails, creating poor performance and destabilizing workloads in other areas, resulting in the end in poor cost-effectiveness for the system as a whole. A failure in sales forecasting, then, may influence materials requirements planning which then results in low product availability of finished goods inventory. This in turn may result in either lost sales or an increased number of back orders which may in turn delay order processing and hence extend the order cycle time. This may result in the need to expedite shipments which increases the cost of service to the customer (Christopher et al., 1979).

Obviously, providing improved customer service will normally incur additional costs for the company. The higher the level of service offered the higher will be the costs. In fact it can be shown that once the level of service increases beyond the 70–80 per cent mark, the associated costs increase far more than proportionately ('service level' being defined for our purposes as the percentage of orders which can be met from stock within a given period).

The implications of this cost function for the distributing company are worth some attention. In the first place, many companies, far from having any explicit service policy, are unaware of the level of service at which they are operating. Even if the company does have a declared service policy it is often the case that service levels have been arbitrarily set. Offering a 97 per cent level of service instead of a 95 per cent level may have only a slight effect on customer demand, yet it will have a considerable effect on distribution costs – for normally distributed demand this 2 per cent increase in the level of service would lead to a 14 per cent increase in safety stock.

Clearly, therefore, it is essential that management recognizes the cost implications of a service strategy. Indeed, by offering logistics service the company is absorbing a cost that would otherwise have to be borne by the customer. For example, if the supplying company delivers twice instead of once a week, it is relieving the customer of a certain responsibility for holding stock – the more frequent the deliveries, the less stock the customer needs to hold. Similarly, if the customer knows that when placing an order with that supplier, the supplier will rarely be out of stock on that item and can deliver it speedily, then again the customer's stockholding can be lower. Because it costs money to hold stock – currently about 25 per cent of its value a year – by offering such a service the supplier is absorbing this customer cost.

WHAT ARE THE COSTS OF DISTRIBUTION?

There has been a tendency in the past for companies to consider only the costs of transport and, perhaps, warehouses, as their distribution costs. Recently, however, more companies have adopted the 'total distribution cost' concept. This concept recognizes that many more costs are incurred through the provision of availability than just transport and warehouse costs. For example, decisions about service level, as we have seen, affect the amount of inventory that needs to be held in the system, thus the cost of holding inventory must be included as a distribution cost. Likewise, order-processing costs are influenced by the distribution activity, so they too must be included; indeed, there is a case for including invoicing costs. The costs of materials handling and protective packaging also form part of the total distribution cost, as should the costs of managing and administering the distribution system.

We could express the total distribution cost concept in the form of an equation:

$$TDC = TC + FC + CC + IC + HC + PC + MC$$

Where

TDC	=	Total distribution costs
TC	=	Transport costs
FC	=	Facilities costs (depots, warehouses and the like)
CC	=	Communications costs (order processing, invoicing and so on)
IC	=	Inventory cost
HC	=	Materials handling costs
PC	=	Protective packing costs
MC	=	Distribution management costs

Various surveys have been made of the relative costs of distribution in industry and their findings seem to suggest that these costs represent about 15 per cent of sales turnover for a typical company. Averages can of course be misleading and, depending on the nature of the business, the figures can be very much higher or lower. Table 23.1 shows one company's analysis of its total distribution costs.

While this company has placed some costs under slightly different headings from those used in the TDC equation above, they amount to the same thing in total.

One of the benefits of being able to identify the specific sources of total distribution costs is that it becomes easier to identify potential 'trade-offs'. A trade-off occurs where an increased cost in one area is more than matched by a cost reduction in another area, leading to an improved situation overall. *391*

Thus, a distribution system with ten regional depots has high warehouse and stockholding costs compared with a system of only five depots, but the savings on trunk haulage and the reduction of stock-outs may more than compensate for the extra costs involved in the ten-depot system. In this case, an increase in warehouse and stock carrying costs has been traded off against a reduction in total system costs.

Table 23.1
A leading food company's total distribution costs

Cost	% of total sales	
Transport inwards		
Materials to factories		1.00
Transport outwards		
Palletization	0.02	
Factories to depots	1.71	
Depots to customer	2.09	3.82
Warehouses, depots		
Clerical wages	0.16	
Warehouse labour	1.29	
Other costs	1.19	2.64
Order processing		
Rental of terminals	0.11	
Operating terminals	0.07	
Computer	0.03	
Sales accounting	0.68	0.89
Protective packaging		2.00
Management		
Management costs	0.17	
Stock auditing	0.02	
Stock planning	0.01	
Training	0.01	0.21
Stock losses		0.26
Interest on capital		
Stocks	0.24	
Building, vehicles, plant	0.46	0.70
TOTAL		11.52

Generally, the effects of trade-offs are assessed in two ways: first from the point of view of their impact on total system costs, and second from their impact on sales revenue. It is possible to trade off costs in such a way that total costs increase, yet because of the better service now being offered, sales revenue increases. If the difference between revenue and costs is greater than before, the trade-off may be regarded as leading to an improvement in cost-effectiveness.

In addition to the possibility of trading off costs between the various elements in the distribution system, for example between depot costs and stock-holding costs, there is the possibility of identifying trade-offs within an individual element. Thus, stock levels of finished goods in the logistics system may be reduced at the expense of the level of service offered, but the reduction in sales revenue resulting is more than compensated for by the reduction in stockholding costs – or vice versa in different circumstances.

TOTAL SYSTEMS MANAGEMENT

For the benefits of such trade-offs to be fully achieved managers must begin to think in terms of total systems rather than in terms of narrow functional areas. A great deal has been written and talked about systems, systems approaches, systems thinking and systems management. While as a generalization it would probably be correct to define anything that converts an input into an output as a 'system', the concept of a logistics system is rather more complex. As we have seen, the logistics system is concerned with the movement and storage of products from their raw state, through various stages of sub-assembly, manufacture, packaging, transportation and delivery to the final customer. Depending upon how widely one wishes to define the 'system' it can be seen that logistics considerations are involved throughout the marketing and exchange channel from the sources of supply to the points of final consumption. To add to the complexity it is unlikely that the same corporate entity will be involved, or will have control, over the entire system. Furthermore, within the company itself many functional areas, or sub-systems, will exist which may have conflicting goals or objectives.

This latter feature is of particular concern to logistics systems management. Table 23.2 shows some of the conflicts that can occur between functions of the firm (that is, sub-systems) when goals are determined by functions without regard to the impact of their actions upon the total system. This very common feature of corporate structures is called 'sub-optimization' by operations researchers – in other words, a failure to recognize that, unless carefully managed, the whole can sometimes be less than the sum of its parts. The ultimate rationale of the logistics concept is that it reduces sub-optimization within the company through a greater integration and co-ordination of connected activities.

Figure 23.1 represents the materials and information flows which must be managed to provide cost-effective customer service.

Many companies fail to recognize that the materials flow through the firm and the related flow of information (that is, orders, forecasts, stock reports and so on) should logically be seen as an integrated system. Typically, responsibility for the various functions involved in those flows is fragmented. At best there will be a partial attempt at integration through the development of a materials management function to manage goods inwards and the procure- *393*

Table 23.2
Situations which can give rise to inter-departmental conflicts

Sub-systems goal	Purchasing	Production	Finance	Marketing	Logistics
Bulk purchases of materials	Advantage /larger discounts		Disadvantage: working capital tied up		Disadvantage: warehousing costs increased
Long production runs		Advantage: low costs	Disadvantage: working capital tied up	Disadvantage: narrow product range	Disadvantage: warehousing costs increased
Broad product range	Disadvantage: discounts small on low volume	Disadvantage: short, high-cost runs	Disadvantage: finished goods stocks high	Advantage: more sales through wider customer appeal	Disadvantage: higher costs through more administration and warehousing space
Tighter credit control			Advantage: greater use of working capital	Disadvantage: possible loss of sales	
Four-day delivery (from seven days)			Disadvantage: higher operating costs	Advantage: more sales because of better service	Disadvantage: system costs increased in order to meet service requirements
Unit loads			Advantage: lower operating costs	Disadvantage: loss of sales to small customers	Advantage: system costs can be lowered by eliminating uneconomic calls

ment of materials, and a parallel distribution management function responsible for the delivery of finished goods. The logistics concept suggests that greater efficiency and effectiveness can be achieved through an even wider, total systems view.

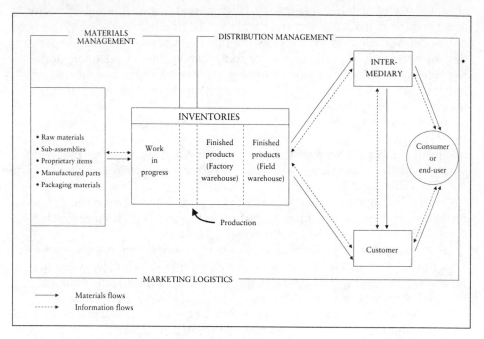

Figure 23.1   The logistics systems concept

Some companies are in fact moving towards the adoption of such an approach to logistics management. Indeed, it has been suggested that there is a process of 'evolution' by which the company might progress on its way to the adoption of a logistics orientation. Looked at broadly there are three stages.

The first of these stages might be described as a *transport management* orientation. In this very basic situation the organization will not have recognized the function of transport except as a means of moving the product from the factory or warehouse to the customer's premises. It will be viewed as a purely mechanical task which does not need senior management attention. Often it will be managed by personnel with little status in the organization and no attempt will have been made to integrate the transport activity with other demand-fulfilling tasks such as warehousing, order processing and inventory control. The emphasis will be on cost minimization, the transport function being evaluated in terms of cost per mile or cost per case shipped or some such similar measure. Many companies have still not moved beyond this stage.

The second stage could be termed the *physical distribution management* or

PDM orientation. This stage reflects a significant transition for the company because it requires a recognition that distribution is more than simply moving goods from A to B but instead is a vital link in the customer satisfaction process. Now the emphasis is on customer service and the use of distribution as a means of gaining leverage in the market-place. A greater status is accorded the distribution manager and the function may even be represented at board level in its own right. Now the functions of warehousing, order processing and finished goods inventory control will probably be incorporated in the total distribution activity and the performance criteria will be as much about delivery as about costs. This second stage is perhaps the most common in British industry today.

Finally comes the third stage: the *logistics management* orientation. The logistics orientation, as we have seen, recognizes that to improve the performance of the system, as measured by the cost-effective provision of customer service, all the interrelated activities in moving materials and goods from source to user must be managed as a whole.

Clearly the logistics concept as we have defined it involves a radical transformation of the way a company faces up to the needs of the market-place in terms of its entire operations management.

What is implicit in this new approach is the recognition of the need to balance the requirements of customer service against the internal management of its resources. Figure 23.2 highlights the integrative nature of the logistics task in bridging the operations gap between source of supply and final demand.

This conceptual framework is analogous to the concepts of materials management and distribution management presented in Figure 23.1. The sugges-

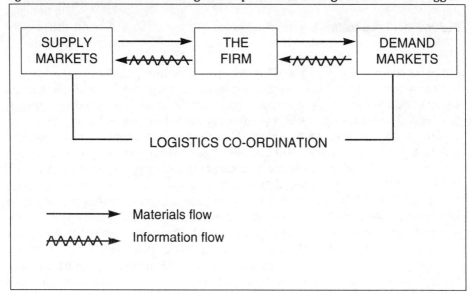

Figure 23.2   Logistics links supply with demand

tion here is that logistics is a *planning framework* rather than a business function. In other words, the management task inherent in logistics is *not* so much concerned with the *management* of materials flows but rather with providing the mechanism for establishing objectives and strategies within which the day-to-day activities of materials management and distribution management can take place.

LOGISTICS' ROLE IN CORPORATE STRATEGY

It is often forgotten that there is an important role for logistics in the development of corporate strategy. Instead a narrow cost-reduction view is taken and as a result many opportunities for improved market performance are missed.

Increasingly, however, more sophisticated organizations are recognizing that logistics has a wider role to play within the business. Decisions taken now on distribution networks, management of materials flow, information systems and so on can be crucial in determining the ability of the company to respond to changed market circumstances or new business opportunities.

A good example of how logistics can have impact at the highest level is provided by SKF, the Swedish bearings manufacturer. Several years ago SKF was facing severe competition in its European markets from Japanese suppliers which were able to supply standard bearings at a price not much higher than SKF's production cost. Analysis of the situation highlighted the fact that while SKF was producing over 50 000 variants the Japanese were concentrating on a very limited range of fast-moving lines. Moreover, SKF had plants in Sweden, Germany, the UK, France and Italy, each of which was generally providing the full range of variants. It became clear that SKF was unable to gain the benefits of scale at the production level because the typical batch run length was so small. The Japanese on the other hand were mass-producing a much smaller number of items and consequently were much lower down the 'experience curve' which was reflected in their lower costs.

SKF's response was essentially logistical. It first reviewed the product range with the object of substantially reducing the number of items manufactured. Beyond this, however, it decided to concentrate the production of certain categories of bearings at individual manufacturing locations. Thus the French factory would make bearings which would be produced only there, Italy had its own unique line and similarly at each of the other manufacturing locations.

The end result was a classic trade-off in logistics costs. On the one hand, the costs of transport involved in distributing finished produce from the plant in, say, Sweden, to a customer in the UK were substantially higher than hitherto when that customer had been supplied from the UK. On the other hand, the production cost savings more than offset this extra cost.

To make it all work SKF installed a sophisticated information and planning system which enabled a centralized control of production and the allocation of inventory to local stocking points. This system, which it called the Global Forecasting and Supply System (GFSS), is essentially a logistics management system.

While SKF has faced severe trading conditions in recent years due to recession in its principal markets, it is probably true to say that its position would
be much worse were it not for the adoption of this radical approach to logistics management.

In a quite different context one of North America's largest wholesale distributors, Foremost-McKesson, revised its logistics strategy to rescue a fast-
deteriorating profit situation. The company was faced with a classic 'middleman squeeze' with more and more manufacturers delivering direct to the
retailer. The company's response was to seek additional ways in which it
could 'add value' to the basic distribution process (*Business Week*, 7
December 1981). Amongst Foremost's responses to the situation it faced were
the following:

1   Taking waste products as well as finished goods from chemical manufac-
    turers, and recycling the wastes through its own plants – its first entry
    into chemical waste management.
2   Creating a massive merchandising service by providing teams to set up
    displays of manufacturers' goods within stores.
3   Acting as middleman between drug stores and insurance offices by pro-
    cessing medical consumer claims.
4   Using the information from its computer to help manufacturers manage
    inventories, collect and analyse market data, and even plan sales and
    new product development.
5   Leasing electronic ordering equipment to retailers, offering shelf-man-
    agement plans, and even providing price labels.

These and other actions have transformed the company's profitability – a
transformation which has been achieved by the recognition that logistics is
essentially a strategic orientation.

One further example underlines the positive impact on the market-place
that a well-thought-through logistics strategy can achieve. The Whirlpool
Corporation is a leading US manufacturer of domestic appliances such as
washing machines, spin dryers and so on. To give some idea of its size, the
company estimates that every day of the year approximately 25 000 customers
buy one or more appliances which have been manufactured by Whirlpool. A
significant percentage of these appliances are purchased from 900 Sears retail
stores and 1 700 Sears catalogue outlets. A further significant proportion of
Whirlpool's annual sales volume is purchased from 13 500 franchised
Whirlpool brand retail and builder outlets which are supplied from 45 wholesale distributors. As might be imagined, the logistics of supplying these various channels of distribution from eight manufacturing facilities located in six
different states are extremely complex. For example, the company estimates
that its daily shipments throughout the system are equivalent to a freight train
seven miles long!

The company recognized some years ago that in a competitive market-place
product availability and customer choice were highly important. Yet given the

size of Whirlpool's product range the cost of holding high levels of inventory throughout the channel would be prohibitive.

To solve this problem the company has installed a 'real time' inventory control and order processing system. If a customer walks into a Sears retail store on, say, Monday and selects a model he or she wishes to buy it can be in the customer's home by Thursday. The way it works is that on Monday evening all the orders for Whirlpool products from that store are transmitted to the nearest Sears regional distribution centre (RDC). On Tuesday morning the Sears RDC combines all orders from its assigned retail stores and transmits their total needs directly into Whirlpool's computer which automatically processes the order, reserves inventory and transmits a shipping document to the appropriate Whirlpool distribution centre by Tuesday afternoon. That same afternoon or evening a trailer is loaded for delivery overnight to the Sears RDC early Wednesday morning from where it is broken into local delivery routes for delivery to the customer's home the following day.

The effect of this is to minimize the total inventory in the system. Apart from the items held in the retail store, which are for display purposes only, the only place inventory is held is in the 19 Whirlpool distribution centres. Not only is inventory reduced through this consolidation but also vehicle space utilization is maximized by shipping complete trailer loads to Sears' warehouses. A further sophistication that has recently been introduced is to offer a greater range of colours for appliances but not actually to hold all these colours in stock. Instead, orders are consolidated by colour and unpainted appliances (which are held in stock) are then sprayed the appropriate colour. This postponement of the commitment to colour allows a further substantial reduction in total stockholding.

The end result of these logistical decisions has been to enhance the customer service offering both in terms of speedy availability and choice and to improve Whirlpool's market position.

These examples demonstrate that companies are increasingly recognizing the importance of distribution and logistics and its impact on their marketplace performance. It seems that the 'dark continent' that Peter Drucker wrote about over 30 years ago (Drucker, 1962) is about to be explored.

REFERENCES

Bowersox, D. (1978), *Logistics Management*, London: Macmillan. (The definition in the text is an amended version of Bowersox's.)

Christopher, M. (1985), *The Strategy of Distribution Management*, Aldershot: Gower. (Chapter 23 is based upon material in this book.)

Christopher, M., Schary, P. and Skjott-Larsen, T. (1979), *Customer Service and Distribution Strategy*, London: Associated Business Press.

Drucker, P. (1962), 'The economy's dark continent', *Fortune*, **72**, April, 103, 265–70.

Shaw, A. W. (1915), *Some Problems in Market Distribution*, Cambridge, Mass: Harvard University Press.

ESSENTIAL READING

Lambert, D. M. and Stock, J. K. (1993), *Strategic Logistics Management*, Homewood, Ill.: Richard D. Irwin.

Christopher, M. G. (1993), *Logistics and Supply Chain Management*, London: Pitmans.

Gattorna, J. (Ed.) (1990), *Gower Handbook of Logistics and Distribution Management* (4th ed.), Aldershot: Gower.

24 Retailing

Stephen Brown

> The British share a love-hate relationship with their retailers. There is nothing they like more than to browse around the shops, but as for shopkeepers... as for shopkeepers, Shakespeare had it right when he wrote that lying becomes none but tradesmen.

Retailing, as the above quotation from Powell's recent history of Tesco (1991, p. 195) amply illustrates, occupies a somewhat paradoxical position in British society. Few would deny that it is an enormously important activity. The retail industry, after all, contributes some 14 per cent of GDP (with distribution) and accounts for approximately 40 per cent of total consumer expenditure. It employs over two million people in 264 000 businesses, ranging from small, independent grocery stores to enormous, multiple organizations like Marks & Spencer, Kingfisher and Sainsbury. And, according to *The Sunday Times'* annual survey of the richest people in Britain, it is now the single largest source of personal fortune, more so even than inherited wealth and property (Beresford, 1993). The retailing system, furthermore, plays a prominent part in our everyday lives. It is something that we encounter on a daily basis, whether it be purchasing a morning paper from the local newsagent, fulminating at its trucks and delivery vehicles as they impede our journeys to work or, quite simply, in our bemused endeavours to comprehend retailers' imaginative sales claims and promotional activities.

Yet despite its undeniable economic and existential importance, retailing has long been considered unworthy of serious analysis, academic or otherwise. This antipathy has been attributed to all manner of factors including the 'triviality' of the subject (Gardner and Sheppard, 1989), its sheer ubiquity (Hallsworth, 1992) and the scholarly caste system which descends from the 'hard' sciences of physics and chemistry, through the softer social and human sciences, to the academic 'untouchables' of business and management (Brown, 1992). The neglect, however, is usually explained in terms of what

401

Porter (1993, p.1) describes as, 'the appalling English snobbery about trade'. The commonplace belief – which is by no means confined to the English – that retailing is a disreputable, distasteful, parasitic, profiteering, untrustworthy, unscrupulous and, ultimately, unwarranted activity.

Marketers, of course, know better and represent a shining exception to this ridiculous rule. Or do they? A glance at the current editions of mainstream marketing textbooks and compendia, reveals that discussions of retailing are often conspicuous by their absence. At best, a single chapter is devoted to the issue and, at worst, retailing is lost in the undergrowth of distribution's 'dark continent'. On reading these analyses, it is difficult not to conclude that many still regard retailers as an impediment to the free flow of merchandise and information, a necessary evil between producers and consumers, a barrier to the implementation of the marketing concept. Academic commentators, admittedly, may not be the best judges of today's marketing realities, but as Morgan (1989, p.544) observed about practitioners in the previous edition of this handbook (a genuine exception to the rule!), 'marketing people liked to think that retailers did not matter, seeing them as an almost mechanical channel of distribution whose only purpose was to allow the wise and seductive manufacturer to make contact with happy and persuaded customers'.

If, as McGoldrick (1990, p.2) acerbically notes, 'much of the literature. . . has seriously understated the power, scope and importance of retail marketing', there is growing evidence to suggest that a transformation in attitudes is slowly taking place. As a result of many recent, remarkable changes in the structure of the industry (see below), retailers now rank among the largest, most sophisticated and dominant business organizations in Britain. Although slow to embrace the marketing concept, with its commitment to adapting a company's product and service offer to the perceived needs of a target market segment or segments, retailers have latterly been lauded as exemplars of best marketing practice (J. Sainsbury, for example, has won numerous 'Marketing Organization of the Year' awards). Consequently, the nature, characteristics and dynamics of the retailing industry are attracting ever-increasing academic interest and retailers themselves are becoming increasingly cognizant of the importance of marketing and the marketing concept. Retail marketing, in short, appears to be coming of age, or, in the words of a recent *Journal of Marketing Management* editorial: 'From being something of a Cinderella of marketing, retailing is assuming increasing attention in the marketing literature, which more properly reflects its importance in the value chain between primary producer and ultimate consumer' (Baker, 1992, p.196).

RETAILING: DEFINITION AND DOMAIN

As any etymologist will no doubt testify, the origins of the word 'retailing' lie in the Old French *retailler* – a piece cut off. It follows that to 'retail' is to engage in small sales, usually to the final consumer for personal, family or household use. This definition, needless to say, is deceptively simple. Retailing involves a host of functions besides mere breaking of bulk (Bucklin, 1972). These include:

1 The physical movement of goods from (usually) a limited number of places of production to numerous and widely scattered points of purchase.

2 The provision of a selection of goods, either within a single product category (for example Toys R Us, Victoria Wine) or across several broad categories of merchandise (Debenhams, BhS), thereby facilitating consumer choice.

3 The holding of stock for instant availability – subject to store opening hours – at relatively stable and clearly marked prices.

4 The acceptance of risk and the transfer of title from producer to purchaser, and the corresponding exchange of accurate and timely payment.

5 The provision of information, advice, after-sales service, credit, car parking, display, delivery, locational convenience, in-store ambience and several other customer services.

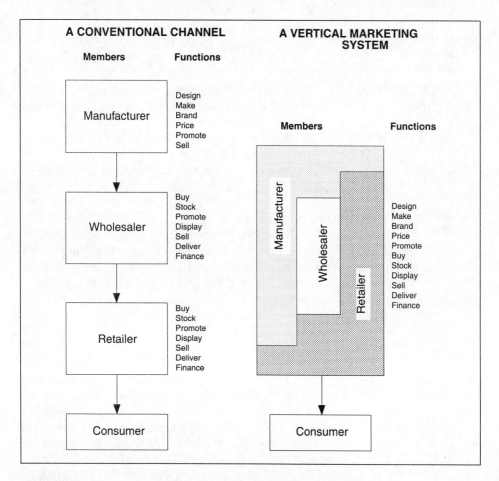

Figure 24.1   The advent of the vertical marketing system

Table 24.1
Reasons for growing retailer influence over suppliers

Factor	Explanation
Size of retailers	Increased retailer buying power for products, equipment, services (e.g. advertising) and finance.
Customer proximity	Closeness to customers means immediate awareness of response to products, changes in demand and so on.
Own label	Growing involvement in 'traditional' domain of manufacturers – new product development, product testing, brand advertising.
Marketing mix	Product, over which manufacturer has control, is no longer sole element of retail marketing mix.
RPM	Resale price maintenance applies to very few product categories.
Space management	Tighter management of space and increased exclusion of manufacturer in-store merchandising.
Physical distribution	Managed by retailer rather than manufacturer.
Management	Retail management more professional than before.
International sourcing	Products sourced from further afield, not dependent on single supplier.
Negotiation	Aggressive short-term negotiation by retailers enforces dependency relationship.

(*Source*: adapted from Dawson and Shaw, 1990.)

The retailing industry, however, is extraordinarily diverse, embracing everything from traditional street markets and modern shopping centres to cigarette vending machines and mail order catalogues. Inevitably, this raises a number of important issues concerning retailing's domain: its *depth*, *breadth* and *classification*.

Depth of retailing

As the other chapters in this section of the Handbook clearly demonstrate, retailing is just part of an extensive distribution system, the organization of which is constantly changing. Illustrated in Figure 24.1, the traditional means of distributing products by means of a wholesale intermediary, is rapidly being supplanted by vertical marketing systems (VMS), where the entire channel of distribution is carefully co-ordinated, operated as a unit and under the direct or indirect control of one of its members, increasingly the retailer (Table 24.1). Given the advent of VMS and retailing's growing dominance over producers and wholesalers, a simple but very important question is: where does retailing stop? Is 'retailing' (and by implication retailing research) confined to the front end of the channel, the point of contact with the public, or does it extend back into the channel itself? And, if so, at what point do we draw the line and say retailing ends here?

Breadth of retailing

Retailing, according to Howe (1992, p.3), can be thought of as 'what retailers do', but the question of who does and who does not 'do' retailing is far from straightforward. An examination of published reflections on and official definitions of retailing reveals a remarkable lack of agreement. In Britain, an optician is regarded as a retailer under the 1950 Shops Act and a filling station is deemed likewise by the Standard Industrial Classification, yet neither rates as a retail activity in the eyes of the Retail Inquiry. Some services, on the other hand, are held to be so similar to shops in operation that they warrant inclusion in the biennial inquiry (television rental for example). Meanwhile, post offices, travel agencies, hairdressers and funeral parlours are considered by town planners to be 'shops', whereas banks, restaurants, public houses and estate agents are not, even though such facilities are often located in shopping centres and regularly used by the public without prior appointment.

Classification of retailing

The intractable question of where retailing ends and non-retail activity begins, with all its implications for even the most basic structural analysis (how many 'shops' are there in Britain?), is compounded by the problem of retail classification. Classification may be necessary in order to make sense of reality, but there are any number of dimensions to choose from, for example:

1 *Form of organization* distinguishes between independent, multiple and co-operative retail businesses, though a variety of sub-divisions, such as between affiliated and unaffiliated independents and large and small multiples, is often recognized.
2 *Sales philosophy* separates retailing into outlets that emphasize cut prices (Poundstretcher, Superdrug, Argos) and those that adopt an exclusive image or service orientation (Harvey Nichols, Jaeger, Ralph Lauren).
3 *Physical size* discriminates between large and small retailing establishments, such as modern grocery superstores and traditional corner shops respectively.
4 *Product range* stresses the contrast between outlets that offer a wide variety but narrow assortment of wares (Woolworth, Littlewoods) and those that sell a comparatively narrow range of goods but compensate with an in-depth assortment (Shoe World, PC World).
5 *Institutional type* attempts to identify and define distinctive retailing formats or techniques – department stores, supermarkets, retail warehouses, catalogue showrooms, mail order houses and so on.

6 *Combined approaches* bring together some or all of the above taxonomic dimensions, such as those summarized in Table 24.2.

Table 24.2
Combined approach to retail classification

Store size	Pricing policy	Product range	Institutional type	Examples
Small	Discount	Narrow	Limited line discount store	Kwik Save, Aldi
Small	Discount	Broad	Catalogue showroom	Argos, Index
Small	Premium	Narrow	Specialist retailer	Next, Laura Ashley
Small	Premium	Broad	Convenience store	7-11, Circle K
Large	Discount	Narrow	Retail warehouse	Toys R Us, Majestic Wine
Large	Discount	Broad	Superstore	Asda, Gateway
Large	Premium	Narrow	Large specialist	Hamleys, Grandstand
Large	Premium	Broad	Department store	Harrods, John Lewis

(*Source*: Brown, 1986.)

Perhaps the best-known classification of retailing is premised on the type of goods sold. A distinction, for instance, has long been made between shops that sell 'convenience', 'comparison' and 'speciality' goods, though these categories are not clear cut, and more detailed type-of-goods taxa are widely employed by government statistical bureaux throughout the developed world. The British retail inquiry recognizes seven broad kinds of retail business – food retailers; drink, confectionery and tobacco retailers; clothing, footwear and leather goods retailers; household goods retailers; other non-food retailers; mixed retail businesses; and hire and repair businesses – and 33 detailed kinds of business ranging from dairymen to jewellers.

RETAIL CHANGE

The basic problem with most retailing classifications is that they are predicated on key criteria which are not only ill-defined but also constantly changing. Change, indeed, is one of retailing's most enduring characteristics, though the pace of change has accelerated considerably in recent years. So much so, that some commentators maintain a retailing revolution, comparable to the industrial revolution of the 19th century, is currently taking place in Great Britain (Dawson, 1982; Sparks, 1989). These dramatic structural changes, which are equally apparent in most other developed countries, can be summarized as follows:

Concentration

Perhaps the most frequently observed feature of the retailing revolution is the relative decline of small, independent, family-run firms and consumer co-operative societies, and the corresponding rise of large-scale, professionally managed, multiple retail organizations (Burt and Dawson, 1990). Although

Table 24.3
Concentration in British retailing, 1988

Sector	Total turnover (£ million)	Largest five groups account for %	Largest ten groups account for %
Food	35 809	41.3	54.1
Drink, confectionery and tobacco	17 189	22.0	33.4
Clothing, footwear and leather	19 901	36.5	49.5
Household goods	27 606	18.5	28.7
Other non-food goods	20 738	23.3	31.9
Hire and repair	1 653	64.6	68.6
Sales by mail order, party plan or automatic vending machines	5 343	65.4	77.0

(*Source*: Institute for Retail Studies, 1991.)

independents still comprise the vast majority of retail businesses in Britain, large multiples (defined as organizations with ten or more retail outlets) account for around 70 per cent of total retail sales, compared to approximately 30 per cent of sales in 1950. This dominance is due to the economies of scale that accrue from centralized administration, managerial specialization, massive buying power and new technology exploitation. An ability to raise capital on the stock market, the operational flexibility associated with a multi-locational presence and, not least, the espousal of strategic planning, have also contributed to the multiples' growing hegemony, as has the inherent weakness of independent and co-operative retail organizations (Dawson and Kirby, 1979). The extent of chain store dominance varies from sector to sector, however, with food retailing and mail order exhibiting a particularly high degree of concentration (Table 24.3).

Nevertheless, the structure of most retail trades is increasingly characterized by a small number of extremely large retail organizations and an extensive tail of small-scale operations. Marks and Spencer, for example, has cornered more than 30 per cent of the UK underwear market. Signet (formerly Ratners), despite its recent difficulties, is responsible for around one-quarter of the jewellery sold in Britain. And, B&Q takes approximately 13 per cent of the country's do-it-yourself business. B&Q, moreover, is but one element of the extensive Kingfisher conglomerate which embraces Woolworth variety stores, Superdrug drug stores and Comet electrical superstores amongst others.

Rationalization

The fluctuating fortunes of multiples, co-ops and independents have unfolded within the context of a dramatic overall decline in the number of retail firms and shops. In 1961, there were some 400 000 retail businesses in Britain operating more than half a million individual outlets. Thirty years later, these totals had fallen to just over 200 000 and 300 000 respectively. This remarkable *407* reduction has been particularly evident in the food sector and among independent retailers, though the latter appear to have held their own in recent years. The historic trend, however, has continued thanks to the merger mania of the mid-1980s, which both reduced the number of large multiple organizations and saw the subsequent rationalization of the new groups' combined branch networks. Amalgamation has also continued apace in the co-operative sector, with the number of societies falling from 216 to 81 between 1979 and 1989 and the number of outlets from 10 000 to around 4 000. The marked decline in goods or product retailing has been offset to some degree by a growth in service retailing – banks, estate agents, fast food restaurants, multiplex cinemas, travel agents, hairdressers, opticians, auto-services, heel bars, health and fitness studios, bowling alleys and so on – though the dramatic appearance of some of these quasi-retail activities in the early 1980s prompted a modicum of short-term concern about their adverse impact on 'proper' retail establishments (Fernie and Carrick, 1983). However, the branch closure programmes of several major banks and building societies indicates that rationalization is taking place in this sector too.

Polarization

Up until the second world war, the British retailing system was largely made up of small shops, with department stores and variety stores comprising the principal large-scale exceptions to the rule. Since then, retailers' search for

Table 24.4
The polarization of retailing: growth formats

Small stores	Large stores
Discount food (Kwik Save)	Supermarkets (Safeway)
Convenience store (Eight Till Late)	Food-based general merchandise (Asda)
Small specialist (Holland and Barrett)	Non-food-based general merchandise (Marks & Spencer)
Brand concessions (Estée Lauder)	Specialist non-food (MFI)
Style shops (Jaeger)	Style superstore (Children's World)
Service shops (Prontaprint)	

(Source: adapted from Sparks, 1989.)

economies of scale and scope, combined with several significant in-store technological developments – most notably self-service – have given rise to progressive increases in average store size. Between 1976 and 1991, for example, the average size of multiple grocery outlets rose almost fourfold, from 3 500 to 13 000 sq. ft. Grocery superstores (defined as outlets with a sales area of more than 25 000 sq. ft) made their first appearance in 1964 and there are now more than 700 such establishments in operation. This large store format has since been successfully adapted to numerous non-food product categories – DIY, furniture, carpets, textiles, electrical goods, sports equipment, garden products, toys, shoes, pets and so on – making superstores one of the most distinctive and characteristic features of the British retailing scene.

Small shops, however, have not been completely swept away by their larger brethren. On the contrary, there is considerable activity at the small-outlet end of the retailing spectrum. As Table 24.4 indicates, several distinctive growth formats can be identified ranging from convenience stores and discounters to style shops and in-store concessions. This has led to the suggestion that a polarization process is taking place where large, mass-merchandising superstores are complemented by smaller outlets targeted at quite specific consumer segments – the discerning affluent, the time poor, the price conscious and so on (Dawson, 1985).

Suburbanization

The advent of food and non-food superstores is closely associated with the pronounced suburbanization of British retailing. Large stores require extensive, low-cost sites for car parking, goods handling and so on, and these are not normally available in congested, high-cost, city centre locations. The contemporaneous process of population decentralization, in which car-owning, high-income groups loom large, has also added to the size and attraction of the suburban market. Thus, despite the misgivings of town planners, who have generally sought to protect the established structure of urban retailing, a substantial amount of suburban and out-of-town shopping development has taken place, particularly in the past decade (Davies and Howard, 1988). Four major types of development can be recognized:

1   *Regional shopping centres*: large covered malls of 400 000 sq. ft or more which contain several major magnet stores, 100 plus unit shops and are usually associated with leisure facilities (for example, Metrocentre, Gateshead; Meadowhall, Sheffield).
2   *Sub-regional shopping centres*: covered malls of between 200 000 and 400 000 sq. ft of floorspace, typically occupied by a food superstore, a non-food superstore and 20–30 unit shops (Cameron Toll, Edinburgh; Hempstead Valley, Gillingham).
3   *Retail parks*: carefully integrated or *ad hoc* clusters of non-food superstores (Greyhound Park, Chester; Olympic Estate, Wembley).
4   *Stand-alone developments*: free-standing grocery superstores, fast food restaurants, department stores and so on (Tesco, Culverhouse Cross, Cardiff; John Lewis, High Wycombe).

Although suburban shopping developments now account for around 20 per cent of total retail sales, the bulk of British retail spending still takes place in   *409*

Table 24.5
Retailer internationalization: push and pull factors

Push factors	Pull factors
Mature markets	Fragmented/underdeveloped markets
Intensive competitive pressures	Corporate philosophy to become a global business
Restrictive trading environment	Presence of overseas niche markets
(Impending) saturation in retail floorspace provision	Establish bridgehead for further expansion
Slow economic performance	To employ more fully existing company skills and strengths
Static population growth	

(*Source*: Treadgold and Davies, 1988.)

traditional town and city centres. Indeed, city centre dominance has been bolstered by the construction of large covered shopping developments (for example Eldon Square, Newcastle; Victoria Centre, Nottingham) and tourist-orientated speciality centres (Princes Square, Glasgow: The Watershed, Bristol). Attempts have also been made to upgrade and improve the city centre environment (pedestrianization, street furniture and so on) in order to maintain its consumer appeal.

Internationalization

Retailers' inexorable advance from city centre to suburb has been paralleled at a much larger geographical scale by the process of internationalization. Although this process is neither new nor one way – Woolworths opened its first UK outlet in 1909 – internationalization has proved to be a particularly popular strategic option among British retailers of late (Table 24.5). In line with the 'psychic distance' hypothesis, much of this investment has taken place in the USA and other English-speaking countries. However, the formation of the Single European Market and the emergence of the market economy in eastern Europe, has led to an increased emphasis on continental opportunities (for example, Kingfisher's £560 million acquisition of French electrical retailer Darty and Tesco's £176 million takeover of Catteau).

Popular though it is proving, the internationalization of British retailing takes a number of different forms (Treadgold, 1991). These include *self-start entry*, where a chain is built up from scratch (Laura Ashley); *franchising*, which reduces capital demands and facilitates rapid expansion (Body Shop); *joint venture*, where partnership with an established organization helps contain the costs and risks of entry (Marks and Spencer with Cortefiel in Spain); and, *acquisition*, perhaps the most common approach, if not necessarily the most successful. Noteworthy examples of the latter include Dixon's difficulties with Silo (USA), Tesco's fiasco with Three Guys (Ireland) and Isosceles' long time albatross, Hermans Sporting Goods (USA). Given the difficulty of internationalizing a retailing concept and the problems encountered by many prominent organizations (for example, Sock Shop's disastrous American foray), it is somewhat ironic that foreign-owned operations today rank among the most successful retailers in Britain – Aldi, IKEA, Toys R Us, the Gap and so on.

Information

The foregoing changes in the British retailing industry cannot be divorced from leading organizations' dramatically increased ability to gather, process store, retrieve, display and, most importantly, manage information. Thanks to the widespread installation of powerful, low-cost, point-of-sale computers and associated developments in laser scanning, product coding, communication networks and decision-support systems, the operations and strategy of modern retailing have been transformed (Dawson and Sparks, 1986). The benefits of EPOS include:

1 *Logistics:* immediate recording of sales leads to enhanced stock control, streamlined distribution, automatic re-ordering and payment of suppliers through the TRADANET electronic data interchange (EDI) network, improved space productivity and precise delivery scheduling.
2 *Productivity*: faster and more accurate check-outs increase labour productivity, reduce shrinkage and help accommodate fluctuating customer flows. Cash management is made easier and the need for item price marking is reduced or removed completely.
3 *Buying*: buyers have constantly updated records of sales trends by product category and store, leading to more accurate demand forecasting and rapid re-ordering or deletion of successful/unsuccessful lines.
4 *Customer service*: out-of-stocks are minimized, queues are reduced, as are check-out errors, and itemized receipts provide shoppers with detailed record of purchases. Promotions can be automatically triggered (money-off coupons and so on) and payment is facilitated when funds transfer (EFTPOS) or credit authorization is linked to the system.
5 *Strategy*: immediate feedback on adjustments to the retail marketing mix gives rise to improvements in store layout, space allocation, new product development and profitability, pricing policies, stock and service levels, sales promotions, supplier performance monitoring and, as Figure 24.2 illustrates, the analysis of store location.

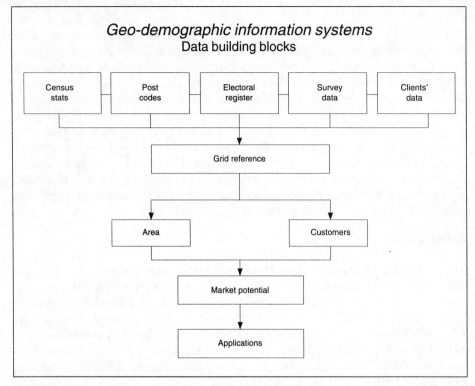

Geo-demographic information systems
Data building blocks

| Census stats | Post codes | Electoral register | Survey data | Clients' data |

Grid reference

Area

Customers

Market potential

Applications

Figure 24.2   IT and store location decisions

Flexibility, however, is perhaps the greatest benefit of information technology. IT enables retailers to deal efficiently with diverse and far-flung suppliers; to exert effective control over hundreds of branches of various sizes, types and trading formats; and, to manage literally thousands of fast- and slow-moving, perishable and imperishable and both seasonal and staple product categories.

MARKETING AND RETAILING

Thanks to the above revolutionary changes, retailing has been transformed from a trade, dominated by small-scale, sales-tactics-driven, entrepreneurial organizations to an industry, characterized by large, complex, strategically orientated, publicly quoted companies (Sparks, 1989). Once the conduits for manufacturer or wholesaler-led marketing, retailers now exert enormous influence over the entire channel of distribution. Not only have they subsumed many of the tasks previously undertaken by traditional wholesalers, though these may be contracted out to third parties (for example, central warehousing and physical distribution), but manufacturers' once exclusive hold over pricing, product development and design, branding, advertising and so on, has also been effectively eroded. Marks and Spencer, for example, is renowned for its very close control over suppliers' product development, quality control, package design and distribution procedures. So much so, that the company is often described as a manufacturer without factories (Tse, 1985).

The inexorable rise of retailing and the shifting balance of supplier-retailer relationships has had major implications for the practice of marketing in Britain. As the relative decline of the brand manager and rise of the trade marketing/key account function clearly indicates, retailers are no longer *part* of the manufacturer's marketing mix. Increasingly, they are the *object* of the manufacturer's marketing mix. Retail organizations, what is more, are now able and willing to employ the full arsenal of marketing tools and techniques in pursuit of their strategic objectives (Randall, 1990).

This dramatic increase in retailer power and influence is reflected in industry's growing awareness of marketing and the marketing concept. A recent study of 70 of the largest retail organizations in Britain found that two-thirds described themselves as marketing orientated; more than 90 per cent possessed marketing departments, most of which were newly established but growing in size; marketing intelligence was widely gathered; the locus of strategic marketing responsibility was believed to reside with the retailer rather than the supplier; and marketing was usually represented on the board of directors. As a rule, however, the responsibilities of the marketing department did not cover the entire retailing mix, nor in many cases were the companies' marketing activities particularly well co-ordinated (Piercy and Alexander, 1988).

Several subsequent studies, employing a variety of research approaches, have painted a broadly similar picture of retail marketing in Britain (Greenley and Shipley, 1989, 1992; Hogarth-Scott and Parkinson, 1993). Although some retailers thus stand accused of adopting the trappings rather than the substance of marketing – although in this they are hardly alone – it is undeniable that many leading British organizations are adopting a more formal approach to marketing and becoming more marketing orientated than before.

THE RETAIL MARKETING MIX

When discussing marketing in a retailing context, most commentators agree that the *elements* of the retail marketing mix are not dissimilar to those that obtain in marketing generally, nor are the fundamental procedures of market analysis, segmentation, targeting, positioning, planning and so on (Walters and White, 1987; Collins, 1992; McDonald and Tideman, 1993). However, the *emphasis* that is placed on the various elements of the mix differs somewhat in a retailing context, as it does from sector to sector – for example between supermarkets and department stores – and from time to time. The principal elements of the retail marketing mix, the changing emphases that have occurred and the differences between retail and 'mainstream' marketing, if such a thing still exists, can be summarized as follows.

Product

Although most manufacturing firms produce a range of different products and many possess extensive product portfolios, few manufacturers' product   *413* ranges compare with the enormous number of items sold by leading retailers. The larger department and variety stores, for instance, carry up to 50 000 lines and modern grocery superstores normally stock a range of 20–25 000 products. Even 'limited line' retailers, such as Aldi or Kwik Save, would typically have 500–1 000 different items on sale. Yet, despite this product proliferation, shelf space tends to be strictly limited, potential suppliers are many and varied, and a plethora of inducements to potential stockists is invariably on offer. The management of retail product offerings is thus a fraught and complex undertaking, though advances in information systems – most notably direct product profitability (DPP) – have helped ease the burden somewhat (Harris and Walters, 1992).

The situation is further complicated by the advent of retailer own-brands, which now account for approximately one-quarter of total retail sales in Britain and about one-third of the market for packaged groceries. The extent of retailer commitment to own-brands varies considerably from company to company and sector to sector (Marks and Spencer, the Body Shop and the footwear sector score highly, for example, whereas Woolworth, Asda and the domestic appliances sector still rely heavily on manufacturer's brands). Nevertheless, from being widely regarded as a cheap and cheerful alternative to manufacturer brands, retailer brands are now seen to offer all manner of marketing advantages and one of the keys to meaningful differentiation in an increasingly competitive retailing environment (de Chernatony and McDonald, 1992).

Service

Fashionable though it has been, the development of an own-brands policy is by no means the only route to successful differentiation in retailing. The provision of value-added customer services has proved to be a particularly popular strategic option for retail organizations in recent years (Sparks, 1992). Retailing, of course, is a service industry and most of the functions of retailing, described earlier, can be regarded as a form of customer service. Examples include locational convenience, product assortment and product availability during opening hours. What is more, improved customer service comprises some of the 'softer' benefits of the IT revolution – fewer out-of-stocks, faster check-outs, itemized receipts and so on. Within the industry, however, customer service is often taken to mean the physical set of service facilities provided within or around the store itself (as opposed to the product related services of 'mainstream' marketing).

Itemized in Table 24.6, the types of service on offer are remarkably diverse, though as might be expected they differ considerably from sector to sector and between self-service and personal-service-based retailing propositions. In self-service dominated DIY outlets, these range from the provision of car parking, home delivery and information desks to timber cutting, tool hire and advice on kitchen or bathroom design. In personal-service-orientated department stores, by contrast, customer services invariably include charge cards, changing rooms, gift wrapping, wedding lists, goods on approval, a fitting and alterations service and so on. Although this apparent preoccupation with the 'tangibles' of customer service, rather than the 'intangibles' of improved staff–customer interaction, has been severely criticized, as has retailers' un-coordinated 'pick-and-mix' approach to service provision (Sparks, 1991), it is undeniable that British retailing in the 1980s was characterized by an increased awareness of customer service issues and a marked improvement in overall standards of customer care.

Table 24.6
Customer services in retailing

Typical department store services	
Credit	Bridal registry
Delivery	Interior designers
Alterations and installations	Car parking
Packaging (Gift wrapping)	Telephones
Complaints and returns	Mother and baby rooms
Gift certificates	Toilets
Trade-ins	Restaurant
Trial purchases	Beauty salon
Sales for regular customers	Information desk
Extended store hours	Shopping bags
Mail and telephone orders	Fur storage

(*Source*: adapted from Berman and Evans, 1992.)

Promotion

Closely associated with the proliferation of customer service provision is the increased sophistication and rapid growth of retailer advertising and promotion. Although the traditional forms of promotional activity – store openings, seasonal sales, games and competitions, price promotions, sports sponsorship and co-operative advertising inserts – are still in widespread use, retailers' heightened appreciation of image building, customer loyalty and

415

marketing generally has prompted a marked change in the nature and style of retail communications. The emphasis is increasingly placed upon such factors as quality, service, the in-store environment and, not least, the retailer's own-brand. Indeed, the size of the major multiples is such that they can indulge in the type of company branding exercises that were once the preserve of manufacturers like Unilever, Mars, Kelloggs and Ford. So much so that retail organizations now tend to dominate the annual rankings of top ten advertised brands.

Yet, despite the dramatic growth in paid retailer advertising and promotion, the store itself remains the principal means of communication employed by retail organizations. Unlike 'mainstream' marketing, in which product benefits messages have traditionally taken precedence over the communication of contextual issues, much of a retail organization's success in the market-place hinges on the appearance, layout, atmosphere, image and personality of its outlets. In fact, of all the elements of the retail marketing mix, overall store design has attracted most attention from practitioners in recent years (see Table 24.7).

Table 24.7
Elements of store design

Store environment	Merchandise presentation	Customer communications
Facade	Layout	Signs
Decor	Presentation methods	Tickets
Walls	Assortment organization	Product information
Floors	Category co-ordination	Graphics
Ceilings	Sample displays	Sound
Lighting	Featuring	Textures
Fixtures	Lighting	Education
Heating	Colours	Promotions
Atmosphere		Personal services
		Cash points

(*Source*: adapted from McGoldrick, 1990.)

Thanks to the evangelical fervour of pioneers like Terence Conran (Habitat) and George Davies (Next), the 1980s was very much the designer decade of British retailing, with enormous sums being spent on design-led refits, especially in the fashion goods sector. However, this over-indulgence has since been superseded by a more disciplined approach and the growing realization that store design must be integrated with the other elements of the retail marketing mix (McGoldrick, 1990).

Pricing

If the 1980s were characterized by an increased emphasis on value-added customer services, sophisticated, image-building advertising and high quality, designer interiors, the early 1990s has seen a renewed price orientation among British retailers, grocery retailers in particular. In line with the wheel of retailing theory (Figure 24.3), a new generation of cut-price, low-cost discounters, such as Aldi and Netto, has emerged to challenge the sophisticated, high-cost, superstore-based operations of Tesco, Sainsbury, Argyll and their ilk (Brown and Quinn, 1993). Although the market leaders have responded vigorously to the threat, with Asda in particular reverting to its original price-led retailing format, it is predicted that – perhaps optimistically – by 1995 the discounters will be responsible for 15 to 20 per cent of the British grocery market.

The growing price orientation of British retailing generally, after a decade of essentially non-price-based competition, has prompted renewed interest in retail pricing and an appreciation of its sheer complexity. In certain sectors, admittedly, retail price maintenance still prevails and the pricing decision

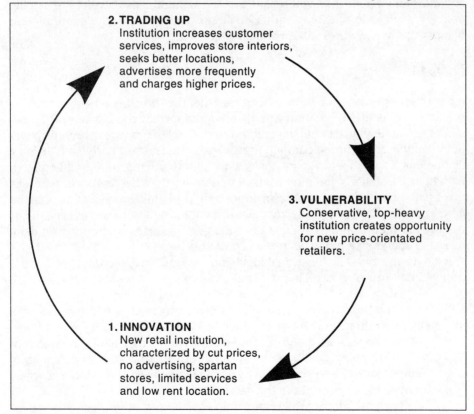

Figure 24.3   The wheel of retailing

rests with the manufacturer, though even here changes are occurring (for example, the discounting of new books by Dillons and other multiple book-sellers). In other sectors, such as motor cars and major household durables, the task of retail pricing has much in common with manufacturer pricing, in that the transaction involves a single, specific product, list prices are often negotiable and purchasers are likely to be reasonably well-informed. In the majority of sectors, however, retailers are required simultaneously to price literally thousands of different products, haggling is rare and consumers are not particularly well-informed about the price of individual items, though they may well have an overall price perception or image of the establishment in question.

This complexity, as McGoldrick (1987) points out, is compounded by geographical, temporal, comparative and assortment considerations. In geographical terms, many retailers alter their prevailing price structures to suit local and regional circumstances. Temporal price changes range from weekly 'specials' to the annual, seasonal and mid-season sales. Comparative issues concern the adjustments that are made in response to the prices set by direct and indirect competitors, whereas the assortment dimension refers to pricing policies, such as loss leading and price lining, which involve the manipulation of mark-ups across the entire product range.

Location

It has often – perhaps too often – been said that the three secrets of success in retailing are location, location and location. Important though the other elements of the retail marketing mix undoubtedly are, the most scrupulous product planning procedures, competent sales assistants, imaginative advertising campaigns, sophisticated store designs and astute pricing policies all come to naught if a retailer's locational strategy is flawed. What is more, whereas errors in pricing, promotions, product range planning and so on can be adjusted comparatively easily, mistaken locational decisions are not readily or rapidly rectified, and only then at considerable expense, disruption and damage to a retailer's carefully nurtured reputation.

If anything, indeed, locational decision making has become even more important in recent years. This is attributable to a number of factors:

1   The growth of motor car and refrigerator/freezer ownership has conspired to alter the nature and timing of consumer shopping expeditions. People are now able and prepared to travel further afield in search of better shopping facilities and to buy both in bulk and less frequently than before. The captive geographical markets that retailers once enjoyed no longer exist to the same extent.

2   The costs of failure are greater than ever before. A new grocery superstore represents a £25 million investment and turns over some £50 million per annum. Dependent as they are on the continuing support of the financial community (for example, Tesco's £572 million rights issue in

1991, which was used to fund their superstore opening programme), major retailers simply cannot afford to make mistakes when taking locational decisions.

3   A much wider choice of locations is now available to retailers. The relaxation of hitherto restrictive town planning controls in the 1980s, coupled with experiments in deregulation (Enterprise Zones for example), led to the proliferation of exploitable locational options, thus adding to the difficulty of retailers' location decisions (see Table 24.8).

4   The emerging marketing orientation among retailers and the development of tightly focused retail formats necessitates the selection of locations that are within easy reach of the target market segments. The problem is compounded by the fact that many retail conglomerates operate several different store formats, each of which has its own specific set of spatial requirements.

Table 24.8
Novel locational options

Types of shopping area	Locational characteristics
Purpose-built regional centres	Town and city centres or out-of-town locations
Purpose-built sub-regional centres	New towns and vast estates
Purpose-built district centres	Outlying housing estates
'Speciality' shopping centres	Edge of town centre, historical district or waterfront
Bulky-goods stores	Variable locations:
Superstores and hypermarkets	• Free-standing on periphery or on industrial estates.
Discount retail warehouses	
DIY/home improvement centres	• Integrated with new purpose-built centres.
Nurseries	
	• Larger traditional centres; retail warehouse 'parks'.
Service centres (motel, garage restaurant)	Alongside main roads in outer areas
Mini-markets; modern convenience stores	Alongside main roads, petrol stations or within large new housing estates

(*Source*: Davies, 1987.)

The difficulties of selecting and managing hundreds of locations (in many cases) have been eased somewhat by what McGoldrick (1990, p.169) describes as 'the rise of the data men'. Thanks to the availability of computerized databases and appropriate interrogation techniques, geo-demographic information systems provide a rapid, low-cost means of assessing, profiling and comparing market opportunities, screening potential sites and defining catchment areas (see earlier Figure 24.2). The call for sophisticated locational analysis, however, varies substantially from sector to sector. Although it has become a virtual prerequisite in the grocery and DIY trades, it is less incumbent upon high-street fashion and speciality goods retailers, where the time-honoured guideline 'as close as possible to Marks and Spencer' still holds sway.

FUTURE DEVELOPMENTS

Predicting the future is difficult at the best of times, but in an industry as mutable as retailing, prognostication is next to impossible. A mere decade ago, for example, many commentators maintained that the traditional, fixed shop was about to be rendered redundant by teleshopping services – only to be proved categorically incorrect. Others held that the growth of high quality, customer-service orientated retail outlets had consigned the 'pile-it-high, sell-it-cheap' strategy to the dustbin of retailing history. Discounters, needless to say, made a dramatic and high profile reappearance. Yet others contended that the central shopping districts of British cities were facing incipient dereliction due to the 'out-of-town exodus', the 'megacentre madness', of the mid 1980s. Most of the mooted mega-scale shopping centres failed to materialize and town-centre retailers responded energetically to the perceived threat with late night opening, improving car parking, promotional activities and so on. In a similar vein, the death of independent retailers, co-operative societies, department stores, village shops, home delivery, customer service, trading stamps and so on has been foretold at one time or another, only for the patient to demonstrate unmistakable signs of life. It thus appears that the only predictable thing about retailing is its unpredictability.

Despite the difficulties and potential embarrassments associated with crystal-ball gazing and the futility of making specific predictions, it is possible to identify some of the broad forces that will affect retailing in the final few years of the 20th century. In this respect, Parker (1991) has identified six key 'environments', some of which are external to the industry and over which retailers have little control. Others impinge directly on the sector or reflect retailing responses to perceived environmental opportunities and threats.

1 *The business or economic environment*: consumers' standards of living and propensity to spend, which are predicated on changing employment prospects, fiscal policies, inflation, interest rates, economic growth/recession, indirect taxation, availability of credit, mortgage rates, attitudes to saving and so on. Real incomes, according to Parker, are likely to continue to increase and living standards improve, albeit fitfully, and the marked contrasts between the 'haves' and 'have nots' will continue to widen.

420 2 *The demographic environment*: changes in birth rates, death rates,

increased longevity and the ageing population structure have major implications for retail organizations. So too does the inexorable increase in household numbers, the decline in average household size, the advent of the dual-income family, and national, regional and local patterns of population migration (north to south, rural to urban and city to suburb).

3   *The consumer environment*: as a consequence of changes in the socio-economic and demographic environments, people's attitudes and lifestyles are being transformed. Consumers are more mature, sophisticated, discerning, cosmopolitan, individualistic, health conscious and environmentally aware. They – the employed, that is – have come to expect increased choice, variety, service, innovation, convenience, exclusivity and, not least, creature comforts from the retail outlets they choose to patronize.

4   *The retail environment*: comprises the retailing industry's response to the opportunities created by the foregoing trends. The emergence of discounters, for example, is a manifestation of the economic recession of the early 1990s. The repositioning of youth-orientated retailers to older target markets (for example Dorothy Perkins) and the suburban shopping centre are largely a reflection of demographic trends. And longer opening hours, healthy eating initiatives, convenience stores, eco-friendly products, fast food outlets, health food shops, customer service provision and so on, are all consequences of changing consumer lifestyles.

5   *The technological environment*: affecting both consumers and retailers alike, technological change is taking place at an increasingly rapid pace. For the consumer, technological transformations have tended to emphasize temporal efficiency – time saving and time management. Examples include microwave ovens, video recorders, food processors, fridge freezers, ATMs, teleshopping services and so on. Technology, as noted earlier, is also transforming the operations and strategy of forward-thinking retail organizations, ranging from space management systems to self-scanning check-outs.

6   *The future environment*: for Parker, information is the key to the future of retailing. Understanding who the customers are, who they are not, where and why they spend, and the service/product offerings necessary to attract or retain them will become increasingly critical in the years to come. At present, technology can provide the customer databases that are required, but the manipulation and management of this information, the avoidance of 'analysis-paralysis' will become the all-important source of competitive advantage.

Irrespective of the accuracy of Parker's overall analysis, the essential points are, firstly, that retailing is shaped by its environment. Changes in economic, demographic, societal circumstances and so on are reflected in the industry, whether it be the emergence of video hire shops, discount computer ware-   *421* houses or eco-friendly cosmetics retailers. Second, retail organizations themselves shape the environment in which they operate. Retailers help mould – not merely respond to – environmental awareness, health consciousness and, as the Sunday trading, resale price maintenance and in-town versus out-of-town debates clearly demonstrate, their own legislative context. Third, and most importantly perhaps, retailing is a highly competitive industry where innovations, being unpatentable, are quickly identified, evaluated, adopted, adapted or negated by inter- and intra-type competition. To cite but three examples: Marks and Spencer's decision to go out-of-town in 1984, stimulated a veritable stampede to the suburbs; the NEXT 'look' revolutionized fashion retailing and spawned all manner of inferior copies; and, the arrival of foreign cut-price grocery retailers led to retaliatory action from the indigenous organizations that had earlier dismissed discounting as passé. It has often been said that the only constant in retailing is change. It is equally true to say that nothing about retailing is inimitable, except imitation.

CONCLUSION

Although introductory textbooks continue to treat retailing as a comparatively minor component of the marketing system, the organization, technique and environment of the retail industry has changed enormously in recent years (Dawson, 1988). In organizational terms, the multiples have grown at the expense of independent retailers and co-operative societies, and coalesced into enormous commercial conglomerates trading under a host of different fascias. With regard to technique, the proliferation of large-scale retailing formats – superstores in particular – and the ready acceptance of the fruits of information technology have transformed the operations and strategy of modern retailing firms. Environmentally, moreover, the layout and design of retail outlets have been revolutionized, international expansion is the order of the day, customer service and (latterly) cut prices have come increasingly to the fore, and once pre-eminent city centres have been challenged by the construction of large-scale suburban shopping complexes.

The upshot of these dramatic changes is that retailing is no longer the preserve of small, independent shopkeepers relying on the marketing muscle and expertise of their sophisticated suppliers. Retailing is now characterized by large, efficient and expertly managed firms with a strategic outlook and marketing orientation. Retailers dominate the channels of distribution; they are powerful brands in their own right; they engender enormous customer loyalty; and, they utilize the full range of marketing mix elements in their pursuit of competitive advantage. Retailing, in short, is no longer one of the *components* of a manufacturer's marketing effort, but the *centre* of its marketing endeavours. Given the inherent dynamism of the retailing industry, the continuation of this dominance cannot be taken for granted. Nevertheless, the genie of retail marketing has escaped from the bottle and, no doubt contrary to the wishes of manufacturers and wholesalers, it is unlikely to be apprehended in the foreseeable future.

REFERENCES

Baker, M.J. (1992), Editorial, *Journal of Marketing Management*, **8**, (3), 195–7.

Beresford, P. (1993), 'Britain's rich: the top 400', *The Sunday Times Magazine*, 4 April, 13–53.

Berman, B. and Evans, J.R. (1992), *Retail Management: A Strategic Approach*, (5th ed.) New York: Macmillan.

Brown, S. (1986), 'Retail classification: a theoretical note', *The Quarterly Review of Marketing*, **11**, (2), 12–16.

Brown, S. (1992), *Retail Location: A Micro-scale Perspective*, Aldershot: Avebury.

Brown, S. and Quinn, B. (1993), 'Reinventing the retailing wheel: a postmodern morality tale', in P.J. McGoldrick (ed.), *Cases in Retail Management*, London: Pitman.

Bucklin, L.P. (1992), *Competition and Evolution in the Distributive Trades*, Englewood Cliffs: Prentice-Hall.

Burt, S.L. and Dawson, J.A. (1990), 'From small shop to hypermarket: the dynamics of retailing', in D. Pinder (ed.), *Western Europe: Challenge and Change*, 142–61, London: Belhaven.

Collins, A. (1992), *Competitive Retail Marketing*, Maidenhead: McGraw-Hill.

Davies, R.L. (1987), 'Urban change in Britain and the retail response', in A. Metton (ed.). *Geographical Research on Commercial Activities*, 35–55, Paris: IGU.

Davies, R.L. and Howard, E. (1988), 'Issues in retail planning within the United Kingdom', *Built Environment*, **14**, (1), 7–21.

Dawson, J.A. (1982), *Commercial Distribution in Europe*, London: Croom Helm.

Dawson, J.A. (1985), 'Structural change in European retailing: the polarisation of operating scale', in E. Kaynak (ed.), *Global Perspectives in Marketing*, 211–29, New York: Praeger.

Dawson, J.A. (1988), 'Futures for the high street', *Geographical Journal*, **154**, 1–12.

Dawson, J.A. and Kirby, D.A. (1979), *Small Scale Retailing in the UK*, Farnborough: Saxon House.

Dawson, J.A. and Shaw, S. (1990), 'The changing character of retailer–supplier relationships', in J. Fernie (ed.), *Retail Distribution Management*, 19–39, London: Kogan Page.

Dawson, J.A. and Sparks, L. (1986), 'New technology in UK retailing: issues and responses', *Journal of Marketing Management*, **2**, (1), 7–29.

de Chernatony, L. and McDonald, M.H.B. (1992), *Creating Powerful Brands*, Oxford, Butterworth-Heinemann.

Fernie, J. and Carrick, R.J. (1983), 'Quasi-retail activity in Britain: planning issues and policies', *The Service Industries Journal*, **3**, (1), 93–104.

Gardner, C. and Sheppard, J. (1989), *Consuming Passion: The Rise of Retail Culture*, London: Unwin Hyman.

Greenley, G. and Shipley, D. (1989), 'Dimensions of product planning in retail marketing', *Irish Marketing Review*, **4**, (1), 53–62.

Greenley, G. and Shipley, D. (1992), 'A comparative study of operational marketing practices among British department stores and supermarkets', *European Journal of Marketing*, **26**, (5), 22–35.

Hallsworth, A. (1992), *The New Geography of Consumer Spending: A Political Economy Approach*, London: Belhaven.

Harris, D. and Walters, D. (1992), *Retail Operations Management: A Strategic Approach*, Hemel Hempstead: Prentice-Hall.

Howe, W.S. (1992), *Retailing Management*, Basingstoke: Macmillan.

Hogarth-Scott, S. and Parkinson, S.T. (1993), 'Who does the marketing in retailing?', *European Journal of Marketing*, 1993, **27**, in press.

Institute for Retail Studies (1992), *Distributive Trades Profile 1991: A Statistical Digest*, IRS, University of Stirling.

McDonald, M.H.B. and Tideman, C.C.S. (1993), *Retail Marketing Plans*, Oxford: Butterworth-Heinemann.

McGoldrick, P.J. (1987), 'A multi-dimensional framework for retail pricing', *International Journal of Retailing*, **2**, (2), 3–26.

McGoldrick, P.J. (1990), *Retail Marketing*, Maidenhead: McGraw-Hill.

Morgan, E. (1989), 'Retailing', in M.J. Thomas (ed.), *Marketing Handbook*, 544–54, Aldershot: Gower.

Parker, A.J. (1991), 'Retail environments: into the 1990s', *Irish Marketing Review*, **5**, (2), 61–72.

Piercy, N. and Alexander, N. (1988), 'The status quo of the marketing organisation in UK retailing: a neglected phenomenon of the 1980s', *The Service Industries Journal*, **8**, (2), 155–75.

Porter, R. (1993), 'A great tradition: shoppe till ye droppe', *The Times*, Saturday 27 February, 1.

Powell, D. (1991), *Counter Revolution: The Tesco Story*, London: Grafton Books.

Randall, G. (1990), *Marketing to the Retail Trade*, Oxford: Heinemann.

Sparks, L. (1989), 'The retail sector', in P. Jones (ed.), *Management in Service Industries*, 43–65, London: Pitman.

Sparks, L. (1991), 'Retailing in the 1990s: differentiation through customer service?', *Irish Marketing Review*, **5**, (2), 28–38.

Sparks, L. (1992), 'Customer service in retailing – the next leap forward', *The Service Industries Journal*, **12**, (2), 165–84.

Treadgold, A. (1991), 'The emerging internationalisation of retailing: present status and future challenges', *Irish Marketing Review*, **5**, (2), 11–27.

Treadgold, A. and Davies, R.L. (1988), *The Internationalization of Retailing*, Harlow: Longman.

Tse, K.K. (1985), *Marks & Spencer: Anatomy of Britain's Most Efficiently Managed Company*, Oxford: Pergamon Press.

Walters, D. and White, D. (1987), *Retail Marketing Management*, Basingstoke: Macmillan.

ESSENTIAL READING

Davies, G. (1993), *Trade Marketing Strategy*, London: Paul Chapman.

McDonald, M.H.B. and Tideman, C.C.S. (1993), *Retail Marketing Plans*, Oxford: Butterworth-Heinemann.

McGoldrick, P.J. (1990), *Retail Marketing*, Maidenhead: McGraw-Hill.

25 Door-to-door distribution

Shelley Radice

One of the fastest growing advertising media, with its full potential still not realized, is door-to-door distribution. This is a medium which is able to stimulate four of the five senses: sight, smell, taste and touch; arouse and satisfy curiosity, and elicit response.

The size of the market is estimated at 5 billion items going through the letterbox every year, valued at about £100 million. Furthermore, 35 per cent of all items coming through the letterbox are unpersonalized.

Household distribution, door-to-door, or letterbox marketing, as it is variously called, is a way of reaching consumers. Advertisers in every category, whether multi-national FMCG companies, local authorities, charities, financial services, restaurants, schools, local stores of every description, tourist attractions and consumer durables, to name but a few, are all happy to use the medium.

This chapter will define letterbox marketing, explaining how it differs from other available local media. The features it offers for marketing, advertising and promoting products and services will be discussed, and recommendations and ideas will be given on how to use it under varying circumstances.

HOUSEHOLD DISTRIBUTION: DEFINING THE MEDIUM

A local medium for national advertisers

Door-to-door distribution of leaflets, free newspapers, coupons, brochures and samples is the most directly local and personal way of reaching potential customers. Items which fall on to the doormat through the letterbox must be individually handled. It is a means of local communication, providing the householder with local information.

Because the distributions have to be mapped, in order to carry out deliveries, specific geographies are used, and related to quantities. This aspect, which relates place to volume and inevitably to time, gives the medium its unique position in direct marketing.

Free newspapers, the most successful of household-distributed products, now taken for granted throughout the UK, are well-read and carry both parochial news and advertising. Their establishment could not have taken place without distribution networks of reliable, regular door-to-door deliveries for at least 51 weeks of the year, and this has provided the foundation for one of the methods for the delivery of other materials, such as leaflets.

A quantifiable medium

Above-the-line media are said to 'deliver an audience' to an advertiser. This can be in the audited circulation of a periodical or newspaper, or as a sampled audience tuned in to a particular programme, even though their attention to the advertisement cannot be judged. Direct marketing delivers the item to a quantifiable audience: in fact not a random audience but one with certain documented characteristics.

With door-to-door, there are two ways of measuring the impact of the message. First, if the marketing proposition contains a response device, actual numbers of respondents and other personal data can be collected. Second, research can be carried out into the householders' recall of the door-dropped item. These features will be examined in more detail later.

A cost- and time-effective medium

An advertising or promotional campaign using the medium can be tailored to fit a budget. During the recession of the early 1990s the use of the medium boomed. It has been seen as a cost-effective way of continuing to promote products and services because the actual distribution costs are so competitively priced.

Further, not only can the material vary in quality without necessarily losing impact, but the size of the distribution, the timing and coverage can all be closely focused to suit the advertisers' fulfilment abilities.

As with everything else, the better the quality of the household-delivered material, the more likely it is to be memorable.

A welcome medium

Direct marketing has had to contend with the derogatory term 'junk mail' for too long. Anything is considered to be 'rubbish' if it is not wanted by the recipient. The Mailing Preference Service (MPS) was set up to halt mailings to those people who do not want to be offered any products. But the majority of people in the UK have not joined this scheme, even when they are aware of it, because they are open to offers, some of which they do want and which they certainly would not consider 'junk'. It is offers made by local companies, for products or

427

services which are nearby, convenient and interesting which are especially welcomed into the home. Into this category also comes mail-order activity – shopping from the home.

It has been shown that leaflets which householders perceive as relevant are pinned up in the home in order to be used at a later date. And although on the whole, memory decay is a factor in recalling receipt of an item, the recall level of catalogues which are perused at leisure actually increases over time.

Product samples have been shown to be particularly popular. An in-depth study of consumer attitudes to sampling, conducted on behalf of Circular Distributors Ltd (1991), found that

> in comparison with other media, sampling seems to be welcomed by its target audience with open arms, and with a complete lack of the usual reserve and cynicism. Sampling, because it breaks through the normal 'bargain' of manufacturer/consumer transaction, evokes surprise, enthusiasm and pleasure, with responses such as 'It's like getting a present.'

Some consumers have become suspicious of addressed direct mail, and feel anxious about 'where did they get my name'. With the unaddressed medium, the question does not even arise.

From the point of view of the advertiser, use of door-to-door distribution means that they do not need to go to the expense of purchasing lists of names and addresses, nor do they need to be concerned about Data Protection legislation, or the MPS.

Research has shown that, on the contrary, the general public find that the most obtrusive form of direct marketing is telephone marketing. Qualitative research conducted by the HPI Research Group (*Consumer Attitudes to Direct Marketing,* 1991) concludes that consumers feel that telephone selling is an invasion of their privacy.

A targeted medium

Although the medium of door-to-door has been available since the early 1970s, it was the technical advances firstly in computing and then, in the late 1980s, of the geo-demographic companies, which enabled this medium to make qualitative advances.

The geographical basis was driven forward by the Post Office, now the Royal Mail, which needed a nationwide alphanumeric system to describe areas in such a way that mail could be mechanically and electronically sorted. Firmly established by the early 1980s, the whole country was given postcodes, the smallest viable unit used by direct marketing being a postcode sector, containing about 2 500 households.

The principal targeting companies – CACI, which produced ACORN; CCN Systems, with their MOSAIC; Pinpoint, with PiN and FinPiN and lifestyle systems such as NDL – can all order and relate their demographic selections back to postcodes, thus creating the geo-demographic solutions for targeting consumers through their letterboxes.

However, door-to-door is by no means confined to post office delineations. One of the most well-used boundaries used for new store openings and special offers in the retail market are 'drive-times'. These can take into consideration the appropriate mileage, for example, 3 miles for a local shop, but 10 miles for an out-of-town superstore, or a 15-minute walk for a fish-and-chip shop but 15 miles to a high-class restaurant, and can also manage the road system, with main roads extending the reach, and one-way systems shortening it.

In some cases even more precise areas can be prescribed, such as particular streets. This is possible using one of the methods of distribution, called solus delivery, which delivers a client's material on its own.

The free newspaper publishers have developed a way to offer advertisers a much smaller target unit than a postcode sector. They have classified their newspaper delivery rounds into different property types, each round containing on average 250 dwellings. The advertiser will soon be able to select these smaller numbers within delivery rounds.

A unique feature of this classification, the AHD Property Classification, is its analysis of age of property into three bands: pre-1919; 1920–1965, and post-1965. This, together with a description of the type of property (detached, semi-detached, flat, council-owned and so on) and the general description of location (city, town, rural) gives common-sense access to targeting, ideal for local or regional advertisers, but also amenable for incorporation into national campaigns (AHD Property Classification, 1992a).

Other local geographies are well within the scope of the household distribution company. These are local authority boundaries, wards and electoral areas, utility company areas and so on.

Probably the most under-used boundaries are those of independent television and commercial radio; more of this in later sections.

A medium to select targets

Advertisers may not always know whom to target. This is an area in which door-to-door can offer cost-effective answers. Manufacturers do not always necessarily know who is buying their product because product purchase in some cases may be aspirational. For example, an up-market alcoholic beverage may not be bought by up-market consumers in the leafy suburbs, but by residents of a council estate who aspire to the lifestyle evoked by television advertising. A special offer coupon, requiring a postcode, will soon enable the manufacturer to find out more.

A creative medium

There are limits to what can be delivered door-to-door. They are principally concerned with the safety and legality of the items, and their conformance to the self-regulatory systems of the UK, namely the British Code of Advertising Practice and the British Code of Sales Promotion Practice.

Mostly, they also have to be able to fit through a standard-sized letterbox, *429* but there are even delivery methods to overcome this obstacle for shaped or large items.

Apart from that, there are no bounds to creativity. All the production gimmicks used for direct mail are appropriate, plus sales promotion techniques and sampling innovations. There is enormous potential for using the print medium to achieve exciting and memorable doormat impact. Glossy paper or card; full colour, and shapes to echo the message, for example, egg-shaped leaflets at Easter time . . . anything is possible.

Differs from other local media

Leaflets can stand out from on-the-page advertisements in the local press because of their colour, size, shape and ability to position the message more effectively. They can take advantage of the wide penetration of a free newspaper, which few paid-for titles offer.

Leaflets inserted into paid-for newspapers will sometimes inevitably land on newsagents' floors. Increasingly it is possible to mechanically insert items into free titles, although advertisers still tend to prefer their leaflets to drop separately on to the mat.

Local radio advertising is not yet widely accepted, and is one-dimensional compared with the written word. Nor is it as easy to elicit a response directly through the medium as the listener has to be alert, with pen at the ready, in order to take up offers. Similar arguments can be put forward with regard to direct response to television viewing; the actual costs involved form another case, as does the penetration. The more focused the targeted audience, the less cost-effective is the use of a broad-brush medium.

Door-to-door is different from direct mail in excluding the purchase or copying of lists of names and addresses, and the higher costs incurred by using the mail.

THE MONITORING OF LETTERBOX MARKETING

The advertiser may feel that he has a problem with door-to-door, because it is intangible. So much has to be taken on trust. Unlike direct mail which can be seen to be posted or display ads which can be filed, thousands and thousands of leaflets are handed over, in order to disappear.

The occasional 'dumping' of a couple of hundred items, although a minute quantity, can arouse feelings of anxiety, and these kinds of problems have no doubt hindered the full development of the medium. In recent years, however, there have been several innovations which should allay the fears.

The first has been the establishment of a trade body for the industry – the Association of Household Distributors – which maintains a Code of Practice, and establishes practical Guidelines. Only well-established distribution companies which meet the criteria can join, and if advertisers have any problems, they can address them to the Association. Not all companies offering household distribution are members, so caution is urged.

Secondly, the checking of deliveries has become standardized, and in one method there is an independent body which regularly checks, and certifies, that the systems for leaflet distribution are satisfactory. This is Verified Free Distribution, part of the Audit Bureau of Circulation (ABC), which is implementing the VFD Leaflet Verification scheme for free newspapers to run alongside the VFD certificate of average distribution.

Third, there is at least one research company which offers to validate a distribution on behalf of an advertiser. It independently reports the recall levels, and by inference the distribution levels, achieved for their particular promotion.

Case study: Stepcheck report

In a presentation to a seminar (AHD, 1992b), the results of nine validations were analysed by Arthur Thompson, of Thompson Beaty, which has developed the package called Stepcheck. The statistics were aggregated to ensure confidentiality.

During the validation of the nine individual items, 1 319 hours of interviewing took place, a total of 26 398 interviews. Using methods of control cells, in which 100 per cent distribution was guaranteed, and asking householders if they recalled receiving the items, it was found that 79 per cent of those estimated as having received the items were able to recall it, and 61 per cent had read it. Recall on one particular item reached 93 per cent.

Arthur Thompson stated that recall varies much more than distribution levels. This he attributed to a variety of factors: the perceived value of the item; a latent product interest; the age of the recipient; memory decay over time, and the accompanying material.

THE DISTRIBUTION TECHNIQUES

There are five different techniques by which consumers can receive items through the letterbox. They are: solus, shareplan, with free newspapers, mechanically inserted into free newspapers, and with the Royal Mail.

Solus

Solus delivery means an advertiser's item is delivered on its own, to highly selected areas, on specified days. This technique is especially valuable for large items, or smaller distributions, or those where perhaps street-level targeting is required rather than postcode sectors.

It must be remembered, however, that the item would not necessarily be found on its own on the doormat by the householder as other distribution companies may be delivering on that day too.

Shareplan

This is the most cost-effective method, but one which usually involves a longer planning stage and less flexibility about the dates. Shareplan is a regular monthly or bi-monthly service offered by the major distribution companies who undertake to deliver no more than five, non-competing items within a two-week period. It is possible to target towns and postcodes.

With free newspapers

All over the UK, the local free newspapers are very much part of the local communication system. In the last ten years they have established themselves in over 18 million homes. Readership research is available from JICREG Limited based at The Newspaper Society. Items accompanying the free titles can benefit from the positive association householders and their families have about their local 'free'. Because they are delivered every week, the advertiser using this method has immense flexibility. The papers usually go out on Wednesday, Thursday or Friday, before the weekend shopping expeditions. The free newspaper distribution method is cost-effective at reaching centres of population and many villages.

Mechanically inserted

Leaflets which are mechanically inserted into free newspapers have the advantage of guaranteed inclusion within the paper as well as the wide coverage offered by the blanket distribution area. Targeting to postcodes is not usually offered with this method, which however may be ideal in some circumstances.

Royal Mail

For those advertisers who need total coverage, including rural areas, Royal Mail Door to Door offers an unaddressed service delivered by uniformed postmen. The time-span for delivery is two weeks, although 80 per cent of items are usually delivered within the first four days.

Case study: *The Independent on Sunday*

'A highly targeted door-to-door campaign in 1990 helped us to successfully launch the newspaper. It was very cost-effective, and enabled us to reach 2.5 million households', Rob McMenemy, marketing manager, *The Independent on Sunday*.

Distribution took the form of solus door-to-door distribution to maximize the impact of the leaflet as it arrived through the letterbox. A total of 2.5 million ABC1 homes throughout the UK were distributed two weeks prior to 28 January 1990. 'The sampler [was] very successful in creating awareness of the launch with the target market'.

MARKETING SOLUTIONS THROUGH DOOR-TO-DOOR

Direct response

The American direct marketing guru, Herschell Gordon Lewis, defines direct marketing as 'causing someone to perform a positive act as a direct result of having received a message'. Door-to-door is the supreme medium for this, especially if there are time constraints. In fact, the experts say that there always should be time limits on offers, so leaflets with an invitation to visit the local health club, money-off coupons for a selection of products at the local grocery shop, or the six-monthly catalogue from the nearest do-it-yourself chain are all invitations to the householder to act, and to act soon.

Every campaign which uses direct response should have built in at the beginning the methods by which the results should be analysed. At the very least, the following should be used:

- Percentage cost per conversion of enquiry.
- Cost per enquiry.
- Cost per order.
- Sales per order.
- Percentage conversion of enquiry to order.

Brand building

Research has shown (Circular Distributors, 1992) that although advertising people differentiate door-dropped material from above-the-line advertising, the public does not perceive it differently. Consumers regard it all as advertising. It can therefore be used like other media, or in strategic combination, for building brands.

Case study: Guinness

Guinness collected names and addresses through a leaflet drop. The leaflet also asked whether the consumer drank any Guinness varieties, and the type of beer drunk at home and in the pub. The leaflet offered a 50p discount on a purchase of Guinness Draught Bitter. The coupon redemption was very effective at generating trial in its test market, and distribution of a further 3 million items was carried out.

List building

Ever Ready, the overall battery brand leader, had a requirement to boost sales. After a well-tried period of piloting and testing, they found that the most fruitful way of reaching potential buyers was by building up their database, and this they did by using direct mail to reach those people who had previously responded to their promotions, which included door-to-door distributions. As the marketing director, Martin Burch, wrote 'the database has been invaluable in providing a wealth of demographic and regional profiling, which is also being used to enhance above-the-line media selection' (Precision Marketing, 1992).

Sales promotion

FSIs, or Free Standing Inserts, are very big business in the USA. They are a collection of coupons in magazine format and were first introduced to the UK in the 1950s as the Household Shopping Guide. There have been recent attempts to repeat the format, but it has not been sustained in the door-to-door format – perhaps a niche yet to be exploited.

Coupons are welcome in the home. Research from NCH (1989) shows that 48 per cent of respondents preferred coupons which had been loosely delivered, nearly double the next preferred type, the on-product category. In addition, redemption levels for the door-to-door delivered items were much higher.

Product sampling

If the item is non-toxic and fits through a letterbox, there are various methods by which it can be delivered, usually the solus or shareplan method, but sometimes with free newspapers.

The premium method of personal call sampling overcomes any weight or bulk problems because the deliverer hands over the items in person. It can be used for specific targeting, for example sanitary items for women only, or pet food to dog-owners. It can be used for high-value items, and enables the manufacturer to collect valuable market information at the same time.

The trade bodies whose members are involved in the distribution of product samples have drawn up guidance notes to be read in conjunction with the British Code of Sales Promotion Practice, emphasizing the safety to the consumer.

USING DOOR-TO-DOOR TO INCREASE IMPACT

With television

One of the earliest integrated media approaches – and now a classic marketing story – is Bonusprint's nationwide door-to-door distribution of photo-processing envelopes, timed to coincide with a national TV campaign telling people to look out for the distinctive envelopes coming through the door. It was expensive, but it worked.

Other more recent users of the TV/door-to-door campaigns include detergents, round-shaped tea-bags and DIY outlets, especially around Bank Holiday time. For an easy route to door-to-door distribution within TV areas consult *The Letterbox Marketing Handbook,* which is arranged by independent television area.

With radio

Elida Gibbs was the first to realise the potential of radio for generating awareness for direct marketing and stimulating first purchase. As part of the marketing mix for Dimension 2-in-1 shampoo and conditioner, a national door drop campaign was devised to reach 2.5m targeted homes. The door drop was co-promoted on 17 participating independent radio stations nationwide, who each ran four-week campaigns on-air, combining sponsorship messages with a week long competition. Part of the door drop leaflet comprised a competition format which required listening to the radio to win cash prizes – and a link to product purchase (Hoy, 1993).

The targeted coupon redemption level was 8 per cent , but in fact 12 per cent was achieved, helping to give a brand share 20 per cent higher than expected.

The on-air promotion was devised to suit the door-drop, pre-alerting listeners to the pending arrival of the mailing, incentivizing retention by explaining its purpose, and encouraging listeners to explore its contents.

With sales promotion

The opening of a new ethnic food outlet, Mexican Tacos, posed a number of interesting problems, for which door-to-door supplied the answer.

Research from the USA has shown that if restaurants can persuade patrons to come through their doors three times, then they will probably continue to be loyal customers. It was considered that continued visits were necessary for customers to familiarize themselves with the unusual taste of the food, and to have a pleasurable experience in the venue itself. The programme selected was, briefly, as follows: Potential customers living within a 2 mile radius of the restaurant were profiled geo-demographically, and this yielded postcode sectors for targeting. The local press was used, in display advertising, but so was a door-to-door leaflet, and the latter achieved a very much higher response to the special offers. These offers varied according to the affluence of the areas in which the restaurants were situated. Once in the restaurant, diners were given vouchers, to encourage repeat visits, and towards purchase of a T-shirt (Johnson, 1993).

Case study: Vernons Pools

Vernons Pools launched a massive campaign to reel in young people as new pools players and bring lapsed players back. The campaign included a door-drop to all 22 million UK households through Royal Mail Door to Door, a 1.5 million direct mailing and national press, consumer magazine and poster advertising.

Marie Ashurst, Direct Marketing Executive, Vernons Pools, said, 'Door-to-door is one of the primary methods by which we recruit clients; we place 66 million items through letterboxes each year'.

RESEARCH ON THE DOOR-TO-DOOR MEDIUM

Letterbox marketing has, to date, not been subject to a great volume of in-depth research, other than that commissioned by some of the leading companies in the field. Recent research, carried out by RSGB and The Human Factor for one of these companies (Circular Distributors, 1992) does help to fill in some of the gaps.

Examples of the major findings are: 95 per cent of adults claim to remember receiving advertising leaflets through the letterbox. Both men and women take a similar interest in the medium. Contrary to what might be expected, the medium is biased slightly up-market. At least half the population read some of the leaflets they receive. This attention compares very favourably with direct mail and mail order offers, and is similar to the proportion claiming to pay attention to television and print advertising.

Coupons are popular among householders, with 54 per cent of adults using at least one that they receive. Also rated as useful and interesting, by a quarter of those questioned, was information about local stores, new product information, and, for women, recipes.

Two-thirds of all respondents claimed to have taken some action specifically as a result of receiving an advertising leaflet. This includes sending off for more information, store visits, product selection and product purchase.

Research into product sampling was conducted in 1991, through RSGB, with a sample of 900 housewives. The results show a highly positive consumer attitude (Circular Distributors, 1991). Key findings are:

- 71 per cent give product sampling as the main reason for switching to another brand.
- 79 per cent give product sampling as the main reason for purchasing a brand new product on the market.
- 94 per cent believe in sampling far more than any other medium.
- 72 per cent 'often' use the sample they have received.
- 75 per cent use them within a week or two.

HOW TO GO ABOUT USING LETTERBOX MARKETING

Define the target audience

Contact either a geo-demographic company or a national distribution company to assist in ensuring that the message goes to the people most likely to respond. Or, to a general market in order to elicit further information.

Place the printing with a reliable printing company

Unless the correct number of items are produced, it will be impossible to ensure complete distribution. A simple but vital point to note is that the number of items should be written on the outside of the packaging. Because packages will inevitably be broken up for dispersal, labelling adds an extra level of security.

CONCLUSION

It would be difficult to think of an advertiser who would be unable to use the unaddressed direct marketing option. As a local medium it is ideal for directing consumers towards locally obtained products and services, and yet it is also capable of generating response in a nationwide campaign.

It links in with targeting, varied geographies and other media. It is capable of measurement, as well as of enormous creativity. Letterbox marketing appears deceptively easy; everyone thinks they know about it because all are recipients. As demonstrated in this chapter, it is a highly sophisticated medium in its own right.

REFERENCES

Association of Household Distributors (1992a), 'AHD property classification: Implementation document', Gloucester: AHD.

Association of Household Distributors (1992b), 'Report on the autumn seminar', Gloucester: AHD.

Burch, Martin (1992), 'The power surge', *Precision Marketing,* June 29, p.24.

Circular Distributors Ltd (1991), *Door-Drop Sampling,* Maidenhead: Circular Distributors Ltd.

Circular Distributors Ltd (1992), *Door-to-door Distribution Media and Research Fact File*, Maidenhead: Circular Distributors Ltd.

Hoy, Janet (1993), 'How to get a direct response from radio advertising', *Adline,* February, p.30.

HPI Research Group (1991), *Consumer Attitudes to Direct Marketing,* London: HPI Research Group.

Johnson, Wunderman Cato in Paul Rowney (ed.) (1993), *The Case History Collection,* Hertford: Brainstorm Publishing Ltd.

NCH Promotional Services (1989), 'A study of consumer usage & attitudes to coupons', Oxford: A.C. Nielsen Company.

Newspaper Society, JICREG Readership Data.

Radice, Shelley (ed.) (annual publication), *The Letterbox Marketing Handbook*, Gloucester: AHD.

ESSENTIAL READING

Radice, Shelley (ed.) (annual publication), *The Letterbox Marketing Handbook*, Gloucester: Association of Household Distributors.

Wells, Nick (1992), 'Door-to-door: direct marketing's new weapon', in Bryan Halsey (ed.), *The Practitioner's Guide to Direct Marketing*, London: The Institute of Direct Marketing.

26 Agents

Bernard Katz

A distribution channel, in marketing terms, is a pathway from the supplier of a product or service to the buyer. An agent is one form of distribution channel; a distributor is another. There are a number of different channels. A supplier makes use of one or more distribution channels as appropriate to the business.

THE DIFFERENCE BETWEEN AN AGENT AND A DISTRIBUTOR

The roles of agent and distributor are frequently thought to be the same. But although the terms are loosely interchanged, each has a specific function.

An agent is a person or company who sells goods and services on behalf of a principal. Goods are delivered by the principal directly to the customer – agents do not usually carry stocks. Payment is made by the customer directly to the principal. Remuneration is obtained by way of commission achieved on sales made to customers.

A distributor buys for his or her own account from a supplier and holds stocks. The distributor then sells on to the end-user. The manufacturer or supplier does not necessarily know the identity of the final purchaser. The distributor is responsible for securing payment for deliveries sold to his or her own customers.

Figure 26.1 illustrates how agents and distributors service a market. The operation of agent and distributor is the same in the home market and the export market; overseas, factors of language and business practice intrude. For example, in the Middle East agents and distributors carry stocks. Both are called agents.

In selling through agents and distributors, each method has advantages and disadvantages.

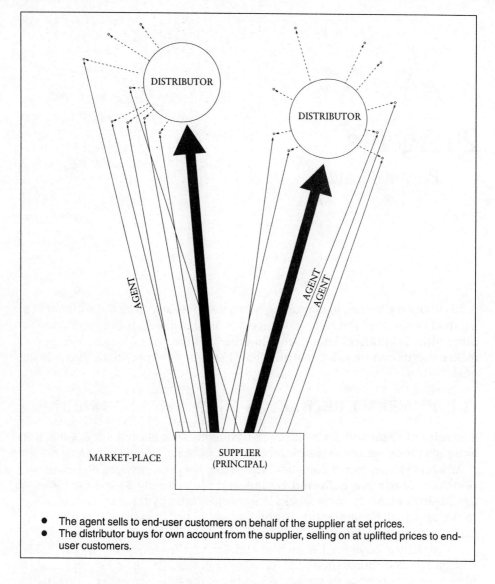

Figure 26.1   How agents and distributors service a retail outlet market

Advantages of selling through agents

1   The principal has direct contact with each customer. If the services of
the agent are discontinued, the relationship with established customers
can be maintained.

2   A full selling price is chargeable to all customers. Agent and principal
must agree on whether commission is payable on the ex-works factory

price, on the delivered site price or, overseas, on the FOB or CIF or any other export contract price. If it is payable on the CIF price, commission is being paid on the insurance and freight charges. Commission rates vary with the industry. On fashion goods the commission rate may be 10 per cent. In the steel industry it is 2 per cent or less.

3 Selling costs are minimal. There are the initial setting-up costs of attracting and screening applicants; the costs of interviewing prospective agents, with travel and hotel costs if the selection is made overseas. When appointed, an agent must be provided with samples of the product, either free or at a substantial discount. There are also printing costs for literature, visiting cards or special instructions. Overseas printing is in the local language. Theoretically, after the set-up costs, agents begin working at their own expense and orders start to flow in.

4 Selling through agents requires little initial investment. That is why it is seen as an easy pathway to new business by companies wanting to grow. But all too often agents are appointed and the principal then waits and waits for orders that never come. The principal/agent relationship is rather like a marriage: as such both parties must work to achieve success. The principal's sales manager must visit the agent regularly to provide support and motivation. Every such visit can be merchandised by the agent setting up customer appointments.

5 There are opportunities for securing ongoing feedback from the marketplace. This requirement should be built into every agency agreement. An agent must report on progress regularly at weekly intervals. Overseas, particularly, agents are well-placed to provide news of impending changes in legislation, demand, fashion trends and new product usage. The agent with his or her ear to the ground is often the first to encounter competitive action and strategies. This important market intelligence must be relayed to the principal.

Disadvantages of selling through agents

1 The unit order size is small rather than large.
2 Credit control management is necessary for a large rather than small number of customers.
3 Packaging and delivery costs are necessary for many small consignments.
4 The principal has no control over the sales effort exerted by the agent for the product.

Advantages of selling through distributors

1 Orders are large rather than small.
2 There are savings in packaging, delivery charges and insurance by making container-sized deliveries.
3 The opportunities for bad debts are reduced by having a small rather than large number of buyers.

4 Established distributors are often prepared to make prompt payment for their purchases to benefit from the maximum cash discounts.

5 When sales are contingent on pre- or after-sales service, distributors are in a position to provide such service. They also have the organization to maintain spare parts stock.

Disadvantages of selling through distributors

1 When bad debts do occur they can be substantial due to the volume of business transacted by distributors.

2 Distributors demand a large discount off list prices because of the size of the orders placed. Margins vary with industries, but distributors require a high return to compensate for their risks, investment and input. Overseas, distributors clear the goods through customs at the port or airport of entry, unpack and store them, and process them for sale to customers.

THE OBLIGATIONS OF THE PRINCIPAL TO THE AGENT

From the agent's point of view there are good and bad agencies. The agent lives by selling – from the sales, commissions are earned. Possession of an agency does not automatically guarantee that the agent earns money. An agent will require the following:

1 *A good product to sell.* Products that are new to a market and demand much groundwork before being accepted by customers are unattractive to agents. The time required to gain consumer acceptance might more profitably be spent selling readily saleable products from other principals.

2 *Reliable early deliveries.* Commission is not usually earned until the goods have been delivered. If the delivery time is extended the agent must wait for the commission.

3 *Favourable commission terms.* Commission rates are frequently stable within an industry. The payment of larger than usual commission rates diminishes profitability for the principal. A higher than usual commission sometimes is offered to an agent for an introductory period, to launch a product new to a market. This is designed to compensate for the additional effort required. Careful consideration must be given to the demotivation factor, if a commission rate is to be reduced after an agreed period to that considered appropriate for normal sales.

The time at which commission payments are to be made requires thought. Agents would like payment immediately the principal receives the orders. This system is open to abuse by sending fictitious orders to claim commission, which orders are subsequently cancelled. One option is for payments to be made when the principal receives payment; another – when regular business is sent by the agent – is monthly payments on a set day, subject to appropriate safeguards.

One situation where a higher than normal commission rate is payable is in a *del credere* agency. Here, the agent agrees to take financial responsibility for customers' orders, in the event of their default. Due to this commitment the agent will make the effort to ensure that there are no bad debts. *Del credere* agencies are not common. Usually they are created in export markets where credit and financial control by the principal is difficult.

4   *Favourable credit terms for customers*. The more attractive the deal for the customer, the easier it is for the agent to build up sales.

5   *Advertising and promotional support*. In distant areas of the home market, and overseas, the agent is often better placed than the principal to advise on promotional input appropriate to the territory – outside, that is, of judgements made by specialist advertising agencies. Most agents ask for and expect the principal to bear the cost of advertising and promotion. Full support or a negotiated compromise is a matter of judgement for the principal.

6   *Training in product knowledge and product usage*. Without doubt, a sound knowledge of the product is a precursor to effective selling. Whenever appropriate, the agent is invited to the factory for indoctrination and training. Any activity that reinforces a relationship between agent and principal is to be encouraged.

7   *Competitive prices*. Non-price competition is a marketing activity: it is quality, it is reliability, it is innovation – and it is something every manufacturer should explore and achieve. From the agent's point of view this is a complication. In general terms, agents believe that if the price is competitive, that is, low, they can sell. If it is high, it is difficult or impossible to sell.

THE RESPONSIBILITIES OF THE AGENT TOWARDS THE PRINCIPAL

The agent/principal relationship is two-way. Both principal and agent have expectations. When they are fulfilled the relationship is mutually rewarding. This does not always happen. Agents sometimes seek relationships in order to prevent a principal from competing against the products of another of the agent's principals. The agent is expected to fulfil certain obligations:

1   *Attract customers*. The agent's task is to find new customers with whom to do business. The agent must be a self-starter, continually motivated to find new business from existing and new customers.

2   *Have a thorough product knowledge*. Incomplete knowledge inhibits sales. It also diminishes the credibility of the principal's image and products in the market-place.

3   *Know all the regulations*. In the home market this means the implications of the Trades Descriptions Act; the current VAT regulations. Overseas, the agent must keep the principal informed of changes in tariff regulations, exchange control, health, safety and local legal requirements.

4 *Acquire and maintain a thorough knowledge of the market.* The agent should identify all the different segments into which the goods can be introduced.

5 *Report regularly.* Market intelligence is the life blood of a marketing plan. The agent must report regularly. A weekly report on the agent's activities helps the principal plan production and identify promotional help that could be made available. The report has two essential ingredients: what the agent has been able to achieve; and the constraints, in the form of external market forces, impeding progress.

For many agents paperwork is unpalatable. Their strengths lie in their selling skills. Filling in reports is felt to be unproductive and the task is delayed or ignored. Figure 26.2 illustrates an agent report form. A structured form eases the task for an agent and should always be provided.

Agent _____

Territory _____

Week No.	Date	Customer contact Old	Customer contact New	Business Taken	ACTION
1					
			Total	£	
2					

Figure 26.2 Agents' weekly report form

6 *Maintain regular contact with customers.* An understanding of customers' needs and problems, reliability and regular contact are the ingredients of good business.

7 *Deal with complaints.* This aspect of the agent's work is often resented. It is not felt to be productive. The same resentment is felt towards filling in report forms. The time spent does not directly generate new business, but it is an integral part of the agency function. Overseas, delays at the docks and airports, and difficulties in customs clearance are problems local agents are better placed to deal with than their principals. In the home market, the agent who has taken the customer's order usually has a closer relationship with the customer than the principal, and is in a better position to understand, pacify and resolve the customer's complaint.

8 *Identify appropriate training requirements.* The agent's perception of training needs reinforces the principal's marketing approach to meet customer needs precisely. Product usage training is particularly important.

9 *Stockholding.* Strictly speaking, an agent is not called upon to carry stocks. In certain trade sectors agents do, particularly in the Middle East. Title to the goods does not pass to the agent, but remains with the principal. The agent provides storage and handling facilities on an expenses basis, and earns commission in the usual way, from sales. Commissions are increased to reflect the additional obligations.

A variation of this situation, usually in export trade, is when business is increased through *consignment trading.* The principal decides, in consultation with the agent, that there is the potential business additional to the orders already placed. So goods are sent by the manufacturer and stored in a bonded warehouse until called forward against fresh orders taken by the agent. The principal then authorizes their release, and they are delivered to the customers. Bonded warehouses are used because only storage and transport charges are incurred; customs duty and import taxes are not payable until the goods are despatched from the warehouse.

SELECTING AN AGENT

The problems of selecting an agent able to generate good business are considerable, particularly in small or specialist markets. Agents with a good track record are already committed. There is usually no shortage of would-be agents, but how does one identify which inexperienced agent will be able to overcome the problems of customer resistance and disinterest? Figure 26.3 provides a checklist of points to be considered. Other items can be added which are pertinent to specific industry and market requirements.

Would-be agents are invariably optimistic. They are certain that good business will ensue. They are also determined to wrest a sole agency agreement from the new principal – for as large a territory as can be secured. Exclusive rights are a powerful marketing tool, when business goes well. Such rights should not be granted lightly. Performance-related safeguards can be introduced.

	YES	NO
Are there live contacts in the market-place?	☐	☐
Is there a sound knowledge of the market?	☐	☐
Is there evidence of a good business reputation?	☐	☐
Is the agent financially sound?	☐	☐
Has the agent provided details of other agencies held?	☐	☐
Does a cross-check with the agent's other principals confirm that the information given is complete?	☐	☐
Is there evidence of the agent's competence technically?	☐	☐
Is there evidence that the agent can sell?	☐	☐
Is there evidence that the agent can cover the projected territory effectively?	☐	☐
Is the agent able to justify his or her projection of future business if the agency is granted?	☐	☐
Overseas, does the agent have adequate language capability?	☐	☐

If the answer is *yes* – OK. If *no*, probe to discover the extent of shortcomings.

Figure 26.3   Criteria for agent selection

Territory demarcation is an important issue. It relates both geographically to a market and to specified products or services supplied. How and when commission is paid on business obtained from a territory must be precisely defined, or circumstances may rise where two agents claim commission on the same transaction, each believing the claim valid.

To give an example, agent Smith sends in an order from a multiple retail outlet customer, whose head office is in his territory. Some of the goods are for a retail outlet in the territory of the adjacent agent, Jones. Jones claims commission on all goods delivered within her territory. Smith claims commission on all goods delivered against his original order.

LOCATING A NEW AGENT

There are various channels for finding an agent. Each may be employed concurrently, to generate a pool of names from which selection is made. The channels are described below.

Personal contact

Suitable candidates may be found from the spectrum of contacts and acquaintances built up in the course of business. Experience of the trade develops a repertoire of knowledge and skills helpful in resolving agent selection needs.

Recommendations

There is a difference between recommendation and personal contact. Existing customers are asked to recommend an agent likely to be interested in handling the principal's goods.

The customer is often willing to do this when he or she is satisfied with the service provided by an agent already calling for another firm. A local agent keen to meet a customer's specific needs offers attractive commercial benefits when the principal's factory or warehouse is remote from the customer.

Advertisements

Advertisements inviting contact from agents are placed in the national or local press, and in the trade press. A useful directory is *British Rates and Data* (BRAD), obtainable from:

> British Rates and Data
> McLean Hunter House
> 1a Chalk Lane
> Cockfosters Road
> Barnet
> Herts
> EN4 0BU
> Telephone: 0181–441 6644

It provides details of every trade publication listed by title and by product or service. Help overseas for the names and addresses of suitable publications is available from:

Department of Trade and Industry
1 Victoria Street
London SW1H 0ET
Telephone: 0171–215 7877

If an advertisement is translated into a local language overseas, it is essential that the text is colloquially and grammatically correct. This criterion applies to all translation. An appropriate check is to use three stages:

Agent _____ Market _____ Date _____ Controller _____

	Weak 1	2	3	4	5	6	Strong 7
PROSPECTING SKILL							
by phone							
letter							
cold canvass							
SALES REPRESENTATION SKILL							
Visual aids							
Qualifying customer needs							
Passing benefit messages							
Overcoming customer objections							
Closing							
Increasing order size							
NEGOTIATING SKILL							
Preparation							
Tactics							
Ability to create variables							
Bargaining skills							
GETTING REPEAT BUSINESS							
Post-delivery visit							
Regular visit							
By telephone							
By referrals							
PLANNING							
Call cycle							
Personal time management							
Report writing							

Use the training audit prompt questions to probe agent's performance and abilities. Evaluate on a scale from 1 to 7. Enter mark by ticking appropriate column.

448 Figure 26.4 Training audit grid

1 Translate from English into the local language.
2 Translate from the text back into English, by a third party.
3 Compare English translation with the original text.

Chambers of commerce

Agents who are members of a chamber of commerce use the services of the chamber to further their activities. Contact with chambers may therefore produce names and contacts wishing to be considered. As a general rule chambers supply lists of names and addresses to anyone who asks, if it will promote the business of the members of that chamber. There is less co-operation if the objective is only to promote the business of the person or company making the enquiry. It is sometimes expedient, particularly overseas, to take out membership of a chamber of commerce – provided that research shows the potential for business in the particular market is good.

Department of Trade and Industry representative service

When seeking overseas agents the department is able to provide help. For a fee it provides a short list of businesses in the market-place. They will all have been screened, and are specifically interested in working with the exporter's product or service.

IDENTIFYING THE TRAINING NEEDS OF NEW AGENTS

At the selection interview it is important to identify the competence and selling skills of the agent. This can be evaluated by probing methodically into the different activity areas.

Figure 26.4 illustrates a training audit grid. The interviewer marks the response at each level on a scale of 1 (weak) to 7 (strong). The mark is a subjective judgement based on the agent's responses to the prompt questions listed below, which follow the format of the grid.

Prospecting

By telephone

- Do you use the telephone to sell?
- Do you use the telephone to make appointments?
- Do you use the telephone to advise if you are late for an appointment?
- How do you eliminate calls having little chance of success?
- Do you use a script for the telephone calls?
- What do you do when the customer says 'No'?
- When the call is not succeeding how do you pave the way for future contact?
- Do you maintain careful records of all prospecting calls?

By letter

- Do you have the resources to prospect by letter?
- Do you have an effective format for a prospecting letter?
- Do you confirm business appointments by letter?
- Is your correspondence with customers businesslike and efficient?

By cold canvass

- How frequently do you make cold calls?
- Is block canvassing likely to generate good business?
- What target number of cold calls per customer visit is practical?
- Have you evolved an effective introductory gambit for the cold call?
- Do you maintain records of all cold calls made?

The sales presentation

Visual aids/samples

- What visual aids/samples do you normally use?
- How can visual aids reinforce your sales presentation?
- At what stage of the presentation should samples/visual aids be introduced?

Qualifying customer needs

- What questions identify customer interest?
- What questions pinpoint customer needs?

Product benefit messages

- What contribution do benefit messages make to winning sales?
- What techniques are useful in passing benefit messages?

Overcoming customer objections

- How do you overcome a customer's 'No'?
- What do you do when a customer says 'I'll think about it'?
- How do you identify whether a customer's objection is the real objection?
- What important rule or rules apply when countering a customer's objections?

Closing

- How many closing techniques do you know?
- How many closes do you use?

- How often do you use the trial close?
- What do you do when the customer says 'No'?

Increasing the customer's order size

- When should one attempt to increase the order size?
- How is the order size increased?
- How frequently should pressure be applied to the customer to give bigger orders?

Negotiating skills

Preparation

- What is the difference between negotiating and selling?
- How does one prepare for negotiations?
- What do you understand by the three negotiating positions:

  - Must achieve or deadlock?
  - Intend to achieve?
  - Would like to achieve?

Ability to create variables

- What is the value of the variable in negotiation?
- What can be termed variable in respect of the products we are discussing?

Tactics

- What different tactics are effective in negotiation?
- How can you create time to think in a negotiation when the other side takes you by surprise?

Bargaining skills

- What questions should be asked before granting a concession?
- What do you consider to be the most important rules of bargaining?
- What is the effect of the other side linking all its issues together?

Getting repeat business

Post-delivery visit

- What are the objectives of calling on a customer after a delivery is made?
- What is an appropriate pattern for a post-delivery visit?

Regular visit

- How frequently should regular visits be made to customers?
- Is it feasible to sell the idea of a telephone call instead of a visit, to save the customer time?
- What is the approach you adopt on a regular call to a customer?
- What innovations are likely to increase the volume of business obtained?

Telephone call

- Is it possible to take repeat business by telephone?
- Should the telephone be used to make an appointment before calling for repeat business?
- Has a script been developed to secure repeat business by telephone?

Referrals

- Have you ever asked customers to recommend other buyers?
- When is the best time to ask for a referral?
- Have you ever asked a buyer to introduce you to another buyer?
- What form of incentive should motivate a buyer to recommend another buyer?

Planning

Call cycle

- Taking into account your other commitments, how frequently would our customers be called on?
- How frequently would potential customers be called on?
- What proportion of business is likely to come from what proportion of customers – that is, would, say 80 per cent of orders come from 20 per cent of the customers?
- How frequently do you call on the most important customers?
- How much time do you consider is necessary to build up a satisfactory customer base?

Personal time management

- Do you achieve everything that you set out to do?
- Do you plan your day?
- Would you like help in improving the management of personal time?

Report writing

- When do you write up your notes on performance?

- What records do you keep?
- What is the most common cause of interruption to your report-writing programme?
- What is your understanding of the reason why we insist on receiving regular reports from you?

PROTECTION FOR THE PRINCIPAL AND THE AGENT

When business is good there seems little need for protection. Agent and principal can work together without any formal agreement: orders are sent; deliveries are made to customers; commissions are paid.

Sometimes the relationship is soured by problems arising from disputes. For example, an agent passes an order to the principal for specialist equipment for urgent delivery by a particular date. The order is accepted. Due to incomplete delivery instructions, the subsequent delivery is misrouted, the equipment arrives late, and delivery is not accepted by the customer. The agent claims commission on the order value which the principal is reluctant to pay, considering that the non-acceptance is the agent's fault for providing incomplete delivery instructions. There is also the loss to the principal in having to dispose of the rejected equipment.

One method of resolving disputes before they occur is to enter into a binding agreement constructed to deal with all matters of dispute likely to arise. When a problem arises, the agreement provides the solution. The absence of a formal contract safeguards neither agent nor principal. Performance can be evidence that a contractual relationship was the intention of the parties, whether or not an actual document is signed.

Whether an agreement is intended to cover all likely areas of dispute or simply the most important, there are a number of essential considerations. The following aspects should be discussed by both parties and incorporated in a principal/agent agreement.

1 *A statement of the parties to the agreement.*
2 *The purpose of the agreement.* One party agrees to appoint the other as agent. The other agrees to act as agent, subject to the terms and conditions stated.
3 *The territory.* Geographically the territory may be a country, a county or region, a town or, say, all land north of a given river. The description must allow precise understanding of the territory limits. The boundaries may also be political, for example the EU, so long as the understanding is clear.
4 *The product range.* Sometimes a manufacturer employs more than one agent in the same territory, selling different items produced by the organization. The products are usually differentiated by value added, for example a textile manufacturer sells piece goods and made-up garments from those piece goods into the same territory.

453

5 *The principal's discretion to accept orders.* The agent's duty is to obtain orders but not to enter into binding contracts for the principal. The principal confirms all orders placed. This is a safeguard against orders being placed which cannot be executed for reasons of inadequate production capacity, time limitation or exhausted stocks.

6 *Commission.* The basis on which commission is paid is clearly stated – when, how frequently, subjected to what exclusions, and whether on orders received directly or indirectly.

7 *House accounts.* There are often existing clients within a territory before the agent is appointed. When very strong personal relationships exist between the principal and a client, such clients are nominated as falling outside the agent's sphere of activity. No commission is payable for goods delivered to these clients, notwithstanding arrangements for commission payable on all direct and indirect business.

   A new agent appointed to an existing territory expects to inherit live accounts. House accounts are likely to be few in number.

8 *Consignment goods.* The terms are given under which consignment deliveries are made, how they are to be insured, and how to be disposed of on termination of the agreement.

9 *Term of agreement.* The period for which the agreement is binding must be stated, together with the period of notice of termination to be given by either party. Termination is to be notified formally in writing.

10 *Duties of the principal.* The main duties of the principal are: to pay the agent's commission due; to pay expenses, where agreed, and provide an indemnity if loss is suffered.

   The principal's right to deal with other agents or to make sales to the territory other than through the agent is to be clearly defined.

The final document reflecting the needs and objectives of both parties should be ratified by appropriate legal advisers.

APPENDIX: FORM OF AGENCY AGREEMENT

This document sets out the terms of the agency agreement prepared and sold by the Manufacturers' Agents' Association, 1 Somers Road, Reigate, Surrey RH2 9DU, Tel: 0737–241025.

[copyright of the Manufacturers' Agents' Association]

This contract is in accordance with the EEC-Council Directive of 18 December 1986 on the coordination of the laws of the Member States relating to self-employed agents.

1 Messrs: .... (principal)

of .... entrust

Messrs:.. (commercial

agent) of ....

with their sole agency for the territory

....

....

....

for the sale of the following products:

....

....

....

....

....

2 The agent shall endeavour to obtain business for the principal and is bound to serve the interests of the said principal to the best of his ability. He will do his best to provide all information necessary for the purpose of promoting business, and to inform the principal immediately about every order received. He may not deviate from the prices, delivery and payment conditions of the principal without his consent.

3 The principal will provide the agent with all necessary samples as well as printed and advertising matter free of charge, custom duties and carriage. The samples remain the property of the principal, provided that they are not intended for consumption, and will be returned by the agent on request and at the expense of the principal.

The principal will supply the agent with all information of importance for the conduct of business. Furthermore he will inform him without delay of the acceptance or refusal of orders. He will also inform the agent without delay if there is a possibility that he can only accept orders to a limited extent. This includes information about all contacts with companies within his territory. The agent will be supplied with copies of correspondence with firms in his territory and of all invoices.

4 The agent is only entitled to collect money from the customers in the case of express authorization.

455

5 The commission will be ....%

(in words ....%)

....

....

....

....

of the invoice amount for all business, both direct and indirect, transacted with customers in the territory mentioned under 1.

The principal will furnish the agent with a statement of commission due upon all deliveries made during the month/quarter of the year not later than the 15th of the following month. The commission, to which according to such statement the agent is entitled, falls due on the day the statement is forwarded.

The agent's claim to the commission expires only in respect of any delivery for which it is certain that the customer will not pay. Commission amounts that have already been received by the agent will be taken into account in the next commission statement.

The agent is also entitled to commission if it is certain that the principal has failed to complete a transaction or has not executed it in the manner agreed upon. This shall not apply if the principal can show that he is not responsible for the non-execution.

6 The principal will reimburse the agent for the following expenses:

....

....

....

....

7 All claims that might be brought against the agent because of a violation of a patent, a utility model, a trademark or a copyright, or because of defective products shall be the exclusive responsibility of the principal. He has to make available to the agent the necessary advances of the costs of the case, and at the agent's request to advance them and to give all such information as may be required for the defence of the case. The principal has also to reimburse the agent for his own expenses. He warrants to the agent his compliance with those legal provisions for the protection of end-users in force in the contractual territory relating to the nature, labelling or packaging of the products. The principal shall be exclusively responsible for all claims and obligations arising in the event of violation of such provisions.

8   The contract shall come into force on the ....
    and shall be valid

    *a   for a fixed period until the   ....
    *b   for an indefinite period

    Where the contract has been agreed for a fixed period, it shall be extended
    for the same period provided that notice of termination shall not have been
    served, by registered letter, at least six months before the end of a calendar
    quarter.

    Where the contract has been agreed for an indefinite period it may be ter-
    minated by either party thereto giving, by registered letter, six months
    notice on the end of a calendar quarter.

9a   For agents, with domicile within the European Community, the provision
     of the EEC Council Directive of 18 December 1986 on the coordination of
     the laws of the Member States relating to self-employed agents
     (86/653/EEC) apply to this agreement. In other cases the law of the domi-
     cile of the agent is applicable.
9b   After termination of the agency contract, the agent shall be entitled to
     goodwill compensation if he/she has brought the principal new cus-
     tomers or has increased the business with existing customers and the
     principal continues to derive benefits from doing business with such cus-
     tomers.

     If termination is caused by the death of the agent, the estate shall be enti-
     tled to the goodwill compensation. No goodwill compensation shall be
     payable where the termination is caused by material breach of contract
     on the part of the agent, nor shall it be payable where the agent has termi-
     nated the contract unless such termination is justified by circumstances
     attributable to the principal or on grounds of age, infirmity or illness of
     the agent.

     If, and to the extent that, the provisions of this section are in contradic-
     tion with mandatory provisions in the laws of the state/state of the agent,
     such mandatory provisions shall be taken into account without invalidat-
     ing the remaining provisions of this contract.

10   Any disputes arising out of or in connection with this agreement shall be
     decided by the court in the area of which the plaintiff has his residence or
     registered offices.

11 Amendments and supplements to this contract must be confirmed in writing in order to be valid.

....

....

Place: ···Date: ···

....

(signature of principal)   (signature of agent)

[*] Please cross out not applicable.

ESSENTIAL READING

Katz, B. (1987), *Managing Export Marketing*, Aldershot: Gower.

Kotler, P. (1991), *Principles of Marketing*, Hemel Hempstead, Prentice-Hall.

Hibbert, E.P. (1985), *Principles & Practice of Marketing*, Oxford: Heinemann Professional Publications.

27 Reaching overseas markets
Kate Prescott

Internationalization by any firm, whether it be a large multinational enterprise seeking to penetrate a new market or a small firm contemplating selling its products or services abroad for the first time, involves a highly complex decision-making process. The starting point is deciding which markets offer opportunities to the firm, a decision which necessitates analysing the environment and the competition in much the same way as is required for domestic marketing efforts. Where the international challenge differs markedly from domestic operations is in the choice of strategy to penetrate and service overseas markets – the 'foreign market servicing decision'. While at face value this may appear a relatively straightforward task, the strategic planner is faced with a myriad of alternative options, some of which may offer far greater benefits to the firm than others. This chapter outlines the complexities of the process, offers some suggestions for rational decision making and throughout attempts to pinpoint certain key factors now emerging in the international business environment which are having a profound impact on foreign market servicing trends.

THE RANGE OF OPTIONS AVAILABLE TO FIRMS

Those new to the area of international business may be forgiven for assuming that exporting (trade) equates with international business activity. So much emphasis is placed on trade flows (imports and exports) that it is often a surprise to learn the volume of overseas sales for a country arising from strategies other than exporting. For example, the UK between 1975 and 1983 derived, on average, over 30 per cent of its foreign sales from investments based in overseas markets and around 10 per cent from contractual arrangements (Buckley and Prescott, 1989).

At its most simple, foreign market servicing can be divided into three *459* generic strategies: exporting, licensing and other contractual arrangements, and foreign direct investment. However, these three generic options are only the tip of the iceberg; within each generic group there are numerous operational strategies available to firms. While it is not practicable to discuss all of these in detail, the main 'types' will be addressed. The alternatives are summarized in Table 27.1.

Table 27.1
Summary of major market servicing options

Generic option	Intra-mode strategy

Exporting	*Indirect*
	· Export houses
	· Confirming houses
	· Buying houses
	· Piggybacking
	
	Direct
	· Via an agent
	· Via a distributor
	· Direct to end-user
	  – from domestic market
	  – from foreign sales office

Licensing and other contractual arrangements	*Contractual/Licensing* · Licensing · Franchising · Management contracts · Contract manufacturing
Foreign direct investment	*Manufacturing* · Full production · Off-shore · Limited product range *Strategic Investments* · Sales/marketing · Research and development

Exporting

Exporting can be sub-divided into two principal groups: indirect and direct. The former relates to passive exporting options where the exporter relies, almost exclusively, on third parties handling the export business on their behalf. Documentation, handling, physical distribution and sales effort are all conducted by the third party, the exporter taking little to no active part in the sale of their goods in foreign countries. Operations of this kind usually result from manufacturers reacting to unsolicited orders, although there are exceptions to this rule.

Indirect exporting modes may take a variety of forms: export houses buy from the company and then sell the products abroad on their own account, taking full control of the operation and bearing full risk. While the exporter may contact the export house in the first instance, this tends to be the extent of their active involvement. Alternatively, exporters may contact confirming houses. These institutions, acting on behalf of the buyer, guarantee payment to the exporter and usually undertake all insurance and transportation arrangements. Unlike export houses, however, confirming houses merely act as intermediaries, the contract being between the manufacturer and the foreign buyer.

Buying houses provide a third option. These are overseas organizations operating on behalf of buyers to secure supply contracts with foreign manufacturers. They tend to serve a particular country or group of countries and are prevalent in the Far East and Continental Europe. The final alternative, piggybacking, allows firms to sell their goods abroad through the established distribution networks of other firms. Established exporters may identify synergistic benefits in handling the products of other manufacturers particularly where products complement their existing portfolios and allow them to lower unit costs through scope economies. While the domestic firms' products may be less actively promoted by the incumbent firm, rapid access to an existing distribution network and relatively low risks make the option attractive.

Direct exporting options necessitate a genuine commitment to exporting – dedicated personnel, careful management and the investment of resources. Three main alternatives exist: exporting via a foreign-country-based agent who sells on behalf of the exporter without taking title to the goods (that is, without taking ownership of the products he sells); exporting via a distributor who takes title to the goods and sells them on through the channel of distribution or straight to the final customer; and direct exporting wherein the exporter sells directly to foreign customers either from the domestic market or a country-based sales office.

In strategic terms, the key distinguishing features between the alternative modes of exporting concern the degree of control afforded by each option and the amount of necessary resource commitment. In simple terms, the more a company is prepared to dedicate to its exporting activities, the more control it will ultimately have over the operation. This relationship is shown graphically in Figure 27.1.

Control here is linked with access to information which is fundamental to strategic planning. Knowledge of the market – economic conditions, competitive activity, political and legal environment and customers – is central to

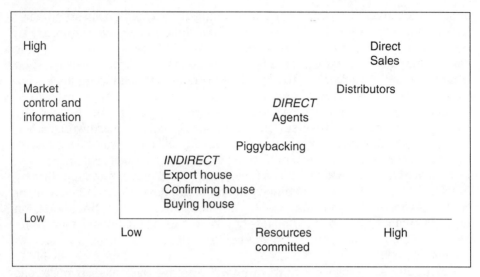

Figure 27.1   Market control and information versus resource commitment in alternative export strategies

Source: Young et al., 1989.

proactive exporting designed to enhance the overall competitive position of the firm. Therefore, organizations which opt for indirect strategies due to lack of risks and low resource commitment not only sacrifice control over their operations but also the potential actively to learn about the foreign market and plan for future development. Alternatively, firms utilizing the services of market-based intermediaries may exploit this business link to gather relevant market data.

While it is generally agreed that exporting involves the least risk of the three generic market servicing alternatives, involving low resource commitment in both financial and management terms, the wide variety of exporting alternatives means there are distinct intra-mode differences. Assuming that all export alternatives are an 'easy' option is to ignore the challenges posed by the various strategies. Problems of managing intermediaries (agents and distributors) are manifold, not least because there is so much scope for conflict. Rosson (1984) identifies three factors which can give rise to disagreements between manufacturers and their foreign representatives:

1   Divided loyalties, resulting from distributors selling a range of competing product alternatives can be highly frustrating for manufacturers. The intermediary's salesforce is most likely to sell most of those products which are either easy to sell or which earn them greatest commission. This may give rise to a continuing round of out-bidding on commission levels or price, ultimately detrimental to the overall profits of the firm. To avoid such a situation, firms may prefer to concentrate on promotional effort ('pulling' the products through the channel of distribution), product differentiation or providing a better service package.

462

2   Where the distributor is treated as a customer by the manufacturer there is a tendency for the two parties to assume the roles of buyer and seller. It is this kind of atmosphere which gives rise to sub-optimization, with the buyer attempting to bid down prices and assuming that once he has title to the products he has control over where and how they are sold. A lack of trust and understanding between the two parties may result which can have a profound impact on the intermediary's willingness to gather and filter market information on the manufacturer's behalf, negating the potential for market learning so frequently associated with this form of market servicing.

3   Because the use of foreign intermediaries often serves as a precursor to firms undertaking their own exporting activities, foreign representative firms are often wary of the future intentions of their suppliers. This can lead to their underperforming as a way of concealing market potential.

Specific strategic issues may also give rise to conflict, particularly disagreements over elements of the marketing mix – product features, price, promotion and forward channels of distribution. Because intermediaries are close to the market they often feel they know best when it comes to determining which strategies best fit market conditions. Failure by the manufacturer to act on advice and recommendations frustrates intermediaries who may consequently be deterred from working hard on the producer's behalf.

Overcoming conflict can be achieved in two ways: co-operation and control. Control involves manufacturers setting targets and quotas, offering rewards and imposing sanctions, and while this can raise sales and improve performance it does little to foster good relations and mutual trust. Munro and Beamish (1987) argue that good performance from the intermediary is best achieved by providing additional support (such as sales and service training and promotional literature). This view is supported by Valla (1986) whose research work for the Industrial Marketing and Purchasing Group uncovered some key findings regarding strategies for success in international industrial marketing. He highlights the positive results which stem from investing more human resources into the operation, basing staff from the supplier organization in the target market to assist the intermediary, demonstrating positive commitment and encouraging the agent to work harder on the principal's behalf. Similarly, encouraging personnel to become involved with their counterparts in the customer organization at various functional levels strengthens the bond between supplier and final customer and raises the level of trust and understanding. Here, bilateral relations between supplier and intermediary are extended to tripartite relations where the manufacturer is also in direct contact with the final customer, working in conjunction with the intermediary.

With such a degree of involvement being proposed for strategic success it is important not to assume that exporting is, for the most part, a hands-off option. Excepting those firms which are content to take a passive approach to their overseas activities (following indirect modes of exporting), success centres on commitment, direct involvement and support – all of which require significant investment of time and money.

463

Another frequently held misconception about exporting is that willingness to commit financial resources and gain more control increases with firm size and international orientation. It is not uncommon to find large multinational enterprises involved in indirect modes of exporting and strategies involving market-based intermediaries. Financial resources and international experience are not, therefore, sufficient to explain choice of alternative option.

Licensing and other contractual arrangements

This group of options also comprises a wide array of alternatives. One can distinguish between licensing contracts (in their various guises) and strategic alliances. Licensing refers to a market sale of embodied knowledge to an independent producer, in an international context to a foreign-based manufacturer. Licensing often centres on patents and trademarks which are legally binding forms of protection, affording firms a monopolistic position for a fixed period of time (often in the region of 20 years). It also extends, however, to less formally defined types of intellectual property which give the licensor a competitive advantage. This may concern both product and process technology and management know-how. The option combines the expertise and skills of the entrant with the local contacts and knowledge of the licensee, usually with clear synergistic benefits.

One of the greatest risks associated with licensing is misuse of intellectual property by the licensee and the possibility of creating a competitor. Careful selection of licensees, the drawing up of watertight contracts and ongoing policing of the license therefore figure large in the management of such strategies. Thus while the option involves little capital or management commitment, the establishment and ongoing monitoring costs must not be overlooked.

Franchising is a specific type of licensing in which the contract tends to cover the total business concept as in the case of Holiday Inns and Kentucky Fried Chicken. Here the contract incorporates common elements such as colour schemes, layout of premises/facilities, promotional activity, brand image and staff training. This commonality allows firms to establish international brands and a standardized approach to their business through contractual control rather than direct ownership, rapidly and cost effectively.

Management contracts involve the devolvement of control of an operation, by contract, to an independent firm which carries out the necessary management duties in return for a fee. The independent firm operates in much the same way as a multinational firm's subsidiary although it is rare for it to be afforded the freedom to develop the business in any substantial way. Turnkey contracts involve the contractor establishing a manufacturing unit or physical facility in the host country, providing all services up to the point of start-up (such as design, managing the building, and installing equipment). In recent years, provision of ongoing support has become common, particularly personnel training and maintenance, in an effort to overcome operational problems experienced after hand-over. Finally, contract manufacturing (international sub-contracting) refers to the production of final goods or components in offshore sites. Design and quality specifications are tightly controlled by the contractor who often ensures standards by providing know-how, equipment and training (usually under licence). This practice typically takes place in developing countries where contractors take advantage of lower costs (particularly for labour and raw materials).

The above three options, although not licensing *per se*, share one important common element: they all centre critically on the establishment of contracts with independent operators. Control is therefore achieved via contractual arrangement rather than ownership, with a great deal of importance being placed on the choice of organization, establishment of good, legal, workable contracts and on ongoing monitoring and maintenance. This clearly distinguishes this group of strategies from strategic alliances and joint ventures which are usually based on the mutual development of co-operative solutions. Part ownership in the case of equity joint ventures and strategic collaboration in strategic alliances mean that co-operation supersedes control as the key management focus. Many observers note the failure to co-operate effectively in collaborative ventures as the main cause of their demise:

> The partnership may be starved of know-how, each partner using its control over know-how transfer as a bargaining tool towards the other: each partner is tempted to restrict the flow of know-how it provides to the partnership in order to increase its own bargaining power. . . Such escalation of partnership dependency may drastically curtail the effectiveness of partnerships and the scope for joint activities (Doz et al., 1990, p.126).

Joint ventures, as typically described, are co-operative business activities formed between two or more partners for strategic reasons. They involve the creation of a separate business entity under joint control and ownership, spreading the risk and rewards of the venture between the partners. While many joint ventures involve equal shareholdings between the various partners, this is not always the case. Equally, some joint ventures involve 'passive' partners who invest money in the venture without taking any active managemental control.

As with licensing, joint ventures permit the sharing of critical assets between partners, in particular technology from the entrant and local market facilities, knowledge and contacts from the incumbent firm. Nevertheless, there are many other resources which may add to the synergy of the business linkage: existing customer franchise, complementary product portfolios, service networks, entrenched distribution network, brand names, complementary research projects. The list is extensive. However, joint ventures are not without risk, in particular: conflicting objectives leading to disagreements in management direction; conflicting business cultures which cause problems in the way the venture is to be managed; hidden agendas wherein one partner attempts to use the joint venture for purposes other than those agreed upon; takeover of small firms by large multinational partners; creating competitors once partners are privy to previously undisclosed intellectual property. Careful selection of partner is essential to the success of a joint venture as is

465

the willingness of both partners to co-operate. Failure to disclose information, pursuit of hidden agendas and a reluctance to dedicate enough time and attention to the operation are all likely to result in its demise.

Strategic alliances are variously defined. Many use the term where the alliance between the partners does not involve equity investment while others use the term to describe co-operation in areas other than manufacturing. However, the most useful method of distinguishing strategic alliances is provided by Doz et al. (1986). They see strategic alliances as being different in a number of key respects: firstly, while other collaborative ventures are between firms of different sizes and capabilities, strategic alliances tend to be formed between organizations with similar capabilities and capacity, usually from industrialized countries. Second, companies involved in strategic alliances are often competing directly with each other in the same product/geographic markets. Finally, they are usually entered into for reasons other than market access or pooling of resources. Because many of the firms involved in the formation of such ventures are large, dominant multinationals, these coalitions are able to change the competitive focus of global markets in significant ways. They can determine which firms are permitted access to new technologies, they can control the rate of technological development in global regions and they can operate outside of the formation of economic unions.

Foreign direct investment

Foreign direct investment options share one common element: they all involve 100 per cent ownership of overseas facilities. These may be established for manufacturing purposes or for a variety of other strategic reasons.

Manufacturing subsidiaries can take several forms: they may produce a full range of products for sale in the foreign market – replicas of the domestic manufacturing unit. These investments permit the firm to produce goods in close proximity to the market, adapting products according to local market needs and monitoring changes in demand and competitive conditions at first hand. They also raise company profile in the market which can enhance overall demand and raise confidence among buyers of their ability to deliver products on time and provide adequate levels of service. Alternatively foreign manufacturing facilities may be established to produce components or finished products for final assembly or sale in other countries (offshore production) usually for the purpose of reducing costs. Finally, manufacturing investment may focus on a limited product range for sale globally or in a number of regionally designated markets. Such rationalization of production into specialized units can also provide cost savings by eliminating the duplication of effort and ensuring business focus in independent units.

Strategic investments, on the other hand, comprise sales and marketing activities – dedicated company business units designed to promote local business effort, and research and development investments intended to tap into local resources (local expertise in particular) to facilitate the development of products for the global market. This kind of investment activity is becoming more prevalent in international business as firms increasingly search for strategies which permit both responsiveness to local markets and economies of scale. This unbundling of the value chain into its constituent processes provides for the most appropriate strategies being formulated for each function.

Continued high growth in sales/marketing investment in developed countries is an active response to growing competitiveness in leading global industrial centres, often necessitating dedicated sales, marketing and service provision by the manufacturer. This trend is particularly evident in the Single European Market (Buckley, Pass and Prescott, 1992) where economies in manufacturing offered by the larger market are being complemented by sales/marketing investments on the ground designed to cater for cultural nuances in the 12 member states.

An interesting development in multinational activity in recent years has been the internationalization of research and development departments. While in the past, many firms pursued scale economies in research by centralizing R&D activity, growing numbers of organizations have seen the need to locate research in centres of technological excellence (countries which have highly qualified technical research staff and which have, as a result of their economic development, witnessed an aggregation of particular industries). A multi-research centre approach also offers potential for deriving new development ideas from different market demand conditions.

Whatever form foreign direct investment takes, there is a further important strategic decision accompanying the choice of option: firms are faced with the 'build or buy' decision. That is, they must decide whether it is more profitable to buy an existing operation or establish their own greenfield facilities. Greenfield facilities are generally favoured by host governments as they provide additional competition, employment and skills. Indeed, many governments offer incentive packages to firms for investment in depressed regions as a means of promoting economic welfare in areas of decline. Greenfield strategies may also permit freer choice of location, investment of the most up-to-date technologies and management practices, and financial commitment in line with market potential.

One of the biggest problems associated with takeovers and mergers is calculating the value of the organization to the firm. It is often the case that firms buy, as part of the overall takeover package, business elements which are not deemed necessary or desirable resulting in a spate of divestments and closures after purchase. This can obviously raise the risks involved with the purchase and can cause political difficulties with existing staff. Equally, the takeover may mean taking on existing problems which can complicate the process of integrating the new business into the international organization. Nevertheless, takeovers allow firms rapid access to markets as acquirers hit the ground running with a currently operating business. Where short-term financial returns are considered important, this can be a key factor in the financial decision. Perhaps more importantly, however, takeovers often involve as part of the package the acquisition of critical assets: brand names, distribution networks, trained personnel, R&D facilities, technical expertise, business contacts, access to raw materials or an existing customer franchise.

467

Although the various strategic alternatives have been clearly categorized for the sake of analysis, there is a high degree of overlap both between and within the generic groupings. Joint ventures, for example, may also be considered as a form of foreign investment, and exporting via a sales office or a wholly owned subsidiary involve both elements of exporting and FDI. It is also common for firms to employ more than one strategy in the same market, possibly because different products in the portfolio demand a different approach, but also because it is possible to establish options which complement each other in achieving a strong strategic position in the market. For example, a joint venture with an incumbent firm may be supported by a locally placed sales and marketing subsidiary, or a foreign manufacturing plant may sell its products via a local wholesaler whose distribution networks and contacts would be hard to replicate.

Within the category of licensing and other contractual arrangements, different options often occur simultaneously. Licensing of technology to a joint venture from one of the parent firms or to a management contractor or an international subcontractor by a multinational is commonplace, making simple definitions and categorization of options highly complex. Similarly, once established, collaborative ventures often take on a life of their own extending beyond simple contractual development in the first instance, to long-term cooperation and mutual reliance. This again complicates the analysis of strategies and places emphasis on longitudinal study of the ongoing models of market servicing rather than simple market entry observation.

THE DYNAMICS OF MARKET SERVICING

The choice of foreign market servicing option is not a once and for all decision. Market conditions, the firm's resources and international experience, and the content and scope of the product portfolio are all prone to change. It is important for firms to continually review the effectiveness of their strategies in the light of these changes. Several models have been developed to explain the dynamics of market servicing. The first emerged from the work of Vernon (1966) who developed a model of the international product life cycle which attempts to explain the process of new product introduction. Briefly, the model is based on the experiences of US firms in the late 1950s. It suggests that after domestic product testing and introduction, demand for the product appears abroad leading to a period of exporting by the original innovator. As overseas volume increases, it is possible for firms to justify investment in foreign markets, investments which are also partly reactionary as foreign firms begin to compete with the market entrant. Intense price competition in both the domestic and foreign markets served ultimately leads to firms locating production in offshore, low-cost sites as a way of preserving profit margins. Ultimately, therefore, firms are seen to import products into their own domestic markets, with overall demand declining as product technologies become outdated.

468   This step-wise process of domestic sales, exports, strategic market invest-

ment and offshore investment has been highly criticized over the years. Firstly, as multinational enterprises have developed complex international business networks, it is more likely for new products to be introduced through extant business facilities. Second, the contention that price competition dominates the mature stage of the cycle before global product demand declines belies the evidence that competition in today's markets more usually centres on differentiation which serves to promote longevity of the life cycle and preserve demand. The reason for this is the trend towards global oligopolies in many leading industries which are now dominated by large multinationals headquartered in the developed world. A classic example of this is the television industry. While the internationalization of black and white televisions adhered closely to Vernon's model – being first produced in the United States, exported to other developed countries, produced in final target markets and then manufactured in offshore sites and re-exported to the United States – the introduction of colour televisions has spawned a highly oligopolistic world industry where product differentiation characterizes global competition.

In response to the changing organization of world industries, Vernon revised his model in the late 1970s in line with the trend towards global oligopolies. The mature stage of the life cycle, rather than focusing on price competition suggests cartel-like behaviour and differentiation. The decline stage of the cycle, senescent oligopoly, rather than featuring a reduction in volume, suggests potential for new market entry which is characteristic of markets where differentiation is a key to competitive success. Small firms, unable to enter markets where price competition and the pursuit of scale economies is dominant, are able to concentrate on specific differential niches. These assertions more closely resemble the current world environment where many industries display a distinct polarization of organizations – a small number of dominant multinationals operating in the main stream and a large number of small specialist producers concentrating on specific product niches.

Other step-wise models have also been developed to explain the dynamic process of market servicing. The stages theory of international expansion which more specifically concentrates on intra-mode exporting strategies suggests that firms gradually increase commitment to export markets moving from indirect to direct modes of exporting as they acquire knowledge of the foreign market. Johanson and Wiedershiem-Paul (1975), the originators of this theory, based their research on the experiences of four large Swedish multinational organizations. Later research has extended their theories beyond the scope of exporting to support the move to investment in foreign markets (Cavusgil, 1980).

Similarly, this theory is not without its critics. Research by Turnbull (1987) of 24 firms operating in France, Germany and Sweden and featuring 72 separate international ventures concludes that many companies skipped stages in the process with several moving directly to foreign direct investment. The main reasons for the divergence from the proposed model stem from the different requirements of various industries and target markets. In some sectors foreign investment and a closeness to the market is a prerequisite of gaining a competitive position. Simply basing internationalization on an incremental learning process is not therefore sufficient.

An alternative approach to internationalization is proposed by Buckley and Casson (1985) who suggest that the timing of the switch from exporting to foreign direct investment can be explained by examining the cost structures of the alternative strategies. Exporting, which has low fixed costs (due to the lack of capital investment in the export operation) features high variable costs as transportation costs, management load, variable production costs and tariffs all increase with volume. Conversely, foreign direct investment has high fixed set-up costs, but lower variable costs. In the example shown in Figure 27.2, it can be seen that at a certain volume of business it is cost-effective for the firm to switch from exporting to foreign direct investment. In this example, licensing never appears as the preferred option. With higher fixed costs than exporting (due to search for an appropriate licensee and the complex process of drawing up contracts and agreements) and lower variable costs (because of the absence of transportation costs and tariffs) this option is ruled out. Nevertheless, this is the general case and in certain industries the picture may prove very different.

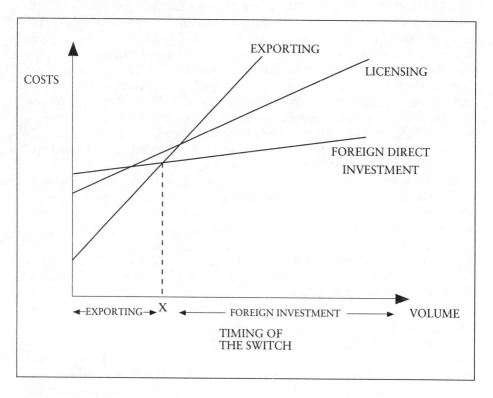

Figure 27.2   The timing of the switch to FDI

Source: Buckley and Casson, 1985.

Buckley and Casson's model is the only one to attempt to include licensing and other contractual arrangements which is a distinct flaw in the other two alternatives. However, simply basing the explanation of internationalization on cost considerations ignores cases where firms enter markets through investment in order to be close to their customers, continue exporting despite large sales volumes because of political uncertainty, or enter into joint ventures or licensing contracts because government stipulations prevent alternative options being followed. Neither, then, is this model sufficient to explain the complex process of servicing foreign markets.

All the models offer something to understanding the whys and wherefores of switches in international strategies over time. Conspicuous flaws, however, make them all of little practical use when considered in isolation. None are prescriptive, although they offer some insight into elements of the process. With such a large number of variables impacting on both the original decision of how to enter a foreign market and the ongoing reassessment of strategies, these simplified models fail to offer anything substantial to the practitioner except – and this should not be overlooked – that foreign market servicing strategies change with market conditions, company capabilities and changing industry structures.

A further limitation of these models is that they are based on the experiences of manufacturing firms. Although, theoretically at least, the same range of options is open to international service firms, various features of service make the internationalization process somewhat different. Boddewyn, Halbrich and Perry (1986) classify types of services according to their tradability based on the extent to which services are embodied in physical goods and the degree of inseparability (that is the extent to which the supplier and customer need to be present at the point of delivery):

1   Service commodities which are distinct from their production process are tradable across international boundaries and thus exportable.
2   Where production cannot be separated from consumption as in the case of legal advice, a foreign presence is essential.
3   Where services comprise a mix of distinct commodities and location-bound service elements, some location substitution is possible.

Because of the inseparability factor, pertaining in many services, incremental internationalization may not be a viable proposition (Enderwick, 1989). This restricts the scope for service firms to learn about the market by following low-investment export strategies and utilizing foreign-market intermediaries ruling out the stages of development approach to internationalization. Similarly, cost and market-volume related switches from exporting to foreign direct investment proposed by the Buckley and Casson model are not feasible, meaning that for many service firms the initial move, restricted to foreign direct investment or collaborative agreements, involves higher risks than is the case in manufacturing. Joint ventures, which permit the sharing of financial risk, may prove the most attractive first move. This has proved the case in *471* the retail financial service industry in Europe where a spate of joint venture activity has resulted from liberalization of the financial service sector.

As more service industries are liberalized on a global scale there is potential for rapid international expansion of services in the future. Nevertheless, the strategic difficulties resulting from the specific nature of services should not be overlooked.

DECIDING ON THE MOST APPROPRIATE OPTION

Referring back to Table 27.1, it is clear that firms are faced with a very complex decision-making task. The obvious question is how, given the numerous available alternatives, firms decide upon the most suitable strategy for their organization in the chosen foreign market? Some kind of strategic audit is necessary for working through the various pros and cons of the alternatives. Figure 27.3 provides a useful overview of the factors to be considered.

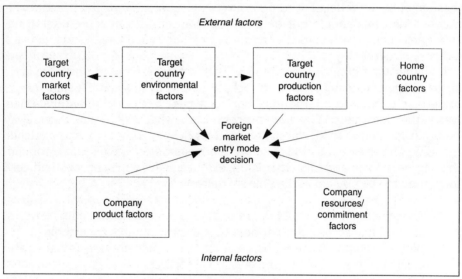

Figure 27.3   Factors in the entry mode decision

Source: Root, 1987.

Analysing these factors in more detail, we can generate a fairly comprehensive checklist of factors which the firm must consider when deciding on foreign market servicing options.

Target country market factors

These relate to the competitive environment of the customer market and include such factors as market size and growth, competitive structure, and power balance between buyers and suppliers.

Market size and growth is a central feature of the stages of development view of international expansion with the suggestion that the larger the market (or the greater the potential for rapid growth) the more resource commitment is necessary to secure a strong competitive position. Root (1987, p.8) asserts: 'Small markets favour entry modes that have low breakeven sales volume (indirect and agent/distributor exporting, licensing and some contractual arrangements). Conversely, markets with high sales potentials can justify entry modes with high breakeven sales volumes (branch/subsidiary exporting and equity investment in local production)'.

This cost-based view of market potential and entry strategy may hold true in some sectors although there are possible exceptions: product specialization in small volume markets means that price discretion can yield high margins and consequently the set-up costs of a foreign production facility can be borne. With growing potential for flexible specialization in manufacturing with the introduction of computer-aided design and computer-aided manufacturing systems foreign investment may be of a relatively small scale. Size and growth therefore need to be considered in conjunction with potential profit contribution.

The competitive structure of the market – atomistic, oligopolistic, monopolistic – can constrain choice. Where the market is dominated by a large number of small players it is possible to enter via indirect exporting or distributors, whereas markets which are dominated by large multinationals may presuppose more direct involvement if market share is to be taken away from such powerfully entrenched organizations. Local visibility and presence may be the only means of convincing local customers of the firm's commitment, ability to supply and to provide adequate service. In the most extreme cases where markets are dominated by large powerful firms, the barriers to entry may be so high that collaborative ventures may emerge as the only feasible option. Much depends on the distinctiveness of the product and the extent to which it is differentiated from currently supplied alternatives. Where products are designed to serve a specific niche in the market, out of mainstream competition, intermediaries may still be used even where large-firm dominance is apparent.

The power of suppliers and buyers, along the lines suggested in Porter's familiar model (1980) of the forces driving competition in an industry, may be influential in determining strategy choice. This applies equally in foreign market servicing strategy considerations. Where suppliers in a host country wield power over manufacturers, firms may prefer to export from the domestic market – either because they can gain a differential advantage by offering lower prices if domestic suppliers are not as dominant, or because they are best served by continuing to add volume to domestic supplies in an effort to earn discounts where similar supplier control exists. Where buyers in the host country have power over manufacturers, foreign production facilities, sales marketing investment or collaborative arrangements may prove the most favourable alternatives. This is due to the need to develop good customer relations and display long-term commitment, made easier through a physical market presence. However, there is growing evidence of firms with industrial customers entering into joint ventures and collaborative arrangements with their foreign customers, developing mutually co-operative business programmes and tying themselves, contractually, into foreign-market sales potential. These kind of linkages are becoming increasingly popular in sectors where customization of products for individual clients is necessary or desirable. Rather than continually bidding for short-term contracts, there is greater scope for long-term competitiveness in developing quasi-partnerships.

Target country environmental factors

Factors here include geographic distance, cultural distance, economic and political factors as well as the physical environment.

Geographic distance has an important bearing on cost considerations. This is where Buckley and Casson's (1985) cost-based model of the timing of the switch to FDI may be practically considered. The greater the geographic distance, the higher the variable costs associated with exporting. The further the market from the domestic manufacturing unit the more cost-effective it is to consider foreign direct investment. It is no accident that approximately 60 per cent of UK firms' sales in the USA between 1975 and 1983 were derived from foreign direct investment activity with only 40 per cent coming from exports (Buckley and Prescott, 1989). The distance between the two markets makes foreign investment more economically attractive than exporting.

Cultural distance, although sometimes overlooked in international strategy development, should be given careful consideration. Entry into markets which are culturally dissimilar involves a high degree of risk in the sense that it is easy to get things wrong. Misunderstanding business practices, the behaviour of managers, consumer buyer behaviour, attitudes and beliefs can all lead to firms making mistakes when dealing with foreign firms and developing marketing strategies for foreign customers. It is therefore advisable for firms to rely on the services of market-based intermediaries or local partners at least in the first instance. Investment is only advised after a period of learning. Many firms, commenting on their international business practices, cite cultural distance as one of the major reasons why they avoid investment in Japan. Complexities in the Japanese distribution system, alien work practices, and lack of language skills all feature as highly as governmental protectionist measures in the low incidence of direct investment in Japan even by multinational firms with vast international experience.

Even where markets appear to be culturally similar, firms should be careful not to assume that they are the same as the domestic market. The repercussions of failing to identify cultural nuances can be as serious as misunderstanding the fundamental character of a nation and puts firms at a disadvantage vis-à-vis indigenous firms. Where firms lack international experience and have not developed systems for reading and adapting to cultural differences, employing the services of market-based intermediaries is again advisable. Alternatively firms may employ local personnel as a way of bridging the cultural gap.

Fundamentally linked to culture is the need to adapt products for the foreign market. Where needs and wants of overseas customers differ from those in the domestic market, product, service and even business-practice adaptation may be a prerequisite of doing business abroad. This has important ramifications for production as there are few scale economy benefits of adding capacity to domestic production providing additional incentives for foreign direct investment. Here, closeness to the market permits greater understanding of the form adaptations need to take for products to be competitive in the local environment.

The economic environment includes exchange rates and tariffs which have historically played a powerful role in shaping international business flows and determining the incidence of exporting and foreign direct investment. Tariff barriers, in the past, were frequently cited as one of the major factors persuading firms to invest abroad. Foreign investment was therefore viewed as an effective means of jumping the barriers thus imposed. While this incentive for foreign direct investment still persists, the ongoing work of GATT (the General Agreement on Tariffs and Trade) to eliminate tariffs and open up world competition has gone a long way to making this a less important consideration in international business activity. Nevertheless, tariff restrictions still exist in politically sensitive industries and with the growth of large dominant trading blocs in the global arena (such as the North American Free Trade Area and the Single European Market) there is some fear that there is a move away from multilateralism, so actively pursued by GATT, to bilateral bargaining between regions raising tariff restrictions once again, and introducing new, highly restrictive, non-tariff barriers such as Voluntary Export Restraints and reciprocity agreements. Where these kinds of restrictions prevail there is great incentive to 'get behind' the barriers, investing in the target market.

Exchange rates have continued to dog export activities for many years. Changes in rates and the time lags inherent in receiving export payments can make a profitable venture into a loss-making exercise overnight. This increases the risks associated with exporting as it implicitly means a high degree of uncertainty in planning. There are ways of minimizing these risks through bankers' letters of credit or payment terms arranged in basket currencies although acceptance of these methods may depend on the customer's preference. In the USA for example, there is a tendency for buyers to stipulate open credit terms which leaves the exporter at risk and subject to adverse changes in exchange rates. Unfavourable exchange rates for UK exporters to the USA through the 1970s and early 1980s may therefore be seen to have acted in conjunction with geographic distance to raise the propensity of firms to invest in the market. Firms may, however, prefer to deal with export houses because they are domestic organizations and do not involve the problems of foreign currency exchange.

The Exchange Rate Mechanism (ERM) of the Single European Market is designed to eliminate the problems caused by exchange rate fluctuations and ensure that European firms are permitted a degree of certainty when planning for exports. It has the potential, therefore, to reduce the incentive for investment for participating countries.

475

Other, more general, factors related to the economic welfare of the nation may also have a bearing on the decision-making process. Stagnant economies offer less incentive for investment, usually because growth rates are low and future potential limited. Noncommittal export activities may consequently be preferred. Conversely, dynamic economies showing high growth rates and rapid change may be attractive investment destinations. Not only does rapid growth support an investment commitment, the dynamism of the market suggests an investment on the ground is better placed to adapt to market developments and change. Very high growth rates in Spain following its acceptance into the European Union gave rise to a vast amount of multinational investment, not only from other EU-based firms, but also from Japan and America.

Political factors also play a central role. Political stability is fundamental to the market-entry decision. Where countries are unstable the least-risk option is always advised – which suggests indirect exporting or perhaps licensing. Firms making capital investments do so with the risk of expropriation of their assets. Government intervention can also have a pervasive influence on strategy. Various restrictions apply to investments: local content rulings dictate firms use foreign suppliers in local production of goods. This ensures that investments are not made for exploitative reasons but help to promote the local economy. Such rulings are prevalent in the Single European Market Initiative and the North American Free Trade Agreement where governments have attempted to rule out, in particular, Japanese screwdriver plants (locally-based investments designed to overcome tariff and non-tariff barriers but relying totally on Japanese-produced components). Because such operations fail to add value locally they are seen as detrimental to the economic welfare of the regions and have been severely restricted through the insistence that a proportion of the components included in the finished product are locally produced. These restrictions become preclusive when suitable suppliers cannot be found.

In some countries, 100 per cent ownership of subsidiaries is not permitted, governments actively promoting joint ventures (or licensing agreements) as a way of promoting technology transfer. This is particularly prevalent in developing countries intent on pursuing import substitution policies for the development of a strong technology base as well as improving their balance of trade. Many East European governments are also taking this stance, fearful that Western firm investment will simply exploit the low-cost production sites without offering any real benefits to the local economy.

Other restrictions imposed to prevent anti-competitive behaviour similarly apply to licensing agreements: stipulations that components and raw materials are supplied by the licensor; limitations on the volume of outputs, prices or export market destinations; prevention of other technologies being licensed-in during the term of the contract; automatic reciprocal access to information by the licensor.

In terms of exporting strategies, governments may impose vertical trading restrictions (prohibiting such things as territorial agreements and price fixing) as well as protecting local intermediaries through demanding compensation for the termination of the relationship. This makes careful consideration of the implications of pulling out of a market as important as calculating the profit potential of a successful operation.

One other important role played by governments is in their capacity as buyers. In order to gain access to government procurement contracts it is often necessary for firms to manufacture in the foreign country, displaying commitment and contributing to the local economy through employment of local personnel and utilization of local raw materials and components. To this extent they are more likely to be regarded as local and thus considered in major procurement contracts. Preferential treatment of domestic producers in procurement contracts is being actively deterred in the European Union under the Commission's Competition Policy initiatives as it is seen as detrimental to economic efficiency and anti-competitive. Theoretically at least this has the potential to reduce the number of investments made for procurement access reasons, although there is continuing potential for governments to favour locally based firms on quality rather than lowest-cost contract grounds.

Market infrastructure considerations, although not paramount in developed markets where physical facilities to support all business arrangements are generally available, may come into play in less developed countries where firms must consider such factors as communication links (transportation as well as telecommunications), workforce (in particular skills and training), financial facilities and the existence of suitable intermediaries. Where infrastructure is poor, exporting or licensing should normally be favoured in order to avoid ongoing logistics management difficulties. However, where a lack of suitable intermediaries and poor distribution facilities are apparent, some form of locally based investment may be essential to support the overseas business.

Host country production factors

This array of variables includes availability and cost of raw materials, and the availability and cost of staff. Obviously lower production costs in the host market as compared with the domestic market favour overseas production and higher costs encourage exporting or collaborative arrangements. Such strategies are not, however, inevitable. Higher production costs abroad may be acceptable if they include highly qualified specialist staff whose experience and knowledge are advantageous to the firm. Conversely, where lower costs of production can only be achieved at the expense of quality control and service levels, exporting may be preferable. Lost sales resulting from late delivery from domestic stock must be considered in any cost analysis of the potential attractiveness of alternative options.

This is, however, an oversimplistic picture. Weighing up the costs of establishing an overseas facility extends beyond simple raw material and labour cost comparisons. Adding export volume to domestic production capacity can offer increased scale economies (assuming a standardized product and longer production runs) and the establishment of foreign facilities may involve substantial duplication of effort. The need for local product and business adaptation once again figures large: where adaptation is critical, duplication of effort may be justifiable for marketing reasons. This is weighed against the economic reasoning behind domestic production for standardized products. It may be, however, that domestic capacity is not sufficient to cater for export demand (or future potential demand) supporting an early move to foreign investment.

Domestic country factors

Market structure and potential often give rise to the initial decision to internationalize with limited growth opportunities, intense competition and depressed markets at home leading to a search for new markets and new potential overseas. Their influence, however, also extends beyond the early impetus to pursue sales opportunities abroad. Government attitudes towards overseas expansion and consequently support of internationalization strategies have a pervasive influence on strategic decision making. Viewed simply, governments tend to support export operations over foreign direct investment as they promote the local economy, add to the country's balance of trade and balance of payments. Overseas investment, on the other hand, takes employment away from the local economy and does little to support key economic variables. Active promotion of exporting activities is therefore common, with government-supported agencies providing information, guidance and financial support to exporters. The sources of these provisions should be investigated by all potential exporters, particularly those new to exporting, as they can dramatically simplify the daunting complexities of selling into overseas markets. (A list of UK organizations assisting exporters is included at the end of this chapter.) Certain of these agencies may also be able to provide support to potential overseas investors, although here the options are more limited. Some governments even go as far as deterring foreign investments through capital flow restrictions in an effort to promote trade flows.

Company product factors

Technological issues, service elements, the extent of differentiation, and the need for product adaptation all feature here.

Technology contributions to competitive success promoting internalization of operations is desirable (that is retaining the technology within the organization rather than selling it by market-transaction to an independent producer). This is for reasons of protecting technologically based competitive advantages from competitors and preventing 'leakage' of technologies to organizations who can use the technology for their own ends. Here, then, the least favourable strategic alternative is licensing (and other collaborative arrangements). Even where licensing agreements are strictly adhered to, the bought technology or skills of the licensor can, and sometimes do, provide the licensee with competitive advantages which they can exploit with other products and in other business areas in direct competition with the licensor.

478

Equally the licensor's intellectual property can provide the foreign licensee with a strong foundation for future research and technological developments and enhanced competitive advantage. This leaves foreign direct investment and exporting as potential alternatives, although in the latter case leakage of product technology may also occur via the agent or distributor who, invested with technological knowledge in order to promote the technological features of the product, is in a position to pass on information to other manufacturers. (Process technology is exempted from these limitations.)

A clear distinction must be drawn between collaborative agreements which are entered into for the purpose of market entry and penetration and those which are specifically designed for the purpose of technology collaboration. Where collaboration is in research and development of new products and processes, failure to disclose information to the contractual/co-operative partner is detrimental to the success of the operation and breeds mistrust and misunderstanding.

Technological issues also extend to decisions concerning appropriate mechanisms for selling products. Products which are invested with high levels of technology require technical specialists for their sale and servicing. Training support staff to this level of specification is time-consuming and costly which makes selling via agents and distributors a difficult task. As intermediaries salesforces are often responsible for a range of competing products, time for their training is limited and creation of specialists is problematic due to their involvement in alternative technologies. While this does not preclude operating by way of intermediaries, it reinforces the need for co-operative management, high levels of support and potentially direct contact with customer organizations as a way of enhancing sales effort or employing exclusive distributors working solely on the company's behalf. Consequently the establishment of sales and marketing facilities may provide the best option, employing company-dedicated personnel to sell and service the product in the host market. Collaborative arrangements cannot be ruled out although much depends on the extent to which the technology provides the firm with key competitive advantages. The licensee's salesforce can be more readily trained and motivated to the selling of the company's products than can those of an agent or distributor as the financial gains to be made by the product tends to give licensees more incentive to actively promote the product.

The level of product differentiation is a further contributory factor. Generally, products which are highly differentiated from the competition do not compete 'head-to-head' with others and satisfy a particular segment in the market with a well-defined set of needs and wants. Selling via market-based intermediaries may therefore be sufficient to serve the market demand for the identifiable benefits. As differentiated products also frequently offer up opportunities for differential pricing it may also be that they can sustain the cost of exporting. The major limitation, however, of operating at arm's length with highly differentiated products is the limited potential to monitor changes in demand and competitor activity, necessary to ensure that differential advantages are maintained. This places heavy reliance on the intermediary's willing-

479

ness to gather and pass on market information, reaffirming the importance of good co-operative relationships being developed with intermediaries. Thus choice of option depends on whether the development of good relations with the intermediary is preferred over the establishment of a company-run sales office or subsidiary.

Some observers (in particular Anderson and Coughlan, 1987) assert that where differential advantages are great, there is a tendency for firms to protect their competitive advantage by internalizing operations and conducting their own sales and marketing in the foreign country. Where differential advantages centre on technological factors (which is common) then the factors described above come into play – supporting their proposition that internal business structures are a preferable solution. Undifferentiated products, on the other hand, where competition centres on price, demand the employment of the most cost-effective mode of market servicing. Volume of business, host and domestic country production costs, potential for scale economies in domestic production along with adaptation and production capacity issues must all be considered in this respect.

Some mention must be made of branding. Established brands need little active selling effort as they are 'pulled' through the channel through promotion and advertising effort. For the most part, therefore, investment in advertising supersedes strategic investment in local production or even sales facilities (although volume-related cost considerations may make local manufacturing more cost-effective). More importantly, however, while technology and product-feature differentiation permits market entry by new specialist producers, branding and heavy advertising expenditure acts as a major barrier to market entry. In industries where branding dominates competitive activity, takeover of existing firms is often the only viable means of market entry, establishing new brands from scratch proving preclusively expensive. Extensive takeover activity in the food and drink industry, for example, confirms that the best (or indeed the only) strategic alternative is the acquisition of an established brand with an extant consumer franchise.

Service considerations arise as products are rarely simple tangible units; they involve associated service provisions which can pose specific challenges for market servicing strategies. Products which require a large amount of pre- and post-sales servicing make arm's-length market servicing options problematic. Proximity to the market through local production or the provision of local sales, marketing and servicing offices or subsidiaries is usually advised. As service provision is increasingly being used as a means of adding value to the product package one can observe a growing trend towards functional specific foreign investments (stockholding to prevent late delivery, local offices and subsidiaries employing servicing engineers) in many industrial sectors.

This is not to ignore the role that intermediaries can play in providing service to customers, many being well-placed to offer rapid and efficient servicing as part of the overall distribution arrangement. Regional stockholding facilities can be far superior to single, central-distribution warehouses which is often the affordable limit for market entrants. It is important to weigh the

Table 27.2
Relative costs of licensing overseas (Australian licensors)

Breakdown of total costs of licensing overseas	%
Protection of industrial property	24.8
Establishment of licensing agreement	46.6
Maintenance of licensing agreement	29.0
	100.0
Breakdown of establishment costs	
Search for suitable licensees	22.8
Communication between involved parties	44.7
Adoption and testing of equipment for licensee	9.9
Training personnel for licensee	19.9
Other (additional marketing and legal expenses)	2.5
	100.0
Breakdown of maintenance costs	
Audit of licensee	9.7
Ongoing market research in market by licensee	7.2
Back-up service for licensee	65.0
Defence of industrial property right in host market	7.1
	100.0

(*Source*: Carstairs and Welch, 1981.)

advantages of developing good links with distributors to foster the development of servicing networks against the additional control, but perhaps limited coverage, of wholly owned operations.

Adaptation was raised in relation to cultural distance and planning production for overseas markets. To recap, where the extent of the product adaptation precludes additional capacity being added to domestic production schedules, there is greater freedom to consider establishing dedicated overseas production units and, in so doing, benefit from proximity to market advantages. This tends to make operations more responsive to local market conditions, and allow market-by-market planning for cultural differences. Trends towards more responsive marketing techniques, in particular relational marketing supported by flexible specialization in manufacturing, arguably raise the importance of locally-based production units as a means of developing competitive advantage. Failure to observe these trends and pursue an approach of standardization for economic reasons may undermine the competitiveness of a firm's strategies. With this at issue, attention to strategic objectives is fundamental to the success of the final operation.

Company resource/commitment factors

These quite obviously centre on the available resources of the firm but also extends to include access to knowledge and company objectives.

Transaction cost analysis and the assessment of the relative costs of strategic alternatives simplify strategic choice for many firms as they constrain the number of options available. Referring back to Buckley and Casson's model of the timing of the switch to FDI, the analysis of relative costs acts as a useful starting point for cost-based research. All strategies involve three types of cost: a non-recoverable set-up cost incurred as soon as the option is adopted; a recurrent fixed cost (independent of the rate of output) due to the indivisibilities of the factor inputs hired in connection with the market servicing activity (such as staff salaries); recurrent variable costs related to transport, materials and so on. While the internationalization model restricts examination to the three generic modes of market servicing, this can be extended to intra-mode options.

Modes of exporting via intermediaries typically have low set-up costs as it is not necessary to establish physical facilities. Search, training and relationship management costs characterize the set-up of operations. More direct types of exporting, particularly where offices are established abroad, give rise to higher costs of this type because of the establishment of dedicated export departments or overseas offices. Recurrent fixed costs also rise in these cases due to greater managerial capacity. In all modes of exporting, variable costs are high as they include transport costs and tariff payments.

By contrast, foreign direct investment options have high set-up and fixed costs, but lower recurrent variable costs. The greater the physical assets and indivisible personnel required, the greater will be these fixed costs. It is presumed that fixed costs of sales subsidiaries, assembly subsidiaries and production subsidiaries rise in ascending order of this ranking due to rising levels of autonomy. It is also assumed that locating production abroad reduces recurrent variable costs. With marketing and sales subsidiaries involving both variable costs of exporting as well as fixed set-up and ongoing costs, this can prove an expensive alternative.

Foreign collaborative arrangements can be analysed using the same tools. Non-recoverable set-up costs can be high as they include the search costs of the licensee. There may also be costs incurred in identifying and embodying the knowledge to be transferred in a form which reduces costs of firm-to-firm transfer. As Table 27.2 shows, establishment costs of the licensing agreement (roughly equivalent to fixed set-up costs) amount to 46.6 per cent of the total costs of a sample of Australian foreign licensors. Within this, search costs amount to 22.8 per cent of the establishment costs. Protection of industrial property (recurrent fixed costs) account for 24.8 per cent of the total. The ongoing (variable) costs account for only 29 per cent.

In the general case, licensing appears to offer a best-of-both-worlds option in foreign market servicing, combining the skills and technology of the entrant with the local market knowledge of the licensee. In practice, additional costs are incurred compared to foreign direct investment due to the problems of transferring knowledge via the market. These costs include:

1 Identifying the knowledge.
2 Embodying the knowledge.
3 Firm-to-firm transfer costs.
4 Problems in the market for information:

   – Finding a licensee.
   – Buyer uncertainty: the buyer does not know what the knowledge is worth until he is in possession of it; when he is, there is no need to pay for it. This may lead to complex contingent contracts.

5 Costs of maintaining the relationship between licensor and licensee.
6 Policing costs – maintaining the behaviour of the licensee to make sure the technology is not used in ways that have not been paid for.

These additional costs may explain the relatively low incidence of licensing (collaborative) activity – accounting for, on average, less than 10 per cent of total British foreign sales over the period 1975–83 (Buckley and Prescott, 1989). An alternative explanation may lie in the loss of control over operations in licensing agreements which are not compensated by low fixed costs as is the case with exporting strategies.

Similar problems may be proposed for non-contractual collaborations (excepting joint ventures) although here costs relate more to the maintenance of co-operation as opposed to commercial transactions for knowledge. In addition, ongoing renegotiation costs can be added to the bundle as firms develop co-operative solutions to mutual problems. Equity joint ventures, on the other hand, involve relatively high fixed costs in the form of up-front capital investments as well as ongoing relationship management commitments. While the capital risk may be lower than is the case of 100 per cent ownership, the ongoing maintenance and development costs may be far higher.

Generally, across all modes of market servicing, firms are prepared to invest additional funds in the short term to attain greater control over activities by internalizing operations. Cutting across this decision is that of acquiring market-based knowledge.

Local market knowledge and organizational implications

Local market knowledge is often fundamental to strategic planning. Possibly because of cultural distance or simply because there are perceived differences in the local needs and wants of the market-place, licensing – which implicitly includes, as part of the contract, collaboration with a local firm – may be attractive. Nevertheless, such formal contracts are not the only means of attaining market information. Intermediaries serve as an external market for knowledge and, if motivated to do so, can provide accurate and comprehensive local market data, although the communication links between the manufacturer and the market are more tenuous and depend more on coercion and co-operation than control. Ultimately, direct presence in the market provides the most comprehensive means of collecting market information and monitoring changes in demand patterns and consumer behaviour.

Transferring knowledge throughout the organization and exploiting skills developed through the acquisition of knowledge requires that firms establish good international communications networks for filtering and processing information. It may be assumed that host-country personnel with direct experience in the foreign market better understand the information required for effective decision making. There are three options facing manufacturers in this respect: forward integration through acquisition; buying-in the knowledge from outside or utilizing the services of intermediaries perhaps at the expense of high quality information; in external business transactions intermediaries may be regarded as either facilitators or bottlenecks for the flow of information. Nevertheless, cross-fertilization of knowledge through internal systems is not automatic. The growing complexity of many multinational enterprises makes the management of internal markets for knowledge a difficult task. This is particularly the case in institutions which have devolved a high degree of power to overseas subsidiaries (decentralized decision making) who plan and manage their affairs independently. Systems have to be developed to facilitate the transfer of knowledge between divisions of the firm in order that knowledge is effectively utilized. This requires investment in sophisticated information technology systems as well as generating a business culture which automatically reports and shares information with the head office and other divisions. Equally, the structure of the organization plays a key role, determining the power balance between head office and subsidiaries and the consequent direction of information flow.

The existence of foreign networks, be they sales/marketing or production, means that for many established firms, business strategy decisions focus on reassessment of options and organizational design rather than market entry *per se*. The models of the dynamics of market servicing go some way to explaining the fluidity of the process although none of these models describe the challenge of adapting inter-firm relationships to improve global competitiveness. The common dilemma of developing global strategies versus adapting on a market-by-market basis faces many multinational organizations. On the one hand, firms which opt for a global approach are able to benefit from scale economies across a wide array of functions by centralizing business activity in large scale units. On the other, adaptation to the local market offers flexibility and responsiveness, and the ability to satisfy specific wants of customers. This suggests that strategy is a trade-off between cost management and marketing effectiveness although in increasingly competitive markets, firms see the need of achieving both objectives.

Achieving this complex balance of objectives requires reassessment of traditional organizational formats. Replacing the multinational hierarchy (where head office power controls subsidiaries) with a more flexible structure can permit cost management and market responsiveness to exist side by side.

Table 27.3
Checklist of factors impacting on the choice of foreign market servicing
strategy

Target country market factors	• Market size and growth • Competitive market structure • Power of buyers and suppliers

Target country environmental factors	• Geographic distance
	• Cultural distance
	• Economic environment:
	   – Exchange rates
	   – Tariffs
	   – Market dynamism
	• Political environment:
	   – Stability
	   – Government intervention
	   – Actions against anti-competitive practices
	   – Public procurement
	• Market infrastructure

Domestic country factors	• Support provided for exporting • Attitudes towards FDI

Company product factors	• Technology:
	   – Contribution to competitiveness
	   – Levels of technological sophistication
	• Product differentiation
	• Service content
	• Need for adaptation

Company resource/commitment factors	• Transaction cost analysis • Access to local market knowledge • Company objectives

Hedlund (1986) believes that the most effective multinational organizations are heterarchies rather than hierarchies, structures characterized by looser control systems, managerial autonomy of subsidiaries and lateral communication between subsidiary divisions. This provides the local responsiveness necessary to effectively adapt to foreign markets. The head office takes on a co-ordination role, setting and promoting objectives through the establishment of broad directives and organizational culture. This approach appears to favour an adaptive approach to international business organization although co-operation across international divisions in the form of task forces and project teams can augment cost management objectives by developing mutually beneficial strategies between international departments.

Although these kinds of multinational firm observations and recommendations are relatively new, the continued unbundling of elements in the value chain in many multinational organizations (sales/marketing investments, R&D specific investments and strategic alliances, collaborative distribution agreements) is testament to a growing trend of this nature in successful multinational business management. Multinational firms can no longer be content to derive advantages from simple static decisions concerning the location of various business functions and the internal versus external development of their markets. They are increasingly being forced to concentrate on deriving effective inter-organizational balances and co-operative business practices.

Certain skills are more easily transferred. The experiences of conducting one type of market servicing strategy and the consequent learning process involved can be transferred to other ventures. Although some problems and challenges may prove very different from one business operation to another, the learning curve of managing a particular kind of operation is, to a degree, common between ventures. This leads some firms to pursue the same types of strategic options in a variety of markets. Learning-curve advantages must not be overlooked, although there is a danger of firms becoming myopic in their international strategic development, sticking to what they know and do best rather than developing appropriate strategies for specific circumstances.

Company objectives

Company objectives cannot be omitted from the considerations involved in choosing a strategy for servicing foreign markets. Much of what has been suggested so far assumes that firms choose the most appropriate and efficient strategy which is within their financial means without much regard to the underlying intentions behind the business venture. It is very rare for any business undertaking to be made for a single reason: multiple objectives including profit and performance targets, market-specific considerations such as building or maintaining market share, the pursuit of a stronger competitive position by matching the activities of competing firms or attempting to build barriers to entry and serve customers from a proximate location, along with strategically motivated goals such as improving technology or reducing risk to the company, all figure in the firm's overriding decision to enter a new market or adjust its strategic position in an existing overseas market. These considerations have a pervasive influence on strategic choice, making the overall decision far more complex than simple, rational, decision-making models suggest.

The question of efficiency versus effectiveness should be addressed. Not only should firms manage their business operations in such a way as to utilize their resources in the most efficient manner, they should also ensure that their objectives are appropriate to the competitive challenges facing them. Simply assuming that a firm has chosen the correct market servicing strategy in the light of their overall objectives ignores the possibility that the stated objectives were insufficient in the first place to improve the competitiveness of the organization, further compounding the complexities of strategy choice.

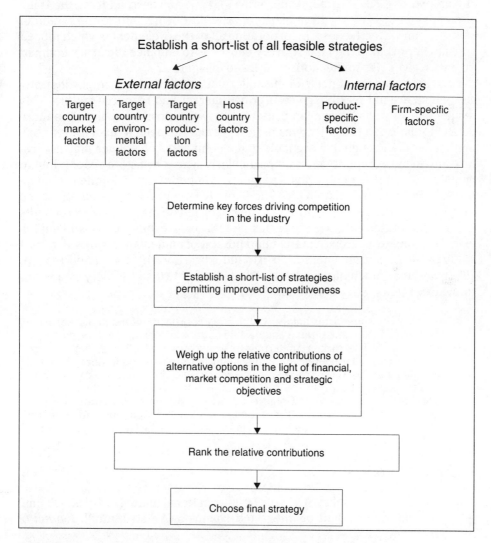

Figure 27.4   Choosing the right market entry and development strategy

The decision-making process

Table 27.3 summarizing many of the key factors under consideration provides a framework (albeit highly simplistic and generalized) for analysis but fails to offer a means for choosing a specific strategy. Assessing different options along these dimensions will suggest various lines of action dependent on specific elements. The question still remains: how does a firm choose the most appropriate market servicing strategy?

Various models have been proposed to answer this question, featuring such techniques as transaction cost analysis, stages of development suppositions and business strategy research (focusing on the relative profit contributions of employing feasible strategy alternatives). Few, however, address the issue of company objectives with a dearth of attention being paid to the notion of efficiency and effectiveness. Incorporating all of these elements, which indeed appears important if the final strategy chosen is to enhance the firm's competitiveness, gives rise to the model proposed in Figure 27.4.

This filter process of decision making rules out at an early stage all strategies which are not feasible given product, market and resource factors. This results in a short-list of available alternatives which can be analysed in more detail in relation to the objectives of the firm and the need to manage for competitiveness. Although it is arguable that a company's objectives may not feature enhanced competitiveness – particularly where firms are responding to unsolicited orders or enquiries – to ignore competitive development presupposes that firms are planning for the short term without thinking about the longer-term strategic implications of their decisions. This can make later shifts in foreign market servicing strategies difficult or preclude options being followed for long-term growth in the blind pursuit of immediate returns. A recent study of the competitiveness of British industry (Buckley, Pass and Prescott, 1992), adduces much of the competitive failure of British industry to a short-termist mentality. They conclude:

> Above all, even where firms have a well defined approach to foreign market servicing the need for a long-termist and flexible outlook is considered to be particularly important. The former underpins learning-curve effects (understanding local cultures and customer needs, establishing harmonious and mutually beneficial supplier and distributor relations) and encourages the firm to seek long-term rather than short-term profit returns; the latter emphasizes (given the different nuances and characteristics of different markets) the need to approach each market separately – looking to the optimum mode of servicing individual markets, rather than attempting an holistic, global strategy (Buckley et al., 1992, pp. 322–23).

REFERENCES

Anderson, E. and Coughlan, A.T. (1987), 'International market entry and expansion via independent or integrated channels of distribution', *Journal of Marketing*, **51**, 71–82.

Boddewyn, J.J., Halbrich, M.B. and Perry, A.C. (1986), 'Service multinationals: conceptualisation, measurement and theory', *Journal of International Business Studies*, **16**, (3), 41–57.

Buckley, P.J. and Casson, M. (1985), *The Economic Theory of the Multinational Enterprise*, London: Macmillan.

Buckley, P.J., Pass, C. and Prescott, K. (1992), *Servicing International Markets: Competitive Strategies of Firms*, Oxford: Blackwell.

Buckley, P.J. and Prescott, K. (1989), 'The structure of British industry's sales in foreign markets', *Managerial and Decision Economics*, **10**, (3), 189–208.

Carstairs, R.T. and Welch, L.S. (1981), 'A study of outward foreign licensing of technology by Australian companies', Canberra: Licensing Executive Society of Australia.

Cavusgill, S.T. (1980), 'On the internationalisation process of firms', *European Research*, **8**, (6), 273–81.

Doz, Y., Hamel, G. and Prahalad, C.K. (1986), 'Strategic partnerships: success or surrender: the challenge of competitive collaboration', paper presented at joint AIB–EIBA meeting, London, 20–23 November.

Doz, Y., Prahalad, C.K. and Hamel, G. (1990), 'Control, change and flexibility: the dilemma of transnational collaboration', in C.A. Bartlett, Y. Doz and G. Hedlund (Eds), *Managing the Global Firm*, London: Routledge.

Enderwick, P. (1989), 'Some economics of service sector multinational enterprises', in Peter Enderwick (Ed.), *Multinational Service Firms*, London: Routledge.

Hedlund, G. (1986), 'The hypermodern MNC – a heterarchy?' *Human Resource Management*, Spring, 9–35.

Johanson, J. and Wiedersheim-Paul, F. (1975). 'The internationalisation of the firm: four Swedish cases', *Journal of Management Studies*, **12**, (3), 305–22.

Munro, H.J. and Beamish, B.W. (1987), 'Distribution methods and export performance', in Philip J. Rosson and Stanley D. Reid (Eds), *Managing Export Entry and Expansion*, New York: Praeger.

Porter, M.E. (1980), *Competitive Strategy: Techniques for Analyzing Industries and Competitors*, New York: Free Press.

Root, F.R. (1987), *Entry Strategies for International Markets*, Lexington, Mass: Lexington Books.

Rosson, P.J. (1984), 'Success factors in manufacturer–overseas distributor relationships in international marketing', in E. Kaynak (Ed.), *International Marketing Management*, New York: Praeger.

Turnbull, P.W. (1987), 'A challenge to the stages theory of the internationalisation process', in P.J. Rosson and S.D. Reid (Eds), *Managing Export Entry and Expansion*, New York: Praeger.

Valla, J.P. (1986), 'Industrial firms in European markets: the French approach to Europe', in Peter W. Turnbull and Jean-Paul Vall (Eds), *Strategies for International Industrial Marketing*, New York: Croom Helm.

Vernon, R. (1966), 'International investment and international trade in the product cycle', *Quarterly Journal of Economics*, **80**, 190–207.

Young, S., Hamill, J., Wheeler, C. and Davies, R. (1989), *International Market Entry and Development: Strategies and Management*, Hemel Hempstead: Harvester Wheatsheaf.

ESSENTIAL READING

Dicken, Peter (1991), *Global Shift*, London: Paul Chapman Publishing.

Porter, M.E. (1990), *The Competitive Advantage of Nations*, London: Macmillan.

Young, S., Hamill, J., Wheeler, C. and Davies, J.R. (1989), *International Market Entry and Development*, Hemel Hempstead: Harvester Wheatsheaf.

UK AGENCIES PROVIDING SUPPORT TO EXPORTING (AND INVESTING) FIRMS AND KEY FACILITIES OFFERED

Chamber of commerce

- Authentication of documents (prices higher to non-members).
- Up-to-date libraries.
- Monthly export newsletters.
- Location and appointment of agents.
- Buyers lists.
- Information on import regulations.
- Export marketing missions.
- Legal advice.
- Standards and codes of practice.
- Translation and interpretation.

Trade associations

- Market information.
- Trade opportunities.
- Tariff, finance and documentation services.
- Organizing exhibitions and fairs.
- Missions (overseas visits to check out market opportunities).

Banks

- Finance.
- Payment.
- Credit.
- Currency exchange
- Pricing advice.

The Small Firms Service (DTI)

- Market information.
- Advice on planning.
- Consultancy services (at very reasonable rates).

Local authorities

- Trade missions.
- Training for exports } discretionary
- Providing contacts.

British Overseas Trade Board

Its role is to:

- Advise the government on strategies for overseas trade.
- Guide and develop the government's export promotion services.
- Encourage and support industry and commerce in overseas trade with the aid of appropriate government and non-government organizations at home and overseas.
- Contribute to the exchange of views between government, industry and commerce in the field of overseas trade and to search for solutions to problems.

Their export intelligence service provides the following information to sub-scribers:

- Specific export opportunities.
- Short market pointers to new trade opportunities.
- Market reports.
- Overseas agents seeking British principals.
- Calls for tender (including invitations to pre-qualify).
- Successful bidders and awards for contracts.
- Overseas business visitors to the UK.
- Outward opportunities for co-operation with overseas firms.
- Inward opportunities for co-operation with overseas firms.
- Changes in overseas tariffs and import regulations.

491

- Aid and loan agreements.
- Trade agreements.
- National and other development plans; general economic reports.
- Lines of credit opened by the Export Credit Guarantee Department.
- Notification of overseas trade fairs, exhibitions, missions (inward and outward).
- World economic comments and quarterly trading reports.

The simplification of Trade Procedures Board (SITPRO)

Specifically offers support on export documentation alleviating the burden for small firms.

Educational institutions

- Language training.
- Information.
- Advice.
- Consultancy.
- Special projects (student-based).
- Market research.
- R&D.
- Business libraries.

Part V
THE PRACTICE OF MARKETING

28 Market segmentation

David Tonks

> I keep six honest serving-men
> (They taught me all I knew);
> Their names are What and Why and When
> and How and Where and Who.
>
> ('The Elephant's Child', from *Rudyard Kipling's Verse:*
> *Definitive Version*, Hodder & Stoughton.)

Market segmentation is the sub-division of a total market into useful component parts. For managers, it is a process where the act of sub-division must not be an end in itself. The resulting components, or market segments, must be *useful*. This may be measured according to customer satisfaction, competitive advantage, managerial efficiency and effectiveness or, ultimately, by reference to corporate objectives. Market segmentation must be implementable and must provide results.

The process and the associated techniques of market segmentation are central to the marketing activities of most supplying organizations even if the underlying concept of market segmentation is left unarticulated. That process is now firmly established in consumer markets for both goods and services. It is widespread, with different techniques, in industrial markets. The process applies to mature as well as to emerging markets. It is relevant to non-profit as well as profit-making concerns. The notion if not the formal process of market segmentation is usually the keystone for small businesses.

The theme of market segmentation can run through the entire organization. At the 'top level', it might exist within a statement of the business mission. At the immediate operational level, the fine detail of assembling and implementing an appropriate marketing mix will be determined by segmentation policy. Between these extremes, market segmentation exists as *the* strategic issue which converts the marketing concept into the practice of marketing.

Some organizations may still see themselves as providing one thing for all their customers. For an even smaller number, this may still be the best approach. However, most marketing organizations are faced with choices in terms of which many possible markets and sub-markets they can decide to target.

Consumer markets in particular have become much more varied during the course of this century. This is directly associated with greater pluralism in society and a trend towards fragmentation. The general rise in disposable incomes, higher standards of education and more intricate social structures have all contributed to complex arrays of wants and needs and to more discerning customers. Such demand-side factors are notable not only for the extent of change but also the speed of change. On the supply side, the extent of competition varies but as a general rule, changes in economic circumstances have resulted in many markets becoming 'buyers' markets'. Simultaneously, changes in the distribution and communication processes have allowed and also required closer attention to individual segments. If the organization is to ensure long-term success and survival then it must recognize the existence of a number of market segments and choose from amongst them so as to create and maintain competitive advantages.

One-to-one relationships might exist between supplier and consumer. This is often the case with specialist services and with products in business-to-business markets. It may become more prevalent elsewhere as technology facilitates and competition requires a closer relationship between the supplier and individual customers. More common, particularly with consumer goods, is the need to disaggregate a large mass and the practical impossibility of dealing with individual consumers. Market segmentation and the managerial policy of target marketing are the outcomes of this conflict. The mass is too diverse, the individual is too expensive to reach.

ALTERNATIVE APPROACHES

Like marketing itself, market segmentation is far from new. It is one of the older rituals of trade. The term 'mass-marketing', in vogue during the 1960s, reflects a brief period when the emphasis shifted towards very large aggregations of consumers served by undifferentiated products. That shift was driven by the quest for economies of scale, lower supply costs and lower prices. Amongst more developed economies, the idea of 'mass markets' is now only encountered in the case of basic commodities. Even a simple consumer product such as salt is differentiated with various brands targeted to particular market segments.

Product-differentiated marketing is effectively a variation on the theme of mass-marketing. With product differentiation, a number of product variations are offered to appeal to more or less the whole market. Product-differentiated marketing can have the appearance of target marketing but it is very different.

With target marketing, the approach is led by the customer so that the organization identifies the individual market segments within the total market, evaluates their worth and only then provides a marketing package designed accordingly. Target marketing – the common operational outcome of market segmentation – is the concern of this chapter.

TARGET MARKETING

Target marketing requires attention to focus on a particular market segment, or segments. There are two common forms. Where the organization concentrates on one segment, this is typically termed 'concentrated marketing'. 'Multiple market segmentation' describes a policy of providing each of a number of identified market segments with a unique marketing mix.

The central concerns of target marketing are to decide how to segment the markets of interest, how to assess their worth and then how to position the organization amongst the segments. Identification, evaluation and then implementation are therefore the key stages. The first two are more concerned with analysis so that the intrinsic desirability of the segments can be determined. The third is more the decision-making stage when differentiation at the product/market level and a suitable marketing mix will have to be determined. Table 28.1 provides a simple summary of these three important stages in developing a policy of target marketing.

Table 28.1
Stages of target marketing

Identification

- Which behaviour variables can be used?
- Which general variables can be used?
- Which mix of behaviour and general variables can be used?

Evaluation

- Which segmentation variables should be used?
- Which of the segments are actionable?
- Which of the resulting segments are the more desirable?

Implementation

- Should the strategy be concentrated or multiple-segment?
- How should the product(s) be positioned for the target segment(s)?
- What marketing mix is desirable for the target segment(s)?

Note: Answering these questions is the concern of this chapter. The emphasis is on larger organizations supplying consumer markets.

497

IDENTIFICATION

The main questions concerning segment identification are provided in the opening quote from Rudyard Kipling – who buys what, where, when, how and why? Putting some structure on this, market segments can be identified using a mix of variables which can be grouped into two categories: 'general' and 'behaviour'.

The term 'general' is used for those variables which define and describe the customers but which do not identify in a direct way acts of purchase, acquisition or consumption. They answer the question 'who?' For example, TV region is a general variable which may or may not be associated with some aspect of buying, owning or consumption.

'Behaviour' variables answer the remaining questions – what do people buy and where, when, how and why do they buy it? Usage rate for a given brand is a behaviour variable because it concerns a particular characteristic of consumption.

Table 28.2

Alternative variables for market segmentation

General variables

- External   e.g. Geography, demographics
- Internal   e.g. Personality, lifestyle

Behaviour variables

Antecedents

- Benefits sought   e.g. Needs, wants
- Perceptions of attributes   e.g. Cheap/dear
- Assessment of attributes   e.g. Important/unimportant

Inclinations

- Preferences   e.g. Better/worse than
- Readiness stage   e.g. Awareness/interest

Actions

- Role   e.g. Buyer/user
- Consumption   e.g. Heavy/light user
- Occasion   e.g. Social/business
- Ownership   e.g. Owner/former owner
- Loyalty   e.g. Switcher/loyal
- Location   e.g. Mail order/superstore

Further classifications of variable types are possible. Table 28.2 takes a closer look at different types of 'general' and 'behaviour' variables.

In the case of general variables for market segmentation, these can concern the 'external' circumstances of the individual or segment, such as geographical location. Alternatively, they can be more concerned with 'internal' characteristics such as personality type. Both external and internal variables may be associated with or may cause buying behaviour.

Behaviour variables can be classified according to the process that leads to purchase or ownership. The early stages in this process provide 'antecedents', such as the underlying benefits sought by an individual. Those behaviour variables concerned with 'inclinations' move to the stage of assessment of alternatives, such as levels of awareness or preferences. The final stage in this simplified process and classification is that of 'actions' – how do people behave? Examples in this final category, often of greatest interest to marketing managers, include usage and user status.

General variables alone are of limited value although the assumption is frequently made that buying behaviour is associated with such descriptions of customers. Quite often, the relationship is known and quantified. For example, if the interest is in heavy users of a brand and those heavy users are known to be in a certain age group and tend to live in a certain area, then they are easier to access when identified using such general variables.

Some confusion can result when this distinction between general variables and behaviour variables is not made clear. The former attach convenient labels to the latter, types of customers who buy, consume or possess in certain ways or for certain reasons.

Which behaviour variables can be used?

A first-level scan of a market to identify suitable variables for market segmentation should take the form of an audit to establish all significant possibilities. In most circumstances, the following list of questions will provide a comprehensive set of options.

1 *Benefits sought:*

- What particular benefits or needs do they expect from the product?

2 *Perceptions and attitudes:*

- How is the product perceived and what are the attitudes towards the product?

3 *Product preferences:*

- What do they prefer and how do they choose between brands?

4 *Product usage/purchase rates:*

- Are they non-users, medium users, heavy users?
- Are they solus users in that they only buy one brand?
- Are the purchasers of interest as well as the users?

5 *User/buyer status:*

- Are they current users, former users, non-users, potential users, regular users, first time users?
- Are the buyers of interest as well as the users?

6 *Loyalty status:*

- What degree of brand loyalty do they display? Is it strong, medium, weak?

7 *Marketing factor sensitivity:*

- How do they respond to the various marketing influences?
- Are they susceptible to price or to advertising?

8 *Purchase situation and occasion:*

- Is it an impulse or considered purchase? Is the context social or business? What is the setting for the purchase?

9 *Media habits:*

- What media are they exposed to?

The final category, Media habits, is a behaviour variable which does not concern, at least not directly, the product in question. It is this category which provides an important link with the general variables.

From such an audit, a target segment for men's aftershave/splash-on lotion might be identified as potential users with low brand involvement and loyalty, who buy on impulse, who are price sensitive and who read particular specialist magazines. Many permutations are possible and at this stage, the choice can be overwhelming. For a broad understanding of the market and its component parts, benefits sought, purchase and usage patterns and brand loyalty will be important.

Which general variables can be used?

These variables, the labels which are attached to important target markets, have received considerable attention as well as use. Again, there is a mix of measures. The more 'objective' of these measures are by far the most wide-spread.

Geographical region

Very common in marketing is the use of geographical region to identify market segments. TV regions have the particular advantage of allowing relatively easy and perhaps cheap access to the desired target audience. More importantly, some buying behaviour does correlate strongly with region.

Of some interest here is the notion of 'global' brands or 'Eurobrands' where market segments are identified within but also across national or other geographic boundaries.

Demographics

Demographics as a sub-group contains the familiar variables of age, sex, social grade, family size, family life cycle, income, occupation, terminal education age, religion, race and nationality. All these variables have at least three advantages in common with geographical area. First, they are relatively easy to measure compared with some other variable types. Second, they are easy to understand and third, they are well-established. However, the issue is the extent to which they can discriminate buying behaviour in some way which is useful to the organization implementing a policy of target marketing. For example, if the concern is with differentiating between users and non-users of men's after shave/splash-on lotion then taking a demographic such as age will be of little value if the age profiles of users and non-users are identical.

Worthy of special mention are family life cycle and social grade as general descriptive variables.

Table 28.3
Life-cycle segments

	Population (000s)	Profile %
Pre-family	2333	11
Young family	3082	14
Older family	3189	15
Young, post-family	3531	17
Older, post-family	4794	22
Single elderly	4473	21

(*Source*: Establishing Survey, Broadcasters Audience Research Board (BARB), 1990.)

While age alone will often discriminate buying behaviour, the presence of children in a family unit will be a prime determinant of lifestyle and subsequent buying behaviour. Table 28.3 provides a typical breakdown of the popu-

Table 28.4
Social grade in the UK

Group	Status	Occupation	% Adults
A	Upper middle class	Higher managerial, professional or administrative	3
B	Middle class	Intermediate managerial, professional or administrative	13
C1	Lower middle class	Supervisory or clerical and junior managerial administrative or professional	22
C2	Skilled working class	Skilled manual workers	32
D	Working class	Semi and unskilled manual workers	21
E	Subsistence	State pensioners or widows (no other earner), casual or lowest grade workers	8
			100

(*Source*: adapted from National Readership Survey, NRS Ltd.

lation into conventional life-cycle segments. With this classification, the 'young, post-family' segment could be of interest to many organizations. This segment is currently characterized by high discretionary income as earnings peak, children leave home and mortgages are paid off.

In the UK, social grade is very often encountered as a way of classifying consumer markets. Social grade is based on the occupation of the head of household. The classification is given in Table 28.4.

There has been extensive debate about the value of social grade as a method of segmenting consumer markets. Many have suggested that the method conceals more than it reveals and, in particular, that the implicit assumption between social grade and income is often incorrect, giving the classic example of a coal miner (Group D) and a vicar (Group A or B). The groups are very large so that the popular combination of C1/C2 contains 54 per cent of the adult population. What may also be a consideration is that while social grade, as a rough and ready general descriptor variable, is probably as good and as bad as it always has been, marketing people are now attracted to more sophisticated and more powerful systems for segmenting markets.

Geodemographics

The techniques and the applications of geodemographics have emerged over the last 15 years. In some areas, the applications have become very popular. Dissatisfaction with more conventional methods, effective marketing and the availability of cheaper computing power have all contributed to this growing popularity.

One common feature of geodemographic 'brands' is that they are all based on multivariate approaches where a large number of general variables are employed. Given the complex, multi-dimensional nature of consumer behaviour, it seems reasonable that univariate segmentation of markets will sometimes be inappropriate. With geodemographics, segments are identified according to similarity and dissimilarity across a wide range of variables. Most systems include at least some data on demographics and household composition variables taken from the census. Some systems also corporate additional data such as financial information from county court judgments. Modified geodemographic 'brands' based on the 1991 census are now available.

The most well-known of the geo-demographic brands are ACORN, MOSAIC, PIN and Super Profiles. In the case of MOSAIC, 58 'types' are identified using

Table 28.5
MOSAIC groups by population, 1989

MOSAIC Lifestyle Group	*GB* %	*Morecambe* %	*Index*
Prosperous pensioners	4	23	646
Older couples/leafy suburbs	7	3	37
Families in inter-war semis	10	20	194
Older communities	17	27	159
Singles and flat dwellers	8	9	119
Worse-off council tenants	13	7	51
Older council tenants	9	4	43
Go-getting council tenants	9	2	23
Young mortgaged families	16	5	28
Country dwellers	7	2	25

(*Source*: CCN Marketing.)

data from census, the electoral register and other sources on demographics, housing type, and financial characteristics.

The 58 MOSAIC 'types' are summarized into one of ten life-style groups and these are shown in Table 28.5. The profiles in this table are for the GB population and that for Morecambe in 1989. As might be expected, the profile for Morecambe is very 'irregular' with an index of 646 for the lifestyle group 'prosperous pensioners', meaning that the proportion of people in this group is more than six times the average for Great Britain. MOSAIC type M1 is described as 'High status retirement areas with many single pensioners' and this is grouped with three other types to give the MOSAIC lifestyle group 'prosperous pensioners' which receives the not surprising thumbnail description 'where wealthy retired people gather together, normally by the seaside'.

The notable advantage of geodemographic systems such as MOSAIC is that the market segments that result can be linked to postcodes thus allowing more efficient access to appropriate market segments within or across specified geographical area or areas. Such systems become very powerful for particular applications of target marketing such as with direct marketing and store location. They are also connected to databases such as TGI (Target Group Index) and NRS (National Readership Survey), allowing comprehensive portraits of target segments to be identified.

Developments in this area can be expected to continue. When in-house customer databases are linked to geodemographic analysis, the potential for refined target marketing and other applications becomes considerable. If the classifications do discriminate buying behaviour, then the particular advantage of geodemographics is the ready access to customers.

Lifestyle

This is the final category of general variables. Many attempts have been made in the past to link personality type with buying behaviour. For example, the extent of 'innovativeness' might well be connected with brand choices. Success has usually been limited and this has been attributed very often to the methods used. The future may hold more promise for this approach but in the meantime, it has been overshadowed by the relative popularity of an associated segment descriptor – 'lifestyle' sometimes known as 'psychographics'.

With lifestyle segmentation, people are classified according to dimensions such as activities, interests and opinions. In this way, the impact on buying behaviour of the broad cultural setting and the more immediate social milieu is captured. Typical of this method is the VALS2 (Values and Lifestyle) created by SRI International which disaggregates markets according to the self-orientation of individuals, classified into 'principle', 'status' and 'action' coupled with their available resources. The VALS2 classification has eight typologies such as 'achievers', 'believers' and 'strugglers'. A similar scheme is that of McCann-Erickson illustrated in Table 28.6.

The use of lifestyle has a very obvious appeal in that it is likely to be linked, at least in some way, to fundamental benefits sought and subsequent buying behaviour. The problems encountered are at the operational level.

Table 28.6
Male lifestyle segments – McCann-Erickson

Segment		% adult males
Avant guardians	Concerned with changes and well-being of others, rather than possessions. Well-educated, prone to self-righteousness.	13.5
Pontificators	Strongly-held, traditional opinions. Very British, and concerned about keeping others on the right path.	15.0
Chameleons	Want to be contemporary to win approval. Act like barometers of social change, but copiers, not leaders	11.5
Self-admirers	At the young end of the spectrum. Intolerant of others and strongly motivated by success and concerned about self-image.	15.0
Self-exploiters	The 'doers' and 'self-starters', competitive but always under pressure and often pessimistic. Possessions are important.	13.0
Token triers	Always willing to try new things to 'improve their luck', but apparently on a permanent try-and-fail cycle. Includes an above average proportion of unemployed.	10.0
Sleepwalkers	Contented under-achievers. Don't care about most things, and actively opt out. Traditional macho views.	13.0
Passive endurers	Weighted towards the elderly, they are often economically and socially disenfranchised. Expect little of life, and give little.	9.0

(*Source*: McCann-Erickson)

Lifestyle segmentation across national boundaries has attracted a lot of attention over the last decade, associated with the emergence of the 'global' brand or the 'Eurobrand'. The essential idea is that identifiable lifestyle segments exist in many countries, share similar existences and have similar wants and needs. Eurostyles, developed by CCA (Centre for Advanced Communication) takes a multivariate approach to identify six major segments amongst European consumers. These 'Eurostyle' segments include 'The Contestors', some 8 per cent of the population of Europe, who are given a summary description identifying them as: 'young, highly educated, holding executive positions . . . favouring innovative products . . . permissive intellectuals . . . motivated by personal expansion and self-expression'.

Which mix of behaviour and general variables can be used?

Combinations of behaviour and general variables are more likely to give useful market segments – segments which discriminate behaviour and which can be reached. Thus, the segment of interest might be brand-loyal users with high usage rates who are known to be males, aged 35–44, living in the South East, who belong to social grade D and who read the daily tabloids. This kind of information may come from routine in-house information collection, from primary research into a market or from an agency service.

There are many agencies which supply data on actual or potential customers classified in a variety of ways. Perhaps the best known of these is the British Market Research Bureau (BMRB) offering a number of specialist services including the Target Group Index (TGI). TGI is compiled on an annual basis from 24 000 respondents who return a self-completion questionnaire that covers 2 500 'fast moving' brands and 150 other brands in the financial sector and leisure. A full range of standard demographics is collected on the respondents along with responses to attitudinal questions for the creation of lifestyle classification. Conversion of the data into geodemographic groups and types is provided. In addition, data on media habits are collected from respondents. This permits the classification of usage rates and media habits against demographics, geodemographics and lifestyle classifications – behaviour variables against general variables.

Table 28.7 gives an example of the combinations made available by TGI which analyses, amongst other things, market segments for products and brands. The data concerns solus users of one brand of aftershave/splash-on lotion in 1992. Solus users are those who use the one brand and no other – 'brand-loyal' customers. The data, a very small extract from one page of one volume, also indicates the danger of data overload when exploring alternative bases for segmentation and target marketing.

In this example, the first column gives the number of adult males in the various categories, 21.8 million adult males in total. The second column, column A, gives the absolute number of men in the various categories who are solus users of the brand – 353 000 in total. Column B gives the profile of solus users against the various categories, such that 23.1 per cent are aged 35–44, 27.3 per cent are in social grade C2 and 29.6 per cent read *The Sun*. Column C provides the proportion in each category who are solus users of this brand. Thus, 1.6 per cent of all adult men, 2.1 per cent of adult men aged 55–64, 3.1 per cent of those in social grade E and 2 per cent of those who read *The Sun* are solus

Table 28.7
Target Group Index data: one brand of aftershave/splash-on lotion – solus users

	Population '000	A '000	B % down	C % across	D Index
All men	21 819	353	100.0	1.6	100
15-19	2 024	28	7.9	1.4	85
20-24	1 989	15	4.3	0.8	47
25-34	4 417	41	11.7	0.9	58
35-44	3 834	82	23.1	2.1	132
45-54	3 249	56	15.9	1.7	107
55-64	2 753	58	16.3	2.1	129
65 and over	3 553	74	20.9	2.1	128
AB	4 133	51	14.5	1.2	77
C1	4 973	66	18.8	1.3	82
C2	6 421	97	27.3	1.5	93
D	4 002	67	18.9	1.7	103
E	2 290	72	20.4	3.1	194
Daily Express	1 810	29	8.2	1.6	99
Daily Mirror	4 351	79	22.5	1.8	113
The Sun	5 263	104	29.6	2.0	123
Daily Telegraph	1 380	15	4.2	1.1	67
Sunday Express	2 186	43	2.1	2.0	121
Observer	946	14	4.1	1.5	94

Source: adapted from TGI, 1992.

users of the brand. Finally, column D provides an index which identifies the frequency of solus users in the various categories in relation to the frequency encountered amongst all adult men. Thus, the frequency amongst men in social grade E is 94 per cent greater than the frequency amongst all adult men.

From this example, it is clear that the general variables of age and social grade do discriminate amongst the defined category of solus users. In addition, the data on media habits also discriminates. Target markets can be identified with these variables, and can also be reached.

Such information from TGI takes the notion of target marketing from the more conceptual level to the data-driven reality of implementation. Problems in applying market segmentation are often caused by an absence of data, sometimes by a surfeit of data and perhaps also by misuse of data.

Choosing from amongst the many possible variables for segmenting a consumer market can be something of a problem. Of ultimate concern is the extent to which the variables and the segments which result are of some use but in the case of a new approach, this may well be speculative. Some forays into segmentation of the market will be based on the premise that segments do exist and can be identified with particular behaviour and general variables. Important questions will include the track record of any one variable in identifying useful target segments for similar products, the extent to which the approach is understood and accepted, the complexity of obtaining worthwhile data and the cost of obtaining that data. The choice of general and behaviour variables may also be intuitive, driven by convention – or simply arbitrary.

All this applies equally to industrial markets. End-use as a behaviour variable and geographic location as a general variable are very popular. Other behaviour variables include buying situation (straight rebuy, modified rebuy and new purchase) and other characteristics of the buying process such as the nature of the buying centre and the buying criteria employed. Other general variables focus on the broader characteristics of the organization such as size, and SIC classification. The principles of market segmentation and of target marketing apply equally to consumer and to industrial markets.

EVALUATION

So far, the concern has been with possibilities for market segmentation and target marketing in terms of identifying possible segments for special attention. The next stage in the process of target marketing is the evaluation stage. Before implementation, the inherent worth of the segments has to be considered.

Which segmentation variables should be used?

There are two considerations when considering the intrinsic worth of any one segment for a policy of target marketing – data availability and segment discrimination.

Data availability

It may well be that a precise audience could be identified as a desirable target market but if data are difficult or costly to obtain, then the extent to which that knowledge can be used will be restricted. On cost grounds, particularly with small businesses, the scope for a formal policy of target marketing may be limited and the use of local knowledge, experience and judgement become critical.

Segment discrimination

Should good data exist, there are certain standard requirements of market segments but chief amongst these is the extent to which the segmentation variable chosen and the segments which result do in fact discriminate amongst consumers. Each segment should include consumers who display homogeneity of needs and preferences, and should contain consumers who are significantly different in these respects to consumers in other segments.

If the approach taken does not stand up to the 'so what?' question at this level then there is little point in proceeding. For example, should TGI profile and penetration data for solus users of a brand be more or less the same across a given general variable classification, such as age, then there may be little point in taking this line of enquiry any further.

For some applications, it is also necessary to go beyond demonstrated association and seek to identify causation. Knowing that solus users of a brand of aftershave/splash-on lotion can be discriminated by age could be a sufficient starting point. In other cases, such as with product design and media messages, knowledge of why the association exists will be required.

Which of the segments are actionable?

If data or judgement indicate that segments do exist, the initial determinant of whether or not a segment is actionable is the accessibility of that segment. This takes evaluation of the segments into the area of operational significance.

One of the main reasons for redefining a key target segment such as solus users by superimposing general variables is so that they can be reached using appropriate communications as well as in terms of physical delivery. Some general variables hold up very well against this criterion. Geodemographic variables display the marked advantage of having their databases linked to postcodes so the target audience becomes very accessible. No doubt the marketing information revolution which is taking place will further enhance the precision which is possible with these methods. Conversely, other general variables present some problems. If the target audience is defined or redefined using some of the lifestyle variables, reaching the audience with an effective communications mix may be extremely difficult, or perhaps expensive and wasteful.

Which of the resulting segments are the more desirable?

The segments are known to exist and can be reached. These are the two primary prerequisites of target marketing. Assuming this point is reached, there are two additional issues concerning the inherent desirability of the identified segments: segment size and segment stability.

Segment size

While it may be that a target segment meets the above requirements, the desirability worth of that segment and the justification for assembling a marketing package for it will be a function of segment size. The segment may simply be too small to warrant any special marketing effort. Markets can be over-segmented or they might be too small in the first place to justify any attempt at target marketing.

Segment stability

The stability of the target segments over time will be important. Ideally, the target segment will be of adequate size and will also have potential for substantial and steady growth. In times of rapid change, emerging segments may be especially attractive in terms of future potential. However, in some markets, underlying benefits sought can shift radically and rapidly. If change cannot be predicted, or at least estimated, then a policy of target marketing can become unduly risky.

IMPLEMENTATION

The segments have been identified and evaluated as being worthy of interest – in terms of their inherent characteristics. The implementation of target marketing now moves from assessment of the customers to assessment of the environment, the company and the competition. This requires consideration of marketing strategy and marketing tactics, covered elsewhere in this book. Some of the major issues are presented below.

Should the strategy be concentrated or multiple-segment?

Whether selecting one or a number of market segments, the capacity of the organization and the activities of the competition will determine appropriate strategy. Embracing both considerations will be broader 'macro-environmental' concerns. In some circumstances, there may be statutory restrictions surrounding a policy of dominating a particular target segment.

The business mission, the strengths and weaknesses of the organization and the revenue/cost/volume implications of target marketing will have to be addressed. On the cost side, target marketing may well result in increased production and marketing costs. Consideration of risk will be an input into the choice between various options, including those of concentrated or multiple-segment approaches.

As for external issues, the competitive position will also drive the decision on segment selection. Segments in which intense rivalry already exists or can be expected will be less attractive than those where the organization has greater freedom to manoeuvre. Associated with this, actual or potential barriers to entry may increase or decrease the appeal of a potential target segment. Exit barriers may also be important. Established and stable organizational networks would well be disrupted through radical changes in target marketing.

How should the product(s) be positioned for the target segment(s)?

Having identified, evaluated and selected target segments, the products have to be 'positioned'. This requires an assessment of the significant dimensions along which the product can be differentiated for the customers and also with respect to any competing products. Such differentiation will usually require assessment of the needs, benefits sought, attitudes and perceptions of customers in the target segment.

What marketing mix is desirable for the target segment(s)?

Identification, evaluation and selection of target segments is nothing without subsequent action. The devil lies in the detail and it is here that rational appraisal and sensible strategy formation can easily come unstuck.

The marketing mix of product characteristics, price, communications and distribution must be assembled to create the desired positioning, to satisfy the needs and wants of the target segment(s) and to establish a competitive advantage. In a perfect world, the response elasticities of the targeted segments with respect to changes in the marketing mix elements would be known. In practice, such responses are assessed by reference not only to the available data but also to experience and to inspired guesswork.

Finally, the implementation stage is incomplete without regular monitoring of the results of target marketing. Where possible, marketing information should identify the profitability of the segments. In practice, other measures are likely to be used.

CONCLUSION

To summarize, when target marketing is appropriate – and this is usually the case – *identification* is necessary first of all. The market segments are defined with an appropriate combination of behaviour and general variables. Then, *evaluation* requires the resulting segments to be assessed according to their inherent desirability. Data availability, discriminatory power, accessibility, size and stability are the main criteria. At the strategic level, *implementation* of target marketing reflects the goals and the capacities of the organization and the configuration of the competition. At the tactical level, pursuit of target segments requires differentiation to position the product in accordance with the needs of the target segment(s) and to secure the competitive edge.

ESSENTIAL READING

Beane, T.P. and Ennis, D.M. (1987), 'Market Segmentation: A Review', *European Journal of Marketing*, **21**, (1), 20–42.

Dickson, P.R. and Ginter, J.L. (1987), 'Market Segmentation, Product Differentiation, and Marketing Strategy', *Journal of Marketing*, **51**, (2), 1–10.

Tonks, D.G. (1990), 'Pinning Down Geodemographics', *Marketing Intelligence and Planning*, **8**, (2), 4–10.

Various authors (1993), *Research Plus: The Magazine of the Market Research Society*, Market Research Society, December.

Weinstein, A. (1987), *Market Segmentation*, Chicago, Illinois: Probus Publishing.

29 Advertising

Charles Channon

Advertising is typically one element in the persuasive presentation of a product or service to its buying or using public. For many of those involved in it, whether as advertisers, agencies or consumers, it is *the* communication element in the marketing mix. What we really mean by this is that it is the most obvious and separately identifiable.

ADVERTISING AND THE MARKETING MIX

In fact, the whole of the marketing mix contains potential or actual communications and all of them, when they are found, are designed to be persuasive to purchase and consumption. A cleaning product may contain coloured particles to highlight certain claimed ingredients and their benefits; a small electrical good may have design elements which highlight its suitability for youth or that it is fashionable; in most instances a pack does far more than simply 'protect' what's inside – it will 'brand' the contents at the very least, and sometimes a great deal more.

Even distribution can 'say' something about a brand. So can price: whether our price is higher or lower than the competition is, potentially, a communication to our market about things other than price. As a relative price it can produce, say, lower margins and higher volume or higher margins and lower volume and either route may mean more or less total profit. But as a communication it can say something about our quality, our market segment, our end-use, and so on. In this respect it must be consistent with our strategy as expressed through the rest of the marketing mix, including, of course, promotion, of which advertising is a part.

In this sense the whole of marketing strategy, directly or indirectly, is a communication with the market-place. It must be so because in most developed market-places the buyer, the customer, the consumer is usually free to choose   *513*

– to buy or not to buy, to buy our product or service or someone else's. To make that choice, consumers need 'information' – information which they have in some way processed and responded to at the rational and/or emotional level, consciously or unconsciously. The response may be as vague as a heightened sense of familiarity or as definite as a feeling of total satisfaction with previous trial or the belief that the product contains added fibre or is selling for 20p off at Tesco's. Of course, as we have seen, this information which is being used and responded to does not just come from advertising. In the last analysis, the response is to the whole of the marketing mix. So, advertising is not unique as a tool of marketing; rather it is like the other communication aspects of marketing, only more so. Its sole function is to evoke a response through communication in paid-for space – usually from the consumer, often (indirectly) from the trade as well, and sometimes from other audiences.

What it communicates may be a claim about value for money or a product performance benefit. It could equally be just a reminder or it could be an association or an image in which words as such, let alone claims, have little significant role to play. Whatever it is will be (or should be) determined by the nature of the product field and the consumer needs within it and by the part that advertising can play in the context of the rest of the marketing mix.

We should never think of advertising as isolated from the rest of marketing. It plays just one part in helping to solve a marketing problem or exploit a marketing opportunity, and to be effective the part it plays must be right. If the marketing problem is distribution, advertising may be able to contribute only a little to its solution; if the problem is price, advertising as such may contribute even less. And if the problem is the product itself, advertising may even be counter-productive. Advertising which generated widespread trial of an unsatisfactory product could well render a later 'new improved' version unsaleable. On the other hand, if the problem is awareness advertising can be very powerful, and even more powerful (because the effect lasts longer) if the problem is positioning, that is, if potential consumers have not grasped where your brand fits in to their needs or lives in a way that is different from the competition.

Where advertising fits, it will work to *simplify* consumer choice in your favour, provided that *the advertisements themselves also form a fit between the brand and the consumer in the real world.* Implicit in this statement of the obvious are some important fundamentals about the nature of advertisements and of the advertising process.

First, advertisements relate products or services to people. To do this effectively, they must be appropriate to the former and relevant to the latter *in a way that helps to express and sustain competitive advantage.* This, if you like, is the generalized or generic version of the strategy to which any advertisement is written (whether consciously or unconsciously). The specifics of the brand, the specifics of consumer needs in the product field, and the specifics of competitive advantage will determine the strategy to which a particular advertisement or campaign is written. Yet, however specific the strategy, *it will not write the advertisements* (though there are still some advertisers and some product fields where it can appear to come very close to doing so). For every given strategy there will be, in principle, an *in*definite number of possible creative solutions.

This gap, as it were, between strategy and execution is not unique to advertising. Nevertheless, it is particularly evident in advertising and helps to explain the high profile of the creative function within it. What matters is the response. Strategy will define the response we want but it is a creative execution – an advertisement – which must elicit it. In some cases the content of the strategy and the literal content of the advertising message will be almost identical; in others this will not be so, due to the nature of the required responses and the way such responses are achieved – emotions, imagery, involvement, and values must be recreated, not just stated.

Target consumers and their needs, however, are only one side of the connection an advertisement makes. The other side is the product or service, which we often speak of as the *brand*.

ADVERTISING AND BRANDING

At the most basic level it is obvious that the one thing an advertisement must do is to identify what it is selling. However, a well-branded advertisement is no more than the final link in a whole process of *differentiation* from the competition, which good marketing will attempt to achieve in the market-place wherever it can. It is a process to which advertising is peculiarly well-suited to contribute and, indeed, it is this power in advertising which has historically accounted for its prominence in the marketing of fast moving consumer goods.

We talked earlier of advertisements relating products to their target consumers in a way that helps to express and sustain competitive advantage. Looked at more closely, this statement can be seen to be almost a redefinition in communication terms of the ultimate operational objective of the whole of marketing. Although the concept of profit is not explicit in this definition, we would do well to remember that it is there by implication as the *business* objective for which all good marketing is simply the strategy: *profit defines the purpose for and constraint under which competitive advantage is created and sustained*.

Competitive advantage can take many forms but, whatever it is, the consumer needs to know about it and needs to know that it belongs to us. It could be a price advantage; it could be a performance benefit like 'washes whiter', 'gets stains out', 'kills 99 per cent of all known germs', or 'kind to hands'. Or it could be a generalized promise of reliability and value which adds up to 'the name you can trust'. It could concern *authenticity* – 'the real thing' – or be a form of social gratification like an enhancement of the role in which the product is used or of the end-use (or end-user) to which (or to whom) it is addressed. It could be that our brand is easier to identify with, or has a more distinctive identity or more attractive personality – or just more fun. Being a better advertiser can sometimes constitute our competitive advantage. But whatever it is will be relevant at some level to consumer choice and the link between it and our product will be forged by branding.

515

Branding links a reputation to a name and creates an *owned difference in the market-place* which is relevant to consumer needs. It provides a focus for interest, credibility and loyalty and, of course, it can be used to identify and reinforce any form of stimulus to sales. It is a powerful aid to the simplification of choice and to the creation of a *protected* franchise among your target consumers.

Branding works by counteracting the erosion of advantage which is the natural tendency of any competitive product field. It creates a sort of patent in the mind or, if you prefer, helps to build what accountants call 'goodwill', which, properly supported, has a good chance of surviving attempts by our competition to match or equal us on our own ground. Successful branding can be very valuable: it becomes our differentiated asset in the market-place and may be worth more to us than any other assets the company has.

In this sense a brand is a unique identity, a whole which is greater than the sum of its parts. You *can* build a brand *without* advertising, but many products need advertising to help them do this because the experience of the product in use will not by itself be enough to establish its unique identity without the projection, the associations and the amplification which advertising can provide.

ADVERTISING AND ADDED VALUES

Most consumers will admit that there are many products which mean something more to their users than simply what they deliver in terms of pure performance. This is most obvious in personal purchase product fields like, say, lager or fragrances, where what we buy is also a statement about ourselves. Yet most household purchases which are not retailers' own-brands make some statement, even if only the residual reassurance and guarantee that the product in question will deliver up to expectation. Even own-branding will have a meaning in this context either because it means something anyway (Sainsbury's wines, for example) or, negatively, because we have decided that this is a product field where price alone ought to be decisive.

All these 'meanings', except the last, constitute in some sense an *added* value. For reasons that will now be obvious, added values help differentiation in the market-place, are a natural product of the creation of a brand and are usually very suited to projection and reinforcement in advertising, although, as with everything else, there are other ways of doing it.

We need to be clear that added values are not a marketing invention but are fundamental to our social nature as human beings. As anthropology has shown, we use goods to define our values, reinforce them, and express them to other people. In this perspective, if, as has been said, money is information in circulation, then *goods are information delivered and received*. Gifts, such as a box of chocolates, are obviously like this but so are houses, furnishings, cars, holidays, clothes, what we serve at a meal and even savings and insurance. All these things serve a functional or rational purpose, but to us as human beings in society they often mean more than the purpose they serve – more to ourselves or to our families and friends or to the world at large. This does not mean that consumption behaviour is necessarily *irrational* but rather that 'rationality' must not be confined to a limited functional and economic meaning.

VALUES, ECONOMIC VALUE, AND EVALUATION

The importance and legitimacy of values and meanings in consumption behaviour have some practical implications for the relationship between marketing and advertising on the one hand and the science of economics on the other. In the end, economics can deal with *values* (that is, all the various consumer needs and satisfactions which marketing and advertising must address in the market-place) only in terms of their *economic* value, expressed in the form of such relationships as the price elasticity of demand (what percentage change in demand will result from a 1 per cent change in price) and so on. This type of analysis can be very useful *retrospectively* in evaluating what marketing has achieved but necessarily gives very little guidance on how you might set about achieving it in the real world in the first place.

The assessment of what has been achieved can still be very valuable, however, and it can be particularly valuable for an *optional and controllable* marketing cost like advertising. It is not easy to achieve because the marketing mix is not just a mix as far as sales and profit are concerned but a *blend*. It requires us to *isolate* an effect due to advertising over and above the effect of the rest of the mix (to which, of course, advertising may also have contributed – if, for example, there is an *underlying* long-term upward trend in sales). It must not only isolate an advertising effect from the rest of the mix which *we* have created but also isolate it from all those other influences on purchasing which we do not control, such as competitors' activities, and a variety of economic, social, technological and even political pressures.

It *can* be done, as the IPA Advertising Effectiveness Awards have shown, and done more rigorously than simple-minded arguments like 'advertising went up and then sales went up' which used to be the staple and inadequate basis of such demonstrations. It is easier to do if planned for in advance and the case histories of the published books of the Awards provide extremely useful models of how to do it. The analyses they deploy, of course, are not solely those familiar from economics textbooks, indeed rather the reverse, but they do go a long way towards demonstrating how in practice advertising helps to convert values into economic value, and economic value into profit.

The bottom-line accountability of advertising will become more important as markets become more competitive and as the *business* objectives of marketing activity come into sharper and sharper focus through the stock market and its analysts. But this is only one aspect of a changing competitive environment for advertising which has tended to shift the aims of advertising activity away from the long-term brand-building effects, which can be inferred but not separately quantified (at least on a consensus basis), to strictly short-term effects where, in certain circumstances, other means of promotion may appear to be equally or more efficient.

ADVERTISING AND THE COMPETITIVE ENVIRONMENT

Two of the most important changes of this kind, apart from the ever-increasing pressure on financial performance as such, have been the growth of retailer power and the shortening life-cycle of many markets.

Historically, brand advertising developed as a weapon of the manufacturer against the retailer and wholesaler. In 1964 the abolition of resale price maintenance in the UK began a process whereby retailers of packaged goods could begin to wrest some of this power back into their own hands. They could, as it were, stimulate demand (by cutting the price of brands at the expense of the manufacturer's margin rather than their own), concentrate demand (by creating larger and larger outlets whose volume would give them economies of scale), and differentiate demand (by creating own-brands and, latterly, by making the stores themselves into an added value 'brand' which could compete on a basis other than price alone).

The effect of this in the UK over time – in the USA the relationship and its consequences have been rather different – has been a tendency to reduce the resources available for supporting manufacturer brands in ways other than cutting the price (or some equivalent incentive to stock) to the retailer. It has also created a double jeopardy for brands which are not brand leaders; the retailer can 'afford' not to stock them but they cannot afford not to be stocked. Other things being equal, it is clear that in a situation where three or four retail chains control half the sales of a brand which itself holds less than 0.1 per cent of those retailers' sales, marketing must shift its emphasis to *pushing* the product through (that is, getting product into stock) and, to that extent, less into *pulling* product through (that is, differentiating demand among consumers).

There are other reasons too why classic packaged goods advertising has begun to be less dominant in total advertising activity than it used to be. For one thing, there has been a growth in service markets generally and in financial services markets particularly. In many of these markets there is a tendency for the advertising task to polarize between highly generalized 'corporate' support and highly specific support and promotion for often short-lived products. Another factor is the quickening pace of the life cycle of a number of advertised products. This applies both to the financial services products which we have already mentioned and to other product fields like consumer electronics. Shorter product life cycles mean that there is less time to recover the initial investment. With manufactured goods there is also less likelihood that the economies of scale potentially open to those first into the market could offset the steep decline in the general manufacturing costs of the technology which so often characterizes technological markets. In these situations there may well be less to allocate to advertising but, equally important, what is allocated must 'move a lot of boxes' before price and distribution-led competition absorbs most of marketing's resources.

There is also a broader thrust at work in many *high* frequency-of-purchase markets whose implications are harder to predict. This thrust comes from the information revolution particularly as it has affected data capture and data analysis. With (or even, on occasion, without) barcoding of goods, it is now possible to retrieve information about sales as they occur at the till and analyse these so as to control stock, facings, reordering and pricing, and, of course, to provide an up-to-the-minute information base for the buyer at head office doing a deal with the manufacturer. One effect of this is greatly to reduce the scope for traditional manufacturer influence on *in-store* marketing, but as these activities have traditionally competed with media advertising for a share of the marketing cake the result may be to increase the importance of advertising in the mix.

A stage further on (quite a bit further on) in the use of electronic point-of-sale (EPOS) data would be the ability *to cross-analyse sales by purchasers by media exposure* as the ultimate form of instant single-source data. Ad-lab data of this kind obviously have huge potential though it should be noted that generating them is one thing and using them effectively is quite another – most information systems in marketing and advertising have been significantly underused. Be this as it may, it seems reasonable to suppose that it would increase and sophisticate the dialogue on media policy between client and agency, provided that the client could have access to these largely retailer-generated data. This is not to say that it would always tend to increase total media spend.

With or without the ad-lab development, EPOS is part of the evolution of the retail sector towards higher margin strategies and away from price competition (in which the lever to profit is sheer volume). In principle, this should make manufacturers' added-value brands (and the advertising that builds and maintains them) more attractive to the retailer. Equally, however, it highlights the fact that switched sales between brands, which change brand shares but not margin or total volume in the product field, are of no particular interest as far as the retailer is concerned. Switching sales, gaining share, are what advertising does best; it can also help to expand the market, if there is room for growth. In future, manufacturers' marketing objectives may need to be at least as much margin-led as they are share-led. Added-value competition at a price premium is more difficult than at price parity and represents a challenge both to new product development and advertising. It could also imply fewer winners unless there is a more effective segmentation of the market.

On balance, this particular development looks as if it will tend to maintain the importance of brand-building advertising, but it may also make it even more competitive for the agencies concerned as the *real* index of performance becomes sterling 'margin share'.

Increasingly, distributed computer power will also greatly expand the potential for applying statistical modelling to markets – and not only to packaged goods markets. This will, as noted earlier, sharpen the element of accountability in the client–agency relationship, but it is a long haul, requiring good data and a long time series over which the data have been collected. It also has one disadvantage, not unknown elsewhere in advertising, which is that the data are very difficult to communicate *with all their proper qualifications* to those who have to act on them. The 'boffins' should not be asked to bear the responsibility for this problem on their own – marketing and advertising management must advance half-way to meet them.

MARKETING AND THE ADVERTISING PROCESS

With one significant exception the whole thrust of this review so far has been to emphasize the necessarily close relationship between the ways marketing and advertising work. Yet whatever the focus, short or long term, just moving unit sales or building a consumer franchise, this symmetry between the tasks and objectives of marketing and advertising is very easy to lose sight of in the real world of the client–agency relationship and the agency's way of working.

One factor here is that clients can be concerned about the confidentiality of key financial performance data, so the agency may not know, for example, the client's margin, other costs and so on. While understandable this is also limiting, not only on the agency's ability to offer general advice but also on the extent to which the agency can really understand the total context of its work as when, for example, it recommends an advertising budget.

Two other necessary factors that arise in the translation from a marketing problem to an advertising objective however are just as important. One of them is the 'gap' we have already mentioned that exists between the advertising strategy and the actual advertising recommendation. Most, if not quite all, advertisements have to be based on an advertising *idea*, which is *not* the same as the advertising strategy. It will be based on the strategy of course, and designed to achieve the consumer responses which the strategy says will help the sell, but it is not created *by* the strategy: it is created *to* the strategy. The ideas that the agency's creative department devise may or may not contain words or claims that reflect the strategy in a literal and direct way.

Creative ideas and their treatment in advertisements constitute the 'language' of advertising. That language has its own conventions, resources and skills. It can draw heavily on the style and typical content of the medium in which it appears (for example, when television advertising uses a 'sit-com' idea as the basis of a campaign). It has its own conventions, too, which arise out of all those approaches, devices, and techniques which are the natural armoury of simplifying communications and persuasive communications – like product demonstration, product endorsement, analogy, imagery, humour and wit. Not every advertisement, of course, uses these resources to the same extent – an 'earpiece' advertisement (those you sometimes see either side of the name of the newspaper on its front page) may simply repeat the brand's 'logo' – this will depend on the job the advertisement is trying to do. But every advertisement, even the simplest, will be trying to have an impact on its audience and leave an 'impression' (consciously or unconsciously) about the product. How effective an advertisement is at doing this job will depend in part on how many target consumers it reaches (its coverage) and how often it reaches them (its 'frequency') but it will also depend on how well it uses the resources of the language of advertising which we have been discussing.

Advertising as a *craft* – the craft of the creation and production of advertisements – is, therefore, unlike many other marketing tasks in its specific skills and in its product. Both are decisive for the character of an agency, for the work satisfaction of all those employed in it (not just the 'creatives' themselves), and for its success in winning and keeping business. So, although in the multi-disciplinary world of the agency there are many relevant skills and resources which to a greater or lesser extent overlap those in the client's marketing department, there are other *defining* elements in it which make if different and mark out its operational goals as in many ways peculiarly its own.

Good advertising is one such goal, and good media planning and buying another. Indeed, media planning and buying, though it receives in its own right less attention from the general public, is the other distinguishing activity of an agency and the other service which its clients are buying, apart from advertisements themselves. They may buy these services from separate sources rather than from one full-service advertising agency but, whether they buy their media from the same source or separately from a media independent (as 'media only' agencies tend to be known), media planning and buying is a craft in its own right with its own special skills and resources. The world of media with its audience research data, its comparisons of cost-per-thousand (the cost of reaching 1 000 of a given audience or circulation), its analysis of reach and frequency, its schedules (the media chosen for a campaign together with the timing – and size or length – of the ads to appear in it), and its optimizations (maximizing what can be obtained for a given campaign cost against specified criteria of coverage and frequency) is also a very different world from that of marketing and, it should be said, from that of creating and producing the advertisements themselves.

We have spoken of these distinctive outputs of an agency as its operational goals to distinguish them as activities from the marketing ends which they both serve. It would be more accurate to speak of them as the distinctive *operational activities* of the advertising business which in their turn have their own distinctive operational goals. If this sounds like mere wordplay on a sort of Russian dolls basis (when each doll opens to reveal another doll which opens to reveal another doll. . . and so on) that is because in any multi-disciplinary and multi-stage business *one person's strategy is always likely to be another's objective.*

For example, a company's business objective may be growth in profits and its strategy to milk existing brands in saturated markets while expanding brand share for its brands in growth sectors. In the light of this the marketing director and his or her brand people may have an objective of increasing share while maintaining margins in their growth markets and a strategy of achieving this by increasing distribution and advertising support. The agency may, therefore, have the objective of stimulating trial among non-users of the brand and a strategy of doing this by increasing awareness and emphasizing its suitability for certain end-uses to which product quality is particularly relevant. The agency's creative department will have the objective of increasing awareness and improving perceptions of quality along with the salience of certain end-uses, and the creative recommendation will in effect constitute its strat- *521* egy for achieving this. The final 'strategy' in this chain of objectives and strategies is the advertisement or the campaign. In the agency part of the chain, the objectives and their strategies are framed in terms of what advertising can achieve *per se* (for example: increase awareness, modify attitudes, stimulate trial – not gain share, increase volume) so that, in this respect, the disciplines of thought which guide the advertising process are distinctive of that process just as much as the craft skills and activities which constitute its end-product to the client.

This contrast between marketing's and advertising's common pursuit of differentiation in the market-place, on the one hand, and their distinctive differences in craft skills, operational goals and disciplines of thought on the other, is nothing special or unusual. Similar contrasts will be found wherever there is specialization within a common endeavour.

One other aspect worth noting, however, is how the search for differentiation in the creative product of advertising leads to a great deal of stress on the new and the original. This is *not* to say that original and creative thought are not found in the rest of the marketing mix – they are and they should be – but the importance of originality in the creative idea and the skills which make that originality work in terms of television, press, radio, posters or cinema, bring into sharp focus a necessary connection between the craft of advertisements and the arts, entertainment and editorial skills of the media in which advertisements appear.

Emphasizing this aspect of the business must be done with care. It can all too often seem like a covert plea for self-indulgence by the agency and an excuse for weakening the need for relevance. That it should neither be like this nor have this effect goes without saying. Equally, however, it is not to be despised simply because it can be abused. It can make an extremely valuable contribution to the sales effectiveness of advertising in the market-place, as is shown by the number of cases in the IPA Advertising Effectiveness Awards where the advertisements concerned win creative awards as well.

THE ADVERTISING CYCLE AND THE AGENCY ACCOUNT TEAM

Advertising is a cyclical process of which advertisements and media schedules are the recurrent product. The cycle starts with what might be called a planning baseline; this leads to the development of a strategy, which leads to the development of a creative brief and a budget, which leads to creative and media recommendations, which lead to running the advertisements, which in turn lead to monitoring our apparent progress in the market-place, which will, sooner or later, become the new planning baseline, with the cycle starting all over again.

As described, the process sounds simple enough. In practice it can be a complex process, which is feedback-intensive, prone to error, and as dependent on sound judgement as on good data. Of course, advertising accounts can differ enormously in their complexity and in the scope and nature of the feedback which is provided, while agencies themselves differ in how they are organized to apportion the various responsibilities to which the process gives rise. For this reason it may be most useful to distinguish the responsibilities as such prior to any consideration of who fulfils them.

In fairly simplistic terms the responsibilities can be listed as follows.

1 *Agency responsibilities to the clients:*

- To advise them generally in their own best interest.
- To provide creative and media recommendations which are relevant and appropriate to the client's business and marketing objectives and strategy.
- To effect this at an appropriate level of quality, professionalism, timeliness, and cost-effectiveness.

2 *Agency responsibilities to the brand and to the consumer:*

- To relate the brand to the target consumer through the advertising so as to help the sell.
- In such a way as to be true to the heritage, character and performance of the brand *and* relevant to the current needs and satisfaction of the target consumers.
- To do this as far as possible so as to protect *future* sales of the brand.

3 *Agency responsibilities to itself:*

- To keep the business and handle it profitably.
- To ensure so far as possible that the client not only receives the best advice but is persuaded by it.
- Not only to produce but to run work which merits the respect of its peer group agencies in the business.
- To attract and retain good talent and, as far as possible, to provide the scope and incentive for its development at every level in the agency.

At first sight such a list may seem somewhat surprising in its structure and emphasis. It is not, of course, a list of legal responsibilities so it says nothing about the fact that an agency is a principal and not an agent when it acts on behalf of its clients. It does not tell whether the agency's remuneration will be commission-based or, as is increasingly the case, fee-based. It gives little indication of the terms of business to be agreed with the client. Furthermore, it appears to draw a surprising distinction between the interests of the client and those of the brand, and an invidious distinction between both of these and the agency's own interest.

In reality, of course, all these interests overlap: they are complementary rather than contradictory, but it is important to remember that they are not identical. They *can* clash when things get out of kilter. The advertising management task which is shared between a good agency and a good client is to ensure that all these critical responsibilities remain in their proper complementary relationship to one another.

For example, it is not in the client's long-term interest that good agency service should remain unprofitable to that agency, any more than it is in the long-term interests of consumers that a good brand should not make any money for its manufacturer. Again, clients with a portfolio of brands may well be tempted to improve the bottom line by a short-term policy of under-supporting one brand or purely price-promoting it in a way that undermines its long-term franchise, securing sales today at the expense of sales tomorrow. If the agency doesn't 'stand up' for the brand in this situation, who will?

Similarly, it is the brand's relationship to the consumer's needs and perceptions, not to those of the production manager or sales manager, that matters. Production may want to stress features or ingredients (or even, according to agency folklore, the factory) rather than consumer benefits or uses or social gratifications; sales may want to emphasize the logo, the value for money, and a slogan they think will appeal to the trade.

Again, agencies cannot best serve their clients through glorious failure. Good work which doesn't run is a loss to the client and a blow to the agency. True, not all 'good work' (in the agency's eyes) is necessarily sales-effective and not all 'dull work' is sales-*in*effective, but in a situation of trust such a dichotomy should be resolvable by research feedback and judgement. It can always be argued that if dull work can sell n boxes then good work *of the right kind* should be able to sell $n+$ boxes.

Not all agencies and not all clients could be induced to underwrite all the responsibilities stated here. Some on both sides set their face against creative awards, for example, as a permanent temptation to self-indulgence and irrelevance. Others, by contrast, believe the real temptation to be in the other direction: work that is nominally relevant in that you can match all the points in it against the strategy, but which never in fact comes to life and never engages the consumer such that its relevance becomes meaningful and effective. There is obviously a question here of balance and fitness for purpose, and a different balance may have to be struck in different situations.

All these responsibilities involve issues and different areas of expertise which have to be handled within the resources of the account team, drawing where necessary on internal agency resources or from outside. Leadership and the primary interface with the client will lie with the account director, media and creative responsibilities with the appropriate members of the team. In respect of those responsibilities which we have described as being to the brand and to the consumer, practice is more variable: they can be handled by the account director working with either an agency researcher or outside research suppliers when research is called for. Increasingly, and particularly in larger agencies in the UK, they will be separately identifiable as the proper sphere of the 'account planner' in the team.

The account planner in this situation will be responsible for generating the advertising strategy in the first place, and for any research-based creative development of the creative ideas produced to that strategy. The account planner will, therefore, be responsible for selecting and interpreting the research evidence both at these stages and at the final stage of evaluation in the market-place, which leads to the next planning baseline and the next round of the advertising planning cycle. In this sense, *as the representative of the consumer's needs and perceptions* the account planner gives a separate and independent voice to the marketing principle as adapted to the agency's own specific product and way of working.

Throughout the advertising cycle, feedback in the form of research or other data has potentially a large and important role to play. The kind of research that is deployed will have much to do with the particular stage in the cycle that has been reached – at the beginning it may tend to the exploratory, the 'open-ended' and the qualitative; at the end to the structured, focused and quantified. It will also have much to do with the respective philosophies of the agency and the client and with the way they have respectively understood the marketing and advertising task. In a nutshell, *how you think the marketing works will influence how you think the advertising works which in turn will influence how you think the research works.* This symmetry is perfectly proper and many of the arguments about research technique and methodology simply conceal a lack of congruence between the way the client and the agency understand the fundamental task. Here, as elsewhere, it would often be more fruitful to bring the assumptions out into the open and see why they differ rather than argue, often fruitlessly, about the methodological consequences that simply follow from them.

In the end there are as many models for marketing and advertising as there are types of differential advantage. Certainty is rarely attained and even more rarely held on to, because solutions wear out and problems change. In any case, the 'how' and 'why' questions, which are so important to consumer choice, do not give *actionably certain* answers whether or not we *count* the answers to them across a representative sample or simply listen to them in group discussions. So advertising decision, however well or extensively informed, is always, in the end, based on judgement, which is why respect and trust between all the parties to it, including the client, are the foundation on which everything else is based.

THE CONTROL AND REGULATION OF ADVERTISING

Advertising in the UK is carried on within a regulatory framework which acts to curb abuse and to make advertising responsive to the public consensus as well as to the letter of the law.

It has not always been so. Nineteenth-century patent medicine advertising in the UK, as elsewhere, was singularly free of any regard for the truth, however laxly defined. The gradual application of legal controls and a rising standard of education in the market-place as a whole were two important pressures in raising standards. The present regulatory system can be regarded as the product of the culmination of these two pressures in the development of consumerism in the 1960s, accelerated by a new consciousness of the potential power of advertising which followed the introduction and spread in coverage of commercial television from 1955 onwards.

Promotion is formally regulated in three ways in Britain:

- By legislation.
- By statutory authority.
- By self-regulation.

No major laws relate directly and only to advertising but more than 50 regulate it as a *by-product* of more general control of marketing (in the lawyers' quaint jargon, 'consumer trade practices'). The most significant of those are the Trade Descriptions Acts of 1968 and 1972, and the 1973 Fair Trading Act, passed during the heyday of 'consumer consciousness'.

Control by statutory authority is exercised over broadcast advertising. In 1964, the Television Act charged the Independent Television Authority, itself set up by Act of Parliament ten years earlier, with the duty to draw up a mandatory code of standards governing the content of television commercials and a mechanism for enforcing it. The outcome was The ITA Code of Advertising Standards and Practice and a sophisticated process of *pre-clearance* implemented on the Authority's behalf by a secretariat. The ITA was later replaced by the Independent Broadcasting Authority and its control remit extended to commercial radio. In 1990, the Broadcasting Act separated the two media again, set up an Independent Television Commission and charged it with the duty to draw up and enforce a code of standards relating to 'standards and practice in television advertising and the sponsoring of programmes'. The outcome was a virtually unchanged successor to the previous code, which had proved effective in practice. This ITC Code of Advertising Standards and Practice and the subsequently developed ITC Code of Programme Sponsorship are the instruments of regulation today.

The General Principle of the first is that 'television advertising should be legal, decent, honest and truthful', a basic requirement elaborated in 43 clauses and five appendices relating specifically to advertising directed at children, financial advertising, health claims and related matters, charity advertising and religious advertising. The Code makes it clear to advertisers and their agencies that those detailed rules 'are intended to be applied in the spirit as well as the letter'. The second Code sets out the rules for programme sponsorship under three headings: Principles, Specific Requirements and Further Guidance.

The pre-clearance mechanism is operated for the ITC by the Broadcast Advertising Clearance Centre. No proposed television commercial may be aired by any of Britain's television stations until it has secured the formal approval of this secretariat. The system is not violated in practice, not least because the ITC is also highly instrumental in the awarding and renewing of the station owners' franchises.

The ITC further allocates 20 minutes of every working day to the viewing of newly aired commercials, to detect any cleared by the BACC which might nevertheless be construed to contravene the Code. It also discharges a second statutory duty to receive and investigate complaints against commercials made by members of the viewing public or by other advertisers, between two and three thousand of which are received each year. The commercials in question are withdrawn for the duration of the deliberations, which place the onus on the advertiser or agency responsible to show why the complaint should not be upheld or to modify the commercial and re-submit it for approval. A Television Advertising Complaints Report is published monthly, adding the sanction of adverse publicity to the ITC's armoury.

In 1991, the newly created Radio Authority, also charged by the Broadcasting Act of 1990 with the duty to draw up and enforce a code of practice, published its Radio Authority Code of Advertising Standards and Practice and Programme Sponsorship. Its main Advertising Principle is familiar: radio advertising should be legal, decent, honest and truthful. That basic requirement is this time elaborated in 30 Rules and seven appendices relating to financial advertising, alcoholic drink advertising, commercials directed at children, advertisements for medicines and related products, charity advertising, environmental claims and religious advertising. Programme sponsorship is governed by a further eight Rules. This Code also makes it plain to advertisers and their agencies that the Authority's rules are to be applied in the spirit as well as the letter.

The mechanism of control is slightly less rigorous than that for television advertising. 'Local' and 'regional' commercials can be approved by designated staff at individual radio stations, whose responsibility is to satisfy themselves that the requirements of the Code have been met. 'National' advertising must be pre-cleared by the Broadcast Advertising Clearance Centre in the same way as television commercials, as must any regional or local commercials dealing with 'investment and complex finance; consumer credit; alcohol; government/COI (includes anti-AIDS, anti-drugs and family planning services); advertisements containing references to political, industrial or public controversy; medicines/treatments/health and related claims (includes slimming treatments/clinics, pregnancy-testing services/kits, contraceptives, feminine hygiene and sanitary protection products); environmental claims; charities; religion'.

The third element of Britain's tripartite advertising control system is the self-regulation of all forms of non-broadcast advertising exercised by the Advertising Standards Authority.

The ASA was set up in 1962 by the Advertising Association, with the remit to receive and investigate complaints from business and public and to publicize the existence of its control system and the mechanism for using it. It was to judge complaints according to the criteria of acceptability contained in the British Code of Advertising Standards drawn up by the Advertising Association a year earlier. This articulates the familiar general principle that 'all advertisements should be legal, decent, honest and truthful', elaborated in 80 pages supplemented by appendices relating to tobacco products and alcoholic beverages. In 1980, the ASA published a separate British Code of Sales Promotion Practice.

Financing of the Authority's activities and its own advertising campaigns, to   *527* discharge the second part of its remit, is achieved by a 0.1 per cent levy on the cost of advertising space, routinely added by media owners to the invoices sent to advertising agencies or direct advertisers.

The most important characteristic of the ASA control mechanism is that it does not demand pre-clearance but requires a complaint to set it in motion. Indeed, it would hardly be practical to pre-clear all non-broadcast advertising, let alone other forms of promotion, for the ASA has estimated that about 25 000 000 distinct and separate examples appear in Britain each year.

If the ASA upholds a complaint, it first asks the advertiser to withdraw and amend the advertisement, in the name of collective responsibility. If that fails, it will issue a Media Notice calling upon media owners to take action against the offending advertiser by:

- Denying advertising space in future.
- Denying media commission in future.
- Refusing future advertisements from the same source unless pre-cleared.

It simultaneously informs the news media and consumer-interest organizations by means of periodic *Case Reports*. The evidence is that most advertisers give in when this happens, so the ASA very seldom has to resort to referral of a case to other elements of the control system. After the event, regular post-checks guard against surreptitious attempts to reinstate the banned material.

Twenty-five million non-broadcast advertisements per year normally generate about 8 000 complaints, which fare as follows:

- 50 per cent not pursued.
- 10 per cent no case to answer, in the ASA's judgment.
- 30 per cent case to answer, but not upheld.
- 10 per cent upheld.

Complaints are not pursued for such reasons as a lack of sufficient information, that they have already been dealt with or that they concern broadcast advertising.

In 1978, the Advertising Association, the Office of Fair Trading and the Consumers' Association jointly commissioned an independent assessment of 3 000 press advertisements, which found that 93 per cent 'conformed to the spirit and letter of the British Code of Advertising Practice'.

Other elements of the promotional mix have been subject to formal regulation only comparatively recently. The standards and content of sales promotion campaigns are subject to the Advertising Standards Authority's British Code of Sales Promotion Practice, which requires users to 'provide substantiation for the conformity of their promotions' with the familiar basic principle that 'all promotions should be legal, decent, honest and truthful'. The nature of that conformity is elaborated in sections relating to protection of privacy; exaggeration; suitability and availability of promotional products; participation in promotions; administration. The ASA monitors promotional campaigns, spontaneously investigating 'any that appear questionable', and investigates complaints received which 'make out a prima facie case for thinking that the Code may have been contravened'.

Direct marketing initiatives come under the scrutiny of the Direct Marketing Association, which issued its first Code of Practice in 1993 as 'an instrument of self-discipline for Members', all of whom have accepted by formally adopting it that any 'breach of its conditions may be considered a disciplinary matter' and are obliged to support it in spirit as well as in the letter. Their obligations are defined as 'the use of selling methods that are consistent with the public interest, promises that are honest and intelligible, performance that matches promises, terms that are fair and equitable and products that match claims' and to 'respect the reasonable privacy and personal notions of taste of consumers'. They are furthermore required to comply with the British Code of Advertising Practice, the Advertising Association's Code of Practice on the Use of Personal Data for Advertising and the Direct Selling Association and the Video Standards Council, and to subscribe to the Mailing Preference Service and (when it becomes available) the Telephone Preference Service. Overt self-regulation has thus been finally extended to the area of promotion most likely to have been generally suspected of lax standards.

It seems fair to conclude from the considerable detail in this section that a comprehensive and effective system of formal regulation is applied in Britain today across the whole promotional mix.

EDITOR'S NOTE

The Institute of Practitioners in Advertising (IPA) continue to hold their biannual competition for Advertising Effectiveness. *Advertising Works 5* (London: Cassell) edited by Paul Feldwick was published in 1990, *Advertising Works 6* was published by NTC Publications in 1991 and *Advertising Works 7* was published in 1993 edited by Chris Baker. These publications continue to provide very substantial insights into how advertising works.

ESSENTIAL READING

Baker, C. (ed.) (1993), *Advertising Works 7*, Henley-on-Thames: NTC Publications Ltd. This is the 7th volume of case studies describing the IPA Advertising Effectiveness awards, a unique source for those interested in good advertising practice.

Broadbent, S. (1975), *Spending Advertising Money*, London: London Business School.

Corstjens, J. (1990), *Strategic Advertising: a practitioner's handbook*, Oxford: Heinemann.

Crosier, K. (1994), 'Marketing communications' in M.J. Baker (ed.), *Marketing: Theory and Practice*, 3rd edn, London: Macmillan.

30 Sales promotion

Tom Brannan

Special offer – Money off next purchase – 2 for the price of 1 – Buy now and get the optional widget free – Win a trip to the moon – Free fitting – 0% finance – Buy X: get a free Y!

All banner headlines which can be found on every high street, in any newspaper. All testimony to the burgeoning sales promotion industry – and all witness to both the fearsome level of competition in most market sectors and the unrelenting pressure on marketers to produce this week's/month's/quarter's sales, circumstances which have fuelled the growth of this specialist field.

The Institute of Sales Promotion defines the activity as follows: 'Sales promotion comprises a range of tactical marketing techniques designed within a strategic marketing framework to add value to a product or service in order to achieve specific sales and marketing objectives.' The key point of the definition lies in the phrase 'to add value'. That is the primary characteristic of sales promotion activity.

Published estimates suggest that sales promotion, in all its forms, represents the biggest single area of expenditure within marketing – the ISP suggests a figure of around £7 000 million a year. It is a powerful tool, it can be an expensive tool, and, on mercifully rare occasions, it can be dangerous enough seriously to threaten a company's health. But it is a tool with which every marketer should be familiar because it has a potential role for any product, in any market – and it can be aimed at any point in the distribution chain. Indeed, it is a major strength of sales promotion that it can be effective both at selling product into the chain and at pulling it through into the hands of consumers.

TYPES OF PROMOTION

The apparent multitude of promotional variants evident in the market-place can be classified into a relatively few broad categories: price promotions, extra product, premium offers, charitable contribution schemes and prize promotions.

Price promotions

These split into two sub-categories which might be described as discount offers, and added-product offers.

Discount offers are particularly prevalent in selling to distribution. In this sector of the market, common approaches include short-term discounts per case, price lists giving specific volume discounts – constructed so as to encourage higher average-order quantities, and discount structures based on total volume purchased over, typically, a 12-month period. Other variants are generally tailored to individual major accounts; for example, a discount given as an advertising allowance or in exchange for specific in-store display commitment by a retailer. Such tactics can be extremely useful both for winning and maintaining distribution.

As is evident in any High Street, price discounting is no rarity in consumer promotions either. In its simplest form, it consists of a reduction in the retail price of the product concerned. This can make eminent sense for a manufacturer which has achieved a production-cost breakthrough in advance of its competitors; the computer market has shown many examples in recent years. The marketing benefit can be increased market share, in effect at no damage to profits since the cost reduction balances the price reduction. Profits may in fact increase, at least until competitors' production techniques catch up.

On-pack price reductions are perhaps the most common manifestation of price cutting. They are most effective when the reduction is off the pack carrying the relevant flash. However, they can also work well as a 'money off next purchase' promotion. There is a cost to the greater effectiveness of the former in that all packs sold will be discounted, whereas in the latter form only a percentage of the flashed packs will result in a cost on the subsequent purchase. Either requires a fair amount of planning because of the need to print special packaging carrying the offer.

The third option in this area is the use of discount coupons which can be distributed by a number of methods such as leaflet drops door-to-door and coupons to be clipped from press advertisements. Coupon promotions are subject to specific regulation including declaration of a closing date and conditions of redemption. They can be launched fairly quickly since there are no production or packaging implications. One aspect of coupons has been much covered in writings on the subject, what is usually referred to as mal-redemption; namely when the retailer ignores the redemption conditions and allows the consumer the discount irrespective of whether the relevant product has been bought. This undoubtedly happens but not on a scale which invalidates the technique. A computer programme designed to match returns with retailers' stock positions (and advised to the trade in advance) can act as a meaningful deterrent though not necessarily an absolute control.

The last major form of cash discount is the cash-back offer, seen in everything from domestic house sales to schemes involving the collection of a given number of proofs of purchase such as bottle tops. This option is most often used to build consumer loyalty and repeat purchase. Payment will only be made on a percentage of the product sold since not every purchaser will collect the necessary elements to qualify. The scheme is fairly easy to administer since it does not involve third-party products as premiums yet it does deliver many of the benefits of other types of build-up promotion.

Extra product

One method of delivering additional value is to give more product for the same price. It is attractive to the manufacturer particularly because giving away £1 does not cost £1. There are two principal forms.

A larger amount at the same price is the first. Supermarket shelves frequently feature packs offering '25% extra, free'. Evidently, the extra product adds only production cost, not retail value, to the manufacturer's bill. So, perceived value is higher than the cost of creating it.

The second is the 'banded' pack: the additional quantity is literally banded to or packaged with the original product – the classic '2 for the price of 1'. Such an offer shares the cost and value perception advantages outlined above.

Extra-product offers do carry additional cost, in the shape of specific packaging in the former case and of special banding and outer cases in the latter. For that reason, both require considerable advance planning.

Premium offers

Premium offers also come in a variety of guises, from free offers to paid-for premiums, from on-pack offers to collection schemes. They can be based on the main product, on a second product from the manufacturer's range or on third-party products specifically purchased to support the promotion.

The simplest form of premium offer involves giving product away, with no purchase required. This is used to encourage trial by potential users. It may consist of delivering small test packs to households, or offering shoppers the opportunity to test or taste the product in-store. Free trial is often seen in airport duty-free areas where its objective is an immediate conversion to sale of the full-sized product.

An extension of the above is the banded offer, where a second product is banded to the main product. Using its own product, a manufacturer might offer a free bottle of fabric conditioner with its washing powder. As with any extra-product offer this creates high value at relatively low cost. It can also be extremely useful for encouraging trial of the second product.

Extensive use is also made of third-party products in premium offers. The offer can be banded (the free window cloth banded to the bottle of window cleaner), included in the prime pack (the free model car in the breakfast cereal), collected at the check-out point (the ubiquitous free glasses with petrol) or obtained by post in the case of collection promotions.

Each method of delivery has advantages and disadvantages. The banded offer shows well on the supermarket shelf and may even steal space from competitors. However, the packs can suffer from significant pilferage. In-pack offers suffer much less from pilferage but can cause real problems with packaging, especially when food products and their accompanying stringent regulations are involved. Check-out collection obviates the packaging issue but retailers generally dislike the inconvenience which it causes them. And postal redemption lacks the immediacy of the others but does eliminate the other problems.

An interesting aspect of premium offers which has shown considerable growth in recent years is the use of the pack itself as the premium: children's toys are sold in a free storage box, coffee comes in a free storage jar. A paradoxical development is the product without a pack. In this case the original product packaging is re-usable; only refills need be purchased subsequently. The premium is the lack of a pack!

Finally, there is the mis-named self-liquidating offer. The principle itself is straightforward: the manufacturer buys in a premium at a substantial, negotiated discount on retail price and passes that saving on to those prepared to buy the requisite quantity of the manufacturer's product to qualify for the offer. The costs of promoting such offers, the need to buy in more than the amount strictly estimated for redemption and yet to hold the price down in order to maintain a high-value perception mean that they rarely genuinely pay for themselves. Recent experience shows that redemption rates are generally low and the effect on sales very limited, hence their rapid decline except in cases where budgets are so tight that there are very few alternatives.

Charitable contribution schemes

Like refillable containers, such schemes are becoming more numerous in response to changing mores. They involve the promoter making a specific donation to a named charity for every product purchased. The 'premium' can be described only in emotional terms; it is the feeling of lending support to a worthy cause by the purchasing decision.

These schemes are attractive from the promoters' viewpoint in that they are simple to administer and associate very positive values with the brand concerned. However, as with the on-pack discount, they are relatively expensive since there is an additional cost to every unit sold.

Prize promotions

English law splits prize promotions into the four categories of lotteries, draws, games and competitions. And regulates each with a fairly iron fist. Few areas of marketing labour under the weight of as much legislation as these types of promotion.

A lottery involves the sale of opportunities to enter a random draw for a specific prize. Premium Bonds are a well-known example. In truth they are of little interest to most promoters since legislation restricts them to being used only for small, local, non-commercial schemes.

533

Prize draws are identical to lotteries with the exception that no entry fee is charged. Indeed entry cannot even be tied to a product purchase qualification.

The regulations for prize draws also apply to games; the two are essentially the same since neither requires any application of significant skill or judgement.

Competitions demand that the entrant use skill or judgement as part of the entry. In this case a purchase may be a condition of entry.

The differences between the types of prize promotion are best highlighted by example. The tombola stall at the local village fair is a lottery since participants pay for the tickets which give them the opportunity to win. The exhibitor at the NEC with the sign saying 'Drop in your business card for the chance to win a bottle of champagne' is running a prize draw. The travel agent offering a holiday to the person who can identify pictures of five cities and give the best tie-breaker phrase is running a competition. The newspaper Bingo promotion is a game.

ANY PRODUCT, ANY MARKET

Several myths surround sales promotion: it is only for consumer products, it only works on low-priced items, it is a very down-market approach. Vestiges of the 'plastic tulip' image live on. Such misconceptions are readily and objectively refuted by examining some of the many successful promotions run in recent years.

The sheer level of promotional noise in the computer press indicates just how widely sales promotion is used in selling to businesses. Both manufacturers and retailers frequently offer bundled packages of computer plus peripherals and software at a discounted, package price. Airlines are avid users of frequent-flier programmes aimed directly at the travelling business executive. Charities are increasingly sophisticated users of all marketing techniques, including sales promotion.

The 'low-priced products' belief is easily dispelled by reference to the free test drive or sun-roof at no extra cost offered by car manufacturers. Or by considering the free carpets and curtains – or even the guaranteed trade-in price used as an incentive in the housing market.

And those old plastic tulips were not quite in the same quality league as one recent promotion by British Airways where Garrads crystal was the incentive to fly First Class.

TACTICAL OR STRATEGIC

In its infancy, sales promotion was almost exclusively a tactical weapon. Its function was to generate short-term sales boosts as and when such were needed. In this role it continues to be a useful and potentially powerful part of the marketer's armoury. But, as the concept of the 'brand' grew, so did the recognition that promotional activity cannot be treated as if it were working in a vacuum apart from the rest of the company's marketing effort.

The critical nature of brand value to corporate well-being is now widely (if not quite universally) understood. The brand image which gives rise to that value must therefore be carefully nurtured both now and in the long term. And short-term, tactical activities must be conceived with that very much in mind. For, whether consciously or subconsciously, sales promotion will have a strategic effect; it will influence brand image.

Finding the strategic fit

There are two keys to effective strategic use of promotions. The first is to ensure they have a clearly identified role which is set in a context of the jobs to be done by other elements of the marketing mix. To illustrate using an earlier example, British Airways might use advertising to achieve overall image objectives, direct mail to encourage trial use of new routes and services, and sales promotions to encourage upgrading and develop passenger loyalty. The second key is to submit each proposed programme to rigorous scrutiny against the target brand image.

Protecting the brand

While both are important, the latter is crucial. A carefully grown brand commanding a price premium over its rivals will soon lose its cachet if it is seen to be subject to constant price-cutting. The BA promotion with Garrads worked because the right associations existed between the products. Substitute Ratners for Garrads and consider whether the same effectiveness would have resulted. Free carpets may be right for promoting house sales but a substantial discount offer will devalue the remainder of the development.

Marketing magazine, in April 1993, published a checklist used for guidance on promotions by Toshiba. The first item read: '*Don't bet the company*'. This was in the immediate aftermath of the Hoover fiasco in which a free flights offer had gone disastrously wrong, to the extent that it cost Hoover around £20 million of unbudgeted expenditure to meet its obligations. Yet the true cost may not be accurately measurable since it is the damage done to the reputation of the company and the values which were inherent in its brand name. The Toshiba maxim sums up the potential risk succinctly.

REDUCING THE RISK

There are two main risk areas in any promotion: the legal and the financial. There are, likewise, two elements to reducing the risk: know the relevant regulations and don't leave sales promotions under the exclusive control of the marketing department!

Staying legal

A whole panoply of regulations touches on sales promotion. They range from

535

what might be called general business law, including the Sale of Goods Act, the Supply of Goods and Services Act, and various Trade Descriptions acts, to more specific law such as the Consumer Credit Act, the Gaming Act, the Mail Order Transactions Order, the Price Marking (Bargain Offers) Order and the Lotteries and Amusements Act. It is not difficult for the inexperienced to get lost in this legislative maze. If the company does not have in-house expertise in this area, that alone would be good reason to use an experienced agency for guidance.

Promotional concepts can be checked for legality in advance of execution. A number of stages should be followed:

- Obtain a copy of The British Code of Sales Promotion Practice from the CAP Committee, Brook House, 2–16 Torrington Place, London WC1E 7HN and ensure the concept complies.
- Contact any trade associations in your sector and obtain any relevant codes of practice.
- Submit the concept together with any promotional copy and visuals, and relevant written conditions of the promotion to the CAP Committee. The CAP offer a free and fast copy-checking service.
- If in any doubt, take advice from a specialist in sales promotion law.

The issue becomes a great deal more complex for the company considering international promotions. Even within the European Union there is enormous variation in the types of promotion allowed within specific countries. This really is a time to take expert advice, ideally from a specialist agency with offices in all relevant countries.

Calculating the finances

The ideal team working on a sales promotion project would include representation from marketing, finance, legal and commercial departments.

Marketing's job is as team leader and guardian of the brand. He or she is responsible for agreeing the objectives, judging whether the proposed concepts can meet them, ensuring that the final proposal is in keeping with the brand values, and for executing the project.

The finance expert is there to confirm that the numbers make good business sense – and as devil's advocate to the normally optimistic views of the marketing department!

The legal representative provides expert opinion on the issues mentioned earlier. Finally, the commercial specialist must tie up clearly defined contract terms with any other parties to the promotion, whether agencies, handling houses or suppliers of products to be used as premiums. Only with such expertise on the team can all areas of risk be effectively covered.

The major cost areas which must be given detailed attention fall into four key areas:

- *The product:* includes an evaluation of the physical product to be used, the cost of any discounts, any special packaging requirements and an estimate of any disruption costs on the production line.
- *The sales promotion:* covering agency fees, the purchase and stockholding of any premiums (and of the possible subsequent disposal of any excess), the administration and fulfilment of the scheme with attendant handling, coupon redemption and postage costs, and the cost of in-store display materials.
- *Promoting the promotion:* covering all advertising development and media costs and any others related to maximizing the effectiveness of the scheme.
- *Evaluation:* of the results is the final key area to be taken into consideration. Sales promotion can be a valuable tool if well used. A fundamental part of using it well is the process of learning from each effort and applying that learning to the next promotion. Full, objective and rigorous evaluation is an essential element of any promotion – and must be funded sufficiently.

DEVELOPING THE RIGHT PROMOTION

As with any aspect of marketing, successful sales promotion is invariably the result of a combination of clear objectives, good planning, meticulous execution – and a healthy dose of creativity. So setting the objectives is the start point.

Setting the objectives

One important aspect of promotional work is its intrinsic measurability. Clearly, that only becomes of value when standards of measurement are set. Therefore the role definition developed as part of the marketing strategy must be distilled into defined, quantified and time-limited objectives for each specific promotion. It is also likely that part of this exercise will be a re-confirmation of the particular promotion's tactical job within the overall strategy.

The following would constitute typical, and valid, objectives:

- To boost sales of Brand X by 10 per cent above the seasonal norm in Week 26.
- To smooth out monthly production by selling Y units into the trade during the normally quiet months of July and August.
- To achieve 15 per cent more shelf space in at least five major retailers during the peak season in November and December.
- To persuade z000 non-users to test Brand X by the end of March.

The above all share the essential characteristics of any promotion objective, except one. There is one further element: the budget. The promotions team must calculate what the value of achieving the objective is to the company, then decide how much of that sum it is prepared to invest. This is where financial expertise really comes into play, for the calculations can involve analyses of warehousing cost, the cost of money, the penalty cost of inefficient, off-season production, and a dozen other factors.

Determining the candidate tactics

Each type of promotion has particular strengths and weaknesses. Air miles schemes, for example, are very good at building customer loyalty but are generally weaker at creating a short-term increase in sales to new customers. However, a short-term 'promotion within a promotion' which offers, say, double the normal number of miles on a specific route can have an immediate effect. Charity promotions are strong on supporting advertising in building corporate or brand reputation but do not tend to work across the whole population in raising sales. Price discounting can be fast and effective but its effect on brand values needs close watching.

For those not totally familiar with the options, the advice of a reputable sales promotion agency is invaluable at this stage, both from the point of view of determining the correct tactic and from assessing whether, from their experience across a wide range of promotions, the objectives are achievable within the confines of the given budget. Their thought process will start from the objective set and compare the available methodologies to identify those which are the strongest candidates to meet that objective. The following is a somewhat simplified analysis of how various promotion types are suited to some of the most common promotional aims. Naturally the analysis starts with the objective in each case.

Objective: short-term sales increase

Price reductions – whether straightforward on-pack offers or price reductions, or disguised as free-product offers – are more powerful in this arena. They offer an immediate reward to the purchaser and are thus most likely to provoke a positive change in purchasing habits. Delayed price reductions such as 'money off next pack' promotions or collector schemes are probably the next most powerful techniques for boosting sales volume quickly. Charitable contribution schemes can also work, but probably only with a section of the population. It stands to reason that, if the target market has a strong affinity with the benefiting charity, this can be a highly effective approach.

Objective: building loyalty

There are several candidate approaches to keeping existing customers and encouraging further purchases. Delayed offers and charity schemes can both be effective as can 'club' concepts. These range from the relatively simple offer such as might be found when buying a new version of a piece of computer software (upgrade to version 4.3 for just £XX), to fully set-up clubs giving access to cheap and/or exclusive products. The book and wine markets feature numerous successful examples. One intermediate version of the club approach is the collectable promotion; this offers many of the loyalty-building benefits without the administrative structure needed for a formal club. Conversely this fails to create the sense of belonging which is a critical element of the genuine club.

The increasing sophistication of database marketing has given added impetus to a raft of new opportunities for loyalty-building activities. Thus holders of credit cards from the major stores are offered 'private' viewings of new season stock, and we witness the burgeoning growth of in-house magazines designed to maintain regular communication – and selling opportunities – with existing customers.

Objective: encourage trial purchase

Free sampling must inevitably be the most successful approach since it guarantees to put the product into the consumers' hands. It is frequently used in the software market in an interestingly modified form: the user is given a trial disk with a working demonstration version of the programme so they can use the 'real' product and be encouraged to buy the full version.

Other effective techniques include on-pack price offers and banded offers (the latter are of course a variation of sampling but to a smaller, self-selecting audience). Games and prize draws have also been shown to generate trial.

Generating the creative idea

The vast majority of companies do not have in-house creative teams and will turn at this point to a specialist consultancy. The consultancy team will only produce good work from a good brief which must contain the following information:

- The objective, as defined earlier, covering the business problem or opportunity, the job of the specific promotion in dealing with that, the quantified target and the time-scale in which it must be achieved.
- The details of the budget allocated for the exercise.
- The history of the brand including sales figures and patterns, and all relevant research into consumer perceptions and attitudes related to the brand.
- Details of the target market, describing people not statistics. Creative teams do not deal in the abstraction of 'markets'. They create concepts to prompt a reaction in ordinary consumers, so make every effort to help them understand the views, needs, aspirations and motivations of the target customer.
- Information on the competitive environment and competitors' recent and current activity.
- Details and evaluation analyses of any previous promotions on the brand.
- Details of all current other marketing activity on the brand.

- Finally, any relevant guidelines or restrictions on items such as logo use, copy style and so on.

The creative team will digest this information prior to going through a series of brainstorming sessions to produce a first raft of ideas. By a process of distillation and development, the agency will arrive at a proposal to the client.

Assessing the proposal

Judging any creative proposal is a skill which is partly innate but is, in the main, learned. Its key element is the ability to put yourself into the role of a member of your target market, so you can view the work, as far as possible, through their eyes. That particular skill is essential to sound assessment of the proposal; the marketer in the client team should have that skill.

The process has several stages:

- Note your first reaction – it is the closest you will come to reacting like a consumer. Is it positive?
- Review the work against the brief. Does it address the brief fully?
- Are you convinced that it is capable of achieving the objective?
- Is it appropriate to the brand?
- Is it relatively original – at least in so far as it does not resemble work done by a competitor?

If the proposal has survived thus far, it has real potential. It is time to look more closely at the mechanics. Check the scheme for any legal pitfalls. If it clears this hurdle, then examine the practical aspects of implementation such as any implications for production, packaging and administration. Finally, define precisely how success will be measured bearing in mind the particular technique being recommended.

Tying up the details

This last phase lies in the hands of the commercial specialist in the team. All necessary third-party involvement in the promotion must be defined in detail, those companies found and watertight contracts drawn up and signed.

At last, you can run the promotion!

PROMOTING THE PROMOTION

As must be evident by now, successful promotions do not just happen; they result from a great deal of thought and effort. Yet, even after all the work so far, we are not finished since a promotion can only work if it actually reaches the market at which it is aimed. Like any marketing message, it must be communicated.

The first target for communications activity is the trade. If distributors or retailers are not enthused by a promotion, they can make it very difficult for a manufacturer to succeed. The converse is equally true: if a manufacturer takes exception to a retailer's promotional use of its products, it can make things tough for the retailer – often in spite of legal constraints aimed at preventing such hindrance. In either case, a big, nationally powerful brand will inevitably find distributor support easier to obtain than will a lesser-known brand. In the latter's case, it is advisable to use types of promotion which involve the minimum of inconvenience to the trading partner.

Promotion to the trade generally uses a mix of media which ranges from advertising in specialist press right down to arming the salesforce with the right presentation materials to sell the concept.

Communicating with the end-consumer can involve significant expenditure. Sales promotion uses all conventional advertising media including television, press, radio, direct mail, telemarketing and posters. It also has a whole range of media which are virtually exclusive to itself. These include door-to-door sampling and in-store demonstrations.

The consumer communications programme is critical from two aspects: it is a major influence on how well distribution will support the promotion, and it is fundamental to ultimate achievement of the objective amongst consumers.

Particularly notable promotions can create a great deal of additional publicity at relatively low cost, through press coverage. An imaginative promotion can generate high journalistic interest. But, a word of warning, a badly run promotion can generate even more!

FULFILLING THE PROMISE

Which brings us to the final and perhaps most important aspect of any promotion: the need for the delivery to live up to the expectation created of it.

A great man once said, 'You can fool some of the people some of the time...'. But, in sales promotion you cannot afford even to do that. The consumer is not a fool; he or she is you. In the UK, consumers are slow to complain when they have received inferior service (although that too is changing). However, they will and do vote with their feet. It is a foolish company which uses as a premium a product which does not match the quality and value perception of its own. Or which fails to guarantee its sources of supply before launching a promotion. The promise made must be met, in every aspect – or the real cost of the promotion may be devaluation of the brand.

ESSENTIAL READING

Circus, P. and Painter, A. (1989), *Sales Promotion Law – A Practical Guide*, London: Butterworth.

Lawson, R. (1987), *Sales Promotion Law*, Oxford: Blackwell.

Riso, Ovid (ed.) (1982), *Sales Promotion Handbook*, 7th edn, Chicago: The Dartnell Corporation.

Toop, A. (1992), *European Sales Promotion – Great Campaigns in Action*, London: Kogan Page.

31 Direct mail

Derek Holder

If direct mail did not exist modern marketers would have to invest billions of pounds to invent it, such is its importance and uniqueness in today's marketing mix. The fact is, no other medium (direct mail *is* primarily a medium) offers marketers anything like the combination of benefits available through direct mail, or the versatility which those benefits afford.

For a start, how many other advertising media can separate regular customers from likely customers, lapsed customers from resistant prospects – and treat each to a truly personal advertising message, with its own product, offer, tone of voice, timing and budget? And which other advertising medium, having identified its target audiences, can appeal to them with all five of the senses through which human beings communicate: sight, sound, touch, taste and smell?

By now, astute readers may already have answered 'telephone' to the question of selective media and 'sales promotion' to the question of versatility. But direct mail remains indisputably the only medium capable of both individual targeting *and* conveying the most complex five-dimensional message.

That, in a nutshell, is what makes direct mail unique.

THE ADVANTAGES

Before looking at direct mail's many and diverse uses, let us briefly remind ourselves of its chief features and advantages.

Selectivity

Whatever the nature of an organization, or its size, one of its goals should always be to concentrate its marketing investment on its better customers and prospects, whilst simultaneously reducing or eliminating waste elsewhere.

Lord Leverhulme is often quoted for his observation that half of his advertising budget was wasted, but since he did not know which half, he dared not trim it. Had he been able to use direct mail he would have been even more successful.

Today, far from being a theoretical ideal, the selection and promotion of best prospects is a reality for serious users of direct mail. Several British insurance companies regularly mail their best prospects with tailor-made proposals which take into account individual prospects' age, marital status, intended retirement date, affordable monthly outlay, and so on – data either given them by prospects for the purpose or otherwise gleaned from customers' prior transactions. Laser printing permits these personalized entries in what are otherwise stock letters and application forms.

True, conscientious sales representatives have always been able to supply a similar level of personal service. What direct mail does so effectively is lower the cost and increase the range of their selling efforts – whether or not other channels of distribution are also employed.

Communication unlimited

Most advertising media are subject to constraints of size, space, lack of colour, or some other restriction. Direct mail, properly used, suffers almost no such constraints. It is an ideal communication vehicle.

Earlier the five senses were referred to, and doubtless a few eyebrows were raised at the notions of smell and taste as advantages of direct mail. It may surprise dyed-in-the-wool adherents of press and television advertising to learn that several of marketing's all-time success stories have made heavy use of direct mail precisely because of its ability to convey taste and smell.

What better way to extol the virtues of cheese or coffee, for example, than by sending a small sample of the product itself to known gourmets? One British copywriter claims to have created the world's first edible mailing by printing the entire text of a letter about catering equipment using food dyes on rice paper!

In the USA, Giorgio perfumes chose direct mail and loose inserts in magazines to disseminate scratch-and-sniff samplers, as well as real samples, and in so doing took itself to national brand leader in barely three years.

At its simplest, direct mail is salesmanship in print. Typically a mailing comprises a letter, brochure, order form and reply device (envelope or card) in an outer carrier. But even at this most basic level it offers communicators several important benefits. For example, there is virtually no limit on the length or complexity of message that direct mail can convey (far more helpful and communicative than the average shop assistant). Should an aural or moving demonstration of a product or service be required, then why not simply enclose a video or audio cassette?

One of the most conclusive demonstrations of direct mail's scope is the catalogue. A catalogue can display and extol the virtues of literally hundreds, even thousands, of product lines – more than a medium-sized department store let alone a mere advertisement.

Accountability

The most frequently cited appeal of direct mail among business managers is its accountability. This stems from the ease, accuracy, and speed with which mailing costs can be compared to responses to produce the vital direct-mail yardsticks of profit and loss, for example cost per order, cost per enquiry, average order value, enquiries-to-sales conversion percentage, estimated life-time value of customer, and so on. The likely outcome of a mailing carried out one week can often be accurately predicted the next, even though replies continue to arrive for several weeks or even months.

Linked to the subject of accountability is another direct-mail benefit: on-line testing. No other medium offers so much scope for split-sample comparisons and fine-tuning, often at nil cost, since the tests are carried out as part of the regular mailing programme. Reliable estimates of future customer behaviour can frequently be deduced directly from test results.

Controllability

Just like the flame in the British Gas commercials, direct mail activity can be switched on and off at will. If business is booming, mail activity can be quickly halted to allow production to catch up; if the warehouse is bulging, additional mailing activity can be mounted to take up the slack. Not the best example of efficient planning, maybe, but very real in practice.

Mailing activity, unlike space advertising, can also be readily contained within geographical areas, and these areas can be further refined by the application of demographic data. An area can be as small as a single postcode, no more than 15 houses. The result – low volumes, high responses – is a realizable goal for the skilled direct mailer.

In contrast, enquiries and sales generated by press and television advertisements, and public relations activity in particular, frequently overwhelm advertisers and lead to complaints, lost orders, escalating fulfilment costs, lowered staff morale, and so on.

In many other areas of control – quality, costs, timing, legality, and so on – direct mail is eminently controllable. Another resultant benefit is that centralized mailing campaigns can be directed at end-users over the heads of agents, stockists and so on – activity which, if left to the intermediaries, might never happen. This is especially useful when directed to overseas prospects, thus avoiding interminable multi-language negotiations with recalcitrant agents and distributors which often characterize this type of initiative.

Privacy and convenience

The personal and private nature of direct mail is appreciated by buyers and marketers alike. To the buyer or end-user, direct mail offers the ideal means of weighing up and ordering products or services which, for whatever reason, they do not wish to discuss or order in a shop or showroom. The concept of   *545* privacy always arouses visions of dubious products in the proprietary medicine and self-improvement fields, and of course the embarrassment factor does account for some direct mail applications. But there are numerous other occasions when customers prefer to deal anonymously with a direct mail marketer – not necessarily for reasons of privacy but also for convenience, and sometimes because direct mail offers better value, having eliminated several layers of middlemen.

It is easy to overlook the convenience that direct mail offers when one lives in a well-stocked city. For many people in rural communities, the elderly, the shift worker, expatriates and so on, direct mail can be a welcome contact with the outside world. One reason often given for its success is that, for some, a friendly sales letter is infinitely better than having the postman pass them by completely.

To the marketer, direct mail offers a means of advertising, selling, and research which is virtually impossible for competitors to monitor, copy or sabotage – simply because they never know when or where it is taking place, or what levels of success it is attracting.

Low outlay

Make no mistake, *prima facie*, direct mail is an expensive method of communication. On a per-capita basis it is possibly *the* most expensive medium after telephone marketing, (although it has a long way to go to match the £200 plus reckoned to be the minimum cost of a personal sales visit).

However, in terms of actual outlay, direct mail can be operated on the smallest of budgets. For example, a mailing to 2 000 prospects for a specialized product valued at thousands of pounds, may cost as little as £2 000 – and still be far more effective than ten times that budget scattered across an assortment of technical and business magazines. One international mailer in the computer field reckons direct mail to be 30 times more effective than the equivalent weight of press advertising.

It works!

Direct mail is a powerful, proven medium. It carries carefully targeted messages into the homes and on to the desks of selected prospects; it tells a full, convincing story; it provides for an immediate response – and it works. Whatever ill-informed critics may say, direct mail delivers.

Take, for example, the case of the well-known publishers, Reader's Digest. Direct mail incorporating large full-colour broadsheets enables the promoters to fully demonstrate the quality, value and sheer size of their excellent reference books. Coupled to worthwhile and genuine incentives, directed to prospects known to enjoy such books, direct mail delivers sales volumes for the Digest's reference books that many paperback fiction writers envy.

So delighted were Midland Bank with the results obtained from their first forays into direct mail, they were encouraged to press ahead with the launch of First Direct, a bank which transacts virtually all its business with customers by direct mail and telephone – a method which permits advantageous terms when compared with bricks-and-mortar banks.

On the international front, Gillette launched its Papermate 'Non-Stop' propelling pencil entirely by direct mail. How? Simply by despatching free samples to the chief executives, secretaries, and stationery buyers of Europe's largest companies. The samples were supported by a superbly illustrated letter (no brochure), written in the prospects' own languages – and accompanied by a questionnaire. What better demonstration of direct mail's power than this £150 000 campaign that opened up massive markets in no less than 13 countries simultaneously, using a campaign entirely directed from the UK?

WHAT IS DIRECT MAIL?

Direct mail, as already noted, is a medium – in other words a vehicle for delivering advertisements direct from advertiser to potential buyer or end-user. The advertisements themselves can take many forms amounting to almost anything that can be transported by mail – literally from a postcard to a stuffed elephant.

One of the alleged weaknesses of direct mail is its frequent 'sameness' and general lack of flair and excitement. There is really no excuse for this since direct mail offers more scope than any medium other than television, and even that is arguable. The fault often lies in the unimaginative minds of those who set the budgets, not realizing that having spent £250 to post a thousand mailings, it is a false economy to allow only £10 per thousand for the actual contents being despatched – but it happens.

APPLICATIONS

Direct mail applications can be categorized according to two brief pairs of objectives:

1 Direct selling *or* sales support.
2 Customer acquisition *or* retention.

All direct mail activity can be further described as either consumer or business-to-business. 99 per cent of applications fit at least three of those criteria, as shown in Figure 31.1.

Direct sales

Historically, direct mail has been the favoured medium of the direct-sell organizations: the 'Big 5' catalogue companies (GUS, Littlewoods, Grattan, Freemans and Empire Stores), the subscription publishers (for example, Reader's Digest, Time-Life), the collectables (Franklin Mint), and, since about 1980, the huge financial services sector comprising banks, building societies, insurers and investment houses.

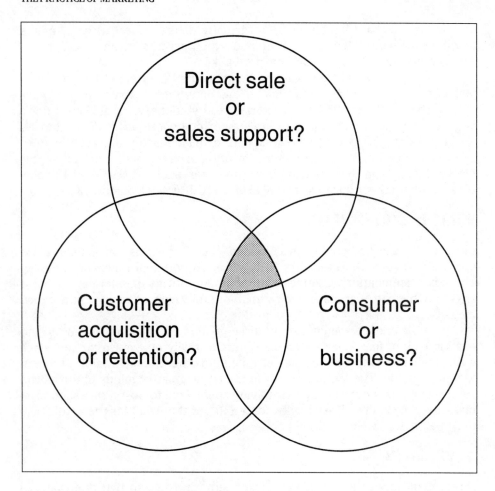

Figure 31.1   Direct mail: the three pairs of applications

More recently, large-scale direct selling by mail has been adopted by computer and office equipment suppliers, housewares specialists (for example, Kleeneze) and specialist clothing suppliers (Lands' End and Racing Green) – all of whom employ comprehensive catalogues. Smaller specialized traders have, of course, relied upon direct sales for decades, one reason being the refusal of retailers to stock their products. Usually they will use advertising to identify prospects initially before following up with direct mail.

Direct selling used to be termed 'mail order', an outdated and misleading term that still frequently haunts exponents of advanced direct mail. The solicitation of funds by charities (mail order in reverse) accounts for a further slice of direct mail activity – as does the solicitation of votes by political parties.

One of the chief advantages of selling via the mail is that it dispenses with the need for, and overcomes the drawbacks of, intermediaries – for example, agents, distributors, retailers and, it must be said, one's own salesforce, who may not always be the best advocates of every product in their company's repertoire.

Support

When not deployed as a direct-sales medium, direct mail is an ideal support activity for other forms of advertising and distribution. In this respect it has much in common with large areas of modern sales promotion practice, and so close have the two activities grown that there is often virtually no dividing line. A new term – 'direct promotion' – has emerged in recognition of this overlap. If a dividing line is sought, it lies between sales promotion's concentration on short-term results and direct mail's potential to engage customers in a lifelong dialogue.

Direct mail to customers and end-users, not forgetting specifiers (such as architects, doctors and so on), may be employed to promote awareness in much the same way as space advertising, but with a sharper focus. Other important applications include: generating enquiries and sales leads for follow-up by further mail, telephone or personal sales calls; directing prospects to stockists, exhibitions and the like; and, increasingly, postal research, a new development in direct mail expertise.

A very effective application of direct mail is in conjunction with other direct-response media. One of the best UK multi-media response campaigns was that conducted by British Gas for its privatization offer which used television, press advertising, direct mail, and public relations to enhance and support each other for maximum synergy.

Other regular direct mail users have successfully tested its booster effect when coupled with newspaper and magazine advertising, television, radio, door-to-door, point-of-sale and on-pack offers.

Acquisition

The acquisition of new customers by direct mail, in truth, is not always cost-efficient. Many established and committed direct-mail users enrolled most of their first-time buyers through couponed newspaper and magazine advertisements, retail outlets, guarantee cards, telephone surveys, promotion redemptions, and the like.

What direct mail excels at in the case of consumer marketing is maintaining the on-going relationship once it has been established, which should be every marketer's long-term goal. However, in the case of business-to-business marketing, the position reverses. There is little doubt that direct mail is the most cost-efficient means of recruiting new business customers and end-users, and of influencing specifiers and opinion-formers (such as purchasing officers and politicians). The ensuing dialogue will almost certainly be maintained through personal sales visits and the telephone as well as direct mail.

Direct sales do, however, occur in the business arena. Books, conferences and seminars, for example, are best sold via direct mail. Several successful 549 operators (for example, Inmac) attract large volumes of phone and mail orders for computer peripherals from catalogues and brochures mailed direct to prospects.

Retention

Direct mail is the ideal medium through which to maintain an ongoing dialogue with customers and prospects, whether consumer or business, once these have been identified. Frequently mail will be used in conjunction with an inbound telephone facility through which customers can check on deliveries and the status of their account, as well as ask questions and air their concerns about an organization's products and service.

Many exponents report excellent results from the periodic despatch of newsletters and bulletins which dispense information and ideas as well as represent customers' news and views. The aim, clearly, is to ensure the advertiser is not forgotten between purchases which, in the case of cars for example, may be several years apart. Sometimes simply recording one's thanks for past support is enough to keep a relationship alive. Once a newsletter reaches a worthwhile level of penetration into a market it can be as effective as advertising bought in publishers' media, at a fraction of the cost and with no direct competition.

Direct mail is also widely used to induce a more mechanical form of loyalty; for example frequent-buyer reward schemes are sometimes offered by direct mail and kept refreshed through follow-up communications featuring special offers, discounts, and other incentives.

'Pampers' is perhaps the best, and certainly one of the earliest, consumer applications of loyalty direct mail. Beginning with the registration of mothers-to-be, Procter & Gamble maintain a constant dialogue with parents throughout their nappy-buying years. Although many collect-and-reward schemes are administered at the point-of-sale (for example, Esso petrol vouchers), P & G prefer to conduct the Pampers scheme directly with their customers, and direct mail is the only medium that can unite seller and buyer in this way. The actual product is bought and sold through the usual retail stockists – only the reward scheme is operated direct.

In the business market-place, direct mail and telephone are used to maintain contact with customers who cannot be visited regularly by salespersons. At considerably less than £5 per contact (perhaps as little as 50p), direct mail is the perfect means for maintaining a dialogue with customers whose business does not merit frequent sales visits and who may not be readily contactable by telephone.

Retention is not, of course, simply about 'staying in touch'. Regular communication may be the vehicle through which incremental sales continue to be made – including the cross-selling of related merchandise and up-selling of higher value alternatives to goods already purchased. The renewal of periodic contracts (for example, subscriptions, licences, annual premiums, and so on) is greatly assisted by well-timed anti-attrition direct mail, and specially attractive offers designed to head off any chance of the customer deciding against renewal when it falls due.

LISTS

Direct mail is distinct from other forms of advertising and promotion in that it is always addressed and almost always carries the name or job function of the intended recipient. Not unnaturally, therefore, the planning process often begins with the list.

Lists can be obtained from many sources. A company's own customer records (house list) may be the start point. Lists can also be purchased or rented from list companies, or compiled from directories. By far the most responsive lists in consumer marketing are those compiled from buyers or enquirers for related merchandise. Any evidence that a person enjoys direct mail and responds to it bodes well for further mail activity. Connections, however, are not always obvious. The skilled list consultant may suggest, for example, that shareholders who own stock in several companies are ripe for an offer of fine wines, and so on.

Lists are also compiled from lifestyle data volunteered by consumers – lifestyle, in this case, meaning essentially shopping habits, hobbies and general interests. Excellent lists can also be arrived at by comparing readily-available lists with criteria established for customers, a process known as 'profiling'.

Business lists tend to be based upon highly segmented subscriber data made available by the specialist publications – one of the main reasons why business direct mail is so effective. For example, the readers of a technical magazine can be segmented by industry, job function, size of business, location, and much more. This is why direct mail to selected subscribers is usually far more cost-effective than advertising in the same journal with its unavoidable waste.

Both consumer and business lists arranged specifically for mailing purposes will already be properly formatted, whether on disc or tape, or offered as ready-prepared labels. Lists made up from miscellaneous sources, for example unprocessed coupons or guarantee cards, require expert computerization before they are usable for mailing in any quantity above the low hundreds.

Direct mail may look simple to produce but the opportunities for error are legion. One common error is to mail new-customer offers to people whose names are already in your best-customer file. For this reason a process known as merge/purge is an essential step if one is mailing several lists which may contain duplicated names or the names of one's own active customers. Merge/purge itself requires expert list preparation before it can be carried out, chiefly because of the many and varied formats which people use for their own addresses.

THE DATABASE

Since the 1960s computers have revolutionized the business of direct mail. At the least sophisticated level they enable mailing lists to be rid of duplicates, or merge/purged as discussed. Computers also enable envelopes and letters to be personalized in conjunction with laser printers, and allow names to be selected according to any combination of pre-determined characteristics (for example, mothers aged 25–40 living in Wolverhampton and known to enjoy armchair shopping).

On-line computers have brought about the development of true databases: complete customer records which are constantly updated and which are accessed not only by marketing personnel but also by management generally. Databases can be set up to take management 'decisions'; for example, when a customer's record reaches a pre-determined status, a campaign can be automatically triggered including the timing, choice of product and so on to be mailed.

The terms 'database' and 'list' are frequently confused but, however one defines them, it is impossible to carry out a direct mail campaign until a satisfactory list of names has been output by one means or other. Thus it is as well to consult a list consultant or reputable broker before contemplating a direct mail programme for the first time.

Just as lists can sometimes be inadequate, it can also be a mistake to invest in an elaborate and expensive database when the real need is a simple list of prospects' names. Consultants tell of several international organizations who have invested millions of pounds to build databases which have never been used for their intended purpose, but have delivered only lists at the end of the day.

CREATIVITY IN DIRECT MAIL

Direct mail, without doubt, presents a golden opportunity for creatives to break out of the one-dimensional strait-jacket that affects many other advertising media. At its most basic, direct mail offers the skilled writer a chance to exercise his or her persuasive skills in the all-important letter. Many *very* successful direct mail campaigns have been conducted with only a letter. Usually a letter will boost response to other enclosures. Letter-writing is a skill which can be learned, although many entrepreneurs produce first-rate letters for their own businesses simply because of their product knowledge and enthusiasm.

Beyond the letter (subject to the budget, of course), the sky is the limit. Direct mail campaigns have been carried out employing the most spectacular and bizarre of formats. One case, possibly apocryphal, talks of homing pigeons being employed instead of reply envelopes! Pop-up folders, coins, litmus tests, working models, lace handkerchiefs – these are just a small selection of the added-interest enclosures that can make direct mail appealing to receive. On a more serious note, business mailings often contain valuable industry reports and surveys. In business and consumer direct mail, incentives such as prize draws have also found a permanent role.

Nevertheless, some age-old rules of direct mail, born in the heyday of mail order, still apply. For example, the chief weakness of direct mail is that it calls for a commitment from recipients even though they may never have seen or spoken with anyone from the sales company. Despite the best copy and illustrations, buyers may well not be able to envisage the true worth of a product or a service before ordering it – which might be too late. So a great deal of creative effort in direct mail is devoted to providing reassurance, answering unspoken questions, offering guarantees, and so on. Some direct mail users devote as much as 70 per cent of their sales effort to providing reassurance. If an offer is accompanied by a request for cash with order, reassurance is not only desirable but paramount and required by law. The result is frequently long copy. The direct mail creative's task is to make that long copy not merely palatable but enjoyable.

Another important quality of effective direct mail is the ease with which respondents can understand and act upon it. The skilled creative quickly develops an eye and an ear for ways of encouraging response and for overcoming lingering objections from potential recruits. Encouraging response may entail applied psychology as in persuasive copy, or simply making responses easier, for example by the layout of an order form or reply coupon.

THE MECHANICS

Once a suitable list has been acquired and the components prepared, direct mail is usually processed by a mailing house or lettershop. Here letters may be personalized by laser printing, and then inserted into outer envelopes along with between two and 22 or more other components. It is not unusual for a mailing to include ten or more separate enclosures, so efficient organization at the mailing house is vital. A large mailing house will have special machines for folding, nesting and inserting components into envelopes (Phillipsbergs) and for attaching labels (Cheshires). Small mailing houses may engage teams of outworkers instead.

Suffice to say, for the uninitiated contemplating a direct mail campaign for the first time, it may be unwise to try and carry out all the operations in-house. First time users are often shocked to discover how much paper is involved in a large mailing. A large consumer mailing, for example, running into millions, will often amount to a lorry-park full of juggernauts stacked high with paper – a real headache if space has not been set aside for it.

When responses to a mailing are received, it is essential that these are processed efficiently. For this the services of a fulfilment specialist should be sought – who may, incidentally, also be the mailing house. Again, complications await the unprepared, especially if money is changing hands, or if respondents have been given reason to expect an instant response when 28 days is more likely to be the case. Other basics will need attention, such as what to do with the inevitable 'gone-aways'.

THE COSTS

The costs of direct mail campaigns derive from the number of components involved and the stages through which they must travel. Below is a basic checklist of costs likely to be involved:

- List rental, purchase or compilation.
- List cleansing and deduping (merge/purge).
- Materials, for example, letter, brochure, order form.
- Laser printing of any personalization.
- Premia, prizes, and so on.
- Handling (enveloping, posting and so on).
- Fulfilment.
- Creative and artwork.
- Postage.
- Return postage.

As already indicated, postage is by far the most expensive cost in the average direct mail campaign. However, large savings can be effected by making use of the various Royal Mail bulk discount schemes available. Anyone contemplating entry to direct mail is well advised to contact their local Royal Mail Business Centre whose excellent advice is free.

List costs at 1994 rates, in Britain, range from an average of £65 per thousand to £100 for established consumer lists, and £95 to £160 for business lists. Remember, however, that if several lists are to be merged, and duplicates are purged, whilst this produces savings in postage and materials, the processing costs can be relatively high. Laser printing is another relatively costly process – unavoidable if the message is to be personalized. There is still considerable debate, even among direct mail consultants, as to the desirability of personalization in every mailing. In business mailings, particularly, it can be preferable to address respondents by job title only, for example 'The Stationery Buyer', rather than use a name – because of the frequency with which people move jobs or change responsibilities.

GROWTH AND POPULARITY

We have discussed the benefits of direct mail to marketers and recipients, but how does this basis for growth and popularity show itself in industry statistics?

Between 1983 and 1991, consumer mailings per head of population in Britain doubled from 20 items annually to 40. Self-evidently this figure is much higher for the more attractive market segments (for example, stable, high-income families) and also when related to households rather than individuals. Especially high among users are financial service organizations, responsible for up to a quarter of all campaigns mailed in 1991–2 (*Precision Marketing*, 11 January 1993). Nevertheless Britain's use and receipt of direct mail is still lower than for most comparable countries in the industrialized world, suggesting that saturation is still a long way off.

As for the acceptability of mail, research suggests this continues to increase gradually. Between 1989 and 1991, those saying they would *not* buy anything by post fell from 21 per cent to 15 per cent (*Precision Marketing*, 2 September 1992). And, of course, a great deal of direct mail does not solicit direct orders.

The chief users of consumer direct mail, besides financial services, are charities, general mail order traders, holiday and tour operators, publishers, motor manufacturers and the utilities (Water, Gas, Electricity and so on) – again suggesting the field is wide open for a wide variety of advertisers outside these categories. Conditions are certainly ripe for further growth as the social, economic and business factors which have helped fuel the growth of mail continue unabated.

Turning to the business sector, according to the Direct Mail Information Service (DMIS), mailing activity grew by 22 per cent between 1988 and 1993, and now accounts for 27 per cent of all direct mail postings. Among the most prolific business-to-business mailers are computer, IT, and office equipment suppliers, financial services, manufacturers, hotel, travel and catering organizations, and conference and educational establishments.

Other statistics compiled by DMIS are encouraging for users and potential users: 43 per cent of business managers describe received direct mail as either 'very useful' or 'quite useful' and 36 per cent keep literature for future reference. But a word of caution: 34 per cent of business mail is intercepted before reaching its intended recipient, an obstacle which skilled marketers have learned to overcome – by treating secretaries and office staffs as integral parts of the decision buying unit and mailing them their own personalized campaigns.

The DMIS reports £904 million spent on direct mail in the last reported year (1993), equal to 9.9 per cent of all UK advertising expenditure. These figures represent an increase of 70 per cent in six years. Not bad for a medium many advertisers profess to know little or nothing about.

SUPPLIERS

In the UK direct mail, the medium is currently in the hands of the Royal Mail. Although very similar in appearance, loose inserts (operated by publishers) and household delivery (door-to-door) do not qualify as direct mail since they are not addressed and cannot be personalized. The Royal Mail has a legal monopoly, at present, on addressed mail posted in the UK – although some large users post into the UK using overseas post offices to take advantage of their lower costs.

Clearly the Royal Mail is a useful source of advice. For the practical work of enveloping and posting direct mail, however, a qualified mailing house (or lettershop) is recommended. They will be able to help with all aspects of mailing including obtaining bulk discounts from Royal Mail. (The current scheme is termed Mailsort.)

Suppliers of direct mail creative and production work include specialist advertising agencies and consultants and some large mailing houses and printers. Even printing for direct mail is a specialized business, and it is advisable to find a printer who knows about suitable papers, formats and printing methods, particularly if laser-printed items are to be included. The way in which paper is folded can present major obstacles to mechanical handling if not planned with mailing in mind and, of course, paper weights are a significant factor in costs.

A multi-piece mailing, including many different printed and manufactured items sourced from a variety of suppliers, calls for organizational efficiency of the highest order. For prospective users contemplating direct mail, it is advisable to hire one expert and let him or her choose the suppliers, rather than take on a team of people none of whom has the necessary experience. Direct mail is advertising and marketing with a huge additional mechanical and technical aspect.

LAWS AND REGULATIONS

In this chapter numerous references have been made to the ways in which direct mail relates to, and differs from, other advertising media. Finally, therefore, it is appropriate to address the issue of laws and regulations since direct mail is subject to many restrictions not applicable to other forms of advertising and marketing. English law being what it is – subject to endless interpretation – no attempt is made here to explain the relevant statutes; instead reference is made to them so that would-be mailers can seek further advice.

There are three broad categories of law which British direct mailers should be aware of:

1 General laws relating to selling and advertising, which apply equally to direct mail, for example, Trade Descriptions Act.
2 Laws relating to specific industries and professions, for example, Financial Services Act.
3 Laws relating specifically to privacy and the control of computer-held information, for example, Data Protection Act.

Statutes closely allied to direct mail, and therefore possibly not familiar to general advertisers, include:

• Unsolicited Goods & Services Act 1975
• Consumer Protection (Cancellation of Contracts concluded away from Business Premises) Regulations 1987
• Mail Order Transactions (Information) Order 1976
• Data Protection Act 1984
• Post Office Act.

Much of the area covered by the above laws is policed by the appropriate trade bodies, the chief of which are the following:

- Direct Marketing Association (UK) (DMA–UK).
- Direct Mail Services Standards Board (DMSSB).
- Mail Preference Service (MPS).
- British Code of Sales Promotion Practice.

THE FUTURE

The prognosis for direct mail is good. It fulfils marketing's need to reach ever-smaller niches as markets fragment under the strains of competitive pressure and widening media choices. It offers marketers greater control and account-ability. It is growing in acceptability, albeit gradually. It offers greater creative freedom than even its practitioners realize. And, as we have seen, it works.

But there is one large cloud on the horizon: the junk mail millstone. Junk mail is a label given to direct mail by the traditional media to whom it represents a threat. This label is encouraged by some elements in the environmental lobby which assume, wrongly, that Brazilian hardwood trees are being destroyed to make the paper used. Unfortunately direct mail practitioners themselves have given ammunition to the enemy in the form of poor to non-existent targeting, ugly cheaply-produced materials and, especially, a cavalier regard for customers' correct names and addresses.

So what is the future? Undoubtedly the need for all direct response media will continue to grow and those who desire its benefits will have to conform to the required standards, or be excluded. Several Codes of Practice are now in place with this aim in view.

With more attention to detail, greater generosity in what is offered, and continued improvement in selective targeting, there is no reason why direct mail should not continue to edge its way to the top of the advertising media league.

ESSENTIAL READING

Burnett, Ed (1988), *The Complete Direct Mail List Handbook*, Englewood Cliffs, NJ: Prentice-Hall.

Harper, Rose (1986), *Mailing List Strategies*, New York: McGraw-Hill.

Hodgson, Richard (1980), *Direct Mail and Mail Order Handbook,* (4th edn), Chicago: The Dartnell Corp.

Lewis, Herschell Gordon (1984), *Direct Mail Copy That Sells!*, Englewood Cliffs, NJ: Prentice-Hall.

Robinson, J.F. (1989), *The Secrets of Effective Direct Mail*, Maidenhead: McGraw-Hill.

32 Telephone marketing
Bernard Katz

We mostly take the telephone for granted. It is always there. But used efficiently, as part of a planned marketing campaign, the telephone can be an extremely cost-effective tool. It has many uses in business. They fall into four distinct categories:

1 *Generating new business:*

- Prospecting for new customers.
- Selling.
- Order taking.
- Prospecting for repeat business.
- Converting enquiries into orders.

2 *Customer service:*

- Generating good PR.
- Answering the phone efficiently.
- Dealing with complaints and with angry customers.
- Dealing with enquiries.
- Debt collection.

3 *Communication:*

- Transmitting and receiving messages.
- Transmitting and receiving telex and fax messages (through a modem and appropriate equipment).

4 *Research:*

- Collecting data.
- Linking with a viewdata system (via a modem and computer terminal or micro computer).

This chapter provides practical techniques, in the form of checklists, examples, and sets of rules for what to do and what to avoid, for prospecting action within category 1. It provides also a constructive approach towards achieving effective customer service from category 2. Other marketing applications of the telephone are beyond the scope of this chapter.

GENERATING NEW BUSINESS

When prospecting for new business there are a number of questions to be answered: Who to telephone? How to find names and numbers of potential customers? What is it that the prospects really need? What is the best way of telephoning? What is the best time of day to telephone? What records should be kept? How frequently should calls be made? How does the caller get better at telephoning?

The answers to all these questions are incorporated in a set of rules, the 'operating rules for prospecting by telephone'.

Rule 1: Identify the existing principal categories of customer. Select a spectrum of potential customers from within these categories.

Cold canvass in selling is the process of starting at a given point, and making contact with every consecutive prospect. The starting point is the beginning of a road, the top of an office building, or the top of a page in a directory. Cold canvass generates some successes. But it involves much wasted effort, because contacts are made that have no chance of success. By restricting telephone calls to potential customers similar to those with whom business is already transacted, the opportunities for failure are restricted.

If five or six categories of customer are selected – and there is no magic number – the distribution of calls should be weighted in accordance with the volume of business received from each category. For example, ten prospecting calls made by a print shop might be made to:

- local retailers – 3.
- insurance companies – 3.
- professional firms – 1.
- transport companies – 1.
- local manufacturers – 2.

It is productive to prepare a simple prospective customer control grid. An example is illustrated in Figure 32.1.

Prospective customer categories					
1	2	3	4	5	6

Prospective customer needs					
1	2	3	4	5	6

Figure 32.1   Customer control grid

Rule 2: Compile a prospecting file of names and addresses of potential customers falling within the major customer classifications.

Most businesses advertise themselves, if only by a one-line entry in a directory. If they are anonymous to the extent that their name does not appear in any published form it is unlikely that they qualify as a potential customer. The names of companies also appear in journals, magazines or newspapers.

A useful directory giving much detailed information is *Kompass* (Kompass Publishers Ltd, Windsor Court, East Grinstead House, East Grinstead, West Sussex RH19 1XD, Tel: 0342–326972). It segments its data against many criteria – product type, distribution channels, turnover, resources employed, geographical locations and so on. Another useful and readily available directory is *Yellow Pages*, providing a general company classification of industry and trades. If the prospective customer is a private person his or her name and address are to be found in the electoral rolls. All persons living at an address are recorded, and there is therefore an indication of the size of a family in any dwelling. But no other information is provided. Information about private persons must be gathered from announcements and classified advertisements in the national and local press.

Rule 3: Identify the main needs of the different prospective customer categories.

Customers are rarely motivated to buy unless their needs are satisfied. Occasionally a purchase decision is made on impulse because the product or service is wanted. Generally the seller must identify and match the buyer's needs. At the telephone there is little time for research – after one or possibly two questions there is a danger that the interest of the person spoken to begins to wane. So the seller's call must talk from the outset about matters likely to interest the customer. The second column in Figure 32.1 is headed 'prospective customer needs'. The grid is a planning document, from which the caller prepares to make the prospecting call.

Rule 4: Set objectives for the prospecting call.

It is essential to be aware of what must be achieved. Does the caller want to take an order? Advertising space can be sold at the telephone, as can office equipment, spare parts or a number of personal services. In such cases, the caller must plan in advance the procedures to be adopted: a telex or letter is to be sent by the buyer, a deposit or the full cost of the product or service is to be paid into an account, or sent to the caller, or made available on delivery of the product. But with some products or services it is not possible to take an order from a cold prospecting call. Jewellery cannot be sold, or houses or life insurance. No one will buy a car without an opportunity for inspection and a test drive.

This does not mean that sellers of these products or services should not make prospecting calls. The level of communication in the prospecting call is inadequate. The objective is different. A meeting is necessary to allow further information to be provided to the customer. The customer must be in a situation where the benefit messages received from the salesperson are reinforced by seeing, touching, hearing or tasting the product. So the objective is to make an appointment.

Taking an order, or making a firm appointment, are the prime objectives of the prospecting call. But there is a secondary objective too. It is to create the opportunity to have a second attempt at success when the first attempt is seen to be failing. The person spoken to is manipulated. A particular effort must be made because if there was interest, the original prospecting call would not be failing.

'Mr/Ms Prospect. I am sorry you do not see how our product can increase your company profits. However, what I will do is put our company literature in *561* the post to you. I never send it cold, because I imagine you are bombarded with unwanted literature. Is that right?'

'Yes, I do get a lot of junk mail.'

'The literature sets out clearly the specification and benefits of our equipment. I will phone you again in three or four days' time to answer any queries that arise. Thank you Mr/Ms Prospect. Goodbye.'

The prospective customer is *not* asked whether literature may be sent *or* if the caller may telephone back. The natural tendency of courteous people is to ask rather than tell. Such questions invite a 'no' response. The action which will be taken is stated briskly and the call closed. The caller has then created a marginally favourable opportunity for a second chance. It is a better situation than attempting to speak again following an emphatic and possibly hostile rejection.

Rule 5: Write the script for the prospecting call, incorporating the 'golden rules for speaking at the telephone'.

A script is always used for the prospecting call. Many salespeople and business executives with track records of success reject the suggestion of using a script. After all, they know their business thoroughly. But the script is of immense help in preventing the caller moving off at a tangent from the call objective. Unless controlled, this frequently happens whenever a detailed aspect of the product or service is being discussed.

The prospective script is a planned pathway from the initial intrusion into the prospective customer's space up to the closing of the objective. Responses are projected in advance to the probing and persuasive questions to be asked by the caller. The first question is worded so that the response is 'yes' or 'no'. This type of question is called a 'neutral closed question'. Different follow-up questions are prepared, to be used depending on whether a 'yes' or 'no' answer is received. The prospecting script is an algorithm or flowchart of stimulus and reaction. Figure 32.2 illustrates a script in block format. The person telephoned is being led carefully and efficiently along a preplanned path. He or she is unaware that this is happening. The caller must not sound as though the call is being read.

Getting the script right takes time. And different scripts are necessary for different categories of customer because the needs and the product or service benefits are different. A script is written and used. One or two calls soon disclose topic areas or customer objections that have not been considered. So the script is then adapted to accommodate the different responses.

'Golden rules' influence and guide the telephone prospecting script.

Golden rule 1: Always smile when speaking to the prospective customer.

Smiling is relaxing. Smile inhibits aggression and tension. An effort should be made to adopt the habit of smiling every time the telephone is picked up. Even at the end of a long tiring day, a conscious smile helps to impart a friendly courteous manner.

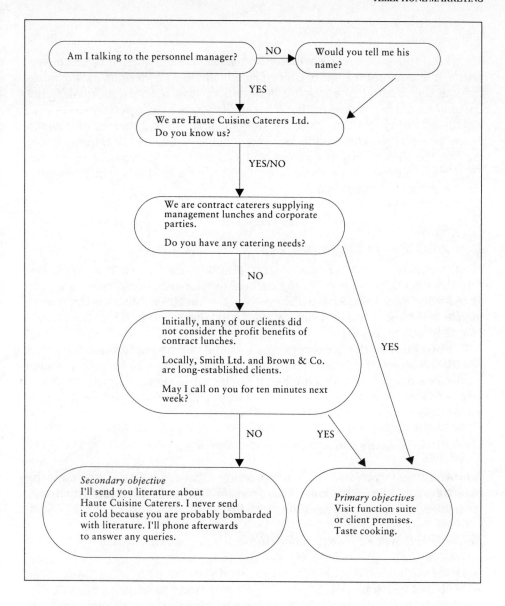

Figure 32.2   Example of script for a prospecting call showing 'block' format within the conversation

Golden rule 2: Involve the customer in conversation as early as possible.

On no account should the caller talk *at* the customer. If the telephone has to be held at arm's length to avoid the torrent of words pouring out, the objective will never be reached.

563

Golden rule 3: Ask frequent questions.

Asking questions brings the person who has been telephoned into the conversation. It is a reinforcement of Golden rule 2. But in its own right, asking questions is the method of obtaining information. It is the way to 'qualify' the customer's needs, to ensure that the call is with the right person – one who has the authority to make decisions – and to establish that there are no identifiable constraints against the objective being achieved. Examples would include the lack of any remaining budget allocation preventing purchases being made currently, or absence on holiday or a business trip preventing appointments being arranged.

Golden rule 4: The prospective customer listens only as long as he or she is interested.

Most people are courteous and will not abruptly tell a caller to go away. But this is not licence for the caller to ramble. The prospective customer does not necessarily want to receive a stranger's views on the weather or the performance of the local cricket team, or even a detailed description of the caller's company and successes.

The objective of the prospecting call can be reached only when the caller has the full attention of the other person. That attention may be held when the customer's needs and wants are being discussed. The caller's product or service can be the best in the world but if it does not satisfy the prospective customer's needs or wants, it will not be of interest.

Golden rule 5: Always aim at achieving the objective.

A pleasant easy conversation is no guarantee that the caller will achieve the objective. At all times the caller must remain aware of the set task. He or she must steer the conversation in the right direction.

Golden rule 6: When the prospective customer says 'no', start selling.

A person with limited selling experience is disheartened by a 'no'. Most of us want to be liked. If we persist in selling to a prospective customer after being told 'no', any friendly relations established during the conversation are likely to be extinguished. Furthermore, the other person may become resentful and irritated or, worse, hostile. Withdrawal, with apologies for any disturbance caused is one option. But a pleasant conversation is not in itself productive – it does not increase profits in either the short or medium term. Another option for the caller is to treat the 'no' as an objection – an objection to be countered. The objection may take the form of:

- Not now . . .
- Next time we buy . . .

- Too much stock . . .
- Business is bad . . .
- No money . . .

The objections might be a smokescreen. They may be product criticism, or there may be a lack of product information. 'No' is a signal for the caller to redouble his or her efforts to identify the real needs of the customer in order to match them with appropriate benefits.

WRITING THE SCRIPT

The script is written to deal with all the different stages of the prospecting call:

1 Contact is established with the correct person.
2 A reason for calling is provided.
3 The prospective customer is qualified to make sure that it is worthwhile to proceed.
4 Benefit messages are given to satisfy the needs of the customer.
5 A trial close is made.
6 If the close is unsuccessful, customer objections are identified and countered.
7 Additional benefit messages are given.
8 Close for the prime objective.
9 If unsuccessful, close for the second objective.

Example of a script

Haute Cuisine Caterers Ltd supplies management lunches in-house, or at its own elegant premises. The company caters for business functions and parties of all kinds. The greater part of its business comes from existing customers. New business is found through telephone prospecting calls to potential customers falling within existing customer categories.

> *Caller:* Hello. I want to speak to the person who deals with company catering please, but before you put me through, would you please tell me the name?
> *Customer:* Pardon? We don't have a company caterer. Who do you want to speak to?
> *Caller:* Oh. In that case I'll speak to the personnel manager. What is the name, first, please?
> *Customer:* We don't have a personnel manager. What is the call about?
> *Caller:* My name is Peter Renwick of Haute Cuisine Caterers Ltd. Please put me through to your managing director.

The opening moments of a prospecting call are often not straightforward. In bigger companies there is a catering manager. In some companies the catering function is looked after by the personnel department. Sometimes there is neither a catering manager nor a personnel manager, but this information is not known until contact is made. The opening question is designed to establish the name of the potential contact before speaking. On occasion the telephonist ignores this request. At other times the telephonist compounds the problem by putting the call through to someone having no possible interest in catering or the authority to take decisions.

Getting past the employees protecting the decision makers requires confident authority. Often there is a direct question: 'What is the call about?' Such questions are ignored. The caller persists in trying to establish a convenient time to call back to speak to the person concerned.

If it is just not possible to get through, the best way to deal with the matter is to say authoritatively and courteously, 'Well, I'll call back at 4.30. Please advise that Peter Renwick is calling at that time. Thank you. Goodbye.'

Customer: Deborah Long.
Caller: Ms Long? Am I talking to the managing director?
Customer: Yes. I am the managing director.
Caller: Ms Long. My name is Peter Renwick of Haute Cuisine Caterers Ltd. Do you know us?

People like to hear their own name mentioned – so 'Ms Long' is repeated. 'Do you know us' immediately brings the potential customer into the conversation.

Customer: No. I am afraid I can't say that I know the name.
Caller: Haute Cuisine Caterers is a local firm specializing in contract catering for management lunches and company functions. Do you employ your own catering staff?
Customer: No. Apart from a few kettles we have no cooking facilities.
Caller: We have a lot of experience in delivering a varied luncheon menu to customers' premises on a daily basis: as well as catering dinners and parties of up to seventy guests in our own elegant suites. We know that we are extremely competitive. Will you come and see us, one day next week, to sample our cooking and discuss how our service may be of benefit to your company?

Product information is given with implied benefits, and the first trial close is made.

Customer: Thank you for that invitation. It is kind of you to offer. But we have no plans for catering activities at the moment.
Caller: I understand. One question please. What arrangements do your management team make for their daily lunches?
Customer: My colleagues and I use a pub or restaurant or bring sandwiches – whatever is appropriate. Thinking about lunchtime has low priority in this company.

The customer is losing interest and is closing the caller out. The caller must offer significant benefits immediately to rescue any opportunity of doing business.

Caller: Ms Long, I get that reply from many of the successful companies I talk to. Happily, a number of them are now our customers. Haute Cuisine lunches take away the need to think about finding restaurants and pubs. There is only one cuisine standard, and that is excellent. May I call and see you for ten minutes next week? Our services are designed to help busy companies restrict their non-productive activities to a minimum.

Customer: Thank you again for your offer. But I am sorry such discussions are not appropriate at the moment. Goodbye.

Caller: Ms Long. I'll tell you what I will do. I'll put our literature in the post describing the range of services, and how they contribute to customer profits. I never send out literature cold, because I imagine you are bombarded with unwanted mail. Is that right?

Customer: It certainly is.

Caller: OK. I'll phone you a few days after you receive the literature to answer any queries that arise. Goodbye Ms Long.

Rule 6: Prepare and maintain a simple records system for all prospecting calls made, particularly to show the *action* result of the initial call.

Leads gathered at the outset of a telephone prospecting campaign appear great in number. If a call is abortive because of difficulties in getting through to the right person, it is tempting to shrug and move on to the next on the list. This temptation is to be resisted. There is a finite number of leads, even from unused directories.

Every prospective customer lead is valuable. If a prospective customer is called and he or she is not in, the call must be made again, later. If the person answering says that Mr Smith or Ms Jones will be available on Tuesday at lunchtime, that is when the second call is to be made.

Figure 32.3 illustrates an effective format for an index card system. Alternatively, the columns can be drawn into an exercise book. Before every call each column should be completed. The action column is completed afterwards. Even though the task is tedious, records must be kept. Memory is unreliable and is not a substitute for keeping records.

Every day the records are looked through to see which calls back must be made. When a decision is made that a prospective customer does not warrant further effort the name should be scored through. It should not be erased or obliterated. When the lists are checked later it is necessary to know which companies have already been contacted.

Contact name	Company name	Telephone number	Prospect address	Action

Figure 32.3   Format for index card system

Rule 7: Establish by trial and error the best time of day to telephone different customer categories.

The time of day at which to make a prospecting call varies with different industries. It is also a function of the caller's own work schedule. At any time of day the prospecting phone call can be considerably more cost-effective than a personal visit.

There is no best time to call applicable to all customers. If there is a valid reason to call: call. The worst that can happen is that the receiver is slammed down in anger. But one is circumspect, so that whatever the time of the call, the 'worst' situation is never reached. Winning business by telephone is a combination of courtesy and the persistence, despite customer resistance, to identify and match the customer's real needs.

Rule 8: Establish the pace of a telephone prospecting campaign with an initial one-week trial period.

A serious pitfall of a telephone selling campaign is excessive enthusiasm. When the great potential of the telephone as a marketing tool is accepted, it is dangerous to dispense with all other approaches to securing business. Prospecting by telephone works, but if too much is expected there is failure, and with failure telephone selling is rejected in its entirety.

For the novice caller, it is helpful to send a prospecting letter first. The caller then telephones and asks if the person has received the letter. In this way, there is no basis for apprehension. The caller is talking about something that is known.

Telephoning cold is difficult and fearsome for most people at the outset. With practice the difficulties and fears are overcome. Some, even with considerable success in face-to-face selling, find the idea of selling at the telephone daunting. If the secretarial resources and the cost of these resources are avail-

	Target dates	Number of prospecting calls	Objectives reached	Number of prospecting letters/calls	Objectives reached	Total successes
Target actual						
Target actual						

Figure 32.4   Target record grid

able, telephoning as a follow-up to the prospecting letter is an excellent method of self-training to use the telephone for prospecting and selling. With practice one is weaned off the prospecting letter.

To establish a benchmark for prospecting activities, make use of the initial week's programme as a trial. Establish the number of prospecting calls it is realistic to make, taking into consideration all other prospecting and selling activities. For half the calls, arrange to send a prospecting letter in advance of the call. Prepare a target grid as illustrated in Figure 32.4. Identify the number of successes from the calls made cold, and from those following a prospecting letter.

When the trial period is over decide:

1   A realistic target number of calls to be made each week.
2   A realistic number of prospecting letters to precede the telephone calls, until total confidence in using the telephone by itself is achieved.

Rule 9: Periodically monitor prospecting call performance by recording calls on a tape recorder and evaluating against an analysis grid.

Prospecting at the telephone can work for everyone. If the results are not good, or not good enough, something is wrong. Is the call deviating from the script? Is the principal customer need identified? Have the 'Golden rules' been followed? Figure 32.5 gives a checklist of likely faults.

	YES	NO
Is the prospective customer brought into the conversation early enough?	☐	☐
Is the prime customer need identified?	☐	☐
Are the objections identified?	☐	☐
Are correct benefit messages given in relation to the customer needs?	☐	☐
Is the close effective?	☐	☐
Is the script amended each time after analysis of an unsatisfactory call?	☐	☐
Is the call allowed to deviate from the script?	☐	☐
Are the prospective customer categories realistic?	☐	☐
Are the calls made at the right time of day?	☐	☐
Have the 'Golden rules' been followed?	☐	☐
Are the follow-up *action* requirements scrupulously observed?	☐	☐
Is the call continued after the customer says 'no'?	☐	☐

Figure 32.5   Checklist of faults

To record a call on a tape recorder, an inexpensive microphone is required, obtainable from most reputable audio equipment shops. The recorded call is then carefully analysed against the checklist of faults, using the analysis grid illustrated in Figure 32.6.

CUSTOMER SERVICE

The telephone has an important contributory role to play in the provision of efficient customer service. In many cases expectation of service is itself a factor of the purchase decision process. The buyer of a car, a computer or a

Early prospective customer involvement			Frequent questions asked			Attainment of objectives				Interest sustained		Termination of call			Objections handled		Benefits messages	
						Sale demos		Literature										
Correct	Too early	Late	Correct	Too many	Too few	Yes	No	Yes	No	Yes	No	Correct	Early	Late	Well	Badly	Correct	Incorrect/ insufficient

Figure 32.6   Telephone prospecting analysis grid

photocopier needs reassurance that operating service is available promptly, whenever there is machine downtime. So important is service in marketing terms that it is helpful to upgrade the concept of the marketing mix – the variables in the control of marketing management – from four Ps to four Ps and an S (product, price, place, promotion and service).

The telephone call often provides the first contact with a company. There is an immediate example of customer service. Many companies fail to observe when levels of service drop because of everyday familiarity. So an audit of telephone performance, periodically arranged through a third party, is an indicator for management of the image perceived by customers. A telephone effectiveness audit checklist is set out below. A simple evaluation scale (*inadequate – acceptable – good*) is sufficient to identify problem areas.

Checklist

1 How quickly is the telephone answered when the company is called?
2 How efficiently is the telephone answered, during lunchtimes and at the beginning and end of the day?
3 How reliably are messages transmitted?
4 How patient is the person answering when there is sound distortion, or a message given is disrupted?
5 How supportive is the person answering when the command of the English language is limited?
6 How efficient is the giving of advance warning when delays in a service call visit occur?
7 How frequently is a contact name given to a customer with a service requirement, to help when making contact again?
8 How competently are customer complaints handled?
9 How effectively are customer enquiries converted into orders?

The courtesy call

The courtesy telephone call has an important role. Its value is disproportionately greater than the effort required to make the call.

'Hello, Ms Gordon. It is John Weston of Patchwork Products Ltd. We have now made the delivery of all goods against your order xb223. Everything matches the specification given, and the delivery was made on the due date. I am just phoning to make sure that you are satisfied?'

'Yes. As far as I know.'

'Good. We have built our business by making sure that our customers are always supplied with what they ask for. Many thanks. Goodbye.'

ESSENTIAL READING

Katz, B. (1987), *How To Win More Business By Phone, Telex and Fax*, London: Business Books.

Stone, B. and Wyman, J. (1989), *Successful Telemarketing*, Lincolnwood, Illinois: NTC Business Books.

Weitzen, H. Skip (1984), *Talk Again*, Maidenhead: McGraw Hill.

33 Franchising
Martin Mendelsohn

Franchising is a method of marketing goods and services which has had an impact on and between all levels in the chain from manufacturer to consumer. Many of the traditional routes to the consumer are discussed in other chapters and include distribution networks and agencies. Franchising is far more integrated than those more traditional methods, but at the same time many of their elements will be found in franchising methods.

Franchising as a concept goes far beyond the traditional approaches; it may help to go back to basics.

TRADITIONAL METHODS

First let us examine the position in relation to products starting with the inventor or creator. He has two options; either he will manufacture the product himself or he will enter into an agreement with someone who will manufacture. He may sell the invention or products concept outright or he may license the other party to manufacture using his process. The product may be identified by a trade mark and if that is owned by the inventor or creator he will license its use as part of the manufacturing licence.

Whichever choice is made the product when made will follow a route to the consumer. The traditional route is manufacturer to wholesaler to retailer to consumer. This route can involve different techniques.

Distributors

There may be a distribution agreement whose terms will vary according to the nature of the product. The more sophisticated the product, the more product knowledge in selling is required; the more important after-sales support is; the closer one gets to what is called 'selective distribution' where distributors are chosen for their knowledge or their willingness to learn and to make the necessary investment. These arrangements have become increasingly the subject of the attentions of competition law authorities (particularly the European Commission) to ensure that they are not used as a cloak for anti-competitive conduct calculated improperly to limit the number of distributors and hence reduce competition in the market-place.

There are other distribution arrangements where the distributor may well carry a range of competing products produced by different manufacturers. Distribution rights may exist in respect of large areas, sometimes a whole country or more than one country. Distributors may be wholesalers or may supply to wholesalers or retailers and in some cases direct to the ultimate user of the products. There is clearly a high degree of flexibility.

What is clear about these arrangements is that the distributor:

- Is an independent business.
- Operates under its own name.
- Runs its business as it thinks fit.
- Invariably controls completely the nature and range of products with which it deals.
- Develops its own skills for the business which it runs.

Agents

Another method of getting the products to the consumer is achieved by the employment of agents. Agents in the strict legal sense are the *alter ego* of their principal. They have defined authority to perform certain duties for the principal who is bound by what they do. It is possible for an agent to go beyond his authority and still bind the principal on the basis that his 'apparent' authority goes beyond his 'specific' authority. An agent is a business getter; he also

- Is an independent business.
- Operates under his own name but as an agent for his principal.
- Runs his business as an agent as he thinks fit but each agency assignment will be subject to the specific authority he receives.
- May control the nature and range of products and the principals whom he represents.
- Develops his own skills for the business he runs.

It will be seen that these basic issues are virtually the same for both types of arrangement.

FRANCHISING

Franchising is simply another method of reaching the consumer. It developed over a long period largely in response to problems for which specific solutions were sought and which resulted in a particular application of already known   *575* principles which include elements of the licensing, distribution and agency arrangements to which reference has already been made.

The birth of franchising

It is generally reckoned that the modern concept of franchising was first introduced in the USA by the Singer Sewing Machine Company, which developed a network of franchised dealers just after the American Civil War. At the end of the 19th century the soft drink bottlers introduced the 'industrial' franchises and what are now called first generation franchises, when they entered into agreements with 'wholesalers' who purchased syrups, combined them with water and bubbles and put them in bottles (now cans) and distributed them. This system is still operated.

In the first decade of the 20th century the motor manufacturers introduced franchised dealers and laid the foundations for the present system of car dealerships. They did so in order to:

- Get the products on sale closer to the consumers rather than from the factory.
- Ensure that the salespeople knew and understood the cars.
- Provide local suppliers of spare parts.
- Provide local mechanics who knew how to repair and service cars.
- Obtain payments in advance to assist them in the financing of their operations.

Around the same time a man called Leggatt who had a drug-store business interested other drug-store operators in joining forces with him to secure better buying terms. This was extended to establishing own-brand manufacturing of products and the participating stores operated under the brand name of Rexall – they still do.

In the 1930s Howard Johnson established his well-known chain of restaurants and a number of other businesses were set up, which some 20 years or so later, chose to expand using franchising as their method of achieving their goals.

It was in the USA during the post-war period from 1946 to 1960 when the first franchising explosion took place; from a handful of operators which were identifiable in 1946 there were over 700 by 1960. That was at the time when the concept was relatively new and there needed to be a fast learning curve. During that period many businesses which are now household franchising names emerged. They include ServiceMaster; BurgerKing; McDonalds; Holiday Inn; Budget Rent-a-Car; Dunkin Donuts; Pizza Hut; Midas.

The growth since then has been remarkable and the statistical evidence from the USA indicates that all types of franchising accounts for some 34 per cent of all retail sales and have had a share of retail sales in excess of 30 per cent for some 20 years. There are now more than 550 000 franchise system outlets.

Franchising has spread throughout the world and it can now be found in varying stages of development in approximately 140 countries, many of which have mature franchise communities.

The reason for franchising's success

Why is it that franchising has achieved such success? The reason is that it combines the success of the innovator in establishing a successful business format under the banner of a well-known brand with the financial and manpower resources of motivated operators. It also provides a level of initial and ongoing services to the operator which are unique in business relationships.

Franchising really developed from the desire of the creator of a business branding and system which was successful to grow coupled with the desire of those with financial resources and ambition to own and operate their own business but who lacked the confidence to do so without help.

The early pioneers developed their businesses – many involved the provision of services rather than product distribution – but they did not have the financial resources to grow as quickly as the demand indicated was desirable. Many started franchising because customers or friends, impressed by what they were achieving, asked if they could be assisted into the same business.

That in essence is what franchising achieves, but in addition to that the franchisee is given the right to use the brand name, is required to use the franchisor's business system, is subjected to quality controls, and is given the benefit of a supporting and continuing relationship. Essentially the franchisee owns the business which he conducts, albeit under a controlled form of licensing arrangement. From this simple structure an infrastructure has to be developed as well as the techniques for dealing with the franchisor/franchisee relationship.

FRANCHISING CONTRASTED WITH TRADITIONAL METHODS

From this explanation it will be seen that franchising differs from the other traditional methods described above except that the franchisee is an independent business person. However:

- He or she operates under the brand name of the franchisor.
- He or she runs the business according to the system established and laid down by the franchisor.
- The range of products and/or services will be controlled by the franchisor.
- He or she will not be carrying any competing products or providing any competing services.
- He or she will acquire the necessary business skills from training provided by the franchisor.
- He or she will pay the franchisor probably an initial fee and some ongoing fees, which may take the form of a product mark-up for the rights granted and the services provided in ongoing support.

Franchisee benefits

These elements constitute a fundamental change from the other methods. The franchisee obtains benefits from this arrangement which may be summarized as follows:

- The risk inherent in establishing a new business is considerably reduced. All non-franchised new businesses have to go through a period of trial and error during which the margin for applying remedies is restricted by the amount of the owner's financial resources. All too often those resources run out before the problems are solved. In franchising, the franchisor must first establish a viable business which is sufficiently successful to attract the investment of others. The franchisor carries the business development risks.
- The franchisor trains the franchisees and assists them in all aspects of setting up and opening their businesses.
- The franchisee has the benefit of the reputation in the branding which grows as the network grows.
- The franchisee will benefit from the bulk purchasing power which the size of the franchise network commands.
- Franchisees' resources are pooled for advertising and promotional activities.
- The franchisor provides continuing research and development and market testing of innovation.
- The franchisor provides a range of 'head office' type support services which makes available to the franchisee a team of people with focused relevant skills as well as field support.

Franchisor's motivation

Obviously there are also good reasons why franchisors choose this method of expansion, apart from the powerful reason that the manpower and financial resources of the franchisee are being used. These include:

- Franchising produces scope for rapid growth.
- The franchisor needs fewer staff than if the outlets were all company owned.
- The franchisor's capital needs are lower.
- Franchisees provide better-motivated management of outlets than employed managers.
- The lower risk of failure has attracted the provision of competitive financial support for franchisees from all the major banking institutions.

The downside

No one would suggest that franchising for all its advantages to both parties does not present its problems. For the franchisor, the biggest challenge is coping with the franchisee and managing the relationship in all its aspects. For the franchisee, the biggest risk factor is the quality of the franchisor, how well it has tested its concept and how well it will perform its ongoing responsibilities to its franchisees.

Franchising criteria

There are some criteria to which consideration should be given in seeking to establish whether or not the basic ingredients for franchising exist:

1 There must be a tried and tested and proved successful business.
2 The branding must be distinctive.
3 The business system must be distinctive.
4 The business system must be capable of being taught to others within an economically sensible time-frame.
5 The financial returns for the franchisee must be sufficient to enable the franchisee:

   – To obtain a reasonable return on the assets employed in the business.
   – To earn a reasonable reward for his labours.
   – To make payment of fees to the franchisor.

6 The income generated by the franchisor must be sufficient to cover the franchisor's overheads and to enable it to make a reasonable profit.

ESTABLISHING A FRANCHISE

In seeking to establish a franchise there are a number of sequential steps to be taken:

1 The development of the concept.
2 The proving that the concept works in practice by pilot operations and the establishment of the franchisor's business system and branding.
3 The development of an operational manual which represents the franchisor's know-how relating to the operation of its system.
4 The preparation of the franchise package which will comprise the elements of what the franchisor will be selling as a franchise, for example, up-front services (including training), ongoing services, research and development and so on.
5 The marketing of the package and its sale to franchisees.
6 Developing the techniques for identifying the right people as franchisees and making franchisee selections.
7 Developing the franchisor's business infrastructure to cope with the growth of the business from perhaps a single pilot operation to a franchisor organization capable of the necessary growth.

Franchise development is not restricted to growth of small newly-emerging businesses. It is a method which has been employed by established businesses with varying degrees of success. There are difficulties for established and large companies in seeking to develop a franchise network since the franchising concept and its implementation is usually alien to or difficult to reconcile with corporate cultures. Even a mature business will need to follow the above sequence to ensure it is dealing correctly with its franchising approach.

THE USE OF FRANCHISING

Apart from the franchising of retail operations as the proven method of expansion the method has been used by:

1 Manufacturers to secure outlets for products.
2 Wholesalers to secure outlets for products and to enable them to make more economic use of storage and distribution facilities.
3 Existing chains of stores to:

- Continue expansion by adding franchised stores.
- Convert existing stores to franchised stores to raise capital.
- Convert existing marginally-profitable or loss-making stores to franchising. By a combination of increased turnover by having the owner run the business and reduce overheads by removing head-office and staff-support costs from the profit and loss account, it is possible to achieve profitability.

SCOPE FOR GROWTH

The UK has had experience of franchising for many years with some early growth in the 1950s, but development was and is much slower than has been experienced in the USA as well as many other countries. There are now reckoned to be some 396 franchisors with 24 500 outlets and annual turnover of £4.5bn.

The growth and extent of market penetration achieved in the US is considerable. In judging the prospects for growth in the UK, it is worth noting that taking franchise network outlets on a comparative per capita population basis there would need to be at least an additional 106 000 franchise network outlets in the UK to catch up with the US. This same exercise carried through into the Member States of the EU produces a shortfall of 375 000 network outlets. This suggests that the growth prospects in the UK and in Europe are considerable: indeed, between them McDonalds and Kentucky Fried Chicken have more outlets worldwide than there are franchised network outlets in the UK.

THE LEGAL ISSUES

There are no franchise laws in any part of the UK. The relationship is governed by the general commercial law as relevant to the particular elements of the franchise contract. There are two particular legal considerations which can impact the way in which franchise systems are structured:

- *The Fair Trading Act 1973* contains provisions relating to pyramid selling schemes which can affect a franchise system if it is desired to split the country into areas with area franchisees who are permitted to sub-franchise. That sort of structure which is uncommon in indigenous franchise systems is often sought to be imported particularly by US franchisors. Great care is needed in such cases to comply with the relevant legal requirements.
- *The Treaty of Rome* contains in Article 85 rules affecting anti-competitive agreements. The European Court of Justice has held that franchise agreements which often contain anti-competitive elements may infringe Article 85. The European Commission has adopted a regulation which grants exemption to franchise agreements which comply with the terms of the regulation. In practice this means that most franchise agreements will follow the regulation and the arrangements between franchisor and franchisee will invariably not be adversely affected.

The contract

Most franchise agreements are founded upon the trade mark, service mark or trade name, business system know-how and trade secrets of the franchisor. The agreement will be very detailed and should reflect the services to be provided by the franchisor from signature through to the opening of the franchisee's business and the continuing relationship. The agreement will also detail the controls to be imposed upon the franchisee. Of particular sensitivity will be the following clauses:

1   *Fee payments* including the method of calculation and the supporting reporting requirements.
2   *The sale of the business* by the franchisee. This will always be a qualified right, since the franchisor must always retain control over who joins the network as a franchisee. When a franchisee seeks to sell a franchised business it is the only time that someone other than the franchisor is recruiting a franchisee. That is no reason for the franchisor's selection criteria to be compromised. In practice a franchisor does not have a vested interest in preventing franchisees from selling to approved purchasers, since it enhances the value of membership of the franchise network which increases its marketability.
3   What will occur in the event of the *death of the franchisee* or, if the franchisee is a small proprietorial company, the death of the owner of the company? Normally one would expect sympathetic provisions which will enable the family to seek to qualify as franchisee or to assist in a disposal so that the business value will pass on to the franchisee's dependants.

581

4 *Termination:* the circumstances in which the agreement will be capable of being terminated. One would expect that an opportunity would be given to a franchisee to remedy any breach before termination can be effective.

5 *The consequences of termination* will need to be set out in full and will be quite drastic to prevent the franchisee from unfairly making use of the franchisor's name, reputation, branding, know-how, system and trade secrets after the agreement is at an end. A post-termination restraint against competition will invariably be found.

In addition to these factors there are two other relevant considerations:

1 The NPA have a vetting procedure before its newspaper members will allow franchisee advertising.
2 The British Franchise Association has adopted a Code of Ethics with which all its members are required to comply. The members of the Association comprise a significant proportion of the leading franchisors in the UK.

Licensing contrasted

This chapter began with licensing of the manufacture of products. Licensing is often confused with franchising for the very good reason that at the heart of every franchise there is a licence (in legal terms) to use a trade mark, service mark or trade name and other industrial and intellectual property rights. The confusion is understandable, but while franchising is a method of marketing goods and services, licensing is invariably dealing with the manufacturing stage and the production of goods which subsequently enter the marketing sphere.

In technical terms also the expressions 'franchise' and 'licence' mean something quite different. The expression 'licence' is invariably used in relation to the grant of the right to exploit a patent or to carry out a manufacturing

Table 33.1   The main differences between
a franchise and a licence

	Franchise	Licence
Manufacturing process	Rarely	Yes
Previous experience in performing necessary activities	Rarely	Essential
Uses trading name of franchisor/licensor	Yes	No
Uses business system of franchisor/licensor	Yes	No
Uses premises designed and laid out according to franchisor/licensor requirements	Yes	No
Part of a network of identical operations	Yes	No

process which may also involve the use of trade marks and will almost always include the use of the know-how used in carrying out the manufacturing process. Table 33.1 illustrates the main differences.

Franchising provides a dynamic approach to the marketing of products and services which has offered a route to successful business operations for many with money and ambition, but lacking the confidence to try to establish their own venture.

ESSENTIAL READING

Mendelsohn, Martin (1992), *The Guide to Franchising*, 5th edn., London: Cassell.

Mendelsohn, Martin (ed.) (1992), *Franchising in Europe*, London: Cassell.

34 Exhibitions

W. S. Richards

This chapter highlights the benefits of exhibitions as a sales and promotional medium and offers advice on how to approach exhibiting and some of the disciplines involved to achieve the optimum benefit.

WHAT CAN AN EXHIBITION DO FOR MY PRODUCTS AND SERVICES?

There are two parties to be satisfied in the course of an exhibition: the exhibitor trying to promote their product and to increase sales, and the visitor, the one on whom the exhibitor hopes to make an impression and from whom a sale can be won.

For the exhibitor there are unique benefits, namely:

- Exhibitions attract dedicated and specifically targeted audiences drawn by a promotion focused on clearly identified market sectors.
- A very high proportion of visitors at trade shows have buying authority.
- Exhibitions generate a high level of quality sales leads with excellent conversion to sales ratios.

For the visitor, or potential buyer, there are also unique benefits which the exhibitor should exploit to the full:

- A valuable opportunity to have face-to-face contact with the personnel of the company promoting the product or service.
- Products can be seen, handled and demonstrated.
- A wide range of products can be viewed and compared at one time (this also includes your competitors' products).

- Visits are used as a prime source for information on new products, services and equipment.

Types of exhibition

Basically an exhibition is a market-place, little different in concept from those events that started in medieval town squares so that farmers could exchange produce for money. In the UK there are roughly 700 exhibitions held every year and there are various types of exhibition, each of which can help to fulfil a range of marketing objectives.

The majority of exhibitions take place on an annual basis and an exhibition will usually only move its location when the event has outgrown the venue. Some trade shows take place every other year and more rarely, every three, four or five years. Occasionally trade shows in the same industry sector, but promoted by different organizing companies, will take place on alternate years, each event having a slightly different emphasis.

Trade exhibitions

These are events to which only the manufacturers and buyers within a fairly well-defined trade or industry sector are invited to attend. Events such as Computers in Manufacturing, International Junior Fashion Fair, and Wine Trade Show are quite specifically aimed at defined markets. Titles are not always quite so clear and events are often promoted by the initials of the title with 'ex' as a suffix, so care should always be taken to find out exactly which market the event is aimed at.

A large number of events are aimed at niche markets, for example, British Luggage Show, Electromagnetic Compatibility, Fibre Optics Exhibition, International Golf Equipment.

If your sales are aimed at wholesalers and distributors, trade fairs and exhibitions are the best way to meet them. If you want to make export contacts it is important to know which exhibitions attract the largest numbers of overseas visitors.

Consumer exhibitions

Events which attract large numbers of the public from whom orders can be taken and, in some cases, sales made at the exhibition, the Daily Mail Ideal Home Exhibition being a good example of this type of event. However, in recent years the equivalent of continuous exhibitions have emerged in the form of specialist hypermarkets which has meant that organizers of consumer exhibitions have had to create a 'family day out' type of event in order to attract and sustain large visitor numbers.

Trade and consumer exhibitions

An example of this type of event is the Motor Show, which is open to the public   *585* and members of the motor trade. Trade buyers may be invited to attend on special days or at special times and would not be expected to pay an admission charge, whereas the public will invariably be charged for admission.

Conference-related exhibitions

These are usually small in terms of the number of exhibitors and the number of visitors that might be available to be influenced. Such events can offer highly targeted markets but can often fail in delivering what is sold as the captive audience might prefer going to lunch rather than visiting exhibition stands.

Conferences and seminars are often an added feature of trade exhibitions and are usually organized to attract a wider audience and to give increased publicity to the event by using public figures whose speeches and comments might be worthy of press comment.

Agricultural shows

Are what they say, but the majority offer an agricultural trade market-place and a consumer event at the same time. In recent times, the UK agricultural industry has contracted and the agricultural show has become the equivalent of a country-fair day-out for the consumer.

Overseas exhibitions

Used to introduce products to export markets, to support overseas agents and representatives in the field or to seek out and appoint representatives in overseas markets. The main German cities probably host the largest number of truly international trade exhibitions which attract large numbers of overseas buyers and exhibitors and can be good events at which to meet potential overseas agents and representatives from markets worldwide.

There are often government financial contributions available for attendance at overseas exhibitions that can help to increase export trade; these are sometimes known as joint ventures. Much depends on the actual government handing out this largesse as to the terms and conditions associated with the financial help. Usually it requires that the individual company exhibitor promotes themselves from within a national pavilion or national corporate identity stand.

Private exhibitions

This is where you do it yourself; hire the venue, set up the exhibition and invite the guests/visitors that you want at a time that suits you, or more effectively at a time that suits the target visitor.

Such events require a certain amount of expertise to execute and confidence in the fact that your invitees will actually attend. Some organizers of private exhibitions will involve their regional offices, agents, wholesalers and possibly suppliers in the event, either to spread the financial risk or to increase the size and impact of the event.

Whilst private exhibitions include product launches, not all are 'private' since they may be held, for example, in a shopping mall to promote a range of electrical goods or other household products and services.

Where do I find out about exhibitions?

A full and regularly updated calendar of UK exhibitions together with listings of major exhibitions worldwide can be found in a monthly publication entitled the *Exhibition Bulletin*. For ease of identification of suitable events there is an industry sector classification. It is usually available at most main public reference libraries. Information on overseas exhibitions can also be obtained from the commercial attaché or trade promotion department of most overseas embassies.

Dates, and sometimes venues, can change unexpectedly and so it is important to contact the named organizers or their representatives to obtain information about the event, dates, costs, and conditions of exhibiting. You will also want to know what space in what positions is available, and what the anticipated visitor numbers and visitor job status profile will be.

The organizer should also give you some details of the methods by which they are intending to attract visitors.

WHICH TYPE OF EXHIBITION SHOULD I CHOOSE?

The answer to this will depend on three critical factors: the first is to know precisely what objectives you are intending to achieve by exhibiting; the second, to identify the right exhibitions in your industry sector that will meet your objectives in terms of attracting the target market; and the third, to be aware of costs.

Objectives

Although the underlying objective in exhibiting will almost inevitably be to increase sales, some further specific objectives might be to:

- Introduce new products, new designs.
- Sustain relationships with existing clients.
- Meet prospective clients.
- Make your industry and its customers aware of your strengths and innovations.
- Meet and appoint agents and representatives.

The objectives will also have a bearing on the choice of exhibition, for example, you might want to expand a regional market or test-market a product.

Without objectives you cannot set a benchmark against which success can be measured, nor will you find it possible to inspire staff to make a positive effort in their people-contact to achieve any significant results.

Selecting the exhibition

Obtain all the information you can from the organizer and examine the visitor profile to see if it matches the market sector or audience that you want to influence. Then speak to one or two of the exhibitors from the previous event to find out what they believe they achieved by exhibiting.

If it is a first time event, check with other companies in your industry sector for their opinion and ensure that the exhibition contract states that your space rental deposit is returnable if the event is cancelled for any reason.

Costs

Exhibitions, although they can undoubtedly be cost-effective, are not inexpensive. This means that you must weigh the cost of investment in the exhibition against the likely gross profits from the conversion of sales leads to sales that will be generated.

If you have never exhibited before, there will be an element of risk taking involved in this calculation and it is wise always to audit the results of every exhibition.

A rough guide to likely costs and the way in which the budget will be spent if you book free space is shown in Table 34.1. If you have booked a shell stand, then the space rental and stand construction costs which are now joined together are likely to be a lesser percentage of the overall expenditure.

Table 34.1
Breakdown of likely exhibition costs

	% of budget
Renting stand space	25–30
Design and stand construction	40–45
Stand running costs, electricity etc.	7–10
Publicity	7–10
Staff expenses	15–20

The direct costs are all the visible and invoiced items of expenditure, but for true costing the indirect costs should be accounted for. These are staff time, company materials, brochures used and so on, otherwise the real cost of the exhibition promotion will be lost.

In cash-flow terms, a non-returnable deposit on the space rented will be required on booking the space, the balance falling due usually two months before the opening date.

Obviously costs vary with the type and style of the exhibition. Major trade shows held in national halls will be the most costly and there may even be waiting lists for stand space, whilst regional and niche market events appealing to smaller markets and attracting smaller visitor numbers are likely to be less expensive.

BEFORE YOU START

A successful exhibition is the result of the concerted and co-operative activity of a number of people with a range of responsibilities, and different companies offering a wide range of services and skills.

A background to the exhibition industry

The UK exhibition industry comprises three distinct sectors:

- Venues.
- Organizers.
- Contractors.

The venues such as Earls Court, National Exhibition Centre, Birmingham, and G-Mex, Manchester provide the halls in which the event takes place, together with a range of supporting services such as catering, hospitality and meeting facilities.

The exhibition organizer, certainly in the UK, is usually a private sector company, the larger organizers often combining their trade magazine publishing interests with exhibition promotion. In other parts of Europe it is more common to find that the organizer is an operating arm of the publicly-owned exhibition venue. Sometimes the organizer is a trade association promoting the interest of its members.

The organizer is a promoter and the primary risk taker. They are responsible for the overall logistics involved in mounting the exhibition – contracting with the venue, securing exhibitors, publicizing the event to attract target market visitors. The organizer defines and publishes regulations governing the conduct of the exhibition and defines the exhibitors' obligations.

The contractor is hired by the exhibitor to make the physical aspects of the exhibition stand come true. The contractors supply the services element, stand design and construction, electrical fittings, floor coverings, furnishings, freight handling, floral displays and cleaning.

It is up to the exhibitor to appoint their own designer and contractor if they are renting free space, and it is quite normal to issue a tendering brief and obtain quotations for the design and construction from two or more competing contractors. If you do not know any contractors, a list can be supplied to you by the British Exhibition Contractors Association whose members are required to follow a strict code of conduct and are all bonded.

Usually there are separate contractors appointed by the exhibition organizers or venue for the supply of furniture, floral decor, telephones and cleaning.

Shell stands or free space?

Most exhibitions offer the exhibitor the choice between a standard 'box' or shell stand provided by the organizer or a clear space in which you can build your own display. It is assumed that, overall, it is less expensive to rent a shell stand than to build your own display on free space. Generally this is true, but the apparent cost saving has to be weighed against the freedom to express and promote your own image and to be able to design the space to display and demonstrate your products in a more imaginative way.

The smallest shell stand usually has a 3-metre frontage to the aisle and is 2 metres deep, so that you are renting 6 square metres of space with three walls. The price charged will often, for the sake of conformity, include a fascia board on which your company name and stand number will be sign-written in a standard typeface. In addition the price may include a certain amount of display lighting and limited furniture items.

However, shell stands come in all shapes and sizes, offering differing amounts of wall-space, sometimes occupying a corner site or being exposed to two aisles with no walls at all. The many ways in which a shell stand can be used to display your products are only limited by the breadth of your imagination and the organizers' regulations. You can divide them into sections for products and divide sections up so that you have interview and private entertainment areas.

Free space does not always mean that you will have an 'island site' and may mean that you and your contractor will have to negotiate with neighbouring sites to ensure that the design and construction matches and does not leave any unsightly and possibly dangerous gaps since overall appearance and safety precautions at exhibitions are paramount.

Almost everything you plan to do in your free space will be governed by the organizers' regulations and it is important that you read them thoroughly for each exhibition you attend before committing yourself to a design, construction materials, double deck stand, private entertainment areas and working machinery demonstrations.

Site selection

Assuming that you are not grabbing a last-minute cancellation site, the selection of your location is as important a factor as choosing a location for a high street shop.

Whilst it is critical that as many visitors as possible are made aware of your presence and visit your stand, there are other factors to be considered such as the location of competitors. For good marketing reasons, you may or may not wish to be close to them. It is quite common for the organizer to group similar products in the same aisles or areas to make it easier for visitors to identify and find types or ranges of products in which they have a particular interest. Some exhibitors ensure that they have the same location every year so that their regular customers will be sure to find them.

Study the exhibition hall plan carefully. Do you want to be near the entrance – or adjacent or close to bars and refreshment areas – or even toilets for a steady flow of visitors – or in a quiet area? If you have working exhibits, you may have to site your stand adjacent to special service points such as gas, water, drainage, or close to good access if you have a very large exhibit. Watch out for pillars cutting through your stand space and make sure you understand what any strange devices marked on the plan actually mean.

If your choice of location is limited and you want to attract attention, this is where a good designer can help to enhance your display and make it stand out among all the others. This may be especially important if you are at a distance from the main entrance, in a remote corner, or where the venue has a gallery and visitors might have an overhead view of your site.

GETTING UNDERWAY

Make somebody wholly responsible for the venture from start to finish, giving them a task checklist and schedule at the top of which your objectives are clearly stated. This will help to ensure that nothing is overlooked and that the reason why it is all being created and implemented is not forgotten.

How much time have you got? You need plenty. Last-minute grabbing of space because it was at a special price may not be such a bargain if there is not enough time for proper planning and execution.

Plan a schedule

The following represent the key tasks that must be built into the exhibition preparation schedule. They are more or less in order of sequence:

- Select site, sign contract, note payment schedule.
- Plan space layout.
- Prepare written brief for contractors to obtain rough visuals and quotations.
- Appoint stand fitting contractor, agree contracting schedule.
- Brief designer and read exhibitors' regulations together, noting build-up and breakdown periods for inclusion in this schedule.
- Develop the brief and obtain full working drawings, detail specifications and finalize costings.
- Agree who will provide house-style material and graphics.
- Agree on which suppliers are to be used for services and include ordering dates in this schedule.
- Agree on furniture provision and supplier.
- Contract with lighting and other services contractors if necessary.
- Agree dates of work in progress review meetings with contractor and designer.
- Arrange for products to be delivered to site or to contractor in accordance with the contractor build-up schedule.

591

- Plan, design and schedule delivery of promotional literature and any competition material.
- Agree method of assessing results and brief selected independent consultant.
- Brief and begin training stand staff and if appropriate allocate responsibilities for various tasks.
- Book advertising space and design advertisement; note copy-date requirements.
- Prepare public relations activity schedule.
- Brief catering contractor on requirements if entertaining on your stand or holding off-stand receptions. Arrange credit facilities with caterer if required.
- Check insurance position: does your company insurance fully cover staff travelling to and attending exhibitions, and the company property exhibited? Advise them anyway.
- Agree exhibition catalogue entry; provide copy to organizer.
- Obtain and circulate free admission passes to selected customers.
- Order floral decor if required from appointed contractor.
- Contract and brief the cleaning contractor.
- Read proofs and inspect artwork before graphics are produced and mounted.
- Attend at site regularly during build-up period to check progress and agree any last-minute adjustments.
- Obtain adequate number of staff exhibitor passes and car-parking passes.
- Organize transfers of equipment and working material from own office/company stores to exhibit stand.
- Pre-opening staff briefing and rehearsal, day before opening; agree rest and working arrangements with staff during exhibition.
- Agree exhibit breakdown procedure with stand fitting contractor and allocate responsibility for the safe removal of your products and other company material.
- Put sales lead follow up procedures into action.
- Analyse results of sales lead conversion to actual sales.

Plan the layout

What are you going to include in the stand area? Will it all fit into the space available? And will the overall design and its impact on visitors achieve the objectives? The following are some of the items and considerations that must be taken into account when you brief a professional designer or contractor:

- Working demonstrations (check health and safety regulations).
- Audio-visual displays (check lines of sight, access for sound level changes, repairs and replacements).

- Static exhibits and product displays including plinths mountings and so on.
- Graphic displays, promotion copy and supporting artwork. (Is it visible? Will it get damaged by visitor contact?)
- Private interview/entertainment areas, visitors and staff coats, personal possessions and secure storage.
- Visitor access and circulation space.

A certain amount of the space planning can be achieved by drawing up a scaled plan and using scaled cut-outs to represent the items that you want to accommodate. Resist overcrowding, introducing counters to keep the visitors away, and discard anything that is not vitally necessary or will not enhance the image and value of your product.

What will the stand look like?

Careful consideration must be given to the way in which the company house-style, logos, and brand names will be exposed, and, just as importantly, how the visual presentation will appear from the visitors' point of view on the day, no matter from which direction they approach, how crowded the aisles or how gaudy, noisy or subdued are your neighbouring exhibitors' presentations.

In this context the way that the stand staff are positioned and presented must be taken into consideration. Should they be uniformed as part of the overall design and where will they stand to be able to win the most advantageous contact with the visitors? Is there enough space for staff to demonstrate the product in a way that can attract further visitors on to the stand?

Most exhibitors distribute promotional literature at exhibitions. Clearly such printed material must be written and designed to achieve the marketing objective. It should be eye-catching, desirable and placed in easy to pick up positions. Just as important is to see that any literature made freely available does not become litter in the aisle. This will not enhance your image.

Extra things to think about

Have you used all the promotional opportunities offered by the organizer – entry in the catalogue, advertising in the catalogue, supplementary advertising in trade magazines, news items for the exhibition daily newsletter, interesting colour and black and white photographs to go in as well?

How are you going to collect and record the names, job titles and contacts of visitors to the stand, and details of their inquiries?

What have you done to ensure that your displayed products and staff property are secure at all times?

Did the organizer give you an allocation of admission tickets and how are you going to distribute them to your best advantage?

How are you going to get everything under your control out of the exhibition hall within the given breakdown time?

WORKING THE SHOW

Exhibitions are people-to-people events. The visitors have to be persuaded to physically get on your stand, to talk to your sales staff, and if it is important to your product promotion, to your technical staff as well. Only careful forward planning and good management will enable you to achieve the best results.

Stand management

The way in which your stand is managed is a direct and continuous reflection of your company image. Staff must be trained for the task and there are at least two excellent training videos that can be hired from Video Arts which point out the obvious in an amusing, entertaining and memorable way. There should be at least two training and briefing sessions organized to include everyone that is to be involved in the exhibition. One should be about six to eight weeks before the event, and the other the day before opening, with a visit to the exhibit stand for staff to get acquainted with the layout and for a role rehearsal session.

One person should be the stand manager, and every other member of staff should be given a list of their responsibilities, tasks and operating rules in writing. If it is a large company with many subsidiaries, it is also important that stand staff are made familiar with what the company produces, its mission statement, the names of its key directors and executives, and the objectives to be achieved at the exhibition. Stand staff should be scripted and rehearsed in what to tell prospective customers about the products or services and what will happen next if the prospective customer shows an interest in purchasing, how they will be contacted, invoiced, credit control and facilities if appropriate etc.

One of the rules has to be that no staff leave the stand without saying where they are going, for how long, and how they can be contacted. Visitors to stands sometimes ask for members of staff by name, or need special technical assistance, and they will not wait very long.

This leads to the use of mobile telephones which some organizers and venues ban on the exhibition floor. They should not in any case be used on the stand public areas.

Only if there is an obvious reception desk or area should stand staff be given the opportunity to sit whilst in the public eye. Stand staff are there to meet prospective customers, introduce themselves, the company and the product and rarely can this be done well or graciously from an inferior position to your guest or visitor.

It is very tiring, standing all day, hopefully continuously talking to sales prospects. Ensure that there are adequate staff and plenty of regular rest periods. Produce a staff rota and make sure that, as near as possible, it is followed.

The staff must have somewhere to put their coats and personal possessions that is secure. They should be briefed about the facilities for refreshments at the venue. Staff must not eat or drink in any public areas of the stand.

The stand must be kept clean, not just tidied up at the end of the day, but all day. Somebody must be made responsible for clearing ashtrays, and everybody for picking up dropped litter.

Using staff hired especially for the exhibition

There are a number of agencies who supply professional exhibition stand staff. When properly briefed, they can often be more effective than your own staff at buttonholing visitors and getting them to come on to the stand or to take literature. You will quickly know if they are qualified professionals because they will ask important leading questions about their responsibilities, the product, who is who in your company and what they are expected to achieve. They will also expect proper rest breaks and to be treated as though they are your own staff.

Promotion

Advertising and public relations at exhibitions should be thought about and planned in relationship to the overall company marketing strategy not as a one-off event. The exhibition is a good opportunity to advertise new products and innovations, often in specially prepared newspaper and trade magazine supplements. It is also a prime opportunity to win editorial copy, comment, and pictures of your product in trade and other relevant newspapers and journals. Feature journalists should be appraised well in advance of your attendance and what you are promoting.

Prepared photographs of products, stand personnel, even human interest stories about the stand staff should be prepared in advance so that any suitable public relations opportunity can be seized effectively.

There will normally be a press office at the exhibition which should be stocked with your literature to which is attached a press release highlighting the most interesting features. The press office should be visited at frequent intervals to ensure that your promotional material is always available. The press office staff should know your publicity contact and where they can be reached at any time.

You should think of an exhibition like a fairground where the loudest barker gets the biggest crowd, except the organizer will not allow you to make that sort of noise!

A technique used to draw regular attention to your exhibit stand and to gather business cards from visitors is to organize a competition that requires the participants to visit your stand. Such a competition properly planned can get extensive publicity in the organizers' promotional literature, daily newsletter and sometimes through regular public address system announcements.

WHAT REALLY HAPPENED?

We all had a good time, met lots of people and went home tired – but was it a success? There is no point in having spent all that money and energy without making sure that the end-results in terms of sales resulting from the exhibition are properly recorded.

There are a number of companies who will undertake an exhibition audit for you during the show. They will guide you on the way in which to prepare forms to record customer-contact conversations, and they will independently interview visitors to the show at random to assess the impact of your exhibit, staff and product, and report the results to you. This need not be an expensive exercise and will allow you to have an independent opinion of your success that can act as a guide to future tactics. It will indicate the changes that you might need to make to the stand design, staff training and management systems to increase the impact next time.

Further, it is vital to introduce a discipline that follows through all the activity after the exhibition that converts sales leads into sales in order to calculate the cost effectiveness of the exercise.

Follow-up

All the sales leads collected need to be followed up either by direct mail or sales calls. The method will depend on the type of product or service that you are promoting, the size and locations of the salesforce, and the general marketing strategies in force.

In some cases the organizer will sell exhibitors a mailing list of registered visitors which can be used to follow up your initial contacts and to reach those visitors who might have missed your stand.

CONCLUSION

Exhibitions are a marketing tool with unique advantages, reaching a targeted market with very little wastage. Visitors to exhibitions tend to be more receptive as they can make direct personal contact with the exhibitor.

To benefit from the exhibition opportunity it is necessary to draw up careful plans for the exhibition stand that creates a visual impact, highlights your product and projects your image. It is also necessary to have trained and properly managed staff to meet and impress the customers.

Exhibitions are a cost-effective promotion and sales medium when they are introduced as an integral part of the overall marketing and sales plan.

Building on the exhibition experience can only be achieved if sales leads are properly followed through and an evaluation of the conversion of sales leads to sales is maintained and recorded.

ESSENTIAL READING

British Exhibition Contractors Association (1993), *Successful Exhibiting*, London: BECA.

Cotteral, Peter (1992), *Exhibitions and Exhibitors Guide*, London: Hodder & Stoughton.

Northover, John (1990), *Exhibiting Handbook*, London: Kogan Page.

Waterhouse, David (1987), *Making the Most of Exhibitions*, Aldershot: Gower.

35 Customer service and customer care

Michael J. Thomas and W. G. Donaldson

In this chapter the management of customer service will be considered on three levels: the strategic level, the systems or organizational level and the people or operational level. According to Albrecht and Zemke (1985), customers rate a service throughout its performance. They hold a kind of mental 'report card' and assess the company for all the types of contacts they have with it (for example, telephone enquiries, sale, after-sales and so on). These mental report cards are the main constituents of a company's image. Customer service relates to the identification and management of the 'moments of truth' (Normann, 1991) when customers come into contact with the organization and form their impressions of its quality and service.

Customer service is often considered to apply only to service industries which have higher levels of customer contact and personal involvement. This usually means greater emphasis on what constitutes customer service. However, this emphasis is the result of a focus on the people and situational factors (the operational level) which offers only a partial solution, ignoring the strategic and organizational problems (see Figure 35.1).

For this reason the term 'customer care' will be adopted here to avoid limiting the discussion to service industries, although the terms can be interchangeable. The characteristics of service marketing such as intangibility, inseparability, heterogeneity and perishability (Zeithaml et al., 1985, 1985b) and the direct contact and social interaction in services mean a higher profile for customer care in the service sector. However, the artificial nature of the product/service dichotomy is clearly shown in situations where the physical product has a high service element, such as design services, delivery performance and after-sales service. There are a variety of diverse and unpredictable 'moments of truth' in such situations. For example, a company in double glazing (or any home improvement) may be selling a product but also operates a service where product qualities cannot be tested in advance and where the customer is usually present.

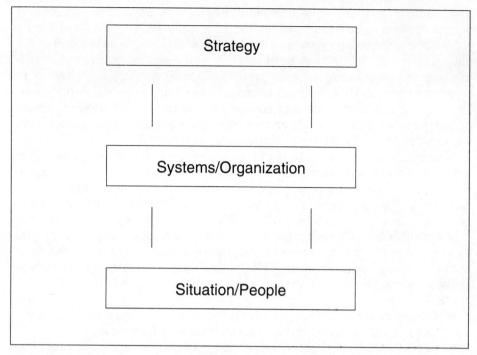

Figure 35.1   Concepts of customer care

There are many situational and product-specific aspects which will affect the resources allocated to customer care. These factors inhibit a universal approach to customer care but may apply equally well to product or service marketing situations. Albrecht and Zemke (1985) suggest therefore a continuum of these moments of truth. This continuum will move over time as motivational and hygiene factors vary in importance. Customer care involves different aspects of a firm's offering and different time-spans. Central to this theme is recognition of individual customers (bespoke rather than mass-marketing), of expert help when needed prior, during and following the purchase and efficiency in execution of the product (delivery) or service (moment of truth). Customer care incorporates core and peripheral activities and in increasingly competitive environments it is the number and quality of these peripherals rather than the core benefit which provide the competitive advantage and differentiation. Many professional buyers will continue to favour an existing supplier despite objective product or price disadvantages, at least in the short term. This inertia is a reflection of various dimensions of continuing customer care and attention.

Customer care is therefore important in differentiating between suppliers in competitive environments but is not an absolute. The level of service will always be affected by situational factors. What applies in personal computers is inappropriate for steel tubes, what is appropriate for crude oil not so for domestic soap powders and what is the norm in Nigeria will be different from that required in Japan. Where competition is intense, buyers' perceived level of customer service will vary. An additional complication is that the dynamic nature of many markets means that customers' views on acceptable service change over time. While it can be observed that the general level of the service component is increasing for most products in most markets, companies can penetrate niche markets with an alternative product, price and service mix. The implications of this are that constant re-evaluation of customer service must take place and trade-offs against, first, the demands of the market and, second, the relative position of competitors are essential.

Customer service and customer care mean the same and represent seller-initiated effort which has value for the buyer thus increasing customer satisfaction and encouraging patronage and loyalty to a supplier. Customer care can be classified in terms of pre-transaction, transaction and post-transaction activities (LaLonde and Zinzer, 1976). This is helpful in structuring customer care activities but still suffers from being a partial solution to a more general and interesting problem of how to make an organization customer-driven. A follow-up study (LaLonde et al., 1988) reached eight conclusions about how customer service has developed:

- Customer service has moved from the descriptive/reactive to a proactive management activity and indeed from an activity to a process.
- Service performance expectations are evolving into a window of acceptable performance rather than a specific point or hurdle. The result: low levels of service lose business but higher levels may not always have an effect.
- Information has moved centre stage in providing efficient and effective customer care.
- A significant amount of change in logistics systems is buyer-driven rather than seller-driven.
- Contractual-driven systems rather than transaction-driven are becoming the norm.
- There are significant differences in service practices and performance by industry.
- The scope of customer service activity in many firms has extended from the domestic to the international sphere of operations.
- The pressure on customer service performance will continue to increase for the foreseeable future.

The issue of how far the customer is prepared to trade-off price for service means it is necessary for management to evaluate customer care as part of marketing and corporate strategy, integrate service with other elements in the marketing mix and evaluate its contribution and worth in obtaining and sustaining business.

Customer care is not only a source of patronage and a revenue generator but a cost whose limits must be carefully monitored – no service is free though some elements of service are more cost-effective than others. These cost aspects of service can be identified internally and estimated with accuracy. Many organizations have concentrated on minimizing or strictly controlling these costs, and this can be myopic. Revenue arising from customer care is much more difficult to assess. Successful companies will allocate resources to this measurement problem and modify their customer care programmes.

INFLUENCES ON CARE LEVELS AND POSSIBLE BENEFITS

A variety of factors, both internally and externally generated, contribute to the growing importance of careful planning of customer care. First, as organizations increase in size there is a problem of a lack of understanding of customers' wants and needs and the real benefits offered by an organization's product/service capability. Second, as economies are achieved by standardization and increased scale of production, it becomes difficult to meet individual customer needs at a reasonable cost. Third, where personal contact is important there is variable quality. Fourth, communications from salespeople or advertising can lead to differences in expectations of what was expected and can be delivered. Pressures on sales and profits exacerbate these problems.

Externally generated reasons for careful planning of customer care may be even more compelling. Increasingly consumers seek higher-order benefits; Maslow's self-actualization needs begin to predominate as lower order needs are satisfied. Consumers are more demanding and more sophisticated. At the same time more is on offer from other suppliers, home and overseas, competing for disposable income. Yesterday's luxuries are today's necessities. Some service features which were considered as a plus or as motivational factors at the point of purchase may become mere hygiene factors as customers get used to them. Punctuality, which was Scandinavian Airline System's selling proposition in 1982, is not listed in the customers' choice criteria any more. Today, punctuality must be offered by airlines as a minimum level of quality and is not an incentive for customers to choose one particular airline over the others. Legal reasons, consumerism, environmental changes and international competition are all contributing factors to changing standards. Successful companies in the future will anticipate such trends, welcome the raising of standards and reap the benefits from providing real customer satisfactions and improving the quality of life.

Other reasons why the customer care movement should be welcomed are the benefits which accrue. First, there is the rather altruistic benefit of higher levels of customer satisfaction. This becomes a highly practical reason since greater satisfaction leads to customer loyalty commensurate with greater sales stability, more effective planning and lower levels of uncertainty. A second benefit is employee satisfaction and loyalty, enhancing job satisfaction and reducing employee turnover. Customer care also provides a competitive advantage not always easily imitated, usually highly cost-effective. Superior customer care can form the basis of promotional themes (for example British Airways). Effective customer care results in positive word-of-mouth communi-   *601*

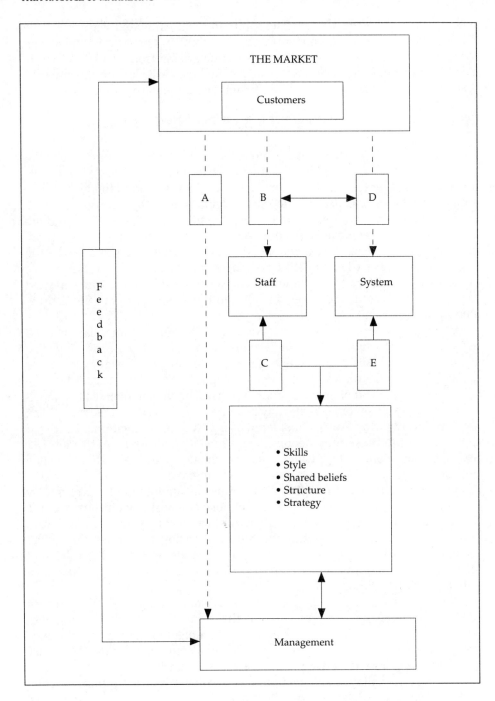

Figure 35.2   The customer care model
Source: Thomas, 1986.

cation from existing to potential customers. This is a most potent means of advertising, which contributes greatly to a company's improved image and reflects itself in improved sales and enhanced profitability. This is the most compelling of all reasons for a competitive enterprise – higher sales and profits and the achievement of corporate objectives.

A CONCEPTUAL MODEL OF CUSTOMER CARE

To reflect the importance of customer care and translate this to effective management it may be useful to model the three levels – strategic, organizational and operational – and consider the interfaces such a system may create. This is shown in Figure 35.2. The interfaces depicted by the model are labelled A to E. These are discussed below.

The management-customer interface (A)

Management does not often come into contact with most customers. However, when dealing with key accounts there is contact. Such accounts are normally the sole prerogative of top management. The logic of such a system, whereby a company distinguishes between customers, comes from Pareto's rule, which suggests that 80 per cent of a company's business comes from 20 per cent of its customers. While these percentages vary from one company to another, the general rule that the bulk of a company's business comes from a small number of customers still applies. By taking responsibility for key accounts, top management can control the bulk of the business.

The low level of contact which management has with customers calls for an efficient feedback system. The external component of this involves the operation of a carefully planned market research programme. This is the most effective way of determining the customer's 'service report card' referred to earlier. To ensure customer satisfaction top management clearly needs to know the elements of the report card. The internal aspect of the feedback system involves the monitoring of customer complaints. From this management can develop complaint profiles. These will help to identify areas of weakness within the organization enabling the adoption of corrective measures.

Management needs to create a service strategy which distinguishes the company's service offer from that of competitors. This needs to be clearly communicated to both the employees and the customer. Furthermore, the service strategy needs to highlight the critical importance of the customers.

Management must ensure that the organization structure is customer-orientated. To achieve this the primacy of the marketing department must be acknowledged, especially in the case of service organizations. In a product organization the marketing department's role can be clearly distinguished from the production process. However, in the provision of a service, the customer is involved in the process. As a result of this the customer is seen both as a consumer and as a producer – a 'prosumer'. It is for this reason that marketing cannot be something done only by a marketing department. The marketing department needs to have control over the salesforce and have considerable control over all employees who influence the provision of the service. To ensure this the marketing department needs to have a line as opposed to staff function. Unfortunately, this is not the case with many organizations.

The staff-customer interface (B)

Undoubtedly, the front-line staff have most contact with customers. The staff should be aware of and understand the customer needs and expectations on an individual basis. Customers will assess the company's service on the basis of the staff they come into contact with. The staff are the ambassadors of the company and should reflect the 'managed image'. As such they need to display a high degree of skill. This includes a professional approach, good interpersonal skills, ability to communicate, a positive attitude, good product knowledge and an ability to sustain this image even under pressure.

The staff who do not come into direct contact with customers need to realize that they are supporting those who do. The staff themselves can therefore be viewed as customers. This highlights the need for a team spirit among the staff. Clearly this will ensure flexibility in their performance. The staff need to understand the system and know how to use it to meet customer requirements. Since they make daily use of the system and know its strengths and weaknesses they could contribute significantly to its improvement.

The management-staff interface (C)

The quality of the service offered by a service company is only as good as the calibre of its staff. Staffing and recruitment, evaluation of performance, the operation of a welfare policy, feedback and shared beliefs or culture are vital. Given that the service industry is people-intensive, management needs to understand people. This underlines the need for management to adopt a participative stance. To demonstrate its commitment, management needs to adopt a high visibility profile, for example, by the adoption of an MBWA (manage by walking around) style.

In manufacturing industry where the quality of the tangible product and its competitive price are also vital, customers often rate service elements such as delivery reliability and the quality and responsiveness of support personnel as of equal and in some cases more importance. In many industrial organizational relationships, the key role of the marketing manager may be to orchestrate, match and manage the interaction of personnel from the supplier with those of the buying organization. In both product and service businesses it is the responsibility of management to see to the training of the staff. Training enhances the skills held by the staff and their confidence in dealing with customers. Furthermore, the staff would feel that management cares and this maintains their enthusiasm.

The customer-system interface (D)

The service strategy must extend to the system in use. This needs to be user-friendly. The design of the system must therefore take into account how the customer will use it. It must not be designed primarily to suit the company, a feature often forgotten in the headlong rush to adopt new technology. A basic reason for improving information systems and procedures should be the positive effect on customers. Leading-edge companies use new technology not only for administrative and operational activities but as a source of strategic competitive advantage (Domegan and Donaldson, 1992).

The management-system interface (E)

Management must continuously seek to make improvements in the system. Traditionally, this could be achieved through work study and organizational and methods departments. Today organizations must be open, flexible and responsive to their customers. Delegation of responsibility to staff, empowerment to manage the total customer contact is another characteristic of the service-driven organization. Management need to better understand their own systems, identify the elements of the task which must be performed in the customer's presence and ensure that non-essential elements are carried out away from the customer. Furthermore, the staff who are the main system users need to be involved. This requires different leadership skills from the traditional manager–subordinate role. For example, management should provide for breakdowns and for the maintenance of the system. To ensure continuity of service, adequate back-up/standby systems need to be available.

The layout of the premises has a profound effect on the atmosphere which is created within the service organization. It should create a comfortable atmosphere for its customers. As Winston Churchill once noted: 'We shape our buildings, and afterwards our buildings shape us.' The layout influences the image which a company can build. The clearing banks spend considerable sums of money to change their interiors to move away from their traditional image. Previously they were perceived as imposing, rather unfriendly institutions. Now they are moving towards a user-friendly stance. While important, these trappings of customer care must also be supported by a more genuine and substantial managerial and organizational commitment to customers.

THE COMPONENTS OF CUSTOMER CARE

Marketing research in customer care lags behind product and advertising research yet is as fundamental to a company's long-term success. Further, even where identification of these service components is well made, translation into operational measures may suffer distortion. Since customer care is aimed at the individual rather than the market, individual channel members or disparate members of a buying-decision unit may have quite different perceptions and expectations of what is required in terms of the service component.   *605*

The organization has no real alternative to identifying the most important sources of power and influence in the purchase decision and giving these priority. Again, the higher the absolute standard of service the less the problem in customer terms, subject to cost constraints.

Identification of the components of customer care has been made using the classification shown in Figure 35.3. These are grouped as discussed below.

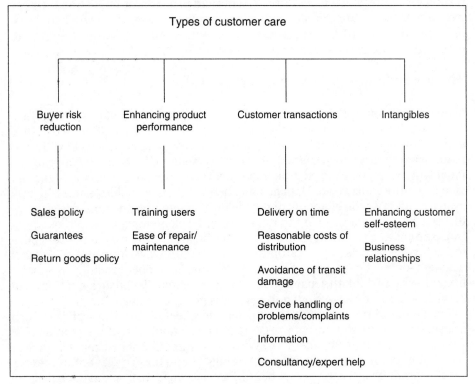

Figure 35.3   A classification of the components of customer care

Buyer risk reduction

In some countries this element is partly covered by legal obligations but companies which believe in their product's viability can offer extended periods of warranty. Companies which promote this service dimension must be aware of the costs of excessive claims and consumers must be confident that the warranty promise will be honoured. Some companies establish a service reputation by a declaration of their returned goods policy – UK retailer Marks and Spencer is an obvious example. Such policies contribute to the source effect in a company's reputation. Price guarantees such as 'if you can buy cheaper we will refund the difference' are also examples of an added service dimension.

Enhancing product performance

Various service components can be built on to the physical product which improve the benefits customers derive from the purchase. Easily repaired or maintained equipment with minimum downtime for users may be preferred to alternative products. Companies which offer training for users or temporary support staff may gain significant competitive advantage far outweighing the cost. Some computer suppliers who have made available such services find a new market demand for support staff as an optional extra. In addition to enhancing reputation such service becomes a profit-generating centre, such as the development of software support to augment machine hardware in the machine tool industry.

Customer transactions

In the customer transaction category are the traditional dimensions of customer service in terms of order processing and the physical distribution function (Christopher et al., 1979). Again, these elements vary with different situational factors affecting the exchange process. The premise here is that well-managed organizations will take a cost-effective, proactive approach to these elements and will have as part of their marketing plans written expectations on:

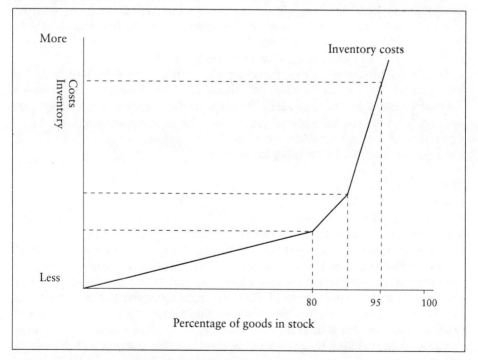

Figure 35.4   Cost of stockholding and service levels

- Delivery time and reliability.
- A competitive cost of distribution to sales.
- A responsibility for minimum damage in transit and handling.
- Speedy handling of enquiries, queries and delivery problems.
- Information on out-of-stock items or unfulfilled orders.
- Translation of order and product service levels into operational standards.

Some companies offer too high a level of service, increasing costs and reducing the distributor's stockholding function. The net effect may be that the service level to the end-user is unaffected while the cost of increased service has been transferred between channel members. Companies may use percentage figures for product service levels (out-of-stock items) or order service levels (number of orders incomplete). The cost of maintaining such levels is a crucial dimension of business efficiency (see Figure 35.4).

Customer care is perceived at a lower level where delivery is slow, a product is out-of-stock or an order incomplete. However, it is the speed, efficiency and courteous manner in dealing with such problems which impress a customer and achieve a higher score on his or her 'mental report card'. If the customer is ill-treated, antagonized or inconvenienced at least two outcomes are possible: one, the customer is dissatisfied and the business is lost with the supply company often unaware of this outcome; or two, the customer takes the trouble to complain and the problem is corrected. One study suggests those who do complain are more likely to remain customers in the future (Priest, 1984). Another writer claims that it costs five times as much to attract a new customer as it costs to keep an existing one (Sellers, 1989).

The moral must surely be that it is incumbent upon suppliers to identify levels of satisfaction or dissatisfaction among existing, potential and previous customers using a variety of marketing research techniques such as attitude surveys, lost order analysis and some form of customer service audit. Many firms now encourage customer comments and actively seek customer feedback rather than merely reacting to complaints.

Intangibles

A factor often suggested as discriminating between product and service marketing is the intangibility of service *vis-à-vis* products. This intangibility extends to services which enhance products. These provide the buyer with greater self-respect and self-esteem – the so-called higher order needs. An example would be new machinery which exposes buyer ignorance, reduces self-esteem and lost orders result. This feature is recognized in the reluctance of certain groups to adopt new products. Suppliers who offer guidance and training and 'free' expertise enhance potential buyers' confidence in new products, perhaps enabling them to 'sell the idea' to other members of the buying organization.

An extension of buyer confidence is the long-term business relationships which are built up between organizations and between individuals. Such relationships are vital in the exchange process over the longer term.

THE MANAGEMENT OF CUSTOMER CARE

The management of the customer care function within an organization requires consideration across the three dimensions – strategy, systems and people – referred to in Figure 35.1 and the interfaces in Figure 35.2. If this function does not achieve separate status, inter-functional co-operation and co-ordination are required. Does the customer have a number of contacts in different functions at different levels and is 'the story' the same? If there is just one point of contact, is this person a specialist in product knowledge, in production and stock control or distribution methods or technical information and advice? Customer care programmes require effective management and therefore a planned approach is advocated. This is outlined in Figure 35.5.

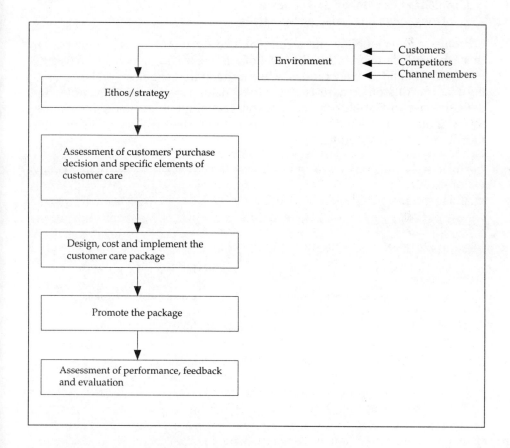

Figure 35.5   The process of managing customer care

Stage 1: The strategy of customer care

The starting point for any customer care plan is the ethos of the organization, usually established by the founder, the chief executive or the board of directors' consensus. In some cases this ethos is formally stated, while in others no formal statement exists but the ethos is understood via operational measures. These measures can either be implicit – high capability, advanced technology, integration of activities, highly qualified, trained and motivated staff – or explicit, such as product service, distribution standards, goods returns policy. In today's environment the customer care concept is typified by what is called 'new culture companies' (Normann, 1991). Characteristics of such organizations are:

1 An orientation towards quality and excellence.
2 Customer orientation.
3 Investment in people orientation.
4 Small is beautiful on a large scale.
5 Strong focus but broad perspectives.

Customer care is a policy, not a concept. Great attention needs to be paid to this aspect since overstating the level of customer care may lead to dissatisfaction at unfulfilled expectations, while understatement clearly misses a selling feature. Customer care is difficult to define, is usually intangible, and difficult even with sophisticated research technique to evaluate in customer terms. If our definition of customer care is too wide it will be ineffective, too narrow it will be restrictive.

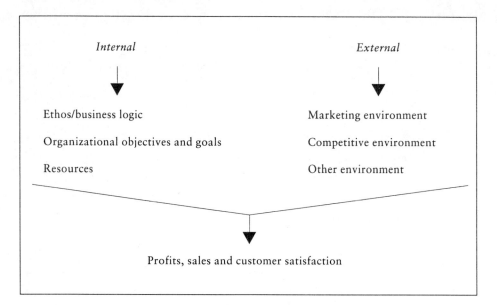

610 Figure 35.6 The strategy balance

Evaluation of customer care can be more easily established by operational measures such as quality control levels, items out of stock or the number of complaints, but also needs evaluation by senior management as to what they say, what they do and the price attached to care levels. This is more than a slogan such as 'the people who care', 'happy to help' or 'technology you can trust' but such slogans are a useful expression of this ethos.

Ethos is such an important part of corporate strategy that it may require elaboration or a separate statement. This ethos or business logic has then to be translated into a corporate core benefit or unique selling proposition which provides the enterprise with its identity in relation to its markets and by comparison with the competition. It is also a means of creating shared values throughout the organization, a unifying direction for management and service priorities for staff. Although ethos can be expressed as a slogan, strategy requires a careful analysis of environmental factors matched with company resources (see Figure 35.6).

Part of the difficulty with this strategic process is controlling both systems and people to implement the strategic role. Consistency with other elements such as product quality, advertising and personal selling is crucial and the integrated effect most important. There is also a tendency with customer care to consider levels as absolute when in fact they are relative. That is, levels of care will change over time and change in particular in relation to competitor activity. To some extent these organizational and situational factors may be more crucial.

Stage 2: Assessment of the customer's purchase decision and definition of the specific elements of customer care

Purely quantitative measures such as sales volume, growth or profit are the intended result of increased levels of care but, as indicated in the conceptual model, this statement is too simplistic. Part of the problem is shown in Figure 35.7 – sales and profits may be increasing in the short run as a result of a superior product or growth market. Yet customer care ratings are low, affecting not only what could be achieved but threatening long-term survival as existing customers are lost to new entrants.

Information regarding service-related purchasing criteria is vital to effective management of the customer care function. This information can be collected in different ways from a variety of sources. The following three are most commonly used.

Unsolicited customer response

The difficulty of using such response is that it can be particularly biased and unrepresentative. Usually those complaints which reach the chief executive get the most attention irrespective of their worth. Such corrective action is also after the event and therefore treats the symptoms not the cause. *611*

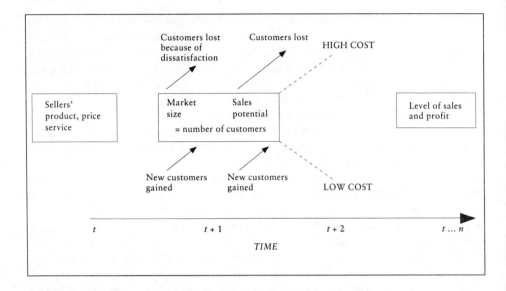

Figure 35.7   The hidden costs of poor customer care

However, formal recording of any negative feedback can identify possible problems at the earliest stage so that corrective action can be quickly implemented.

Solicited customer response

Having identified customer service to be important it is necessary to manage service effectively. For this to be achieved feedback is required from customers, members of the distribution channel and those people in the organization such as salespeople who are in contact with customers.

   The difficulty in using these sources is the lack of objectivity in their responses. Salespeople, for example, may report customers' views inaccurately so that they are seen not to have failed in their persuasive skills. Other salespeople may exaggerate customer service problems as an excuse for poor selling effort. Distributors too may exaggerate customer problems or use competitors as a source of blackmail to force manufacturers to increase their service and costs for their own ends. To be too generous in improving service may create additional problems. Customers are clearly desirable sources of information but, again, how objective and representative are their comments at one point in time for a given situation?

Marketing research surveys

The use of research is necessary to assess accurately the need for customer service and to measure existing performance *vis-à-vis* competitors. Such surveys can take a variety of forms. Where possible, outside agencies should be used to maintain objectivity although qualified in-house personnel can also be considered. Such surveys cannot be one-off exercises and if not necessarily continuous should at least be regularly updated. These surveys should reveal:

- A rating for the level of service provided by the organization.
- A comparative position with competitors.
- The relative importance of different service elements.
- The possibility of additional improvements in service.

Stage 3: Design, cost and implement the customer care package

Armed with an organizational philosophy, an understanding of buyers' decision processes and marketing research input, management must design, cost and implement the service elements. This is the systems or organizational level and is similar to that applying for product or promotional decisions – a sub-section of marketing activity. The quality of the package will be most effective using a combination of marketing research, trading flair, customer contact and innovation. Also required are adequate information systems, efficient order-processing facilities and clear communication. This may mean investment in computing capability, technical facilities and trained people and a policy of after-sales service. Recruitment, training and motivation of staff are essential, backed by top management involvement.

Improved service and customer care do not necessarily increase costs. For example, better quality control, formal reporting procedures and increased automation may both improve customer care and reduce costs. The implication of service both as a cost and a revenue must be carefully assessed. If the costs of improved service levels become excessive, leading to a comparative cost and price disadvantage, some compromise will be required. Some diminishing returns to increased service levels will result. Trade-offs must be made between more and better levels of service and other customer benefits. A separate issue, although one which can be evaluated at the same time, is the competitive advantage which does or does not accrue from the service package.

Stage 4: Promoting the package

The efforts to obtain an advantage in terms of customers through care programmes must be fully exploited in promotional and selling effort. Any marketing advantage must be confidently and repeatedly sold to the buyer.

Stage 5: Performance evaluation

Figure 35.8 outlines the process of service performance evaluation and feedback. As stated in Stage 2, the establishment of standards for service performance is often quite challenging. This is because it requires the involvement of the customers in the production process. Preliminary market research is, therefore, mandatory because the evaluation factors that customers use for rating the service performance must be identified. This is a basic step in the customer research process.

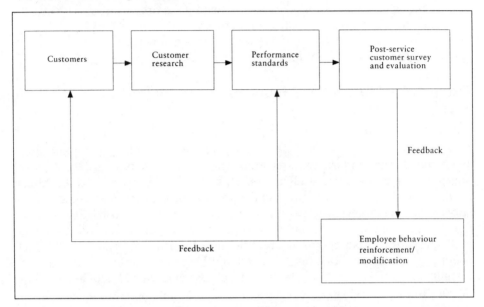

Figure 35.8   Service performance evaluation and feedback process

The service performance standards are then established on the basis of the identified evaluation factors. These are incorporated in the service strategy and communicated to the front-line people.

The measurement of performance is done via post-service survey through customer and attitude tracking. Such research can be both continuous or discrete. Results obtained will indicate to management how customers view the organization's service performance. BT is doing this via its Telecare programmes and British Airways uses customer surveys. Post-service research provides feedback to management. This will be used to evaluate the performance of employees. If the feedback is positive, management will consolidate its performance standards and engage in employee behaviour reinforcement. If the feedback is negative, the company would review its performance standards and engage in employee behaviour modification. Feedback would also entail informing the customers of significant improvements undertaken by the organization to enhance service performance standards. A company which follows the service performance evaluation procedure described above would be one that responds proactively to its environment.

Stage 6: Operations and people

It is imperative that the customer care training programme has the support of top management. This will ensure their involvement and that the necessary resources are made available. Lower-level management and staff must know that their performance will be judged by their superiors. This ensures a motivating climate. Otherwise nothing is likely to result no matter how hard the personnel department tries. It is a feature of companies which have undertaken customer care programmes that the instigators have in fact been top executives. At SAS the strong personality of the president, Ian Carlzon, was instrumental in injecting a service culture to the organization. He ensured he talked to everyone and clearly put forward his commitment to service. The same can be said for British Airways. Their programme of 'putting people first' came about with the arrival at British Airways of Colin Marshall as chief executive. He was the prime mover, setting new objectives and ensuring that the service culture penetrated to all levels of the organization. Top management commitment was underlined to employees by Marshall making an appearance at the end of each course in the retraining programme. As Sasser and Arbeit (1976) note: 'the successful service company must first sell the job to employees before it can sell its services to customers'. This in effect involves an internal marketing exercise with the objective of ensuring motivated and customer-conscious personnel.

Effective management support can come about only if management has a means of receiving feedback from employees. The importance of operating a feedback system has been recognized at American Express, where staff at all levels report to management about problems they have encountered with their jobs and in dealing with customers. Another method aimed at obtaining feedback with a view to taking corrective action has been the setting up of quality circles which are usually based on groups of genuine volunteers whose task is to examine ways to better customer services. Quality circle programmes are based on the assumption that employee participation leads to valued outcomes, such as intrinsic satisfaction and recognition, and that it also results in changes which enhance productivity and satisfaction. Management is also responsible for establishing standards of quality.

The result of customer care programmes ultimately depends on the attitude and motivation of the employees. Individuals must be aware of the company philosophy, trained in interpersonal skills and in providing expert help. In some cases personnel may be high in engineering skills and technical ability but are different from customers in temperament, lack a sense of shared values with the corporate ethos or simply do not understand the extended role they must perform. Role ambiguity may be exhibited where individuals do not know or care about what is expected when dealing with customers. It is as crucial that the management–subordinate interface is managed on the basis of consistency and clarity of role, as well as the company–customer interface.

REFERENCES

Albrecht, K. and Zemke R. (1985), *Service America! Doing business in the new economy*, New York: Dow Jones–Irwin.

Christopher, M., Schary, P. and Skjott-Larsen, T. (1979), *Customer Service and Distribution Strategy*, London: Associated Business Press.

Domegan, C.T. and Donaldson, B. (1992), 'Customer Service and Information Technology', *Journal of Information Technology*, **7**, 203–12.

LaLonde, B.J., Cooper, M.C. and Noordewier, T.G. (1988), *Customer Service: A Management Perspective*, Chicago: Council of Logistics Management.

LaLonde, B.J. and Zinzer, P.H. (1976), *Customer Service: Meaning and Measurement*, Chicago: National Council for Physical Distribution Management.

Normann, R. (1991), *Service Management: Strategy and Leadership in Service Business*, 2nd Ed, Chichester: Wiley.

Parasuraman, A., Zeithaml, V.A. and Berry, L.L. (1985), 'A conceptual model of service quality and its implications for future research', *Journal of Marketing*, **49**, (4), Fall, 41–50.

Priest, A.A. (1984), 'Service departments become marketing adjuncts when they're used to field more than complaints', *Marketing News*, 7 December, p. 10.

Sasser, W.E. and Arbeit, S.P. (1976), 'Selling jobs in the service sector', *Business Horizons*, **19**, 61–65.

Sellers, P. (1989), 'Getting customers to know you', *Fortune*, **119**, (6), 26–33.

Thomas, Michael J. (1986), 'Customer care', a research report, University of Lancaster.

Zeithaml, V.A., Parasuraman, A. and Berry, L.L. (1985), 'Problems and strategies in service marketing', *Journal of Marketing*, **49**, (2), Spring, 33–46.

ESSENTIAL READING

Christopher, M., Payne, A. and Ballantyne, D. (1991), *Relationship Marketing: Bringing quality, customer service and marketing together*, Oxford, Butterworth–Heinemann.

Gronroos, C. (1990), *Service Management and Marketing: Managing the Moments of Truth in Service Competition*, Massachusetts: Lexington Books.

Lele, M.M. and Sheth, J.N. (1991), *The Customer is Key: Gaining an Unbeatable Advantage Through Customer Satisfaction*, New York: John Wiley & Sons.

Zeithaml, V.A., Berry, L.L. and Parasuraman, A. (1990), *Delivering Quality Service*, New York: Free Press.

36 The legal framework
Jane Hancock

In marketing any product, whether goods or services, there are a wide range of legal issues which must be taken into account. Without consideration of these issues, at the very least you may have dissatisfied your customer whilst at the opposite extreme, you may be facing prosecution in the criminal courts and action in the civil courts. It is therefore vital to get it right. Prime concerns are to ensure the product is properly described, of an acceptable quality and safe. There is a plethora of consumer and business law which should be considered in any marketing exercise. Limitations on space prevent coverage in detail of all UK laws relevant to marketing activities, but of prime concern are those that keep the customer protected whilst ensuring that your image (or that of your client) is not tarnished.

SAFETY

Many years of careful marketing can be eroded overnight by a single adverse press report or a warning given on the main television or radio news. Heavy fines can be imposed by the courts on companies which sell unsafe goods, together with equal fines and possible imprisonment of directors and senior managers. In addition, awards and damages can be made to individuals by the civil courts in cases where a product has caused injury.

The implementation of the Consumer Protection Act 1987 introduced the concept of the all-encompassing General Safety Requirement (GSR), making it an offence to sell any goods which are not reasonably safe. A similar requirement has subsequently been included in the General Product Safety Regulations 1994 (EGSR), which impose a requirement only to place safe products on the market. In deciding whether a product is safe the circumstances in which the product is presented, together with the instructions and labelling which are to be provided, must be considered. Marketing is thus inextricably

617

linked with safety of the goods; marketing and consumer safety therefore go hand in hand.

General Product Safety Regulations 1994

The Regulations are now the main source of public law controlling consumer safety. They are restricted to *consumer goods* although some sectors, antiques for example, are exempt. The Regulations act as a catch-all for safety problems not covered by specific safety legislation. The principal requirement of the Regulations is to require producers to place only safe products on the market and distributors to act with due care not to supply unsafe products. Products should not present any, or only a minimum, risk compatible with the product's use, including duration. In particular account should be taken of:

- Product characteristics, including composition, packaging, instructions for assembly and maintenance.
- The effect it may have on other products.
- Product presentation, labelling, instructions for use and disposal.
- Categories of consumers who may be at risk through use of the product, particularly children.

These circumstances are also equally applicable to sales promotions. When considering marketing any free gift these must also be 'safe'. Consumer safety is an emotive issue and any injury is likely to reverse the benefits of the promotional drive.

In addition to the all-encompassing EGSR, there are approximately 90 specific safety regulations covering the safety of a wide range of products from toys to anoraks, electrical appliances to machinery. The requirements of these regulations, which often call up safety standards, must also be considered in the marketing of any consumer product. It is not possible within the remit of this book to include details of all regulations but any marketing department should ensure that, in conjunction with product development and technical colleagues, all legal and non-legal safety aspects of the product in question have been addressed.

Product liability

Part I of the Consumer Protection Act 1987 deals with 'product liability'. People injured by defective products may have the right to sue for damages. 'Product liability' is the term given to these rights. Until the implementation of Part I of the Act, an injured party had to prove a manufacturer negligent or to show there had been a breach of contract before they could successfully sue for damages. The Act, in removing the need to prove negligence, imposes what is known as a *strict* liability on the following:

- The producer (manufacturer) of the defective product.
- The 'own brander'.

- The importer into the EU.
- The retailers who cannot identify the previous three categories.

It provides the same rights to anyone injured by a defective product, whether or not the product was sold to them, thereby removing the problem of 'privity of contract'. Here, only a person party to the contract can sue, which often deprived an injured person of the opportunity to seek redress. A child who is electrocuted when touching an appliance whilst visiting the home of a friend is an example.

Liability under this Part of the Act if not restricted to consumer goods although unprocessed agricultural products are specifically excluded. All other goods, including those used at work, are included.

What is 'defective'?

A defective product is defined as one 'where the safety of the product is not such as persons are generally entitled to expect'. The definition provides an objective test of 'defective' and refers neither to the particular injured person nor to the particular producer. A product will not be considered defective simply because it is of poor quality or because a safer version is subsequently put on the market. Once again, as when deciding whether a product is 'safe', the Courts will take into account all the relevant circumstances including:

- Any instructions or warnings that are given with it.
- What might reasonably be expected to be done with it.
- The time the producer supplied the product.

And, of most importance to marketing personnel:

- The manner in which the product is marketed.

A person can sue under the Act for compensation for:

- Death.
- Personal injury.
- Private property valued above £275.

The plaintiff must be able to show that on the balance of probability the defect in the product caused the damage.

QUANTITY

Nearly all goods are required by the Weights and Measures Act 1985 to be sold by reference to quantity, for example by weight or volume. The quantity must be marked clearly and legibly on the pack. Markings used must comply with regulations both in relation to the type of units used and size of the marking.   *619*

Some products, mainly foods, are required to be sold only in specified or 'prescribed' quantities. Even if the pack weight is correct it may be illegal to sell the product if it is not made up in the correct prescribed quantity.

Quantity control

It is particularly important to consider these prescribed quantities in relation to 'extra value' packs or special promotional packs. Where a product is required to be made up in a prescribed pack size there is a danger that a pack with a certain amount extra may not fall into the next highest prescribed pack size. For example, jam is required to be made up in quantities of 2oz, 4oz, 8oz, 12oz, 1lb, 1½lb or a multiple of 1lb. Packs of less than 50g are exempted. If it was decided to offer10 per cent extra on a 12oz jar, the new jar would be 13.2oz and thus not a permitted size. The jar would be unlawful.

Average quantity

The concept of 'average quantity' was introduced in the UK in 1979. Pre-packages must be marked with the weight or other measurement of their contents and packers and importers must comply with the three 'Packers Rules':

1 The contents of the packages must on average be as declared on the pack.
2 Not more than one package in 40 may contain less than the declared quantity by more than an amount known as the 'tolerable negative error'. This varies according to the quantity stated on the package.
3 No packages are allowed to contain less than the nominal quantity by more than twice the tolerable negative error.

Regulations specify which goods must be packed to the average system. Certain items such as ice cream, cakes and fresh fruit and vegetables are excluded, as are goods packed in very small and very large packages. However, packages not included in the Regulations may be voluntarily packed according to the average system if they are made up within the range of 5g to 10kg or 5ml to 10 litres and marked with the EC mark, that is, they must bear the 'e' mark.

Goods, irrespective of whether or not they are required to be packed to the average system, may continue to be prepacked to a minimum declaration where all quantities must be at or above the declared weight. Compliance with the minimum system ensures that the packers rules are met, although in practice this will result in far more checking.

The 'e' mark

The EC mark is a small 'e' which may be put on packages in the same field of vision as the nominal quantity. It must be at least 3 mm high and is shown in

Figure 36.1. The 'e' mark constitutes a guarantee by the packer or importer that packages have been made up in accordance with the average system and acts as a 'passport' throughout the whole of the EU.

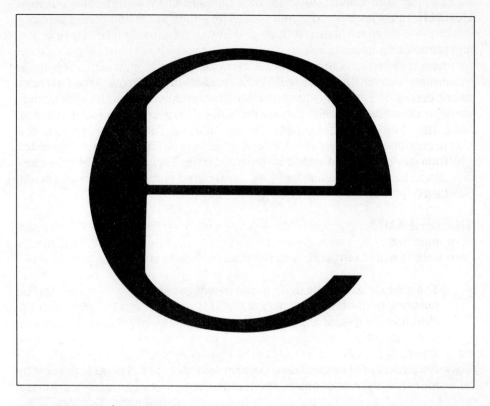

Figure 36.1   The 'e' mark

Short weight

Certain offences are created by Weights and Measures legislation. It is an offence to sell goods that are short weight, of an 'inadequate quantity' where average packs are involved or where a wrong indication of an amount is given. It is also an offence to give a lesser quantity than corresponded with the price charged. As such it would be an offence to advertise a product as £2 per litre, then charge the customer £2 but serve 750 ml.

QUALITY

There is an implied condition set out in the Sale of Goods Act 1979 that in relation to the sale of any goods to consumers they must be of *merchantable quality*. This means that they must be of reasonable quality likely to be acceptable to ordinary consumers, taking into account the purchase price and any other description given to them. In addition, the goods must be *fit for their intended purpose*. If the buyer requires goods for a specific purpose, or if the advertising or labelling of a product suggests that they are fit for a particular purpose, then they must be fit for that purpose. The goods must also conform to any description given to them. It follows that any description in labelling or advertising must also be accurate.

If any of these conditions are not met, the buyer is entitled to reject the goods and recover the money paid via a civil action. In summary the customer is entitled to be supplied with goods which correspond with the description, are of merchantable quality, and are fit for their purpose. Other legislation also introduces the concept of quality. For example the Food Safety Act 1990 creates the offence of selling food (or giving it away) which is not of the nature, substance or quality demanded by the purchaser. This is an example of a criminal statute where a trader could be prosecuted and fined for selling 'unfit' food.

DESCRIPTION

'Any person who, in the course of the trade or business:-

(a)   Applies a false trade description to any goods, or
(b)   Supplies or offers to supply any goods to which a false trade description is applied, shall, subject to the provisions of this Act, be guilty of an offence'.

So states Section (1) of the Trade Descriptions Act 1968. The Act makes it an offence to misdescribe goods or services in the course of a trade or business, and is intended to protect consumers from such misleading statements.

What is a trade description? This is comprehensively defined in the Act and includes such categories as quantity, size or gauge, method of manufacture or production, composition, fitness for purpose, strength, performance, behaviour or accuracy, other physical characteristics, place or date of manufacture, production, person by whom manufactured or processed, and any other history, including previous ownership or use.

A false description is one which is false to a material degree. In addition, the definition includes those descriptions which although they may not actually be false, are misleading. Case law has clarified that this means misleading to a typical consumer, not an expert in the field. The description must be applied in the course of a trade or business.

Property misdescriptions

Until the implementation of the Property Misdescriptions Act 1991, in April 1993, those involved in the sale of property were in the fortunate situation of being able to misdescribe property without running the risk of prosecution.

The act has now brought into line descriptions applied to property in the same way as other legal sanctions over goods. Misdescription of other goods is controlled by the Trade Descriptions Act 1968.

PRICE

Control over misleading prices is exerted by Part III of the Consumer Protection Act. The Act prescribes an offence as to give, by any means, in the course of a business an indication which is misleading as to the price at which goods, services, accommodation of facilities are available. A second offence provides that a person is guilty who has given to consumers in the course of a business an indication which has become misleading and there has been a failure to take all reasonable steps to prevent consumers relying on the indication.

Guidance as to what is or is not misleading is given in a Code of Practice for Traders on Price Indications, issued by the Department of Trade and Industry. The Code is not mandatory, and thus traders need not follow the Code. However, compliance with the Code may constitute a defence of 'all reasonable precautions and all due diligence' as provided by section 39 of the Act. Due diligence is discussed later in this chapter. Furthermore a court may have regard to the recommendations in the Code in determining whether or not a particular price indication is unlawful.

The Act defines the meaning of misleading: a price is misleading if it indicates that the price is less than it in fact is. In addition, a price indication can become misleading after it is given. The indicated price for goods which are offered with incentives can all too easily be caught by this offence.

STATUTORY DEFENCES

Most of the legislation discussed so far, that prescribes offences and which has a direct impact on marketing, contains what is known as a 'due diligence defence'. The defence is: 'In any proceedings for an offence under this Act, it shall be a defence for the person charged to prove that he took all reasonable precautions and exercised all due diligence to avoid the commission of an offence by himself or any person under his control.'

Though the words differ from Act to Act, the general principles are the same. If the defendant can prove to the Court that he has a due diligence defence, he will be acquitted; furthermore, if he can satisfy an enforcement officer that he has an adequate defence, the case is unlikely to proceed further.

Statutory defences have developed gradually during the past 120 years following the introduction in trading legislation of criminal offences of strict liability, that is those in which it is not necessary for the prosecutor to prove the defendant intended to commit the offence. Mere commission of the unlawful act is sufficient to secure conviction. Accordingly, the law seeks to redress the balance by the provision of such defences. Over the years there has been a great deal of judicial interpretation laying down what a defendant must do in order to establish the defence. The following principles should be considered: *623*

1 'All reasonable precautions' means setting up a control system. 'All due diligence' means taking steps to ensure that the system is working.
2 The system must be tailored to the company concerned. It is not possible to buy an off-the-shelf or blueprint system.
3 The system must be under the 'directing mind and will' of the company, but it is possible to place responsibility for day-to-day running of the system with senior employees or agents.
4 The degree of control required depends on the risk posed by the firm, its size and resources, and all other relevant circumstances of the case.
5 The system must be comprehensive, covering all relevant legal risks discussed in the preceding chapters.
6 The system must include the means to cross-check and obtain written confirmation of crucial details from vendors.
7 The due diligence system must be written down, with adequate instructions and training being given to staff. Records must be kept of the checks made to demonstrate that the system is working properly.
8 Staff should receive detailed instructions as to their duties and responsibilities within the system, together with adequate training. The responsibilities of directors, managers, and employees should be stated in writing and acknowledged by them. Job descriptions are an ideal vehicle.
9 Supervisory staff should be similarly trained and instructed, with particular emphasis on their responsibility for making the system work.
10 The system should be both proactive and reactive, that is it must be capable of preventing faults from occurring and of correcting them when they do occur.
11 Consumer complaints should be built into the system so that they are properly resolved and any problem areas or trends indicated by them are taken into account.
12 The system should be reviewed by senior management at appropriate intervals and be monitored, adjusted or amended as required.

The value of a due diligence system

Much has been said about the value of due diligence in dealing with prosecutions. However, it should not be overlooked that possession of a viable system will make it very difficult for local authorities to commence proceedings. It is not necessary for the system to prevent all offences from occurring; the operation of a good system which can withstand the scrutiny of the courts will be sufficient for acquittal even in cases where the facts clearly show that an offence has been committed.

SALES PROMOTION

There are diverse legal controls over many of the familiar techniques used to promote sales, some of which have been discussed in this chapter, for example, draws and competitions offering prizes, the offer of free goods and the collecting of tokens to offer in exchange for products. As such, promotions must contain no false descriptions, must give no misleading price indications, and goods supplied must be safe in all respects taking into account both the GSR and any other relevant regulations. Issuing tokens, vouchers and the like is a familiar and popular technique. Trading stamps law must also be considered and, in the case of competitions, care must be taken that the competition does not inadvertently become an illegal lottery. Great care and thought must therefore be given to any promotion to ensure its legal compliance. In addition, any promotion should also comply with the self-regulatory British Code of Sales Promotion Practice, which can be obtained from the CAP Committee of the Advertising Standards Authority.

Prize draws

Care must be taken to ensure that any prize draw or competition does not inadvertently become a lottery and thus illegal. The Lotteries and Amusements Act 1976 outlaws all lotteries other than several defined types such as private lotteries and local lotteries which are beyond the scope of this book.

The term lottery is not defined in the Act but case law over the years has clarified the meaning of lottery. In the case of *Reader's Digest Association Ltd* v *Williams* [1976] 3A11 ER, 737, the Lord Chief Justice said:

> There are really three things one must look for in deciding whether a lottery has been established. First of all the distribution of prizes; secondly, the fact that that was to be done by means of chance; and thirdly, that there must be some actual contribution made by the participants in return for their obtaining a chance to take part in the lottery.

In other words, any game of total chance in which there is an award of prizes and people pay, directly or indirectly, to participate, is a lottery. General legal opinion is that if one of the three elements is defeated, a lottery cannot result. Thus, a promotion in which participants are requested to send in their name and address together with a product label as proof of purchase would be illegal if the winners were to be picked at random. However if an element of skill were introduced, such as a tie breaker, in which the winner was selected based on the aptness of the tie breaker, or where there was a blank paper entry, the promotion would not be a lottery as one of the elements has been defeated.

Gaming

Care must also be taken to ensure that promotion does not stray into the realms of gaming. Gaming is defined by the Gaming Act 1968 as meaning the playing of a game of chance, or of chance and skill combined, for winnings in money or money's worth, whether any person playing the game is at risk of losing any money or money's worth or not. It has been held that the expression 'playing a game' involves the participant in some form of activity. Mere *625* passive participation is not 'playing'. Unless gaming takes place in private in purely domestic circumstances, it is unlawful unless permitted by both the Gaming and Lotteries and Amusements Acts. This is a complex area of law and when considering this type of promotion it would be prudent to check its validity before pursuing the matter.

Free gifts

Free gifts are a commonly used promotional tool. In any free offers it is vital that the product or service offered is *actually* free of any charge and, unlike so many failed sales promotions, genuine. Failure to do so could lead to possible offences under Part III of the Consumer Protection Act and the generation of adverse publicity. The unqualified use of the word 'free' in a promotion means just that – no charges of any kind. The British Code of Sales Promotion practice requires that offers should not be described as free if there are any direct costs to the consumer, other than a charge not exceeding, as appropriate:

- Current public rates of postage.
- The actual cost of freight or delivery of the promotional goods.
- The cost, including incidental expenses, of any travel involved in the consumer profiting from the offer.

In all cases, the consumer's liability for such costs should be made clear, and there should be no additional charges for packing or handling.

In addition, the Code of Practice for Traders On Price Indications stipulates in relation to free offers:

1 It should be clear, at the time of the offer for sale, exactly what the consumer will have to buy to get the 'free offer'.
2 If any indication of the monetary value of the free offer is given and the sum quoted is not the trader's own present price for the product, clear details of the source should be given.
3 If there are any conditions attached to the 'free offer', the main conditions, with the price indication should be detailed, together with details of where full details can be obtained.

In addition the code states that a free offer should not be claimed if:

- Additional charges have been imposed which would not normally be imposed.
- The price of any product the consumer must buy to obtain the free gift has been inflated.
- The price of goods will be reduced to consumers who do not take up the free offer.

626 A recent phenomenon is the offer of free travel and/or accommodation in relation to the purchase of goods. Such schemes can sometimes be unstructured and cause major problems for clients. The Hoover free flights promotion in 1993 is a salutary lesson for those marketing executives striving for the ultimate promotion. Utmost care should be taken to ensure that such schemes are viable, as adverse publicity can have devastating effects on the company. If these simple rules are followed, there should be no problem with the legality of the promotion of 'free' goods and services.

OTHER LEGAL CONTROLS

This chapter would be incomplete if some mention were not made of the legal controls you need to consider in order to protect your own rights in respect of any marketing issues, for example an innovative packaging design, snappy slogan or interesting photographic advertisement.

Patents

Before launching a new product it is essential to consider whether there are any original aspects which may be patentable. A patent is essentially a monopoly granted for a limited period by the government (Patent Office) for a new and inventive industrial idea. Once granted, a patent prevents anyone else from copying your design for a period of 20 years. Not all inventions are patentable. To be patentable an invention requires four things:

1   It must be original.
2   It must involve an innovative step.
3   It must be capable of industrial application.
4   It must not be of an excluded type, for example scientific theory, of music or literary work, mental scheme, computer program, presentation of information, offensive, immoral, antisocial, plant variety, or be of mere discovery.

Design registration

Your new product or its packaging may have a particularly unusual and interesting appearance. Provided the appearance does not depend on the method of construction of the article or the job it has to do, one should be entitled to the grant of a design registration. Once registered, no one may use the same design, and you can stop anyone from doing so even if the imitation of your design was inadvertent.

Design right

Where an article has an unusual internal or external shape which does not depend on the method of construction of the article or the job it has to do, it can be entitled to a design right. There is no registration procedure for this.   *627*

Copyright

Where an article has an original shape and involves an element of artistic craftsmanship, then it may qualify for protection under the law of copyright. Again there is no registration procedure for this. Copyrights are enforceable against people who trade in the works where they ought to have known they were unauthorized copies. Copyrights may also be granted to prevent deliberate copying of artistic works, for example a copyright may cover films, photographs, written words and so on.

Trade marks

A trade mark is a badge by which one commercial enterprise distinguishes its products or services from those of another. A trade mark can take a variety of forms; usually it is a word or an invented word such as Rentokil, Bovril, Kodak. Shapes and pictures can also be trade marks. Registration of a trade mark is optional; there is no legal requirement to do so. However, anyone who neglects to register a mark is misguided, as registration can prohibit anyone else from using that mark in the classes for which registration has been granted.

THE CITIZEN'S CHARTER - WHAT PROTECTION DOES THIS AFFORD?

The answer to this question is in effect very little in regard to legal marketing issues. It may be arguable that false claims made to the effect that a business has met a Charter would contravene the Trade Descriptions Act. Essentially the Charter is a programme to improve the services of public sector and provides the 'citizen' with the right to be informed and choose for themselves. For those professionals involved in the marketing of public utilities there is clearly a need to be aware of the relevant Charter and care should be taken that any claims made, or requirements under, any Charter are met.

A FINAL WORD

Many legal controls are often ignored either through design or ignorance. Very little is done by way of 'taking reasonable precautions', thus illegal schemes abound. By exercising forethought, investigating legal risks and introducing controls *your* marketing exercise will be legal and, hopefully, successful. Remember, if the 'legal' wheel does come off, the resulting disaster can be horrendous.

ESSENTIAL READING

Rowell, R.A., Gresty, G.S. and Turner, A. (eds) (1992), *Practical Food Law Manual*, London: Sweet & Maxwell.

Parry, D.L., Rowell, R. and Harvey, B. (eds) (1994), *Butterworth's Trading and Consumer Law*, London: Butterworth.

O'Keefe, John A. *The Law of Weights and Measures*, ed. A.A. Painter and Brian Harvey, 2nd edn, London: Butterworth.

Index

database 552
definition 547
edible printing 544
future outlook 557
growth statistics 554–5
legal considerations 556
lists 551, 596
low cost outlay 546
regulations 556
trade bodies 556–7
typical form 544
use of consultant or other expert 555
use of mailing house or lettershop 553
UK total expenditure 555
volume of paper involved 553
see also Letterbox marketing
Direct marketing
Code of Practice 529
definition 433
see also Target marketing
Direct Marketing Association 529, 557
Direct Selling Association 529
Distribution
consideration of in agenda for marketing
change 5
costs 391–3
in international markets 272–3
maximizing return from 107
overseas *see* Exporting
physical distribution management 396
see also Logistics
Distributor-owned brands 146
Distributors
advantages of selling through 441–2
disadvantages of selling through 442,
462–3
role compared with agents 439–40
role compared with franchising 574–5
DOB *see* Distributor-owned brands
Donovan data systems 26
Door-to-door distribution *see* Letterbox
marketing
Doran, L. 105
Doyle, Dayin and Burback 88
Doz, Y. 465, 466
Drucker, P. 107–8, 388, 399

Eastern Europe 105–6, 109, 345, 476
EC *see* European Community
EC mark 620–1
Echikson, W. 107
Economist Intelligence Unit 20
EDI (electronic data interchange) 28
Effem Management Services 27
EFTPOS 411

Ehrenberg, A. S. C. 253
Elida Gibbs 435
Enterprise Zones 419
Environmental analysis *see* Market
environment analysis
Environmentalism 105
EPOS (electronic point of sale) systems 1,
22–3, 411–12, 519
ETOP profile 67
Ernst & Young 122
EU *see* European Union
Euro-Brands 268, 349, 501
Euromonitor 20
European Commission 581
European Community 97, 109, 467, 475
geographic, demographic and economic
centres 100
pedigree of 101
position in World trade 101
see also European Union
European Management Education Guide 169
European Union directives and legislation
273–4, 303–4, 476, 477, 536
Eurostyles 506
Ever Ready 433–4
Exchange Rate Mechanism (ERM) 475
Exchange rates *see* Foreign exchange rates
Exhibition industry 589
Exhibitions
agricultural shows 586
audit 596
benefits for products and services 584–5
choice of 587–8
conference related exhibitions 586
consumer exhibitions 585
contractors 589
costs 588–9
follow-up 596
information sources 587
key tasks to plan 591–3
layout planning 592–3
mail list compilation 596
objectives 587
organizers 589
overseas exhibitions 586
private exhibitions 586–7
promotion 595
retrospective review 595–6
site selection 590
stand appearance 593
stand management 594–5
stand type 590
timescale 591
trade exhibitions 585
use of hired stand staff 595
venues 589

Total systems management 393–7
Toyota 83
TRADANET 411
Trade Description Act 1968 443, 526, 536,
    556, 622
Trade exhibitions *see* Exhibitions
Trade marks 628
Training *see* Customer training *and* Staff
    training
Treacy, M. 95
Treadgold, A. 410–11
Treaty of Rome 581
Trotman and Company 153
Tseng, J. 108
Turnkey contracts 464

UK 146, 162
Unfair Contract Terms Act 1977 381
Unilever 2, 89, 142, 143, 159, 347
Unisource alliance 115
United Biscuits 354
University of Warwick Statistics Service 25
Unsolicited Goods and Services Act 1975
    556
US 125, 151
    see also America
Utterback, J. 365

Valla, J.P. 463
VALS2 (Values and Lifestyle) 504
Value added
    advertising 516–17
    application of 229
    contribution to profit 228–30
    impact of managing 230
    influences on 229, 237
Value Added Tax 109, 443
Value delivery 10–11
Value in terms of consumer needs 517

Van Herk, M. C. 270
Van Westerndorp, P. 335
Vernon, R. 468
Vernons Pools 435
Vertical marketing system 403, 404–5
Virgin Airlines 85
Virgin Company 86
Virtuous *versus* vicious circles 166–7
VHS video format 85–6
Video Standards Council 529
Vocabulary of graduates, fall in standard
    157
Voluntary Export Restraints 475

Walker, J. 232
Webster, F. E. 4
Weights and Measures Act 1985 619–21
Which? magazine 252
Whirlpool Corporation, logistics strategy
    398–9
Wiersema, F., 95
Wilkins' Tiptree brand 345
Wind, Y. 261
W. L. Housewares 345
Women in marketing jobs 143
Wright, Peter 61

Xerox 88

Yellow Pages 560
Yves Rocher 107

Zemke, R. 598, 599

4Ps 116
30Rs 117–21
100 Club 114